Corporate Control
and Accountability

Corporate Control and Accountability

Changing Structures and the
Dynamics of Regulation

Edited by

Joseph McCahery,
Sol Picciotto,
and
Colin Scott

CLARENDON PRESS · OXFORD
1993

Oxford University Press, Walton Street, Oxford OX2 6DP

Oxford New York Toronto
Delhi Bombay Calcutta Madras Karachi
Kuala Lumpur Singapore Hong Kong Tokyo
Nairobi Dar es Salaam Cape Town
Melbourne Auckland Madrid
and associated companies in
Berlin Ibadan

Oxford is a trade mark of Oxford University Press

Published in the United States
by Oxford University Press Inc., New York

British Library Cataloguing in Publication Data
Data available

Library of Congress Cataloging in Publication Data
Corporate control and accountability: changing structure and the
dynamics of regulation / edited by Joseph McCahery, Sol Picciotto,
and Colin Scott.
p. cm.
Includes bibliographical references.
1. Corporate governance—Congresses. 2. Corporate governance—Law
and legislation—Congresses. I. McCahery, Joseph. II. Picciotto,
Sol. III. Scott, Colin.
HD2741.C77 1993 658.4—dc20 93-19420
ISBN 0-19-825827-5

Set by Hope Services (Abingdon) Ltd.
Printed in Great Britain
on acid-free paper by
Biddles Ltd
Guildford & King's Lynn

Preface

This book resulted from a Workshop on Corporate Control and Accountability held at the University of Warwick in July 1991. We would like to thank all those who made the workshop, in the general view of all involved, an enjoyable and stimulating occasion. For administrative help which ensured that it ran extremely smoothly, we would like to thank Helen Beresford, Dorothy Hyams, and Claire Newman. For advice, encouragement, and support we are grateful to Anthony Carey, Paul Edwards, Paul Marginson, Brendan McSweeney, Tony Steele, and Chris Whelan. We are especially grateful to the organizations which responded speedily and helpfully to our requests for funding, without which essential conditions for the success of the workshop, such as precirculation of the papers, would have been impossible. These were the Nuffield Foundation, the Research and Innovations Fund of the University of Warwick, the Institute for Chartered Accountants of England and Wales, and the Legal Research Institute of the School of Law at the University of Warwick, which sponsored the workshop. Finally, the active involvement of all the participants was the vital ingredient which produced such stimulating ideas. We were unfortunately unable to incorporate in this volume all the themes covered at the workshop, which meant that some excellent papers could not be included, but we would like to thank all the authors of papers, commentators, and chairs of sessions for their contributions. Finally, for help in the preparation of this volume for the press we would like to thank Simon Curran, the School of Law at Warwick University, and our editor, Richard Hart.

J. McC.
S. P.
C. S.

October 1992

Notes on Contributors

Theodor Baums, Professor of Law, University of Osnabruck.

Phillip I. Blumberg, Dean and Professor of Law and Business, Emeritus, University of Connecticut School of Law.

Caroline Bradley, Lecturer in Law, London School of Economics and Political Science.

William W. Bratton, Jr., Professor of Law, Rutgers Law School.

David Campbell, Reader in Law, City Polytechnic of Hong Kong.

Hugh Collins, Professor of English Law, London School of Economics and Political Science.

Yves Dezalay, charge de recherches au C.N.R.S. (Centre National de la Recherche Scientifique), and associate, C.R.I.V. (Centre de Recherches Interdisciplinaires de Vaucresson).

Tom Hadden, part-time Professor of Law, Queen's University of Belfast.

Neil Kay, Professor of Business Economics, Strathclyde University.

Joseph McCahery, Lecturer in Law, University of Warwick.

Paul Marginson, Lecturer in Industrial Relations, University of Warwick.

Sol Picciotto, Professor of Law, Lancaster University.

Michael Power, Lecturer in Accounting and Finance, London School of Economics and Political Science.

D. D. Prentice, Allen & Overy Professor of Corporate Law, University of Oxford.

Colin Scott, Lecturer in Law, London School of Economics and Political Science.

John Scott, Professor of Sociology, University of Leicester.

William H. Simon, Professor of Law, Stanford Law School.

Katherine Van Wezel Stone, Professor of Law, Cornell Law School and Cornell School of Industrial and Labor Relations.

Gunther Teubner, Otto-Kahn-Freund Professor for Comparative Law and Legal Theory at the London School of Economics and Political Science.

Contents

Table of Cases

Introduction: Corporate Control: Changing Concepts and Practices of the Firm

JOSEPH McCAHERY, SOL PICCIOTTO, AND COLIN SCOTT

This volume brings together lawyers, accountants, sociologists, and economists to explore some central themes of the legal and organizational accountability of the public corporation.

The papers collected in this volume also offer the first sustained attempt to transcend the new institutionalist and contractarian visions which, during the 1980s, became the mainstream perspectives in academic and policy-oriented discussions of the corporation. Founded on theoretical approaches of a much earlier vintage, these came to the fore in a period when the upheavals in financial markets and the boom in mergers and acquisitions (M & A) focused attention on the relationship between the constraints and disciplines of financial markets and the strategies of firms. This provided a very different basis for consideration of important issues such as the regulation of M & A, the definition of creditors' rights and directors' duties, obligations of disclosure and prohibitions of insider trading, and corporate governance and the role of banks and institutional shareholders.

However, as the excesses of the market for corporate control reached their peak at the close of the 1980s and attention shifted to regulatory failures and the need for enhanced corporate accountability, the limits of the existing theoretical approaches became apparent. Based on a simplistic dualism of the firm and the market, and failing to draw on the richness of contemporary social theory, the predominant law and economics approaches are in many respects inadequate, especially to tackle the 1990s agenda.

First, there is an awareness of the greater variety of patterns of economic and social relationships institutionalized in the corporate form. The frequently complex and decentralized structures within corporate groups and the great variety of links and networks between firms have made it hard to draw a clear distinction between market and hierarchy. The wave of corporate restructurings has produced not only buy-outs and divestments, but also the formation of new concentrations and conglomerates—for example, the backward integration of electronics firms such as Sony moving into the entertainments industry. Hybrid forms such as franchising have produced spectacular growth for many firms, such as Benetton, especially in service and consumer goods industries. Similar hybrid networks have been created in established industries, such as auto, power-plant, and heavy electrical, by co-operative arrangements between firms to help fund the enormous costs of research and new product development, and even for production of key components.

Secondly, financial markets entered a new era, often referred to as the Big Bang, in which the increased velocity, complexity, and volatility of the markets disrupted existing forms of regulation and broke down barriers separating professional groups, while increasing competition for professional services. This led to a continual process of regulatory renewal, often entailing greater juridification and bureaucratization. At the same time, new regulatory arrangements were found to be necessary also for newly privatized utilities and other former state monopolies.

Finally, and perhaps most importantly, a new phase of globalization has created greater awareness of contrasts between national patterns of financing and managing business activities, as well as styles of regulation. The dismantling of non-tariff protective walls has not only created new competition between firms in industries (especially in services and utilities) previously substantially shielded from world markets; it has also called into question the adequacy of existing international arrangements for the co-ordination of business regulation.

I. HISTORY AND THEORY OF THE CORPORATE ECONOMY

For over a century, the public corporation has been one of the primary institutions of capitalism. It has provided an enduring framework for the ownership and control of assets, the investment and accumulation of capital, and the organization of production in the broadest sense. This organizational framework facilitated a process of concentration of corporate ownership, first in the USA and then in Germany, the UK, and other leading capitalist countries in the period prior to 1914; and a surprisingly high proportion of the major corporate groups established at that time still exist, in one form or another, today. This process of concentration was the subject of substantial public and popular debate in the period 1890–1914. In the USA, despite considerable populist rhetoric, the development of antitrust laws and regulatory commissions did not blunt corporate power, but integrated it into a regulated corporatist consensus (Kolko 1963; Sklar 1988; Weinstein 1968). In Europe, anti-corporate populism was less strong, and the policy consensus favoured direct state regulation of cartels and industry groups. The stronger socialist variant advocated nationalization, which, it was envisaged, would realize the potential for socialized production relations embodied in the high degree of development of means of production through large-scale corporate organizations (Renner 1904; Hilferding 1910).

The consolidation of the giant firm in the 1920s, and the survival and recovery of such firms following the crash and great depression, were the basis for the development of managerialist theories (Berle and Means 1932; Chandler 1962). The dispersion of share ownership and legal changes introduced the flexibility necessary for management to organize large, multi-divisional companies, subject to minimal constraints on managerial behaviour. Managerialist theories emphasized the logic of size in terms of scale economies, and focused on the rationality of corporate decision making in hierarchical bureaucracies. Critics argued that the lack of accountability of management undermined efficacy and rationality, but they did not challenge the managerialist consensus.

The managerialist theories were at their pinnacle in the post-war period of growth and relative stability, and it was perhaps not surprising that, with the transition to greater volatility in the financial markets in the 1980s, contract-based theories should come to the fore.

The managerialist perspective was not challenged until the 1970s, with the rise of the new institutionalist theory of the firm. Based on Coase's pre-war essay revising the micro-economic theory of the firm in terms of transaction costs, the new approach opened up the 'black box' of the firm to an analysis of the patterns of contracting between the various actors (managers, investors, workers, etc.). The internalization of such relationships in a regulated structure within the firm, rather than by market-contracting, is justified if firms are able to produce goods or services more efficiently internally. The important insight offered by this approach was that institutional structure and internal governance are key elements in the firm's strategy, which in turn determine its competitive success.

The micro-economic theories of the 1970s paralleled the managerialist theories, however, in that both emphasized the separation of risk-bearing and management functions. Nevertheless, they differed in that the new neo-classical theory treated management as agent for the shareholders, and emphasized that internal and external monitoring devices (e.g., non-executive directors, external auditors, disclosure to capital markets) are necessary to ensure convergence of interests within the firm. The managerialist theories had already emphasized the asymmetries of information due to diffusion of share ownership and managers' expertise and superior access to information, especially about the firm's assets. The new approaches entailed a further re-evaluation of the neo-classical assumption of perfect information; but this essentially reinforced the neo-classical model of utility-maximizing economic actors by focusing on decisions under uncertainty.

This new neo-classical approach split between the institutional and the agency strands. The former emphasizes transaction costs, and concentrates on designing governance structures to deal with contractual hazards and the problem of bounded rationality (Williamson 1985). Agency theory (Alchian and Demsetz 1972; Jensen and Meckling 1976; Fama 1980), more radically, views the firm as a legal fiction serving as a nexus for a set of contracting relations among factors of production. It insists on abandonment of the notions of power and hierarchy within the firm, and sees management as a 'continuous process of negotiation of successive contracts' (Alchian and Demsetz 1972: 794). Since managers' functions of interpreting objectives and formulating plans may have given them considerable discretion for acting in their self-interest, and given also the self-interest objectives of other agents, the task is to devise a set of incentive structures which avoid efficiency loss. Such pursuit of self-interest, or 'shirking', becomes a dominant theme as a typical cost associated with the agent–principal relation, and provides a different slant on the analysis of the firm's structures, including hierarchy, as essential to reconcile the role of managers and others in the firm in relation to the residual risk-bearers.

In the 1980s, agency cost theorists argued that one of the primary mechanisms for disciplining managerial agents is the market for corporate control. The effectiveness of this mechanism has been the subject of considerable debate within the legal, industrial relations, and finance literatures. The theory of corporate control is based on the proposition that where agents have specific human capital investments in the firm, their firm-specific wealth is threatened by a hostile acquisition of the firm which may bring in a new management team. The threat of take-over is itself sufficient to induce managers to co-ordinate their strategic actions to meet the interests of the residual risk-bearers. However, the empirical evidence on the market for corporate control is contradictory, and contains many ambiguities. In the first place, it has concentrated on the issue of whether the threat of hostile take-over reduces the non-value-maximizing actions of agents: but post-merger studies in the UK and USA show only slight differences in profitability between companies that became take-over victims and those that did not. There has been much less attention given to the extent to which take-overs provide an avenue for managers to maximize self-interest by value-reducing defensive strategies, such as 'poison pills' and other forms of dilution of capital.

Despite little evidence backing the claim that mergers lead to significant improvements in internal efficiency, there is another major problem with the market for corporate control: it fosters short-termism. According to this critique, short-termism is manifested in companies' reduced investments in R & D and other long-term growth strategies. The threat of hostile take-over may deter management from making strategic investments to bolster dividends. The stock-market as a mechanism for corporate control is largely a US and British phenomenon, and does not yet exist to any great extent in Japan or continental Europe. The claim is that these latter systems, which support stability of ownership and management by restricting voting rights, may provide a better basis for economic growth and long-term efficiency. Some empirical studies show that managements which fear take-over do not necessarily reduce investment in R & D, but the evidence is limited and inconclusive (Hall 1990).

The issue of controllability of management also suggests that the relationship between management and labour requires renegotiation. An important question is how to introduce controls over management which alter the balance of power between management and labour while maintaining the interests of shareholders. This suggests a new slant on the question of workers' control and a perspective for discussion of policy issues such as two-tier boards, the European Company statute, and the Social Charter; or, in the USA, union buy-outs and bargained concessions.

Financial markets have clearly played an increasing role in mediating the restructuring of capital. The parallel trend to privatization, first in mixed-economy countries and finally in centrally planned economies, could also be placed within a corporate control hypothesis. Transfer from the public to the private sector of entitlements to residual profits implies a change in the relationship between the persons responsible for making decisions and the beneficiaries of the residual profits. The general problem is how to establish for the 'agent' a set of structures which contribute maximally to the interest of the 'principal' (Laffont and Tirole 1991). Privatization entails a shift in the objectives of the principal, since the ownership changes now link rewards to the share price. Thus, like the market for corporate control, the new ownership arrangements must consider the type of managerial governance structures which will induce performance in a new regulatory and competitive environment. Again, this provides a perspective on the policy issues debated in key areas such as communications and utilities.

Conversely, there has been a process of more overt politicization of the fields of corporate regulation: for example, in both Europe and the USA the tensions between the political and regulatory criteria in decisions on mergers and take-overs are increasingly evident. A politics of corporate regulation can be seen to be emerging, which purely economic approaches cannot easily comprehend. In particular, important aspects of cultural differentiation are often neglected, especially in economic accounts.

2. CONTRACTARIANISM VERSUS ENTERPRISE CORPORATISM

Corporate theorists looked to the new economic theories as a framework for analysing the conflicting interests within the firm. Contractualists also emphasize that there is no single, a priori governance structure which is appropriate for all businesses. Rather, the claim is that entrepreneurs must decide which combination of rules will attract the highest level of corporate investment by interests outside the firm. Failure to locate the right mix of rules will result in higher costs relative to other firms, and in the long run only the least-cost corporations will survive. This approach, advanced by Easterbrook and Fischel (1991), combines two related theories (agency costs and the efficient markets hypothesis), and states that managers have an incentive to create legal rules and corporate structures that mimic the market. In general terms the function of corporate law, on this account, is to design an efficient set of default rules (to deal with the potential for informational asymmetries and barriers to collective action) to govern the rights and duties among directors, shareholders, and investors. It follows, therefore, that an efficient set of governance structures would include those background rules to which most parties would agree after a complete round of bargaining.

The move to conceptualize the firm as contract has several conceptual advantages. It offers a framework for assessing the efficiency of alternative governance structures, the economic properties of the different forms of contracting, and the behaviour of private parties operating in a complex environment of uncertainty, complexity, and bounded rationality. In particular, the contractualists accept that there are different interests within the firm, and that shareholders can protect themselves through designing rules, bonding mechanisms, and incentive structures to limit, to some degree, moral hazard and adverse selection. The conceptual power of the contractualist paradigm has been applied in different corporate law fields, including insolvency, commercial contracts, securities, and financial regulation (R. Clark 1989; Macey 1984; Charny 1991).

However, the contractualist perspective is not a unified theory, and several critics have argued that it is not an adequate theory, because its results are not easily subject to empirical confirmation (R. Clark 1985; Bratton 1989c). Other theorists have argued that the nexus of contracts theory is inadequate because, by choosing to characterize the corporation as a standard form contract, it reduces the corporate entity, which is a complex social phenomenon, to a single mode of organization (Bratton 1989b). Moreover, these critics contend that corporate law operates in areas outside conscious agreement; that is, the relationship between shareholder and manager is contractual only in the metaphorical sense (Kronman 1989).

From this point of departure, William Bratton, in the first contribution to this book, states that 'corporations are complexes of diverse elements that resist reduction into neat rationalized blueprints of legal and economic theory'. In his account, corporations contain simultaneously both discrete and relational contractual elements, which result from free contract, but also entail empowerment and dependence. Rejecting a vision of the firm based on one foundational principle—that is, wealth maximization—anti-foundationalists such as Bratton contend that there is not just one positive image of the firm, and that different conceptions of the firm must be 'synchronized in time and circumstance'. A reconfigured theory of the firm would focus on the firm as a complex organization involving a consensus element, which permits external values such as an ethic of goodwill to be incorporated, in order to enhance the legitimacy of corporate actions, as well as a business purpose which is based on wealth maximization. Bratton argues that what matters is to accord the twofold values of wealth and public value an equal footing within the corporation and to embrace a vision of corporate law which is mediative. A mediative theory of corporate law transcends contractualism. Since corporate law is not easily reduced to a single, narrow foundation, a mediative approach offers more access to a richer legal description of the corporation, and provides greater access to more theories of the firm, as well as a normative basis for guiding practical action.

The issue of complexity of social and economic relationships embodied in the corporate form is also explored, from a different perspective, by Gunther Teubner. He also finds the modern contractualist approach unsatisfactory, since it levels the distinction between contract and organization: 'Organizations, too, should be seen as contractual arrangements through which payment flows pass smoothly.' Such approaches are constrained by economic thinking, 'interpreting every social arrangement as a hypothetical contract between rational actors'. Although the 'more moderate' institutional variants accept the importance of the organization as providing internal governance structures and co-ordination, their limited notion of 'bounded rationality' provides a slender basis for an adequate understanding of the dynamics of either market or organizational relations, and certainly none for the important hybrid form of networks.

For Teubner, the firm should be understood as a collective actor or macro-entity. By emphasizing the distinctive organizational nature of the firm, based on communicative modes, Teubner seeks to demonstrate that an adequate evaluation of the rules governing such networks should not be based on the assumptions of either organization or contract. Utilizing both contract and organization elements, Teubner argues that the evolution away from the entity mode to the inter-organizational mode requires a change in our legal and sociological understanding of the firm. The organizational firm, for Teubner, is premissed on a theory developed by Luhmann, which states that the firm is an evolutionary entity which learns through hyper-cycles of autopoietic reproduction of communication. Applying insights from autopoietic theory, Teubner argues that the network of franchise contracts represents a higher-order evolutionary entity, because its structure provides greater flexibility and intermediate levels of control for the franchisor. Arguing against contractualists, Teubner insists that the form of the company does not always specify the economic borders of the firm. He contends that the organizational pole, based on the concept of the firm as a network of communications, breaks down the internal versus external contractual relations distinction. The communication-based firm, then, involves the interpenetration of hierarchical and relational organizational elements, which provide the basis for greater flexibility, learning, and change in the firm. The emphasis on intercommunication also provides a different perspective on regulation, suggesting that the firm or network is capable of internal regulation by virtue of communication among the nodes, resulting in adjustments reflecting risks and liabilities and the system's capacity for learning. He rejects a functionalist view of the efficacy of external regulation, arguing that the response of a system to the external environment is indirect, depending on the interaction with the internal communicative system.

The next chapters continue the discussion of contract and organization. The merger wave created large wealth transfers to shareholders from a variety of stakeholders in the firm, such as creditors, managers, employees, and local communities. A portion of the wealth transferred to shareholders included the gains achieved from breaching the long-term implicit contracts between shareholders and stakeholders (Shleifer and Summers 1988). The breach of trust not only involves the transfer of wealth to shareholders, but also changes the environment of contracting, which is reflected in stakeholders adopting risk-adverse strategies in order to limit the hazards of expropriation. Implicit contracts are important, because they provide an incentive for employees to invest in acquiring firm-specific capital in exchange for delayed compensation. One of the leading reasons for a hostile take-over was the existence of firm-specific labour, which constituted an important component of the transfer gain to shareholders. Katherine Stone's general point is that the breach of trust requires regulatory intervention to protect the expropriation of stakeholders' firm-specific capital. Employing insights from contractarianism, Stone argues that workers have an implicit contract of job security which they exchange for deferred income. While the implicit contract is a non-enforceable promise, Stone contends that respect for implicit contracts is necessary to convince stakeholders to make firm-specific investments. In evaluating the regulatory structure necessary to uphold implicit contracts,

Stone defends collectivist regulation, such as statutes which constrain the power to wield control of an acquired firm against other stakeholders, to protect labour's entitlements in the firm.

Hugh Collins challenges Stone's contractualism. Collins argues against a broad view of corporate governance based on the implicit contracts approach to collective enforcement of labour's entitlement in the firm. At the outset he states that the implicit contracts model is theoretically suspect, since it relies solely on the forces of supply and demand to explain internal wage patterns, and does not explain the persistence of the discriminatory wage. Collins argues that implicit contracts probably do not exist, and that even if they do exist, parties in interest could avoid respecting them. Moreover, Collins points to a logical problem in Stone's argument. In Stone's theory, it would appear that respect for implicit contracts is governed by common law considerations, although her concern with the breach of promises made by management to stakeholders suggests that her approach is grounded in moral theory. Stone's response to Collins, in the addendum to her paper, shifts the ground of the debate, in that she clarifies that in speaking of the 'implicit contract' she was not arguing for a contract to be 'externally' implied, but rather that the law should recognize the terms of an agreement which is often explicit in unilateral promises made by management. However, this still leaves open the question of whether contractual terms are ever fully specifiable, and on what basis the 'gaps' are to be filled (discussed further in chapters by Bratton, Bradley, and McCahery).

In place of the implicit contracts model, Collins adopts an organizational model of corporate governance, based on the view that the modern corporation is a set of structures which reflects the attitudes and beliefs of its members. Addressing the problem of corporate restructuring, Collins argues that an organizational paradigm is superior, since it mandates owners to respect a social obligation to minimize the social costs of dismissals, and requires that directors recognize employees as members of the organization, who should be treated with respect and consulted with regard to decisions of the corporation and their consequences, especially as they pertain to redundancy. Having sketched out an alternative theory, Collins' emphasis on communication and contradictory interests implies that a different welfare logic might be found outside the considerations of contract and the market. Collins's approach to the firm is similar to Bratton's mediative theory of corporate law, since both theories depend on mediative structures and practical reason as the basis for organizational decision making.

3. REASSESSING MARKET FAILURE AND TRANSACTION COSTS THEORY

Part II addresses the institutional theory of the firm, as it has been developed by Coase and Williamson. The transaction costs framework explains economic transactions and complex organizations, based on the economic costs of processing the inputs and co-ordinating the outputs of the firm. For the last ten years, this has been the dominant approach to the study of economic organizations, and has been applied to analyse the economic effects of corporate restructurings, take-overs, mergers, and buy-outs.

David Campbell offers a historically informed and theoretically challenging contribution to the debate over the efficacy of the transaction cost and market failure approach. Arguing that the transaction cost framework is a deeply flawed account of the modern firm and its regulation, Campbell begins by pointing out that corporations are not 'aberrant products of the market' but, rather, organizations which developed to suppress it. Three arguments are offered against the transaction cost framework. First, the concept of 'market failure' fails to capture the historical development of the *laissez-faire* system. That is, Campbell contends that the firm, which is allegedly a cheaper mechanism to organize inputs and outputs of production, is insufficiently theorized as a result of Coase's twofold failure to offer a historically informed account of the market and the role of the firm within the market system. Coase's analysis of the origins of the market system is, paradoxically, based on the very market assumptions—that is, the existence of a perfect market—which he is attempting to displace with his theory of market failure. While Coase correctly demonstrated that the assumption that markets exist everywhere is false, Campbell argues that Coase erred by attempting to provide an explanation for its existence while simultaneously ignoring the conditions of its realization. This theoretical and historical blindness undercuts Coase's theoretical project.

Offering a reconstruction of the historical development of American capitalism and the firm, Campbell argues that Coase's work should be understood as a rationalization for the development of the American economy in the earlier part of the twentieth century. Campbell offers historical evidence which shows that an earlier generation of economists was highly influential in guiding the restructuring of the American corporate economy. In contrast with Coase, these economists understood that the market is structurally prone to over-production, and that departures from the price mechanism are justified in order to retain the market institutions and property relations. Campbell contends that these early economists endorsed the use of corporate mechanisms which suppressed prices, reduced competition, and encouraged inequalities in distribution, in order to maintain the property rights system. On this account, the corporation is characterized in terms of its ability to suppress *laissez-faire* capitalism's tendency towards over-production. Campbell concludes that theories of corporate regulation, based on market failure, are self-defeating, since they attempt to refer corporations back to a free market which does not exist and to a sub-optimal system of corporate regulation. This self-defeating framework is best expressed in the case for privatization.

Neil Kay focuses specifically on Williamson's transaction costs framework. Williamson's theory, which is a complex combination of the insights of Coase and Simon, stresses that the problems of bounded rationality, asset specificity, and opportunism govern the choice between contract or vertical integration. The choice of the organizational form has implications for the level and costs of producing the output. Williamson argues that the existence of any one of the three conditions referred to above creates problems for economic organizations, and the problem for owners is to select a system of governance which is most efficient in organizing the economic activity in question. Williamson's fundamental insight is that economic activity will be constrained in processing information when all three factors exist. Williamson argues that, under these circumstances, the one clear solution is for the principal to internalize the economic activity in order to reduce transaction costs. Under certain conditions, internal organization will be more efficient than market contracting. However, the move to internalize is not sufficiently costless, since administration involves costs and limits the power of the market to control the process. In offering a critique of Williamson, Kay argues that Williamson strains the concept of transaction and distorts the notion of hierarchy. Using a series of analytical examples, Kay contends that Williamson employs two mutually inconsistent concepts of the term 'transaction'. Further, Kay argues that Williamson's model falters to the extent that he analyses the transactional properties of external markets and compares them to internal markets, but fails to concentrate on the distinction between markets and hierarchies. The latter distinction, which is the central theoretical focus of Williamson's work, is never developed, and this point is demonstrated in terms of Williamson's analysis of the multinational firm. Asset specificity is far from being an adequate explanation for the development of the multinational firm, since the specificity of assets can be the basis for contractual solutions such as licensing.

Turning to management–labour relations, Paul Marginson offers a sustained and critical treatment of the efficiency theory of the firm, while pointing also to the limitations of alternatives based on power relations. Recognizing that the efficiency perspective values hierarchy, as a means of ensuring the common over individuals' goals, radical theorists such as Bowles and Gintis argue that the efficiency perspective's attempt to reconcile the collective action problem through socially necessary voluntary coercion is inadequate. The radical theorists argue that the hierarchy model has a weak empirical basis, since there is little evidence to support the claim that generally workers will act opportunistically and managers will act to secure the common good. Thus, the existence of the hierarchy, for radical political economists, creates conflict over the employment contract: the open term in the contract is the intensity of work performed, which is dominated by management. The radical theorists, according to Marginson, insist that the supervision of labour is costly, because it involves the incorporation of structures within the firm which create a drag on productivity. Following up this line of argument, Marginson contends that these arguments are further supported by the fact that, contrary to institutionalists' claims, workers organize into unions in order to reduce employer opportunism and to enhance their bargaining position. Taking together insights from both the radical and the institutional perspectives, Marginson argues that managers' actions are constrained, on the one hand, by the shareholders' desire to maximize profits and minimize labour inputs and, on the other hand, by the workers who organize to secure an adequate wage and to assert their own control over the pace and content of work. Managers use not only coercion but a range of influences to secure the optimal work effort, and their aim is not only efficiency but also the enhancement of their authority and maximization of private returns.

The broader question of workers' control is addressed by William Simon through a discussion of the role of pension funds in redistributing risk and control over the corporation. In the 1970s the debate over 'pension fund socialism' was conducted in terms of 'reform versus revolution' and whether the social-democratic wage-earners' fund based on contributions from corporate profits could provide a mechanism for social transformation. Simon notes that the Swedish experience is not a hopeful model for an 'engine of redistributive transformation', since the trade union trustees of pension funds preferred high returns to socially desirable investments, and resisted their use to gain leverage in wage bargaining. The central dilemma is whether to take on additional risk through concentrated investment or to reduce exposure through diversification. Simon addresses this concern by assessing the comparative advantages of the defined benefit and defined contribution plans; he observes that workers have a preference for security over risk, as reflected in their choice of defined benefit plans and the state insurance of these plans (in the USA, through the federal Pension Benefit Guaranty Corporation). Nevertheless, Simon believes that the defined contribution plan more closely approximates egalitarian goals, since it spreads risk more fairly. Its effect is to balance the commitment to older workers, while giving lower levels of security to younger workers. Simon acknowledges the limitations of private pension funds for redistribution in relation to wage differentials. However, he argues that a well-funded social insurance plan could achieve the macro-economic and political effects of redistribution. The second part of the chapter explores the various conflicts of interest (retired versus current employees, senior versus junior workers, managers versus rank-and-file, etc.) and the prospects for ameliorating disunity. Simon explores in detail the possibilities, within the framework of US employee retirement laws, for overcoming sectional interests. Turning to the problem of redistribution, Simon rejects the populist views that the tax subsidies for employee stock ownership plans could turn the country 'from a nation of plutocratic absentee investors to one of yeoman worker-owners', since such plans are regressive, being paid for essentially by workers through lower wages and higher taxes. Instead, he prefers the Swedish trade union proposals to finance wage-earner funds from a profits tax rather than wage-based contributions, embodying a vision of the gradual social ownership of capital.

4. THE KINETICS OF CORPORATE CONTROL

Part III explores the changing features of corporate regulation in symbiosis with the changing structures and practices of corporate activity. An important theme emerging here is the developing competition between regulators and among professionals on shifting regulatory territory.

The problem of internal control of the firm's financial accounts is one of the most important corporate control topics to emerge in the last five years, especially in the wake of prominent cases such as Maxwell Communications, BCCI, Polly Peck, Ferranti, and Dunsdale Securities. Michael Power offers an important and timely essay on the politics of regulatory control in the UK financial services sector, arguing that the recent growth of monitoring activities reflects a significant displacement of trust from management to auditors. With relocation of trust to the auditor, Power points to the growing concern that there are certain economic activities which, by virtue of their complexity and elusiveness, escape the regulatory net, and are therefore ungovernable. Turning to the Financial Services Act 1986, Power shows that the regulatory framework is itself *ad hoc* and that the 'regulatory space' in which the auditor works is inherently competitive, and that reporting is as much a political process as a technical matter. The insertion of the competing regulatory agents into a contradictory regime creates an interdisciplinary field which makes internal control virtually impossible. Hence, Power views auditing as a political technology which, like other elements within the financial field, is responding to the demands placed upon it, and argues that the professional guide-lines, such as those of the APC and APB, provide the basis for different interpretive strategies. It is this interpretive looseness, however, which offers auditors the room to deal with the different constituencies, providing the basis for their own competitive advantage over other professionals. Here he follows Bourdieu, who has provided a theoretical basis for breaking with functionalist accounts of the social role of professionals in mediating state regulation, by emphasizing the constitutive role of professional competition in the formulation and legitimation of law.

This theme is developed by Dezalay, who explains how globalization has created a new competition between regulatory regimes, and has thrust professionals to the forefront of the attempt to legitimize regulation. The disruption of national systems of regulation resulting from the globalization especially of financial markets has deprived national states of their legitimacy, and professionals have become more than mediators. They now 'find themselves responsible for the management of the symbolic capital represented by the legal order'. Thus, the emergence of the global mega-firms, which have commercialized and bureaucratized professional practice, is paradoxically accompanied by their massive investment in scholarly symbolic capital, which gives the new mandarins both their legitimacy and their competitive edge. Dezalay's account has moved far from the simplistic model of firm–state–market, and focuses especially on the role of professionals acting on behalf of corporate clients in shaping and structuring regulatory fields. For example, the 'comfort letter' in European Community competition law can be seen as an adaptive mechanism developed by the interaction of regulators and corporate professionals, mediating between the logic of the legal rules regulating competition and the dynamics of corporate agglomeration.

The changing dynamics of financial markets in the 1980s involved major transformations of regulatory arrangements, raising fundamental questions about the extent to which orderly markets require external regulation and the form and style that such regulation should take. In the UK one of the major City dramas was the Guinness affair, leading to the prosecution and imprisonment of the managing director, Ernest Saunders. An important sub-plot was the litigation involving the issue of fiduciary duties and directors' compensation (*Guinness* v. *Saunders*, 1990), based on the improper conduct of Saunders in the take-over bid by Guinness PLC for Distillers in 1986. Caroline Bradley argues that the case reveals the limitations of a paternalistic or 'consumerist' approach to regulation. Employing a contractualist perspective, Bradley contends that regulation is justified only if it increases efficiency, which is generally better achieved by bargaining between private parties rather than by *ad hoc* and selective interventions by regulators or courts. This is illustrated by analysing the approach of the House of Lords in considering whether the board could delegate powers to a special committee to authorize a highly remunerative contract for services with a sitting director. In her view the question is, did the shareholders of Guinness consent to paying Thomas Ward, the American lawyer and adviser, more than five million pounds for advice in the context of the take-over of Distillers. Bradley points out that the House of Lords went against the clear and express language of the agreement in deciding that the directors' committee of Guinness did not have the power to bind the shareholders to the contract with Ward, on the grounds that Guinness's Articles did not empower a special committee to authorize special remuneration to a director for services to a company, as only the board was authorized to grant special authority. The House of Lords, according to Bradley, also ignored the express provisions of the Articles, as well as the expectations of the shareholders, and enforced its own version of the Articles in the belief that it was protecting the interests of Guinness shareholders. Bradley argues that a consumerist approach to corporate contracts, as evidenced in *Guinness*, is likely to prove unsatisfactory, and that shareholders are capable through their own actions—that is, ratification—of protecting themselves.

However, the Guinness case involved much broader considerations, illustrating also the internationalization of corporate regulation as part of the globalization of financial markets. In the build-up in Britain to the new regulatory framework formalized in the Financial Services Act, 1986, the breaking of the Guinness scandal was one of the widening repercussions of the growing Wall Street crisis, symptomized by the confessions of Ivan Boesky to the Securities and Exchange Commission, which culminated in the disgrace of Michael Milken and the collapse of Drexel Burnham Lambert (Moran 1991: 82; Stewart 1991). Information and encouragement from the US authorities, as well as concern to ensure that London retained and developed its place as a prime financial centre, motivated the British authorities to initiate action in cases such as *Guinness* and to establish a more formalized regulatory regime. The diffusion of concepts of regulatory control takes place through cross-jurisdictional co-operation arrangements, as well as through competition between regulators and market-places, nationally and internationally.

A major feature of the fiscal and financial landscape of the 1980s was the global movement of national liberalization and privatization. While governments thereby granted greater legitimation to market mechanisms, paradoxically the transition to private ownership thrust regulation increasingly to the fore. The legal and financial processes involved in this restructuring of ownership have also further fuelled the growth and importance of the professional mega-firms, which in turn have helped to supply the necessary legitimation for the ownership transfers and the new regulatory regimes.

The political-economic justification of privatization is the claim that private ownership creates greater efficiency incentives for managers, by focusing on the goal of profit maximization. Privatization is said to introduce new levels of technical efficiency, by introducing market incentives and monitoring devices which operate to align the interests of managers with the residual risk-bearers' interests in maximized profits. Privatization is also designed to produce changes in the firm's efficient use of resources, by improving allocative efficiency through enforcing competitive pricing. Taken together, the introduction of allocative and technical efficiency constitutes the theoretical justification for a government's liberalization policy. The wave of privatizations in the 1980s had led to both an economic assessment of the allocative and technical efficiency of the newly privatized companies and a legal analysis of the decisive influence that regulation plays in monitoring the newly privatized industries.

Colin Scott commences his examination of the control and accountability of the privatized sector with the observation that transfer of ownership is not necessarily accompanied by a wholesale transfer of all control and accountability functions to the private sector. Focusing on the public utilities sectors in the UK, Scott attempts to show the complexity of the mixture of control and accountability structures in the product and capital markets and through new regulatory structures. From this analysis it is possible to derive the conclusions that initially the position of the utility companies in the product and capital markets arises not spontaneously, but rather in a way planned for and fashioned by government. But following on from this, these market forms of control, when taken together with public regulation, create a layering of control and accountability mechanisms so complex as to defy the ability of the companies themselves, the regulators, or the Government, to plan for optimal decision making. As experience of the delicate balance of market controls and regulation has developed, we are beginning to see the utilization of alternatives to direct regulation, such as franchising and common carriage regulation, which on the one hand seem to demonstrate a more pragmatic and functional approach to the privatized sectors, but on the other tend to make more visible the continuing role of government.

The issue of how far markets can act as control mechanisms was most directly posed by the arguments that the take-over frenzy of the 1980s represented the operation of a 'market for corporate control', implementing the judgment of shareholders over the actions of management. This is explored by Joseph McCahery, who initially considers whether the control market is an effective mechanism in terms of its capacity for wealth creation and as a disciplinary device for aligning managers' interests with those of the residual risk-bearers. To this end, he considers Coffee's (1987) differential risk hypothesis, that the asymmetry of risk between managers and shareholders explains in part the rapid changes in the market for corporate control in the 1980s, and suggests that it offers an incomplete explanation for the expansive wave of take-overs. McCahery attempts to counter Coffee's hypothesis by challenging the assumption that there is a fixed risk asymmetry between managers and shareholders, and argues that the balance is a dynamic one, which depends on the ability of managers either to offset risks through *ex ante* bargaining or, alternatively to use firm-specific assets to further entrench themselves. McCahery argues that the conflict between shareholders and managers is an unsteady game, and can be altered by the introduction of external devices such as managerially biased anti-take-over statutes and stakeholder statutes.

The failure of market mechanisms to control management conduct is widely acknowledged. With the increase in institutional ownership in the 1970s and 1980s, the corporate governance issue has moved away from the question of ownership and control, and concentrated more narrowly on the problem of development of internal and market structure forms of control, which are less costly and dramatic than regulation. Recently there has been some academic discussion concerning the introduction of lower-cost regulation, although most of the recent proposals have centred on the potential role of the institutional investor to offer a solution to the corporate governance problem. American and European theorists have looked to the governance structure of Japanese or German corporations, which provides expert monitoring and retains the market model of shareholder power, as an alternative model.

Against this background, Theodor Baums offers a careful review of the 'housebank' relationship between firms and banks in Germany. Employing a law and economics approach, Baums asks whether bank control is effective in reducing moral hazard. Baums argues that the currently popular notion that the housebank may be better able to reduce moral hazard by obtaining improved information is questionable. While the bank may not obtain better information earlier, certain theorists contend that banks, by virtue of their equity holding, may be in a position to reduce moral hazard through their enhanced powers to monitor and influence management. Baums rejects this argument, claiming that few banks would take a large equity position to influence management and noting, furthermore, that there is little incentive to absorb the transaction cost involved in additional monitoring and controlling for moral hazard. Baums contends that banks act like other shareholders, in that their acquisition of shares is usually a transitory action, and that the shares give them less than an equity stake in the firm. In the last part of the chapter, Baums considers whether intermediaries can efficiently provide the function of delayed monitoring. This question cannot be easily answered, for a number of complex reasons traceable to agency problems within banks, although Baums does cite some evidence that banks are efficient institutional custodians. He observes that the supervisory board of a bank, through appointing a member on the supervisory board of a company, is able to exert influence and assist in setting the agenda for meetings of the board. In terms of the importance of the German experience for the future of corporate control, Baums claims that while a comparison of different legal systems is impossible, it is likely that the role of institutions such as banks will be important in both limiting take-overs and ensuring efficiency.

5. THE REGULATION OF CORPORATE GROUPS

The treatment of corporate groups is one of the most complex areas of corporate regulation. In the opening paper of Part IV John Scott deploys some of his extensive research into British corporate groups and networks to demonstrate the complexity of social factors which must be taken into account to evaluate such linkages and which elude simple contractarian and managerialist perspectives. Amplifying upon the distinction between legal ownership and structural control of corporations, he introduces the concept of the 'rulers', who constitute the dominant coalition within an enterprise and determine its strategy within the constraints set by the structures of control. This provides a footing for the analysis of financially based business empires in which inter-corporate shareholdings establish control structures. Through the examples of the Kylsant and Hill Samuel groups, Scott shows that British investment trusts built empires similar to those of the Japanese *zaibatsu* (a modern equivalent might be the Hanson Trust). But in general, British enterprises, as they outgrew family wealth, did not become tied to a single source of capital, especially as institutional capital was strengthened by the growth of welfare provision through pension and insurance funds. Nevertheless, as is shown by Scott's own previous research, institutional shareholders form 'controlling constellations', which exercise a negative power of constraint within which the managers and rulers of enterprises must operate. The conflicting interests within constellations provide a space for managerial independence; but the central institutions dominate the overall flow of investment capital in the economy, while key directors involved in control networks also dominate corporate affairs. Hence, corporate groups must be understood as emerging within social and financial networks. This broader, sociological perspective stresses the importance of the class relations, embedded in the complexities of legal ownership and financial power, within which corporate management functions.

The next three chapters offer diverse evaluations by company lawyers of the legal problems entailed in taking account of the complexities of corporate groups. Philip Blumberg offers a historical and theoretical analysis of the decline of the entity view of the corporation. Blumberg argues that entity law, which was supplemented and strengthened by the principle of limited liability, has become 'hopelessly anachronistic' in an era of multinational corporations. Through a nuanced discussion of the specific application statutes, Blumberg offers an analysis of the problems of regulating economically integrated groups, based on enterprise principles. A more comparative perspective is provided by Tom Hadden, who argues that the emergence of the corporate group or network suggests that flexibility of form is an important consideration for the development of the corporation. While Hadden recognizes the evolutionary potential of the group, he is concerned that the group form may be employed for regulatory avoidance and anti-competitive gains. Hadden surveys the different forms of groups in advanced capitalist countries, and argues that, while regulation of groups is necessary to prevent abuses, the complexity of the group form requires a broad range of regulatory instruments to ensure accountability. Hadden concludes that, although some structural constraints may be desirable on group arrangements (especially corporate cross-holdings), regulation must generally be specific and focused on abuse in particular transactions. Prentice, in his brief comment, is even more sceptical of the possibility or desirability of a general or conceptual approach to the regulation of corporate groups. Nevertheless, as he points out, there is plenty of law about corporate groups; Blumberg, however, remains confident that it can and should be rationalized into a law of corporate groups.

In the last chapter, Sol Picciotto explores many of the themes of the book by focusing on a specific area of corporate regulation, the taxation of international corporate income. He provides a detailed account of the international framework within which corporate taxation emerged and developed and of the interaction between the processes of legitimation through the national state and the technicist administrative arrangements for international co-ordination. His account highlights how power is split between jurisdictions and control becomes a complex struggle fought over shifting terrain. In this context, an important factor in the growth and strength of transnational corporate groups has been their ability to take advantage of regulatory differences and lacunae, although they may also be vulnerable to the competitive conflicts of state regulators. Picciotto shows how the deployment of intermediary companies formed in convenient jurisdictions exploits the indeterminacy both of the legal rules and of the legitimacy of the political basis for state jurisdiction. While some stability can be achieved by regulatory modes which supplement general formal rules with informal bargaining processes and understandings, it can be upset if a crisis in the social regulatory process is expressed in the politicization of the issues. Picciotto argues that the growing national fiscal legitimacy crisis and the political campaign against 'the multinationals' from the late 1960s led to an internationally orchestrated attempt, led by the USA, to revamp and juridify the taxation of transnational corporate groups. However, national regulators, as well as the representatives of international business, remain committed to the allocation of tax rights between states on the basis of the arm's length principle, which purports to treat affiliated companies as if they were independent. Although the alternative of formula apportionment has a long history, there has been great hostility to its global application, due to the lack of adequate international legitimation processes. Such processes are necessary in order to underpin common definitions of taxable income, as well as the apportionment formula. However, the diversity of corporate groups also makes it hard to agree as to what constitutes an integrated group, and likely that apportionment could not be achieved by a general formula, but would entail an *ad hoc* decision for each firm. Paradoxically, however, Picciotto shows that attempts to establish functional, internationally co-ordinated arrangements for taxing such groups are groping towards such a solution, through the simultaneous examination of related entities and the negotiation of agreements among regulators and firms establishing methodologies for the pricing of intra-firm transactions (transfer pricing). What is still lacking is an adequate basis of political legitimacy.

The wide range of issues and subject-areas explored in this book reflect the paradigm shift in the study of the modern corporation and its economic and social environment. Earlier approaches relied on an insufficiently theorized view of the firm–state–market triad, and thus failed adequately to capture the dynamic shape and evolving forms of the business enterprise and its regulatory context. To appreciate the complexity and diversity of those forms, it is crucial to understand their evolution within the regulatory processes under the umbrella of the state. Several contributors have pointed to the limits of any functionalist view of what can be achieved through the state and regulation. This is especially the case in the present context of globalization, in which the multiplicity of overlapping regulatory fields, partly co-ordinated and often competitive, seems to stimulate increasing diversity of corporate forms. This book is an attempt to harness the wide resources of diverse disciplines to help construct a social theory of the business enterprise.

PART I

Corporate Theory beyond Contract

2

Public Values, Private Business, and US Corporate Fiduciary Law

WILLIAM W. BRATTON, JR.

Legal theorists and legal decision-makers deal with the same corporations. But they deal differently. The theorists aspire to provide objective answers to all questions. Their theories tend to pose clear-cut, determinant choices among alternatives. Legal decision-makers share the theorists' aspirations. But, in the world of cases and legal practice, the subject-matter of legal debates never seems to be determined once and for all by reference to an objective theory or a meta-ethical scheme. Though legal decision-makers aspire to theoretical certitude and consistency, in the end they tend to mediate between the alternatives.

This chapter takes this aspect of corporate law—its tendency to mediate—as the starting-point for an exploration of its capacity to endorse and incorporate values originating in the world outside corporations. A question at the frontier of corporate fiduciary law is addressed: namely, can fiduciary constraints that lack a base in either the expectations or the values of actors within corporations legitimately be imposed to vindicate values important to actors outside corporations? Or, restating the question in economic terms, can we justify corporate fiduciary rules that entail no cost saving or entail net costs? Stated either way, it is the hard political question respecting corporate fiduciary law.

In this chapter the possibility of an affirmative answer is entertained. I will experiment with arguments for regulating internal corporate conduct based on community values and process, drawing in particular on the concept of communicative action. In so doing, I will project a framework for public justification of fiduciary constraint that avoids reliance on the moribund notion of the corporation as a delegation of sovereign authority.[1]

---

[1] Concession theory asserts that corporations must derive positive authority from the state. Sovereigns have made this claim since Roman times (Dewey 1926: 666). The theory enjoyed vitality in the USA during the first half of the 19th century. Thereafter the practice of ministerial incorporation by states caused the theory's imagery to lose plausibility (see Bratton 1989c: 433–6; but cf. Hessen 1979: 3–33).

I. CORPORATE LAW AS MEDIATION

In practice, corporations are complexes of diverse elements that resist reduction into the neat rationalized blueprints of legal and economic theory. They have a complex of foundations. They are welfarist instruments. They also are nexuses of interpersonal relationships with ethical implications. They advance each participant's self-interest. But they also demand individual sacrifices to collective goals. They are nexuses of contract relationships. At the same time, they are separate entities with identifiable, albeit reified, contents. They include relational contracts and discrete contracts. They result from free contract, and yet entail empowerment and dependence. They amount to hierarchical power structures in some respects, and artefacts of arm's length contracting in others.

Corporate law's mediative aspect follows from sensitivity to this practice. The doctrine draws on all the foregoing conceptual bases. In so doing,[2] it avoids the foundationalist error of excluding one basis as a function of respecting another. Instead it mediates between the various components and norms in the complex, toward the end of mediating between and among the people involved with corporations.

Corporate law thus stems in part from the actions and values of the actors involved and in part from the state. It is partly mandatory and partly enabling. To structure corporations, it draws both the model of trust and the model of agency. It also draws freely on both contract and fiduciary principles. Following the practice, it does not adhere to any single positive theory of the firm. It leaves even definitional matters unsettled and subject to mediation.[3] Different conceptions of the firm, instead of being synthesized in law, are synchronized in time and circumstance. An accurate description of corporate law must account for this mediative, anti-foundational aspect.

A mediative approach provides a basis for a satisfying theory only if we reduce our expectations about what a theory can achieve. To many, good legal theories consistently apply a single or limited foundation. Those employing economic paradigms, for example, evaluate their expla-

---

[2] It does not lapse into relativism thereby, because it accords recognition to each basis as an objective force.

[3] The definitional question of whether corporations should be conceived and treated as entities that transcend the presences of individuals who participate in them receives different answers in different legal contexts. In some contexts entity treatment makes normative and practical sense. In others, firms seem better conceived as aggregates of relationships between participating actors. The positive choices have a normative aspect. Entity treatment may 'make sense' in a given situation, because of a decision that duties to the group 'ought' to obtain. Even the legal definition of the corporation, then, remains a matter of ongoing normative discussion, resting on ethical presuppositions. For detailed discussion of the contingent nature of our positive conceptions of firms, see Bratton 1989c: 407.

nations of law in terms of instrumental rationality based on the economic welfare goal. To an observer steeped in a methodology of this sort, a mediative description of law at best amounts to a theoretical failure.

Against this reproach can be ranged several advantages. First, methodological correctness does not necessarily enhance a theory's descriptive accuracy. Legal practices, viewed as a whole, are unlikely rationally and consistently to manifest one or another limited conceptual basis. Corporate law has certainly resisted reduction to neat articulations from narrow foundations. Its many apparent inconsistencies persist with undiminished strength despite many attempts to eliminate them through theory. A mediative approach, therefore, provides access to a more sensible legal description of the corporation. Second, a mediative approach also opens access to corporate legal theory. It lets us draw on the strengths of different theories even as they compete. Corporate law may be legitimately conceived as a positive law template for corporate organization with an accompanying rule book. It may also be conceived as a set of contract terms. Given a mediative approach, neither conception is accorded foundational status. Yet neither is disregarded. We admit the insights of both. Third, a mediative approach facilitates normative responsiveness. Legal mediation uses practical reason to synchronize the competing demands and values of actors through the appeal to legal principle (Cornell 1990: 1705). Legal principles, while they do not lead us down a track to a single right answer, do offer guidance. They isolate wrong answers (ibid. 1704), and inform us of the values at stake in the decision between competing solutions.[4]

A mediative conception of the law can thus be useful, despite modest theoretical aspirations. It encourages better understanding of the 'tough questions'. Where two valid, but inconsistent, normative directives come to bear on a problem, mediation is required. The choice between the two is a matter of judgment. By articulating the reasons behind a doctrinal inconsistency, rather than ignoring or suppressing them, we learn something about the properties of these legal judgments.

The great normative decisions in corporate law occur at these mediative junctures. These are points at which decision-makers breach enduring conflicts for situational resolution. Closed and consistent legal theories are ill suited to identify and explain them. And if deep and hidden rationalities inform the law, they do so at these points.

So, the assertion is that we can look at corporate law and find legitimate, ongoing, normative conflicts. Given a legitimate conflict, we can only try to mediate; our theories cannot offer directive signals with surety. But, by identifying the conflict's sources and parameters, including

---

[4] The proposition in the text is the operative assumption of the traditional law teacher, who seeks to teach students to be 'comfortable with ambiguity'.

its economics and the other values at stake in its resolution, we can accomplish a great deal. A legal decision-maker, thus briefed, could render a judgment of high quality.

2. PUBLIC VALUES AND CORPORATE FIDUCIARY LAW

Now let us employ a mediative conception of corporate law to assess the extent to which public values can be brought to bear to regulate the internal conduct of corporate affairs.

To concretize the question for discussion with a hypothetical case, imagine a pair of fiduciary rules. The first tightens the corporate opportunity constraint to bar all outside business pursuits by officers and directors of public corporations (Brudney and Clark 1981: 1022–42). The second applies the majority to minority fiduciary duty so as to impose a 'business purpose' standard that discourages a small class of cost-saving mergers (*Singer* v. *Magnavox*, 1977). Both rules have been imposed as a matter of public policy to protect investors. Either one could be modelled as wealth-maximizing, given the right assumptions. But in this exercise, different assumptions will be made. Although neither rule significantly impairs the conduct of business, neither follows from the values or transactional expectations of the average manager or investor. The first regulation is stipulated to be cost-neutral, the second to have a slight cost. Can one, the other, or both be justified under any legal theory plausible at this time?

2.1 Strategies for justifying cost-neutral and costly fiduciary law

a. The contract paradigm and the traditional concept of the Fiduciary

Both hypothetical regulations are hard to justify. Certainly, no support can be found under the 'contract paradigm' that dominated corporate legal theory in the 1980s. The paradigm qualifies fiduciary regulation only on proof of wealth-maximizing consequences (Jensen and Meckling 1976), and requires a showing of contract failure to make the proof. A thick stack of articles make this proof, and 'contractually' justify the traditional fiduciary bar against management self-dealing.[5] But the hypothetical facts stated here include no contract failure between management and investors. Nor do they stipulate any externality reducible to dollars and cents that might justify intervention on behalf of economic interests out-

---

[5] Albeit a narrowly construed version of the traditional fiduciary bar. The story is that information imbalances and barriers to collective action prevent dispersed shareholders from substituting a more effective contractual set of conflict of interest regulations (see, e.g., Bebchuk 1989; Coffee 1989; Easterbrook and Fischel 1989; J. Gordon 1989).

side the corporation (Ayres and Gertner 1989: 88–9). In short, neither regulation serves an economic welfare function.

The traditional doctrinal conception of the fiduciary does not provide much support for the hypothetical regulations either. Corporate fiduciary law, as traditionally conceived, rests on an ethical case against abuses of position by self-interested managers. But, at the same time, it recognizes that the self-interested pursuits of corporate actors are necessary and legitimate in many circumstances. Tensions arise between these concomitant considerations. The doctrine mediates the tensions with a rule-and-exceptions approach. It thereby pursues the generally shared goal of wealth maximization, all the while trying to protect the trust in the goodwill of others that suffuses complex economic relationships (Bratton 1992).

We can describe a conceptual tie between the hypothetical regulations and the ethic that motivates traditional fiduciary doctrine: the regulations impose business sacrifices on managers in favour of the interests of shareholders to protect trust reposed in the managers.[6] This description lacks justificatory force, however. On the facts stated, the shareholders do not expect or rely on the particular constraint that the regulations impose.[7] Traditional doctrine protects only the interests of actors inside the corporation, and looks to those actors to define their own interests. The regulations, by contrast, follow from outside ethical instructions as to appropriate conduct inside corporations. Furthermore, a justificatory base in traditional fiduciary goodwill would be debatable even if the regulations' origins in outside values presented no problem. Ethical considerations do not support fiduciary constraint under the traditional conception without reference to economic welfare (Bratton 1992). When ethics and economics conflict, the doctrine offers no programme to direct and legitimate results.

b. Community standards and process

Without backing from fiduciary doctrine, the proponent of regulations has to fall back on the values of members of the outside community. This public justification presupposes a consensus behind the values that motivate the regulations. The argument goes as follows. Corporate affairs are conducted not as a matter of juridical right. Corporate behaviour may be

[6] The entire class of shareholders in the first case, and a more narrowly defined class of minority shareholders in the second.

[7] In contemporary commentary in the conventional mode, strong, anti-managerialist fiduciary regulations tend to be justified as protections of shareholder expectations, based on casual empirical assumptions. Here the stipulated facts block these assumptions. See ALI 1986: sect. 2.01, comment h (management may not take ethical considerations into account if doing so 'would be likely to violate the fair expectations of the corporation's shareholders taken as a group'); (also Phillips 1979: 219–20; Brudney 1966: 299).

restricted even in the absence of a concrete economic externality. In such cases the externality that prompts the regulation is one of values. Sordid business spectacles, enforced in law, inflict non-pecuniary injury. If prominent business people pursue self-interest according to values materially different from those held outside the corporation, legal endorsement of their conduct injures the community's wider sense of itself.

This public justification is problematic, of course. Wealth maximization is a community value also. We only suffer corporations to benefit from low-cost production in the first place (Coase 1937).

At this point, a distinction opens between the cost-neutral and costly regulations. The community consensus assertion is more plausible empirically, and carries more justificatory force with respect to the cost-neutral regulation. All other things being equal, the community will support vindication of its values. With a cost-neutral regulation, we can even expect the acquiescence of actors inside the corporation. We can ascribe to them a desire to 'harmonize' (cf. MacNeil 1980: 67–9) their relationships with values prevalent outside. With the costly regulation, all other things are not equal. The insiders' urge to harmonize diminishes as constraints become costly. Impairing the wealth of those inside the corporation solely to vindicate outside values comes across as a weak exercise of distributive justice. The 'external' community justification must be stronger.

c. Possibilities for cost-neutral regulation under the trust model

Although cost-neutral regulation is thus justified in theory, the question is whether the cost-neutral fact pattern ever shows up in practice. The economic paradigms insist that it does not. They include a presumption that regulation is always materially costly, in the absence of a strong and precise showing to the contrary (Gilson 1987: 843; Butler and Ribstein 1990: 64).

But the point can be argued the other way, given the usual absence of empirical proof. First, we look behind the stipulated cost neutrality of the hypothetical corporate opportunity prohibition. It turns out that a 'cost-neutral' prohibition cannot exist without some consonance with the interests of actors inside the corporation: since regulation is intrinsically costly, cost neutrality implies a cost/benefit stand-off; some economic benefit must result. Such a stand-off is easily posited for a corporate opportunity bar. On the one hand, the regulation causes costs in cases where managers would otherwise pursue individual entrepreneurial projects about which their investors would be indifferent.[8] But benefits would follow to the extent that the rule caused managers to pursue investor-

---

[8] Also, some talented people, discouraged by the directive to serve others, might pursue careers only in closely held corporate enterprises, avoiding executive positions in public corporations.

beneficial results in a more single-minded way. Arguably, this actualized professionalism would result in improved production and a lower cost of capital. At this point, the traditional conception of the fiduciary strongly comes to bear in support. And the point carries, even if shareholders do not expect the protection *ex ante*. Shareholder expectations have an inchoate aspect. The law helps shape them, and can have cost-beneficial consequences as it does so.

Since we now have plausible arguments on both sides, the matter comes down to the usual contest between regulatory and anti-regulatory burdens of proof. Today, a stronger case can be made for stepped-up fiduciary regulation under a trust model of the corporation, and against the economic presumption against regulation, than at any time in the last decade. The failure of market mechanisms adequately to control management conduct is once more widely acknowledged. Academic policy talk, however, remains in a deregulatory mode. Current work looks to institutional investor self-help for solutions (Gilson and Kraakman 1991; Black 1991). Avenues toward less costly legal regulation remain unexplored. Yet such avenues exist. Corporate fiduciary law always has had a tentative, experimental pattern of application (Bratton 1992); today, it can even have a conditional pattern.

A decade of contractual thinking about corporate law has left us with the tools to create statutes that regulate corporate conduct but also leave open paths for contractual innovation within particular corporations. Conditional regulation subject to opting out in particular corporations by shareholder vote is now everyday business.[9] It is the great gift to regulation from the 'nexus of contracts'. Unfortunately, up to now, the device has been used to legitimate management-protective innovation. It would be better used in the service of a more professionalized model of management conduct. The regulatory improvements pursued piecemeal by today's institutional investor activists—for example, secret ballots, independent director majorities on compensation committees, constraints on golden parachutes (Wayne 1991), and limits on compensation schemes lacking ties to corporate performance results (Gilson and Kraakman 1991: 891, n. 22)—should also be pursued as law reform suggestions

---

[9] The most dramatic and widespread legislative movement toward opting out concerns the duty of care. This reform movement began in 1986, when Delaware amended its corporation law to permit corporations to amend their certificates to exclude directors' liability for breaches of the duty of care. (Del. Code Ann. tit. 8, sect; 102(b)(7) (Supp. 1988)). By now, at least 35 states have followed (Branson 1989: 381).

These amendments respond not to the contractarian law review commentary, but to a controversial decision of the Delaware Supreme Court, *Smith* v *Van Gorkum*, 1985. The Court took the duty of care in an unexpected and potentially expensive direction, finding a board of directors liable for negligent approval of a corporate control transaction. Coming at a time when insurance markets were already in a state of disruption, due to expanding legal liabilities, this case precipitated a little corporate insurance crisis.

under the fiduciary rubric. Liberal use of the opting-out device can minimize the risks attending such regulatory experiments, and put the burden of justification on management, where it ought to be under the traditional fiduciary concept.

d. The process case for costly fiduciary regulation

Returning to the hypothetical costly rule, we find it in some trouble. It comes up against independent ethical objections. When the state imposes a fiduciary rule on unwilling subjects, the regulation's sentimental grounding becomes attenuated. Here outsiders want to impose their conception of appropriate business relationships with wealth-constraining effects. But, as the motivating values are transformed into legal constraints, their sentimental roots atrophy. The values become a construct, a reified ethic of goodwill toward other corporate participants operating as law. Imposition of the construct can even mask an expression of ill will from one group to another. What started as an aspiration for the ethical conduct of business becomes not only a construct, but an oppressive one.

A related political objection also comes up. Without a manifest and compelling consensus behind it, the costly rule looks élitist (Kronman 1989: 1754–5). It makes its subjects worse off in order to vindicate values of importance to a subgroup of actors with power in the law-making process. We tend to find open pursuit of self-interest in business contexts more consonant with democratic values than business regulation to vindicate ethical values, at least in the absence of the cleansing effect of a democratic process (cf. Leubsdorf 1982: 1026–35).

These ethical and political objections can be answered, if not categorically rebutted. On the ethical point, it can be noted that state-imposed morality is more tolerable in business contexts than in other contexts. The stakes go only to small amounts of wealth and not to significant components of other people's identities. A strong political consensus may therefore ameliorate the ethical objection: we may, as a community, decide to be less well off in order to pursue a notion of the good.

The political objections lead to inspection of the regulatory process. Let us assume that the costly regulation is judge-made law that carries no opt-out privilege. It is imposed by a state court acting within our existing institutional system of corporate law making. This system, despite its bad reputation (see, e.g., Carey 1974), carries process guarantees—particularly in the rare case where it rouses itself to constrain self-interested management conduct. In the system, state and federal authorities interact with one another and with the various communities inside and outside business (Black 1990: 564–6). Delaware law-makers paid special heed to management and capital interests (Manning 1987: 783–6), subject to the implied constraint of federal pre-emption in the wider public interest. Management and capital also make their interests felt in federal law-making processes. Professional organizations, scholars, and other commentators all provide a background of discussion. All quarters accord considerable respect to economic welfare concerns.

Viewed cumulatively, this law-making process supports a positivist defence of the costly regulation. As a practical matter, it is unlikely that any regulation emerging from this system could present a cognizable threat to democratic concerns or to long-run economic welfare. So long as the underlying conflict between welfare and the competing ethic is controverted and discussed, it cannot be said that the regulation's cost is imposed in disregard of anyone's material needs. The facts of controversy and discussion also imply the presence of legitimating 'consensus' views. Finally, given the historic pattern of experimental applications of legal constraint in corporate fiduciary law, the regulation implies no permanent, universal, theoretical assertion of right. Born of controversy, the regulation amounts to a judgment made at a given moment in reference to perspectives particular to that moment. It remains subject to revision.

Although problematic in the abstract, then, the costly regulation has ties to a system and, through the system, to a wider consensus. In effect, the regulation manifests a mediation of a conflict of values within the system. If we see it as a mediation, rather than as a wider assertion of the primacy of values conflicting with economic welfare, its legitimacy need not depend on a perfect fit with a welfarist theoretical construct.

2.2 Public fiduciary law as communicative action

a. Instrumental and communicative action

The foregoing lawyerly appeal to the mediative force of process in the defence of the costly regulation carries weight. But, taken alone, it looks uncompetitive as an intelligible justification when compared to today's well-articulated theories of welfare and contract (Van Zandt 1989: 13). We can strengthen the process case, however, by reference to dialogic theory[10] and its constituent concept of communicative action.

---

[10] Ethical theory centred on dialogue is surprisingly well suited to legal theory. Like most legal theory, it presupposes a sceptical view of substantive ethical theory. Observe the competing substantive claims made by the several philosophical paradigms operating today. The ideal of rational justification can be pursued within the utilitarian paradigm. It can also be pursued in the Rawlsian paradigm—i.e, rationality as guided by the principles that rational and self-interested persons in a hypothetical situation of equal liberty would agree to accept (see Rawls 1971: 11-12). It can be pursued too in other paradigms (see Macintyre 1988: 2-3; Ackerman 1989: 13-15). In legal theory today, the others are essentialist; they employ what Ackerman characterizes as the 'trumping' strategy, isolating a single generally accepted

We can look to the work of Habermas[11] to find a more capacious concept of action and power than the concept that informs most American
legal theory. The usual model of action is teleological; an individual or
group pursues a set purpose. In this model of 'instrumental action',
power follows as the possibility of forcing one's will on others (Habermas
1983). Habermas, drawing on Arendt (1958: 199–205), identifies a
different source of power—power as the capacity to agree in uncoerced
communication on some community action. This power may also be realized in action, but the model of action is different. In this 'communicative
action', the participating subjects voluntarily agree (Arendt 1958: 173).
Habermas articulates a theory of rationality based on this communicative
action. He says that instrumental or strategic action and rationality inter-
mix in society with action and rationality based on reciprocal understanding, shared knowledge, and mutual trust (Handler 1988: 1029, 1067,
1079). Within this framework, he sets out a procedural ethical theory. He
posits an ideal ethical discussion that includes the identities and perspectives of all sorts of people. Under this, valid norms must meet a strict
standard of acceptance by all participants.[12]

value and focusing on its political implications so as to solve our disagreements (Ackerman
1989: 13).
  No agreement results from the discourse between and among all these paradigms. In the
end, therefore, the paradigms provide a means 'for more accurate and informed definition
of disagreement rather than progress toward its resolution.' (MacIntyre 1988:3). Nor does
any theory seem to answer practical ethical questions. We are unable within our culture to
unite conviction and rational justification' (ibid. 6).
Dialogism accepts the shortcomings of the competing substantive theories and turns to the
process of discussion. It posits participants taking roles in an ideal conversation. Then it
constructs theoretical pictures of these actors as they disagree about ethical principles but,
nevertheless, through dialogue, derive bases of agreement. We get a variety of ideal conversations: different dialogic theorists shape the roles in ideal conversations with different
norms.

[11] According to Habermas (1989: 52), moral theory should 'clarify the universal core of
our moral intuitions'. It cannot make any substantive contribution.

[12] First, all concerned must consent to them in their role as participants in the discourse.
Second, the consequences and side-effects of the general observance of the norm for the satisfaction of each person's particular interests must be accepted by all participants
(Habermas 1989: 40). American legal theory offers contrasting pictures in this dialogic
mode. Cornell discards Habermas's procedural limits. The result is dialogue in pursuit of an
ideal of the good (see, e.g., Cornell 1990: 1696–1700, 1709). Ackerman (1989: 8) describes
an ideal conversation with a practical imperative behind it. His actors disagree on ethical
questions, but nevertheless seek to solve problems of living together. Ackerman (ibid. 10)
makes dialogism an obligation of the citizen in the liberal state. The obligation to talk
about moral disagreements arises precisely because the liberal state avoids imposing a
morality. The participants exercise conversational restraint: they stick to the available public
premises and filter out inappropriate personal moralities (ibid. 19). Habermas's participants, says Ackerman (ibid. 19), look to ultimate conversational victory in some far-distant
ideal speech situation. His participants concentrate on getting things done in this world
without compromising their moral beliefs. The result is an ideal of dialogue with a direct tie
to the juridical, political, and economic conversations familiar to American law teachers.

b. *Communicative action and corporate law*

The distinction between instrumental and communicative action can be brought to an everyday legal subject like corporate law with instructive results. The exercise helps explain and justify the doctrine's diverse substance and mediative operation.

Corporate law guides and constrains instrumental action. It directs corporate actors, and makes available a structure in which corporate actors can exercise directive power over one another. Corporate law also includes, and results from, conversations. In our society, corporate power depends to some extent on ongoing consent. This approving consensus stays in place in time as corporations' many constituents make and deal with corporate law. When people talk about how corporations should be governed and what the duties of corporate actors should be, they take part in the ongoing endorsement of corporate power.[13] Corporate law, viewed as a result of this conversation, is a residuum of events of communicative action. It may be conceived as a dialogue, in part.

Since assent to corporate institutions manifests itself through communication over time, in practice it never coalesces around a permanent and universal set of ideas. Accordingly, the law and legal theory connected with the consensus cannot be expected to take the form wholly of tight and consistent deductions from first principles. The law nevertheless contains extended sequences meeting the standards of instrumental rationality. These follow from the ever-present corporate marching order to go out and produce cheaply. But this basic order is executed in a multitude of contexts and among a multitude of participants. In a democratic environment we therefore also expect to see routine departures from the instrumental pattern, and may be able to justify them with standards of communicative rationality.

We begin to see why diverse principles persist in corporate law and theory, and why corporate law has a mediative aspect that follows from sensitivity to this diversity. And we hear an unexpected note of consequentialist urgency. Corporate law, by accepting disagreement on norms as an integral part of social and economic life, thereby helps us live with institutions despite disagreement. Corporate law must encompass entity and contract, fiduciary and contract, state and contract, trust and agency, self-interest and co-operation, welfare and goodwill, mandate and facilitation, so as to serve as a nexus of communicative action that contributes to corporate institutional stability.[14]

---

[13] The objective of this conversation, ultimately, is general assent to a vision of appropriate corporate conduct.

[14] Reference to communicative action also reinforces the traditional conception of the fiduciary duty, which amalgamates welfarism and an ethic of goodwill. The picture of instrumental and communicative action presupposes a human actor oriented towards

This dialogic justification of conventional corporate law has obvious limitations. Perfect consensus occurs only in theory. Legal conversations, moreover, are a far from ideal vehicle even for an imperfect consensus. Conversations about legal doctrine proceed subject to substantial restraints. First, participants in doctrinal conversations take limited, tradition-bound roles. They assume a posture of neutrality, treat reifications as realities, and so on (Ackerman 1989: 12; 1980: 61–2, 333–4).[15] Ethics operates in these conversations, but shows up only indirectly.[16] Second, the stylized and professional nature of the conversation limits opportunities for participation. But, despite the constraints, the talk nevertheless includes a range of perspectives and goes on in a number of venues. We have a proliferation of law-making agencies, governmental and quasi-governmental. In academic venues, corporate legal theory now includes some economics. In other venues, we seem to have a lot of corporate lawyers talking to clients about corporate law. Corporate matters also figure into popular politics.

c. Primary and supplemental elements of doctrine

Let us return to the hypothetical costly fiduciary constraint, and assume that for most people most of the time economic welfare determines the appropriate regulatory decision. In nine out of ten such cases the welfarist result obtains, and no noticeable controversy follows. Given the normative power of consensus, a question arises. Why not change the result in the tenth case, and erase all elements of fiduciary law that do not work as instruments in the production of maximum wealth? We thereby achieve consistency. And, even though the result in the tenth case now fails to garner a consensus, in the long run views may change.

A number of responses meet this proposition. For one thing, dialogue remains valuable in all ten cases. The members of the hypothetical welfarist consensus may need to participate in the dialogue to reconfirm their position as times change and events occur. Furthermore, those outside of the consensus are nevertheless members of the polity that makes this welfarist law. Like a judge rendering a written, reasoned opinion, the consensus has to explain and justify its position to the outsiders through this

agreement with others as well as pursuit of self-interest (see Habermas 1989: 179). The conventional fiduciary duty presupposes a similarly modelled person.

[15] 'Neutrality' here refers to the character of the conversation, not to that of consequences (Ackerman 1980: 61).

[16] Thus the corporate law judge making an ethical assertion will probably cite Cardozo's 'punctilio of an honour the most sensitive' language before sermonizing directly (see *Meinard* v *Salmon*, 1928). Our ambivalence toward business morality results in a division of function. Sermonizing about the good is professionalized, and assigned to places of worship. There, moralizing proceeds without the force of positive law and without immediate financial consequences for dereliction of duty.

conversation. In so doing, it recognizes the legitimacy of the outside position and those who hold it.[17]

People may also have inner conflicts that need sorting out through conversation. Law, to the extent it stems from political communications, has a wide base of values and principles. Participants on both sides of a legal issue may subscribe to all the principles that diverge over it. In the case of corporate duties, for example, cost does not become the sole pertinent value, because of the constant political possibility of a situation in which the public chooses to sacrifice wealth in favour of some other value. By thus opening the law to the whole body of values, we sacrifice its consistency. But we do so in order to make law cohere with the values in play in the outside political community.

The result is that a complex of primary and secondary or 'supplemental', normative elements can combine to make up an area of law. The supplemental elements accompany the law's primary norms. They do not often determine results; but they do cause many dialogues. And the dialogues have consequences, even if they do not change results.[18]

Corporate law has several notorious and problematic supplemental strains. One is its internal public interest component. This has only two generally accepted zones of outcome determination, the charitable contribution privilege (see, e.g. *A.P. Smith Manufacturing* v. *Barlow*, 1953; ALI 1984 and the duty to obey the law (Ryan 1991:413). Otherwise you can find it cited in the outcome of only a handful of famous cases (*Schlensky* v. *Wrigley*, 1968; *Herald Co.* v. *Seawell*, 1972; *Paramount Communications* v. *Time, Inc.*, 1989; Millon 1990: 251–61). But, performing a critical function, it persists and gets a lot of attention. Corporate law's persistent but ineffectual strain of creditor-protective doctrine is another supplemental strain (Bratton 1989b). The duty of care can also be cited. A negligence directive, it works well in its accepted sphere only to the extent that it almost never results in liability. In effect, then, it operates as a legal formality that includes a negligence liability principle in a supplemental, largely rhetorical position.

In the case of fiduciary duties, ethical values can be seen in this supplemental posture in the subgroup of situations in which no easily articulated co-operative wealth-maximization story supports restraint of self-interested pursuits. Sovereign enforcement of an ethic of goodwill is problematic in these situations. But, so long as the ethical value is left in a supplemental posture, the only thing mandated is a legal conversation: the law makes us talk about the good, but does not force us to impose

---

[17] Habermas (1989: 45) rightly argues that the degree of solidarity and growth of welfare are not the only indicators of the quality of communal life. He notes that equal consideration to the interests of each person is also important.

[18] Constancy of enforcement is not a cogent normative standard (cf. Handler 1988: 1026).

it.[19] The regulatory 'consequence' is that the lawyers become ministers to a congregation of business persons. The business actor who turns around and engages in questionable maximizing on Monday morning has already been deemed culpable, even though no one imposes the violent apparatus of legal enforcement.

The anti-business activist makes an understandable objection to all this: fiduciary sermons without enforcement consequences have no point. Two responses can be made. First, the supplemental doctrine lends normative legitimacy to the activist's cause. In business contexts it takes a very strong consensus about the culpability of conduct to support enforcement. Such a consensus supports most applications of corporate fiduciary law. The ongoing presence of ethical values in fiduciary law, albeit in a posture short of enforcement, serves the activist by making change conceivable and legitimate. If the activist builds a new consensus, the law's normative structure easily accommodates it. Second, doctrinal conversations can be seen as nascent events of sovereign constraint. Where the law has a complex texture, the cautious, self-serving actor who approaches its edge has to consult a lawyer. Depending on the actor's aversion to legal risk, actual constraint may occur at this point. Even if the actor is counselled to go forward, the attorney-client encounter has resulted in a dialogic playing out of the ethical problem, albeit one couched in terms of legal uncertainty.[20] The maximizing actor, forced to suffer this conversation in order to get a full risk-return projection, is disempowered.

3. PUBLIC VALUES AND PRIVATE BUSINESS

The hypothetical costly fiduciary restraint presupposes a conflict of values inside and outside the corporation. Such conflicts arise because corporate relationships tend to be informed by different values than are relationships in outside communities. Corporate associates share common ends, and corporate associations give rise to feelings of goodwill with ethical implications. But corporations are, for the most part, instrumental associ-

[19] The proxy rule on shareholder proposals might also be discussed at this point and in this framework (Rule 14a-8, 17 C.F.R. sect. 240.14a-8 (1990). This rule mandates access to proxy statements for purposes of encouraging dialogue on ethical and policy questions. It does so at a cost (Securities Exchange Act, Rel. No. 19135 (1982) (Appendix)), with no immediate beneficial consequences.

[20] An analogy can be drawn to the division of lawyers' rules of professional conduct into disciplinary rules and ethical considerations. Simon notes that the ethical considerations perform the valuable function of acknowledging the appropriateness of conduct left within the zone of autonomy (Simon 1988: 1133). Couching the lesson in doctrinal terms may lessen its momentary force as an ethical performance while enhancing the power of the operative ethic. Lodged as a presupposition to a 'legal' conversation, the ethic avoids the debilitating effects of lying on the moral side of the law/morality distinction.

ations. They do not give rise to strong community ties constitutive of the member's self-understanding. Very little of anyone's personal identity becomes staked in investor–manager relationships, for example.[21] In contrast, relationships in stronger communities define the participant's identity (Sandel 1982: 146–50), at least to some extent (Handler 1988: 1071–2). And they do so dialogically;—the individual finds himself or herself through dialogue with others. We should expect participants in these stronger communities to value solidarity more highly than participants in less closely intertwined associational situations. The upshot is that the same standards of loyalty that operate outside corporations may not operate inside. Moreover, outsiders not fully conversant with differences between corporations and outside communities may easily over-react to self-interested behaviour by corporate actors.

But it does not follow that corporate law should follow only from inside values. Corporate law is not an entirely 'private' proposition, even though it tends to lie on the private side of the broader continuum of public and private law. No corporate legal matter is 'inside' in an absolute sense. Corporate actors ask for public endorsement of their arrangements when they turn to courts for enforcement. Corporate law conversations, like all legal conversations, are public events.[22] The legal context and public audience transform the discourse, even if the substance may be plausibly characterized as contractual. This public aspect results in inspection in terms of public values. This extends even to the insular Delaware-based corporate law system.

Viewed from this public perspective, corporate law exists for its participants as regulation and dialogue, and for the rest of the public as performance. It is at this performative level that corporate law does or does not integrate smoothly with the fabric of life in the stronger communities outside. Corporate cases, statutes, litigation documents, law review articles, and legislative discussions interplay with the values of actors outside.

---

[21] The particular 'community' relationship operating within a corporation will depend on the position of the particular participant. Bondholders and stockholders of public corporations, looking for return on investment and nothing else, will see their participation as instrumental. Stockholders or creditors of close corporations may have personal ties that transform the relationship into one of common endeavour.

Officers and employees of public corporations presumably have a shifting combination of instrumental and sentimental ties. Here the question arises as to whether the employment relationship is constitutive in the strong sense. Assumptions along these lines inform the movement to constrain employment at will (see, e.g., Cornell 1990). A normative individualist might respond that no one should permit so much self-respect to be tied to a particular position as to permit the relationship to become constitutive. At least since the disappearance of the 'realist' theory of corporate existence current during the first three decades of this century (see Bratton 1989b: 1490–91), corporate law and theory have stayed close to the individualist norm.

[22] And, of course, we continue to hold to the formality of state creation. On the public/private distinction and corporate law (Bratton 1989c: 436–38).

When people look at law, any law, they expect it to confirm their sense of the right and the good. A performance of corporate law that has this effect has enhanced legitimacy. Contrariwise, the proponent of corporate legal performance that offers no recognition of values strongly held outside bears an additional burden of persuasion. The ethic of goodwill may survive in corporate doctrine in part due to outside community notions of loyal behaviour in co-operative situations. On this theory, the mandatory aspect of fiduciary rules contributes to a harmony of values. In the long run this enhances the political legitimacy of corporate ventures.

Of course, acknowledging that the law recognizes public values does not 'decide the case' of a particular costly constraint. But the acknowledgement assists the analysis. The welfarist position against the regulation also draws on public values. The implicit assertion is that people want wealth; any value-laden regulation that inhibits wealth creation subverts the public choice for wealth. And it does so in order to recognize the values of an élite group (Kronman 1989: 1754): if we block action that maximizes wealth, we deny recognition to those who lack wealth. This connection between wealth, public values, and production assures that most internally generated corporate norms do not conflict with outside community values.

But noting a connection between wealth and public values only begins discussion of the matters of identity and recognition at stake in the public law of corporations. In a world of scarcity, we each lack wealth in different degrees. Therefore, distributional questions come up whenever wealth maximization is advanced as a public value. Economic welfarism, pursued in the institutional context of American corporate law, accords full recognition only to those situated inside the structure of corporate production as beneficiaries and to those who identify with those thus situated. This leaves, potentially, a large number of people on the outside of a purely welfarist corporate law system. Many outside may still hold values which privilege maximization, exclusive of distributional concerns. Many outside may also be satisfied with the present structure of distribution. But obvious room for discussion remains. Depending on the distribution and, importantly, the public's sense of the distribution, an outside consensus plausibly could coalesce for a constraint that disempowers corporate insiders over a contrary rule that maximizes wealth.[23]

[23] Disempowerment may be one of the 'public' values. Those outside experience an enhancement of their freedom when they watch insiders being constrained. Significantly, 'freedom' and 'autonomy' do not come up as values in many contemporary corporate law discussions (see Kronman 1989: 1753). But they have an implied presence. Sufferance of corporations implies an acceptance of diminished freedom in producing relationships in exchange for more wealth. The alternatives set out in corporate jurisprudence offer different concepts for integrating the constraints of organizational participation with political values, democratic or liberal, as the case may be.

Tensions between corporate values and outside values will persist. So long as wealth creation depends on peoples' drive to maximize for themselves and distribution remains uneven, the business corporation will not be an institution fully satisfactory to those outside it. Corporate law mediates this difference. As it does so, it accords considerable respect to those who invest their financial and human capital in corporations. Corporate actors have a substantial zone of discretion. Occasional costly reductions of this discretion do not necessarily negate the base of respect.

3
The Many-Headed Hydra: Networks as Higher-Order Collective Actors

GUNTHER TEUBNER

I. FAR-EASTERN SECRETS

Alarm about the Japanese invasion of Western markets has been exacerbated by the realization that the Japanese are using downright organizational monsters. Evidently the Japanese strategies operate not only through prices and quality, but at the same time through new types of 'organizational weapons'. Western observers, taken aback, record the use of hybrid organizations—'something between market and organization' (Thorelli 1986)—that cannot be fitted into the usual organizational patterns of Western practice and theory. The Japanese *keiretsu*, an aggressive group of vertically co-operating Japanese firms, behaves as a hybrid between organization and market. Here a core firm controls tightly linked supply and distribution networks without having any equity ownership in the supply and distribution firms (Imai and Itami 1984; Gerlach 1989). Such intermediary organizations operate in Japan not only in the production sphere, but particularly in the R & D sector, in the relations among banks and other firms, and even in the links between government and private firms (Dore 1987). The secret of Japanese success seems to depend in no small measure on this 'third arena of allocation', which is of enormously greater scale in Japan than in the West (Twaalhoven and Hattori 1982; Imai, *et al.* 1985; Kaneko and Imai 1987; Wolf 1990: 106.).

In the West there has been increasing interest in such hybrid organizations, both in organizational practice and in academic analysis (see the surveys in Jarillo 1988; Hollingsworth 1990; Lorenzoni 1990; W.W. Powell 1990). Some of these networks have a long tradition in 'organized capitalism', but some, such as 'just-in-time' supply networks (see Nagel 1989), have come about only as a direct response to the Japanese challenge. Today decentralized conglomerates, multi-divisional firms with autonomous 'profit centres', joint ventures in the R & D area, strategic

Translation from the German by Iain Fraser, Florence. I would like to thank Dirk Baecker, Hugh Collins, Michael Hutter, Renate Mayntz, Sol Picciotto, Fritz Scharpf, Philip Selznick, Sean Smith, and Oliver Williamson for their constructive critique.

alliances, franchising networks and other distribution systems, contractually organized supply systems, systems for cashless transactions through banks, major building projects on a subcontracting basis, organizational networks in the energy, water, transport, and telecommunications sectors are some prominent Western correlates of the Japanese 'interpenetration of market and organization'.

Renate Mayntz even goes so far as to identify networks as a key factor in societal modernization: 'Obligatory and "promotional" networks in the economy, political and infrastructural networks—these parallel developments suggest that the emergence of interorganizational networks is a concomitant of structural change in modern societies; it seems to be a basic characteristic of societal modernization' (Mayntz 1992: 21).

Though network research and transaction cost economics have since done yeoman service in investigating the specific features, causes, and consequences of such hybrid organizations, there are still major questions left open. What has been gained if networks are merely described metaphorically as 'complex arrays of relationships among firms' (Johanson and Mattson 1989) or as 'managed economic systems' (MacMillan and Farmer 1979)? Is it sufficient to locate them along a continuum between contract and organization (Williamson 1985: 83; W.W. Powell 1987)? And if we characterize them, by contrast, as being 'neither markets nor hierarchies' (W.W. Powell 1990; Williamson 1991*a*), what is their *differentia specifica*? Does one do justice to their organizational nature simply by stressing the relational character of contractual arrangements? Should one speak only of networks among corporate actors (Schneider 1988), or could one also speak of networks as corporate actors? And how is one to deal in both theory and practice with negative externalities that are characteristic of networks?

I will attempt to employ the theory of autopoiesis, as developed by Humberto Maturana and Francisco Varela (1980), Heinz von Förster (1985), and Niklas Luhmann (forthcoming), to find answers to these questions. This theory explains the appearance of new organizational forms as an emergence of self-referentially constituted units. I shall set up the following three theses for discussion:

(1) Networks constitute themselves as genuine emergent phenomena, not *between*, but *beyond* contract and organization. The self-organization of networks as higher-order autopoietic systems is accomplished through 're-entry' of the institutionalized distinction between market and organization into the area which that distinction defines. A 'double attribution' of action results from this as the *differentia specifica* of networks.

(2) Networks are not just relations between several autonomous corporate actors, but are themselves 'corporate actors' of a special nature. As

'polycorporate collectives', they are in fact personified webs of relationships with a special capacity for collective action which is constituted among the nodes of the nets.

(3) Networks, whose efficiency gains are based on an intelligent combination of market and hierarchy, also have a dark side. They create specific transactional risks. Their externalization brings them (illegitimate) cost advantages. Appropriate internalization seems possible through novel legal mechanisms of simultaneous multiple attribution of responsibility.

2. EMERGENCE THROUGH SELF-ORGANIZATION

In what sense is it possible in the case of communicative networks to speak of 'emergence through self-organization'? The term 'emergence' is commonly used to denote the appearance of something new in an evolutionary process, or to express the fact that the whole is more than the sum of its parts (Hastedt 1988: 175, and sources cited there). According to Popper and Eccles (1977: 22), emergence refers 'to the fact that in the course of evolution new things and events occur, with unexpected and indeed unpredictable properties'. The theory of self-organization breaks with this tradition of 'emergence from below'. The idea of emergence from below, which presupposes that new properties emerge from the interaction of given elements, is discredited simply by the fact that properties and interactions are not separable (Roth and Schwegler 1990: 39). But if this is so, then emergence becomes trivial: everything is emergent. Moreover, the idea of elements existing 'in themselves' is presumably untenable too. In the theory of self-organizing systems, the concept of an element makes sense only in relation to a system. It specifies the ultimate unit only for that system, which in no way excludes its being broken down in other system contexts (Luhmann forthcoming: ch. 5, sect. 1).

In the theoretical context of self-organization, emergence takes on another meaning. Emergence appears when, in a given constellation, self-referential circles loop together in such a way as to form new elements which constitute a new system. The theory of self-organization thus gives a specific answer to the central question that has remained unanswered even in the recent ambitious emergence theories of Popper and Eccles (1977) and Bunge (1980); namely, how a process of gradual change makes the qualitative leap into autonomy (Hastedt 1988: 186). The answer is self-reference. Self-reference leads to the regrouping of given material in such a way as to allow both new elements and new systems to come about which are autonomous *vis-à-vis* the previously existing constellation. The evolution of self-referential relations is to be understood as a gradual process leading to the formation of new and at the same time autonomous systems (on this gradualization, see Roth 1987: 400; Stichweh 1987: 152.; Teubner 1987a: 430.; Teubner 1993: ch. 3; conversely, Maturana and Varela 1980: 301; Luhmann 1985: 22).

I will analyse the emergence of communicative networks in the framework of the theory of autopoiesis, which separates different levels of emergence (organic, neuronal, mental, and social autopoiesis). I cannot discuss the background here in detail (see Luhmann, forthcoming: ch. 1, sect. II). The ultimate elements of networks are, correspondingly, not human actors, as is mostly assumed in theories of personal networks (Tichy 1981; Birley 1985: 113; Mueller 1986; Kaneko and Imai 1987), but communications. And what is involved in the emergence of networks is the autonomization of social processes not *vis-à-vis* human actors, but within the sphere of social phenomena themselves (Sapelli 1992: 89). Communication systems become autonomized from other communication systems. This means asserting that even within the same phenomenal sphere, the formation of higher-level self-reproducing systems is possible (cf. Roth 1987, on the one hand, and Teubner 1987a: 430, on the other). This requires distinguishing within a phenomenal sphere among autopoietic systems of different orders. Society as the ensemble of human communications is to be regarded as a first-order social system. Second-order social systems emerge when specialized communications within society become differentiated and linked up in systems with their own identities. If a further interlinking of specialized communications comes about within these systems, then third-order social systems form, and so forth. The phenomenon of emergence will be demonstrated in the case of networks at the level of the second- and third-order differentiation of autopoietic systems.

3. BEYOND CONTRACT AND ORGANIZATION

The currently dominant conception of networks and other hybrid arrangements (such as relational contracts and joint ventures) certainly looks rather different. Generally it is used to denote a decentrally regulated relation of co-operation among autonomous actors (Schneider 1988: 9; Kenis and Schneider 1991: 26). These loose forms of co-operation are no longer mere transient interactions; but at the same time, they do not yet display the dense co-operation of formal organizations. This concept of 'no longer, but at the same time not yet' was already dominant in the 'organization set' with which sociologists studied inter-organizational relationships (Evan 1966; Aldrich and Whetten 1981). In group sociology, concepts such as 'personal networks' were used to refer to forms of co-operation that do not have the density, nor the bureaucratic drawbacks, of formal organization (Tichy 1981; Mueller 1986). Their influence can again be found in the idea of 'policy networks' used by political scientists to analyse, among other things, neo-corporatist forms of co-ordination (Hanf and Scharpf 1978; Trasher 1983: 375; Lehmbruch 1985: 285–303, Sharpe 1985: 361; Marin and Mayntz 1991*b*).

The ideas in economics are not much different. They start from the position that actors select institutional arrangements according to cost/benefit calculations. 'Act so that the maxims of your will can always at the same time serve to minimize transaction costs', runs the new categorical imperative. 'Minimize transaction costs!' decides whether actors conclude a contract or set up an organization (Williamson 1985). There are no fundamental differences between contract and organization, since organizations, too, should be seen as contractual arrangements through which the payment flows pass smoothly (Grossman and Hart 1986). According to the extreme neoclassical version, organizations do not differ 'in the slightest degree from ordinary market contracting between two people' (Alchian and Demsetz 1972: 777). According to the more moderate institutionalist version, they differ only in the governance structures, which are intended essentially to control opportunistic behaviour (Williamson 1985). Recently, this version has become even more moderate, stressing the difference between contractual 'autonomy' and organizational 'co-ordination' as a reaction to environmental disturbances. However, networks are still seen as intermediate between contract and organization. (Williamson 1991*a*: 277, 281). Hybrid arrangements are chosen at a point on this scale where, on the one hand, market controls are weak because of the asset specificity of the transaction, and on the other the transaction costs of fully integrated organization are too high (Williamson 1985: 83; Thorelli 1986; W.W. Powell 1987).

I do not object to the practice of comparing institutional arrangements from cost viewpoints—but I object strongly to an attempt to level the distinction between contract and organization! Here it is the constraints of economic thinking that prevail, interpreting every social arrangement as a hypothetical contract between rational actors. This explains the almost compulsive subsumption of formal organizations under the category of contract (organization as a nexus of contracts) and the concomitant claim that the organization 'has no power of fiat, no authority, no disciplinary action any different' from contracting (Alchian and Demsetz 1972: 777). The result is, as Herbert Simon claims, an irresponsible reductionism: 'The attempts of the new institutional economics to explain organizational behaviour solely in terms of agency, asymmetric information, transaction costs, opportunism, and other concepts drawn from neoclassical economics, ignore key organizational mechanisms like authority,

identification, and coordination, and hence are seriously incomplete'
(H.A. Simon 1991: 43).

By contrast with such reductionist positions, it is here assumed that
'contract' and 'organization' each represent separate second-order
autopoietic social systems, which differ from each other in principle, and
not merely in the degree of intensity of their governance structures.
'Networks' too, then, are not merely an intermediate, but a stepped-up
form of a special nature. Networks 'are neither fish nor fowl, nor some
mongrel hybrid, but a distinctly different form' (W.W. Powell 1990: 299).
But why does it make sense to see them as 'symbiotic contracts', as an
institutional arrangement of a third type clearly differing from classical
contract and classical organization (Schanze 1991)?

For formal organizations, I have shown elsewhere in detail how their
self-reproductive autonomy comes about through processes of spontaneous self-organization (Teubner 1988a; 1988b). Accordingly, here only
the result will be mentioned. Organizations emerge from diffuse interaction where communication processes in the interaction itself reflexively
constitute the components of boundary ('membership'), element ('decision'), structure ('norm'), and identity ('collective'). If these components
are linking together in a hypercycle, especially if 'membership' and 'norm'
and if 'collective' and 'decision' are mutually constituting each other, then
the formal organization has developed into a self-producing system. By
comparison with simple interaction, formal organization is an emergent
phenomenon, since formal organization constitutes self-referentially new
types of system components, and links these up with each other in circular fashion.

Contracts are in turn not simple building blocks of organizations, as
institutional economics suggests. Rather, they are built on a fundamentally
different type of action, and the two cannot be reduced to one another:
exchange is distinct from co-operation (Teubner 1979: 719; 1993: ch. 7,
Sect. II, see also Luhmann 1988b: 101; forthcoming; ch. 9, Sect. VI). While
organizations are formalized relations of co-operation, contracts are formalized relations of exchange. In contract, too, there is a process of gradual autonomization from a merely informal interaction to a highly
formalized arrangement. In simple interactional exchange, there is as yet
no duty of performance on the partners that can be said to exist 'in itself'.
It is only with the first performance by one of them that the expectation of
exchange on the other's part, on the basis of diffuse social norms, arises.
The great achievement of modern formal contract lies in the fact that it
has self-generated duties of performance that arise without prior performance by the other party. They arise on the basis of the conclusion of the
contract, as an act that self-referentially constitutes itself in the interaction
(on the sociology of the contract, see Köndgen 1981: 97; Schmid 1983).

Contract as a self-reproductive unit emerges via self-referential constitution of its components. Elements of contract are no longer mere diffuse communications of social exchange, but become reflexively defined as formalized 'contractual acts' (conclusion of the contract, breach of contract, change of contract, completion of contract). They emerge against the background of normative structures that have become autonomized from mere general social norms into self-generated 'contractual norms'. The identity of the social relationship is no longer determined by mere presence of the participants in the interaction, but is temporally extended through their definition as 'parties to the contract'. The process is no longer determined by the mere course of the interaction, but by the life history of the contractual relationship itself (for a systemic interpretation of contract, see Parsons and Smelser 1956: 104, 143; Teubner 1980: 44; Schmidt 1985, 1989; and for its autopoietic radicalization, see Deggau 1987; Teubner 1993: ch. 6).

Hypercyclical linkages can also be shown in contract. Of prime importance is the self-reproducing linkage of 'contractual act' and 'contractual norm', which constitutes a separate type of modern norm production alongside mere co-ordination of behaviour, legislation, judge-made law, and rule making in formal organization. In contrast to formal organizations, however, contracts do not have other forms of hypercyclical linkage. In contract there is no comparable autonomy of the social relation as such *vis-à-vis* persons, which is achieved in formal organizations through linking boundary and structure. By comparison with changing the members of an organization, changing contractual parties is very much harder, even in highly formalized contracts. And completely absent in contract is any collectivization, such as would be achieved in an organization through the cyclical linkage of identity and action.

Contract and organization are, then, second-order autopoietic systems based on different types of action—exchange and co-operation. Hence, it is no longer sufficient to locate networks between contract and organization, characterized by 'semi-strong' incentives, by an 'intermediate' degree of administrative apparatus, by 'semi-strong' adaptations, and by a 'semi-legalistic' contract law (Williamson 1991a: 281). Networks are higher-order autopoietic systems beyond contract and organization. Their intrinsic logic can be seen only once networks are viewed not as transitional forms in a grey area that throws doubt in principle on the clear distinction between contract and organization, but instead as enhanced forms of them that presuppose their clear distinction. Such enhanced forms can be organized only where the distinction between contract and organization that underlies them is solidly institutionalized, and can then be used to build up the system of the networks. Their principle is not de-differentiation of market and hierarchy, but maintenance of their differentiation plus an internal reduplication.

4. NETWORKS AS HIGHER-ORDER AUTOPOIETIC SOCIAL SYSTEMS

Our approach finds its starting-point in a specific form of 'market failure' and 'organizational failure' (Imai and Itami 1984: 298) that refers to the precarious relation between variety and redundancy. 'Variety will be used to denote the multiplicity of the elements of a system, and redundancy for the extent to which once one knows one element one can guess others without being dependent on further information. These are two different but not strictly opposite measures of complexity'. (Luhmann 1987: 47–8, 1988*a*; taking up from Atlan 1979).

Purely market-based contractual relations display relatively high variety with relatively low redundancy. On the one hand, they are extremely flexible, changeable, and innovative; on the other, they develop little long-term orientation, forcefulness, coherence, and accumulated experience. While the invention of formal organization was able to solve such problems of insufficient redundancy, this was done only at the expense of variety. Rigidity, bureaucracy, problems of motivation, lack of innovation, and high information costs are notorious problems, not only of government organizations, but also and specifically of private firms. The redundancy failures that plague large organizations are 'inability to respond quickly to competitive changes in international markets; resistance to process innovations . . . and systematic resistance to the introduction of new products' (W.W. Powell 1990: 319).

The sense of having missed opportunities, then, is the most important stimulus to a new experiment with institutional arrangements. It is not the calculated action of rational actors, but the uncoordinated interplay of evolutionary mechanisms—variation by trial and error; selection by competition and power; retention by institutionalization—which evaluates this experiment and its success. It is at this point that networks emerge. They bring about the re-entry of an institutionalized distinction into that which it distinguishes (Spencer Brown 1969). Networks, as third-order autopoietic systems, result from a re-entry of the distinction between market and hierarchy into market, on the one hand, and hierarchy, on the other. In the words of the Japanese masters Imai and Itami: 'Market principles penetrate into the firm's resource allocation and organization principles creep into the market allocation. Interpenetration occurs to remedy the failure of pure principles either in the market or in the organization' (Imai and Itami 1984: 285).

Contract and organization are based on the institutionalized distinction between market and hierarchy. Organizations are defined by their boundary to the market; contractual arrangements are defined by their contrast with formal organizations. Problems in the mix between variety and redundancy mean that contracts seek to make up for their shortage of redundancy by incorporating organizational elements into themselves. Similarly, formal organizations experiment with the introduction of market elements. In this experimental interplay of de-differentiations and fluid transitions, networks in a narrower sense are an interesting special case (W.W. Powell 1990; Mayntz 1992: 24). They steadfastly hold to the arrangement chosen, but at the same time, and on the basis of this arrangement, firmly institutionalize the counter-principle. Within the arrangement defined by the institutionalized distinction between contract and organization, the distinction between contract and organization is institutionalized once more. Contracts incorporate organizational elements into themselves, and organizations are permeated by market elements. Networks are thus in a position to distinguish institutionally between the language of organization and the language of contract. The result is the 'dual constitution' of contract and organization in one institutional arrangement.

	DIFFERENCE	RE-ENTRY
MARKET	contract	market network (e.g., supply systems, franchising, bank transactions)
HIERARCHY	organization	organization network (e.g., conglomerates, joint ventures)

It is this dual constitution that comprises the emergent phenomenon. The decisive step towards the self-organization of networks is the production of a new self-description of their elementary acts and then to link these up operationally. A 'network operation' as a new elementary act emerges from the twofold social attribution of actions: every communicative event in the network is attributed both to one of the autonomous parties to the contract and simultaneously to the organization as a whole. My consumption of a juicy hamburger is accompanied by this sort of magical double act: the transaction of the franchisee on the motorway and that of MacDonalds themselves. And the local manager in a multinational firm speaks with a double tongue: on behalf of the national subsidiary and at the same time on behalf of the headquarters in the far-off USA.

'Network operations' are thus emergent phenomena, by comparison with mere 'contractual acts' on the one hand and mere 'organizational decisions' on the other, in so far as they refer to contract and organization at one fell swoop. They can be reduced neither to market transactions nor to organizational decisions. If the dual attribution of action enters into the self-description of the social arrangement and is also used operationally there, then the network has constituted itself as an autonomous system of action via the constitution of new elementary acts.

The dual constitution which we found in its elementary acts is repeated in the network structure. Every network operation must simultaneously meet the structural requirements of both the contract between the individual actors and of the network organization as a whole. The resulting dual structure governing individual operations constitutes the specific feature of the 'network system'. By contrast with contract and organization, networks are higher-order autopoietic systems, to the extent that they set up emergent elementary acts ('network operations') through dual attribution, and link these up in circular fashion into an operational system.

This makes simultaneous enhancement of the contractual and the organizational dimension possible. We are used to treating the interplay between contractual and organizational components as a zero-sum game, in which one side always wins at the expense of the other. In moving from short-term spot-market transactions, via relational contracts and loosely organized partnerships, to integrated large organizations, we regularly observe that organizational elements gain weight precisely to the extent that contractual elements lose it. Networks cannot be accommodated along this scale, since in them contractual and organizational components gain importance simultaneously. As the example of franchising shows, in networks both the collective nature (system character, marketing co-operation, unity of image, competitive unity) and the individual character (local autonomy and profit orientation of the selling points) can be simultaneously heightened to the extreme (see Martinek 1987: 121).

The result of this enhancement of contrary principles is a remarkable self-regulation of the network, based on the twofold orientation of action. In economic terms, all transactions are oriented simultaneously towards the network's profit and the profit of the individual actor (profit sharing). This double orientation works as a constraint, since all transactions must pass the double test. At the same time it works as an incentive, since network advantages are bound up with individual advantages. Through cleverly devised incentives and penalties, individual contractual clauses seek to ensure that the double orientation actually affects the actors' motives (Dnes 1988; 1991: 135). The economic nub of franchising, by comparison with, say, distributive networks in an integrated firm, even with internal incentive programmes, lies in the franchisee's 'residual claim' (for a particularly clear, empirically based study, see Norton 1988). Due to savings on monitoring costs, the residual claim is regularly higher than comparable incentives in distribution networks of integrated firms (see Rubin 1978; Brickley and Dark 1987: 411; Dnes 1991: 134). Economists analyse this twofold orientation in terms of 'principal–agent incentives' and 'information incentives' (Norton 1988: 202; see also Klein and Saft 1985; Mathewson and Winter 1985).

Correspondingly, in a network one must start from the co-existence of collective and individual goals (Sapelli 1992: 98). This is in clear contradiction to the idea widespread among lawyers that the participants have either contrary interests—an exchange contract—or else common interests—an association (e.g. Larenz 1987: sect. 60 I). In networks, individual actions are simultaneously and cumulatively oriented both to the common goal and to the individual goals of the members, though no normative primacy of one orientation or the other can be assumed. Networks pursue collective goals 'through collaboration without abrogating the separate identity and personality of the cooperating partners' (W.W. Powell 1990: 315). Here lies the decisive distinction from relational contracting, on the one hand, which gives primacy to the pursuit of individual as against joint goals, and to loose forms of co-operation, on the other, where common goals are given primacy. Polycentrism and multi-polarity are, then, characteristics of the unified network (Lorenzoni 1990).

The advantages of double attribution become especially relevant when the problem arises of how to adapt to outside disturbances. If one does not take double attribution into account, hybrids seem to be very weak in their adaptability. The reason is that 'hybrid adaptations cannot be made unilaterally (as with market governance) or by fiat (as with hierarchy) but require mutual consent' (Williamson 1991*a*: 291). The opposite result is to be expected, however, if one takes double attribution into account. Double attribution gives hybrids a synergistic advantage in adaption to disturbances, which makes them superior to both contract and organization. The reason is that the proportion of the blend of market and organization is not fixed. It can vary according to strategic viewpoints. In the case of outside disturbances, network management can choose—and can change this choice over time—whether the hybrid should react as a whole or whether the nodes should react autonomously. In contrast to both contract and organization, which dispose of one stabilizing mechanism, this pattern characterizes the network as a multi-stable system (Pausenberger 1975: 2243). In networks, market and hierarchy can be used alternatively as well as complementarily (Kirchner 1985: 226). A 'navigational rule' which is not available either to contract or to organization becomes a principle built into the hybrid organizational form. To change organizational form, as a chameleon changes its colour, is an adaptive mechanism of the hybrid. Choosing the colour that fits the environment is one of the main tasks of network management.

5. ORGANIZATION NETWORKS AND MARKET NETWORKS

Two types of networks can be distinguished, according to which side of the basic distinction, market or organization, is primary. 'Organization networks' emerge where formal organizations repeat within themselves, inside their own boundaries, the internal differentiation of the economy into a formally organized sphere and a spontaneous sphere. Decentralized corporate groups of the multi-divisional form are the most significant innovation in this sphere, the latest form of which is developing into 'network groups' (Sapelli 1990).

As stated above, they respond to shortfalls of redundancy in large organizations by seeking to increase the extent of variety within the organization through three strategies (for more details, see Teubner 1993: ch. 7). (1) Direct hierarchical control is replaced by indirect contextual control of autonomous sub-units by the centre (general group policy, management personnel policy, indirect profit control; see Hedlund 1981; Scheffler 1987: 469; van den Bulcke 1986: 222). (2) Long hierarchical chains are replaced by markets within the organization: the relationship between the group centre and a group company simulates a sort of capital market, alongside which there emerge within the group labour markets, manager markets, resource markets, and product markets. (3) A functional differentiation of the overall organization, leading to inadequate maximization of functional units, is abandoned in favour of segmental differentiation in which the autonomous profit centres have a twofold orientation: their own profit and the profit of the overall organization (Dioguardi 1986; Lorenzoni 1990; Wolf 1990: 114).

'Market networks', by contrast, emerge in the contractually organized sphere (on the interpretation of franchising as a network, see Teubner 1991). They react to shortages of high variety in market-controlled contracts, and seek to increase redundancy by building in elements of organization. The emergence of franchise systems, for instance, can thus be explained by the fact that purely contractual arrangements do not meet the requirements of sales organization (central advertising, supraregional unity of image, decentralized sales, strong local variations) (see Rubin 1978: 223; Mathewson and Winter 1985: 503; Dnes 1991: 134). They provide insufficient incentives to the franchisor to build up and control a unified sales system, and have inadequate control mechanisms against opportunistic behaviour by the franchisees. Additionally, there exist informational asymmetries in respect of local conditions, which cannot be removed by purely contractual mechanisms. These market failures suggest the enhancement of internal incentives and controls and reduction of information asymmetries, by building organizational elements into the contract.

Market networks repeat within their boundaries the differentiation of market and hierarchy. They not only sporadically insert organizational elements into the contract, but systematically build up the contractual nexus itself as a formal organization. Only rarely can such networks be organized spontaneously and without co-ordination. Regularly there is a 'hub firm', a 'focal firm', an *impresa guida*, that plays the leading role in setting it up and in ongoing co-ordination. This specialization in strategy and co-ordination by one of the firms involved may, but need not, be based on a presumed market-power gap (e.g., between market levels: industry-commerce or industry-suppliers). However, network centres which have their basis in an equal division of labour are equally wide-spread (Jarillo 1988; Lorenzoni 1990).

The result of this re-entry of organization into contract is:

Strategic Networks. In these, a hub firm has a special relationship with the other members of the network. Such relationships have most of the characteristics of a hierarchical relationship: relatively unstructured tasks, a long-term point of view, and relatively unspecified contracts. They have all the characteristics of investments, since there is always a certain asset specificity to the know-how of, say, dealing with a given supplier instead of a new one. And yet, the contracting parties remain independent organizations, with few or no points of contact along many of their dimensions (Jarillo 1988).

Contractual networks. These take advantage of the interaction between mechanisms that enhance variety and those that enhance redundancy. It is not a question of a precarious compromise, a balance between the two principles, but one of enhancement. This is presumably where the secret of their success lies, though it can be conceived by economists, in their rich *Weltanschauung*, only as a transaction cost advantage.

By contrast with the usual definitions of networks as loose forms of co-operation, as decentralized co-ordination of autonomous actors, or as transitional forms between contract and organization, we have now arrived at a narrower and at the same time more exact concept of a network. The term should be used if and only if an institutional arrangement is constituted simultaneously as a formal organization and as a contractual relation among autonomous actors. The empirical test for a network is a positive answer to the following two questions: (1) Can twofold attribution of actions to the organization and to the contractual parties actually be shown? (2) Is action subject to the twofold normative requirements of the total organization and the contractual relationship? To assess this, the easiest methods to use are survey techniques measuring attitudes and individual knowledge about the attribution of actions and about the effectiveness of organizational norms and of contractual norms.

A more rigid test would be directly to observe the attribution procedure in cases of both failure and success, and thus to deduce structures of attribution and expectation from actual acts.

It need not be disputed that alongside these very closely defined networks there are other empirical phenomena of loose forms of co-operation that do not meet these strict conditions (W.W. Powell 1990: 305; Mayntz 1992: 24). The point is not the terminology (network, symbiotic contract). The decisive factor is the characterization of a specific empirical phenomenon through the simultaneous twofold attribution of actions to contract and organization. And one should clearly separate the two phenomena: it is one thing to orient action toward an environment which is non-competitive, co-operative, and based on trust; some people call such a non-competitive market a network. It is another thing to formalize an interactive relation which combines contractual and organizational elements. I would prefer to limit the term 'network' to denote this kind of hybrid arrangement.

6. NETWORKS AS CORPORATE ACTORS?

But are networks collective actors? Are decentralized groups of companies capable as such of social responsibility? Can franchise systems develop a corporate identity? Should bundles of mere contracts themselves appear as collective units? Are 'decentralized and informalized organizations . . . emergent collective actors *sui generis*' (Geser 1990: 405; Ladeur 1992: 209)? Do we need a new conceptual tool kit for the collective nature of networks 'when the relations are so long-term and recurrent that it is difficult to speak of the parties as separate entities' and when 'the entangling of obligation and reputation reaches a point that the actions of the parties are interdependent, but there is no common ownership or legal framework' (W.W. Powell 1990: 301)? All these are questions as to the capacity of networks for collective action. They are directed primarily at empirical social research, and of course at the same time at social theory. At any rate, this is not only a problem of legal construction.

The political and moral explosiveness of the collective character of networks should not be underestimated. In no way can it be reduced to cultivating the image of corporate identity. A few years ago the news was splashed across the papers that the Daimler–Benz group was again being confronted with its Nazi past. In the war years, concentration camp inmates had been detailed to the group, and were now demanding financial compensation and political and moral satisfaction. 'Without recognizing any legal obligation', the Daimler–Benz group finally, after painful public debate, paid a symbolic sum. Is this a *de facto* social recognition of 'collective guilt' by a big conglomerate? Or is it rather the case that after the death of those managers who had been involved, the group no longer had any responsibility? Is it possible to deny political and moral responsibility of the network for the behaviour of its sub-units? And can private institutions deny any responsibility for such political matters and displace it to state institutions? (see for the Siemens case *Die Zeit*, No. 36, 31 Jan. 1990, and for the Volkswagen case Siegfried 1987). These, of course, are all normative questions of moral and political evaluation, but at the same time questions addressed to sociology, about the social reality of networks and their capacity for collective action.

But in the contemporary social sciences, the idea of a suprapersonal collective with a supposed capacity for action on its own is extremely controversial. It is flatly denied by economists. Their methodological individualism leads them into such contradictory statements as the following:

The private corporation or firm is simply one form of legal fiction which serves as a nexus for contracting relationships . . . it makes little or no sense to try to distinguish those matters which are 'inside' the firm (or any other organization) from those matters that are 'outside' it. There is in a very real sense only a multitude of complex relationships (i.e. contracts) between the legal fiction (the firm) and the owners of labour, material and capital inputs and the consumers of output . . . the 'behaviour' of the firm is like the behaviour of a market, i.e. the outcome of a complex equilibrium process. We seldom fall into the trap of characterizing the wheat or stock market as an individual, but we often make this error by thinking about organizations as if they were persons with motivations and intentions. (Jensen and Meckling 1976: 311; similarly Williamson 1985: *passim*; Easterbrook and Fischel 1989: 1426).

Such statements are contradictory since, on the one hand, they strictly deny the social reality of a collective capable of action ('trap', 'error', 'fiction'), but, on the other hand, find themselves forced to assume the reality of this sort of fiction as a contractual party ('nexus'). Furthermore, why should one elide the distinction of market and organization as far as their capacity for social action is concerned? It is only for organizations that capacity of action is claimed. And their critique of the distinction between 'inside' and 'outside' only makes inconsistencies in the theory of the firm stronger ('outside': firm as rational actor on the market; 'inside': firm as contractual nexus among individuals; unsolved problem: how does a nexus become a rational actor?).

Sociological theories are often no better, particularly since Max Weber's authoritative verdict (1978: 13) denying collectives the capacity for action. The most advanced concepts still identify collective actors with resource pooling (Coleman 1974, 1982, 1990; Vanberg 1982: 8ff., 37). However, this refers only one-sidedly to the static structural aspects, and leaves out the dynamic aspects of collective action.

The theory of social autopoiesis, by contrast, allows a conceptual grasp of the collective actor that can escape the traps of fiction theories and the mystifications of theories of real associative personality (Teubner 1988a: 133ff.; Knyphausen 1988: 120; Hutter 1989: 32; Ladeur 1989; 1992: 186.; Vardaro 1990; Luhmann forthcoming: ch. 5, sect. VI). Put briefly, collective actors are neither fictions of the law nor the 'mind–body unity' of real associative personality nor autonomized bundles of resources. Even the concept of system—indeed, even that of formal organization—does not give us accounts of collective capacity for action. Instead, corporate actors have their social reality in the communicative self-description of an organization as a cyclical linkage of identity and action. The nub of the collective lies in the fact that the organization produces a self-description ('corporate identity'), and that social processes attribute individual actions to this semantic construct. As Scharpf (1989: 13) puts it, collective actors are a 'useful fiction controlling the rules of attribution', not only of the law and the state, but of social practice itself, which produces the capacity for self-commitment, for collective action, and for actor identity (cf. Geser 1990: 402).

Now we come to the real question: Are networks 'collective actors' in this sense? At first sight, no. For in their decentralized mode of operation they are diametrically opposed to the image of a hierarchical organization that acts through its centre (central management). Sales networks, for instance, do not act through the distribution centre; instead, the capacity for action is distributed decentrally over the individual outlets as autonomous actors. And were one to interpret groups of companies as unitary enterprises in which the mother company acts for the daughter companies, one would, in view of the characteristics of group organization —contextual control, market internalization, decentralized dynamics—be acting counterproductively.

Does this mean, then, that networks have no collective capacity for action? That is hard to swallow. Does Daimler–Benz as a large corporate group have no 'corporate identity'? Is MacDonalds not an 'image unit'? And how! MacDonalds is simultaneously a 'marketing community' and a 'competitive unit' (or whatever the economic euphemisms for franchising systems are). At any rate, empirical research on franchising led to the conclusion: 'Franchising is more like an integrated business than a set of independent firms' (Dnes 1991: 141). Ought one, then, not to ascribe to networks at least a sort of underdeveloped collectivity? This could do justice to the decentralized autonomy of the sub-units, and still let the hierarchical centre, the group leader company or the hub firm of network organizations, represent the whole.

But the constructions of social practice are far more radical than is dreamt of in our philosophy. The self-organization of networks in the real world has long burst the seams of our anthropomorphic notions of 'corporate actor', of the 'associative person' acting with the help of 'organs'. Anthropomorphic thinking in terms of collective 'persons' has always forced us to conceive collectivities as unitary centres of action, which will serve as a focal point for the attribution of acts, rights, and responsibilities. Since the Christological analogy of the 'King's Two Bodies' made social systems, in particular the state, but also firms and associations, capable of action themselves (Kantorowicz 1957), we have become used to associating collective capacity for action with their 'personification'. Our social practices have to date regarded particular social formations as 'persons', and have equipped them, on the model of the human person, with their own centre of the will, interests, capacity for action, and even 'general human rights' (for a critique of this, see Dan-Cohen 1986; Röhl 1990: 266).

Networks break definitively with such all-too-human personifications. They bring out a new form of collective action that abstracts from the parallels with the human individual. No longer does the associative person endowed with a unitary centre of will seem the appropriate metaphor. The new metaphor is the many-headed hydra. It is no longer personification, but polycentric autonomization; no longer unitary attribution, but simultaneous multiple attribution, that can do justice to the collective logic of networks. The collective capacity for action is maintained, but fragmented into decentralized sub-units, among them the centre as *primus inter pares*. Networks act collectively, not through a single action centre, as is typical for the classical corporation, but through a multiplicity of nodes. The network itself is a collective actor whose actions are accomplished not in one node, but in all nodes, without the nodes themselves thereby losing their capacity as collective actors.

7. NEGATIVE EXTERNALITIES

What, then, does the metaphor of the many-headed hydra mean for the social responsibility of networks? Are there negative external effects that are specific to networks? And should they be internalized by equally network-specific mechanisms of responsibility? The sociological and economic literature celebrating the efficiency gains of network organization is remarkably silent on this question (cf. MacMillan and Farmer 1979: 277; Kaneko and Imai 1987; Jarillo 1988; Lorenzoni 1990; W.W. Powell 1990). They limit themselves to highlighting their sophisticated combination of contractual and organizational elements. But apart from only a few legal scholars (Nagel 1989; Collins 1990a, 1990b; Hadfield 1990; Joerges 1991b; Macaulay 1991), nobody talks about internal power relations, exploitation of the internal members, opportunistic behaviour of the core firm itself, collectivization of action without concomitant collective responsibilities, shifts of risk to third parties, artificial contractual restrictions of responsibility, and synergies of risks for other people. Is this somewhat dirty work to be left to the lawyers who here seem to receive surprisingly little help from law and economics and the sociology of organizations?

In both market networks and organization networks there undoubtedly are phenomena, well known in the case of formal organizations, which have to be termed 'illegitimate transaction cost savings' or more brutally, 'organized irresponsibility' (in general on this, see Coleman 1982: 79; Röhl 1987, 1990; Beck 1988: 96; Perrow 1988: 267). Indeed, by comparison with other formal organizations, hybrid arrangements are distinguished by particular network-specific externalities. Collins (1990*a*: 737) calls this the 'capital boundary problem' in 'complex economic organizations': 'Because the firm determines its own size, it also chooses the limits of its legal responsibilities, which in turn provides an open invitation for the evasion of mandatory legal duties.' The practice of corporate groups of creating autonomous profit centres, in order to secure, alongside (legitimate) efficiency advantages, at the same time (illegitimate) risk displacement and liability limitation, supplies ample illustrative material here (e.g., Hommelhoff 1990: 761). But this phenomenon occurs also in supply and distribution networks, such as the contractual networks in transport, banking, and telecommunications; socially desirable transaction cost advantages from the intelligent mixing of contract and organization go hand in hand with socially questionable shifts of risk to third parties and artificial contractual restrictions of responsibility (here, for the case of franchising, see Teubner 1991; for other contractual networks, see Collins 1990*a*).

These negative external effects are network-specific for two reasons. First, they arise out of the segmentation, through division of labour and isolation, as far as responsibility goes, of co-ordinated chains of action. 'Where the work is organized through numerous separate legal entities rather than a single firm, the limits of legal responsibility set by reference to the boundaries of capital units establish the conditions for potential injustice' (Collins 1990*a*: 736). Second, they are attributable to the above-mentioned capacity of networks to change the organization's colour chameleon fashion—contract, organization, network, contract, organization—according to what the environment and the profit require (Pausenberger 1975: 2243; Kirchner 1985: 226). Networks have the 'power to manipulate capital boundaries in order to reduce or eliminate potential legal liabilities' (Collins 1990*a*: 738).

If this is to be opposed by legal policy, then in principle two control mechanisms are required. One involves a high flexibility of mechanisms of legal responsibility, which cannot be nailed down to the chosen arrangement, but respond just as opportunistically as the chameleon-like shifting network itself. The other requires the simultaneous multiple attribution of corporate responsibility. Responsibility should not be confined to the nodes of the network; it must simultaneously go to its centre and to the co-ordination system of the network itself.

What was said above about the orientation of objectives and about allocation of responsibility applies equally to the political responsibility and legal liability of such hybrid arrangements. Simultaneous multiple attribution of responsibility to the collective, the centre, and the individual unit distinguishes the network from organization, on the one hand, and contract, on the other. Even if present-day law is still far from treating corporate groups, still less contractual systems, as legal subjects, in socio-economic practice tightly organized distribution systems and corporate groups (even if decentrally co-ordinated) are 'observed' as a paradoxical *unitas multiplex*, as a unit of action and at the same time as a multiplicity of actions (cf. Martinek 1987: 121). Practice makes possible without further ado what today still looks like a contradiction in law: assigning responsibility for one and the same act simultaneously to the network, the centre, and the individual unit.

And this threefold responsibility which appears in social practice should also provide the model for a network-adequate political and legal responsibility. Such a political-legal concept of multiple responsibility would treat hybrid forms as third-order ones, beyond contract and organization, which need specific network-adequate regulation. If their specificity lies in the unity of an organization with decentralized action units, then the following would be the guiding principles.

External liability of networks. External liability of the network itself and not only of the individual units should be provided by the law. Such a piercing of the contractual veil should result, however, not in the unified collective liability of company law, but in a decentralized, multiple, and selectively combined liability of the network and the concretely involved nodes. As against liability of fully collectivized formal organization, this would result in a relative re-individualization of collective liability in networks. Moreover, if networks realize increased synergy risks for other people, this would have to be compensated by increased liability of the net. Due to the increased risks, in these cases the level of protection to outside creditors would need to exceed the level of protection in both contract and organization (for some details, see Teubner 1991).

Minority protection for members in the network. Internal minority protection in networks should be provided by the law, and not only the rudimentary protection of weaker parties in contract law. However, the guiding model should not be the dependence of labour law, but the semi-autonomy of decentralized action centres. Not the classical sanctions of labour law, but new protective rules are needed, that safeguard their autonomy, status, and reciprocity (for some details, see Collins 1990b: 376; Hadfield 1990: 978; Joerges 1991b: 33, 66; Sciarra 1991: 251; 258).

Collective interest representation in networks. Collective interest representation should be provided by the law which would go beyond the minimal participation requirements of contract law. However, it would be inappropriate to follow the unified collective representation of corporation and co-determination law in rigid institutions. Rather, countervailing power centres need to be created by law that do not lay down a rigid catalogue of competencies, but utilize flexible quasi-contractual arrangements for legitimation and control (see Teubner 1993: ch. 7).

Such indirect regulation via rules for external liability and for an internal constitution will 'hit' the self-regulating nerve of the network if it is capable of 'irritating' the multiple orientation of network action (on the model of indirect regulation of autonomous systems, see Luhmann 1988b: 345; on the questions of network regulation in corporate groups, see Teubner 1990a: 266). New liability rules that simultaneously influence the cost/benefit calculations of the network, of the centre, and of the nodes can give outside regulation some chance of irritating the network's behaviour. The decentralized character of the network suggests that we go beyond the dichotomy of collective and individual, and establish the threefold responsibility of collective, centre, and individual unit.

4

Labour Markets, Employment Contracts, and Corporate Change

KATHERINE VAN WEZEL STONE

The decade of the 1980s witnessed a revolution in the practices and theory of the business corporation. The dramatic wave of take-overs, buyouts, mergers, and bust-ups rippled through our institutional and conceptual world, and left behind a new topography of economic and power relationships. At its most immediate level, the wave of corporate restructurings produced unprecedented wealth for corporate raiders, enormous commissions for investment bankers, and substantial gains for many stockholders. At the same time, it left devastation for employees and the communities in which they live.

In the United States hundreds of thousands of employees lost their jobs as a result of the merger mania of the decade.[1] In addition, the new jobs created and the newly reorganized jobs offered lower wages and fewer benefits than the jobs they replaced (Mishel and Frankel 1991: 69–127; Levy and Murnane 1992: 1346–51). Thus the decade was one in which there was a redistribution of wealth from employees to corporate raiders, stockholders, and upper management. Indeed, some scholars have argued that there was not merely a passive wealth redistribution, but a coercive transfer (Coffee 1986: 70; Shleifer and Summers 1988: 41–2).

Further, in the 1980s, new norms of economic life arose to accompany the new forms of business behaviour, norms which celebrated rugged individualism and denigrated collectivist solutions to social problems. As a result, a legal climate emerged which made it difficult for the labour movement to protect its members or its own organizational survival in the face of business change.[2]

[1] The AFL-CIO estimates that over 500,000 jobs were lost in the 1980s as a result of take-overs and corporate restructurings (Hostile Take-Overs: Hearings before the Senate Committee on Banking, Housing, and Urban Affairs, 100th Congress, 1st Session, 262 (8 Apr. 1987) (testimony of Thomas P. Donahue, Secretary-Treasurer, AFL-CIO). See also Shleifer and Summers 1988: 41–2). Some economists have disputed the claim that take-overs led to lay-offs or otherwise harmed employees, but all such studies to date suffer from serious methodological flaws (see generally Stone 1991: 45–47 and n. 4).

[2] See, e.g., Modjeska 1985: 131 (describing 'the [Reagan Era] Board reversals [which] profoundly alter the pre-existing balance of labour management relations'); Atleson 1985:871

Two statistics tell the story. First, despite the unprecedented boom on the financial and real estate markets in the decade, the wages of production workers in the United States declined 8 per cent between 1979 and 1987.[3] Second, in the same period, union membership in the United States declined, in absolute numbers, by 25 per cent. By 1990 only 16 per cent of the non-agricultural work-force belonged to unions (Bureau of Labor Statistics 1991: January). Thus the decade of the 1980s signified a deterioration of workers' standard of living and a demise in their collective organizational strength.

There are several attitudes one could adopt toward these developments. One is that the job loss that follows corporate restructurings is not a problem, because an employee who loses her job will get another one at a wage equal to the value of her marginal product. In the meantime, according to this view, everyone is better off because production has been made more efficient. Maybe employees pay some slight costs in terms of transitional unemployment, but it is short-lived, and more than offset by the net gains from capital mobility.

This is the view of neo-classical economic theory. While it fits the theory, it does not fit reality. The evidence of extensive and lengthy job loss is too convincing, and the stories of human suffering too poignant, to gainsay the fact that corporate transformations and restructurings have imposed serious costs on employees.

There is another view which says that employees pay a price for corporate transformation, but that it is ultimately for the greater good. Someone has to pay, so why not employees? In this Darwinian world, it is said, if employees want to strike a better deal and shift the costs to someone else, they should try to do so. For example, they could unionize and bargain collectively for provisions that ensure that the costs of corporate restructurings are not borne by them. Alternatively, they could invest in human capital, and learn valuable skills or even a profession, thereby enhancing their labour market power. If they cannot or do not choose either to unionize or to invest in human capital, then they will be the ones to pay the price of economic restructuring, and deservedly so. Neither sentiment nor law should aid the weak, the lazy, or the mealy-mouthed. I call this the Darwinian view (see, e.g., Epstein 1984; Macey 1989: 194–5).

(arguing that recent Board and Supreme Court decisions have weakened union power, and that these decisions both reflect and further the growing imbalance of power between unions and corporate structures); W. B. Gould 1986: 939 (arguing that the Reagan Board has exhibited a pronounced hostility to unions and collective bargaining). See also Stone 1988 (detailing recent legal decisions that have restricted the power of unions to influence strategic decision making).

[3] Private non-agricultural weekly earnings for production and related workers, indexed in 1977 constant dollars, have been as follows: 1978: 183.9; 1979: 183.4; 1980: 172.7; 1983: 171.3; 1985: 170.4; 1987: 169.3 (*Statistical Abstract of the United States*, 1989, p. 404, table 663).

Both the neo-classical view and the Darwinian view draw support from the new contractual theory of the firm (discussed in depth by Bratton 1989c). Fifteen years ago, Jensen and Meckling deconstructed the concept of the business firm, announcing that the firm only exists as a metaphor for the contractual relations between a set of constituent parts (Jensen and Meckling 1976: 311). These parts include capital (which is subdivided into equity, capital, and debt), labour (which is subdivided by various levels of skill, from unskilled to professional to managerial labour), suppliers of raw materials, customers for output, and the communities in which the firm operates. The different parts come together to form what we know as the modern business firm. The parts are interdependent in so far as each is better able to pursue its interests if it does so in conjunction with the others. The way that the parts come together is defined by private contracting and external law. That is, contract and legal regulation define the relations of dependency, power, and advantage between the various constituencies of the firm.

The contractarian theory of the firm contains an embedded normative assumption about the terms of the contract itself. It suggests that by making a contract, each side expresses its own priorities and preferences, and bargains to its best advantage. In the end, both sides benefit from the making of the deal—otherwise it would not have been made. This provides a justification for the terms of the deal and a powerful reason to reject all public intervention into its terms (Epstein 1984: 953–5).

The deconstructed view of the firm provides a vantage-point from which to evaluate employees' position in the firm. It says that employees' relationship to the firm, like that of the other parts, is defined by private contract and by the legal regulations that constrain or delimit those contracts. As applied to employees, the normative message of the contractarian framework is that employees who are laid off in response to corporate change have experienced the consequences of a contract to which they knowingly and willingly agreed. They chose to contract for present wages instead of job security, and therefore risked the consequences. They bought a ticket, and lost the lottery.

Here I want to challenge the neo-classical and the Darwinian views about the impact of corporate restructurings on employees, and to propose a different view of the labour contract and of labour–capital relations, one that provides employees with some protections against corporate restructuring and with a role in corporate governance. To do this, I also want to contest the normative message contained in the contractual theory of the firm.[4]

---

[4] For purposes of this discussion, I am accepting the broad contours of the contractual theory of the firm and using it as a descriptively useful starting-point for analysis. I do not thereby intend to enter into the metaphysical debate about the absolute truth value of the

My argument has four parts. First, I argue that there is no such thing as a free market for labour that is not itself the product of regulation. Bargaining outcomes are not a simple function of pre-existing power relations: they are mediated, shaped, enhanced, or diminished by law. Thus we cannot treat the outcomes of bargaining as normatively privileged. They are merely the bargaining outcomes within a given set of public policy choices about which groups to favour. So, even if all dimensions of labour–capital relations within firms can be described in the language of contracts and markets, we still must confront the public policy choices concerning which background rules to select, and consequently which distributive outcomes to promote.[5]

Secondly, I look at the particular form of the labour contract that prevails in the West today. I show that even within the existing set of background contracting rules, employment contracts are being repeatedly and systematically breached by employers when they undertake mass lay-offs in conjunction with corporate restructurings. It is incorrect to say that employees have contracted for wages instead of job security. Rather, employees have contracted for both, but they are finding that they cannot enforce the security aspects of their deals.

Thirdly, I look at the available means for employees to enforce their promises of job security. I examine the possibilities both for individual contracting mechanisms and for collective contracting through the mechanism of unionization and collective bargaining. I conclude that under existing legal rules, neither individual nor collective contracting provides adequate enforcement for such promises.

In the last section I examine several different approaches that have been proposed for revising the background rules governing labour relations. I conclude that an expansive conception of collective bargaining, one in which unions are empowered to contend for a greater voice in corporate decision making, is the only one that can effectively protect employees' reasonable expectation of job security.

I. LEGAL REGULATION AND POLICY CHOICES DEFINE THE MARKET

A market is a set of legal rules and institutional arrangements that bring together buyers and sellers (Mansfield 1982: 20–1). Legal regulation

theory as an empirical matter. See Bratton 1989*b* (entity and aggregate views of the firm emphasize different aspects of the legal phenomenon known as a corporation, but do not in fact entail any particular policy implications).

[5] Background rules are the pre-existing legal doctrines of contract, tort, property, and criminal law, as well as statutory laws such as antitrust, that together define the institutional framework of the market. The background rules that define the labour market and their distributional consequences are discussed in part 2 below.

shapes the markets in which contracts are made. In the employment relationship, legal regulation plays a particularly prominent role. Legal rules determine such matters as who can be a party to a wage contract, the permissible terms of such a contract, the compulsory terms, the methods that parties can utilize to improve their contracting position in relation to the other, and the consequences of breach. The particular way that these issues are settled is constitutive of the relative power of employers and employees. And the relative power of the parties determines the bargains they will strike. Thus the particular rules governing the contracting process have distributive consequences (Stone 1988).

Any discussion of employment contracts assumes a great many background legal rules which have shaped their terms. One of the types of rules that have the greatest distributive consequences is that governing the right to strike and engage in economic warfare. For example, without knowing whether or not workers can legally combine and strike, we do not know whether they have enough economic power to achieve their bargaining goals. Similarly, even if workers have a right to combine and strike, we still cannot judge the effectiveness of the strike weapon without knowing whether they also have the right to picket, to engage in a partial strike, to call for consumer boycotts, to engage in secondary labour boycotts, and so forth. Further, to judge the power of the strike weapon, we would have to know whether or not the employer can lawfully carry on operations during a strike, whether the strikers can get their jobs back at the end of a strike, or whether, instead, the employer can permanently replace them. We would also have to know whether those strikers entitled to reinstatement are also entitled to full seniority or merely to reinstatement as new hires, and whether the employer is permitted to use other extraordinary means to procure replacements, such as to offer them premium wage rates or super-seniority. Further, we would want to know whether the replacements would have any rights against the union or the employer if they were to be displaced at the end of a strike. That is, even if workers have a right to strike, we have to know which of the many possible rights that make up the bundle called a 'right to strike' they have, in order to know what the right means and to evaluate its consequences. A right to strike can, and does, take may different forms in different legal systems (Stone 1990). To know the particular form, we need to look at not only the labour laws, but the criminal conspiracy laws, antitrust laws, trespass laws, tort, contract, and property laws as well.

The legal rules governing union organizing also have powerful distributive consequences. Professor Weiler (1990) for example, has shown the impact of legal rules governing union organizing on union success rates. If workers can organize freely, without fear of either discharge by their employer or criminal prosecution by the state, then they can more easily collectivize and enhance their bargaining power. If their ability to organize is subject to legal constraint, then they lose that advantage. Thus, for example, a rule that prohibits an employer from firing a union activist for engaging in organizing activities assists union organizing, and enhances workers' market power. A rule that gives employers free rein to resist union organizing by any otherwise legal means, including dismissing union activists, has the opposite impact. Similarly, a rule subjecting union organizing to antitrust liability diminishes employee market power, while one that permits unions to engage in secondary boycotts in order to pressure employers to recognize and bargain with them enhances it. In the United States there are a myriad of detailed doctrines concerning precisely what employers may and may not lawfully do to discourage their employees from unionizing, and they are all distributive in their impact.[6]

Bargaining rules are also distributive. If an employer is required to bargain before it makes major changes in strategic business practices, then employees have a bargaining chip which they can either play or trade for something else. Thus they enter the contracting arena with more clout than if the rule were otherwise. Conversely, if unions are not permitted to bargain about, or strike about, strategic-level corporate decisions that affect the existence of jobs, then their power is greatly diminished.

Because the background legal rules governing labour relations are not conventional and fixed, all labour law rules involve normative choices concerning the distribution of power and advantage. Each choice of rule enhances the power of one side at the expense of the other. There is no neutral ground, no legal state of nature, upon which contracting can take place. Thus, while the contractual theory of the firm focuses attention on the bargaining between constituent groups within the firm, it does not obviate the need for normative, and distributive, choices.

To be sure, a contract is an expression of individual will and choice, but it is a constrained choice. A contract represents the choice one makes amongst the available options in light of whatever specific constraints and empowerments the background legal rules have conferred. As a delimited and constructed exercise in choice, contract is therefore entitled to only a limited normative claim.

In terms of the employment contract, this analysis says that the terms of the labour contract are largely determined by the legal rules governing organizing, bargaining, and economic conflict. Thus, for example, if workers routinely fail to contract for job security, we cannot conclude that they do not value that goal; it is equally possible that the legal rules make it difficult, or even impossible, to obtain such a term in their con-

---

[6] For a more general statement of this proposition, see Hale 1923: 474–8 (all incomes in society are a function of the amount of coercion one can legally bring against others).

tracts. Therefore, in response to the Darwinian claim that workers who lose their jobs 'got what they bargained for', we can answer, 'They got the bargain that society gave them.'

2. THE NATURE OF THE LABOUR CONTRACT

Even within existing background rules of labour relations, we cannot conclude, as do the neo-classicals and the Darwinists, that employees who suffer job loss as a result of corporate restructuring got what they bargained for. If employees' relationship to the firm is indeed a product of contracting with the others groups that make up the firm, we have to know something about those contracts in order to ascertain whether the risk of involuntary, unprovoked dismissal was part of the deal. That is, we have to ask about the terms of employees' contracts with their firms, and whether those contracts are being performed.

2.1 The conventional view of the labour contract

According to the conventional legal view, the labour contract is not really one contract, but rather a series of discrete contracts for the performance of certain work tasks in exchange for a monetary wage. If the tasks are sufficiently discrete and definite, then the exchange is a money-for-service exchange between two independent contracting parties. Where the tasks are continuous, indefinite, and ongoing, there is not merely a money-for-service exchange, but rather the establishment of an employment relationship. Occasionally this relationship is expressed by means of a written contract of a fixed duration; but, more often, the relationship is based on an oral agreement or understanding, unspecified as to its duration.

In the latter case, the law presumes that the employment relationship is a contract that lasts from moment to moment, each moment signifying the completion of one contract and the commencement of a new one. At the end of each of these momentary cycles, the contract is fully performed, and no further sums of money or other obligations linger. This conventional conception of the labour exchange underlies the American at-will employment doctrine, which says that either party is free to terminate the relationship at the completion of any cycle by merely refusing to enter into another one.

Neo-classical economic theory has a view of the price at which the labour contract will be made that is consistent with the conventional legal view of the labour exchange. It says that the price at which a worker is paid is equal to the value of her marginal product. The value of the worker's marginal product will tend to equalize across firms, each of which are earning the exact same normal rate of profit. Thus there develops a single prevailing competitive wage rate for each type of labour (Reynolds *et al.* 1986: 36–43).

The neo-classical view of wage determination is consistent with the conventional view of the labour exchange because it suggests that the labour–capital exchange is paid the competitive rate at each moment, and is therefore fully executed on both sides as it goes along (e.g., Jovanovic 1979: 973). That is, the employment relationship is an instantaneous, pay-as-you-go exchange. No obligations linger; neither side is creditor or debtor *vis-à-vis* the other.[7]

Thus the conventional theory of the labour exchange, the at-will employment rule, and the marginal productivity theory of wage determination are three mutually reinforcing aspects of the conventional description of the employment relationship. Together they paint a powerful picture of the labour contract as a consensual transaction in which the terms are set by external and inexorable market forces, and each side, by entering into the exchange, stands to benefit.

All aspects of this picture have been challenged many times on many different grounds. The at-will rule has been challenged on the grounds that it ignores factors of power, reliance, duress, inequality, and so forth (see, e.g., Feinman 1976: 132–3). The marginal product theory of wage determination has been challenged on the grounds that it ignores the impact of employment discrimination, imperfect information, sticky wage scales, and other market imperfections, and for not comporting with empirical evidence about wage rates (Kaufman 1988: 146–203; Segal 1986: 389–91). In addition, many scholars have argued that the wage contract is not like other contracts, that it is unique, and is not subject to the rules governing a competitive market in the first place (see below).

In general, it is scholars on the left who argue that labour contracts are not like other contracts. For example, Hugh Collins argues that employment relations are not merely contractual, but are also bureaucratic (Collins 1986). Therefore, he argues, certain 'natural law' concepts like estoppel, reliance, and substantive fairness can be used to judge their terms.

There is another line of left-leaning scholarship which argues that in labour contracts, many crucial terms are left unspecified, so that they cannot be said to be a contract in the usual sense. Claus Offe is a particularly clear spokesperson for this position. In arguing that labour is not a commodity, and thus does not conform to the economic laws of commodity exchange, Offe writes:

---

[7] I refer here not to the frequency at which payment is tendered, but rather to the rate at which pay is said to be 'earned'—i.e., the point at which the worker's right to receive payment is said to 'vest'.

First, unlike genuine commodities, [labour] is not created for the purpose of sale in a market . . . The decision to produce the fictive commodity labour is not reached in market-oriented enterprises but, rather, in families and other agencies of socialization where motivations are largely distinct from that of marketability . . .

Second, labour power differs from conventional commodities because of its market variability and plasticity . . . The employment contract is clearly determined only with respect to pay, whereas the specifications for concrete work tasks—the circumstances of labour exertion, work intensity, etc.—remain relatively under-defined. This gap of indeterminacy is closed in the firm through managerial authority ('command of labour').

Third, the 'commodity' labour power is not clearly separable from its owner . . . Every buyer of labour power must rely on the participation of the worker since, on the one hand, that buyer cannot exclusively control the purchased commodity, and, on the other, the utilization of labour power is linked inextricably to the co-operation of the owners. The worker must also want to work; the fundamental problem in every company or organization consists accordingly in inducing the worker, as the subject of labour power, to co-operate. (Offe 1985: 56–7; see also Bowles and Gintis 1986; Vogel 1983: 133)

The reason some scholars argue that labour contracts are different from other contracts is to escape the *laissez-faire* policy conclusions that seem to flow from the contract and market model of commodity exchanges, and to justify instead some sort of externally imposed regulation to protect labour. While that goal is laudable, it cannot be achieved merely by asserting that labour contracts are unique. All contracts are unique in some respects.

As Stewart Macauley and Ian MacNeil have shown, long-term contracts between parties who have ongoing relationships are very different from those governing one-shot deals between strangers (Macaulay 1963, 1985; MacNeil 1978: 989; 1980: 54; see also Summers 1959: 565–6). For example, a contract to buy ten bushels of tomatoes to be delivered at a certain time and place for a certain price is very different from a long-term contract between a submarine manufacturer and the United States Government to build sixteen nuclear-powered submarines on a cost-plus basis, with specifications to be provided. It is also different from a contract between a restaurant owner and an ice-cream manufacturer to supply all the restaurant's requirements of ice-cream for the next ten years. Contemporary contract law is broad enough to embrace open-ended and partially specified agreements, even those that fail to specify such seemingly important terms as price and time of performance.[8]

---

[8] See, e.g., Uniform Commercial Code (UCC), sect. 2–305(1) (West 1989) ('The time for shipment or delivery or any other action under a contract if not [. . .] agreed upon shall be a reasonable time'); UCC, sect. 2–309(1) (West 1989) ('The parties if they so intend can conclude a contract for sale even though the price is not settled. In such a case the price is a

Therefore, the claim that labour contracts have special features does not automatically justify government intervention. This claim becomes compelling only if we do more than delineate the special nature of the contract. To take the labour contract out of the realm of contracts altogether, one must show how the particular unique quality of the labour contract makes it inappropriate to call such relationships contracts at all.

While there is no doubt that the employment contract has special qualities, it is futile to deny that it is a contract, or that it functions in a market. Rather, I think it is more productive to be precise about the terms of the contract, to examine the background rules against which they are negotiated, and to determine whether contracts are being enforced. Out of this inquiry, we can consider arguments for different types of legal interventions in the wage bargain.[9]

2.2 An implicit contract model of the employment relationship

In the 1970s some labour economists noted that, contrary to neo-classical theory, the terms of the labour contract do not correspond to a process whereby employers attempt to match the marginal costs of labour with its marginal revenues. Rather, these economists suggested that there is a labour market internal to the firm, according to which rewards such as raises, bonuses, and promotions are distributed. This internal labour market is governed by considerations of productivity, morale, and incentives, as well as by considerations of prevailing wage rates and technical efficiency (see Doeringer and Piore 1971).

Since then, a number of labour economists have developed a model of career wage trajectories to explain wages in the internal labour market

reasonable price at the time for delivery'). The UCC also provides for requirements and output contracts, which are contracts in which the quantity term is not fixed. See UCC, sect. 2–306 (West 1989).

[9] In a recent article, Bowles and Gintis have attempted to develop a model of the employment relationship and the labour market that illuminates the factors of power that operate (Bowles and Gintis 1990: 222). They argue that, in competitive equilibrium, workers receive a wage greater than their reservation wage and, in exchange, provide a level of effort which is greater than the minimum required to avoid dismissal for shirking. As a result, labour markets are non-clearing markets; there are always a large number of equally qualified potential employees ready and able to step in, should the employer want to replace any given worker whose performance is not up to par. This fact gives the employer power in the relationship.

This argument is extremely interesting. However, it does not deal with the issue of the legal system's treatment of labour contracts. It proceeds from the altogether reasonable assumption that labour contracts are 'contingently renewable'—i.e., that they are all at-will. Therefore Bowles and Gintis do not consider the possibility of legal rules that protect employees from unfair dismissal. My task is to model the employment relationship in order to formulate appropriate legal rules for its governance. To that end, I ask a somewhat different question, which is: Do the legal rules that currently govern the labour contract adequately protect the contractual understandings and reasonable reliance of the parties?

(see Ehrenberg and Smith 1988: 425–30; Lazear 1979, 1981; R. Hutchens 1986, 1987; Malcomson 1984). The internal labour market of career compensation describes the compensation function for employees through various phases of their employment. By doing so, it demonstrates the way in which employees are vulnerable to expropriation by other groups within the firm.[10]

In brief, the model is as follows. Both companies and workers invest in the acquisition of skills and knowledge on the job, skills and knowledge which are necessary for employees to function productively. Some of this investment in human capital is general, and gives workers an asset they can sell in the general labour market. However, some of this investment is firm-specific, so that the knowledge gained redounds primarily to the firm (see generally Doeringer and Piore 1971; see also Willis 1988: 594; Reynolds *et al.* 1986: 162–71). Employees benefit from acquiring firm-specific capital only if their firm rewards them for acquiring it.

Because some of the investment that employees make in their training is firm-specific, the employees' value to their employer increases over time as they acquire such firm-specific capital, while their value to other employers may not. The interaction between employees' compensation and the value of their marginal product over time is represented in Figure 4.1. This shows that in the first phase of employment, a new employee in an internal labour market is paid an amount that equals or is slightly greater than the value of her marginal product and less than the value of her opportunity wage—the amount she could command in the general labour market. This is because she is acquiring human capital, and both she and her employer are investing in its acquisition. As stated earlier, some of this human capital is firm-specific and some is not.

At some point the employee acquires enough capital to become useful to the employer—that is, the value of her marginal product rises. This is phase II in which the employee is paid less than the value of her marginal product. Hence the firm is already benefiting from the joint investment of phase I.

What is most notable about phase II is that the employee is paid not only less than the value of her marginal product, but also less than her opportunity wage. Why, we might ask, would anyone accept a rate of pay that is lower than she could earn elsewhere? The reason is that in this

[10] This model has been called a theory of life cycle earnings, because it posits a relationship between wages and marginal productivity over a worker's life cycle, rather than at each moment in time (Willis 1988: 594–8; see Ehrenberg and Smith 1988: 245–9, 425–30; Lazear 1979). Some labour economists reject the life cycle earnings theory, and instead argue that each worker is paid the value of her marginal product at each moment in time (see, e.g., Jovanovic 1979: 973). While there is empirical evidence to support both the life cycle earnings theory and the competing human capital theory, 'a clear-cut resolution of this question awaits further research' (Willis 1988: 597–8).

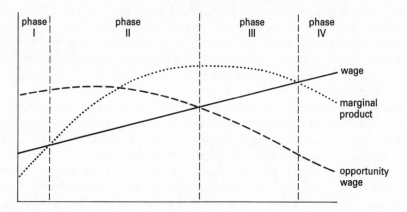

FIG. 4.1. Taken from Wachter and Cohen 1988: 1362. This graph is a variation on a diagram first developed by Lazear 1979: 1265.

phase, the employee has an expectation that the job will be steady and that the wage will keep rising throughout her working career. For that expectation, she defers compensation. The expectation is created by the employer, and is a defining element in the notion of the internal labour market.[11] Thus, in phase II, the employee is investing in acquiring human capital and is deferring compensation.

In the third phase, the firm-specific nature of the human capital that the employee has acquired means that she is worth more to her employer than she is to other employers. Hence, the value of her marginal product to her employer is greater than the value of her marginal product to other employers. In this period she is paid more than her opportunity wage, but less than the value of her marginal product.

And in phase IV—the employee's later years—her productivity begins to lag. However, due to customs, norms, policies, or incentive schemes, her pay is not reduced. Instead, her wage level either continues to rise or levels off. Thus in this period she is paid more than the value of her marginal product and more than her opportunity wage. This is the recoupment stage, in which the employee recoups on her investment in firm-specific training and deferred compensation.

The graph suggests that during the middle two periods, workers have made an investment for which they have not yet been compensated, and for which they anticipate deferred compensation. If they suffer involuntary job loss during that period, their investment is lost. As they

[11] On the origin of internal labour markets and the personnel theory that underlies them, see Stone 1974.

approach the end of phase III and enter the beginning of phase IV, they are particularly vulnerable to involuntary job loss.[12]

Workers' investments in firm-specific capital and deferred compensation are made not on the basis of some explicit contractual arrangement, but rather take the form of an implicit contract. The implicit contract in the internal labour market is that in the early phases of their career, employees will be paid less than the value of their marginal product and less than their opportunity wage in exchange for a promise of job security and a wage rate later in their working lives that is greater than the value of their marginal product and their opportunity wage.[13] Thus, employees are investing in the firm during their training and high productivity periods with the expectation of recouping on the investment in their declining years (Rosen 1985: 1147; see also Segal 1986: 400–1).

This analysis comports with the widely held intuition that it is unfair to lay off workers who have substantial seniority without some form of warning, severance pay, and pension protection (Weiler 1990: 140–1).[14] It shows that middle-period employees have made an investment which they need to protect. If they lose their investment at the point when they are about to recoup as a result of decisions that are made by and for the benefit of other constituent groups within the firm—for example, if their implicit contract to defer compensation is breached and their investment appropriated by managers or shareholders—then they have been treated unfairly, and should have some additional means of legal recourse (Rosen 1985: 1149).

The model also shows that employers have an incentive to renege on the implicit contracts just as workers are entering the recoupment stage. That is, the employment relationship contains a built-in incentive for managers to breach their implicit promises of job security and deferred compensation, and appropriate that investment to the firm or to themselves (Note 1989*b*: 523).[15] This is true regardless of the moral character or personal intentions of the manager. Indeed, frequently the manager

[12] Of course, the amount of investment made in the middle period and the point at which one moves from the middle period of investing to the later period of recouping the deferred compensation depends upon the shape of the particular curve in the particular case.

[13] On the implicit contract in the internal labour market, see Reynolds *et al.* 1986: 171–5; Ehrenberg and Smith 88: 425–6; Willis 1988: 597; see also Williamson 1985.

[14] If employees cannot recoup because their firm fails, then arguably they have made a poor investment, and should suffer the consequences. In such a case, they should have some rights in the bankruptcy context on a par with the other creditors of the firm. Indeed, this analysis suggests that workers should have rights against the common pool that go beyond claims for unpaid wages and pensions. Current bankruptcy law does not recognize such claims (Baird 1986: 130). However, there is no reason in theory why it could not (see Schwartz 1989: 255–7).

[15] Whether that appropriated surplus ultimately redounds to the manager in the form of higher salary or to the shareholders in the form of higher dividends is a function of the contract between those two groups.

who lays off a late-career employee was not even with the firm at the time the employee was hired, and had nothing to do with whatever implicit promise was given.

The incentive for managers to renege on implicit contracts may well be constrained during 'normal' times, when both management and employees share a commitment to their long-term relationship as defined by the internal labour market job structures such as seniority systems, internal promotion ladders, and pensions. However, during 'abnormal' times, such as mergers or buy-outs, management's view of the employment relationship may change. In that situation, the employee may continue to view the relationship as an ongoing one governed by the terms of the implicit promise, while management may view it in short-term efficiency terms. At that point, the incentive of managers to breach, together with the power they have to do so under current legal rules, renders employees particularly vulnerable. To redress this imbalance, employees must find a means to enforce their implicit contracts.

3. THE PROBLEM OF ENFORCING THE IMPLICIT CONTRACT

Because employees' contracts for deferred compensation are implicit, they do not carry the usual legal enforcement mechanisms. Some economists have argued that legal rules to enforce the contracts are not necessary because firms will generally honour such contracts and punish managers who breach them. This argument has two variations. One focuses on the firm's reputation in the outside world, and says that firms which repeatedly violate employees' reasonable expectations of job security will not be able to attract the workers they need. To avoid getting a reputation for engaging in opportunistic firings, firms will honour their implicit contracts (Macey 1989: 192; Williamson 1985: 259–61; see also Epstein 1984: 967–8). However, in large and widely dispersed labour markets this argument is not plausible. In such settings, there is no reliable means by which information about firings can be transmitted on a regular basis, so that reputation factors cannot serve the policing function (Fenn and Whelan 1984: 372–9; Note 1989*b*: 524–5).

The other variant of the argument about implicit contracts focuses on the role of reputation within the firm itself. David Kreps, in his essay 'Corporate Culture and Economic Theory,' argues that in employment relations unforeseen contingencies necessarily arise (Kreps 1990: 90). He argues that in a hierarchical relationship, it is necessary that one party agree to permit the other to exercise discretion in the face of such contingencies, even though that party is vulnerable to the opportunistic exercise of the other's discretion. Using non-co-operative game theory, Kreps demonstrates that in order for the organization to succeed and the relationship to continue, the party exercising discretion must act honourably and honour implicit contracts often enough to develop a reputation for being trustworthy (ibid. 116). Without such a reputation, the inferior party will refuse to trust the other, and will not engage in any more transactions (ibid. 124). The need for firms to develop a reputation for trust and to disseminate it through a multi-layered management structure gives rise to a corporate culture.

The Kreps argument may be a plausible account of firm labour relations during 'normal' times. However, it has no applicability to periods of corporate transformation. During such periods, corporate culture undergoes cataclysmic changes. New managers come to power, and they have no stake in upholding prior reputations. To be sure, they have their own reputations to establish, but in many respects they begin with a clean slate. With new managers, a new corporate culture, and often a substantially new work-force, old implicit promises are history. In that case, implicit promises of job security are not self-enforcing, and employees need some means to protect their investments.

The legal system has set up substantial difficulties for employees seeking to police and enforce their implicit contracts. Some commentators have suggested that employees should make their implicit contracts explicit at the time of hire, and therefore avoid the enforcement difficulties.[16] There are several general problems with this suggestion. First, most employment is at-will, so that explicit terms settled at the time of hire are subject to perpetual renegotiation, *de facto* modification, and implied waiver.[17] Second, given the complexity of employment relationships and the many unknown factors that affect their success, neither employees nor employers are likely to want to contract for whole-career employment at the outset of the relationship. And even if employees were willing to take the risk in exchange for job security, employers are not likely to want to do so. Given that at the time of hire, employees have not yet acquired any firm-specific capital, and hence their bargaining power *vis-à-vis* the employer is at its nadir, the employer's position is likely to prevail.

---

[16] See, e.g., Macey 1989: 192 (arguing that by forming unions, employees can contract to appropriate the firm's capital investment, thereby counterbalancing any danger of expropriation by the other side) and Gavis 1990 (arguing that employees can protect their implicit contracts and investment in human capital by use of explicit contracts for severance payments, successorship clauses, and employee stock ownership plans).

[17] Even if employees could negotiate an employment contract that contains a promise of lifetime career employment, the law presumes that any employment contract that purports to be permanent is at-will. It takes extraordinary expressions of intent to create a long-term contract and to convince a court that an employment contract is anything other than at-will (Brodie 1988: 666–70).

Unable to achieve protection by bargaining on an individual basis, employees often try to gain protection by unionizing and bargaining on a collective basis. Unions can play a role as enforcers of the implicit contracts of employees to defer compensation within the internal labour market. They can do this without forcing both sides to lock into a lifetime employment contract prematurely or unwittingly. Thus, for example, typical union contract clauses which permit an employer to fire an employee only for 'just cause', or which impose a seniority principle to govern lay-offs, function during normal periods to prevent firms from reneging on their implicit contracts and appropriating the workers' investment in deferred compensation.

However, during times of corporate restructuring, unions are not able to police or enforce the implicit contracts. In the United States, the ability of unions to contract to protect themselves against unfavourable strategic-level corporate decisions is severely restricted by specific labour law rules and by the practicalities of labour relations. An examination of some of the most commonly suggested contractual solutions will demonstrate why this is so.

3.1 The duty to bargain

The National Labor Relations Act imposes a duty to bargain in good faith on employers whose employees are unionized.[18] One might think that this legally imposed duty protects employees in the face of corporate restructuring decisions by giving their unions the power to discuss and influence such decisions while they are under active consideration. However, the duty to bargain does not have this effect.

Despite the broad language of the statute, the duty to bargain does not require an employer to bargain about all issues involved in operating a business, or even about all issues which affect employees. In particular, courts have adopted the view that the duty to bargain does not apply to decisions which 'lie at the core of entrepreneurial control'.[19] Under this rationale, the Supreme Court in 1981 held that an employer was not required to bargain about a decision to close part of its operation.[20] The

---

[18] The employer's duty to bargain is found in sect. 8(a)(5) and 8(d) of the National Labor Relations Act (29 U.S.C. §150 et. seq.). Sect. 8(a) of the NLRA says: 'It shall be an unfair labor practice for an employer . . . (5) to refuse to bargain collectively with the representatives of his employees.' Sect. 8(d) defines the bargaining obligation as requiring the parties 'to meet at reasonable times and confer in good faith with respect to wages, hours, and other terms and conditions of employment'. Sect. 8(b)(3) of the statute imposes a corresponding duty on the union to bargain with the employer in good faith.

[19] This language, which first appeared in the concurring opinion in *Fibreboard Paper Products* v. *NLRB*, 379 U.S. 203 (1964), became the position of the majority of the Supreme Court in 1981, in *First National Maintenance* v. *NLRB*, 452 U.S. 666 (1981).

[20] *First National Maintenance* v. *NLRB*, 1981. Much earlier the Court made it clear that

Court said that when making decisions that have a direct impact on employment security, management is required to bargain 'only if the benefit, for labour management relations and the collective bargaining process, outweighs the burden placed on the conduct of the business' (*First National Maintenance* v. *NLRB*, 1981:679). This test says that there is no duty to bargain where an employer can demonstrate that sufficient market factors—'burden[s] on the conduct of the business'—constrained its decision.

The reasoning in this case suggested, and subsequent decisions by lower courts have demonstrated, that the bargaining obligation under American law does not attach to other types of strategic-level corporate decisions that entail massive job loss, decisions such as mergers, take-overs, asset sales, stock repurchases, or management buy-outs. Both the National Labor Relations Board and the courts agree that where an employer makes a decision that involves a fundamental change in the scope or direction of the enterprise, there is no bargaining obligation (*Dubuque Packing Co., Inc.*, 1991; *Arrow Automotive Industries, Inc.* v. *NLRB*, 1985).

Thus for most corporate decisions that threaten to breach employees' implicit contracts, there is no legal bargaining obligation that might enable unions to protect employees at the time such decisions are made. Unions must therefore try to protect against breaches of their members' implicit contracts by negotiating for *ex ante* contractual protection.

3.2 Tin parachutes

The most obvious way in which unionized employees might try to negotiate *ex ante* contractual protection against post-contractual opportunism is to put large severance pay clauses in their contracts. Such clauses have been termed 'tin parachutes' (Ryan 1989: 10 n. 15), the blue-collar analogy to the 'golden parachute' severance pay packages that executives often negotiate. It has been suggested that a tin parachute could give employees comparable protection against job dislocation to that which a golden parachute gives to corporate executives (Ryan 1989: 12–13, Gavis 1990 1479–84).

Despite the conceptual simplicity, however, tin parachutes pose complex negotiation problems. As a practical matter, it is almost impossible to design a tin parachute that would accomplish the goal of protecting employees' investments against expropriation by managers and shareholders in the face of corporate change. While severance pay of nominal amounts is a common feature in collective bargaining agreements,

an employer has no obligation to bargain about a decision to go out of business altogether: *Textile Workers Union* v. *Darlington Mfg. Co.*, 380 U.S. 263 (1965).

severance pay in amounts sufficient fully to compensate employees for their firm-specific investments and deferred compensation would involve a much more substantial sum. It would have to equal the discounted value of the recoupment due on the implicit contract—that is, the difference between the internal labour market wage for the declining years and the opportunity wage in the same period, plus the cost of possible extended job loss. The calculation problems are obvious.

Further, such a tin parachute would involve a substantial amount of money. Studies have shown that many employees who lose their jobs involuntarily as a result of corporate restructuring are often unemployed for several years, and are re-employed at only a fraction of their former pay.[21] A tin parachute would have to give compensation for the present value of those losses. But companies which presently offer tin parachutes and the commentators who advocate them are not contemplating payments of this order of magnitude.[22]

In addition to the calculation problems, there is also a serious drafting problem involved in negotiating tin parachutes. Any contract containing a tin parachute clause would have to specify the events that would trigger its exercise. The drafting problem involves specifying which involuntary job losses warrant opening the parachute and which do not. A narrowly drafted clause that grants parachute protection for some types of involuntary job loss but not others would appear unfair and arbitrary to employees who suffer one of the unspecified types of job loss. However, if a parachute is drafted broadly, such that all involuntary job loss triggers the pay-out, then there will be a problem of perverse incentives and moral hazard on behalf of both employees and employers. If the parachute provides employees with adequate payment for the discounted value of the investment in firm-specific capital and deferred compensation, then employees might be tempted to shirk in order to provoke a staff reduction and thereby obtain the benefit of the parachute. The shirking problem can be solved only by designing a parachute whose pay-out under-compensates employees for their investments. However, such a parachute would unfairly penalize those whose job loss is truly involuntarily.[23]

---

[21] See Flaim and Sehgal 1985 (of 5.1m. workers with 3 or more years experience displaced between 1979 and 1984, only 3.1m. were employed in January 1984, and one-half of those were earning less than they had on their previous job) and D'Amico and Golon 1986 (young workers displaced by plant shutdowns lose on average 7.85% of their income, as well as their fringe benefits, pensions, seniority, and job-specific skills).

[22] See Ryan 1989: 12 (of 19 companies which voluntarily adopted tin parachutes, the maximum payment an employee could get was 2 years' wages.). See also Gavis 1990: 1483 and n. 162 (describing tin parachute plan of Herman Miller Furniture Company, under which employees could be paid up to 2.5 times the employees' annual wage).

[23] It has been suggested that the same moral hazard and shirking problem is created by golden parachutes, and yet the problem has not deterred their use. That is, some claim that

3.3 Enforcing contractual protection

Even if the drafting and moral hazard problems could be overcome, so that adequate tin parachute clauses could be negotiated, unions in the United States would none the less face serious difficulties getting the clauses enforced. In the event of a sale of assets, the labour law successorship rules provide that the pre-existing collective bargaining agreement is not enforceable against the new corporate entity (*Howard Johnson Co.* v. *Detroit Local Joint Exec. Bd.*, 1974; see also *NLRB* v. *Burns Int'l Security Services, Inc,*. 1972; see generally Estreicher 1988; Stone 1988: 102–11). Nor is it enforceable in the context of most mergers.[24] Thus, in either of those types of situations, the very event that triggers the operation of the tin parachute would also relieve the perpetrator of liability. Or, stated differently, the contractual provision would be rendered inoperative by the very contingency against which it was designed to protect.

In the event of a take-over, as opposed to a sale of assets or a merger, a tin parachute offers more protection, at least at the outset. That is, a change in control, unlike a change in ownership, would not normally vitiate pre-existing collective bargaining agreements. However, it is not take-overs *per se* that lead to job loss. It is the restructuring that often occurs either after a take-over or to defend against one. If a take-over is a prelude to a sale of assets, then the protection of a tin parachute clause is short-lived because, as explained above, the clause is not operative against the successor.[25] If there are lay-offs as part of a down-sizing to

the more generously a golden parachute compensates an executive for job loss, the more likely the executive will shirk so as to make the company an attractive take-over target, in order to gain the benefit of the parachute. One commentator has responded to this apparent paradox by noting that golden parachutes are merely one form of compensation for which executives can bargain. Given the close relationship between executives and directors, it is unlikely that executives would bargain for parachutes large enough to give them an incentive to shirk, when they can just as easily bargain for some other item in the compensation package, an item which is payable in the here and now and not in the remote and contingent future (Note 1985: 920). The mechanism to check the moral hazard potential of a golden parachute does not operate in the case of tin parachutes. Tin parachutes are negotiated collectively, not individually, so individual employee preferences regarding the optimal trade-off between job loss insurance and present income will not necessarily prevail. Thus there is no way to prevent a tin parachute from generating perverse incentives for shirking behaviour other than to make the pay-out grossly inadequate compensation for the value of a worker's investment in her firm.

[24] There may be an exception for mergers in which a unionized entity merges with a non-union entity and the former entity ceases to exist. In this narrow situation, the Supreme Court has said that the successor has an obligation to arbitrate under the terms of the predecessor's labour contract (*John Wiley & Sons* v. *Livingston*, 1964).

[25] Recently three states have tried to legislate around the successorship rule by adopting statutes that impose an obligation on a successor to honour a predecessor's collective bargaining agreement; see 19 Del. C. sect. 706 (Delaware successorship statute); 1990 Pa. SB ch. 36 sect. 2587 (Pennsylvania successorship statute); 149 Mass. Code ch. 149. 20E (Massachusetts successorship statute). However, there is a serious question as to whether those statutes are pre-empted by the federal law of collective bargaining (Note 1991).

defend against a take-over, then a tin parachute triggered by a take-over would be of no avail. And a tin parachute which would apply to all down-sizing, regardless of the actuality or threat of a take-over, would pose a severe form of the moral hazard problem discussed above.

3.4 Specific clauses granting job security

Given the difficulties in drafting *ex ante* contract provisions that provide adequate tin parachutes, some unions have attempted to negotiate specific clauses that give employees job security for the life of the agreement. These can take many forms. Some unions have negotiated blanket 'no lay-off' clauses, or rights to confer with management before certain types of adverse decisions are made (see, e.g. *United Telegraph Workers* v. *Western Union* 1985). In one case, a union negotiated with the company for a contractual promise to invest resources in the plant (*Local 461, Int'l U. of Elec., Radio and Machine Workers* v. *Singer Co.,1982*). Its purpose was to ensure that the plant remained viable during the life of the collective agreement.

The problem with these types of clauses is that, in the United States, they have proved hard to enforce. Courts will not enforce them directly; rather, they refer them to private arbitration (Stone 1981: 1529–30 discusses the centrality of arbitration in the post-war system of collective bargaining). Yet arbitration takes time, and arbitrators have limited remedy powers. In particular, they cannot order provisional relief.[26] Therefore when unions try to enforce such specific types of job security provisions, the arbitrator is often presented with a *fait accompli*. The corporate decision has already been made and implemented by the time the arbitrator hears the case, and the arbitrator who finds the company liable must devise a remedy. In most cases, arbitrators are reluctant to undo the decision and restore the *status quo ante*. At best, they try to formulate some kind of after-the-fact monetary relief.

Thus, even with explicit contractual provisions against adverse corporate decisions, unions can only enforce them in arbitration for an after-the-fact damage recovery. And in awarding damages for their breach, arbitrators generally believe that they do not have the power to impose awards for breach of executory contracts or for breach of implicit contracts (Elkouri and Elkouri 1985). Furthermore, arbitrators tend to be conservative on the issue of monetary relief. They will award damages

---

[26] *In re Armour & Company and Amalgamated Meat Cutters*, 1977: (Goetz, Arb.) ('Arbitrator has been unable to find any arbitral or judicial precedent, nor any scholarly commentary, that might lead to the conclusion that the Arbitrator has authority to grant the extraordinary relief [temporary restraining order] requested by the Union'); Elkouri and Elkouri 1985: 291 and n. 298 (arbitrators are extremely reluctant to issue temporary restraining orders pending determination of the merits of a dispute).

only for a specific monetary loss that has been suffered, and only if the injury is concrete rather than speculative (ibid. 401). For example, they are unlikely to award the full value of a tin parachute, as it represents contingent losses in amounts that are speculative as to their amount.[27] Thus arbitral remedies are limited to retrospective back pay for breach of promises contained explicitly in a collective bargaining agreement. As a result, the breach of the implicit contract is not compensated.

Furthermore, some of the other types of contractual clauses that unions have attempted to negotiate in order to protect their members from corporate restructuring have been held to be illegal. For example, unions that have attempted to bargain to limit the practice of 'double-breasting'—the establishment of a non-union subsidiary and transferring to it the unionized subsidiary's work—have been found in violation of the secondary boycott laws (*D'Amico* v. *Painters District Council*, 1985). Similarly, union efforts to bargain to ensure their members the ability to perform new work in the face of automation that eliminates work they formerly performed have been found to violate the secondary boycott laws (see Rosenberg 1984: 148–9 n. 69). Also, union efforts to negotiate clauses that say that if an employer sells or transfers assets during the term of the collective bargaining agreement, he must obtain the transferee's assent to be bound by the labour agreement, have been found unlawful (*Danielson* v. *Int'l Organization of Masters, Mates & Pilots*, 1975).

In all these ways, the labour laws severely restrict the ability of unions to use *ex ante* contractual provisions to protect their members' jobs. Under current labour law doctrines, it is almost impossible for unions to negotiate contractual provisions *ex ante* or to enforce them *ex post* in a way that provides employees with meaningful protection for their investments in firm-specific capital and deferred compensation. Furthermore, since 1981, unions have had very few rights to require their companies to bargain about strategic-level decisions at the time such decisions are being made (Stone, 1991).

4. PROPOSALS FOR PROTECTING EMPLOYEES'S INTERESTS IN THEIR FIRMS

Because the labour law rules, at least in the United States, make enforcement of employees' implicit contracts problematic, it is important to consider what other enforcement means are available.[28] In recent years,

---

[27] Cf. Note 1976 (urging arbitrators to use penalties to protect employees' intangible interests in their labour contracts).

[28] My argument is that an employer has an obligation on the basis of an implicit

scholars and legislators have considered a variety of other proposals to revise the background rules of the labour exchange in a way that would enable workers to enforce their employer's implicit promises of job security and deferred compensation. These proposals can be clustered into three distinct approaches: (1) individual regulatory approaches; (2) collectivist contractual approaches; and (3) collectivist regulatory approaches. I will consider each of these briefly.

4.1 Individual regulatory approaches

In the past two decades in the United States, some state legislatures and courts have tried to find ways to enable individual employees to enforce their implicit contracts of job security. This trend began in the 1970s, when some state courts created exceptions to the at-will doctrine to vindicate important public policies, policies such as serving on jury duty or preventing perjury. In the face of the massive corporate dislocations of the 1980s, courts developed other exceptions to the at-will rule, exceptions that came not from a desire to vindicate some external public policy, but rather from a desire to enforce an implicit promise of job security. To this effect, courts have reached to find such personnel practices as employment handbooks and supervisory reassurances to be promissory in nature and contractual in effect, even when conventional contract law doctrine cannot justify such treatment. In doing so, courts are *de facto* enforcing the employer's implicit promise.

In addition, the federal government, in response to the problem of unanticipated and sudden job loss has enacted a statute that requires employers to notify employees of imminent plant closings (Worker Adjustment and Retraining Act of 1988). This is a legislative acknowledgement and partial response to the problem of policing implicit contracts.

Some state legislatures have gone further, and have revised their corporate laws in ways that help workers protect their implicit contracts in the face of take-overs or other corporate restructurings. For example, over half the states have revised their corporate laws in the past few years to impose fiduciary duties on directors and managers on behalf of employees. These statutes, called non-shareholder constituency statutes, permit managers to take the interests of employees into account when making strategic-level decisions.[29] Considered by some scholars a revolution in

promise which induced employee reliance. Unlike Joseph Singer, who argues that workers have a property right in their plants on the basis of their reliance (Singer 1988), I am attempting to build on, and extend, the idea of contract embodied in the wage relationship. Thus this analysis is akin to modern unilateral contract theory and promissory estoppel in its effort to protect the vulnerable party to a contract.

[29] For a listing of state statutes, see Stetson Law Review Symposium 1991: Appendix; see also Hanks 1988: 1246–53 (App.).

corporate law, the stakeholder statutes redefine the director's fiduciary duty away from the shareholder to other constituent groups within the firm (e.g. Millon 1991). In addition, one state (Pennsylvania) has enacted legislation that requires companies to pay severance benefits to employees who lose their jobs as a result of corporate restructuring.[30]

These measures attempt to limit the ability of employers to breach their implicit contracts. However, for several reasons they are not adequate to the task. First, it is expensive for individual workers to bring the legal actions necessary to vindicate their rights, and therefore despite these measures, many breaches go unremedied.[31] Second, the individual regulatory approach relies on the largess of state courts and legislatures to aid employees in times of distress. What the legislatures and courts can give, they can take away. Third, the corporate stakeholder statutes, which purport to permit directors to take employee interests into account in making strategic decisions, do not actually give employees any meaningful protection. With the exception of Connecticut, all the statutes speak in permissive tones. They say that directors *may* consider the interests of other constituencies. And none of the statutes give employees standing to sue to enforce whatever fiduciary duties the statutes create.

Thus the statutes, as currently written, give employees neither an ability to protect their interests directly, nor a right to insist that corporate decision-makers take their interests into account. Indeed, the statutes do not even give employees a right to ascertain whether their interests are considered in the making of important decisions. Thus these statutes give employees very little. Even if the statutes were amended to provide enforceable rights, given the business judgment rule, the range of stakeholder interests, and the conflicts between them, the statutes would merely amplify managerial discretion (Stetson Law Review Symposium 1991, especially articles by Hanks and Macey).

4.2 Collectivist contractual approaches

Because the individual-based approaches to enforcing workers' implicit contracts are inadequate, it is important to consider whether collectivist approaches might prove more effective. Oliver Williamson has proposed one such approach in his work on corporate governance. Williamson uses transaction cost analysis to address the problem of worker vulnerability

[30] See Pa. Stat. Ann., tit. 15, sect. 2481–2587 (Purdon supp. 1991), which provides that an eligible employee is entitled to a one-time lump-sum payment of severance compensation if the employment is terminated within 90 days prior to, or 2 years subsequent to, a 'control share approval'.

[31] A study by the Rand Institute for Civil Justice of 120 wrongful discharge cases brought in California between 1980 and 1986 found that over 53% were brought by executives or middle management (Dertouzos *et al.* 1988: 19–21).

that results from making investments in firm-specific capital. He presents an analysis of the wage contract that emphasizes the firm-specific nature of employees' investment in their jobs.[32] That is, he argues that workers whose jobs entail substantial investments in firm-specific human capital have developed a means to protect these investments. That means, which he calls an alternative bilateral governance mechanism, is the industrial pluralist system of collective bargaining that exists in the United States. That is, he argues that workers can police their implicit contracts by unionizing.

As we have seen, however, the current rules of collective bargaining in the United States make it difficult, if not impossible, for unions to protect workers against strategic-level corporate decisions that threaten their jobs. Because employees are at risk of employers reneging on the specific promises of job security and longevity-related benefits, the fact that unions are unable to protect jobs in the face of corporate change means that they cannot play the policing role that Williamson ascribes to them.

Instead, we must conceive alternative models of collective bargaining and revised labour law background rules which permit workers to collectively police their implicit contracts. Elsewhere I have advocated changes in the legal rules governing collective bargaining which emphasize union participation in strategic-level corporate decisions (Stone 1988). Such participation would enable unions to influence those corporate decisions that most profoundly affect their members. Even when union influence is not sufficient to change the outcome, it might be able to cushion the impact on their members.

The nexus-of-contracts view of the firm has focused attention on the question of the power of the firm's various constituents within the entity as a whole. Under this view, no group has an a priori privileged relation to the entity as a whole. All use their own particular input and their own type of leverage to strike the best bargain they can. I have used this view to advocate an expanded bargaining model of collective bargaining, in which labour stands on an equal footing with all other contenders for power within the concern. Labour should be able to bargain with the other groups for a governance role, and to utilize its economic weapons and other forms of clout in order to obtain such a role (Stone, 1988).

From this perspective, we can imagine collective bargaining transposed to the boardroom, where unions can then contend not only with management, but with all the other constituent groups that comprise the firm. This is already occurring in the United States in Chapter 11 bankruptcy reorganization proceedings, where unions sit on creditor committees and

---

[32] Williamson shows how employees' investments in firm-specific human capital raises the possibility of opportunistic expropriation of their investment. However, he does not share the analysis of deferred compensation or description of the career wage profile presented here (Williamson 1985).

negotiate with all the different classes of creditors about every aspect of the fate of the enterprise. Similar forms of expanded bargaining are occurring in the capital markets during creditor work-outs and take-over battles (Stone 1988). Collective bargaining is beginning to overspill its borders and claim new roles in corporate life.

The nexus-of-contracts view of the firm assumes that the constituent groups bring to their bargaining position whatever legal rights, powers, and immunities they have under external sources of law. Thus, for example, creditors have various liens, collection procedures, and priorities which are defined under a variety of state and federal laws. These rights form the background against which creditors make their bargains with other groups within the firm. So too, if employees have rights under external law, those rights form part of the definition of the economic clout that employees have and can exercise in their bargaining with the other groups.

This model thus requires reconsideration of the rules governing economic weapons. Unions have clout in negotiations with other constituents of the firm only to the extent they can bring to bear a credible threat of withholding their investment and thereby adversely affecting the others. The ability to withhold investments and the consequence to others—that is, the 'negative market power' of unions—is determined by the legal rules governing strikes, secondary boycotts, picketing, and so forth. Thus this model is incomplete without addressing the background legal rules of economic warfare.

4.3 Collectivist regulatory approaches

There is yet another approach to the problem of enforcing workers' implicit contracts, a collectivist regulatory approach. This approach involves creating rights to collective participation by statute, as is found in some of the Co-determination and Works Councils Acts in some European countries. While this approach seems to hold a great deal of promise as a means of countering the asymmetry in enforcement of promises in the internal labour market, it is not likely to find a welcome reception in the United States in the near future (Summers 1982 describes the problems of implementing co-determination in the climate of American labour relations and suggests solutions). It would have to take the form of statutes enacted at the federal level. Federal laws mandating co-determination or works councils in American work-places would constitute an enormous change in the way labour regulations are regulated. Paul Weiler has advocated that Congress enact a form of mandatory works council in all American work-places having more than twenty-five employees (Weiler 1990). Whether such proposals can receive serious consideration and lead to legislative change remains to be seen.

5. CONCLUSION

I have attempted to analyse the impact of the wave of corporate restructurings of the 1980s on workers. I have argued that in the course of such restructurings, wealth is transferred from employees to other groups within the firm by means of breaches of the workers' implicit contracts for deferred compensation. I have also shown how current legal rules define the employment contract and the labour market in ways that make it difficult for workers to defend themselves against expropriation. I have also presented some of the current proposals to redress the problem of breach of employees' implicit contracts, and have argued in favour of a collective empowerment approach rather than an individual rights approach. Whether or not one agrees with the specific solutions advocated here, it is hoped that by developing an understanding of the problem of worker vulnerability, we can move toward a more socially accountable model of the firm and a more effective means of providing work-place justice.

6. POSTSCRIPT: RESPONSE TO HUGH COLLINS

Hugh Collins, in this volume, provides a useful framework for comparing a conventional contractual approach with an organizational approach to the firm. Collins astutely describes how the two approaches lead to different types of analyses and yield different conclusions on such topical issues as the responsibility of parent corporations for the liabilities of their subsidiaries, the duties of directors, and the role of non-shareholder stakeholders in firm decisions. However, I do not believe that he correctly describes or addresses my attempt to give the contractual approach a new direction. Therefore, in the interests of clarifying my position, I feel obliged to respond.

Collins treats my argument as a conventional contractual approach to labour relations, albeit with a 'novel twist.' Thus he says that I 'accept . . . wholeheartedly the contractual frame of reference with respect to power in the corporation.' However, he misses the essence of my argument.

I argue that in internal labour markets, workers are given an implicit promise of job security, a promise that should be enforceable by some legal mechanism. This implicit promise is not the product of bargaining—that is, its existence does not depend upon the power of the parties to bargain expressly for particular terms in the wage package. If it were a bargained-for exchange, there would be no need to speak of an implicit contract—the contract would be express. Rather, I argue, the implicit promise of job security is a unilateral promise made by employers to workers, not as a result of bargaining, but because it serves their production and organizational goals.

What goals does the implicit promise serve? At least two (see Weiler 1990: 64–7). First, since the beginning of this century, the dominant theory in management and personnel relations in the United States has been that employers should encourage employees to stay with the firm a long time (Jacoby 1985: 115–26). Thus, human relations specialists have advised employers to encourage employee attachment to the firm by offering rewards for long and loyal service. The rewards can take many forms, including corporate welfare policies, longevity bonuses, and so forth. But by far the most important form was the creation of hierarchically arranged job ladders whereby employees were told that they could expect advancement in status and pay if they stayed on the job for a long time. The theory said that by so encouraging employment longevity, employees would tend to internalize the goals of the firm. Such employees would be motivated, their morale and productivity would be high, and their tendency to shirk, sabotage, or unionize would disappear (see, e.g., Bloomfield 1921: 295–8; see generally Stone 1975: 45–54). This view was held and practised by many of the great nineteenth- and early twentieth-century captains of industry, including Andrew Carnegie and Henry Ford.

The second goal that the implicit promises serve is that they encourage employees to invest in firm-specific human capital. Increasingly, businesses require such specialized types of human capital. But without some sort of job security, employees are reluctant to invest time acquiring it. Further, management has long struggled with the problem of how to induce older, more experienced workers to impart their firm-specific, or job-specific, knowledge to new recruits (see Stone 1975: 56–8). Older workers know that if they train their juniors, they may well be replaced as soon as their own speed, dexterity, and strength begin to fade. Yet if they do not provide new workers with such training, years of valuable knowledge and experience are lost to the firm. Personnel managers have used many techniques to solve the training problem, including suggestion boxes, quality circles, and the like. However, the most effective means is simply to promise workers that they will not be fired in their later years, despite some decline in their faculties. The implicit promise of job security and deferred compensation in the internal labour market thus solves the training dilemma as well as the motivation problem.

So, for almost one hundred years, promises of job security have been made to employees. They appear in many forms, such as in explicit oral promises made by supervisors, in self-promotional statements in employment manuals, and in general knowledge transmitted through the in-plant grape-vines. They have served as the fundamental fact of life in most medium-sized and large modern establishments, in industrial and service sectors alike. Thus, to rely on these promises as a basis for protecting employee job security is not to rely on workers' bargaining strength; it is to hold corporate managers accountable for the terms they themselves set in the initial employment contract.

Collins also misses the mark when he says that the implicit promise is ambiguous as to its terms. He says that it could just as well contain a term in which 'the risk of premature dismissal is calculated into the wages from the start'. The implicit promise of which I speak is not an imaginary or hallucinatory one, as Collins seems to suggest. It is a message intentionally and repeatedly conveyed to workers inside internal labour markets, disseminated with the intention that it be believed and that it serve as the basis for worker reliance. It is contained in the ubiquitous employer statements found in words, writings, and deeds to the effect that 'If you work here, if you do a reasonable job and don't cause trouble, you have a job for life.' Are these promises or not? If they are, then let us give them legal status and devise means to enforce them. If they are not, then we must ask, what is their status? Perhaps they are intentional misrepresentations, which in their breach should give rise to a tort-like remedy or at least a promissory estoppel. Again, let us devise a remedy. Otherwise we have, by inaction, perpetuated a fraud.

In addition to misunderstanding my argument about implicit promises, Collins evidences a formalistic understanding of the relationship between moral wrongs, legal rights, and remedies. He says that by basing my viewpoint on an implicit contract, I can consider only conventional contract remedies to redress a breach. 'It seems to follow from the contractual framework of analysis that either the employee should be entitled to financial compensation for the loss of the deferred remuneration expected to arise from continuing membership of the internal labour market, or the employee should in fact be kept in her job in order to fulfil the promise.' While I do not reject either of these remedies, I do not confine my analysis or policy proposals to them.

Over fifty years ago, the legal realists exploded the myth that remedies followed automatically from rights. All modern legal jurisprudence, at least in the United States, assumes that particular remedies are not logically entailed by rights, but rather that once a right is recognized, an appropriate remedy should be devised (Llewellyn 1931: 1244; see, e.g., Fuller and Perdue 1936–7; see generally Horwitz 1992: 193–206).

The realists also demonstrated that legal rights are not transcendent and fixed, but rather embodied society's views of moral wrongs. By engaging in detailed and painstaking analysis in one field of law after another, they showed how legal doctrine is infused with political beliefs, and urged us to recognize this and reshape legal doctrine to fit modern sensibilities (M. Cohen 1933: 580–7; Hale 1923).

Thus, my task here has been to identify a wrong, argue that it is one that the legal system should rectify, and suggest one or more possible remedial avenues. The traditional expectancy remedy, which in this case would be financial compensation for the loss of the value of the implicit contract, is one that I discuss. I also demonstrate the legal difficulties in achieving it and the practical difficulties in calculating it. I then consider other suggestions for remedies—such as changes in the at-will employment doctrine, changes in the laws of collective bargaining, changes in the corporate laws, and mandatory employee participation on corporate boards of directors. All the suggestions I make are appropriate ways to redress the wrong which I identify. They are proposals that must be evaluated, to be sure, but not on the basis of whether they comport with a nineteenth-century view of legal rights, wrongs, and remedies. Rather, we must ask whether the particular remedial devices proposed are feasible, effective, or otherwise desirable as ways to restructure the legal terrain upon which labour–management relations take place.

Collins concludes his piece by touting the superiority of the organizational perspective to the contractual perspective in providing employee job security. He argues that the organizational perspective would force owners of capital to see their firms as public institutions, and would induce them to act responsibly toward their employees and communities. He also says that an organizational approach would lead corporate managers to see employees as members of an organization, and treat them with respect. Part of this respect would involve discussing corporate transformations with them in advance, and helping to provide them with redundancy assistance.

It would be a welcome, but remarkable, turn of events if either of these outcomes came about by the adoption of an organizational perspective. I would take no issue with either of them; indeed, I would applaud. However, Collins has not given us any reason to believe that these outcomes would follow from his approach. Other than hortatory statements of lofty ideals, he proposes no mechanism which would force owners of capital to recognize 'social obligations' to their employees and others. Nor does his approach tell us who will impose 'social costs' on firms, or how those social costs are to be ascertained. Furthermore, under the organizational approach, what will induce corporate managers to treat their employees with respect? Indeed, who is to define what the requirements of that 'respect' are to be?

Collins's attempt to illustrate the superiority of the organizational perspective demonstrates that lofty ideals alone, by any name, cannot solve the difficult problems in labour–management relations. For a long time, scholars have urged corporations to show respect for their employees and to practise social responsibility. But without some structure of legal rules, some definition of legal rights, and some concrete legal remedies, such pie-in-the-sky aspirations remain fantasies at best, and at worst, smoke-screens that pre-empt suggestions for real-world, here-and-now improvements.

5
Organizational Regulation and the Limits of Contract

HUGH COLLINS

This chapter provides a commentary and critique of the previous contribution by Katherine Stone. Before commenting directly on Stone's chapter, I should like to stress the importance of the present exciting conjuncture of scholarly traditions. All the contributions in this work traverse boundaries between academic disciplines and between different fields of legal studies. This is a fitting culmination to an intellectual process which has been proceeding apace during the last twenty years or so. Many authors combine the insights of political economy with aspects of company law, the law of contract, and labour law, developing a new contextual subject, which we might call the law of the productive enterprise. This development has occurred as a result of a series of colonizations of the territories of formerly distinct fields of study.

I. THE LAW OF THE PRODUCTIVE ENTERPRISE

The first invasion came from institutional economists. They realized that the firm could be analysed usefully as a network of contracts (Jensen and Meckling 1976; Williamson 1975). This 'deconstruction of the corporation', as Stone calls it, allows one to see all (or rather, nearly all) the groups involved in a productive enterprise as making different types of contracts with the legal entity of the corporation. These contracts include employment, investment through equity (shares) or debt (debentures), directorships, purchases and sales by creditors/outsiders, and so forth. Institutional economists then examined the different terms of these contracts with an eye to their evaluation by reference to such criteria as efficiency and justice. Following this lead, the company lawyers became contract lawyers (Williamson 1984*a*; but for criticism, see Brudney 1985). Then, in a second invasion, the contract lawyers became labour lawyers.

Taking their lead again from the institutional economists (Alchian and Demsetz 1972; Williamson 1975: ch. 4), some lawyers began to investigate the employment relation as if it were merely another contract like a sale of goods (Epstein and Paul 1985). This permitted them to doubt the desirability of any mandatory regulation of the employment relation, since such regulation would prevent the parties to the contract of employment from reaching a wealth-maximizing bargain. Enacting a statute to give a right to claim compensation in the event of unfair dismissal (discharge without just cause), for example, would prevent employees from making their own choices between job security and high wages in selecting the terms of their contracts of employment. By coercing choices in this way, the regulation of dismissal would prevent wealth-maximizing contracts from being forged. In this phase of development, therefore, labour law became subsumed by contract law. Then the labour lawyers struck back indirectly by encroaching on company law.

Labour lawyers, committed as they usually are to improving the lot of the workers (Collins 1989), realized that the private market solutions of improving the bargaining position of workers in negotiating collective agreements had never achieved any real redistribution of power within the firm (Stone 1981; Collins 1987). The crucial strategic decisions were beyond the scope of collective agreements. The remedy seemed to many labour lawyers to lie in transforming the governance of the corporation to give employees a greater say in how such strategic decisions might be reached. Labour lawyers thus became interested in organizational structures, bureaucratic systems of government in the enterprise, arguing in one way or another that workers deserved a more central role in the decision-making process, a process primarily governed by company law (Stone 1988; Davies and Wedderburn 1977; Wedderburn 1985b.)

What emerges from these three colonizations is a rich subject for investigation: the law of the productive enterprise. At its heart lies the question of the just distribution of power in the corporation. The precise nature of this just distribution is, of course, controversial; but as the title of this book recognizes, in the last resort, it can be realized only through legal techniques designed to ensure corporate accountability and control.

2. COMPETING PARADIGMS

Standing back from the debates about the just distribution of power in the corporation, as exemplified in this book, I suggest that they revolve fundamentally around two competing paradigms of analysis of the problem of power in the corporation. On one side, the contractual model informs the analysis of the arrangements of a productive enterprise, and provides the starting-point for debates about the proper scope and aims of legal regulation. On the other side, an organizational model, one which draws on notions of bureaucracy, governance, and public responsibility, offers a radically different paradigm for analysis and intervention. Each paradigm offers valuable insights, yet seems incomplete on its own. I shall illustrate how these competing paradigms appear in the literature by picking on a few of the themes of this book.

The questions raised by groups of companies can be examined from these two perspectives. The contractual perspective sees the relation between parent and subsidiary as a contractual relation of investment; whereas the organizational framework insists upon the effective unity of the two companies within one organization. The contractual perspective advocates the distinction between corporate entities; the organizational perspective insists that at least for certain purposes the group of companies should be treated as one unit for issues of responsibility and accountability.

Another theme of the book raises the question of the proper responsibilities and advantages of the directors of a company. The contractual framework emphasizes here the freedom of the parties to determine their duties and rewards. By contrast, the organizational perspective favours a view of directors as privileged holders of power who should be subject to special duties and constraints to prevent the abuse of such power.

Another theme concerns the position of persons traditionally regarded as outsiders to the company, such as holders of debt like banks and the local community. The question is what power, if any, over the governance of the corporation these external groups should enjoy. The contractual framework limits their interest to their negotiated rights, which in the case of the local community will usually be none at all. The organizational framework emphasizes how the different constituencies which are dependent upon the way power is exercised in the corporation should be placed so as to permit some influence on how that power may be exercised.

Finally, the example of the nature of the employment relation is a recurring theme. Is this a simple contractual wage/work bargain? Or should we perceive employment as a form of membership in an organization which entitles its members to have a say in how the organization is run and to protect their membership in it?

Having illustrated this contrast between the contractual and organizational perspectives, it becomes apparent that the organizational perspective is at once both more challenging to existing legal arrangements and more obscure. There is good reason for both these features of this paradigm. The organizational discourses fit uneasily into the private law framework out of which the law of corporations has been forged by imaginative legal draughtsmen. It contests the public/private divide which absolves the company from social responsibilities. At the same time it refuses to conceive the corporation as composed of the traditional building blocks of private law in its concepts of contract and trusts. Herein lies one challenge presented to the contributors to this book: to devise a legal discourse which can provide the conceptual structure for the articulation of the organizational paradigm.

3. ECONOMIC DISMISSALS AND THE CONTRACTUAL PARADIGM

With these rival perspectives in mind, I turn now to a more concrete examination of Stone's chapter. It confronts one socially significant aspect of debates about power in the corporation. It asks whether anything can, and should, be done to relieve the position of workers who lose their jobs as a result of capital mobility?

Stone answers this question affirmatively. Her argument gives the contractual perspective a novel twist. Instead of accepting the normal version, which insists that workers have the degree of job security for which they bargained and that any interference in these arrangements will be inefficient and unjust, she argues that the dismissed workers can allege that the contract which they agreed to has implied promises of job security in it which are breached in the event of dismissals due to capital mobility. It follows, Stone argues, that some form of regulation designed to ensure the keeping of these implied promises, or at least compensation for breach of them, is due to workers who lose their jobs.

This is a neat and intriguing argument. But in the final analysis, I do not find it attractive, precisely because it accepts so whole-heartedly the contractual frame of reference with respect to power in the corporation. Let me sketch out the disadvantages of this approach in the context of her particular topic and argument, before suggesting how the organizational perspective can provide a more fruitful paradigm for analysis.

I have to concede that the contractual framework can suggest some plausible arguments for protecting the interests of workers dismissed as a result of capital mobility. These arguments take two forms. One insists that the worker has an investment in the firm—a property right in his job, if you like—and that the coercive taking of this investment by dismissal should be compensated or prevented (Singer 1987; Barron 1984; Davies and Freedland 1984: 428–32). The other suggests that express or implied promises of job security have been made, and that the law ought to ensure that the promises are kept (Note 1989*b*). The arguments differ, because the former focuses on unjust enrichment by seizure of another's property, whereas the latter appeals to the moral principle of the binding force of agreements. The remedy for unjust enrichment lies in restoration of the property or its worth, whereas the remedy for breach of promise lies in compensation for expectations or specific performance. For example, if severance or redundancy pay were mooted as the proper remedy in both instances, in the former case the sum of compensation would be assessed by the value of the lost investment, in the latter by reference to the expectation of a stream of income from a job.

It is not entirely clear which of these arguments Stone really favours. She shifts from the rhetoric of one to other in the course of the chapter. From one angle we can see that the loss of investment in firm-specific human capital can be regarded as a form of proprietary interest which should be compensated if it is expropriated. Alternatively, we can see that by the rhetoric of implicit contracts she is really appealing to the morality of promise keeping, so that the basis of compensation lies in remedying the loss of expected future income. On balance, I favour the latter interpretation. It is true that the investment in firm-specific human capital has been lost, but it is far from clear that the firm has expropriated it, thereby becoming unjustly enriched. The firm no longer has access to this human capital; it has simply been wasted. The real force of the moral claim for intervention seems to me to lie in the idea that some implied promise of job security on a rising wage curve has been broken, so that this expectation should be compensated.

If this is the correct interpretation of the argument, then we should address two further questions. First, how convincing is the moral claim advanced for legal regulation? Second, assuming that it does have moral force, what kind of legal regulation of dismissal does it warrant? I shall consider these questions briefly before returning to my more general criticism of this form of argument based upon the contractual paradigm.

3.1 Moral force

The moral claim rests upon two premises: one concerning wage patterns in the internal labour markets of firms, the other concerning the implied promises made by employers to employees who enter an internal labour market. Both premises are vulnerable to objections, which render them shaky foundations on which to base a moral claim.

With respect to the wage patterns of the internal labour market, I think one must admire the ingenuity of neo-classical economics in adjusting the simple model of labour markets to account for many of the features of internal labour markets. Those economists who developed the model of the internal labour market argued that employers enjoyed considerable administrative discretion in setting wage rates for jobs within the firm's hierarchy, with only port-of-entry jobs being tied to the external labour market (Segal 1986). To resist this suggestion that internal labour markets set wage rates by reference to such social factors as position in the hierarchy of authority within the firm, the neo-classical economists had to wrestle with features of wage rates for jobs which do not conform to some simple spot market depending on forces of supply and demand. To account for such anomalies as wage stickiness and substantial inter-firm differentials for the same occupation, neo-classical accounts of the setting of wage rates introduced such factors as the quasi-fixed costs of hiring and training, the investment in and acquisition of human capital, the significance of firm-specific skills, and of course that old compendium of transaction costs.

The implicit contract literature, on which Stone draws, was devised originally to explain why employers tend to make adjustments to demand by changing quantities of labour rather than its price—that is, use dismissals rather than downward wage adjustments to reduce labour costs (Rosen 1985). But like all good theories, the implicit contract idea can be used for different purposes. Stone uses the concept of an implicit contract to explain one feature of the internal labour market, the tendency of wage rates to rise during lifetime employment with a particular firm to the extent that they clearly exceed external labour market rates. Stone argues that the implicit contract contains a promise of deferred remuneration which will be realized by preserving job security. So a theory invented to explain levels of unemployment from a micro-economic perspective is now employed with admirable job flexibility to demonstrate why this allocation of the risks of unemployment is unfair.

Let me put forward two sceptical observations about this line of argument. In the first place, I confess to an impatience with these elaborate neo-classical theories of internal labour markets. The idea of an implicit contract is yet another device to explain by reference to forces of supply and demand the pattern of wage rates set within an internal labour market. The persistent unwillingness to recognize that wage rates are set in internal labour markets by reference to social and administrative norms, rather than efficiency considerations, seems to me to result from a blinkered perspective of the discipline of economics (Adams 1975). One has only to look, for example, at studies of women's pay to find what I regard as convincing evidence that social norms account to a considerable extent for wage levels (Treiman and Hartmann 1981). The internal labour market justifies itself principally as a meritocracy, and wages are allocated accordingly. As a result, women's jobs become devalued precisely because they are performed by women.

If, as I think, the features of internal labour markets are best explained by reference to social norms, then the elaborate neo-classical explanations of wage rates miss many of the key factors in wage determination. The phenomenon which Stone describes in her chapter, of wages rising with seniority, is in my opinion primarily the product of a social norm which ties wages to experience and status within the hierarchy, not a clever bargain for deferred remuneration; so the justification for some remedy for premature dismissal disappears.

My second sceptical observation about the basis of the moral claim concerns the terms of the implied contract. One of the features of the contractual paradigm is that everything turns on the terms of the agreement between the parties. By alleging an implicit contract, the terms are not open to inspection. But this leaves open the possibility that serious disagreements may exist as to the terms of the implicit bargain. Any argument in this form runs the risk that subtle alterations of the terms of the implicit contract can change the moral outcome.

In Stone's interpretation of the implicit contract, the employer promises to pay higher wages later on in return for the employee's acquisition of firm-specific skills and their use over a long period of employment. Premature dismissal then amounts to a breach of promise of deferred remuneration. But it could equally well be argued, I suggest, that the risk of premature dismissal is taken account in the wages from the start, so that in effect the employee has been paid an insurance premium against the risk of economic dismissal. Evidence for such a premium would be found in higher wage rates in the internal labour market as compared to external market rates from the outset. Such evidence can be found in inter-firm wage differentials for the same job, a phenomenon which provided the basis for the theory of labour market segmentation (Reich *et al.* 1973; Cain 1976). If this is so, then the terms of the implicit contract do not include any promise of job security; the promise is rather for the employer to pay a risk premium to induce the employee to acquire firm-specific skills. Thus the premature dismissals do not amount to a breach of the implicit contract at all; for the risk premium has been paid in the form of higher wages already.

We could no doubt play at length with the terms of the implicit contract. I remain agnostic on both the question of its existence and its terms. My sole point is that the terms of this implicit contract could be formulated in a variety of ways, and most alternatives would undercut the moral force of Stone's argument. The notion of an implicit contract is therefore at best a hazardous foundation on which to base a moral claim for protection of workers against lay-offs and redundancies.

3.2 Remedies

But suppose that the implicit contract idea does rest upon safe and defensible premises, what moral obligation does it suggest? In other words, what kind of legal regulation does it justify? It seems to follow from the contractual framework of the analysis that either the employee should be entitled to financial compensation for the loss of the deferred remuneration expected to arise from continuing membership of the internal labour market, or the employee should in fact be kept in her job in order to fulfil the promise. The legal regulation which the moral argument justifies therefore amounts to a severance payment calculated either on the basis of some future expectation of income above external market rates or on specific performance of the contract of employment (Collins 1992: ch. 7).

In her chapter, Stone strikes a pragmatic tone with respect to remedies. She indicates that in general the most effective remedy will lie in strengthened collective bargaining, and mentions in particular requirements of a warning of impending dismissals, severance pay, and pension protection. I regard this pragmatic approach as a weakness in the argument, for it uncouples the moral justification for intervention from the precise regulatory measures envisaged. For example, the requirement of advance notification of economic dismissals flows neither from the need for compensation for expected rewards nor from the desire to preserve job security. A persistent reservation which I have with such contractual approaches is that they tend to support only limited financial remedies payable to the dismissed employee. They provide scant support for active manpower policies designed to reduce the social costs of plant closure. Once one adds a note of pragmatism, one may discover an even greater dilution of the financial remedy if the social costs of implementing it exceed the benefits achieved (Note 1989b).

4. THE ORGANIZATIONAL PARADIGM AND ECONOMIC DISMISSALS

It is this latter kind of point about the remedies, of course, which leads me ultimately to have grave misgivings about the fruitfulness of the contractual approach as a way of analysing and justifying any alteration in the existing distribution of power within the corporation. Some of its implications seem to me to be wholly unsatisfactory.

The logic of the argument seems to leave out in the cold both all those workers who do not benefit from an internal labour market and senior workers in the firm. The former cannot claim to have been beneficiaries of an implicit contract at all; whereas the latter have reaped the reward of high pay already, so no compensation falls due. In addition, because the local community or the state normally lacks a contractual relation with the firm, it can make no claims on the employer.

Moreover, like other contractual arguments, the terms of the explicit or implicit contract will depend upon the respective bargaining strength of the parties, as Stone acknowledges. My principal objection to these contractual arguments, and indeed to the whole industrial pluralist tradition of labour law which prefers to allocate rights to workers on the basis of collective contracts, is simply that some interests of workers in the corporation are too important to be left to the vagaries of market forces. We accept already, for example, that bargaining strength cannot justify race and sex discrimination; but it seems to me that many other interests connected with job security are too important to be left to depend upon the fluctuations of the demand for labour (Collins 1992: 195, 270). Yet if contracts, whether explicit, implicit, or collective, are permitted to allocate rights, then these market forces will play the dominant role in the distribution of rights, and the rights will be foregone wherever the workers' bargaining power is weak. Thus the exclusion of workers who lack implicit contracts under Stone's scheme is no minor difficulty, but reveals a fundamental flaw in the whole contractual approach to the just distribution of power within the corporation.

What, then, might the alternative organizational paradigm propose as the analysis and justification of legal regulation in this sphere? In outline, I think that it would lead to measures which reflect two considerations. In the first place, the owners of capital would be required to respect a social obligation to minimize the social costs of their action of dismissals. This obligation flows from the perception of the productive organization as a public institution with responsibilities which go beyond the residual claims of owners of capital. A social-cost approach would justify a range of legal measures designed to reduce periods of unemployment, including notice provisions, time off for job search, assistance for retraining, and co-operation in state-run active manpower programmes. The second consideration would arise from the idea that employees as members of the organization should be treated with respect, so that corporate plans should be discussed and a social programme to help with the consequences of redundancy formulated and observed. Notice that these proposals grounded in the organizational paradigm offer little support for severance payments (Collins 1992: ch. 5).

In this brief illustration, I hope to have shown how the rival paradigms of contract and organization lie behind our analyses and justifications for the distribution of power in the corporation. To think within the paradigm of an organization does not require one to abandon the notion of contracts entirely, but rather to recognize that other dimensions of power exist and need to be controlled within the corporation. One can accept, for instance, that the employment relation has contractual dimensions, but also observe that the best way to describe and understand the relation between worker and boss is to recognize that between them personally no contract exists, and that the power relation springs from the organization of which they are both members (Collins 1986). The question then becomes not how to alter the bargaining strength of workers so that they may improve their prospects for job security, but rather how justifiable it is that managerial members of the organization should have in law the exclusive and unfettered power to alter the labour requirements of the firm.

PART II

*Corporate Regulation: Critiques of Market
Failure and Transaction Cost Theory*

6

Why Regulate the Modern Corporation? The Failure of 'Market Failure'

DAVID CAMPBELL

The argument that corporations should be subject to legal regulation of at least some of their actions tends to be couched in terms of 'market failure'. Corporations are recognized to have characteristics, particularly the scale and scope of their operations, which make the market governance of their actions imperfect. The purpose of regulation is to iron out those imperfections and to restore market governance. Now in some cases this may mean very extensive legal regulation indeed, and in exceptional cases, particularly in respect of the so-called natural monopolies, an acceptance that market governance must be abandoned in favour of state governance. What typically is aimed at, however, even in these cases, is a sort of market governance through legally enforcing the effects of such governance when the market itself has lost the power to be self-enforcing.

I will argue that this approach is fundamentally mistaken with respect to the giant corporations which are the principal institutions of the advanced capitalist economy. These corporations should not be understood as aberrant products of the market. They are, at their heart, designed to oust the market, and they have succeeded. It is quite widely conceded that there is little point in attempting simply to restore the market, even if it were possible. As the competitive advantages of corporations would merely lead to them ousting the market again, any such policy stops right where regulation really needs to start (Lenin 1964b: 290). But what is insufficiently appreciated is that the abolition of the market was no bad thing. The typical advocacy of corporate regulation regards the market as the best form of economic governance, and hopes to preserve its sovereignty or even enlarge it against those features of the corporation which threaten to narrow it. But by the last quarter of the nineteenth century, the real market of *laissez-faire* capitalism had entered into such a state of systemic decay that the future of capitalist property seemed to be called into the most serious question. The development of the modern corporation was undertaken as a

I would like to thank the British Council for its financial support of the preparation of this chapter. I should also like to thank Jim Allan for his comments, the editors of this volume for their revisions, and Sue Clay and Rosita Chan for their assistance in the compilation of the footnotes.

necessary response to the limits placed by the market on continued capital accumulation—limits which were being manifested in the most profound economic crises and which were very widely analysed as leading to an impending 'breakdown of capitalism', by both those who hoped for and those who feared this outcome. To hope for the restoration of market governance is to hope for a return to those limits of accumulation; and, of course, no one really wants this.

I will put forward my argument in three parts. First, I will discuss the concept of the 'market' used in market failure arguments. This is the 'perfect market' of neo-classical economics. The use of the perfect market to set up transaction cost explanations of the firm is, of course, associated with Coase (1937), whose perspective directly leads to 'market failure' analyses. Coase explains the firm as a governance structure which minimizes transaction costs in the face of high degrees of risk which distort the ideal typical perfect market. It goes without saying that there is great technical interest in this; but institutional economics are very poor indeed when it comes to explaining the nature of the real corporation's relationship to the real market of *laissez-faire*. Though interesting accounts of the firm can be built on a transaction cost basis, the concept of the market which such accounts use systematically fails to deal with the structural properties of historical *laissez-faire*. This failure makes the idea of restoring analogies to market governance highly problematic.

Second, I will explore the implications of a curious feature of Coase's work, that it was at the very least twenty-five years behind its time. The American economy had already taken a thoroughgoing corporate form by the time the USA entered into the First World War, and Coase's work really stands as a rationalization of developments which we can see had taken place much earlier. What is more to the point—and it is of the first importance—is that this rationalization has very little in common with the perspective of the economists whose views actually guided the development of the corporate economy. An earlier generation of American economists, of whom J. B. Clark, C. A. Conant, A. T. Hadley, D. A. Wells, and C. D. Wright may be taken as representative, held to a view of *laissez-faire* as structurally prone to chronic over-production, a view which is now associated with Marx. These influential bourgeois economists conceived of the corporation as the principal way of dealing with the problems of *laissez-faire* within a broad framework of capitalist property. They did not regard departure from the price mechanism as an unfortunate cost, but as an absolutely necessary shift in the nature of capitalist economics if capitalist property was to be sustained.

Third, following from this, I will show that corporate regulation must necessarily fail to be effective when it is conceived of as a corrective to market failure. It fails because it does not appreciate the size of the problem at hand, and because it puts forward solutions that are so inappropriate that they cannot consistently be implemented. These solutions refer the corporation back to a market which just does not exist, and leave a vacuum just where regulation should be effective. This vacuum represents a huge space free of meaningful public control, in which corporations are obliged to follow the oligopolistic imperatives of the advanced capitalist economy by adopting plans which are, to use the jargon, sub-optimal or, to speak sensibly, appalling.

The inherent absurdity of the goal of this type of regulation prevents its energetic pursuit even within its self-defeatingly narrow limits. With a breath-taking leap into abstraction, capitalism is conceived of as *laissez-faire* without internal contradictions, and economic harmony is held to follow from reducing the corporation to the market governance of this wholly mythical capitalism. But when taken out of the economics textbook and turned into policy, any actual restoration of the market would restore the conditions of capitalist crisis which the corporation was urgently required to solve. Now, of course, none of the advocates of the market want this; indeed, it is the last thing they want. This gives the corporation the ever present excuse for the exercise of corporate power that the real introduction of the market would be disastrous. This argument is hard to defeat because it is correct, and this imposes a further limit on what it is thought appropriate for regulation to attempt.

Regulation is stalled by a debilitating paradox at the heart of current economic policy. The theoretical apparatus of neo-classical economics as a technique for guiding the rational allocation of resources is applied to the modern corporation, and precisely the wrong conclusion is drawn. It is obvious that the giant corporation produces all sorts of outcomes which hinder optimal allocations. The response, especially in the privatization of formerly state-owned corporations, is to approximate to the market by extending capitalist private property. But this is precisely the form of control of the means of production which could be preserved only by the ousting of the market that causes the systematic obstructions to optimal allocations in the first place! The development of new forms of control, whereby governance structures could be implemented which would allow of optimal allocations, is prevented. Indeed, such steps as have been taken in this direction are at present being reversed.

To get beyond this quite paralysing paradox, a full appreciation of the obsolescence of the market in the advanced capitalist economy and a proper recognition of the size of the political task necessarily involved in corporate regulation are essential. The issue is not to approximate a return to the 'market' of capitalist property, but to determine the political structures which will allow the adoption of marginalist techniques for the control of the modern economy.

I. THE CHARGE OF MARKET FAILURE

One should not underestimate the extent to which sufficiently abstract reasoning along neo-classical lines can lend purportedly market-based theoretical support to the actions of even the largest multinational corporations. It is perfectly possible to view present allocations as basically rational by holding that advanced capitalism essentially is a free market (Friedman 1982: 121–3), albeit with minor imperfections (ibid. 128–32). After this, depending on how much one can bite off and chew as a minor imperfection before one chokes, one can identify welfare with unrestrained corporate pricing (Friedman 1977). Having thus forestalled any open-minded attempt to investigate the distance between corporate policy and public welfare (Pigou 1938: pt.2), one can even go on to say that attempts directly to pursue welfare outcomes are totally wrong-headed (Coase 1988: 133–56). I will not address this line of argument, for the evidence against it is quite overwhelming, and, for the purpose of theoretical development, to recapitulate it would be redundant. Rather, I will turn to those approaches which recognize that the corporation systematically limits market governance, and propose regulatory measures to remove these limits. These measures can be grouped into five classes. Let me put forward my grouping; then I will put forward my criticism of them all, together with my alternative approach to the issue.

1.1 Remedies for market failure

The first group of measures are those concerned with ensuring the proper functioning of the stock-market. These measures all seek to ensure a symmetry in the availability of information for potential participants in this market (Pennington 1990: 251–60). Thus, disclosure requirements for corporations seeking investment, ranging from common-law misrepresentation (*Peek* v. *Gurney*, 1873) to the most extensive legislative provisions (Financial Services Act, 1986), are added to an apparatus of rules enforced by the appropriate trade bodies (Stock Exchange n.d.).

The second group of measures are analogous measures within the corporation itself—the province of company law proper. The basic model is that of restraining the corporation within the broad limits of its publicly declared objects (*Ashbury* v. *Riche*, 1875) and of the general meeting, composed of individual shareholders having rights proportional to their holdings (*Borland's Trustee* v. *Steel*, 1901), democratically formulating strategic policy and seeing that the board carries this strategy out (*Automatic Self-Cleansing Syndicate* v. *Cuninghame*, 1906).

This group of measures still constitutes the overwhelming substance of the majority of undergraduate classes in company law. However, though they may have some meaning as an administrative apparatus for the running of a corporation by its management, they are really rather worthless as any guide to its meaningful control, as I think is generally conceded from a wide variety of standpoints (Campbell 1990; Sealy 1984; M. Stokes 1986). If we conceive of the general meeting as a meeting of shareholders who are individual financial investors of disparate interests and whose commitment to the company is through their alienable investments, it is clear that the transaction costs of meaningful supervision by those shareholders are overwhelming, indeed infinite. As this is so, private control on the traditional company law bases of exceptions to the rule in *Foss* v. *Harbottle*, section 459 of the Companies Act, 1985 and section 122(1)(g) of the Insolvency Act, 1986 (Hollington 1990) is more or less irrelevant to the actual conduct of the corporation, at least while it remains in reasonably good health (Farrar *et al.* 1992: pt. 6).

The third group of measures are those concerned to ensure that corporate executives keep within certain bounds of proper conduct, although it is manifest that these bounds cannot be enforced by the legal rules of corporate structure. The possibility of separating ownership and control in the modern corporation (Berle and Means 1968: bk. 1) implies not only the loss of the real entrepreneurial spirit which follows from putting one's own money at risk, which was feared by Adam Smith (1776: 741), but also the general substitution of the good of management as bureaucracy for the good of the shareholder as owner as the goal of the organization (Williamson 1964, 1986: ch. 2). Thus directors are regarded as being subject to a range of fiduciary duties owed to the corporation as a whole (*Canadian Aero Service* v. *O'Malley*, 1974), and the contracts of employment of those in more routine management positions will bind them to the good of their employer in the normal way (*Sec. of State for Employment* v. *ASLEF* (No.2), 1972).

Of all the areas of corporate regulation, the one purporting to set up directors' duties is the woolliest; the space left by the absence of any real concrete content of these fiduciary duties has been filled by resorting to analogies which have viewed directors variously as agents (Fama 1980; Jensen and Meckling 1976), executors of a trust (Berle and Means 1968: ch. 7),[1] or sellers of management services (Manne 1965, 1967). The

---

[1] Berle explored the implications of the trust analogy at length in a long exchange with Dodd (Berle 1931; Dodd 1932; Berle 1932; Dodd 1935). When Berle retrospectively summed up this interesting exchange (Berle 1954: 169), it was in the rather bathetic form of giving up his own vague idea of the shareholder as beneficiary to install the entire public as the beneficiary of the corporation's activities. Such an idea could not even be as concrete as seeing the corporation as a trust; the corporation now had to have a 'conscience'. This idea is an obvious forerunner of the notion of the 'soulful corporation' advanced by Kaysen (1957:

information disclosure provisions I have already discussed simply cannot
be effectively maintained as an adequate basis for regulating management
behaviour in the face of the overwhelming evidence that general meetings
are more or less worthless as expressions of general shareholder control.
Hence the effect of the directors' duties is merely to give some plausibility
to the location of control in the mythical average shareholder of the general meeting, who is regarded as the principal, beneficiary, or buyer.
While it is manifest that these duties work only at the most abstract level,
or perhaps merely as rhetoric (Bratton 1989c; Brudney 1985; De Mott
1988), they must obviously be maintained if there is to be any plausibility
to the market failure rationale for regulation, since there is no other way
to bring the market back into play once it is admitted that the formal
mechanisms of corporate law fail.

The fourth group of measures are those which seek to enforce market
outcomes on corporate policy when it is clear that the market has lost the
power to be self-enforcing. These measures range all the way from piecemeal regulation of the qualities of specific products to the nationalization
of entire industries; but the most discussed example is antitrust after the
US pattern (Neale and Goyder 1980) and its weaker European analogues
(Bellamy and Child 1991). The problem here is that market governance is
regarded as optimal, but the invisible hand has lost its grip. The corporation has the power to set prices, and the state is required to impose theoretical market outcomes by limiting that power within acceptable bounds
which approximate those that it is believed the market would have set.
The panoply of potential measures is vast, and the econometrics of their
application hugely complicated; but all boil down to this essential goal, of
restoring at least an analogue to market governance so far as the situation permits (Posner 1976: ch. 2, appendix).

The twists and turns this imposes on the would-be regulator would be
humorous if it were not that real issues of the greatest importance are
being reduced to a disabling antinomy between the pricing mechanism of
laissez-faire and the efficiency of giant-scale production carried out by the
oligopolistic corporation. Consider the US Federal Trade Commission's
holding that antitrust violations could be shown by 'evidence . . . that the
acquiring firm['s] overall organization gives it a decisive advantage in
efficiency over its smaller rivals' (*Foremost Dairies*, 1962). It is rather easy
to point out that this is no way to view efficiency, and to add all sorts of
apparatuses for giving weight to the efficiency gains of corporate growth
(Turner 1964–5: 1323–8); and this is what has happened in antitrust theory since the time of *Foremost Dairies* (Williamson 1986: ch. 12; 1987a:
ch. 13). But this merely tilts the balance back the other way, and there

311–19) which enjoyed a considerable vogue. The degenerative emptying of any concrete
content out of these accounts is manifest.

are obvious limits to this, the recognition of which was the motivation for the antitrust effort in the first place. It is hardly novel to point out this antinomy (Posner 1976: 35), but my claim is that it is not simply the unfortunate fact of economic life which it is typically taken to be (Bork 1978), but rather the product of a remediable theoretical shortcoming in the analysis of the corporation which follows from framing corporate control exclusively in terms of market failure.

The fifth set of measures are those which recognize that corporate actions will systematically fail to produce outcomes in conformity with the public good, and so impose regulations which run directly counter to normal corporate outcomes. The obvious examples are occupational health and safety and anti-pollution regulations, which are regarded as countering the corporation's typical tendency to cut labour and capital costs in such a way as to harm workers and the environment.

Even these measures, however, can be brought into line with a market failure argument. The problem with pollution, for example, is that from the perspective of the individual corporation the environmental 'costs' of its polluting activities are 'externalities', in the sense that those costs are so remote to the corporation that it would be inefficient to take preventative measures representing the expenditure of a large amount of resources to avoid a small or zero cost (Richardson 1983: ch. 1). It is Coase who takes the market failure approach furthest here. It requires only that a tangible property right be invested in those suffering from the polluting activity—by the law of nuisance, for example—for regulation to be superfluous, as the socially efficient level of pollution will be determined by agreement between the polluter and the harmed, assuming sufficiently low transaction costs (Coase 1988: 95–133).

1.2 The foundations of transaction cost analysis

Ending the above list with reference to 'The Problem of Social Cost' (Coase 1988) is entirely appropriate, for the thinking running through all these measures is very heavily indebted to Coase. The consistent theme of these groups of measures is the identification of market governance as the proper goal of regulation, coupled with the substitution of an idealized market for the real market of *laissez-faire* capitalism. This substitution represents a major loss of realism in the view of the market. At first glance, this seems a strange comment, for, of course, the extraordinary power of Coase's work lies in its claims to be realistic: 'Modern institutional economics should study man as he is, acting within the constraints imposed by real institutions. Modern institutional economics is economics as it ought to be' (Coase 1984: 231). Coase's explanations of institutions purport to be of real structures, classically, of course, of the firm: 'It

is hoped to show . . . that a definition of a firm may be obtained which is
. . . realistic in that it corresponds to what is meant by a firm in the real
world' (Coase 1988: 33–4). The definition we have given is one which
closely approximates the firm as it is considered in the real world' (ibid.
54).

How does Coase arrive at his account of the nature of the firm? 'The
Nature of the Firm' (Coase 1937) puts forward an account of the firm as
a cheaper way of dealing with the risks of complicated production than
the market, as against some contemporary contributions that are not now
widely read. The reasoning involved was made more clear in 'The
Problem of Social Cost' (Coase 1988) in what has come to be known as
the postulate of zero transaction costs. A hypothetical discrete exchange
carried out with zero transaction costs is assumed (ibid. 97–114), and
then the costs ancillary to establishing the exchange are added as externalities (to put it in a way of which Coase would not approve). The
object of the exercise is to keep such costs to a minimum, for they
obstruct or prevent the exchange. Hence the conclusion is the establishment of the least costly appropriate governance structures. This may
mean regulating the market through congenial principles of contract, or
integrating through the firm (or even state governance) (ibid. 114–19).

The consequence of Coase's intention to focus on obstructions to perfect discrete exchange is that such costs are regarded as a type of friction
in transaction cost analysis. The basic assumption remains the perfect
exchange, so that, even in transaction cost analyses pointing to governance structures external to, but essential for, the market, the market is
regarded as being composed of rational, individual utility-maximizers.
Transaction costs are 'the costs of carrying out market transactions' (ibid.
115), and the point is to minimize them, for they are merely obstructions.
Though the zero-sum transaction cost is 'a very unrealistic assumption'
(ibid. 114), this does not alter the character of the effort, which is to
remove costs in order to leave the subsisting, perfect discrete exchange.

For Coase to set up his argument in this way involves a very strong
separation between the realism of his statement of boundary conditions
and the unrealistic nature of his assumptions about the residual exchange.
The reality of zero-transaction-cost exchanges should be this: they could
never take place. For if one really took away all the costs of exchanging,
the exchange would not take place cost-free. It simply would not take
place. But this is absolutely not what Coase means. He does believe—and
claims to identify this belief also in Adam Smith (Coase 1976)—that there
is some residual quality about human beings as such that makes them
exchange or, to use Coase's more modern synonym, choose. 'Economics',
Coase says, is 'the science of human choice' (Coase 1988: 2; cf. Robbins
1935: 16). This is like saying that physics is the science of forces and

objects, in that while it is in a sense true, it is so utterly abstract as to be useless. But Coase is quite sanguine about 'the acceptance by economists of a view of human nature so lacking in content' (Coase 1988: 5); indeed, he celebrates the applicability of economics not only to all human phenomena (ibid. 2; cf. Becker 1976), but also to the 'animal behaviour' of 'the rat, cat and octopus' (Coase 1988: 3; cf. Kagel *et al.* 1981).

If we are to do anything with this idea, we must have some notion of concrete preferences, and, despite his claims of generality, this is just what Coase has: 'I believe that human preferences came to be what they are in those millions of years in which our ancestors (whether or not they can be classified as human) lived in hunting bands and were those preferences which, in such conditions, were conducive to survival' (Coase 1988: 4).

This is complete nonsense, which receives no corroboration from any philosophical or sociological work on the determinate features of human preferences of which I am aware (e.g., Bhaskar 1989; Harré 1979), other than the suspect discipline, which Coase significantly cites in his support to the exclusion of all other social theory, of sociobiology (Coase 1988: 4–5). Ignorance of social theory's conclusions about the nature of human agency and social structure (e.g., Giddens 1984) is essential to Coase. His position, a common enough one (Lukes 1973: ch. 11–13, 18–20), rests entirely on a mistaken identification of capitalism, a specific economic form with a clearly delimited historical provenance (Wallerstein 1974, 1979), with 'choice'.

It is obvious that on this basis Coase could not possibly give an accurate account of the origin or nature of the modern (or indeed any) economic system; nor can he do other than grudgingly acknowledge the structural properties of that specific system. These are very serious shortcomings (Cooter 1982; D. H. Regan 1972), which confront any attempt to expand Coase's work into a general account of the modern economy.[2] Coase correctly observes that 'in mainstream economic theory, the firm

---

[2] In this way, Coase's work centrally involves the closure of some potentially extremely productive explanatory lines in institutional economics which were to the forefront of Veblen's legacy (Veblen 1970). These lines have been developed by other institutional economists, obviously including Commons, but particularly by C. E. Ayres. The flavour of Ayres's institutional economics emerges clearly enough from the following, taken from his last published work:

Surely the species that has found its way from savagery to husbandry, and from husbandry to automation can do better than what Karl Marx called capitalism. The market system was a product of the industrial revolution of the eighteenth century. But we are now approaching the twenty-first century and a world-wide economy. Like the first stone hand-axe, the first fire-brand, and articulate speech itself, computerized automation is a manifestation of the technological process. Human life and well-being depends upon the furtherance of that process now no less than it did a thousand years ago when (as we have lately discovered) the foundations of an industrial economy [were] being laid, or a million years ago when mankind was first embarking upon its technological adventure. The values we seek are those of human life and well-being. The process by which we seek them is an experimental process, as it has always been. By pursuing this process we will go beyond capitalism, as our forebears went beyond the systems into which they were born. This is the message of institutionalism. (Ayres 1973: pp. xi–xii)

and the market are, for the most part, assumed to exist and are not themselves the subject of investigation' (Coase 1988: 5), and his own work undertakes such an investigation. But his accounts are based on the very assumptions of perfect markets which he is trying to refine, and there is a self-defeating circularity about this: 'What differentiates [my writings] is not that they reject existing economic theory, which . . . embodies the logic of choice and is of wide applicability, but that they employ this theory to examine the role which the firm, the market and the law play in the working of the economic system' (ibid.).

Coase's objection to assuming that markets exist is not that he wants to explain the market's existence, for he himself makes this assumption. He objects to assuming that the market exists everywhere, and he goes on to explain instances of its non-existence (forgetting that this is all instances) as a departure from the normal case. Consequently, Coase himself never really examines the market as such; for it is assumed to exist, though certain forms of exchange are examinable. The institutional thrust of Coase's work is effectively undercut in this way, for the principal economic institution, the free market, is never itself explained.

For our purposes, there is a very substantial problem with this, which relates to the peculiar abstraction of the perfect market. This market is typically introduced as a purely theoretical assumption; yet it is to function as an aspiration. The difficulty is that when this type of market reasoning needs to be given a concrete form, the form it is given is that of *laissez-faire*. This is never made explicit (at least in academic writings), for the way it takes place is rather surreptitious. Nevertheless, in this way the ideological equation of efficiency with a mythical view of *laissez-faire*, which is the commonest currency of neo-classical economics (S. Clarke 1991; Therborn 1975), is found at the heart of the realism of transaction cost economics, and indeed, is given probably its most vulgar academic expression in Posner (1986: pt. 3). While this is undoubtedly a purely ideological correlation of two very different markets, I want now to look at how plausible such a correlation was for the development of the form of the corporation and is now for the analysis of that form.

2. *LAISSEZ-FAIRE* AND THE ORIGINS OF THE LARGE CORPORATION

A less blasé account of *laissez-faire* was central to the analyses of those economists who, up to fifty years earlier than Coase, actually guided the corporate restructuring of the international capitalist economy.[3] For,

---

[3] Many of the texts of these economists are now difficult to obtain. In citing references here, I have restricted myself to texts available in the Bodleian Library of the University of Oxford.

while integration with macro-economic concerns is entirely absent from transaction cost accounts of the firm, it was a principal feature of the work of these economists. They were working against the background of the profound crisis in the international capitalist economy between 1873 and 1896, regarding the empirical existence of which there is complete unanimity (Rosenberg 1943). The main place this crisis has had in the history of economic theory is in the explanation of the success of Marxist political movements in the late nineteenth century. *Das Kapital* sets up an account of capitalism as prone to over-production manifested in increasingly acute crises and a secular tendency towards chronic stagnation (K. Marx 1981: ch. 15). When, after Marx's death in 1883, Engels took on the main burden of efforts to popularize Marx's thought and consolidate the political movement largely based upon it, he had the stimulus of putting his arguments forward in the context of this crisis, which he was able to use to show that the limits to accumulation which Marx had identified were becoming ever more pressing (Engels 1976: 113).

The majority of the economists of the Second International, including Engels himself, interpreted Marx's work, which is radically incomplete at this point, along the lines of what is now known as 'breakdown theory': that is, a claim that capitalist accumulation had run up against limits that were making its collapse inevitable (Luxemburg 1973). That this interpretation now seems very seriously flawed (Sweezy 1956: ch. 10; Hansen 1985: ch. 3–4) should not detract from the severity of the economic crises against which it was developed, which gave it an at least plausible empirical background.

I do not wish to pass any sort of judgment on Marx's or Engels's views of the limits to capital accumulation. The consideration of the adequacy of these views as such is not directly relevant here, because I will show that very similar positions have been at the heart of efforts not to bring about the breakdown of capitalism, but rather to ensure its continuance, through the adoption of the corporate form together with the associated formulation of state policies aimed at the provision of domestic and foreign economic environments which will allow continued capital accumulation far beyond the limits of *laissez-faire*. Only the most abstract economist can fail to see that the advanced capitalist economy based on the giant corporation is a very different structure from *laissez-faire* capitalism. It must be fully appreciated, however, that advanced capitalism represents a rejection of *laissez-faire* after that system had come to be considered quite insupportable, and that, accordingly, to criticize the corporation as a market failure greatly underestimates the extent to which that 'failure' is a desirable state of affairs.

Marx, of course, based his account of capitalism on the leading national economy of the nineteenth century, that of Britain (K. Marx

1976: 90). This distinction has now obviously passed to the USA (Baran and Sweezy 1966: 20), so it is appropriate that we should focus on US materials, on what recent historiography is describing as the formation of 'corporate liberalism' in the USA between 1873 and 1916 (Parrini and Sklar 1983; Sklar 1988). This focus crudely overrides many important differences between, for example, US trust formation and European cartelization (Sklar 1988: 154–66). I put it forward in this context, however, as of general application to the understanding of the relationship of the corporation to the real market of *laissez-faire*.

2.1 Over-production

The *First Annual Report* in 1886 of the US Commissioner for Labor, Carroll D. Wright, was addressed specifically to the causes of '[t]he present industrial depression . . . the first of its kind' (Wright 1886: 11), because '[n]o more important and vital question could have been selected for the first work of the Bureau of Labor' (ibid. 13). In a most comprehensive review of the European (ibid. ch. 1) and US (ibid. ch. 2) evidence, Wright concluded:

The family of manufacturing states, Great Britain, France, Belgium, Germany, and the United States, if not also Austria, Russia and Italy[4] are suffering from an industrial depression novel in its kind, and yet having characteristic features of similarity throughout the whole range of states. It seems to be quite true that in those states considered, the volume of business and of production have not been affected disastrously by the depression[5] but that prices have been greatly reduced, wages frequently reduced, and margins of profits carried to the minimum range. Over-production seems to prevail in all alike without regard to the system of commerce which exists in either. (ibid. 254)

Reflection on this crisis was characterized by the remarkable paradox of grandiose celebration of the development of immense economic

---

[4] The Commissioner is not saying that this last group of countries escaped the depression, but that he lacks the confidence to draw conclusions about them on the basis of the materials available to him (Wright 1886: 291).

[5] The Commissioner is contrasting his relatively well-informed account to '[t]he popular idea of the severity of the present depression [which] would lead one to suppose that all branches of business were severely stagnated, and that failures were the order of the day' (ibid. 66). In fact, the popular view, focusing on 8 per cent unemployment in agriculture, trade and transportation, and mining and manufactures, had more plausibility than the Commissioner gave it. The other indicators which he thought showed more 'gratifying results', such as a relatively low rate of business failure and a relatively slow rate of fall in output, show the emergence of the now typical features of the way that the larger corporations schedule their responses to shortfalls in demand according to the availability of credit and the difficulty of defraying various fixed costs. In 1886 labour was a relatively easily defrayed cost. Writing of this period with the benefit of 10 years of hindsight, A. C. Conant (1927: 661) concluded that 'the multitude of failures caused intense alarm for a while and threatened to bring business to a standstill'.

resources, yet thoroughgoing pessimism about their use. An 1889 review of recent economic changes by D. A. Wells, one-time US Special Commissioner of Revenue and a distinguished academic, began as follows:

The economic changes that have occurred during the last quarter of a century . . . have unquestionably been more important and varied than during any former corresponding period of the world's history. It would seem, indeed, as if the world, during all the years since the inception of civilization, has been working up on the line of equipment for industrial effort . . . that this equipment, having at last been made ready, the work of using it has, for the first time in our day and generation, fairly begun. . . . As an immediate consequence the world . . . has never been able to accomplish so much. (Wells 1889: p. v)

But when he describes the tenor of 'The Economic Outlook' occasioned by these developments, one is almost shocked to find him saying that: 'The predominant feeling induced by a review and consideration of the numerous economic changes and disturbances that have occurred since 1873 . . . is undoubtedly, in the case of very many persons, discouraging and pessimistic' (ibid. 326).

The reason is clear enough. The development of productive power has been attended by drastic crises, and the improvements in human happiness that this development occasioned have been offset by profound and enormously threatening manifestations of discontent:

[As] a necessary consequence of these changes [there] has come about a series of widespread and complex disturbances; manifesting themselves in . . . the discontent of labour and an increasing antagonism of nations . . . Out of these changes will probably come further disturbances, which to many thoughtful and conservative minds seem full of the menace of a mustering of the barbarians, from within rather than as before from without, for an attack on the whole present organization of society and even the permanency of civilization itself. (Ibid. p. vi)

There was, of course, a very great deal of diversity in the detailed explanations of these disturbances; yet a surprising degree of unanimity in the broad character of these explanations emerges from a review of contemporaneous works. What first tended to be described was a huge fall in prices, not merely a fall which is part of the normal swing of supply and demand, but a wholly unprecedented and dramatic secular fall: '[T]he recent fall in the prices of the great staple commodities of the world has been in extent and character without precedent in the world's history' (ibid. 115). Comparing the data for 1885–'86 with those of 1866–'76, the decline . . . has been extraordinary, and has extended to most countries . . . the estimate of . . . thirty-one per cent as the average measure or extent of this decline, is not excessive' (ibid. 122).

The overwhelmingly predominant explanation of this fall was based on the idea of over-production. As C. A. Conant, a leading financier, financial analyst, and government adviser, put it in 1901: 'In a practical sense . . . over-production in respect to effective demand is not only possible but has been the actual history of many leading commodities during the last three decades' (Conant 1901: 374). In a first sense, over-production is merely another way of describing the debilitating fall in prices: '[O]ver-production . . . describes what, in the time of a crisis, and in the case of many producers, is a reality, the possession of goods they have made and cannot sell, except at a ruinous sacrifice' (J. B. Clarke 1898: 2.)

But over-production also captures the essence of what was perceived as the extraordinary novelty of this fall in prices. Wells distinguished between the over-production that may 'occur through lack of progress and enterprise' and that which occurs 'through what may be termed an excess of progress or enterprise' (Wells 1889: 71). The former results from the disproportionalities that may occur locally despite the existence of demand which, due, for example, to a lack of transport facilities, cannot be satisfied. But the latter, which now is 'intensified to a degree never before experienced' (ibid. 72), is 'industrial over-production' (ibid. 74) is and it 'is to be found in the results of the improvements of production and distribution . . . [T]he supply of very many of the great articles and instrumentalities of the world's use and commerce has increased, during the last ten or fifteen years, in a far greater ratio than the contemporaneous increase in the world's population, or of its consuming capacity' (ibid. 72–3). The fundamental reason for over-production and the pessimism it generated was the very increase in productive capacity that gave its unique character to economic life in the last quarter of the nineteenth century. It is the unprecedented growth in productive capacity that typically lowers prices and creates the basis for over-production crises by throwing a huge amount of consumer goods on the market:

[A]ll economists who have specially studied the matter are substantially agreed that, within the period named, man in general has attained to such a greater control over the forces of Nature, and has so compressed their use, that he has been able to do far more work in a given time, produce far more product, measured by quantity in ratio to a given amount of labour, and reduce the effort necessary to insure a comfortable subsistence in a far greater measure than it was possible for him to accomplish twenty or thirty years anterior to the time of the present writing. (ibid. 27–8)

Conant, whose viewpoint was principally financial, added to the appreciation of the cumulative nature of the problem when he drew attention to the pernicious consequences of what he called 'the loan fund'. By this he meant the huge and rapidly growing supply of savings available for productive investment, which was greatly in excess of the investment needed for the production of consumption goods:

There was a time when every dollar of available saving was required for productive enterprises in Europe and the United States. . . . But the . . . employment of labor-saving machinery in farming and manufacturing has promoted saving in almost a geometrical ratio from year to year. The saving has been capitalized into increased producing plant, which has greatly increased the saving of another year, until the amount of capital offered annually for investment in new enterprises has reached several thousands of millions of dollars every year.

The great development in modern society of saving for investment has contributed to increase the tendency to a mis-direction of productive power. Overproduction of consumable goods takes place because so large a part of the purchasing power of the community is saved for investment. A better equilibrium would be established between the production of finished goods and the demand for them if the community devoted a larger portion of its purchasing power to obtaining such goods. . . . But so large a part of the earnings of society has been set aside in recent years for investment that the equilibrium between the production of finished goods and the effective demand for them has been broken. (Conant 1901: 380–1).

Under these circumstances, production for profit is forestalled, and, given that commitments to future production have been made on the basis of expectations of profit, a general crisis ensues:

The primitive producer, providing directly for his own wants by his own efforts, occupied a very different position from the modern producer, who produces a large quantity of a single article and produces wholly for exchange. If it turns out that he cannot exchange his product for as much of other products as he expected, his calculations of profit are defeated. If he relies for his income upon the margin of profit above cost of production and finds that he cannot sell them for as much, he receives no return for his labor and ceases to be a purchaser of the products of others. If he holds his products for what he considers a fair equivalent in money or in other goods, but the producers of other goods will not pay this equivalent, he finds on his hands a useless stock of goods. When this condition reaches a large number of producers, and affects the mechanism of credit by their inability to fulfil their obligations to the banks, a crisis occurs. (ibid. 375–6)

2.2 Competition and combination

I do not wish to give here any extended consideration of the adequacy of these views, though I do think that they provide significant indications of the limits to accumulation under *laissez-faire*. The picture that emerges is in large part that which one gains from Marx, of a geometrically expanding distance between the growth of productive forces as private capital and the growth of mass consumption as effective demand. But in Marx, remedies are considered which contemplate the most radical changes in the economy—indeed, in the entire social structure. Growth for reasons other than private accumulation and for directly broadening the possibilities of mass consumption are considered as ways of attacking the fundamental causes of over-production (Marx and Engels 1976*b*).

By contrast, what is essential for understanding the form of the corporation is that capitalist responses to over-production were directed not at its root causes but at its superficial representation in destructive competition. Though the critique of Say's law and other variants of the attempt flatly to deny the possibility of over-production were explored theoretically (Conant 1900: 5–8), the main cause of crisis was, wrongly but understandably from the capitalist point of view (Marx 1981: ch. 50), identified as competition itself. All economists of this period acknowledged the simple returns to scale that underpinned the concentration of capital, but W. F. Willoughby, an economist analysing the concentration of industry for the US Department of Labor, demonstrated the institutional sophistication of these economists by not giving these factors the first importance in his account of concentration: 'The various economies realized by the large establishment are now so generally recognized that it is quite superfluous to comment on them further. We, therefore, turn to a benefit resulting from the concentration of work, which either has been ignored or slighted in all discussions of the question, but which is nevertheless of prime importance' (Willoughby 1898: 85.)

The factor Willoughby had in mind—and I will return to his analysis—was removing the pernicious effects of competition. Willoughby was right, surely, claiming that the avoidance of competition was marginalized in mainstream neo-classical economics; but it was certainly much more in the forefront of the minds of corporate owners and controllers and of the institutionally sensitive economists upon whom I am concentrating. E. S. Meade of the Wharton School of Finance and Economy of the University of Pennsylvania described manufacturers' attitudes to *laissez-faire* thus:

[I]t is not difficult to understand why the regime of free competition was productive of manifold hardships to the manufacturer. Competition might be considered the life of trade, but at the close of the last industrial depression it was regarded as the death of profits. It was highly desirable from the manufacturer's view-point to stop, or at least to abate, this struggle . . . They desired a larger profit without such an effort to get it. . . . In 1898 and 1899 the time was ripe for a change. Men were weary of competition and the era of combination was gladly welcomed. (Meade 1903: 23)

The obvious response to these evils of competition is combination. In the 1886 report which I have already mentioned, the US Commissioner for Labor conveyed the following results of his investigators' interviews of manufacturers:

Many manufacturers have said . . . the course of this investigation . . . that if the employers in any industry would combine under an organization that should have positive coherence there would be no difficulty, so far as that industry is concerned, in regulating the volume of production in accordance with the demand, and that with this regulation of supply on a scientific foundation there would be no opportunity for labour troubles or depressions to occur. . . . The manufacturers, so far as all the facts which can be observed indicate, are correct in their position. . . . Any one great industry, under complete organization, can be regulated by all the forces acting understandingly and together, and it is only through such organization that production can be wisely regulated on the basis of necessity to supply the market. (Wright 1886: 287)

The testimony of sixty-two witnesses, chiefly large capitalists, before an Industrial Commission established in 1898 (Industrial Commission 1900: p. v) was summed up thus, under the heading 'Competition the Chief Cause': 'Among the causes which have led to the formation of industrial combinations, most of the witnesses were of the opinion that competition, so vigorous that profits of nearly all competing establishments were destroyed, is to be given first place' (ibid. 8).

The first thing that can be remedied by removing competition in this way is the principal characteristic of the *laissez-faire* economy, which is precisely its unplanned character, in which sales, or their absence, pass a judgment about investment that is not known in advance:

Future values have been anticipated; men thought they saw amounts of wealth coming to them that appeared ample. If these had only been real, they would have justified large expenditures in them. Orders for large amounts of consumers' wealth have been given, and the mills have been set running in order to meet them. The goods come into existence; but the wealth that was seen in a vision of the future has not materialized. The mills have made the cloth, shoes, furniture, etc.; and the values that were to have paid themselves have resolved themselves into a mirage. (J. B. Clarke 1898: 4–5)

Against this fundamental potential for crisis, extensive combination offers the theoretically most attractive solution outside central planning. If one is apprehensive about the amount of power that this extent of combination would place in a few hands (Conant 1901: 379), this does not diminish the force of the basic case for integration through the large corporation:

Probably the most fundamental benefit resulting to society generally from production on a large scale [after realizing economies of scale] is the influence it exerts in steadying production. Ever since the inauguration of the modern industrial regime, industry has been periodically paralyzed, trade injured, and progress brought to a standstill by what are called 'industrial depressions'. . . . The injury resulting from this unstable condition of industry cannot be calculated. Any device which will to any degree regulate this intemperance, and steady production, must be welcomed as a great gain to society. This the large industry certainly tends to do. The attempt to control production so as to keep their plants in constant operation has been one of the great motives leading manufacturers to consolidate their enterprises and organize such combinations as trusts. (Willoughby 1898: 86–7)

What has become the central theme of later antitrust policy can be seen to have been given expression right at the beginning of the major centralization movements. As A. T. Hadley of Yale put it, 'The Good and Evil of Industrial Combinations' had to be weighed, and a distinction drawn between necessary and valuable integration through the corporation and unwelcome price distortion through unacceptable levels of combination (Hadley 1897: 377). The position at this time seems to have foreshadowed, with infinitely more justification, the basic tendency of the latest directions in antitrust, in that public welfare was seen to inhere more in allowing concentration than in its prohibition (American Academy of Political and Social Science 1900).

The corporations' repertoire of strategies to iron out fluctuations included some which were regarded as quite unobjectionable. These included simple product diversification. 'The large establishment is able to command a larger market; it can offset a falling off in demand in one quarter or in one commodity by the cultivation of trade in another direction or the production of other articles' (Willoughby 1898: 86) and planned purchasing leading to vertical integration downwards 'A large concern can purchase supplies upon a more favorable basis. It can . . . make use of refuse and by-products that are destroyed by the smaller establishments' (ibid. 83).

Some other strategies occasioned a great deal of disquiet, however. The major problem of over-production crises from the capitalists' point of view is the destruction of the value of installed capital because of excess competition. The availability of huge investment funds through the stock-market allows of the very rapid equipping of plant, which may well undercut the competitiveness of earlier installed plant:

The [securities] markets, especially that for transferable capital, afford a constant menace . . . to the producer. He knows that if his profits rise above average, the great loan fund of the world is ready to pour into his industry, create new mills and increase to an excessive amount a production which was probably already sufficient to meet effective demand. He knows also, that if a new invention appears upon the market, reducing by 5 per cent or even a smaller fraction the cost of producing his goods, the loan fund is available for equipping new mills with this invention or enabling his rival to apply it to their old mills. (Conant 1901: 378)

Corporate owners and controllers found it simply intolerable that huge plant installations could be rendered effectively worthless well within their possible productive lifetimes by this gale of competition. The idea that capital of this size can be moved to other employments is simply non-sense: 'Capital once invested in the machinery of production cannot always or easily be withdrawn or converted to other uses. The mobility of capital has greatly increased under the system of banking credits and stock exchange securities, but arguments based upon this mobility refer to the loan fund of floating capital and are not applicable to capital which has become fixed in mills and machinery' (ibid. 377). There can be no doubt that, given restricted markets and the capital stock available through the share, large-scale investment was hugely problematic for cap-italists.

The response that was made is clear. It was hyper-competitive pricing, which cleared out the industry to the point where the remaining corpora-tions, unable to drive each other out of business, agreed on mutually acceptable prices (Lamoreaux 1985). Andrew Carnegie gives what we can take to be a first-hand account of manufacturers' responses to an over-production crisis:

Prices . . . continue falling until the article is sold at cost to the less favorably sit-uated or less ably managed factory; and even until the best managed and equipped factory is not able to produce the article at prices at which it can be sold. Political economy says that here the trouble will end. Goods will not be pro-duced at less than cost. This was true when Adam Smith wrote, but it is not quite true to-day. When an article was produced by a small manufacturer, employing, probably at his own home, two or three journey-men and an apprentice or two, it was an easy matter for him to limit or even to stop production. As manufacturing is carried on to-day, in enormous establishments with five or ten millions of dol-lars of capital invested, and with thousands of workers, it costs the manufacturer much less to run at a loss per ton or per yard than to check production. Stoppage would be serious indeed. The condition of cheap manufacture is running full. Twenty sources of expense are fixed charges, many of which stoppage would only increase. Therefore the article is produced for months, and in some cases that I have known for years, not only without profit or without interest upon capital, but to the impairment of the capital invested. Manufacturers have balanced their books at the end of the year only to find their capital reduced at each successive balance. Whilst continuing to produce would be costly, the manufacturer knows too well that stoppage would be ruin. His brother manufacturers are of course in the same situation. They see the savings of many years, as well perhaps as the capital they have succeeded in borrowing, becoming less and less, with no hope of a change in the situation. It is in the soil thus prepared that anything promising relief is gladly welcomed. . . . Combinations—syndicates—trusts—they are willing to try anything. A meeting is called, and in the presence of immediate danger they decide to take united action and form a trust. Each factory is rated as worth a certain amount. Officers are chosen, and through these the entire product of the article in question is to be distributed to the public, at remunerative prices. (Carnegie 1889: 142)

Of course, the degree of overt collusion that Carnegie postulates would now be unusual (Sklar 1988: ch. 3–4), but the same outcome is reached, after the clearing out of the industry down to a few giant corporations, by mutually conscious oligopolistic pricing by the remaining giants. That outcome is 'the organization of production': 'The tendency to over-production resulting from unrestricted competition has been corrected to some extent during the past decade by the consolidation of industry and the restriction of production. Production has been curtailed in many lines to conform to ascertained or probable demand' (Conant 1901: 379).

It is clear that towards the end of the nineteenth century, continuing to guide production by the price mechanism was becoming a flat impossibility. Competitive production utilizing modern plant required large-scale, immobile investment. The cost advantages that such investment yielded were purely ephemeral, given a low elasticity of demand in more or less all markets and the ready availability of equivalent equipment to potential rival producers. The time-scales for the amortization of investment needed to be longer, because of the disproportion between the size of the investment and the difficulty of opening new markets. But these scales were made unreliable and very often far too short by unrestrained competition. Production for private accumulation cannot take place on this basis (Robinson 1955), and another method of organizing production seemed, both to the capitalists and the socialists of the late nineteenth century, to be becoming a necessity. Socialist solutions ultimately tended towards undercutting private property. The capitalist solutions we have discussed put forward corporate organization as a way of saving that property, and, by concentrating on limiting competition, were able to do so. Production for long-run profit in markets hugely restricted by inequalities of wealth distribution is made possible by replacing price competition with the oligopolistic pricing which is the principal feature of the corporation. Paradoxically enough, the price mechanism was ousted as the cost of maintaining private property or, in the lax way it is typically put, the market.

Capitalism has developed as a system of a limited number (Aaronovitch and Sawyer 1975; Hannah and Kay 1977; P. E. Hart and Clarke 1980; Prais 1981) of giant corporations working on vast scales (Chandler 1990: esp. pt. 1) to bureaucratic plans (Williamson 1970). Price competition is irrelevant to pricing decisions in the influential sectors of the economy (Kalecki 1954: ch. 1; J. Robinson 1969: bk. 1), and has been more or less displaced as a form of competition (Chamberlin 1962: ch. 4–7) by cost cutting while holding prices constant (Steindl 1976: ch. 4) and by the sales effort (Baran and Sweezy 1966: ch. 5). The smaller firms and consumers in the residual areas of the economy must take the production decisions of the large corporate price-makers (Scitovsky 1952: ch. 2) as the crucially determining boundaries of the relatively unimportant decisions they are left to make (J. K. Galbraith 1975; cf. 1974). This is the advanced capitalist economy, which specifically 'is not an exchange economy in which the price mechanism regulates all economic activity'. 'Thus it follows that the invisible hand theorem of classical theory is not applicable to the capitalist economy' (Gerrard 1989: 126.)

2.3 The state

The main focus of this chapter is the corporation, but it is quite absurd to attempt to discuss the advanced capitalist economy by reference to the dominance of corporations alone. One must take into account the other feature that identifies that economy, the huge role in economic management given to the state. Though substantially freed of the price mechanism, corporations are still subject to the fundamental contradiction between their infinite urge to grow and the relatively restricted growth in mass consumption. Of itself, the corporation's ability to set prices actually limits demand in relation to capacity, and that capacity grows at exponential rates through the capital concentration powers of the share (and associated debenture financing) and the growth in the productivity of plant.

The rescheduling of growth to bring it into line with the longer planning horizons of corporations can offer no more than a short-run palliative for the over-productive effects of this contradiction, and it became widely accepted among US economists, arguably by the turn of the century, that state adjustment of aggregate demand was essential. A massive expansion in the state's role in regulating the domestic economic environment has proved to be the principal mechanism for the maintenance of stability in advanced capitalism. But this policy developed rather later, being strongly intimated under Wilson, but rapidly accelerating after the great depression (Fine 1967), and thus is somewhat outside the scope of this chapter. However, the form in which the necessity of state underpinning of the economy first became manifest was a product of the era upon which we are focusing, and that is the foreign policy of economic imperialism. The intellectual analysis of imperialism does not have its origins in Hilferding, Luxemburg, Lenin, or even Hobson, but in earlier, pro-capitalist economic writers (Etherington 1982, 1983; Fieldhouse 1961; Stokes 1969), among whom let us focus on Conant and P. S. Reinsch.

Conant's account of imperialism is a perfectly lucid expression of the views one would have held prior to the experience of underdevelopment as a process of net capital export from the underdeveloped country (Baran and Sweezy 1966; ch. 7, sect. 5),[6] if one organized those views around an inviolable commitment to private ownership. Writing in 1900, Conant described a situation of massive capital saturation in the USA and the other capitalist countries, and saw overseas investment as the only means of relieving this saturation and thus relieving the chronic tendency towards declining returns which follows from it: 'The necessity of sending capital abroad is the salient economic lesson of the closing days of the nineteenth century. . . . The real opportunity afforded by colonial possessions is for the development of the new countries by fixed investments, whose slow completion is the only present means of absorbing saved capital without the needless duplication of existing means of production' (Conant 1900: 22–3; cf. ch. 4, 6).

Conant had a very clear idea that the USA had to turn from being 'absorbed . . . in the development of our industries at home' and must recognize 'that the United States is rapidly approaching the condition of Great Britain, France, Germany, and Belgium, where she will be compelled to seek free markets and opportunities for investment in the undeveloped countries, if she is not to be crowded to the wall by the efforts of the other great civilized powers' (Ibid. 75, 79; cf. ch. 7).

Conant also saw that this meant international difficulties: 'Outlets might be found without the exercise of political and military power, if commercial freedom was the policy of all nations. As such a policy has not been adopted by more than one important power of western Europe. . . the United States are compelled, by instinct of self-preservation, to enter, however reluctantly, upon the field of international politics' (Ibid. pp.: iii-iv).

However, it was Reinsch, Professor of Political Science at the University of Wisconsin, who was the principal formulator of the 'Open Door' policy, the specific formulation of a formally open world investment system which thus falls into spheres of interest determined by the economic power of a particular imperialist nation, rather than a formally closed colonial system based on privileged trade relations within empires. Writing in 1900, just after the end of the US-Spanish war, Reinsch recognized that US isolationism was ended: 'That the United States is to play a leading part in international affairs,—that she is to be one of the five leading world powers,—has been irrevocably decided by the events of the recent past. A nation of our power and resources would be untrue to its vocation if it did not sooner or later realize its duty in this important

---

[6] This description of capital flows under imperialism, which implies a complete reversal of the effect of imperialism expected by Luxemburg (1913: sect. 3) is based on Baran's work on underdevelopment (1973: ch. 5).

position to which it has attained' (Reinsch 1900: 311; cf. 1902: ch. 5–6; 1905).

He coupled this, however, with a fundamental recognition that US expansionism should be distinguished from colonial aggrandizement on the European pattern:

A headlong policy of territorial aggrandizement should be avoided by the United States, as it would entail the danger of burdening our national existence with elements that could not be assimilated and would only weaken the state. It should be the aim of our nation to counteract everywhere, at home and abroad, the ambitions of universal imperialism. . . . Commerce and industry should be developed by establishing trade depots and means of communication, and by upholding the policy of equal opportunity throughout the colonial world, rather than by territorial acquisitions. (Reinsch 1900: 361)

This very brief sketch of aspects of the nascent advanced capitalist economy has tried to show that its basic structure is formed by an attempt to deal, within the limits of capitalist property, with what was generally accepted to be *laissez-faire*'s chronic tendency towards over-production. The abolition of the price mechanism by the principal corporations is regarded as an essential positive step, for it allows such returns to be made as will encourage large-scale, efficient investment to take place. Major crises of disproportionality in the economy are to be overcome by the replacement of market disorder with corporate planning. Alongside this planning, the state will provide the (domestic and) overseas environments in which corporations will be able to expand; for of themselves, even when oligopolistically organized, they are unable to secure a climate of investment opportunity.

As a description of the advanced capitalist economy, this sketch is hardly complete, especially as it leaves out of the account the manifest periodic failures of these strategies to counter over-production (Mandel 1978: ch. 17–18). But I put it forward as having one major advantage over the concept of the market in market failure analyses—namely, that it recognizes the real structural failure in the actual market of *laissez-faire* capitalism. Understanding this failure leads us seriously to reconsider the value of the idea of 'market failure' in the argument for corporate regulation.

3. THE CORPORATION AND THE PRESERVATION OF CAPITALIST PROPERTY

The explanatory shortcomings of the economic writings I have discussed are obvious on even a cursory examination. They are sometimes very great. I have referred above to the 1889 paper in which Andrew Carnegie sought to exorcize contemporaneous public fear of 'The Bugaboo of the Trust'. After having modestly put down the creation of trusts to the work of 'some of the ablest business men the world has ever seen' (Carnegie 1889: 143), he went on to defend those creations by use of a method which is a forerunner of many of the worst excesses of contemporary apologies for the corporation. The method is simple enough: one uses free market assumptions to explain away the specific features of the corporation which have made those assumptions untenable. Thus Carnegie, whose whole paper, we have seen, is a lament about the huge size and vulnerable fixity of the capital investments required by modern scales of production, defends oligopoly pricing by imagining that entry into such production is open to all: 'The people of America can smile at the efforts of all her railway magnates and all her manufacturers to defeat the economic laws by Trusts or combinations, or pools, or "differentials", or anything of like character. Only let them hold firmly to the doctrine of free competition. Keep the field open. Freedom for all to engage in railroad building when and where capital desires subject to conditions open to all' (ibid. 149).

Such arguments are, of course, without any real value, other than providing amusement. In particular, the 'freedom for all to engage in railroad building' is priceless, perhaps bettered only by Hadley giving up part of his *magnum opus* to the following: 'Crises have occurred with tolerable regularity ever since the introduction of applied steam power. They have usually come once in ten or eleven years,—a fact which led some observers to connect them with sunspots which have a period of the same length' (Hadley 1896: 295).[7] The reason I cite these worthless arguments is that, though much of the economic debate of this period parallels Marx, the key aspect of Marx's analysis has no parallel. Marx does not consider capitalist property as ineluctable; indeed, this historically specific form of ownership and control of the means of production is what is mainly to be explained. But these other writers treat this form of property and the control of the means of production it represents as simply a given. All analysis is carried out within limits which are called 'economic', and which are thought to have a more or less natural character, but which are nothing more than capitalist property.

Carnegie, for example, couples what must have been one of the most acute practical awarenesses of the specific qualities of the trust with a belief that the economy will remain essentially the same after tycoon capitalism, because 'economics' will always be the same: 'The great laws of the economic world, like all laws affecting society, being the genuine outgrowth of human nature, alone remain unchanged through all these

---

[7] The principal locus of this bizarre idea is, of course, Jevons 1965: 136.

changes. Whatever consolidations, or watered stocks, or syndicates, or Trusts endeavour to circumvent these . . . the great laws continue to grind out their irresistible consequences as before' (Carnegie 1889: 141).

A particularly picturesque version is given by Conant, who again couples an acute insight into the real reasons for modern economic developments—in this case imperialism—with laughable generalizations: 'The irresistible tendency to expansion, which leads the growing tree to burst, which drove the Goths, the Vandals and finally our Saxon ancestors in successive and irresistible waves over the decadent provinces of Rome, seems again in operation, demanding new outlets for American capital and new opportunities for American enterprise' (Conant 1900: 326).

The explanatory failures consequent upon this are as manifest as they are still common. We have seen them repeated, though articulated in a more modern jargon, in Coase. Specific historical structures are given a quite inappropriate natural explanation which is really no explanation at all. They are the assumptions which underpin such explanations as are given, and as such themselves remain unexplained. For present purposes, a brief indication is needed of the limits these explanations impose on what might be considered appropriate to prevent the systemic decay of *laissez-faire*.

What the corporation preserves, in the face of the crisis of *laissez-faire*, is the capitalist property which is assumed to be desirable in market failure analyses, but which we can see produces systematic obstructions to rational economic planning by preventing the erection of structures allowing free choice. Faced with over-production, there are two main possibilities which flow particularly clearly from Marx's analysis, which of course is not limited by the constraints of capitalist ownership.

One is to undercut the law of the tendency of the rate of profit to fall by removing profit maximization as the overweening goal of economic effort. While the corporation has done this to some extent, by substituting long-term growth for short-term profitability, the difficulty is that, however construed, growth as much as profitability aims at the expansion of private property in either dividends or increased value of stock. The consequences are that rational outcomes from the point of view of the consumer must be subordinated to private wealth. We have seen Meade describe the way that competition came to be seen as an evil by manufacturers; and the context in which he puts this is most instructive:

Invention and improvement are always most active when the lash of competition is applied to the manufacturer, and the consumer profits from the lower values which competition frequently produces and invention confirms. In the interest of public policy, the investment of profits is to be commended; but it should not be forgotten, when the benefits of competition are extolled, that society is a long way from the time when men will labour for the public interest to the relative subordination of their own advantage. Whatever the social and industrial effects of large capital expenditure out of earnings, the manufacturer was not satisfied with the results. . . . It was highly desirable from the manufacturer's point of view to stop, or at least abate, this struggle, which benefitted nobody save the consumer. . . . The producers were tired of working for the public. (Meade 1903: 22–3)

What is at issue here is hardly what we need to do to determine what men will or will not labour for, but rather when capitalists will allow others to labour for them, or, if we get away from this way of speaking altogether, when and in what fashion we can employ the means of production. There can be no doubt that the limitation placed by production for private profit on the volume of economic activity is a major distortion of potential rational outcomes—such as planned reduction in the amount of necessary labour time—and it is the continuance of capitalist private property in the corporation which produces it.

The second possibility is a concerted expansion of mass consumption relative to the growth of the private wealth contained in the capitalist ownership of the means of production. Again, the corporate economy has, especially since Keynes, embraced this; but crucial residual problems remain. The expansion of mass income was put forward as a solution to unemployment of capital and labour by Wright: 'If . . . the standard of living for those whose consuming power is . . . low . . . can be increased . . . the problem of the unemployed would pass away. An increase of $1 per week per family of those living under the lower rates of consuming power . . . would make a market sufficiently expansive to overcome the margin between actual production and productive capacity' (Wright 1897–8: 673–4).

What is entirely missing from Wright's advocacy of 'All efforts . . . which have for their purpose the raising of our people to higher levels of living' (ibid. 674) is any grasp of the necessary political changes that would allow making those efforts central to economic planning. Such efforts require the determination of incomes by means other than competitive wage struggles in the context of a massively skewed distribution of wealth. That is to say, they require the determination of incomes outside the context of capitalist property; but this is precisely what is precluded by the preservation of that property through the adoption of the corporate form.

I hope that it is obvious that I am not suggesting here that these measures are a full solution to over-production problems. What I am arguing is that something like them should be considered as part, and indeed an essential part, of any such solution. But it is the corporation that excludes them. The regulatory initiatives that follow from the market failure approach are bound to be wrong-headed, because they are based on the systematic suppression of the structural problems of the market which the corporation was brought into existence to solve, and therefore they continually run up against those problems as limits. Much of the real significance of the corporation is left out of the account. The ideological correlation of the technical, perfect market and some sanitized view of *laissez-faire* seriously debilitates regulation, because the extension of the former market is identified with the extension of capitalist property, when just the opposite conclusion should be reached (Roemer 1988). If we want to bring corporate conduct under optimal governance, the formulation of the appropriate governance structure cannot always be biased towards private ownership of the means of production. It must be made clear that what is at issue is the end of economics, or rather the recognition that the modern corporation has brought positive economics to an end, and that such 'economic' indicators as now remain relevant to the corporation are the expressions not of productive governance but of our failure properly to bring the corporation under socially self-conscious and responsible control.

4. CONCLUSION: THE FAILURE OF MARKET FAILURE

On the basis of what we have seen of the necessity behind the active restructuring of capitalism into its advanced form, it is only through the most wishful thinking that the criticism of the corporation can take the form, as it predominantly has, of market failure. Every rational capitalist will seek the advantages of monopoly, and will be obliged to do so by the perverted form of competition that prevails under oligopoly; and those advantages continue to be disadvantages for the public (Baran and Sweezy 1966: ch. 11, sect. 1–4). But allowing the largest firms to price on a monopoly basis has been necessary for capitalism to survive. Market failure is not a sad, unfortunate anomaly, but the central feature of the advanced capitalist economy.

If this argument is accepted, what should be said of the sets of regulatory measures proposed under the market failure argument? Hopefully, it should enable a proper grasp of the usefulness of these measures, and indeed of their extension. Apart from the proposals for expanding the number of consumers in the market for corporate control by extending shareholder democracy, which seems to be a fanciful policy in relation to the privately owned corporation and a fruitless one in regard to widening the control of any corporation (Cotterell 1988), all these measures have a strong claim to be implemented, along with other measures derived from marginalist techniques as appropriate (Lange 1960).

My aim here is not to put forward any specific proposals for regulation of a general type, since I am entirely committed to Coase's position that appropriate governance structures must be determined in each empirical case. But I do insist on it being recognized that any such measures, even the construction of 'market governance', must now be conceived not as the remedy of market failure and thus an attempt to return to *laissez-faire*, but as entailing political choices as to the most appropriate governance framework for production. Being political choices, they should be made not by those who have power under the real market, the small élite of capitalists (typically with directorships) and top management (typically with a significant equity holding) (J. Scott 1979: 105–23; 1982; Giddens 1981: ch. 8–12) who, through interlocking holdings and directorships (J. Scott 1979: 83–95; J. Scott and Griff 1984) and overall financial supervision (J. Scott 1979: 95–104; 1986; Coakley and Harris 1983) command the strategic heights of the economy and the economic policy of the state (J. Scott 1979: 155–8; Jessop 1982; Miliband 1983). Rather, these choices should be made in a proper public fashion. This, of course, is to say that choices of governance structure should not have instinctive recourse to the capitalist market, but should pose the fundamental question of the inequity and inefficiency of the present structure of ownership and control of the corporation. Though this is precisely what is obscured by the notion of 'market failure', it is, I submit, the direction that regulatory policy should take.

On the basis of this argument, we should be able to draw up a list of the basic principles underpinning corporate regulation on grounds other than 'market failure'. They are:

The major corporations are not subject to market governance in terms of price competition, and thus the advanced capitalist economy is not a 'market economy'.

Those corporations cannot be subjected to such market governance without wholly unacceptable economic costs, and hence regulation with such a basic aim is quite misdirected.

The real determinants of corporate behaviour are not economic at all, if we take the price-competitive market as the realm of economics, and thus cannot be explained as market failures, but must be explained in terms of the sociology of corporate organization, particularly emphasizing the class structure of corporate control.

A strategy is needed for expansion of the interests represented in corporate control which consciously regards this as a political, not an economic, issue.

The creation of any realm of 'economic' governance by marginalist techniques can only follow from, and not be in opposition to, the democratic resolution of the political issue of corporate control.

It should be clear that I regard the market failure analyses developed from Coase as, in important ways, a regression from the resources of earlier economics of the corporation. It is fitting, then, that I conclude with a passage from Willoughby's 1898 article that, sadly, will do well enough as an account of present scholarship:

The advantages of production upon a large scale are so manifest that it would be unfortunate to retard the movement in any way. On the other hand, the public should not be left at the mercy of a few men. The great evil is the power possessed by a few individuals arbitrarily to fix prices, and this, if possible, should be controlled by the state. As yet the means to do this have not been discovered. It would seem to us that this has been because a radically wrong line of policy has been pursued. Legislatures have failed or refused to recognize the advantages of production upon a large scale. They have looked upon large enterprises as an evil in themselves and essentially detrimental to society. Their efforts, therefore, have been directed toward the prevention of the formation of combination of establishments. In so doing, they have attempted to stem an irresistible economic movement. The true line of policy is to recognize that the consolidation of industrial enterprises is inevitable; and thus instead of attempting to prevent, seek rather to control these combinations. (Willoughby 1898: 93–4)

7

Corporate Governance and Transaction Costs

NEIL KAY

The role of transaction costs in determining the nature and behaviour of different forms of economic organization has emerged as a major issue in recent years in economics and law. Coase's early insights (1937) were developed by Williamson, whose work may be represented by three texts, *Markets and Hierarchies* (1975, henceforth *M & H*), *The Economic Institutions of Capitalism* (1985, henceforth *EIC*), and *Economic Organization* (1986, henceforth *EO*).

The purpose of this chapter is to explore limitations in the transaction cost approach as developed by Williamson. There are conceptual and empirical problems that deserve attention; but Williamson's custom of presenting his version of transaction cost economics as *the* transaction cost approach reinforces the need for a considered examination of its potential contribution.

Section 1 develops a brief description of Williamson's transaction cost approach; section 2 looks at problems in Williamson's framework arising from its contractual foundations; section 3 examines conceptual limitations of the framework; while section 4 examines Williamson's analysis of corporate strategy and structure.

I. THE TRANSACTION COST APPROACH

As summarized in *EIC* (30–2), there are three concepts which are fundamental to Williamson's transaction cost approach; bounded rationality (cognitive and language limits on individual abilities to process and act on information), asset specificity (specialization of assets with respect to use or users), and opportunism (self-interest seeking with guile).

If these three conditions coexist in any transactional situation, then transaction costs may interfere with the efficient operation of the market mechanism. However, Williamson argues that if any of these three conditions are absent in a specific situation, then the market mechanism will still be effective. For example, if bounded rationality does not exist, all future possible contingencies will be specified and built into contracts. The contractual framework may then settle problems arising from asset specificity or opportunism. Also, if asset specificity does not exist in a given transactional situation, then assets can be easily switched in and out of alternative uses, mistakes can be easily rectified, and opportunism does not have serious or lasting consequences. Finally, if opportunism is not a problem and all parties to a transaction are honest and sincere, then surprises and shocks due to bounded rationality can be resolved by agreements in principle to resolve problems fairly and equitably (*EIC* 30–2).

Therefore the absence of any one of these conditions from a given transaction situation means that contract will be an effective method for dealing with resource allocation questions. On the face of it, this would seem to constitute a strong general justification for the market as a tool for allocating resources; but Williamson argues that transactional situations in which all three conditions are present are common. In such circumstances the narrow market imperative is replaced by a broader imperative to: '*Organise transactions so as to economise on bounded rationality while simultaneously safeguarding them against the hazards of opportunism.*' (*EIC* 32, emphasis original)

Williamson builds on this principle to develop a comparative approach to alternative governance structures for resource allocation. In principle, a given transaction can be organized in a variety of institutional forms, ranging from centralized direction through a variety of mixed or hybrid modes to market exchange. The question then becomes which form is the most efficient for organizing the appropriate transaction.

All institutional forms may involve information problems if conditions of bounded rationality, asset specificity, and opportunism are present. In the case of market transactions there may be search, bargaining, and monitoring costs, all of which feed into transaction costs. It may be more efficient in certain circumstances to internalize and use organizational controls to scrutinize the transaction and provide more direct incentives than may be possible in arm's length market transactions. In such cases internal organization may provide lower cost and superior performance over market exchange, by mitigating bounded rationality problems and controlling opportunism more effectively. Transaction costs may therefore lead to the potential domain over which market exchange could operate, being partially substituted by expansion of corporate boundaries.

Such substitution will involve costs such as impairment of incentives (*EIC* 131–62). Williamson argues that the market's high-powered incentives of profits and losses may be softened within the firm. Personalization of internal human relations may dull penalties for adverse performance, and promises to behave responsibly may not be costlessly enforced. Williamson argues that efficiency criteria will enforce choice of the least-cost alternative in individual cases.

These are the foundations of Williamson's analysis. In the following sections we shall consider their application in comparative institutional analysis, beginning with the transactional interpretation of hierarchy in this approach.

2. TRANSACTION AND HIERARCHY

In Williamson's analysis of hierarchy, contract plays a central role. Williamson describes the problem of individuals and institutions 'designing governance structures related to their contracting needs' (*EIC* 87). Only when the coincidence of bounded rationality, opportunism, and asset specificity create transaction cost pressures on market exchange, do circumstances arise in which transactions may be removed from the market. Therefore, 'one of the most attractive attributes of the transaction cost approach is that it reduces, essentially, to a study of contracting' (*EO* 97). This perspective is carried through to the extent of analysing hierarchy in contractual terms; 'if one or a few agents are responsible for negotiating all contracts, the contractual hierarchy is great. If instead each agent negotiates each interface separately, the contractual hierarchy is weak' (*EIC* 221). Williamson acknowledges that hierarchy may also be analysed in decision-making terms (*EIC* 221), but uses the contractual analysis of hierarchy in most of his work.

However, a problem with using contracting as a basis for analysing hierarchical relations is that it transposes a tool designed for analysing market exchange relations to an arena—internal organization—for which it was not designed. This leads to two related difficulties in Williamson's analysis; inconsistencies in the interpretation of transaction and a problematic interpretation of hierarchy. We shall consider both in turn.

Curiously, transaction is not defined in either *M & H* or *EIC*. It is defined in *EO*; but the definition falls into two separate parts, which, as we shall see, are not necessarily mutually consistent.

The costs of running the economic system to which Arrow refers can be usefully thought of in contractual terms. Each feasible mode of conducting relations between technologically-separable entities can be examined with respect to the *ex ante* costs of negotiating and writing, as well as the *ex post* costs of executing, policing and, when disputes arise, remedying the (explicit or implicit) contract that joins them.

A transaction may thus be said to occur when a good or service is transferred across a technologically-separable interface. One stage of processing or assembly activity terminates and another begins. (*EO* 139)

Arrow's costs of running the economic system referred to in the first paragraph above are transaction costs (*EO* 136), and the first concept of transaction described in that paragraph is a contractual or exchange-based interpretation. However, the subsequent definition of transaction in the second paragraph, as transference across a technologically separable interface, is a quite distinct interpretation. We may characterize the two interpretations of transaction as the contractual and interface-transfer definitions respectively. In the cases that Williamson analyses, the contractual and interface-transfer definitions are generally interchangeable. This is because Williamson tends to select a fairly narrow range from the universe of actual transactions. Since *M & H* in 1975, the major focus of Williamson's analysis has been on intermediate product markets and vertical relations, with extensions into employment relations and capital market issues. The interchangeability of the definitions can be illustrated with an example. A publisher and two potential co-authors may make a deal to publish a text. The transaction may be described in contractual terms (agreement to make payment on delivery of manuscript, subject to appropriate qualifications) or interface-transfer terms (physical delivery of manuscript from authors to publisher). They may be regarded as alternative interpretations of this particular vertical transaction.

However, contract does not necessarily imply interface transfer and technological separability. The two co-authors may have worked closely on all aspects of the text to the extent that it is not possible to disentangle their individual contributions from the eventual output. The senior author may offer a 70–30 split on royalties to the junior author. This sub-contract is very easy to conceptualize and describe in contractual terms, though it certainly does not adhere to Williamson's description of transference of good or service across a technologically separable interface, since what the authors are arguing about is of course a joint product.

Similarly, interface transfer does not necessarily imply contract (explicit or implicit). The authors may decide to do their own desk-top publishing rather than make a deal with a publisher. There is still a transaction in the sense of physical transference of the manuscript from the writing stage to the physical production stage. However, there is no longer a transaction in the contractual sense, unless there is resort to the *reductio ad absurdum* of the authors making a deal with themselves.

It should surely be of concern when what must be the central concept of transaction cost economics—the nature of transaction itself—appears so vague and inconsistent in Williamson's analysis. In fact, Williamson usually invokes the contractual interpretation of transaction. This means that both external markets and hierarchies are analysed as characterized by opportunistic contracting parties; and consistent with this, the role of hierarchy in Williamson's analysis is reduced to questions of the monitoring and control of internal markets in capital, labour, and intermediate products. Thus Williamson's approach is really about markets and contracts, not markets and hierarchies, and, consistent with this, *EIC* analyses hierarchy in contractually based terms.

Is there a problem here, beyond the obvious inconsistency in definition of transaction? The answer is yes, because a defining characteristic of hierarchy and organization is the appearance of relations other than exchange and contract to govern resource allocation. The physical transference definition of transaction is the more general of the two, and a census of resource allocation within organizations typically reveals that resource transfers take place through mechanisms other than market contract; for example, as Coase pointed out, 'If a workman moves from department Y to department X, he does not go because of a change in relative prices, but because he is ordered to do so' (1937: 387). Rather than invoke the idea of incomplete contracts, it would make more sense to analyse autonomous decision making and inter personal relations as the dominant influences on resource allocation within organizations. However, Williamson focuses on one narrow and, indeed, rare form of human action—exchange. This may suffice in dealing with market relations; but, as we shall see, it is inadequate in dealing with resource allocation within complex organizations.

3. WILLIAMSON'S TRANSACTION COST FRAMEWORK

As discussed earlier, Williamson's framework is built on the contention that non-trivial transactional problems require the coexistence of bounded rationality, opportunism, and asset specificity (*EIC* 30–2). While bounded rationality may be generally recognized as an integral part of the human (and, therefore, transaction cost) condition, the status accorded to opportunism and asset specificity is highly questionable.

In the case of opportunism, Williamson argues that 'the hazards of trading are less severe in Japan than in the United States because of cultural and institutional checks on opportunism' (*EIC* 122); yet he still claims that 'the same principles that inform make or buy decisions in the United States and in other Western countries also apply in Japan' (ibid.).

Such a perspective is firmly rooted in the cultural origins of the transaction cost framework in the USA. Importing a behavioural framework based on individual opportunism into a culture such as Japan is highly questionable. Commentators such as Patrick and Rosovsky have noted Japan's emphasis on co-operative group decision making, as opposed to individualistic decisions and procedures. Merely asserting, as Williamson does, that the same principles underlie transactions in Japan and the USA is unsatisfactory. However, since Williamson has offered a major hostage to fortune in requiring opportunism as a necessary condition for transaction cost problems to exist, such inflexibility is necessary to defend his framework.

A second major hostage to fortune is offered by Williamson in requiring the existence of asset specificity (specialization by use or user) as a pre condition for transaction cost issues. In fact, contrary to Williamson's argument, asset specificity may actively facilitate market exchanges. Blois (1972) pointed out that dominant buyers could use their monopsonistic power to exercise a high degree of control over suppliers without having to go to the trouble of taking them over. He also found that high-technology areas had a higher degree of intellectual property right protection for producers if a high degree of expertise specificity created mutual dependency between themselves and customers (Blois 1972: 265–6). Joint specificity of transactional arrangements may reduce or even eliminate potential gains from opportunistic behaviour. If both parties are in the same locked room, bomb threats by either party would be unconvincing.

Asset specificity may also create transaction costs, as Williamson claims; but the actual effects are much more complex than Williamson recognizes. However, an even more damaging problem is the lack of recognition by Williamson that transactional difficulties may be a direct consequence of asset non-specificity.

This neglect exists because Williamson (*EIC* 31–2) argues that if there is no asset specificity coherent in a transacting situation, then market contracting will be unproblematic, given contestability and free entry and exit in and out of markets. This ignores the issue that non-specificity of assets is often expressed as property right problems. For example, leakage of knowledge and competitive advantage from innovator to imitator is a direct manifestation of the fact that innovations and resultant profit opportunities may not be specialized by use and/or user. Patenting may be ineffective in protecting property rights, and so a common solution is concealment of proprietary knowledge through internalization. These are well-trodden issues in the areas of licensing and multinational enterprise, and we shall discuss these further in the next section.

It is true that opportunism and asset specificity may influence transactions, and it is not intended to deny that here. However, Williamson's treatment of both phenomena as necessary and definitive features of transaction cost problems is unjustified and problematic. In the next section we shall look at specific problems involved in applying this transaction cost perspective to areas of corporate strategy and structure.

4. CORPORATE STRATEGY AND STRUCTURE IN WILLIAMSON'S FRAMEWORK

In this section we shall look at the application of Williamson's framework to three particular issues: the conglomerate, the evolution of the M-form, and the multinational.

4.1 The conglomerate

The conglomerate strategy has been regarded as a curious and even irrational strategy by many commentators. Since it is based on internalization of unrelated product markets, there are no obvious synergy gains in the form of economies of scale or scope. Williamson (*M & H* 155–75, *EO* 154–8) provides a transaction cost explanation based on the idea that the conglomerate may constitute a miniature capital market.

The miniature capital market hypothesis has two components: gains from internalization and gains from divisionalization. The internalization argument was discussed in section 1 above. The external capital market may have transaction costs impeding or preventing exchanges. Opportunism or potential opportunism on the part of providers or users of funds may be pervasive; and independence of parties may make screening, monitoring, and auditing of parties difficult. Internalization of the capital market within the conglomerate may improve both information flows and degree of control over performance of respective parties.

The divisionalization argument is based on the formation of profit centres as divisions within a multi-division (M-form) organization. Each conglomerate division is measured in terms of the same financial performance standards. The universality and measurability of the profit criterion facilitate the operation of the conglomerate as a miniature capital market.

Williamson's explanation for the conglomerate is that the combination of internalization and divisionalization advantages allows it to operate as a miniature capital market with efficiency advantages compared to the external capital market in certain circumstances. There is nothing wrong with this explanation when used to explain the superiority of the conglomerate over the external capital market supporting separate smaller and independent firms. The problem is that this is not enough. To explain the evolution of the conglomerate, Williamson must demonstrate its superiority over specialized alternatives. This he does not do. We can demonstrate the difficulty here with a simple mental experiment.

Suppose we have nine specialized firms: three textiles, three food, and three electronics firms. For simplicity we assume that they are identical in terms of size, profitability, and all other financial and managerial matters.

Each has been characterized by management as administering existing resources inefficiently and as facing difficulties in attracting new funds. This is consistent with Williamson's analysis of growth problems faced by specialised U-form (unitary form) firms (*M & H* 133–6).

Consistent with Williamson's miniature capital market hypothesis, merger or take-over activity within this group could help to create a larger corporation based on M-form lines with concomitant internalization and divisionalization advantages over the external capital market. The crucial problem is that Williamson's own internalization/divisionalization explanation does not favour conglomerate internalization over specialized internalization within industrial sectors. For example, amalgamation could follow a conglomerate route with a combination of one firm from each sector, or it could pursue a specialized strategy by merging together, say, the three firms from electronics. Both conglomerate and specialized electronic strategies could be based on M-form profit centres and explore internal capital market advantages, the former independent firms now constituting divisions with the respective combinations. In such respects both conglomerate and specialized strategies could exploit similar efficiency gains. However, closer examination of the potential efficiency gains desirable from the respective strategies suggests that the specialized strategy could exploit not only all the internalization/divisionalization gains which the conglomerate could achieve, but additional efficiency gains as well.

First, resource complementarities between divisions in the specialized strategy could provide opportunities for internal exchanges and agreements. Such transactions in the external market between independent firms would be carried out by institutional arrangements such as joint ventures, licensing, and so forth. The internalization of resource swaps or sharing means that senior management 'umpires' may reduce transaction costs in these markets just as they do in the internal capital market. This is simply another way of expressing the traditional gains associated with individual and corporate specialization.

Secondly, similarities in markets and technologies between divisions in the specialized firm facilitate performance comparison compared to the conglomerate, as Williamson recognizes (*EIC* 140). Comparing like with like results in more meaningful and realistic profit comparisons.

In short, there is no efficiency gain provided by conglomerateness which could not also be exploited by specialization, while specialization typically provides further efficiency gains not achievable by conglomerates. Ironically, Williamson's analysis of the conglomerate as a consequence of internalization gains is a more reasonable explanation of specialization than of conglomerateness.

The conglomerate is in fact a highly unusual strategy (Rumelt 1974;

Channon 1973; Dyas and Thanheiser 1976), and where it exists, there are usually special features which make it a one-off phenomenon (e.g., Hanson, Lonrho). Even highly diversified firms typically exploit strong economies of scale and scope within a limited range of markets and technologies. Firms may wish to move away from a completely specialized strategy for a variety of reasons (e.g., market saturation, over-dependence on vulnerable markets and technologies); but when they do, they typically exploit existing market and technological skills as far as possible (N.M. Kay 1982, 1984).

In responding to these arguments, Williamson (1992) brings in additional points such as the role of history and antitrust legislation to explain the existence of conglomerates, but does not adequately defend his internal capital market explanation for the conglomerate. It is also relevant that Williamson neglects related diversification, a curious omission given the prevalence of this form of corporate strategy. In fact, the Williamson approach cannot deal with such internalized strategies at all. By definition, related diversification is based on shared assets which facilitate the exploitation of economies of scope. The idea that assets can be shared between different uses and become a basis for internalization is of course the opposite of Williamson's principle of asset specificity or specialization by use or user as a basis of internalization. If Williamson's approach is applicable to issues of corporate strategy, its dependence on asset specificity of necessity limits it to the special case of the single-product firm and vertical market relations, which is of course the area to which it was first applied. The framework simply does not apply either to unrelated or related diversification.

4.2 The evolution of the M-form

The appearance and development of the M-form corporation has been a major aspect of Williamson's transaction cost economics (*M & H* 132–54, *EO* 65–77, *EIC* 279–94). However, there are difficulties with Williamson's explanation. Williamson argues that U-form firms (i.e., those organized by functional specialism) run into control- and strategy-formulating problems as they expand, these losses being exacerbated by diversification. Centralization creates significant organization costs, with information having to pass through multiple levels, thereby creating control-loss problems, and short-run issues dominating long-run strategies. *Ad hoc* solutions, such as expanding top-level decision making capacity by involving functional heads, bring in additional problems. Thus, U-form expansion typically encounters significant organization costs after a certain point.

Williamson argues that the M-form corporation is designed to cope with these problems. Inter-functional co-ordination is carried out by divisions, reducing control-loss problems. Senior management time is also released to focus on long-run strategic problems. Divisional profit centres may help to create the foundations of an internal capital market.

There is nothing wrong with such *ex post* analysis of the superiority of the M-form structure for the large diversified firm. The difficulties arise when Williamson relates them to the evolution of the M-form. He argues that 'the ability of the management [in the U-form] to handle the volume and complexity of the demands placed upon it become strained and even collapsed . . . the U-form laboured under a communication overload while the pursuit of sub-goals by the functional parts (sales, engineering, production) was partly a manifestation of opportunism' (*EIC* 280–1). Therefore, 'faced with the need either to retrench or to develop a new set of internal contracting relationships, organizational innovators devised the M-form structure' (*EIC* 295).

Williamson is arguing that U-form expansion eventually creates an internal crisis and the resulting development of the M-form to solve these problems; 'eventually the U-form structure defeats itself and results in the M-form structure to solve these problems' (Williamson 1971: 350). The M-form evolution is seen as a process involving natural selection (*EIC* 296), and Williamson generally sees transaction cost reasoning as depending on the process of competition to select the more efficient over the less efficient through natural selection (*EIC* 22–3, including footnote).

However, these arguments are flawed. In particular, it is a reversal of natural selection to argue that the U-form 'defeats itself' through over-expansion resulting in the M-form solution as a response to crisis. In natural selection it is the superior form which generates crisis in the inferior form, not crisis in the inferior form which generates the superior form. Natural selection filters and selects from what is actually available.

As Alchian argues, 'even in a world of stupid men there would still be profits' (1950: 213). Exactly the same points could be made of an industry populated by U-form firms before the introduction of the M-form innovation. Competition favours the relatively efficient, and U-forms could be unqualifiedly inefficient compared to the M-form, but still happily survive and profit as long as the multi-divisional system was not on the market. So where did the U-form 'crises' come from?

The obvious culprit would be competition from smaller more specialized firms. Apart from other U-forms, these were the only other game in town prior to the M-form innovation. In those circumstances the selection process would be expressed as limits to growth of the firm; indeed it would parallel the traditional size limit represented by a U-shaped, long-run, average cost curve, as diseconomies of scale and co-ordination appear. This is consistent with Williamson's weak-form selection, in which the relatively fitter survive (*EIC*: 23 n.).

The main points here are that Williamson's analysis of the evolution of the M-form is unsatisfactory in itself, and also signals the need for a properly developed selection mechanism for alternative institutional choices. Dow (1987) points out difficulties with Williamson's selection mechanisms in the context of diffusion of institutional forms; but these points also indicate problems in Williamson's analysis of organizational innovation.

As Elster (1983: 49–50) points out, evolutionary or natural selection theories provide functional explanation, and contrast with theories of intentional explanation which typically involve either optimizing or satisficing decision making, assuming rationality (ibid. 69). Williamson's functionalist natural selection explanation of institutional development is unsatisfactory, and he is unusual in modern micro-economics in not involving explicit decision-making criteria (optimizing or satisficing) by which institutional choices can be made. Consequently there is no satisfactory functional or intentional explanatory foundation in Williamson's approach on which to build his contention that efficient forms evolve.

In his reply to these points, Williamson (1992) challenges me to suggest an alternative hypothesis to his M-form hypothesis, that 'the organization and operation of the large enterprise along the lines of the M-form (more closely approximates) neoclassical profit maximization than does the U-form organizational alternative' (*M & H* 150). However, the point of my argument was not to query the M-form hypothesis; general adoption of this form among large corporations makes the hypothesis self-evident and obvious. One could equally hypothesize that a Ford Granada is more advanced than a model T Ford without saying anything about how the Granada evolved or how it was constructed. The M-form hypothesis conceals deficiencies in the analysis of choice and selection of institutional form in Williamson's framework.

4.3 Multinational enterprise

We saw earlier the difficulties of extending Williamson's framework to analysis of diversified corporate strategies, and there are also problems in extending the framework to analysis of multinational enterprise. This phenomenon has been generally neglected by Williamson, but in *EIC* he argues that his transaction cost framework can also be applied to this area.

In the context of multinationalism, Williamson again argues that asset specificity represents a necessary precondition for internalization of the market with corporate organization in the form of the multinational enterprise:

A more harmonious and efficient exchange relation—better disclosure, easier reconciliation of differences, more complete cross-cultural adaptation, more effective team organization and reconfiguration—predictably results from the substitution of internal governance relations for bilateral trading under those recurrent trading circumstances where assets, of which complex technology transfer is an example, have a highly specific character. (*EIC* 294).

However, Contractor (1981) provides evidence that specificity of transactional relationships may support the market alternative of licensing, consistent with our earlier arguments in section 4.3. In reviewing the empirical evidence, Contractor points out that the disadvantages of licensing arising from licensee independence are often removed if the licensee is kept dependent on trademarks, foreign market access, technical improvements etc.' (ibid. 78). He also points out that the market solution of licensing may be resorted to if non-specificity of assets in the guise of appropriability problems is not likely to be an issue. Consistent with this, it is non-specificity of assets in the form of leaky intangible assets such as intellectual property which is frequently identified as the major transactional issue leading to internalization and the development of multinational enterprise (Casson 1979; Dunning 1981; Caves 1982). Coombs *et al.* (1987) point out that internalization may help prevent information leakages to other firms (ibid. 161), while Casson (1987) points out that 'because knowledge has the characteristics of a "public good"', the firm with privileged knowledge tends to become multinational' (ibid. 29). Pure public goods are in fact the extreme opposite of asset specificity as described by Williamson.

Williamson's analysis of the multinational neglects links between technology, transaction costs, and institutional arrangements, as Englander notes (1988), and fails to deal adequately with the phenomenon. C. Galbraith and Kay (1986) argue that analysis of the multinational must recognize that technology transfer typically involves bundles of specific and non-specific assets. Again, Williamson's adherence to the role of asset specificity as a necessary precondition for transaction cost problems makes his approach generally inapplicable to this area of corporate strategy.

In his reply (1992) Williamson argues that all the issues discussed in this section are areas to which transaction cost economics can be applied. This is agreed here; the point being made is that the Williamson version thereof is inapplicable because of its dependence on asset specificity as the driving force for internalization.

6. CONCLUSION

In his original article, Coase argued that 'the distinguishing mark of the firm is the supersession of the price mechanism' (Coase 1937: 389), and emphasized that this means the replacement of systems of exchange with internal organization and authority. By way of contrast, Williamson represents the comparative institutional foundations of his transaction cost approach as internal markets versus external markets, whether he is dealing with capital, labour, or intermediate product markets. This is extremely unsatisfactory. While internal transfer prices certainly exist within organizations, to analyse resource allocation within organizations as reducible to a series of internal markets provides a partial and distorted view of hierarchical resource allocation and decision making.

The development of such false hierarchies characterized as contractual frameworks built around internal markets also leads to problems of analysis of corporate strategies and structures in Williamson's framework. The lack of a proper mechanism by which institution selection can be analysed and the adherence to asset specificity as a necessary condition for the existence of transaction cost problems are critical problems. Williamson's analysis of the evolution of the M-form corporation and his explanations for the existence of diversified firms and multinational enterprise are correspondingly flawed.

Williamson (1992) suggests that I neglect property right issues, which is curious, because that is exactly the criticism I make of his treatment of the multinational in section 4.5 above. Property rights are in fact central to transaction cost problems, and frequently involve problems of asset non-specificity, which puts them beyond the self-imposed limit of Williamson's approach.

If there is a fundamental problem in Williamson's approach to transaction cost economics, it is the confusion which arises when he represents his framework as *the* transaction cost approach as set out in *EIC*. The most recent published work cited, his 1992 reply, retained this narrow definition: 'The principal dimensions on which transaction cost economics presently lies for purposes of describing transactions are (1) the frequency with which they recur, (2) the degree and uncertainty to which they are subject, and (3) *the condition of asset specificity*. Although all are important, many of the refutable implications of transaction cost economics turn presently on the last' (Williamson 1988c, emphasis added).

Williamson suggests (1992) that the 'purported shortcomings of transaction cost economics already have been, or can be, dealt with by an extension or refinement of transaction cost reasoning'. Indeed they can, as I have indicated above in different sections. The point is that the extensions frequently involve refutations of *the* transaction cost framework as developed by Williamson—for example, his assertion of the necessity and centrality of the principle of asset specificity.

It is not coincidental that Williamson's early work heavily emphasized vertical integration. As we have seen, extending this version of transaction cost economics beyond this special case of corporate strategy is impractical because of the limitations of the framework. In my view, unless Williamson concedes the role of asset non-specificity as in economies of scope and appropriability problems in transactional analysis, his approach will remain limited to this special case. While there are other problems associated with his approach, notably the lack of an adequate selection mechanism for institutional choice, abandonment of his fundamentalist position on asset specificity is a prerequisite for progress.

I would also suggest that the various problems raised by Williamson's statements as to what constitutes transaction cost economics can be helped by referring to Coase's original article. 'Within the firm . . . in place of the complicated market structure with exchange transactions is substituted the entrepreneur-coordinator who directs production. It is clear that these are alternative methods of coordinating production' (Coase, 1937: 388).

It would be sympathetic to Coase's original analysis and would resolve the ambiguities over Williamson's use of the word, if transaction was limited to exchange relationships. Comparative institutional economics could then be concerned with broader costs of co-ordination in which exchange costs are only one element. Co-ordination cost economics would include costs of organizations as well as exchange costs, and could be a genuinely Coasian framework for comparative institutional research.

8

Coercion and Co-operation in the Employment Relationship:
Efficiency and Power Theories of the Firm

PAUL MARGINSON

The question of why productive activity should be organized within firms has stimulated considerable debate between proponents of two broad paradigms. New institutionalists, notably Williamson (1975, 1980, 1981), have tried to demonstrate that the evolution of the firm from the putting-out system to the large modern corporation has taken place primarily for efficiency reasons. By contrast, radical authors, such as Marglin (1974) and Edwards (1979), have stressed the search for superior means of management control over labour as the underlying dynamic explaining the evolution of the firm (see McPherson 1983 and Putterman 1986 for reviews of the relevant literature). Both approaches signify an important departure from the standard neo-classical theory of the firm, in which the production of outputs from inputs is treated as a purely technical relationship. This is because forms of work organization are considered to affect the transformation of inputs into outputs.

This chapter is concerned with the characterization and analysis of the employment relationship offered by the competing efficiency and power perspectives of the firm. Building on existing criticisms in the literature, the aim is to demonstrate that considerations of power and control, as well as those of efficiency, are essential to an adequate theorization of the firm and the relations between management and labour within it. The efficiency claims of the new institutionalists are subjected to scrutiny. Although a number of scholars have contributed to the refinement of the 'efficient institutions' approach, the argument focuses on the work of Oliver Williamson. This is because Williamson is centrally identified with the development of the approach, and in his many writings he has comprehensively covered the issues with which the paper is concerned.

The chapter starts by summarizing the main features of the efficient institutions approach. Three central propositions are identified. These are then questioned, existing criticism discussed, and counter-propositions

I am most grateful for the helpful comments of Keith Cowling, Paul Edwards, Jean Hartley, and Peter Nolan on earlier versions of this chapter.

developed. An alternative approach to the firm, resting on a recognition
of the importance of power as well as efficiency considerations, is then
sketched. A further section identifies some inadequacies of existing writings from a power perspective, and discusses why the exercise of power
cannot be adequately modelled through coercive means alone, before
some conclusions are drawn.

I. THE EFFICIENT INSTITUTIONS PARADIGM

Williamson (1975) outlines a theory of the firm, and within it the employment relationship, based on transaction cost minimization. Following
Coase (1937), Williamson argues that the co-ordination of economic
activity through administrative units (firms), rather than markets, can be
explained in terms of the costs incurred in transacting in markets. If institutions reduce the costs of transacting below those obtaining in the
market, then they are considered to be more efficient. Transaction costs
are seen to stem from the combination of certain environmental factors
with certain attributes of human behaviour. Williamson identifies uncertainty, complexity, and bilateral or small-universe exchange relations as
the pertinent environmental factors in which two assumed attributes of
human behaviour become important for economic outcomes. First,
human agents are assumed to be boundedly rational, which recognizes
that there are computational limits to human capabilities in processing
information (H.A. Simon 1955). Bounded rationality contrasts with the
usual assumption of global rationality, which implies human capacity to
process an infinite quantity of information. Second, human agents are
assumed to be self-interested or opportunistic. Thus they will pursue individualistic or sectional, as distinct from organizational, goals.

In the context of the employment relation, the existence of uncertainty
over the precise work tasks required to be performed during any particular period, when combined with bounded rationality, makes the negotiation of a complex contract covering all potential contingencies extremely
costly, if not impossible. Hence, Williamson argues, the contract between
employers and workers will necessarily be incomplete. Moreover, the
propensity of workers to behave opportunistically necessitates the conclusion of this incomplete contract within an organization, the firm, where
employers have power, within limits, to allocate workers to tasks, specify
effort levels, and monitor behaviour. Costs incurred by transacting in the
market, such as embezzlement and cheating, are minimized, and an
improvement in efficiency is consequently achieved. The resulting authority relation is assumed to be in the interest of both employers and workers, because organizational performance is enhanced through the curbing
of self-interested behaviour.

The direct employment of workers, is itself associated with certain transaction costs, however. These stem from problems of asset specificity, which is the degree to which skills and know-how are specific to the firm, and hence not tradable on the open market. Where workers have firm-specific skills which are not immediately replaceable, a situation of small numbers exchange relations pertains, and there is scope for opportunistic behaviour. Workers may use the bargaining power deriving from their possession of firm-specific skills to obtain an undue share of the returns accruing to internal organization. Williamson, *et al.* (1975) argue that such problems can be overcome by the creation of a collective organization, involving both employers and workers, aimed at generating an atmosphere of trust, a common frame of reference, and goal congruence between management and workers. In this context they cite the development of the bureaucratic mode of employment relations in contemporary large corporations, characterized by a structured internal labour market with low ports of entry, internal job ladders, on-the-job training, associated promotion opportunities, and deferred compensation.

In creating a collective organization, union recognition and collective bargaining are seen by Williamson *et al.* as important, although not essential, facilitators. Unions assist in elevating organizational goals above opportunistic or sectional ones (Williamson 1984*b*). The argument draws on the application of Hirschman's (1970) exit-voice model to trade unions by Freeman (1976). Workers are likely to develop a collective voice through a union in preference to individualized means of expressing dissatisfaction, such as quitting, only when they have a strong interest in maintaining a continuing employment relationship, by dint of possessing firm-specific skills. Where workers do not possess such skills, they are assumed to have less interest in a continuing relationship with a particular employer, and thereby less interest in joining a union. For their part, employers in firms characterized by high degrees of asset specificity will be interested in promoting a union because of its role in minimizing sectional or self-interested behaviour and its orientation towards organizational goals. Workers and employers in firms characterized by firm-specific skills have, according to Williamson, a mutual interest in developing collective organization.

The foregoing argument utilizes the concept of transaction costs to develop a comparative static perspective to the question of whether markets or firms are more efficient at co-ordinating economic activity. Williamson (1980) has also attempted to demonstrate that efficiency considerations prevail when examining the organization of production in an evolutionary perspective.

Williamson's (1980) method is to compare the transaction costs properties of alternative modes of organizing work, holding technology constant. The efficiency properties of historically earlier forms of work organization, such as putting-out, are rated as poor. Embezzlement and cheating were endemic to the system, which also required large inventories to be held. Eventually putting-out was supplanted by modes of work organization possessing superior efficiency properties in transaction costs terms. The first step was internal contracting, followed by the hierarchical capitalist firm where labour is directly employed. However, as noted above, the direct employment of workers is itself associated with transaction costs arising out of asset specificity. These problems are supposedly mitigated by the emergence of the bureaucratic form of work organization in the large corporation. Williamson concludes that the evolution of the firm is the result of the search for ever more efficient forms of employment organization. Moreover, since later forms of internal organization which vest more power in the managers of firms, through strengthened hierarchy, are also shown to be more efficient, Williamson contends that considerations of power can be set aside.

This outline of the main features of the efficient institutions framework employed by Williamson to explain the organization of productive activity within the firm, and more particularly the employment relationship, embodies a number of key propositions. First, hierarchy is viewed as being in the mutual interest of both workers and employers. Second, workers can act opportunistically, and by implication possess bargaining power, only in so far as they command firm-specific skills. Moreover, trade unions are expected to arise for efficiency reasons, in circumstances where both workers and employers have an interest in a continuing employment relation. Third, to paraphrase Marx, efficiency acts as the motor of history.

2. EFFICIENCY, HIERARCHY AND DOMINANCE

Each of these key propositions of the efficient institutions approach is open to question. First, the authority within the employment relationship may be used in the interests of one party rather than both. Second, workers derive bargaining power from sources other than their possession of firm-specific skills. Allied to this, union organization need not rest on the existence of firm-specific skills. Third, efficiency is not the only consideration driving the historical evolution of forms of work organization. These lines of argument are developed, and then drawn together, in the four subsections below.

2.1 Hierarchy and the mutual interest

According to the efficient institutions paradigm, the role of hierarchy in the capitalist firm is to ensure the prevalence of common goals over sectional or individual goals. Because self-interested behaviour is curbed to the benefit of broader community or organizational goals, hierarchy is viewed as being in the mutual interest of both employers and workers. For Williamson *et al.* (1975), the legitimacy of the authority relation lies in a process of voluntary exchange in the employment relationship. Workers cede limited authority to management over the direction of tasks and the specification of effort levels in return for guarantees relating to wages, conditions, and security of employment.

Bowles (1985) characterizes this and similar approaches as 'neo-Hobbesian', because they focus on the archetypal Hobbesian problem of reconciling self-interested behaviour with the common good. Conflict exists within the firm; but it is conflict between self-interest and the common good. The explanation of the functional nature of hierarchy within the firm 'bears a close resemblance to the original Hobbesian rationale for the state as a socially necessary form of coercion' (Bowles 1985: 16). Workers submit themselves voluntarily to the employer's authority in a manner analogous to the voluntary acceptance by individual citizens of the state's authority. Crucially, the argument rests on the assumption that the employer will act in accord with the common interest.

This involves an underlying asymmetry in the application to employers and to workers of the behavioural assumption of opportunism. Williamson (1980: 7) has claimed that 'except as incumbent workers enjoy advantages over outsiders (by reason presumably of firm-specific experience) there would be no need for supervision and discipline beyond that imposed by the market'. Under this formulation, workers are assumed to act opportunistically whilst employers are assumed to act in accordance with an (undefined) community interest. Only employers are faced by a problem of bounded rationality. As Willman (1983) notes, this is a weak basis on which to erect an efficiency justification of hierarchy. One has only to be consistent in the assumptions made, by also allowing for employers to be opportunistic and workers to be boundedly rational, to see the tenuous foundation of Williamson's argument.

Take, for example, internal labour markets. These are incompatible with competitive hiring, firing, and wage setting. Williamson *et al.* (1975) underline the efficiency benefits stemming from the effectiveness of such an arrangement in curbing workers' ability to exercise their bargaining power in an opportunistic fashion. But they are silent on the scope that internal labour markets provide for employer opportunism. FitzRoy and Kraft (1987) note that where workers possess firm-specific skills, their labour market mobility is impeded. They are therefore susceptible to 'managerial pressure' aimed at eliciting additional effort. The restraints on worker mobility 'give the firm a measure of power over its employees' (McPherson 1983: 363).

Thus far it has been argued that workers and employers should be treated in a behaviourally symmetric fashion. Once this is done, the consequences of opportunism by employers can have much more widespread ramifications. These lie in the possibility that authority itself can be used in an opportunistic fashion. As Dow (1987) observes, authority provides a tool, decision by fiat, which is tailor-made for the unilateral pursuit of self-interest. This is the more so where those able to impose decisions by fiat also possess informational advantages, such as those enjoyed by employers as compared to workers. Williamson himself admits of such a possibility, albeit under 'extreme circumstances':

Internal organization is thus able to adapt more effectively than can inter-firm trading to changing market and technical circumstances. Not only do employment contracts contemplate such flexibility by providing for zones of acceptance within which orders will be implemented without resistance, but orders that exceed the scope of the authority relation can be implemented in extreme circumstances. (Williamson 1985: 249)

But because authority relations create the 'structural preconditions' (Dow 1987: 21) under which employer opportunism can flourish, it is reasonable to presume that such abuses of authority are likely to occur under normal as well as extreme circumstances. It follows that employers are likely to display a preference for hierarchical forms of work organization within which authority can be more readily exercised.

Bowles (1985) demonstrates that this preference for hierarchy results in socially inefficient forms of work organization. Distinguishing between the capacity to work purchased by the employer and the actual labour input, Bowles focuses on the conflict of interest between employers and workers over workers' effort levels. His method is to supplement the traditional production function with a third term representing worker effort. It is assumed that employers are able to compel workers to act in ways that they would not themselves choose, but that the exercise of this authority is costly. This cost takes two forms: the use of supervision and the payment of a wage premium above the market rate. Assuming decreasing returns to both these elements generates a unique profit-maximizing point, which is at a lower level of output than if no such costs arose. The form of internal organization preferred by capitalist employers is thus shown to be socially inefficient.

Historical evidence amply demonstrates that employers are likely to select those forms of work organization which most effectively enable them to serve their own interests. Pollard (1965), E.P. Thompson (1967), and Marglin (1974) all illustrate how the institution of hierarchy through the factory system had its origins in a search by employers for a more effective means of coercing workers to work. Factory organization was associated with working more days of the week, longer hours of the day, and more intensively. Marglin argues that early factories employed the same techniques as those utilized in putting-out, but provided the employer with a more effective means of control over workers' choice between productive time and leisure time. Employers will also prefer technologies that maintain or enhance their authority. Landes (1986), in his response to Marglin, while arguing that factory production remained at a cost disadvantage to domestic industry until power-driven machines were available, concurs that technological choice is dictated by returns not only in money but also in power.

In sum, both theory and history indicate that choices of technology and work organization which most effectively enable employers to pursue their own interests may not be the most efficient in overall terms. The efficient institutions proposition that hierarchy is in the mutual interest of employers and workers is flawed, because it fails to take adequate account of power considerations. Drawing on the arguments above, the following proposition is preferred: Employers select that means of work organization consistent with the objectives of maximizing their own return and maintaining or strengthening their own authority.

2.2 Firm-specific skills, bargaining power, and unionism

The claim that workers' bargaining power is exclusively contingent on their development of firm-specific skills denies the possibility that there may be other bases of bargaining power. However, once these other bases are taken into account, it becomes impossible to subsume the reasons for, and history of, trade union organization within an efficient institutions approach.

An important category of skills which are not firm-specific in character are those, such as craft and technical skills, which are transferable across markets. Workers derive bargaining power from possessing these market skills (Enderwick 1984); specifically from the fact that such skills are relatively scarce, being costly and time-consuming to acquire. Workers acquiring firm-specific skills may suffer a loss of market bargaining power as equivalent employment opportunities outside the firm disappear. But there is no reason why the loss of market bargaining power should be exactly offset by work-place bargaining power associated with firm-specific skills.

Even where workers possess neither firm-specific nor market skills, they may still possess bargaining power. V. P. Goldberg (1980: 262) argues that 'workers acting in concert' can act opportunistically whether skilled or not. Workers possess a degree of bargaining power by dint of their ability to work in a perfunctory manner and thereby impair performance. Hence employers need to encourage workers to perform certain tasks and expend certain levels of effort, even where firm-specific skills are minimal. Goldberg argues that a principal means of doing so is deferred compensation, and in this context cites Henry Ford's $5 day as a prime example (see also Raff and Somers 1987). Goldberg concludes that the existence of a continuing employment relationship, as well as institutional features associated with structured internal labour markets such as age-earnings profiles (see Lazear 1981), can be explained without recourse to firm-specific skills.

Implicit in Goldberg's argument is the notion that workers can derive bargaining power from the mere act of combination. By 'acting in concert', workers with few skills of either a market or a firm-specific nature can make themselves costly to replace. Evidence of this process is provided by Friedman (1977) and Ozanne (1967) in their respective studies of the UK car industry and a large US agricultural equipment manufacturer. The history of workers' organization in the docks in both countries, originating as it did among an unskilled and casual work-force, provides a further example. The point is important. Power does not arise automatically from the possession of certain skills. Although the acquisition of skills may enhance bargaining power, its realization is contingent on some form of independent organization by workers. Organization is a precondition for the effective deployment of bargaining power, as Shorter and Tilly (1974), for example, demonstrate in their historical study of strikes in France. Moreover, action cannot be read off directly from organization; a further factor intervenes: namely, mobilization (Klandermans 1984). Thus bargaining power depends on organization and mobilization, as well as on intrinsic factors such as the possession of firm-specific or market skills. Firm-specific skills are neither necessary nor sufficient for bargaining power to exist.

Williamson (1984*b*) predicts that unions will develop early in industries with a high degree of firm-specific skills (e.g., railways) and late in those industries where skills are differentiated (e.g., farm labouring). But he is silent on the question of union organization based on market skills. Yet the possession of market skills has provided a successful basis around which workers have developed trade union organization. Historically, in both the USA and the UK, the early growth of unionism was based on market, not firm-specific, skills (Edwards 1979; Hyman 1975). An example is the printing industry, in which union organization around market skills across several industrial countries dates far back into the last century. Moreover, this form of union organization does not hinge on a continuing employment relation. Many workers organized into unions in printing continued to be employed on a casual basis. This was equally true of workers at the docks in the UK. A major objective of trade unions in these sectors was to secure a permanent employment relationship. To the extent that they were successful in this objective, and contrary to Williamson's (1984*b*) postulate, union organization preceded, and was not a consequence of, the establishment of a continuing employment relation. In general, union organization cannot be considered as being endogenous to a particular type of employment relation, nor contingent on the development of firm-specific skills.

Although V. P. Goldberg (1980) developed a more satisfactory approach to workers' bargaining power, his analysis remains within a framework in which the primary concern is with opportunistic behaviour by workers. By showing that workers are able to exercise power irrespective of whether they possess firm-specific skills, Goldberg implies that the scope for such opportunistic behaviour is enhanced. Union organization, on this view, still serves to restrain opportunistic behaviour. But why, then, should employers concerned to develop collective organization in order to restrain opportunistic behaviour (Williamson *et al.* 1975) choose unionism as the preferred form? For while unions can provide a 'voice' for workers, their presence is not essential to the 'voice' effect. Prominent non-union firms utilize extensive consultation procedures, suggestions schemes, and participative arrangements, in order to forestall union organization by providing substitute 'voice' channels. In the USA in particular, large employers have had a long-standing preference for collective arrangements of a non-union character.

A very different perspective on unionism arises once account is taken of the possibility that employers act opportunistically, and that in order to protect themselves from the consequences of such employer opportunism, workers organize themselves into trade unions (FitzRoy and Kraft, 1987). On this view, union organization arises as a means by which workers exercise countervailing bargaining power within an employment relationship wherein employers can utilize authority to pursue their own interests.

Once trade unions are seen as exercising countervailing power within the employment relationship, a further possibility arises: namely, that employers will be concerned to shape union organization into forms that minimize any threat to their authority. (Indeed, employers may go further and attempt to eliminate trade union organization altogether.) Employers can shape union organization in many ways. In the UK, Brown (1981), for example, suggests that in some circumstances employers have promoted facilities for shop stewards, including provision for full-time shop stewards, preferring to deal with a union organization that is internally, or firm, based rather than one that is externally based. Recently, successive incoming employers to the UK, most notably Nissan, have demonstrated a clear preference for a particular type of unionism: single union and 'no strike' (Wickens 1987). Employers on 'greenfield' sites have also sought to select which union, if any, their future employees will belong to (Bassett 1986).

In short, the shape of trade union organization itself does not arise out of some efficiency blueprint, but is a product of conflict between employers and workers. Contrary to the efficient institutions propositions, firm-specific skills are neither necessary nor sufficient for workers' bargaining power to exist. Nor is trade union organization contingent on the development of firm-specific skills. The following proposition summarizes the argument of this section: The exercise of bargaining power by workers rests on the formation of countervailing organizations (including trade unions) against the use of authority by employers. Employers will try to minimize the threat to their authority posed by workers' (trade union) organization.

2.3 Historical evolution of the Firm

Williamson claims that efficiency considerations have dominated the evolution of modes of employing labour (Williamson 1980). His immediate concern was to refute Marglin's (1974) proposition that the evolution of the capitalist hierarchical mode of employing labour can best be understood from a perspective that emphasizes employers' aims of exercising control over workers. Williamson's claim has been questioned elsewhere on methodological grounds (Dow 1987). Here the construction of, and conclusions from, his historical comparative exercise aimed at demonstrating that efficiency considerations will win out in the end, are also shown to be open to objection.

A particular problem of method in undertaking such a comparison concerns the definition of efficiency employed. An increase in technological efficiency is usually taken to mean an increase in output for given inputs, or the production of the same output with given inputs. (Economic efficiency takes account of relative price effects as well, and the two definitions may not always coincide.) Importantly for the argument here, employers can minimize costs and gain more for less, without there being a corresponding increase in technological efficiency. Indeed, it is possible that a production system that gives more for less—that is, is more profitable—may be less efficient in technological terms than another, less profitable system. This is because by securing greater effort from workers, employers can increase output and revenues, but the cost of labour inputs remain unchanged.

Thus, a strengthening of the authority relation, such as occurred with the shift from the putting-out system to factory production, could result in more output from the same capacity to labour purchased. But to the extent that the increase in output is secured through employers' ability to extract more labour effort from a given work-force, then labour input has increased as well. Thus, while costs may have been minimized and profits increased, the efficiency implications of strengthening the authority relation are indeterminate; both outputs and inputs have increased.

By focusing on the issue of transactional efficiency and holding technology constant, Williamson side-steps the crucial question of technological efficiency. He formulates his hypothesis in its strongest possible form: 'the best evidence that power [labour control] is driving organizational outcomes would be a demonstration that less efficient modes that serve to concentrate power displace more efficient modes in which power is more evenly distributed' (Williamson 1980: 20). Note, however, that showing that, out of two alternative forms of work organization with equivalent efficiency properties in transaction costs terms, the one selected served to maximize employers' private returns by enhancing their authority would be sufficient to demonstrate the relevance of power considerations.

In his comparison, one form of co-operative organization, based on communal ownership and communal reward, emerges as having good efficiency properties in transaction cost terms, on a par with those of the capitalist bureaucratic mode. This is despite its weak rating in terms of leadership and monitoring properties.[1] If this is the case, why do we observe the capitalist bureaucratic mode of employment relation to be so widespread, while co-operatives are relatively rare? Williamson is silent on this question. A dimension of analysis is missing one that would explain why one form of efficient organization should develop and not another. Putterman (1982) and Dow (1987) cite appropriation considerations as being important. Within a co-operative the benefits of internal organization, as compared to market co-ordination, accrue equally to all the members of the firm. By contrast, within a capitalist firm it is possible for the employer to secure all, or a disproportionate share, of the benefits deriving from internal organization. In societies where there is an

---

[1] This rating is a direct result of Williamson's definition of co-operative, requiring rotation of tasks, including leadership and monitoring—a requirement which in his analysis generates inefficiencies in transaction cost terms. In practice, however, producer co-operatives have been observed to have a permanent division of tasks, including monitoring (Putterman 1984). (Moreover, while rotation may be transactionally inefficient in Williamson's static sense, it may provide a process of learning which results in dynamic efficiency gains.) A centralized monitoring structure does not, of itself, rule out worker control as Williamson assumes. It is not the existence of a hierarchy which defines an organization as capitalist, but the use of hierarchy by one economic agent to exercise command over other economic agents.

uneven distribution of wealth and power, the incentive for individual entrepreneurs to establish a capitalist firm is greater because returns to internal organization within a co-operative have to be shared. Appropriability considerations are, of course, central to Marglin's (1974) argument about the emergence of the factory system. It was precisely the power to appropriate the returns from the organization of production in the factory which, Marglin argues, spurred capitalist employers to embrace that system.

A more limited claim to the efficiency of existing modes of organizing work, which would appear to recognize the force of such points, is made by V.P. Goldberg (1980: 268): 'An efficient institution is one that survives in a particular context. The efficacy of a particular arrangement will depend upon the ability of the parties to exert legal or extra-legal power.' This draws specific attention to the power which employers and workers are able to exercise, and to 'context'. The latter presumably includes not only the legal framework within which the employment relation and firm operate, but also the educational system, the financial system, the political context, and the family. These are unlikely to operate in a neutral fashion. For example, Bowles and Gintis (1976) show how the schooling system in the USA has been fashioned to reflect the dominant, capitalist mode of organizing work. The financial system in the USA and the UK has been shown to mitigate against the development of co-operatives, because equity is provided on less favourable terms (Putterman 1982, 1984; Thornley 1981). And political intervention has been crucial in the USA in affecting the ability of workers to exercise countervailing power through trade union organization.

Given the opportunities open to employers and workers to exercise power, discussed in section 2.2, together with the additional opportunity to influence the context in which power is exercised, it is hard to see how efficiency considerations can win out in any global or historical sense. Contrary to Williamson's claim that efficiency considerations are primary, this section has underlined the salience of power considerations to a satisfactory explanation of the evolution of forms of work organization. The following proposition summarizes the argument: The historical evolution of the firm reflects a series of choices by employers over technology and work organization which served to maximize their own private return; there is no presumption that these choices were technologically or organizationally efficient.

2.4 Employer control and the firm

The argument of the preceding sub-sections can now be drawn together. By paying proper attention to the power aspects of relationships between employers and workers, the propositions developed throw a distinct light on the nature of the firm.

Central to an adequate theorization of the firm is the proposition that employers and workers have an inherent conflict of interest over the utilization of the workers' capacity to work after the labour contract has been concluded. Employers are motivated by the acquisition of profit, which necessitates cost minimization and control over the production process, including workers' effort and task adaptability. Workers are motivated by the need to attain an adequate standard of living and to exert control over the pace and content of their work. Employers do not purchase a specified quantity of work performed through a precise contract, but control over workers' capacity to produce through an incomplete contract. Scope for conflict thus exists not only over the terms of the incomplete contract, but subsequently over the precise labour which workers are required to perform.

More generally, the rationale of the employment relationship in the capitalist firm can be seen as the production of goods and services at a profit to the employer. Additional value is generated in production through securing actual work performed whose value is in excess of the price of labour inputs. This is not a question of cheating or opportunism, because the employer's right to direct workers to tasks and to specify effort levels are, within limits, contractually agreed prior to production commencing. It is in this sense that Marx (1974) maintained that labour and capital engaged as equals in the realm of exchange, but confronted each other as unequals within production.

It is this aspect of the employment relationship which is at the root of the distinction between the capacity to work purchased by employers and actual work performed. For other factors of production, such as capital equipment or raw materials, no such distinction arises. Given quantities of raw materials or capital equipment purchased will have a fixed relationship to productive output. But for labour, the relationship between the capacity to work purchased and actual work performed is variable and unspecifiable before production commences. The transformation of the capacity to work into actual work performed will depend on the employer's ability to direct workers to tasks and to secure worker effort. Both employer and worker have an interest in leaving these unspecified, the employer in order to secure task allocation and levels of effort commensurate with profitable production, the worker in order to secure control over the pace and content of his or her work. These interests inherently conflict.

Employers are able to use the authority which the incomplete nature of the labour contract vests in them to try and secure an outcome to this conflict which is favourable to their interests. Forms of technology and work organization will be selected by employers that they believe best enable them to exploit workers' capacity to work. These will maximize the private return to the employer, but will not necessarily be socially efficient. Workers, for their part, develop their own forms of organization in order to exercise countervailing power against the use of authority by employers. In turn, employers will try to shape the form of workers' organization, including trade unions, in order to minimize the challenge to their dominance. The exercise of power depends on extrinsic factors, organization and mobilization of resources, as well as intrinsic factors, the possession of certain skills or the ability to hire and fire. The wider context, the legal, political, and socio-economic systems, is also an important influence on the exercise of power. Outcomes, in terms of those parts of the labour contract which are left unspecified, are therefore indeterminate.

3. POWER APPROACHES TO THE FIRM AND THE LIMITS TO COERCION

Power or 'control' models of the firm have emphasized the coercive nature of employer authority (Marglin 1974; Edwards 1979; Bowles 1985). The essence of the authority relation is seen to lie in the ability of the employer to force workers to do things which they would not otherwise do. In Bowles's formal model, outlined in section 2.1, labour effort is secured through coercive means, either directly or indirectly. Direct coercion is exercised through supervision and monitoring, indirect coercion through the ability to impose a cost on workers for non-compliance with employer directives. By paying a premium above the market wage, the employer can make job loss, and the threat of it, costly to the worker. Marglin similarly emphasizes the role of indirect coercion arising from the consequences of being thrown out of work, as well as the direct coercion of the supervisory and monitoring systems developed in the early factories.

By contrast, writers taking an efficient institutions approach have emphasized the consensual nature of the authority relation. Workers' voluntary submission to authority is seen to be in the interests of employers as well as workers, in so far as organizational goals are thereby elevated above sectional ones. The inadequacies of this view of authority have already been spelled out. In this section it is argued that it is not enough simply to counterpose coercion to consensus, as writers taking a power approach have tended to do. To focus on the coercive aspect of the employment relationship alone is to ignore that employers secure effort from workers by other means, and their reasons for doing so. The aim is to develop an account of the interplay of coercion and co-operation within the employment relationship.

The starting-point is a recognition that the exercise of employer authority is contractually agreed, and acceptable, only within limits. Workers are voluntary agents who retain rights, most importantly to quit the employment relationship. In this sense workers differ from slaves and serfs, who can be compelled to submit to authority. The fact that authority relations in the capitalist firm 'arise endogenously via the bargains struck among initially autonomous agents, rather than through crude coercion' (Dow 1987: 16) places initial limits on the exercise of employer authority. But these are not the only limits to the use of coercion in the employment relationship. Following the argument in section 2.4, workers enter the employment relationship with their own set of interest, which conflict with those of the employer. Post-contract, the employer is faced with the problem of securing labour effort and task adaptability.

Moreover, employers may be concerned to harness workers' adaptability and creativity, as well as to direct them to tasks. Thus a distinction exists between what has been termed 'perfunctory' and commensurate performance by workers. Perfunctory performance is associated with low levels of effort and task adaptability, commensurate performance with high task adaptability and effort levels. M. Friedman (1977) argues that labour enters the employment relationship in a contradictory manner. Labour is at the same time both flexible in the tasks to which it can be applied and resistant to intensification of effort and direction of tasks. Employers need to enlist the creative potential of labour, as well as overcoming its recalcitrance. Coercion may well overcome workers' recalcitrance, as is the case in Bowles's model, but it is unlikely to harness workers' flexibility and creativity. Coercive means can secure perfunctory, but not commensurate, performance from workers. Employers must to some degree seek co-operative relation with workers in order to harness their creative and productive powers. Workers also have an interest in working effectively. This is because the viability of the firm has implications for their own future employment, security, and pecuniary rewards (Cressey and MacInnes 1980).

The circumstances under which employers are able to secure commensurate, rather than merely perfunctory, performance from their workers have been the concern of a diverse literature. In psychology, an extensive literature is concerned with individuals' motivation. The several theories developed break down into two basic directions of analysis (Nicholson 1981): theories concerned with mobilizing energy or effort and theory concerned with the direction of effort—the values, goals, and purposes for which energy is expended. In economics, various literatures have pointed to the importance of institutional arrangements in securing commensurate performance. In the growing literature on participation, concerned with opportunism by employers as well as workers, it is argued that commensurate performance is more likely to result when decisions on aspects of work organization are taken jointly, rather than unilaterally by the employer (Cable and FitzRoy 1980; McCain 1980; FitzRoy and Kraft 1987). In similar vein, Freeman and Medoff (1984) argue that unionization through providing 'voice' for workers as an alternative to exit, and through shocking management into better practice, can enhance performance.

A different perspective is offered by efficiency wage theories, whose central insight is that employers are able to elicit greater effort from workers by the payment of a wage above the market rate. It is presumed that employers pay a higher wage because it results in higher profits. Thus, employers will pay an 'efficiency' wage where the costs of doing so are less than those incurred through monitoring workers' effort (Raff and Somers 1987). The claim to efficiency is questionable, as, recalling the discussion of section 2.3, higher profits do not guarantee that an increase in efficiency has occurred. Such problems notwithstanding, the central insight of the approach is an important one, and is not contingent on the claim to efficiency.

One variant of efficiency wage theory underlies the work of Bowles (1985) and V.P. Goldberg (1980) discussed above. If there are pecuniary costs to losing a job, workers will be induced to work harder. A second variant emphasizes the importance of workers' norms about what constitutes a fair day's work (Akerlof 1982). In return for a wage in excess of that obtainable elsewhere, workers are prepared to work at levels of effort and adaptability in excess of minimum, or perfunctory, work standards. A similar idea underpins Annable's (1984) efficiency wage model of the firm. Employers are able to secure effort through the payment of a wage premium. The wage premium is determined by reference to a wage norm, which is defined as the 'workers' standard of fair treatment and is rooted in custom and tradition' (Annable 1984: 8).

The use of concepts such as 'norms' and 'conventions' in the analysis of worker effort draws heavily on sociological and psychological models of human behaviour. Sociologists have questioned the assumption employed in economic models that workers are necessarily averse to effort (Cressey and MacInnes 1980). Studies have suggested that rather than seeking 'not to work', workers attempt to control the pace and content of their work (see, e.g., Roy 1969; Lupton 1963; Baldamus 1961). They do this by enforcing norms or conventions about the amount of effort to be expended. Effort is seen as a relative concept, most notably in its relation to pay. Behavioural approaches to effort stress the range of means by which employers can elicit effort from workers (Mintzberg 1983). These range from direct supervision, where effort is secured by issuing instructions to workers and monitoring their actions, to reliance on norms and conventions. The latter extends to professionalization, where workers have internalized values about how work should be performed and about effort levels, requiring no direct supervision. Socialization occurs prior to employment through the training required to perform the work. This contrasts with socialization on the job, associated with the enforcement of effort norms and conventions, referred to above. Mintzberg (1983) notes that most employers simultaneously adopt several approaches to elicit effort from their work-forces, according to such things as the differing nature of the tasks being performed and the extent of prior training.

The argument of this section points to the importance of a complex range of influences whereby labour effort is secured, of which the coercive means emphasized by critics such as Marglin (1974) and Bowles (1985) are only one. In their analysis of how employers secure effort and adaptability from workers, these 'control' models offer only a partial explanation. It has been suggested that institutional and normative factors are also important in securing labour effort. An emphasis on coercion to the exclusion of other factors ignores employers' need to enlist the creativity of workers, or that workers have their own conventions about levels of effort to be expended.[2]

5. CONCLUSIONS

This chapter has argued that issues of power are inherent in the type of economic problem addressed by efficient institutions theories. According to its own assumption of self-interested behaviour, the efficient institutions approach should anticipate that employers will use the authority vested in them by the incomplete nature of the labour contract to pursue their own interests. In which case, employers will select forms of work organization which maximize their own private returns and which are consistent with maintaining or enhancing their authority. It follows that claims to the efficiency of the resultant forms of work organization can no longer be sustained. It has been further argued that workers' bargaining power cannot be reduced to a derivative condition dependent on the possession of firm-specific skills. Workers will try to counter employer authority through their own autonomous forms of organization, and in

[2] Importantly, the strategies for securing labour effort pursued by employers may vary according to the position of workers in the production process or external circumstances. Employers may be more concerned to harness the creativity of some groups of workers than others. What M. Friedman (1977) has termed 'responsible autonomy' strategies are characterized by a degree of work group self-management aimed at enlisting workers' creativity, and contrast with 'direct control' strategies which are more overtly coercive.

turn employers will try to shape worker organization so as to minimize the threat to their authority.

Power or control models of the firm provide a more satisfactory account of the nature and consequence of the exercise of employer authority. But in so doing, they lay too much emphasis on the role of coercion. Little attention is paid to the needs of employers to secure commensurate, as distinct from perfunctory, performance from employees. By contrast, the efficient institutions literature displays a greater sensitivity to the importance of institutions and 'atmosphere' (Williamson 1975) in eliciting commensurate performance from workers.

This reflects a strength of the efficient institutions approach: namely, its sensitivity to the potential contribution of other disciplinary approaches to the analysis of economic problems. The associated concepts of bounded rationality on the part of human agents and complexity and uncertainty in the environment are explicitly drawn from organization studies. But a corresponding weakness lies in the attempt to incorporate such insights as stylized facts into a framework which in other respects has much in common with traditional neo-classical economics. Thus, despite the important collective aspect of the employment relationship, the analysis is largely conducted in terms of the individualistic concept of opportunism. Little attention is paid to concepts that might bind workers to each other or to their employers, such as norms or conventions, or work groups together, such as solidarity.

Perhaps economics is least comfortable when dealing with issues of power (Rothschild 1971). It is well known that situations of bilateral monopoly and small numbers are conducive to the exercise of power. These situations characterize the types of employment relationship with which the efficient institutions approach is concerned. Regard needs to be paid to the limits on the exercise of coercion to secure worker effort and to the importance of normative factors. More broadly, the role of non-coercive means of maintaining power, including socialization and legitimation, requires attention. A more adequate treatment of power within economics is essential to further developments in the theory of the firm.

9

The Prospects of Pension Fund Socialism

WILLIAM H. SIMON

Classical political economy portrayed the function of the capitalist class as saving and investing. This is an undeniably important role, and it seemed implausible to the classicists that, in a capitalist society, the great masses of people with minimal assets and barely enough income for current needs could participate in it. The fact that the performance of this socially valuable role entailed a socially regrettable distribution of ownership and income was seen as either a necessary evil or cause for the rejection of the entire capitalist framework of private ownership and market allocation of capital.

Contemporary developments in economic theory and practice have given us a different vision of the institutionalization of the savings and investment role. This vision locates savings and investment not in the class structure, but in the life cycle. In early adulthood, people tend to save negatively (borrow) to finance education and the setting up of households. As their careers proceed, they save positively, paying back their loans and accruing assets in anticipation of retirement. In retirement, they draw down their savings. This vision has considerably more benign distributive connotations than the classical one. The privileges and responsibilities of saving are distributed throughout the population. And there is no exploitation of savers by non-savers, since the two roles are performed by the same people at appropriate phases of their lifetimes.

If you had to choose between the class vision of capital formation and the life cycle one as a description of contemporary western economies, you would have to choose the class vision. But post-Second World War welfare policies have given some substance to the life cycle vision. A substantial portion of the capital claims in the advanced economies are held by public and private funds that secure retirement benefits for broad segments of the work-forces in these economies. For example, about a quarter of the value of equity securities and about 15 per cent of the value of the debt instruments of American business are held by pension funds (Employee Benefits Research Institute 1990: 43). These portions seem likely to increase in the future.

Moreover, the life cycle vision has served as an inspiration for reform. It has occurred to some that the road to socialism, or some substantial socialization of the investment process, might lie through an expanded, publicly regulated system of pension finance (Drucker 1976; Deaton 1989). In the United States such notions have surfaced occasionally in debates over the 'social investment' of pension funds or over the 'employee stock ownership' type of pension plan (Blasi 1988; Rifkin and Barber 1978). In Europe during the 1970s and 1980s quite ambitious plans for 'wage-earner funds' (not necessarily, but sometimes, tied to pension finance) were debated prominently (Swensen 1989: 129–223). Recently some proposals for the 'privatization' of formerly Communist East European economies have included provisions for the transfer by states of responsibilities for retirement benefits and assets to fund them to private pension plans.

'Pension fund socialism' is probably not the term best calculated to evoke broad enthusiasm for measures of this sort, and it is potentially misleading to the extent that it suggests that these plans are uniformly radical. But the term seems appropriate nevertheless, since, at the most general level, these plans are animated by the traditional socialist ideal of a more egalitarian and democratic economy; and they pursue this goal in a manner long associated with socialism—reallocation of capital ownership. Moreover, the work of the politically centrist management theorist Peter Drucker in popularizing the term may have eroded its more radical connotations.

At a more concrete level, some of the discussions in America and Western Europe were prompted by the economic dislocations of the past two decades. In the USA the large unanticipated employment and wage losses associated with deindustrialization (intensified international competition and technological change) in the manufacturing sector and deregulation in the transportation and communications sectors made the established forms of job and wage security through employment contracts seem inadequate. Forms of worker ownership, especially where accompanied by tax subsidies through the pension system, struck some as a promising response to these inadequacies.

The debates over 'wage-earner funds' in West Germany and Sweden focused on a distinct set of problems. One was the difficulty that the national labour confederations in these countries with centralized, high-density union structures experienced in developing a strategy that maintained productivity-based wage growth without causing job losses or inflation or crippling investment incentives. High wage demands risked inflation or unemployment (or both), but wage restraint might allow capitalists to capture most of the benefits of price stability. The state or the labour movement might try to recapture these benefits through exactions on profits, but such exactions risked an undesirable reduction in investment. The wage-earner fund idea would combine wage restraint with profit exactions, but would have the exactions reinvested on a long-term basis on behalf of the workers, thus in theory offsetting any reduction in investment by capitalists due to the exactions.

In the rest of this chapter, I want to consider the principal constraints on the fulfilment of the egalitarian and democratic aspirations of socialism through pension reform, especially in the United States. These are the constraints of risk allocation, conflicts of interest, control allocation, and redistribution. I conclude that the promise of pension fund socialism is significant, but considerably more modest than many proponents suggest.

I. RISK ALLOCATION

In conventional capitalist theory, both the control and the financial return associated with ownership are functions of risk. Owners get control to limit the risks to their interests, and the return they receive is in substantial part compensation for the risk they bear. Although classical socialism was quite hostile to this idea, both descriptively and normatively, most discussions of pension fund socialism seem to accept it. Pension fund socialism is a form of market socialism, and market socialism seems committed to allocating at least some of the risks that markets create in accordance with ownership.

Perhaps the most fundamental issues of risk in pension plan design are as follows.

1.1 Defined benefit versus defined contribution

A defined benefit plan promises a specified benefit on retirement; for example, an annual payment during retirement equal to 1 per cent of final average salary during the worker's last three years, for each year of service with the company. A defined contribution plan simply promises a specified contribution to the pension fund and guarantees the worker accumulated contributions and earnings (or losses) on them. In a defined benefit plan the worker does not bear any investment risk associated with the fund. The promised benefits are insured by the employer, an insurance company, and/or a government agency. If the fund's investment performance isn't adequate to pay promised benefits, the insurer pays them. In a defined benefit plan, the economic premiss of worker control— worker investment risk—is absent. (At least, this is so to the extent that benefits are completely and effectively insured. As long as workers' benefits are implicitly conditioned on the solvency of the firm or insurance company, they bear some risk. However, in the United States the Pension Benefit Guaranty Corporation (PBGC) insurance system covers about 80 per cent of benefits in most private employer defined benefit plans, and while there remains some risk that it will be unable to pay all insured claims, the system surely alleviates worker concern about employer solvency.) Here the insurer bears the residual risk (and is entitled to any assets above those necessary to fund benefits), and on conventional premisses ought to have control.

It is thus a matter of significance to any ambitious project of pension fund socialism that industrial unions have tended to bargain for defined benefit plans, and have pushed for federal insurance of such plans. Apparently, they have preferred security to control.

But there is a strong case to be made—control considerations apart— that defined contribution plans would be a socially preferable basis for a pension system with broad coverage. First, workers pay for the security of defined benefit with lower expected benefit levels. An employer should be willing to make a larger current pension contribution where, as in a defined contribution plan, she bears no continuing investment risk (or is not required to pay some other insurer to bear this risk).

Second, and far more important, the egalitarian goals of the socialist vision are ultimately more compatible with defined contribution plans. The society as a whole cannot escape investment risk. If some are to be immunized from it, others will have to be saddled with it. If capitalists bear the risk, they will demand compensation for it. If some sectors of the work-force bear investment risk, while others participate in defined benefit plans that immunize them against it, large inequalities between the sectors may emerge. Of course, a system limited to defined contribution plans would still produce inequality; the less successful funds would have lower returns than the more successful ones. But in such a system the high returns would be less socially concentrated and less correlated with other dimensions of social status than they would be in a system where a small class assumes primary responsibility for investment risk.

Moreover, public insurance arrangements for defined benefit plans are prone to unfair cross-subsidization of different classes of workers. Cross-subsidization among the beneficiaries of different defined benefit plans may occur because of the political or administrative difficulty of calibrating insurance premiums to risk. This seems to have been the case with the PBGC system, on which more than 80 per cent of claims to date have come from auto and steel workers, at the expense of workers in other industries. Cross-subsidization of defined benefit beneficiaries as a class by the rest of the population may occur if insurance funds prove insolvent and governments feel compelled to bail them out with general revenues; many fear that this will happen in the case of the PBGC, which is insolvent by some estimates (Ippolito 1989: 41–5).

An approach that spread risk more evenly throughout the population would seem to be more compatible with the socialist equality aspiration. From this point of view, a programme of defined contribution plans (with broad coverage) seems better. On the other hand, paternalist and social welfare concerns weigh against excessive risk bearing. Some fraction of a retired worker's income claims should involve relatively riskless claims of the sort that Social Security and defined benefit plans now provide. The society's ability to honour these claims depends on the performance of its economy; but by giving them a high priority on social resources, the society allocates much of the economic risk to the younger generation. The effect is to give relatively strong short- and middle-term security to older workers, and to make it possible to adjust the retirement system very gradually to economic change.

Whether social or private pension insurance is a better way to provide this baseline of security is debatable. It is easier to redistribute internally to compensate for wage inequality in social insurance and easier to achieve universal coverage. On the other hand, public social insurance tends to be unfunded, with undesirable macro-economic and political effects, especially that of lower savings rates. In theory, social insurance could be funded, though the United States lacks both institutions and public managers to accomplish this on a large scale (though the largest state public pension plans, which are partly funded, may provide emergent models). The key point, however, is that only a fraction of the typical worker's estate should be invested in the type of claims that involve the risk associated with ownership.

1.2 Concentration versus diversification

The second major issue of risk concerns the diversification of the funds that secure workers' pension claims. Funds that invest in a representative variety of businesses are less risky than those that invest in a single business or a single industry. Other things being equal, the economic returns to diversified funds will have less variance than returns to undiversified ones. Concentrated funds will expose more beneficiaries to the risk of large losses, and will produce more inequality among beneficiaries.

On the other hand, diversification dilutes and/or centralizes control in a way that strains the democratic goal. From the democratic perspective, control should be decentralized and focused on the institutions that most affect beneficiaries. This suggests funds concentrated in the industries or enterprises in which the beneficiaries work. But such funds would be riskier, and would produce more inequality (i.e., there would be more variance in their returns).

The point that the efficient allocation of risk creates a trade-off between economic democracy and worker economic welfare has to be qualified, however. There are important non-political reasons why it may be desirable for workers to bear the risks associated with investments concentrated in their own firms. First, only investments focused in his own enterprise are likely to enhance a worker's productivity incentive. Second, even while they increase the employee's investment risk, concentrated investments may mitigate another economic risk—job loss. A fixed-wage employment contract will usually lead to larger and quicker lay-offs in the event of product market downturn than a contract that makes wages contingent on profits. Thus, it may make sense for workers to trade off fixed wages for profit shares; and enterprise-focused funds, such as Employee Stock Ownership Plans (ESOPs) may be good vehicles for doing so.

Nevertheless, the diversification point has substantial force. It will rarely be optimal for workers to concentrate anything close to most of their retirement savings in their own enterprises. Two key variables affecting the viability of such concentrated funds are the (firm-specific) capital intensity of the firm and the age composition of the work-force. The more capital-intensive the firm, the less likely worker savings can play a major role in financing it. Still, even in the more extreme cases of capital intensity, there will often be some role for worker investment. One might have thought that the steel industry would be one of the worst cases for worker finance. It has always been capital-intensive, and recent technological changes have increased capital needs at the same time that they have reduced work-force size. Despite this, Weirton Steel was the outstanding example of the sizeable, 100 per cent employee-owned industrial firm, and about 50,000 members of the United Steelworkers participate in employee stock ownership plans (see Newman and Yoffee 1991). This may be a transitional phenomenon, however, related to the traumatic circumstances of the steel industry in recent years. Having re-acheived profitability, Weirton Steel sold a substantial minority interest to the public. In the long term, the less capital-intensive firms seem the more plausible candidates for the more ambitious worker ownership plans.

Finally, older work-forces are less plausible candidates for worker ownership than younger or middle-aged ones. Workers will typically want to cash in their shares on (or before) retirement, and under the Employee Retirement Income Security Act (ERISA), the firm must enable them to do so. Unless there are enough junior workers to buy out the retirees, the shares will have to be sold to outsiders.

1.3 Background investment risk

The extent to which investments expose workers to risk depends in part on the nature of a country's business environment. Notably, business risk is partly a function of government policy and industrial structure. Government policies that promote or tolerate price and currency exchange rate volatility and unrestricted foreign competition tend to create more business risk than policies aimed at monetary stability and cushioning competitive pressures. Industrial structures in which volatile, impersonal capital markets play the major monitoring role and in which seriously troubled firms are left to a costly, traumatic bankruptcy process involve more risk than structures in which firms linked in consortia monitor each other and provide some mutual insurance against the more traumatic effects of restructuring. In the United States, government policies and industrial structure are of the sort that tolerates a relatively high degree of business risk (see Aoki 1984).

To the extent that the United States adopts economic policies that moderate business risk in general, policies encouraging retirement finance through private investment might become more plausible. By moderating the variance in investment returns, such policies could serve egalitarian goals. They could entail great inefficiency, however, as the examples of the late Eastern European Communist economies attest; but the example of Japan suggests that they don't inevitably do so.

2. CONFLICTS OF INTEREST

The relative roles of fiduciary and voting principles in American pension law is currently a matter of dispute. Many believe that pension plans should resolve policy disputes by beneficiary vote; but the Department of Labor insists that plan trustees sometimes have a duty to ignore beneficiary instructions when they believe them to be patently contrary to the beneficiaries' interests. (US Department of Labor 1988). The fiduciary perspective presupposes a high degree of unity of interest among beneficaries; it does not contemplate separate analysis and action with respect to each beneficiary's interest, but rather a single collective judgment and response.

Although voting permits differential responses among members, it still requires a substantial degree of shared interests. It is theoretically possible to allocate specific assets to individual accounts in a defined contribution fund; but in most such funds the beneficiaries share undivided interests in a single portfolio. Moreover, to the extent that the fund is an ESOP invested in the beneficiaries' work-place, they are all dependent on the success of the enterprise. In such circumstances, a decision by some members (on purchasing or selling or voting stock) will affect others, whether or not they oppose it. Moreover, the idea of using pension funds as vehicles for worker control suggests a further need for shared interests.

Workers cannot constitute a viable political community without a significant degree of shared interests. Conflicting interests can lead to costly squabbling and paralysis. And conflicting interests may lead some worker beneficiaries to defect and ally themselves with other constituencies, such as outside investors or creditors, in ways that subvert worker control.

The more important potential conflicts seem to be the following (see generally Fischel and Langbein 1988).

2.1 Retirees versus current employees

The assets of a defined benefit plan typically secure the claims of both retired workers receiving benefits and current employees who will not receive benefits until retirement. The potential for conflict arises from the fact that the typical retiree will be interested exclusively in the value of the shares in the fund, while the typical employee will be interested in a variety of enterprise policies that affect employment. If wage cuts and lay-offs will improve profitability, the retiree has an interest in implementing them; but for many, and often most, employees the interest in profitability will be outweighed by wage and employment interests.

In the 1950s John L. Lewis had the United Mineworkers pension fund purchase shares in Northeastern utilities, intending to influence them to purchase only union-mined coal, which would arguably have benefited current employees. This was held to be a breach of common law fiduciary duty, presumably to retirees (*Blankenship* v. *Boyle*, 1971). In the mid-1970s New York City's public employee pension plan purchased large quantitites of low-rated bonds from the financially distressed City. Retirees charged a breach of fiduciary duty, arguing that the purchases were motivated by a desire to obviate lay-offs of employees. The court conceded that such a motive would have been improper, but rejected the challenge on finding that the purchase was justified by the fear that, if the bonds were not sold, the City would become bankrupt and default on payments to the fund, thus harming retirees and employees (future retirees) alike (*Withers* v. *Teachers' Retirement System*, 1978). Some, including officials of the Department of Labor, believe that ERISA's fiduciary norms codify the premises of these cases: The trustee's duties are to the shared interest of all beneficiaries in the soundness of the funds; benefits to working beneficiaries through their employment are not legitimate concerns, at least if they require a trade-off in terms of returns to the fund (Lanoff 1980).

This conclusion seems at the least debatable. Proponents argue that the statute is concerned exclusively with retirement security. However, the statute does not interfere with the ability of employers and workers to trade off retirement benefits for current economic welfare in setting the terms of compensation. True, once the terms are set, the statute largely precludes workers from using pension accumulations for current consumption. But it seems unlikely that this effect reflects a legislative judgment that retirement interests should always trump all current economic interests. Legislative concern about worker short-sightedness or self-indulgence might be weaker where the worker wants to trade off retirement security for job security than where he wants to trade it off for current consumption. Moreover, one might generalize the point in the Withers case and deny any clean trade-off between job and retirement security, since a job is a pre-requisite for continued retirement saving as well as for current consumption. At least where a large gain in job-related benefits for workers could be achieved at only a small cost to the fund as a whole, it seems unreasonable to require that it be foregone.

Nevertheless, it is undeniable that a fund designed to exploit the full possibilities of control in the interest of active workers is likely to run into severe conflicts with retirees. There is, however, a solution to this problem. The interests of workers can be severed from the fund on retirement. This is now typically done with defined contribution plans. A retiring beneficiary can take her stock and become an outside shareholder, or she can be given an annuity equal to the value of her interest, or a lump sum in cash. She thus ceases to have an interest in the fund, and the possibility of conflicts with employee interests is avoided. Though defined benefit plan beneficiaries typically remain dependent on the plan after retirement, these plans in principle could be restructured to allow separation on retirement as well.

2.2 Senior versus junior workers

A related conflict is between senior and junior workers. In a mature plan, senior workers will tend to have different stakes and different perspectives than junior ones. Senior workers will be more intensely concerned about preserving and enhancing retirement benefits; they will be less concerned about the long-term prospects of the firm and less fearful of lay-offs (both because seniority protects them and because the value of the job is lower to them because their expected tenure is shorter). Their views on issues such as lay-offs that increase profitability will be much closer to those of retirees than to those of junior workers. Moreover, depending on how the plan is structured, senior workers may have accumulated far larger shareholdings than junior workers. Their interests as shareholders will thus be larger relative to their interests as employees than will be the case for the junior employees. This also creates problems regarding the distribution of control. If control is distributed in proportion to financial stake, senior workers will get much more than juniors. But if control is distributed on a one person–one vote basis, there may be a risk that junior workers will disrespect their seniors' investments (e.g., by voting for excessive wages or highly risky investments).

One response to these problems would be to try to smooth out differences in shareholdings in the employing enterprise by permitting or requiring senior employees to diversify their holdings. The ERISA requirements for ESOPs give workers the option of diversifying after the later of age 55 or ten years of employment. For the first four years after this milestone, they can instruct the trustee to invest 25 per cent of their accounts outside their own companies, and beginning with the fifth year, they can raise this portion to 50 per cent. Such diversification serves two purposes. It responds to the relatively greater risk aversion of the senior employee, and it limits the inequality in shareholdings in the employer company.

2.3 Managers versus rank-and-file employees

A third axis of potential conflict of interest is between highly paid employees and senior managers on the one hand and rank-and-file workers on the other. High earners are more inclined to save and invest than low earners. This general tendency is intensified by the practice of the American tax system of subsidizing pension savings through tax deductions, which are more valuable the higher the bracket of the taxpayer.

In many nominally employee-owned firms, managers have vastly disproportionate financial interests and sometimes complete control. In such situations, rank-and-file workers often experience no difference in their role in the firm following the transition to employee ownership, and labour disputes indistinguishable from those in investor-owned firms have arisen frequently. South Bend Lathe and Vermont Asbestos are well known examples (Bradley and Gelb 1983: 102–5).

Moreover, the most publicized recent adoptions of ESOPs in large public corporations were initiated by management as take-over defences. The managers count on employees to support them in take-over contests for fear that new owners will initiate wage or job cuts. Such considerations are often legitimate employee concerns, but it is disturbing that these ESOPs, while inhibiting assumption of control by outsiders, typically do not effectively reduce management's own ability to initiate wage and job cuts. And while they limit the ability of outside investors to discipline managerial incompetence or self-indulgence, they typically do not give the employee-shareholders the ability to do so.

I will address issues concerning the translation of ownership into control below, but a separate set of problems arises from the bunching of ownership among the work-place élite. The tax code attempts to respond to this problem by constraints on inequality in pension contributions known as the 'non-discrimination' and 'top heavy' rules. For example, under the latter a plan must provide no more than 60 per cent of its benefits to defined 'key' élite workers, or must meet specified alternative standards designed to constrain inequality. There are also fixed dollar maxima on the amounts that can be contributed on behalf of any one employee.

However, these rules constrain inequality only very loosely. They permit the wholesale exclusion of part-time workers, newly hired workers, workers under 18, and workers covered by collective bargaining agreements. (That is, these workers are not even counted in determining whether the plan satisifies the minimum coverage requirements.) Thus, many ESOPs exclude more than half the relevant work-force entirely. For those included, contributions proportional to salary are considered non-discriminatory. In fact, many plans take advantage of the option afforded by the rules on 'integration' of pension and Social Security benefits to make contributions on the basis of larger fractions of salary for higher-paid employees than for lower-paid ones (Blasi 1988: 39–52).

Tightening these rules might mitigate the inequality problem. For example, the inclusion of all non-probationary workers might be required, and contributions at uniform fractions of salary could be required, perhaps with a fixed dollar maximum based on the relevant fraction of the median worker's salary. Changing the tax benefit from a deduction to a credit would equalize its value to high and low earners. Such a system would still be subject to the criticism of the present rules that they make the benefits available to any individual worker turn on the wages of the people she works with; for example, low-wage workers in work-forces with lots of high-wage workers end up with higher contributions than they might like and would get in a work-force where they represented a larger fraction. Obviously, the more equal the underlying wage distribution, the less severe this problem. In addition, the more effectively control arrangements allow workers with diverse preferences to articulate them and have them considered in determining the design of compensation arrangements, the less severe tax distortions will be.

2.4 Division of labour

Finally, we should note conflicts arising from the division of labour. The more rigid and extensive the division of labour, the more the potential for conflicts arising from different work roles. With a rigid, high division of labour, there would be a relatively strong potential for conflict over such issues as relative compensation, technological changes that enhance productivity but eliminate certain work roles, and product choice (where only certain workers are able to work on certain products). Henry Hansmann (1990) argues that the extent of the division of labour is the most important determinant of the viability of worker ownership.

This point may be overstated. (This conflict problem is no less severe within unions, which seem to have overcome it often enough.) Nevertheless, it seems plausible that worker ownership has an affinity with the kind of work organization that trains workers in general and diverse skills and either narrows the range of jobs or rotates workers through the fullest feasible range of them. We do not know, however, what the technologically plausible range of this type of work organization is. Both theory and experience recently have challenged many deep-rooted assumptions on this point and suggest that the range is broader than previously thought (Piore and Sabel 1984).

Note that, while there are plausible mitigating responses to the retiree/employee, senior worker/junior worker and manager/rank-and-file worker conflicts, the responses tend to reduce the pool of savings available for concentrated industry or enterprise-focused funds.

3. CONTROL ALLOCATION

The economic democracy norm contemplates worker control, but pension fund beneficiaries are not necessarily full-fledged owners, and even full-fledged ownership rights to capital often carry very limited control rights.

3.1 Scope of control rights

I noted above that, on the US Labor Department's interpretation of ERISA, the statute imposes a residual paternalistic duty on the trustee that sometimes requires disregarding beneficiary instructions deemed contrary to beneficiary interests. Scandalously, the ESOP tax legislation permits private companies to give trustees (typically managers or management appointees) full voting power except with respect to major 'organic' changes (mergers, sales of all assets, stock exchanges, recapitalizations, liquidations). Thus, private company ESOP beneficiaries can be denied the basic shareholder right of electing the enterprise's directors. (As of 1990, all shareholder voting rights must be passed through for leveraged ESOPs—plans in which the stock is purchased with borrowed money—in private companies, as well as for public company ESOPs. However, in leveraged ESOPs, voting is passed through only to the extent that the loan has been repaid (see generally Rappaport and Cannon 1989, 48–64.)

Moreover, however adequate to protect the interests of outside investors, shareholder rights, even when fully passed on to beneficiaries, look pretty skimpy in the light of any ambitious vision of worker control. Shareholders get to elect the directors and to approve 'organic' changes, but, typically, that's it. Thus, if workers are to be given control over shop-floor issues or over any strategic decisions (investment, marketing, work-force level) other than the basic 'organic' ones, forms of participation other than those routinely accorded shareholders need to be built in.

3.2 Initiation and termination

A failing in some respects more serious than the limited participation afforded by ESOPs themselves is the complete absence of participation afforded in connection with the adoption and termination of the plans. Unless the work-force is unionized, employers can institute ESOPs unilaterally on their own terms, and unless the ESOPs give employees more control than they typically do, employers can terminate ESOPs unilaterally.

One approach to remedying these defects would be to condition the tax subsidy on the creation of more meaningful participatory structures than those associated with conventional stock ownership. Since labour law provides a model of such a structure, one might make the subsidy available only to unionized work-places. Such a measure would have some affinity with 'corporatist' labour law models in which unionization is encouraged and strengthened by conditioning benefits on unionization and giving unions a role in administering them.

This currently would not be a politically viable approach in the United States, despite the recent change in the political control of the Presidency. For reasons that rightly make some suspicious of worker ownership, its new popularity is accompanied by intensified hostility to unions. A more modest measure would provide that the inauguration or termination of a tax-subsidized ESOP could be undertaken only with the consent of a majority of the employees in a vote that met stipulated procedural requirements. The very process of coming together to consider the initiation of the plan might generate employee relations and organization that would persist after its inauguration. Alternatively, the tax code could define and mandate some such organization in terms less ambitious than those defining unions—perhaps an elected workers' council charged with co-ordinating the exercise of share voting rights.

3.3 Distribution of voting rights

Another set of issues concerns the allocation of voting power in relation to shareholdings. Presumptively each share carries an equal vote, so the more unequally shares are distributed, the more unequal the voting power. Some believe, on economic democracy grounds, that even where unequal financial returns are justified, unequal voting is not. Union voting structures are traditionally on a one person–one vote basis (and federal labour law requires this). In unionized settings, an ESOP with unequal voting power would violate the principle of equal voting rights (though not any legal requirements, since the labour law equality requirement applies only to internal union procedures). It would also canalize the shareholder control process outside the union structure.

A further concern is whether workers are to vote individually or collectively. If there are outside shareholders, or management has large holdings, or workers are divided into recognizable constituencies, individual voting may lead workers to divide their votes in ways that are generally counter-productive to their group interests.

Voting trusts have been used to respond to concerns about both equal voting and vote splitting in a few union-led ESOPs (e.g., Rath Meatpacking). For example, the trustee can be instructed to vote all the shares in the manner directed by the union pursuant to a majority vote on a one-per-person basis (Olson 1982: 757–8). Whether ERISA will be construed to permit such arrangements remains to be seen.

3.4 Control in diversified plans

So far, I have presupposed plans focused on the workers' own enterprise, such as ESOPs. What are the control possibilities with respect to diversified plans? Some large diversified plans have beneficiary-elected trustees, including two enormous ones: the California Public Employees' Retirement System and TIAA-CREF, the private teachers' fund. Experience so far, however, does not suggest that beneficiary participation is very meaningful. Voter participation rates are low. Elections are not contested, and candidates do not run on substantive programmes. The investment decisions of these plans seem generally comparable to those without participant voting.

One problem is that a consequence of diversification is that holdings are spread among a wide variety of enterprises, and represent only a small fraction of the equity of each. (ERISA mandates diversification for defined benefit plans.) The issues that will arise in such plans will seem more remote to the worker, and the plan's influence over the issues will seem less than in the case of the typical issue in an ESOP.

There would seem to be two ways of responding to the problem. One would be to narrow the diversification of the fund and focus investments on projects or enterprises that are related to the workers' own. One could focus on the workers' own region, for example, or on local housing investments (to take an example that has attracted several public employee funds), or even housing loans for members of the union (to take the example of a programme of a Florida local of the Operating Engineers Union that survived an ERISA challenge). Or a union plan might form a venture capital fund targeting experimental enterprises of special promise to workers with a view toward selling off its interests once they became successful. (If the fund itself were diversified among a variety of start-ups and were only a small part of a much larger, more extensively diversified pension fund, the high risk associated with new enterprises might be permissible.)

All these efforts would probably entail additional risk. On the other hand, plan fiduciaries might have informational advantages over conventional lenders in areas of local interest that would mitigate or offset the effects of lost diversification. The investments might also generate compensating externalities in the form of, say, worker training or demonstration effects that would inspire private investors to emulate successful projects and thereby create attractive jobs. To the extent that these practices involve additional risk, it is not clear to what extent ERISA permits them. It seems plausible that beneficiaries would take a greater interest in the policies of a more locally focused fund, since the potential of the fund to influence local conditions would give them an interest in the investments apart from financial return.

The other approach would be to link the funds to national institutions engaged in broad economic and political functions, such as labour confederations and electoral parties. The more inclusive labour federations of Sweden and West Germany and the social democratic parties allied with them are examples of such institutions, and the wage-earner fund proposals in those countries seem to have contemplated that the participatory mechanisms of the union would spill over into the decisions of the wage-earner funds. The funds were to be managed by trustees appointed by the state and the unions jointly (Swensen 1989: 156–72, 185–215). Nevertheless, the mechanisms of worker influence on the fund and the types of decision-making contemplated are quite vague in the plans. Moreover, impressive as the Swedish and West German labour federations are, it is quite questionable how effectively participatory they are. Thus, we really don't have a model of any detail of how participation would work in a diversified fund.

The history of the Swedish supplementary ATP pension funding mechanism is sobering on this issue. This mechanism provided for a programme of wage-related pensions supplementing the basic flat grant pension provided under the original Swedish social security programme. Unlike the flat grant programme, the supplemental one was to be funded as follows: employment taxes were to be paid into four funds managed by tripartite boards. Inaugurated in 1959, these funds have been major players in the Swedish capital markets. (In the 1960s, they accounted for between a quarter and a third of new long-term investment and credit; this fraction has declined as the need to pay retiring beneficiaries has caused the funds to cash out increasing portions of its holdings.) Notably, neither the unions nor the labour representatives on the fund boards have shown any interest in incorporating non-financial criteria into fund investment decisions. Indeed, during the 1960s when the Swedish government sought to marshall credit on terms favourable to housing as part of a massive social programme of housing expansion, the funds resisted on the ground that they could get a higher financial return elsewhere (Pontusson 1984). The labour movement seems to have believed that 'social investment' could best be accomplished through the state, rather than the labour movement, and independently of the system of retirement finance.

In the USA the 'corporate campaigns' of some unions, including notably the textile and mineworkers' unions, provide one illustration of how pension fund socialism might be linked to traditional union functions. In a corporate campaign, the union seeks to use its status as a creditor or shareholder or customer of an enterprise it is organizing or bargaining with or of some institution that is a creditor, shareholder, or customer of the target enterprise to increase pressure on the target enterprise. The prospect that worker pension holdings might be employed in this manner on a broad scale has excited some visionaries. American labor law currently prohibits exclusive union control of private sector pension funds, so such strategies would require acquiescence by management trustees in jointly administered funds. Moreover, given diversified funds, such strategies would be practical only if co-ordinated by labour federations with strong central control and broad coverage. Such institutions do not exist in the United States.

More modestly, one might consider establishing for employee groups co-ordinating institutions along the lines proposed by Ronald Gilson and Reinier Kraakman (1991) for mainstream institutional investors. A group of diversified funds might sponsor an independent non-profit corporation to research companies, recommend votes on contested shareholder voting issues, and field candidates for boards. The sponsoring funds would presumptively follow the lead of the non-profit corporation, and when their holdings were aggregated, might achieve considerable influence.

Again, the lack of interest among the stronger European labour movements in using retirement finance to gain leverage in organizing and bargaining is sobering. The most obvious reason for their lack of interest is lack of need. These organizations are strong enough to obtain their organizing and bargaining goals without putting their members' retirement capital at risk. This makes the 'corporate campaign' type of pension fund socialism seem a provisional and tactical response to circumstances of weak union organization and an unsupportive state rather than a model for the ultimate socialization of the investment process.

Of course, there are serious paternalistic and social welfare issues about the extent to which workers should be encouraged to politicize investment decisions in retirement programmes. Moreover, if there is to be politics, it should take the form of general principles legislated by beneficiaries but implemented by disinterested fiduciaries. The funds should not become either slush funds for union leaders or charitable trusts in which claims of sentiment routinely trump interests of fiscal soundness and reasonable return on investment.

4. REDISTRIBUTION

Apparently the United States owes its ESOP tax subsidy to the influence of the theories of the maverick financier Louis Kelso on Senator Russell Long, chairman of the Senate Finance Committee at the time the subsidy was enacted. Like his father Huey, Russell Long was an exponent of a peculiar brand of populism that attacks large corporations in the name of the toiling masses but sometimes performs its most effective services for wealthy 'independent' businessmen. (Among Russell Long's other enduring legacies is a set of oil production tax subsidies for the likes of J. R. Ewing.) Kelso suggested that ESOPs could accomplish massive redistribution, turning the country from a nation of plutocratic absentee investors to one of yeoman worker-owners.

This seems implausible. Of course, workers pay for ESOP shares and other pension benefits through lower wages, higher taxes (the incidence of the tax subsidy is largely regressive), and lower employment. This trade does not itself make workers richer, except to the extent that it creates incentives for greater productivity, and even then, labour does not necessarily capture a greater portion of the increased wealth than lenders, outside shareholders, or managers. Pension policy might encourage a more egalitarian distribution in the long run if it induced the non-rich to save more than the rich. But as I noted above, the thrust of American pension policy is generally in the opposite direction.

The trend toward pension fund socialism has not been accompanied by any marked equalization in the distribution of capital ownership. Thus an ambitiously redistributive pension programme will have to look outside American pension programmes for models, and here the European social-democratic wage-earner fund plans, notably the one formulated by Rudolf Meidner, chief economist of the Swedish blue-collar labour federation (the LO), are of interest. Meidner (1978) proposed funding his wage-earner funds by a profits tax, rather than by wage-based contributions. He argued that this approach had the virtues of avoiding the employment disincentive effects of high wage-based benefits, of avoiding driving marginal firms out of business, and of enabling labour to capture a substantial portion of the rents of more successful firms without abandoning 'solidaristic' wage policies designed to limit inequality in compensation across firms.

The Meidner plan was designed to gradually socialize Swedish capital. It proposed a 20 per cent profits tax on firms above a minimum size. The tax was to be paid in the form of shares held by diversified union-managed funds. The scheme envisaged that eventually the funds would acquire control of all the large private enterprises in the economy. The pace of socialization would depend on the profitability of the firms. In a firm earning 5 per cent a year on its capital, the funds would acquire a controlling interest in seventy-five years; in a firm earning a 15 per cent annual return, the funds would acquire control within thirty-five years. As the funds grew, they would become the major source of investment finance in the economy. Eventually, the funds would own all large enterprises entirely. (Of course, this timetable would depend on the funds' pay-out policies. If the funds were used for retirement finance and there were no population growth, one would expect the funds' growth to level out at the point when the last of the first generation of workers had retired and begun to draw their pensions. At that point, contributions would be roughly balanced by payments.)

In effect the plan socializes investment through a combination of (1) radically differential taxes on capitalist and worker investment (the tax rate on profits is uniform, but the share contribution to the funds rebates the tax on worker investment); and (2) forced savings by workers. In the programmatic repertory of socialism, the Meidner plan is distinctive in its combination of radicalism of goal and gradualism of implementation.

The Meidner plan was not proposed as a form of pension fund socialism. The returns to the funds were to be used for collective consumption, worker training, unemployment benefits, and union organizing expenses. The plan's proponents may have been influenced by the rejection of social investment in the supplementary pension (ATP) plan. Nevertheless, the proposed targeting of investment proceeds in the plan seems odd. If the plan ever reached the ultimate conclusion Meidner envisioned, it would hold a far larger fraction of social wealth than it would be rational to devote to these purposes.

The broader versions of the plan met with political defeat; only a shrunken version was enacted, with little prospect of having significant systemic impact on investment practices. Nevertheless, the plan seems far more plausible than the Kelso/Long approach as an engine of redistributive transformation.

5. BACKGROUND ECONOMIC FACTORS

The viability of pension fund socialist projects depends in substantial part on a variety of background economic factors. Unfortunately, some of these factors as they occur in the American economy make the United States a relatively unfavourable setting for the more ambitious of such projects—at least if considered in isolation from broader economic transformations.

Investment risk. We noted above that investment tends to be more risky in the United States than elsewhere. For that reason, pension fund socialism would require American workers to take on more risk with their retirement savings here than elsewhere, and will thus seem less attractive.

Social insurance. The less generous social insurance programmes are, the less investment risk workers can afford to take with their private savings (though more generous social insurance programmes are likely to require taxation that will leave workers with less income for private savings). American social insurance programme are relatively ungenerous.

Wage inequality. The more wage inequality, the harder it is to design programmmes that preserve the socialist equality goal. Either fund contributions must be subject to progressively more restrictive limits for higher-income people (thus limiting the available investment pool) or control and/or income rights must be detached from wages/contributions (thus limiting the incentive effects of wage differentials). The United States has a relatively high degree of income inequality.

Political infrastructure. Where there is a strong union/party structure with wide coverage that pension fund control procedures can be integrated with, the problem of effectively democratizing control measures is less severe. But the United States has a relatively weak union/party structure, from which most of the population is alienated and excluded.

In many industries, enterprise- or industry-focused funds could probably play a significant role in extending worker control. However, except in the most stable and skilled labour-intensive industries, such funds are unlikely to achieve anything approaching majority control. At the level of larger, diversified funds, the prospects of pension fund socialism depend on developing means to co-ordinate control rights on behalf of large, dispersed constituencies. It seems unlikely at either level that pension reform would obviate the need for non-ownership means of worker control and protection.

PART III

Changing Concepts of Accountability

10

Auditing and the Politics of Regulatory Control in the UK Financial Services Sector

MICHAEL POWER

1. INTRODUCTION

The early 1990s will be remembered as a critical period for the auditing 'industry'. A series of 'failures' in the UK financial services sector received prominent coverage in the national press, notably the closure of the Bank of Credit and Commerce International (BCCI) in mid-1991 and the collapse of the Maxwell business empire. These events added further fuel to continuing preoccupations with the 'expectations gap', understood as the difference between public and auditor perceptions of the role of audit (e.g., KPMG Peat Marwick McLintock 1990; Humphrey 1991). In the UK research has been commissioned to address this problem, and, as an initial measure, a new form of words for the audit report has been proposed (APB 1991), with the intention of bridging this gap by educating the users of audit services. Perceptions of the role of the UK statutory auditor have also been affected by some interpretations of the judgment in *Caparo* v. *Dickman*, 1990 which suggest that auditors have little legal responsibility to those third parties who may place trust in their work. In addition, Labour MP Austin Mitchell has been at the forefront of public criticism of the accounting profession and its auditing activities. With each new company failure (British and Commonwealth Holdings, Polly Peck, BCCI, Maxwell Communications), initial reactions have included the question: 'What were the auditors doing?' (Mitchell 1990).[1] These events and related criticisms of the audit function seem to have stimulated an institutional response; after a noticeably brief consultation period, the Auditing Practices Committee (APC) was replaced by

The author is grateful for the helpful comments of Michael Clarke, Anthony Hopwood, Gary Marx, and Peter Miller.

[1] In the USA there have been similar pressures on auditors, magnified by the collapse of the savings and loan industry and more recent problems in the banking sector. The US accountancy firm of Laventhol and Horwath filed for chapter 11 protection from its creditors in November 1990, largely because of litigation burdens. In the same week Standard Chartered Bank initiated a massive lawsuit against Price Waterhouse based on claims of a negligent audit (*Financial Times*, 29 Nov. 1990). Hence the intensity of enquiry around the external audit function is by no means only a UK phenomenon.

the Auditing Practices Board (APB) on 1 April 1991, and it is evident that questions of auditor ethics and independence are high on the APB agenda.

These developments constitute the background for the principal focus of this chapter upon auditors' extended reporting requirements in the UK financial services sector. While auditing has been widely regarded as a neutral and somewhat dull practice, even by its own practitioners, this 'technicist' view disguises the fact that state and quasi-state regulatory agencies are heavily dependent on the monitoring services that auditing claims to provide. Because of this, the auditors' responsibilities in the financial services sector have a political dimension which requires apparently 'technical' practices to be located within a broader institutional context, a context in which the expectations of state-sponsored regulatory bodies are as important as those of the investing public, the traditional beneficiaries of auditing services. The auditors' reporting responsibilities in the financial sector attempt to establish a new communicative relationship between auditors and regulators. These responsibilities cannot be understood simply as one more technical reporting requirement; they also express a new political and 'regulatory rationality' (Miller and Rose 1990) linking the auditor to the state. Hence the auditor must be regarded as occupying an institutional position within a regulatory network, or 'space' (Hancher and Moran 1989*b*), the stability of which is threatened by corporate collapse and fraud. Within this regulatory environment technical questions of fraud detection have implications for political and regulatory responsibility, and hence for institutional patterns of blame during times of perceived crisis.

The relevant legislation which ties the auditor to state control functions necessarily assumes that enforcement can be delegated to competent agents. Hence, we can say that audit is a 'condition of possibility' for a regulatory programme which distinguishes between policy and enforcement (Baldwin 1990: 332–4). But in any system of regulation the very possibility and nature of enforcement can be misconceived by delegating authorities (G. Marx 1981), giving rise to intra-regulatory 'expectations gaps'. While auditing is a necessary 'institutional myth', a 'rationalized ritual of inspection' (Meyer and Rowan 1992*a*: 41), for the purposes of governmental control, it is also a problematic technology which fails to the extent that it can be 'decoupled' from the organizational contexts in which it operates. Accordingly, a gap may emerge between the symbolic capital provided by audit and perceptions of its actual performance.

Because of this institutional framework, within which auditing provides formal links between regulator and regulated, professional documents (APC 1989*b*, 1989*a*, 1990*b*) addressing (imprecisely specified) reporting responsibilities in the financial sector must be regarded not merely as technical guidance for internal use by the audit profession (indeed, this may be their least significant role), but also as political texts for external consumption by regulators and others. As economic agents (Antle 1982), auditors can be expected to respond to legal initiatives and claims upon their role with strategies both to preserve their credibility as appropriate experts within official 'ceremonies' of inspection and, simultaneously, to translate their own goals into institutional rules. However, responses by auditors to new environmental demands are as much a structural product of the existing norms and abstract routines of audit culture as they are simply a self-interested need to limit an extension of responsibility. In this institutional context we may talk of 'creative auditing' as a response strategy by auditors which decouples professional judgment from formal codes in order to retain 'zones of discretion' and to preserve control of the interpretation of their role. Regulation is therefore not simply an external stimulus to which auditors respond passively, but a stake in a competitive market for the allocation of responsibility. Nowhere is this creative process more evident than in the professional guidance governing the circumstances under which auditors may communicate directly with financial services regulators.

2. THE AUDITOR IN REGULATORY SPACE

Recent developments in the UK financial markets suggest that 'gentlemanly' patterns of motivation and self-control (or at least the myth of such forms of behaviour) have given way to a new generation of amoral, calculating players and their expert advisers (Moran 1989). Accordingly, previous self-regulatory arrangements in financial markets have, under various pressures for reform, given way to an intensification and codification of financial regulation on an unprecedented scale (Moran 1991). The issue is not simply one of an increase in the quantity of regulations, but is also one of the recruitment of new bodies of expertise into the service of the state, resulting in a distinctive form of dependence by the state upon 'professional' regulators such as lawyers and accountants. This professionalization of the regulatory process represents a 'fragmented centralization' of institutional control, in which authority for principles is centralized, but enforcement is widely delegated to agents such as auditors (Meyer and Rowan 1992b).

This systematization of oral traditions of control and the increased levels of bureaucratic surveillance in financial institutions (e.g., via newly created 'compliance' officers) may or may not raise standards of prevention and detection. However, they mark an important change in regulatory style. The shift from invisible, private modes of regulation to more public, explicit and codified patterns of control is especially significant in the UK banking sector; Moran (1986), for example, argues that this shift signified a change in the relationship between the Bank of England and the Treasury during the 1980s. Hence the communicational demands upon auditors under recent legislation must be understood as part of this broader reconfiguration of regulatory responsibilities. The auditor is just one of several actors in regulatory space, understood as a public institutional arena not merely for technical rule enforcement but also for competition and conflict between different regulatory agencies. Financial services regulation in the UK provides a particularly strong illustration of a regulatory pluralism visible, for example, in the multiplicity of bodies concerned with the collapse of Dunsdale Securities (see *Financial Times*, 30 June 1990, 2 July 1990). Such a pluralism inevitably gives rise to competing 'expert' interpretations of the 'disturbing' event in question, which, in turn, imply different allocations of responsibility.[2]

The pressures for reform which usually result from publicly visible fraud of this kind create a demand for regulation of the potentially unregulatable. These pressures do not simply raise the question of which organization(s) will bear responsibility for detection and/or prevention of fraud, but also of how the issue itself is to be articulated and allocated: 'If groups can be organized into, or out of, regulatory space, the same can be said of issues. There are no obvious natural limits of the boundaries to regulation. Notions of what is regulatable are plainly shaped by the experience of history, the filter of culture and the availability of existing resources' (Hancher and Moran 1989*b*: 278).

Financial collapse involving fraud invariably shifts concerns with narrowly bureaucratic and technical regulatory practices into the wider political arena. In this way problems move beyond the orbit of professional control. Questions of how to regulate to prevent fraud (even the presumption at important points in the regulatory system that this is possible) become enmeshed in processes of competition and conflict, or, more accurately, 'perceived' conflict, over the attribution of responsibilities and authority in the regulatory arena. Hence, as one agent in regulatory space, the auditor is not necessarily autonomous in determining his or her own mission, and must compete to establish public understandings of the events in which he or she is involved: 'The definition of the character of a regulatory issue is itself an important part of the process by which it is

---

[2] In system-theoretic terms, this suggests a network of regulatory sub-systems responding to the 'environmental' disturbance provided by the 'event', whose communication with each other is filtered via distinctive and possibly conflicting rubrics. One might therefore suggest that the reception and allocation of these problems is necessarily autopoietic—i.e., relative to discrete bodies of expert knowledge—and hence that expectation gaps are a systemic product of regulatory autopoiesis.

allocated to the domain of certain organizations and removed from the domain of others (ibid. 293.')

Thus, auditors respond competitively and creatively concerning the appropriate definition of the regulatory issue. However, the regulatory dependencies are multi-directional, and auditors will respond to newly defined duties only within an available audit 'technology'. The auditor translates the demands made upon him or her, especially where these are general statutory requirements, into a range of practices that are familiar and possible. This can be described as a creative process of 'rendering auditable', a strategy with the aim of securing both a 'zone of discretion' and the confidence of a regulatory clientele.

3. FRAUD, BLAME, AND THE RECONSTRUCTION OF THE REGULATORY MISSION

In general, large-scale fraud supplies an exogenous jolt to regulatory regimes which invariably react by generating new institutional structures. For example, the consolidation of investigatory resources into the Serious Fraud Office (SFO) added a new interdisciplinary player to the stage on which the auditor operates.[3] Fraud, as an object of regulatory attention, also gives rise to pressures for improved technical guidance to auditors in this area. As a participant in a regulatory politics, a body such as the APC, and its successor the APB, must respond to wider regulatory concerns in a functional area where the very possibility of audit is itself problematic.

There is nothing particularly new about fraud in the financial services sector. The collapse of Barlow Clowes and the Levitt Group in the UK are recent examples of failures which have prompted questions about the role of the auditors. Indeed, the institutionalization of auditing in the UK, in the form of the APC, has, like institutionalization in many other areas, been prompted by public criticism (see Taylor and Turley 1986: 139). For example, the collapse of the Johnson Matthey Bank, and associated criticisms of the supervisory function, initiated the legal arrangements under the Banking Act 1987 for communication and consultation between auditors and banking regulators (M. Clarke 1986: 48; Moran 1986: 163–77), arrangements which are replicated in the Financial Services Act, 1986 (FSA), and the Building Societies Act, 1986.

Because these regulatory developments embody expectations regarding the role of audit as a 'political technology', they have given rise to concerns about the burden of technical expertise demanded by the FSA (see

---

[3] The performance of the SFO has not itself been without critics (T. Smith 1990*a*), and may suffer from its own 'expectations gap'.

Accountancy Age, 6 Sept. 1990). For example, the collapse of Dunsdale Securities precipitated enquiry about the level of technical expertise necessary to audit an SRO (self-regulating organization) member, and particularly a member of the Financial Intermediaries, Managers and Brokers Regulatory Association (FIMBRA). It was argued that the complexity of the rule books for self-regulatory organizations under the FSA generates technical problems in monitoring compliance, and the Securities and Investments Board (SIB) responded by attempting to simplify them. When an event such as the fraud-related collapse of Dunsdale Securities occurs, then auditors and regulators attempt to represent their respective burdens of responsibility.[4] The under-secretary for the APC was reported as stating in response to criticism by SIB that 'there is an awful lot of buck passing. It needn't necessarily land with us' (see *Accountancy Age*, 23 Aug. 1990). Within regulatory space there are therefore different institutional perceptions of responsibility for control. In the Dunsdale case, the auditors were a small firm of chartered accountants, and this triggered speculation that the SIB would propose a more rigorous regime for the regulation of the auditors of authorized investment businesses, such as a panel of auditors along the lines of the Lloyd's market.[5] Similar proposals were made following the SFO investigation into Garston Amherst Associates (GAA) in February 1990. Indeed, SIB displeasure at the Dunsdale collapse seems to have prompted action by the APC in providing a 'practice note' on the audit of client money (APC 1991). This was followed by the expulsion of one and the censure of two of the auditors of Dunsdale by the Institute of Chartered Accountants in England and Wales (ICAEW).[6]

SIB regulations specify that SROs are responsible for ensuring that they have effective arrangements for monitoring and enforcing the principles established by SIB. In the wake of the GAA affair, the chief executive of the Investment Management Regulatory Organization (IMRO) was reported as claiming that 'accounting vigilance was a prerequisite for competent regulation, as SROs simply do not have the resources to be able to cover all the dealings that members are involved in' (see *New Accountant*, 12 Feb. 1990). FIMBRA is also heavily reliant upon its auditors (T. Smith 1990*b*); its retired chief executive, O'Brien, was reported as stat-

---

[4] An example of competitive allocation of responsibilities is also apparent in the case of the Levitt Group. In late 1990 the senior partner of accountants Stoy Hayward, whose role as auditor has been examined by the ICAEW (*Financial Times*, 24 Dec. 1990) after referral by FIMBRA, stated in response to criticism that the problems at Levitt had come to the attention of regulators as a result of their audit process (*Financial Times*, 14 Dec. 1990).

[5] The president of the ICAEW was reported as denying the comparison between the Lloyd's market, which is a small and restricted grouping, and the thousands of small investment businesses which are licensed by FIMBRA.

[6] See 'Institute expels Dunsdale auditor', *Financial Times*, 14 June 1991.

ing that FIMBRA cannot be expected to 'spot' sophisticated fraud, thereby implying that auditors can. It must be recognized that such criticisms of the audit function by SROs are partly for the consumption of the audit profession, but also for SIB and the Bank of England. SROs are subject to expectations as much as auditors, and FIMBRA itself has been subject to extensive criticism (see *Independent*, Sunday, 16 July 1992; *Financial Times*, 24 Dec. 1990). A similar story is emerging both in the aftermath of the collapse of BCCI, although auditor/regulator tensions in this instance are less publicly visible,[7] and regarding the role of IMRO in regulating the investment companies within the collapsed Maxwell empire.[8] While IMRO has criticized its own role in the supervision of Bishopgate Investment Management (BIM), the fund management organization which was apparently the instrument of pension fund theft, it was also critical of BIM auditors Coopers and Lybrand.[9]

These intra-regulatory deliberations concern the very possibility of effective monitoring, and illustrate an important feature of the regulatory network created recently in the UK: namely, the manner in which an intractable problem such as the detection of management fraud becomes translated into a more manageable problem—by appealing to more rigorous licensing or training arrangements. Crisis is thereby deflected from systemic scrutiny of intrinsic procedures towards processes of authorization. Or, to put it another way, problems about the 'how' of audit become translated into the 'who' of audit; technical crisis is addressed as a problem of social credibility. Thus, perceptions of the efficacy of the financial monitoring function must be constantly reconstructed in response to criticism; systemic doubt about the possibility of audit is not a regulatory option. Codification of audit practice is an important element of this reconstructive process. But such a development of official audit knowledge cannot simply be understood as an internal and merely evolutionary technical process. It is part of a broader regulatory politics in which the authority of the auditor as an expert is subject to continuous pressures for reform.

[7] This chapter was written before the publication of the full text of the Bingham Report on BCCI. Early indications suggest that the role of Price Waterhouse as auditors will not be singled out for blame. See 'Abu Dhabi Blamed over BCCI', *Financial Times*, 16 July 1992; 'Bank of England had Early BCCI Warning', *Financial Times*, 18 July 1992.

[8] See Dale 1991 for criticisms of the structure of supervision of BCCI. Also, 'BCCI Collapse: Auditing at the Crossroads' *Financial Times*, 15 August, 1991; 'Watchdogs who did not Bark', *Financial Times*, 15 Nov. 1991; 'A Failure of Supervision', *Financial Times*, 18 Nov. 1991; 'Watchdog Seeks IMRO Explanation', *Financial Times*, 5 Mar. 1992.

[9] See 'Lessons from the Maxwell Collapse', *Financial Times*, 19 Dec. 1991; 'IMRO Admits Failings over Maxwell', *Financial Times*, 10 June 1992; 'MP Seeks Publication of IMRO Report on Maxwell', *Financial Times*, 17 June 1992; 'Maxwell Auditors Criticize IMRO', *Financial Times*, 22 June 1992; 'Pressure over Maxwell Report Grows', *Financial Times*, 23 June 1992.

4. FRAUD AND THE CODIFICATION OF AUDIT PRACTICE

Before we consider auditors' communicative responsibilities in the financial services sector, it is necessary to locate them within broader conceptions of their responsibility for the detection of fraud. Despite repeated claims by auditors that the primary responsibility for the detection and prevention of fraud lies with management, the precise division of duties has never been clear, and has often been subject to public scrutiny. In 1985 an ICAEW working party was established to address the issue of the auditors' responsibilities following various pressures for reform, not least from the Minister for Corporate and Consumer Affairs of the time, Alex Fletcher, who was reacting in part to criticisms of the audit function in the JMB affair (see *Accountancy Age*, 25 Oct. 1984; *Accountancy*, Dec. 1984: 6). The ICAEW working party reported to the Department of Trade and Industry in late 1985, and resisted any extension of the auditor's role on the grounds of cost and feasibility. It proposed a counter-recommendation that large companies should be required by statute to maintain adequate systems of internal control (see *Accountancy*, Sept. 1985: 13). This proposal was rejected at the time, although something like it is now a central part of financial services legislation (and may yet become a general requirement following the recommendations of the Committee on the Financial Aspects of Corporate Governance, the 'Cadbury Committee' (Cadbury 1992)). In 1988 the APC issued an exposure draft concerning the auditor's responsibility for detecting and reporting fraud and other illegal acts. This was subsequently modified and published as a full guide-line in February 1990, five years after the working party had reported to the DTI.

Without doubt the 'visibility' of the APC deliberations were as important as the result. To be seen to be seriously 'addressing' an issue is strategically important in regulatory politics. Evidence of seriousness is also provided by the production of a 'text' which can be regarded as a solution to a problem. The 'guidance' document (APC 1990a) places emphasis upon management responsibility for establishing adequate systems of internal control, while accepting that the auditor must plan his audit to give him a 'reasonable expectation' of detecting material misstatements. The audit industry has continued to maintain this plea for recognition of an effective sharing of liability between management and auditor; the ICAEW submission to the Cadbury Committee is a recent example, and it is reasonable to assume that perceptions of the role of audit are linked to those of the role and responsibility of company directors.[10]

[10] See 'Auditors Look to Pass the Buck as Pressure for Reform Increases, *Independent*, 12 Nov. 1991.'

An issue of more general significance concerns the point at which textual professional guidance defines areas of discretionary judgment. No rule or system of rules can entirely control the conditions of its own applicability without extreme specificity. Hence forms of regulation imply a configuration of explicit guidance which can be codified, but which nevertheless implicitly depends upon undefined discretion. This 'zone of discretion' allows a document to appear to provide detailed operational guidance, while maintaining the specificity of professional judgment. Thereby it serves to link institutional myths of increasing rational control to the realities of technical practice. Creative auditing is the production of such 'technical texts' which both ceremonialize and formalize procedures, but which also simultaneously maintain zones of discretion at critical junctures. These zones of discretion provide a basis for closure of interpretation by appeal to what is professionally 'reasonable'.[11] In this sense auditing can be understood as an example of professional knowledge which must be 'abstract enough to survive objective task change but not so abstract as to render jurisdiction indefensible' (Abbott 1988: 239).

In other words, 'practical' guidance must never be so practical that it is readily replicable or subject to scrutiny by outsiders. By the same token, a strategy of what we might call 'non-codification codification' is visible in the context of auditors' professional guidance. Regarding the question of auditors' general responsibilities to detect fraud, the official text negotiates a balance between transparency, which risks capture of the evaluation process by outsiders, and a silence which threatens the legitimacy of audit practice itself. This negotiation is crucially dependent upon the ambiguity of concepts of 'materiality' and 'reasonable care and skill' which occupy a central position in the articulation of the auditors' responsibilities. The APC guide-line is particularly significant in so far as it does not explicitly deny that the auditor has a duty to detect fraud; rather, it qualifies this within a planning horizon capable of providing 'reasonable expectation' of detecting material misstatement. Thereby it provides a form of words which may be acceptable to regulators and a zone of 'professional discretion' around certain key concepts which, though by no means determining their legal meaning, would constrain outsider attempts to define these terms.

In a rule-intensive environment, it can be argued that there is opportunity for monitoring regulatory compliance as a proxy for management integrity. The juridified and rule-intensive nature of the financial services environment provides the auditor with considerable opportunity to monitor compliance in this way at a detailed level. The auditor's task is

---

[11] This phenomenon is well known to critics of positivistic jurisprudence. For example, Fish (1989) exposes Hart's attempt to 'close' the contestability of 'core rules', and shows that the strategy culminates in an appeal to 'what lawyers actually do'.

therefore located between the possible (monitoring compliance) and the difficult or even impossible (detecting elaborate management frauds). While there is little possibility of specifying a priori a clear cut-off point as regards what could be 'reasonably expected' of him or her, official audit guidance represents a creative strategy of transforming the unfamiliar and intractable into the familiar and possible.[12] This strategy is a key element in the 'low' politics of financial regulation, in which there is competition for control over interpretations of regulatory procedure, and in which technical guidance is both a basis for, and a product of, negotiation with regulators (Baldwin 1990: 322). While these processes of negotiation are largely hidden from public view, their effects are particularly visible in the documents concerning the auditor's responsibilities in the financial services sector.

5. CREATIVE AUDITING: REPORTING TO REGULATORS OF THE FINANCIAL SERVICES SECTOR

Auditing has been implicated in a number of pressures for change in the financial services sector. Accounting firms have become increasingly involved over the years in the growth of internal treasury functions and the development of financial control systems. The FSA, driven by state commitment to investor protection, is a significant factor shaping the future of auditing and accounting (for a detailed analysis of these provisions, see Tattersall 1991; also Cooper *et al.* 1991). In terms of the number of organizations affected, the FSA has a more extensive significance for auditors than the Banking Act, 1987, although the drafting of the latter has provided the model for auditors' responsibilities in other areas.

In the financial services sector, the auditor is now required to report on the adequacy of accounting systems and internal controls more visibly than for a normal statutory audit. At one level, this simply represents a formalization of hitherto implicit audit practice. For many years it has been standard practice for the auditor to ascertain the reliability of internal controls as a basis for determining the necessary amount of detailed work, but there was no explicit reporting requirement.[13] At another level, this change is more than simply a requirement for auditors to be explicit

---

[12] An obvious example of this concerns the auditor's reliance on other experts such as valuers and actuaries. The relevant audit guidance emphasizes the need to audit the social credibility of the expert, rather than the substance of the expert practice. In this way an unfamiliar domain can be 'made auditable'.

[13] The Companies Act, 1985, does require the auditor to report by exception on whether 'proper' books and records have been maintained. 'Proper' is not defined in detail. Though it might include appropriate internal controls, the adequacy of bookkeeping is generally distinguished from that of control systems.

about what they have always done anyway. Such initiatives go beyond a mere codification of practice, and serve to construct a new consciousness and expectation of the role of these procedures in relation to the broader mission of audit. Hopwood and Page (1988: 90–1) suggest in the context of the FSA that 'the auditor seems bound eventually to acquire a responsibility for detecting—and reporting to supervisory authorities—fraud and failures of internal control and other management controls. The cloaks of materiality and disclosure may cease to be available once there is a breach of the "Maginot line"' defence that the auditor's duty is solely to form an opinion on the accounts.'

The auditor's responsibility to report directly to regulators on an *ad hoc* basis illustrates this point, and demonstrates that official guidance in this area functions as a creative response to avoid such a breach of the 'Maginot line' and the implied assumption of new duties. As suggested above, auditors are not passive in relation to generally drafted conceptions of their duties, and react to control their interpretation.

The auditor has similar *ad hoc* reporting duties under section 47 of the Banking Act, 1987, section 82(8) of the Building Societies Act, 1986, and section 109(1) of the FSA. In March 1989 the APC issued revised and extensively detailed auditing guide-lines in response to this new legislation (APC 1989*a*, 1989*b*). Hence, the FSA requirements can be regarded as one part of a broader legislative shift in the financial sector: an intensification of regulation in the name of investor protection and a response to the need for improved communicational structures linking regulators to their agents of enforcement. The APC published a draft auditing guide-line (APC 1988) which was subsequently considered to be too broad, and it was decided to address the FSA in more discrete sections, commencing with the *ad hoc* reporting requirements (APC 1990*b*).

The relevant legislation is very general, and does not specify detailed reporting responsibilities. Rather, it consists of an 'enabling' component and a 'delegating' component. The enabling component is illustrated by section 109(1) of the FSA which states that 'No duty to which an auditor of an authorized person may be subject shall be regarded as contravened by reason of his communicating in good faith to the Secretary of State, whether or not in response to a request from him, any information or opinion on a matter of which the auditor has become aware in his capacity as auditor of that person and which is relevant to any functions of the Secretary of State under this act.' Thus, if the auditor reports under this section to a regulator, and does so in good faith, no other duty is breached. Section 109(2), the delegating component, states that the government expects the various accountancy bodies to make rules or provide guidance on the circumstances under which appropriate matters are to be communicated. The object of the legislation is to create a professional, rather than a statutory, duty to communicate to regulators; if 'adequate' professional rules are not forthcoming, then the Secretary of State is empowered to make such rules, and this would create statutory reporting duties.[14] In addition, section 109(5) states that the matters about which the auditor may communicate are those which are relevant to the regulator's function in determining whether a person is 'fit and proper' to carry on investment business, and whether the conduct of business rules have been complied with.[15]

The audit guide-line developed by the APC is therefore a delegated interpretation of section 109 subject to approval by the Secretary of State. But this document is much more than simply a neutral clarification of reporting circumstances. As Tattersall (1991) observes, the postulated relationship between the auditor and the regulator challenges the traditional basis of the relationship between auditor and client, hitherto premissed upon a near inviolable confidentiality.[16] Hence section 109 of the FSA, although it may appear to lack substance, represents a 'Trojan Horse' and may challenge the traditional organizational culture of audit practice, in which responsibilities to shareholders, rather than depositors, were formerly paramount.[17] Accordingly, an official document such as this auditing guide-line does not merely aim to provide operational guidance to auditors, but also to set boundaries to official interpretations of the audit function by other regulatory bodies. These boundaries are the product of negotiation, and, while it is difficult to obtain evidence of the precise processes, the development of this professional guidance has undoubtedly resulted from detailed consultation with the relevant regulators, particularly the Bank of England.[18]

As far as the substance of the guide-line itself is concerned, paragraph 17 states that the potential scope of reportable matters is very wide, but

[14] It may be that the auditor's statutory right to report to regulators will eventually become a duty. This was the recommendation of the House of Commons Treasury and Civil Service Committee on 'Banking Supervision and BCCI: International and National Regulation', which is likely to be endorsed by the Bingham Report on BCCI. See also 'Tighter Auditing Rules may Follow BCCI Investigation', *Accountancy Age*, 19 Mar. 1992. However, even if a right is transformed into a duty, the weight of interpretation will continue to fall on professional guidance rather than statute, although at the time of writing the APB has deferred any amendments to its guidance on *ad hoc* reporting to regulators. See 'Auditor's Duties to Regulators Defined', *Financial Times*, 29 June 1992; APB 1992.

[15] There has been some debate about what can be understood as 'capacity as auditor'. There are substantive uncertainties concerning whether 'capacity as auditor' includes non-audit activities such as consulting (see Morgan 1989; *New Accountant*, 13 Aug. 1990).

[16] This confidentiality was also a characteristic of the relationship between the Bank of England and the banks under its supervision, a relationship which was forced to change following the collapse of JMB (see Moran 1986).

[17] This culture is by no means universal; e.g. there is evidence to suggest the closer proximity of the French audit function to organs of the state.

[18] This is a matter for empirical investigation, which is in principle possible by examining the APC working party papers which developed the three guide-lines.

that (paragraph 22) this does not require the auditor 'to change the scope of his audit or other work for the authorized business'. Such a qualification also exists in the relevant auditing guide-lines for banks and building societies (APC 1989*a*, 1989*b*). It states that the auditor is not 'placed under an obligation to conduct his work in such a way that there is a reasonable certainty that he will discover a notifiable matter'. This assertion that the scope of investigatory audit work need not change is consistent with auditors' more general assertions of their responsibilities in relation to fraud discussed in the previous section. In effect, the APC is maintaining that the audit function is only passive in relation to 'notifiable matters' such as suspected fraud, provided it satisfies general criteria for reasonable audit procedure.

Auditors have therefore managed to avoid codifying the idea that they are actively engaged in the pursuit of notifiable matters; this guidance document addresses only the auditor's reporting responsibilities which may be triggered by matters of which he 'becomes aware in his capacity as auditor'. How he 'becomes aware' is placed beyond the scope of normal audit procedure. It is in this sense that we may talk of this document providing 'non-guidance guidance'. It concentrates on the processes of communication with regulators, and says very little about the operational processes which may give rise to a responsibility to communicate, other than to state that the scope of audit work need not change. The auditing guide-line therefore gives an impression of providing operational rules, but is in substance a defensive text which maintains professional control over the interpretation of the operational scope of the auditors' work under this part of the FSA. This is not in any way a conscious and deceitful process. It arises quite naturally from the systemic imperatives and tradition of audit practice, which must filter the demands made upon it according to an available body of knowledge. The auditor's *ad hoc* reporting responsibilities are therefore entirely conditional on a process of discovery about which no guidance is given, except, negatively, that the scope of the audit need not be extended. This again is an example of an elaborate 'creative' translation; guidance on an unfamiliar and difficult function (assessing whether investment businesses are run by 'fit and proper persons') is translated into something more possible (the reporting procedures if a reportable matter is found) by conditionalizing the auditor's role.

However, despite this passification of the auditor's detective function, the guide-line contains elements which at least point to broader and more active responsibilities. The auditor is required to take the initiative where he considers that investors have incurred, or are at 'significant risk' of incurring, a 'material loss' at the hands of the regulated persons. The audit guide-line states that in situations where there is evidence of dishonesty, serious incompetence, or serious failure to observe rules, then such an *ad hoc* report would be 'likely' to be required. The guide-line further emphasizes that the auditor's decision to report or not under section 109 may have to stand up to examination at a future date on the basis of the following possible considerations: what he knew at the time, what he should have known in the course of his audit, what he should have concluded, and what he should have done.

Most significant in this statement is the claim that the auditor may be judged in terms of what he should have known. In this sense there are limits to auditors' control over their duties. It is a matter of speculation as to which regulatory agency was responsible for inserting these paragraphs, but their effect is clear; the APB cannot necessarily control *ex post* interpretations of what an auditor should have done—this is ultimately a matter for a court of law or a quasi-judicial forum.

The question this raises for auditors is whether they can, in defence, reasonably appeal to their own official guidance in section 109 within such a regulatory politics. Does it provide them with an appropriate rhetoric of responsibility with which to respond to intra-regulatory blame? The answer to this question is empirically open. The guidance document can be judged only in terms of its actual political effects in generating and restoring regulatory consensus about the function of the auditor. In this sense it is important to bear in mind that official texts are as much an outcome of political negotiation as an input to it. This particular document can therefore be regarded as representing a temporary point of consensus between auditors and regulators, notably the SIB and the Bank of England.

From this point of view, the fact that the guidance is operationally ambiguous is a source of political strength, even if it is strictly a technical deficiency. The APC auditing guide-line may give little substantive guidance to auditors in the financial services sector, but may, by virtue of a technical rhetoric and an underlying negotiated consensus with regulators, play an important political role in securing a form of words acceptable to all parties. The under-secretary of the APC has claimed that the guide-line 'shouldn't introduce any new procedures that competent auditors of any FSA company are not doing already' (*Accountancy Age*, 23 Aug. 1990). But the politics of codifying 'generally accepted practice' is more complex than this statement suggests. Codification is intelligible less in terms of providing 'guidance', and more in terms of negotiating the zone of responsibility within which particular auditor performances will be evaluated by regulators.

A final question which must be posed is whether this APC document, and others like it,[19] serve to allay or intensify expectations around the

[19] The APC has also issued draft guidance to auditors in relation to illegal acts in general (APC 1990c). Cooke (1990) states that this document is important because 'it attempts to

audit process. To the extent that they are deeply dependent on notions of what is a 'reasonable expectation' of fraud detection, they cannot control the interpretations that may be constructed around them; the 'zone of discretion' is fragile and open to appropriation by critical outsiders. Hence the attempt to control the field of regulatory expectations is a hermeneutic impossibility. These extensive guidance texts are drafted in a technical idiom, but whether this can withstand the often hostile external scrutiny that follows financial scandal is always an open question. However, it must be remembered that wholesale condemnation of the monitoring function would undermine the very possibility of financial regulation itself. Hence there are pressures within the regulatory domain to 'particularize' audit failure, rather than to interpret it in any general and systemic sense. In this way, fundamental arguments about the role of audit can be displaced, and substantive questions of extended general responsibilities can be translated into procedural questions of quality control for existing responsibilities. Given the dependence of the regulatory edifice upon auditors, a need to trust those who do not trust, it is reasonable to suggest that official audit guidance not only provides a potential point of negotiation between auditors and regulators, but, in doing this, a basis for securing the legitimacy of the wider regulatory process itself.[20]

6. CONCLUSIONS

Auditing in the financial services sector must be set in the context of a regulatory politics in which regulatory agencies may react competitively in times of perceived crisis. This political process is visible in media coverage, but can also be traced in official texts which both respond to, and enable, that process. A 'sociology of audit knowledge' liberates our understanding of the nature and role of the professional guidance issued by the APC and the APB from a technicist framework. In any event, auditors in the field are more likely to consult heavily practice-orientated

map out auditor's responsibilities in an area where they did not realise that they had responsibilities'. There is an implied acceptance that the auditor now has responsibility to detect illegal acts, subject to 'reasonable expectation', which may be remote from the financial statements or his or her normal range of competence. While the language of this new statement mirrors that of earlier guide-lines, its more general status serves to force a wider field of regulatory vision upon the auditor. Hence it recommends that the auditor must plan his audit to understand the broad legal environment of the auditee. Even breaches of regulations which are apparently remote from effects on the financial statements may indirectly provide evidence of lack of management integrity in less remote areas. The question of reporting to third parties such as the SFO is considered in this document, and the recommendations mirror the FSA context. Whether this draft will eventually become official is uncertain.

[20] Indeed, the arguments concerning 'zones of discretion' could be applied equally to regulators themselves.

texts such as Morgan and Patient (1989) than APC documents. The latter function more as a basis for negotiating and controlling the interpretation of audit practice. In this sense the elaboration of new audit technologies is less significant than the political processes through which they are promoted and mobilized.

Auditing in the financial services sector is a 'political' technology. In other words, it is a technology which is demanded by a regulatory regime which presupposes its own effectiveness and thereby the possibility of effective auditing. As a political technology, auditing is constantly responding to demands upon it, demands which seek to shape and extend its role in the name of various ideologies of control. There is no reason why the politically shaped mission of financial regulation and the enforcement horizon of audit technology should necessarily be congruent with each other. Indeed, rather than a tight 'structural coupling', there is more likely to be a 'looseness of fit' between different levels of the regulatory process—'expectation gaps' by another name. Official texts, such as the guidance on auditors' responsibilities for communicating with financial services regulators, may function as much to preserve an interpretive looseness as a political resource, as to close any perceived 'gaps'. Audit guidance therefore provides a point of focus in which the aspirations of the Secretary of State, regulators, auditors, and an investing public can be represented. The linking of these multiple constituencies is a political act which would be frustrated by complete transparency. In this sense, auditors have a political interest in maintaining enough of an 'expectation gap' to ensure a zone for their own discretion.

11

Professional Competition and the Social Construction of Transnational Regulatory Expertise

YVES DEZALAY

One of the paradoxes of the scholarly discourse on law and regulation is that it is essentially addressed to professionals, although it behaves as if these professionals did not exist; or, more precisely, as if they did not intervene actively in the legal game on the basis of strategic choices determined by their specific interests as much as by the interests of those whom they represent. The 'depersonalization' of this discourse may help law's social credibility. In any case, it means that those who produce it need not ask themselves how far this knowledge is determined by its markets and its conditions of production. But this blindness also prevents them from analysing what is happening in the domain of regulation[1] of economic activity to facilitate internationalization, since these transformations are taking place precisely at the intersection between the field of professional practices and that of the scholarly debates and conflicts which are the process of redefinition of the law and of the position of lawyers (or other experts) in the relations of power.

The regulation of enterprises has become one of the main arenas of confrontation in a politico-economic war in which professional mercenaries, or 'hired guns', fight it out through expertise and specialist knowledge. One of the main factors disrupting the national systems of regulation results from the competitive pressure exerted by the forum shopping for regulatory regimes to which multinationals of expert services incite their clients. At the same time, to occupy positions of strength in this field, the élite of learned professional—and in particular those tied to the great conglomerates increasingly dominating the market for consultancy—are making enormous investments in the fields of knowledge and

Translated from the French by Sol Picciotto.

[1] The term 'regulation' is here understood in the broad sense given to it by economists such as Boyer (1989) the totality of institutional arrangements which contribute to the stabilization of the social relations of production to facilitate the accumulation and reproduction of capital.

of the production of norms,[2] especially at the level of transnational institutions; since it is a matter adapting national regulatory arrangements to this new commercial order. In short, in conformity with the immemorial tradition of the learned clerks who claimed to be both counsellors to the king and defenders of his subjects, these new experts practise the art of double-dealing (Bourdieu 1989) by guiding their clients through the regulatory maze which they know all the better for having been, to a great extent, its designers (R. Gordon 1984).

This trend, which creates competition between modes of regulation, while weakening the boundaries between the roles of regulators and practitioners advising on regulation, and equally between producers and consumers of normative knowledge, also requires us to develop new theoretical approaches.

Since the internationalization of the market for business law is disrupting both the professional fields and the national regulatory systems, it provides a favourable moment to break with this ideological fiction of a law without actors, by analysing regulation as simultaneously a strategic space and the market for a particular type of skill; or, more precisely, as a whole series of spaces and markets which are interrelated and complementary, or even competing: the new arenas in which the newly emerging regulatory arrangements are arising are many and varied, and the competition between these different forums is a strong incentive for innovation.[3]

Researchers can no longer adequately approach this universe in the throes of transformation by analysing the complex poacher–gamekeeper relations which are formed in a 'regulatory space'. They are compelled to take into account the structural diversity of these spaces, because this diversity is now a central element of the confrontations from which new forms or models are emerging. Not only is the object of their research widened, but they confront the additional difficulty of being at the same time observers and actors in this recomposition of regulatory spaces and institutions. Furthermore, these actors are all the more directly implicated by this restructuring, since their autonomy is brought into question by the rival bids of the great firms of practitioners learned in the law.

To clarify the nature of these complex transformations, I propose to consider first the relationship between the state and experts, and then to

---

[2] Thus Alexander and Murray (1992) show that, following the mergers and acquisitions (M & A) boom of the 1980s, the elite of these practitioners became partially reconverted to public service activities: participation in government committees, etc.—perhaps to fill in the time while waiting for a new M & A wave? or, more likely, as a sort of reinvestment permitting them to accumulate a more diversified social and legal authority, which may produce new dividends.

[3] The wave of deregulation of financial markets after the 'Big Bang' and the outbidding of each other in the 'modernization' of national rules relating to international commercial arbitration both provide perfect examples of this institutional competition linked with the delocalization of the market for services.

go on to show how the transposition of the economic war to the terrain of law leads to a fundamental restructuring of the professional fields which disrupts the relationship between practice and knowledge.

I. COUNSELLORS TO THE KING . . . WITH NO KING

While double-dealing by experts is not new, one may still ask whether their relationships with state power are not undergoing a reversal: first, because of the unprecedented nature of the concentration of resources and of knowledge represented by these conglomerates of expertise; but second, because these royal counsellors no longer serve any king but themselves. There is no transnational state, and transnational regulation is still largely a fiction. Finally, the nation-states have lost much of their legitimacy as institutions for regulating the market, to the extent that they can no longer claim to incarnate the general interest, since they have become, in their turn, instruments in a process of international competition which has now engulfed every aspect of economic activity. In short, practitioners of regulation play the role not so much of intermediaries between the state and the merchants, but of mediators between economic interest groups which are all the more aggressive because of their highly diverse geographical and social origins. In this global economic warfare, these new clerks have a special interest in establishing a semblance of order and rationality, since what is at stake is their credibility and autonomy in relation to the entrepreneurs and financiers who are always tempted to reduce them to the status of mercenaries carrying out orders.[4]

In other words, the position of these experts at the margins of economic power leads them to try to structure this international market by making themselves the spokespersons of the general interest. Paradoxically, the weakness of the nation-states thus leads them to 'manufacture the state'[5] or to substitute themselves for the state in reliance on their know-how. This is no doubt one of the sources of the formalism, or juridicism, which is increasingly prevalent in international economic relations, both private and semi-public. But it is also the source of the aggravated competition between experts or between types of expert which even intrudes into the field of knowledge. By moving on to the field of law and regulation, the economic war has also introduced competition and commercial preoccupations into a professional arena which had always striven to bottle them up. There again, this is not a new contradiction.

---

[4] As J.P. Morgan was reputed to have said about his lawyers: 'I pay you not to know whether I can do it, but how to get it done.'

[5] In the sense of institutions which can gain acceptance for a certain conception of the general interest, or at least establish a certain regularity in commercial relations.

The struggle between legal entrepreneurs and guardians of the temple has always been at the heart of the professional game (Dezalay 1991, 1992). The only difference, albeit a major one, is that these sellers of services are now absorbing the guardians of the temple,[6] and hence find themselves responsible for the management of the symbolic capital represented by the legal order. The new commercial order which is emerging thus owes as much to the economism of the financial groups which dominate the economic sphere as it does to the oligopolistic competition between the mega-firms which dominate the market for expertise and inscribe this ideology within the legal order.

2. THE STATE AS INSTRUMENT AND OBJECT OF THE ECONOMIC WAR

This development cannot be adequately analysed in doctrinal terms, nor even by means of a more sociological approach such as the theories of 'capture' or their modern variants (McBarnet 1984). There are two reasons for this. The first, which has already been mentioned and to which we will return, is that they blind themselves as to their own role in these professional confrontations which are power struggles. The second is that they still think in terms of the three-way relationship firm–state–market,[7] as if the growth of multinational firms had not made this relationship highly problematic (Picciotto 1989).

The multinationals were, indeed, for a long period still an exceptional phenomenon. The major oil companies were the prototype for these great private organizations, which were at the same time quasi-states and marginal to states. These firms, in the same way as the colonial companies, carefully preserved their autonomy, yet unhesitatingly resorted, where necessary, to the force or the authority of national state institutions. But such interference in the regulatory process was strictly limited to the sphere in which their direct interests were at stake. Hence, the emergence of this private transnational order did not fundamentally challenge the state system. Further, this type of relationship in which the enterprises could influence the regulatory processes—or at least negotiate with them by playing on the competition between states—was confined to certain sectors of activity such as oil, due to the historical circumstances which had facilitated cartel agreements. Today this bargaining between produc-

---

[6] Judging especially by the number of academics who have been tempted by the siren song of the market and have joined the multinational firms in the service of the enterprises.

[7] This opposition between the state and the market is fairly artificial, to the extent that there can be no market without a certain regularity, hence without rules and the means of enforcing them. In short, there can be no market without a minimum of state-like institutions. On the other hand, these means of structuring relations of production are many, and in rivalry.

ers and regulators has become generalized. The new technologies of production and circulation of information have led to a multiplication of the number of firms which can practise this delocational blackmail and cash in through regulatory concessions. The negotiation takes place less in terms of the control of strategic resources than in terms of the use and acquisition—or preservation—of a dominant position in the field of economic power. But the result is the same: regulation is no longer a given which firms can at most get around in more or less legal (if not legitimate) ways, but a basis for negotiation.[8]

The delocalization of economic activity thus poses a challenge to the very structure of, and the positional warfare within, regulatory space, all the more brutally because it is a cumulative process. The weakening of the state is as much the cause as the result of the internationalization of transactions. At the same time as they are obliged to renegotiate the rules with their enterprises, the states are under great pressure[9] to reduce, or even eliminate, the barriers protecting their national markets from external competition. By increasing the pressures on enterprises, this opening of borders also gives them additional arguments to make to state authorities, which are increasingly reduced to being mere auxiliaries of the 'national champions' in the economic war.

The exacerbation of international competition has meant that states have 'changed their role from shield against the world market to that of transmission station for the latter's demands' (Bihr 1992). The management of the internal equilibrium between supply and demand, characteristic of Keynesian regulation, is replaced by the 'now sacrosanct external constraint of competitiveness . . . Its task will now be to facilitate the emergence of "national"' oligopolies big enough to operate on the world market, while organising the withdrawal and disappearance of those parts of national capital incapable of carrying out such a transformation' (Bihr 1992).

To the extent that the main sectors of economic activity are now affected, directly or indirectly, by international competition, it is the totality of regulation that is in disarray. By the same token, it is the concept of the state itself that becomes one of the stakes in capitalist competition. According to Albert (1992), the 'Rhenish model' of regulation, negotiated under the supervision of the state, is opposed to the Anglo-Saxon model of self-regulation of a financial market, which the state merely seeks to ensure operates freely. What is paradoxical about this transformation is

---

[8] At least for those who are in a strong position to practise this delocational blackmail. For others, the strategy of regulatory avoidance (within the law) or evasion (outside the law) is still necessary.

[9] The pressures are all the greater for those states which are at the periphery of the capitalist system. However, these challenges to the state apply also to the core, if only because of the increased number of core states and the competition between them.

that the various protagonists are each in turn obliged to adopt the weapons or strategies of their opponents. Thus, the advocates of Colbertism have discovered the limits of state interventionism. And for their part, even if they call it by a different name, the heirs of neo-liberalism seem today to have rediscovered the merits of industrial policy. These U-turns suggest that regulatory models make sense only in a strategic context. Loyalty to great principles counts for less than the play for alliances or tactical moves. This does not reduce the fierceness of the clashes between adherents of one or the other model. The building of Europe, like other international arenas, is evidence of this. Like mercenaries, the experts fight with all the more conviction because what is at stake are their interests and those of their principals. Around these regulatory mechanisms are structured networks of power in which they are inscribed. The negotiators and lobbyists devote so much effort to trying to impose their view of the state on Brussels precisely because what is at stake is the prosperity of the entrepreneurs or the financiers who dominate the national politico-economic spaces. It is also because these mercenaries are fighting on their own ground.[10] The outcome of the struggle very directly affects their positions, both in the market for expertise and in the professional hierarchy.

The choice of battlefield also determines the choice of weapons, or at least legitimate weapons. If the economic war is fought on the field of rules, it must bow to the rules of law,[11] even if it means transforming them.

3. THE RESTRUCTURING OF THE FIELD OF EXPERTISE

Owing to this confrontation, the structure of the field of expertise is undergoing a radical transformation. What is at stake is not only the emergence of new rules or a reorientation of the politics of regulation, but a reorganization of the mode of production of rules. By establishing new relationships between knowledge and economic power and by instituting new modes of international accumulation and circulation of expertise, the constitution of great multinational conglomerates of expertise is

---

[10] It is also interesting to note that this opposition between the Rhenish model and the Anglo-Saxon model corresponds to the Weberian dichotomy between the 'Professorenrecht' systems and those dominated by practitioners.

[11] Thus the relative strengths on the legal terrain do not exactly reflect those prevailing at the economic or political levels. The colonial model is no longer acceptable, and, with a few exceptions, the export of legal models is no longer by means of gunboat diplomacy, but in terms of competence or rationality.

poised to bring about a major upheaval in what some have called 'regulatory space,' (Hancher and Moran 1989*b*).[12]

First, this notion of regulatory space should be clarified. At the international level, the plural should be used; for there is considerable diversity between these spaces. What does GATT have in common with regional treaties such as the EEC or NAFTA?—not to mention the proliferating sectoral agreements for the definition of technical standards or for the co-ordination of the work of national bodies regulating markets. The difference is not limited to the scope of the agreement or the number of participants; it is also due to the fact that in each of these forums, the issues, the resources, and hence the protagonists and the strategies, are different. What is more, these multiple initiatives sometimes converge, and sometimes compete. Indeed, how could it be otherwise, since the economic war and professional competition are henceforth waged on the turf of the state and of business regulation? It is no longer possible to talk as if there were a homogeneous space and a unique model of regulation. The fragmentation of the regulatory mechanisms, and hence the creation of competition between them, is the corollary of the internationalization and delocalization of economic activity.[13]

These circumstances call for a pragmatic approach: it is necessary to start from a careful and detailed observation of these multiple, particular, and more or less autonomous situations (S. Moore 1978), which henceforth constitute the mosaic of international regulation. Each time, an understanding of the continual process of evolution and redefinition of these sub-spaces cannot rely on the intervention of external determinations, whether technological or political, but must show how these new factors are reinterpreted and reintegrated through the professional competition—and the learned conflicts—which unfold on the particular terrain and redefine it. This approach represents a break with previous perspectives; instead of privileging the ambivalent poacher–gamekeeper relationship, the emphasis is put on the structural struggles over the redefinition of the fields of confrontation and the means of intervention deployed by the different protagonists.[14]

[12] The innovation may certainly seem a minor one, since it is primarily organizational, and essentially affects the division of symbolic labour; but we should not forget that the invention of the phalanx revolutionized the art of war more than the invention of gunpowder—not to speak of the implications of the factory for the artisanal mode of production!

[13] Thus, the increasing internationalization of the market for corporate control, and hence of mergers and acquisitions, has led the lawyers to involve simultaneously several national bodies regulating competition and take-overs: no fewer than five in the Minorco–Goldfields battle. This had the paradoxical result that the fate of the two largest British M & A operations was decided to a great extent by American judges.

[14] A similar development to that noted by the economists of the regulation school, for whom 'negotiation through the rules has become negotiation about the rules' (Salais and Thevenot 1986: 4).

Paradoxically, this fragmentation of, and increasing competition between, regulatory mechanisms leads to the strengthening of the weight of professional decision making. In fact, the professional field creates the unity of these sub-spaces. That is where the various particular matters are linked together and articulated, if only because the same individuals or the same organizations frequently meet on a certain number of these fields, even if in different strategic positions or configurations. The legal multinationals have even made forum shopping one of their main marketing points. But this movement between spaces is not unique to practitioners. Academics have long played the role of emissaries between legal cultures or spaces, facilitating information exchanges or institutional transplants.[15] The more general character of their knowledge predisposed them to play the part of intermediary. By comparison with practitioners who are too closely linked to particular interests or situations, they represented that rationality and universalism which give law its legitimacy. In moving from one sub-space to another, they helped to break down their separateness by bringing to each institution the know-how, the innovation, or the contacts—in short, the symbolic capital—accumulated in another.

The increasing parcellization of international regulatory space gives ever increasing importance to the key role of these possessors of knowledge and to professional legitimacy. First, because many of these spaces have lost the legitimacy or the political rationality which the nation-state gave them, they must rely all the more on what Weber named 'formal rationality'. Hence, professional knowledge plays a strategic role in the confrontations between practitioners of regulation; it supplies the protagonists with their most legitimate weapons,[16] and allows them to capitalize on their victories.

But in becoming a strategic space in professional rivalries, the field of knowledge becomes an object of power which is too important to be left to academics—at least to academics who cultivate an excessive distance and ivory-tower detachment. The direct interest of business people in the law makes the cultivation of disinterestedness rather difficult.

Scholarly struggles, even when they give the appearance of academic debates, increasingly take on the style of technological battles. In a world in the process of redefinition, the organizations or expert groups which

[15] At least in systems where the Professorenrecht prevailed. Indeed, this was one of the factors which facilitated the diffusion of the continental model. Elsewhere, this same role is played by the more academic practitioners, the QCs who write the legal textbooks and the lawyers who move between the law schools and the law firms.

[16] Thus, during the negotiations to finalize the European Community regulation on mergers, the German model was an easy winner because it was generally agreed that its intrinsic legal rationality was clearly superior to that of the British provisions, which were the product of practitioners more concerned with pragmatic solutions than formal coherence.

succeed in imposing their reading of the enterprise—and more broadly their vision of the social world or of the technical-political stakes— thereby ensure for themselves a situational rent very similar to that won by the industrial and financial groups which succeed, at the cost of substantial investments in terms of research and lobbying, in securing the ratification by the international bodies of their own normative system in respect of telecommunications or high-definition television.

These comments do not aim to challenge the observations of political scientists emphasizing the role of international communities of experts in the globalization process, but simply to underline the point that the structuring of these communities is itself also at issue. Between the model of scholarly associations and that of multinationals offering services to business enterprises lies a whole range of possibilities which would allow variations in the mode of selection of experts, their strategies, and the compromises which result, the circuits of influence and of dissemination—in short, which would influence the type of norm or of transnational regulation which might emerge from these communities, or, more precisely, from the competition between these multiple forums. Here again the increased stakes in play on the market for international regulation stimulate supply and multiply the initiatives. The competition between bodies involved with the production, approval, and dissemination of knowledge has become one of the dimensions of the economic war, for the same reasons as the competition between states. And it is in the professional field, which provides the link between the different poles of power,[17] that one of the keys to this parallel development may be found.

4. THE LAW OFFICES PRE-EMPT THE FIELD OF SCHOLARLY LAW

The professional domain now functions in symbiosis with that of the economy. In it can be seen the same phenomena of concentration, restructuring, and increased competition, even if waged on a field and with weapons which are highly specific. The introduction of competition between laws—and between modes of production of law—is both a result of the economic war and also one means by which it is waged.

The disruption of regulatory mechanisms due to internationalization is thus inseparable from a redefinition of the structures and of the mode of production of practices—and of realms of knowledge—relating to the regulation economic activity. It is because they are machines for

---

[17] Thus, Charles (1989) suggests that the legal professions owe much of their prosperity to their structural position at the intersection of the three poles around which cluster the different fractions of the élite: business, the state, and knowledge.

producing knowledge and institutions that the great conglomerates offering services to business dominate the field of international expertise. This policy of pre-emptive investment in knowledge enables them to put the authority of the law and that of science at the service of their clients; but to the extent that they are the only ones who can afford such massive technological investments, it also reinforces their own oligopolistic positions in the market for expertise.

In contrast to the traditional character of the practitioner, more a man of business (Landon 1990; Sugarman 1991) than a pure professional, and indeed often richer in social capital than in scholarly competence, these great conglomerates claim above all to be groups of experts with a mastery of the most sophisticated knowledge. True, the globalization of markets is causing a growth in the demand for mediation; yet the great international law offices are not satisfied with merely being high-flying intermediaries; cashing in on their address books, they sell knowledge and legitimacy. To have some for sale, they must produce some, and give themselves the means of producing it by investing in this field: by recruiting producers with a legitimacy based on their recognized scholarly competence, by putting considerable research facilities at their disposal, but also by a policy of systematically ensuring a presence both in the places and circuits where legal expertise is produced and approved and those in which the new regulatory mechanisms are elaborated and established. This is indeed the strategy of these mega-law firms which Nelson (1987) rightly calls 'law producing machines'.[18] This systematic policy of investing in law enables them to wield a recognized legal authority which they can capitalize on with their clients: either by offering them new fiscal or financial operations the legality of which they guarantee, or by exploiting their privileged access to the regulatory or adjudicatory bodies.

These strategic choices perfectly correspond to the characteristics and the expectations of their large-firm clientele. Given their size and their repeated use of law and the courts (Galanter 1974), the latter indeed have every interest in investing in law by embarking on judicial or legislative strategies. Such investment in the normative field makes it possible to put pressure on the structuring of their markets in accordance with their specific interests, while helping to protect it from the savage competition of newcomers. The size and wealth of these multinationals is such that they can afford the legal fees based on percentage contributions demanded by this strategy. On the other hand, the very fact that it prevents their less fortunate competitors from following them on this normative field, the price of these 'Rolls-Royce' services constitutes an

---

[18] The same goes for the accountancy Big Six, whose investments in knowledge are all the greater because they are in fields in which the academic tradition is much more recent and less well entrenched.

additional entry barrier helping to close off securely the markets dominated by these large firms. This transformation of law into a commodity
granting the dominant operators in the economic world a privileged
access to juridical authority allows them to make their economistic vision
of social relations prevail by giving it the legitimate form of a legal order.

This integration of law into business—with its corollary, the intrusion
of business logic into the law—is not new: the law-firm model was created to respond to the needs of the 'robber barons'; it was one of the
main tools which allowed them to achieve the first major campaign to
restructure and monopolize the North American economy. And it is certainly not by chance that, almost a century later, the new wave of
restructuring following the oil crisis should coincide with a broadening
and an acceleration of this phenomenon of concentration of expert services available to business. A new generation of mega-firms (Galanter and
Palay 1991) has arisen, with the means and resources needed for a field of
activity and influence which now extends to all the industrialized
economies. The small firms which flourished in the shadows of Wall
Street, priding themselves on preserving the élitist atmosphere of a 'gentle-
men's club', have become multinational conglomerates bringing together
hundreds of professionals and administered by management specialists
more concerned with the level of profit than with good manners. The
difference cannot be measured simply in terms of size or scale. The race
to gigantic size has been accompanied by the generalization of business
rationality under the pressure of increasingly bitter competition. The
opening and the spectacular growth of the market for consultancy have
exploded the tacit agreements which kept the practice of commercial law
separate from business competition and reserved it to a small élite who
were the heirs of the Tocquevillian gentlemen-lawyers. The arrival simultaneously in both the enterprises and in the professional field of newcomers more concerned with efficiency and profits than good manners not
only stimulated the demand for legal services while bringing the world of
business closer to that of the law; it also helped to introduce the economic war into the field of law.

Thanks to the big M & A operations, the new financiers have discovered the tactical advantages of the courts; but at the same time, the entrepreneurs of legal services have let themselves be converted to
management techniques. Like their clients, the more ambitious among
them have realized that take-overs of their competitors offered a quicker
and cheaper route to 'external growth'; but conversely, the less lucky ones
have known the anguish of bankruptcy or absorption. But, although they
are increasingly becoming like other enterprises, these new expertise
multinationals are not abandoning the field of law. On the contrary,
stimulated by the competition of new holders of know-how on the

consultancy market (the famous Big Six), they are even led to make yet larger investments in it, mobilizing the considerable resources they now possess. Paradoxically, the more the business lawyers are sucked into the logic of business, the more they invest in scholarly law, while at the same time introducing to it the rules and the imperatives of the market.

This raising of the competitive stakes also corresponds to the structure of the international market for legal expertise, where uncertainty as to the quality of the products is heightened by the number of operators and the accelerated pace of the transactions. As in cold war situations, this insecurity tends to favour a strategy of deterrence, and hence of over-armament. The legal multinationals are obliged to put on a display of legal authority to reassure their clients and intimidate their adversaries by a show of preventive force. Given that the legal-financial arrangements or tax manœuvres they devise are only rarely tested and authorized by bodies having a legitimate authority, their credibility and validity essentially derive from the authoritative capital linked to the name of a great law office. To nourish their reputation, these large organizations are therefore always obliged to do too much, in order to give the conviction that they would be able to do enough, if necessary, if any brazen person were bold enough to threaten their authority and the interests of their clients. The logic of over-equipment becomes the corollary of oligopolistic concentration.

The competition between legal systems also contributes to this process of escalation. To become established in the markets where the authority of scholarly lawyers is still very strong, the legal multinationals are obliged to resort to the same type of competence, because it is the most acceptable one. Thus, there can be seen in the field of legal practice the same phenomenon of imitation which we noted in relation to the competition between models of state regulation. The logic of confrontation leads each protagonist to borrow the weapons of its adversary. To preserve their positions in a legal field which is internationalizing, the continental academics are led increasingly to give up their ideal of autonomy, so as to become closer to business, or even to transform themselves into intellectual entrepreneurs. At the same time, to extend their hegemony, the practitioner firms increasingly move away from their original pragmatism, and strengthen their intellectual capital.

This combination of internal and external pressures ends in a frenetic competition between these large firms in the legal field, which is reflected in many indicators, such as the systematic enticement of academics and the growth of part-time courses underwritten by practitioners, the funding of chairs and of research work, the proliferation of internal training and publications, and the giving of patronage to conferences, journals, and even publishing houses—in short, a whole series of converging phenomena, which increasingly blur the line between practitioners and producers of scholarly law, and which can be interpreted as either the privatization of the places of production of legal knowledge or the annexation of doctrine, or at least the reduction of its autonomy. The same phenomenon can be seen at the level of the production of norms. Transnational regulatory bodies complain of being literally 'besieged' by these experts offering their services and abilities (virtually) for nothing, based on studies which they have carried out privately. Effectively, in all the fields where expertise can be turned to a profit from enterprises—the environment or industrial property, the regulation of competition or of M & A—the specialist literature today emanates from the big firms. Just as the national public bodies which traditionally took the job of collection and rationalization of the information necessary to keep regulatory measures up to date are at the same time, increasingly pushed to the side, whether because they are confined to the national space or by reason of their lack of adequate resources to cope with a transnational market, so the privatization of expertise and knowledge is gaining pace simultaneously with heightened competition between increasingly numerous and diverse producers. The emergence of an international market for expertise thus appears as both cause and effect of the establishment of a transnational market for goods and services.

12

Contracts, Trusts, and Companies

CAROLINE BRADLEY

I. INTRODUCTION

The conceptualization of corporations as complex networks of contracts between the different interest groups involved has proved to be a powerful tool for the understanding of these entities.[1] The various contracts which are supposed to exist are those involving shareholders, directors, employees, and creditors of the company, but the aspect of this nexus of contracts which has received most academic attention, and which is the subject of this chapter, is that which concerns the relationship between the shareholders and the directors of large companies. The reasons for this focus are clear: a major concern of academic company lawyers and economists is the extent to which corporate management puts, and should be allowed by law to put, its own interests before those of the owners of the company.[2] Manne (1967: 284) has suggested that 'large corporations function in a largely permissive framework and . . . market forces rather than legal ones have dictated their organization and structure' (but cf. Campbell 1990). The courts, however, have recognized that problems arise in relation to large companies involved in public securities markets (see *Caparo* v. *Dickman*, 1990: 376).

The characterization of the relationship between corporate managers and shareholders as an essentially contractual relationship, rather than a relationship the nature and terms of which are determined by laws and regulations, is attractive for a number of reasons (Easterbrook and Fischel 1989: 1444–5). First, statute provides for the existence of a 'corporate contract' in section 14 of the Companies Act, 1985. Although this is a contract between the shareholders *inter se* and the company, the terms of the contract impose obligations on the company's directors, and are relevant to the identification of the limits of the fiduciary duties

---

[1] See, e.g., Coase 1937; Bratton 1989c; Easterbrook and Fischel 1989: 1426; Mueller and FitzRoy 1986. For different views of corporate personality, see, e.g., Bratton 1989c: 433–6; Eisenberg 1989: 1487; Teubner 1988a: 136; H. Hart 1954: 49–60.

[2] Berle and Means (1932) identified a separation between ownership and control of large corporations in the USA. The identification of this phenomenon has spawned a vast literature. See, e.g., Herman 1981; Fama and Jensen 1983; Williamson 1983; Jensen and Meckling 1976; Brudney 1985.

imposed on them. Second, the emphasis on the contractual aspect of the relationship between corporate managers and shareholders should allow judges to protect the legitimate interests and expectations of the parties to the contract (see *Re Posgate & Denby (Agencies) Ltd.*, 1987: 14 (per Hoffmann, J.); but cf. *Re Blue Arrow*, 1987: 590 (per Vinelott, J.)) In addition, emphasis on contract as the source of corporate identity may involve playing down the more traditional idea that corporate personality may be achieved only as a concession from the state, and, for this reason, conceptualization of the company as a nexus of contracts may appear to remove the justification for interference in corporate affairs by the state (Brudney 1985: 1408–9).

The position is not so simple, however. The rhetoric of contract need not involve the courts indulging in blind deference to the apparent terms of an agreement; and there are many examples in relation to non-corporate contracts of a tension between the desire of judges to recognize and uphold party autonomy and their determination to interfere in contracts tainted by an inequality of bargaining position. (Cf. other circumstances where equity is prepared to intervene to amend the terms of contracts: e.g., *Multiservice Bookbinding* v. *Marden*, 1979; *Compaq Computer Ltd* v. *Abercorn Group Ltd.* 1991: 493 (per Mummery, J.).) Is the contract between corporate management and shareholders in a large quoted company a case of inequality of bargaining position? At first sight, it would appear not, because institutional investors such as pension funds, unit trusts, and life assurance companies, which are apparently not consumers in their relations with the companies in which they invest, hold the majority of UK listed equity securities. However, individuals also invest in listed equities, and government has tried to encourage wider share ownership through tax incentives, such as Personal Equity Plans (PEPs), and through the active marketing of privatization issues.[3] It may be appropriate to think of two classes of investors in listed equities, therefore: those who are consumers in their relations with the companies in which they invest and those who are not.

Prospective investors should be able to influence the terms of the contract between shareholders and management by valuing at a low price shares in companies which propose unacceptable contracts or which are established in jurisdictions which imply unacceptable terms into the contract. A management which seeks to raise new capital or to maintain the

---

[3] The selling documents have, of course, contained risk-warnings, but the volume of advertising surrounding the issues has probably been, on each occasion, more noticeable. The standard risk-warning was used in the mini-prospectus for the Regional Electricity Companies share offers, dated 21 Nov. 1990. This stated: 'Before deciding to apply for shares you should consider carefully whether shares are a suitable investment for you. Their value can go down as well as up. If you need advice, you should consult a stockbroker, solicitor, accountant, bank manager or other professional adviser' (p. 1.).

price of its shares after issue in order to protect itself from the risk of displacement through take-over therefore has an incentive to propose to or maintain for prospective investors contractual terms which the latter are likely to accept. However, it is not clear that investors in general are able to understand the meaning and significance of the contractual terms which are offered to them (Brudney 1985: 1411). One problem is that many of the terms of the contract are hidden in statutes and court judgments, rather than being expressed in a document presented to prospective investors; but even the interpretation of express terms by a court may not reflect an uninformed investor's view of the meaning of those terms.

A powerful argument for not worrying about the inability of investors in general to take part in the process of negotiating the terms of the contract between shareholders and management is that the forms of management–shareholder contract used by different companies are relatively standardized, which facilitates comparison of the performance of the different companies (Easterbrook and Fischel 1989: 1435), and investors in general are able to free-ride on the investment decisions of expert investors. Ordinary investors do not need to assess the value of a particular corporate contract, because professional investors will do the job for them (ibid.; see also Posner 1986: 421; Eisenberg 1989: 1487); the market price gives an indication of the value of a share. The ordinary investor's decision to invest in a particular share, therefore, is made on the basis of factors extraneous to the valuation of the share, such as the investor's perception of the company concerned or the way in which the share issue is marketed.

We can argue that it does not matter that investors in general are unable to influence the terms of management–shareholder contracts to which they adhere, because non-professional investors can rely on professional investors to ensure that such contracts oblige management to act in the interests of shareholders and maximize profits. However, professional investors are likely to diversify out of the risk associated with investment in particular companies. In addition, professional shareholders have resources and expertise which they can apply to monitoring the managements of companies in which they invest which are not available to non-professional investors, and, if they hold a large stake in a company, they have the power to discipline management by threatening to sell their stake, which might provoke a decline in the share price. The exit of non-professional investors does not have the same impact on corporate managements, and so their voice is not so loud (Hirschman 1970).

The provisions of the corporate contract governing the remuneration of the company's directors are particularly problematic. Inflated remuneration of directors represents only a fraction of the money directors may abstract from shareholders in various ways. A wide range of equitable

and statutory rules applies to limit the ability of directors to use their
company's money for their own benefit (Companies Act, 1985, sect.
312–22, 330–47; *Bray* v. *Ford*, 1896; *Regal Hastings* v. *Gulliver*, 1942).
Should the courts enforce the terms of the agreement as they appear in
the company's Articles of Association, or should they be prepared to
interfere with the terms of the agreement? The use of contract theory to
describe corporate relationships also imports the idea of *caveat emptor*,
which appears when courts analyse agreements freely entered into by
competent parties. However, even in ordinary contractual relationships
courts are prepared to interfere with the express terms of an agreement.
Two of the reasons used to justify such interference may be relevant to
the analysis of the corporate contract: first, that an inequality of bargaining position has resulted in a contract the terms of which are unfair to
some of the parties, an approach described below as a contractual analysis; or, second, that certain terms of the contract are incompatible with
the duties to which some of the parties are subject apart from the contract, an approach described below as a social control analysis.

2. THE HARM: REMUNERATION PROVISIONS IN CORPORATE CONTRACTS

Table A, the standard form for Articles of Association, provides that the
remuneration of the directors is a matter for the shareholders of the company to determine by a simple majority (regulation 82 of table A in the
Companies (tables A–F) Regulations 1985: SI No. 805). In practice this
provision is commonly amended to allow the board of directors to determine the remuneration of individual directors, and *The Yellow Book*
(Council of the Stock Exchange 1984) does not prohibit this practice.
However, in response to concerns that directors may be tempted to make
irresponsible decisions about their own remuneration, various bodies have
suggested that listed companies should appoint remuneration committees
consisting wholly or mainly of non-executive directors and chaired by a
non-executive director. These independent committees would make recommendations to boards of directors about all forms of directors' remuneration (see, e.g., Cadbury 1992: para. 4.34; Institutional Shareholders
Committee 1991: 4–5); but faith in the ability of outside directors to control the actions of executive directors has not been justified in the past
(Brudney 1982: 597), and is unlikely to be justified in the future (Gilson
and Kraakman 1991).

In 1990, the House of Lords considered remuneration provisions of
Articles of Association which read:

REMUNERATION OF DIRECTORS. 90. The board shall fix the annual remuneration of the directors provided that without the consent of the company in general meeting such remuneration (excluding any special remuneration payable under article 91 and 92) shall not exceed the sum of £100,000 per annum . . . 91. The board may, in addition to the remuneration authorised in article 90, grant special remuneration to any director who serves on any committee or who devotes special attention to the business of the company or who otherwise performs services which in the opinion of the board are outside the scope of the ordinary duties of a director. Such special remuneration may be made payable to such director in addition to or in substitution for his ordinary remuneration as a director, and may be made payable by a lump sum or by way of salary, or commission or participation in profits, or by any or all of those modes or otherwise as the board may determine (*Guinness* v. *Saunders*, 1990: 328)

Article 2 of the Articles of Association defined 'the board' as 'the directors of the company for the time being (or a quorum of such directors assembled at a meeting of directors duly convened) or any committee authorised by the board to act on its behalf, and the definitions in article 2 were to apply 'if not inconsistent with the subject or context' (see *Guinness* v. *Saunders*, 1990: 329). A cursory reading of the Articles of Association would therefore suggest that a committee of the board of directors of Guinness PLC was competent to take decisions about the remuneration of the directors of the company. The House of Lords, however, refused to accept this construction of the provisions of the company's Articles of Association.

The litigation arose from the delegation by the board of Guinness PLC of the conduct of its take-over bid for Distillers in 1986 to a committee of the board. The committee was authorized 'to authorise and approve, execute and do, or procure to be executed and done, all such documents, deeds, acts and things as they may consider necessary or desirable in connection with the making or implementation of the offer and/or the proposals referred to above and any revision thereof' (ibid. 327). The committee of the board had paid £5.2 million to a company controlled by one of its members, Thomas Ward, in consideration of services performed by him for Guinness during the take-over to promote its success. Guinness later sued to recover this sum, and the vice-chancellor ordered that it should be repaid (*Guinness* v. *Saunders*, 1988 (High Court)). The Court of Appeal (*Guinness* v. *Saunders*, 1988 (Court of Appeal)) and the House of Lords upheld this decision, although on other grounds. The vice-chancellor and the Court of Appeal treated the arrangement as a contract between Guinness and Thomas Ward, but required him to account to the company for the profit he had made because of his failure effectively to disclose his interests in the contract to the company. The House of Lords, on the other hand, held that the committee did not have authority to bind Guinness to the arrangement: 'The simple fact emerges, at the end of the day, that there was, in law, no binding contract under which Mr Ward was entitled to receive the money and that, as a fiduciary, he must now restore the money to Guinness' (per Lord Goff of Chieveley, *Guinness* v. *Saunders*, 1990: 343).

The House of Lords decision that the committee of the board of directors did not have authority to bind the company to the arrangement with Thomas Ward was based on the court's interpretation of the Articles of Association of Guinness, which Lord Goff of Chieveley described as 'conspicuous neither for their clarity nor for their consistency' (ibid. 340). In particular, the court was concerned with the provisions in the Articles of Association which gave the power to determine directors' remuneration to the board of directors. Lord Templeman's approach to this problem was to say that 'the law cannot and equity will not amend the articles of Guinness. The court is not entitled to usurp the functions conferred on the board by the articles' (ibid. 331).

The effect of article 2 of Guinness's Articles of Association was limited by Lord Templeman, who said that the language, subject, and context of the provisions of the Articles of Association dealing with special remuneration of directors were inconsistent with the board, meaning anything but the board, and that '[t]he remuneration of directors concerns all the members of the board and all the shareholders of Guinness' (ibid.). Although article 110 of Guinness's Articles of Association provided that the directors could delegate any of their powers to a committee, this provision did not allow the board to delegate the power to decide directors' remuneration.

Article 100(D) of Guinness's Articles of Association did provide that directors could act for the company in a professional capacity and receive payment for their professional services. However, Thomas Ward had not argued that his payment was for legal professional services, and Lord Templeman expressed the view that '[t]he services pleaded by Mr Ward were the services he was bound to carry out and which any member of the board is entitled and bound to carry out as a member of a committee established by the board' (ibid. 330)

Lord Templeman pointed out that Guinness's Articles of Association were different from the provisions of table A, which he described as 'recommended by statute', and which provide for the determination of directors' remuneration by the company in general meeting (ibid. 328; see also table A in the Companies (tables A–F) Regulations 1985; SI No. 805, regulation 82). This reference to table A as being 'recommended by statute' is rather misleading. Sections 3 and 8 of the Companies Act, 1985, refer to regulations providing for the form of a Memorandum of Association and of Articles of Association. However, whereas section 3(1) of the Act requires the form of the Memorandum of Association to be 'as specified . . . by regulations made by the Secretary of State, or as near to that form as circumstances admit', section 8(1) provides that a company 'may for its articles adopt the whole or any part' of table A.

Generally, the House of Lords' idea that certain provisions are appropriate for inclusion in a company's Articles of Association, whereas other provisions are inappropriate, is reminiscent of the interpretation of the statutory provision now to be found in section 14 of the Companies Act, 1985, which means that outsider rights are not enforced as part of the contract constituted by the Memorandum and Articles of Association (see, e.g., *Eley* v. *Positive Government Security Life Co. Ltd.*, 1876; *Quin and Axtens Ltd.* v. *Salmon*, 1909; Wedderburn 1957: 210–15; G. Goldberg 1985; Gower 1958a, 1958b. Cf. *Re J. E. Cade and Sons Ltd.* 1991: 374 (per Warner, J.). There is a serious inconsistency between the courts' insistence that, on the one hand, they will not interfere in a company's internal affairs and will not amend its constitution, and, on the other hand, that they will regard certain provisions as inappropriate for inclusion in the company's Articles of Association. The justification for this approach is the expectations of the shareholders in the company, a body of people who are unlikely to have examined the provisions of the company's Articles of Association in any detail, and who, if they have examined them, will not understand their significance.

The real problem faced by the House of Lords, and by the lower courts in this case, was that Thomas Ward had put himself in a position in which his personal interests conflicted with his duties to Guinness, as one of its directors. As a director, he had a duty to give independent and impartial advice to Guinness; but the agreement he reached with the committee meant that he would obtain a fee if the bid for Distillers succeeded (*Guinness* v. *Saunders*, 1990: 336). Both Lord Templeman and Lord Goff of Chieveley examined Thomas Ward's position using the familiar method of comparing the position of a director with that of a trustee (Sealy 1967), but introduced the idea that the Articles of Association may be treated as a trust instrument (*Guinness* v. *Saunders*, 1990: 331, per Lord Templeman) or as equivalent to a trust deed (ibid. 341, per Lord Goff).

In *Guinness* v. *Saunders*, 1990, Lord Templeman and Lord Goff of Chieveley invoked the languages of contracts and of fiduciary duties in dealing with the apparent consent of the shareholders, through the terms of the Articles of Association, to the payment to Thomas Ward. They resolved this problem by deciding that the Articles of Association did not mean what they said. It would have been preferable for the House of Lords to have explicitly based its decision either on the need for protection of the shareholders in Guinness, as consumers of their shares, or on the need to encourage high standards of behaviour among corporate directors. The shareholders in Guinness do not seem to have suffered as a result of the committee's actions; so it appears that the justification for the decision must lie in a perceived need to make directors in general act properly, irrespective of the effects of their actions on shareholders. If the Law Lords were attempting to promote commercial morality through their decision, they should have made this clear.

3. CONTRACTUAL ANALYSIS: THE CORPORATE CONTRACT AS A CONSUMER CONTRACT

The term 'consumer' is generally used in the context of statutory provisions to identify those who should benefit from the protection of the statute in question. In this context, as Goode has suggested, the definition of a consumer may be complex: 'The task of deciding who is to qualify as a "consumer", and what is to constitute a "consumer" transaction, for the purposes of protective legislation is far from easy. Indeed, the answer will usually vary widely according to the type of protection sought to be provided and the underlying purpose of the legislation' (R. Goode 1989: para. 7.7). However, it is not only through legislation that consumers are protected; inequality of bargaining position or market power are often taken into account in the decisions of courts, even outside a statutory context (see, e.g., MacPherson 1987: 17–18; Craig 1991), although it is arguable that the common law is inadequate to protect consumers in all of the situations where their interests may be prejudiced (Borrie 1991: 562–3).

In order to consider whether it is appropriate to consider shareholders, or some shareholders, as consumers, it is necessary to identify the characteristics of a consumer. How is the term 'consumer' defined in existing rules for the protection of consumers, and do these definitions apply to shareholders? It is clear that shareholders do not benefit from the consumer protection provisions of the Unfair Contract Terms Act, 1977. This statute generally applies where one party to the contract enters into the contract in the course of a business, and the other party does not enter into the contract in the course of a business or hold himself out as doing so (section 12). The definition of consumer, therefore, quite clearly seeks to identify circumstances where there is an inequality of bargaining position between two parties to a contract. Where such an inequality of bargaining position exists, the Act limits the freedom of the parties to contract. However, schedule 1 to the Act contains exceptions relating to contracts of insurance, contracts relating to securities, and:

any contract so far as it relates—
(i) to the formation or dissolution of a company (which means any body corporate or unincorporated association and includes a partnership), or
(ii) to its constitution or the rights or obligations of its corporators or members. (schedule 1, para. 1(d))

Shareholders are excluded by this provision from the protection of the statute; but, of course, companies legislation also contains provisions comparable to some of those in the Unfair Contract Terms Act, 1977 (see sect. 310, Companies Act, 1985). Article 1(2) of the draft EC directive on unfair terms in consumer contracts (OJ No. C 73/7, 24. 3. 92) provides that the directive will not apply to contracts 'relating to the incorporation and organization of companies or partnership agreements'. However, the proposed directive does cover a wide range of services, including many financial services transactions, such as credit, banking, insurance, and professional advice from investment advisers. The scope of the Financial Services Act, 1986, has recently been restricted by the Companies Act, 1989, so that the statutory remedy for damages for breach of rules made under the Act is available only to 'private investors' (sect. 62a). The definition of 'private investor' for these purposes:

means an investor whose cause of action arises as a result of anything he has done or suffered—
(a) in the case of an individual, otherwise than in the course of carrying on investment business; and
(b) in the case of any other person, otherwise than in the course of carrying on business of any kind (Financial Services Act, 1986 (Restrictions of Right of Action), Regulations 1991, SI 1991 No. 489, regulation 2(1))

Institutional investors, for whom the investment process is part of their business, and who are able to take part in the valuation of corporate contracts and influence their terms, and are also able to monitor the activities of corporate management and control these activities, are not consumers for the purposes of these or any definitions. However, other investors would fall within these definitions if they were applied to the context of participation in corporate contracts. Shares are unlike many of the products which are usually described as consumer products, and it has been argued that they should not be regarded as consumer products because 'unlike most goods and services distributed by the economy, stocks have no intrinsic value. They are only instruments representing other, possibly valuable, rights. Investors do not "consume" them. "Producing" securities requires no more than the paper and ink needed to print them' (Stout 1988: 641–2, footnote omitted).

This argument concentrates on the difficulty of perceiving a share as a product. As a 'product', a share is as complicated as a computer; the ability of the average consumer to understand enough about the workings of a computer to make a sensible decision about whether to buy a particular model is probably no greater than the ability of the average investor to make a similar decision about investment in shares. Another problem is that shares 'have no intrinsic value'. Shares involve rights to vote, which are useful only if a shareholder has a large number of them, and rights to receive dividends if they are declared. All a shareholder's rights are contingent. However, this problem of accepting that a shareholder can be regarded as a consumer persists only so long as we consider a share as a product to be consumed. If we concentrate on the idea that the corporate contract is a contract for a service, for one person's money to be managed by other people, similar to the relationship between a customer and her bank, it is easier to accept that the contract is a consumer contract.

Despite these difficulties in construing the corporate contract as a consumer contract, some protective rules do already apply to investment in shares. For example, the need for protection of investors has been recognized in rules which regulate the information provided to prospective investors and the activities of investment intermediaries. The Financial Services Act, 1986, provides for the protection of investors, and, under the scheme of regulations which has been established with this legislation, ordinary investors should receive greater protection than professional or experienced investors.[4]

The first of these areas of consumer protection regulation which may apply to the corporate contract involves the regulation of the contents of investment advertisements and selling documents which are used to persuade investors to part with their money. The disclosure requirements which apply to such advertisements have been subject to much criticism over time (see, e.g., Posner 1986: 421; Kripke 1979; 1975: 293). Although the rules are designed ostensibly to provide adequate information to prospective investors so that they can make properly informed investment decisions, those investors who need protection are unlikely to be able to understand the mandated information (DTI 1990*a*: 13). The greater ability of institutional and other professional and experienced investors to value investments has been recognized by the Department of Trade and Industry, which has suggested that the marketing practice of producing two selling documents, a mini-prospectus and a full prospectus, which has in the past applied to privatization issues, may be applied to other share issues (ibid.; see also DTI 1989*b*).

The DTI's views about the appropriateness of reducing the amount of

---

[4] See, e.g., the Securities and Investment Board Core Conduct of Business Rules issued on 30 Jan. 1991, which distinguish between 'ordinary business investors', 'small business investors', 'private customers', and 'non-private customers'.

information which is made available as a matter of course to non-professional investors reflect the ideas of commentators who characterize such non-professional investors as free-riders on the work of others, such as underwriters, sophisticated purchasers of securities such as pension funds, and financial analysts (Posner 1986: 421). The non-professional investor thus has an 'army of helpers' (see Easterbrook and Fischel 1989: 1435).

The activities of many of these 'helpers' do, however, provide many opportunities for them to benefit themselves at the expense of investors, and the second set of consumer protection rules which applies to investment in shares governs the relationship between a prospective investor and an intermediary involved in the investment process. The Financial Services Act, 1986, requires that anyone who is involved in investment business in the United Kingdom must generally be authorized to carry on that business by the Securities and Investments Board or through membership of a self-regulating organization or recognized professional body. The rules of these bodies regulate the conduct of investment business, and provide, for example, that an investment adviser must recommend only suitable investments to a prospective investor. What is suitable depends on who the investor is. Rules made under the Financial Services Act, 1986, also regulate the activities of those who manage investments on behalf of others (see, e.g., Financial Services Act, 1986, ch. 8).

These two sets of rules are not sufficient to protect the consumer who may invest in shares, however. Investment advisers, who are regulated under the Financial Services Act, 1986, are required to take care to ensure that they only recommend suitable investments to their customers.[5] Investors who invest through investment advisers should therefore be protected against investment in unsuitable corporate contracts, assuming that there is an option of investment in a 'suitable' corporate contract. However, some investors may decide to invest without taking professional advice. The suitability rule imposed on investment advisers is, therefore, a rule designed to protect investors against the misleading advice of investment advisers, rather than a rule designed to ensure the suitability of investment products for investors. One solution to the problem that many corporate contracts may not constitute suitable

---

[5] See the SIB Statements of Principle issued under section 47A, Financial Services Act, 1986, on 15 Mar. 1990, Principle 4: 'A firm should seek from customers it advises or for whom it exercises discretion any information about their circumstances and investment objectives which might reasonably be expected to be relevant in enabling them to fulfil its responsibilities to them.' See also the SIB Core Conduct of Business Rules issued on 30 Jan. 1991, Core Rule 16: 'A firm must take reasonable steps to ensure that it does not . . . make any personal recommendation to a private customer of an investment or investment agreement . . . unless the recommendation is suitable for him having regard to the facts disclosed by that customer and other relevant facts about the customer of which the firm is or reasonably should be aware.' See also section 47, Financial Services Act, 1986.

investments for ordinary investors might be to give to investors incentives to obtain investment advice, or to reduce non-systemic risk through diversification.[6] Another is to interpret the terms of the consumer corporate contract in a way which reflects the inequality of the parties to that contract. It is arguable, however, that this approach only becomes appropriate if a real shareholders' remedy develops, so that shareholders may obtain remedies in damages for breaches of the terms of the contract in which they are involved.[7]

4. SOCIAL CONTROL ANALYSIS: ENFORCING HIGH STANDARDS OF BEHAVIOUR

Fiduciary duties, which are imposed on directors, involve the idea of an inequality of bargaining position, and may be seen as rules which have been developed to protect shareholders as consumers. (For an argument that different rules should apply to close companies and publicly owned companies, see, e.g., Brudney and Clark 1981: 998.) Fiduciary duties are often based on some sort of contract: a contract where the fiduciary has superior information or expertise, or is managing property. The law treats a company's Memorandum and Articles of Association as creating contractual relationships (sect. 14, Companies Act, 1985); yet directors are, because of their position, subjected to fiduciary duties which are similar to the duties imposed on trustees. (See, e.g., *Re Lands Allotment*, 1894. See also Berle 1931: 1074). Of course, the trust relationship is also a contractual relationship. However, it is not always the contractual elements of the trust relationship which take precedence; as Roger Cotterrell (1987: 88) has said: 'The idea of fiduciary obligation of the trustee harnesses to legal doctrine a moral conception of great social significance and induces us to see the trust beneficiary not as the possessor of property-power but as a person meriting protection; a person to whom moral as well as legal obligations are owed.'

Comments such as these, and such as those which judges apply to the characterization of the relationship between trustees and their beneficiaries and between directors and shareholders, suggest that

---

[6] It is worth noting that the managed investment products which provide the easiest access to diversification for individual investors, such as unit trusts, also involve risks similar to those of the corporate contract that those involved in management will benefit themselves at the expense of investors.

[7] See sect. 111A of the Companies Act, 1985, introduced by sect. 131 of the Companies Act, 1989, removing barriers to remedies in damages for shareholders. If a shareholder were to have a personal right not to have the value of her shareholding affected by the unlawful acts of the directors, this provision might allow a remedy in damages. There is some doubt, however, as to how the new provision should be interpreted. See also Wedderburn 1957: 211; Gower 1950: 367; Hornby 1956.

fiduciary duties do not, in the minds of judges, as opposed to neo-classical economists, represent the contractual provisions which investors would choose if they were to address their minds to the issue, or if they were willing to incur the necessary expense of identifying the appropriate provisions. Indeed, it may be more accurate to emphasize the regulatory function of directors' duties and see them as instruments of social control, regulating the conduct of all directors. For example, Lord Wedderburn (1985*b*: 221) has expressed the view that '[f]iduciary obligation is imposed by private law, but its function is public, and its purpose social' (see also Kahn-Freund 1946: 235). Judges have also emphasized the social control aspects of fiduciary duties (*Keech* v. *Sandford*, 1726; *North-West Transportation* v. *Beatty*, 1887: 600 (per Sir Richard Baggallay)).

A view of directors' fiduciary duties which concentrates on their regulatory, or social control, function would limit the capacity of shareholders to modify the duties; whereas the imposition of purely contractual duties on directors would be merely a matter of the relationship between the directors and shareholders of a particular company, therefore allowing for relatively unrestricted modification of the duties by the shareholders. Although it is clear that there are some express limitations on the power of shareholders to exempt directors from liability for breach of their fiduciary duties (see sect. 310, Companies Act, 1985; but cf. *Movitex* v. *Bulfield*, 1988), in practice the likelihood that directors will be sued as a result of breaches of their duties is affected by the limitations on the ability of minority shareholders to bring such actions. Shareholders in companies involved in public markets are unlikely to discover that fiduciary duties have been breached, and the rule in *Foss* v. *Harbottle*, 1843, ensures that litigation regarding breaches of directors' duties is usually corporate litigation, and controlled by the directors. Actions against miscreant directors are likely to result where the company goes into liquidation, and the liquidator acquires the power to litigate in the company's name, or where there is a change of control.[8] Another weakness of fiduciary duties as social control mechanisms is, as Lord Wedderburn (1985*b*) points out, that the shareholders in a company can remove liability through ratification, so that private action prevents control in the public interest.

Courts may interfere with the terms of the corporate contract using a contractual approach, which emphasizes ideas of inequality of bargaining

---

[8] A change of control led to the litigation in *Regal Hastings* v. *Gulliver*, 1942, and a change in the composition of the board of directors led to the litigation in *Guinness* v. *Saunders*, 1990. For an assessment of the effects of the limitations on minority shareholders' actions in relation to the breaches of duty by directors of companies involved in public markets in the context of take-overs, see Bradley 1990: 178–81.

position, or a social control approach, which emphasizes the idea of enforcing high standards of behaviour among corporate directors, or both approaches together, using the rhetoric of contract to disguise social control. Both approaches raise some important questions. First, can shareholders realistically be characterized as a type of 'consumer', in the light of protection provided by the operations of the market for corporate shares and other protection provided through regulation of the marketing of shares and the activities of investment intermediaries? Second, should statutory rules be developed to require prospective investors to obtain investment advice or to diversify or to provide adequate consumer protection for shareholders where necessary? Third, should shareholders be able to obtain remedies in damages for breach of the provisions of the corporate contract?

Other questions are raised by consideration of the social control function of directors' duties. It seems clear that, to judges, the regulatory function of directors' duties is important, but the foundations of control of directors through these duties are weak, because of procedural barriers to litigation by minority shareholders, particularly by minority shareholders in companies involved in public securities markets. In order for fiduciary duties to control the activities of directors effectively, these barriers should be weakened.

13

Privatization, Control, and Accountability

COLIN SCOTT

I. INTRODUCTION

Since 1979 the British Government has initiated a substantial transfer from public to private ownership of nationalized industries. The short-hand term which has been adopted to describe the policy has been 'privatization'. In this context the use of the term 'privatization' refers to the ownership of the assets once publicly owned by the state by various private shareholders and corporations. This process has occurred in a wide range of nationalized industries in the industrial and service sectors, including Rover, British Aerospace, and Rolls Royce, and in each of the main utility sectors—telecommunications, gas, electricity, and water (see generally Veljanovski 1987; Vickers and Yarrow 1988; Veljanovski 1990a). The privatization of ownership, however, need not imply the full transfer of control and accountability functions from the public to the private sector. Indeed, all private companies are subject to a variety of forms of state control, in the form of competition law, company law, consumer protection laws, contract and property laws, and so on. For the public utility sectors, which provide the focus for this chapter, transfer of assets to the private sector has created the risk of permitting private monopoly profits, and so new regulatory issues concerned with the pro-motion of competition and protection of both domestic and industrial users have been raised, which go beyond questions of the regulation of ordinary companies. For many of the former nationalized industries the process of privatization has involved a substantial degree of state plan-ning and continuing involvement of the state in the activities of the industries, most explicitly through new forms of sectoral regulation of the public utilities, but additionally in a variety of less visible ways. It is pos-sible, therefore, that the assumption that privatization, in the form of transfer of ownership of state assets, leads to less state intervention, is misleading. This chapter attempts to explore the range of control and accountability mechanisms to which the former nationalized industries

I would like to thank Chris Whelan and participants in the Workshop on Corporate Control and Accountability held at the University of Warwick in July 1991, in particular Aileen McHarg and Roger Sugden, for comments on earlier versions of this chapter.

are subject, and the new forms of state planning which these mechanisms imply. The implication of this argument, that we should treat government as ever present in monitoring and structuring privatized industry, is to suggest that the new structures we see are contingent principally not upon the requirements of the market, but rather on the decisions of government.

Much of the rhetoric of this policy of privatization has been concerned with addressing the perceived inefficiency of the nationalized industries. At times it has appeared that government has sought to argue that transfer of assets *per se* will increase efficiency. However, it is apparent that ownership is only one aspect of industrial efficiency, and that competition and regulation play an important role. The early public utility privatizations, British Telecom (1984) and British Gas (1986), it has been argued, paid insufficient attention to either the potential for restructuring the industries to promote competition or the design of regulatory structures to address the problems associated with asymmetry of information between regulator and regulatee. What is apparent is that the political economy of privatization is much more complex than just the pursuit of efficiency. Indeed, it could be argued that the transfer of a vertically integrated monopoly from the public to the private sector with only light-touch regulation has little to do with a policy of pursuing efficiency. Other government objectives, which included the reduction of the public sector borrowing requirement through the assets sales, the widening of share ownership, the weakening of public sector unions, the reduction of state intervention in the economy, and the full co-operation of the existing utilities management may have been just as important in the design of the privatization policies (for the official government justifications of the early privatizations, see J. Moore 1986*a*, 1986*b*). It would not be surprising if the pursuit of more competitive and efficient industries did not determine the shape of the policies. More recent privatizations of the water and electricity industries and proposals to privatize rail and postal services have demonstrated greater interest on the part of government in restructuring those industries along the lines suggested by industrial economists. Furthermore, after periods of learning, it appears that the new regulatory offices are pursuing more interventionist and radical regulatory styles which substantially adjust the initial regulatory settlements, which tended to favour the industries and their shareholders. Thus the extensive residual state role in the activities of the privatized utility sectors has become more visible.

In the abstract at least, the choices of industrial organization for government, between public ownership, regulated private ownership, and unregulated private ownership, raise problems of calculating the best instrument for pursuit of industrial policy (Trebilcock and Prichard

1983). A growing body of literature, which draws upon agency costs theory, developed in the context of corporate control, emphasizes the costs and benefits of the use of different organizational patterns in pursuit of government economic objectives. Public ownership involves the integration of policy making and service delivery in government, permitting the pursuit of a broader range of social objectives than might be possible in the case of an unregulated private corporation and greater direct control over decisions in investment and employment policies than might be possible for a regulated private company. However, the public ownership form may create acute problems of monitoring and incentives, where the principals, the public and politicians, have little incentive to monitor the industrial activities, and the agents, the managers of the publicly owned corporations, have few incentives to pursue the objectives of the principals (Trebilcock and Prichard 1983: 26–8; Vickers and Yarrow 1988: 230–2; Sappington and Stiglitz 1987). A government attempting to regulate private enterprise is likely to encounter very similar problems in terms of monitoring and controlling regulated companies as shareholders and creditors find with managers. So regulated firms face incentives to comply less than fully with regulatory norms, or in the case of subsidy to comply less than fully with conditions attached (Trebilcock and Prichard 1983: 27–8; Laffont and Tirole 1991; Macey 1992; McCubbins *et al.* 1987; Noll 1989; Sappington and Stiglitz 1987). In the case of publicly owned enterprises in the United Kingdom the signals as to what the industries' objectives were, were mixed. The loose structure of the relations between government ministers and the industries permitted government to pursue a range of contradictory objectives concerned not just with industrial efficiency, but also with public expenditure, inflation, and employment (Prosser 1986: 136–7).

The basic economic argument for privatization, then, is that it will create greater incentives to efficiency, and therefore result in better service. These incentives may be found in the product market, where it is possible to introduce greater competition. There are also other techniques which employ the product market, such as deregulating entry to create a potentially contestable market or promoting competition for the field through franchising schemes. Where it is not possible to harness these market incentives in the product market, arguments for public regulation may be strong. However, where a degree of monopoly continues, monitoring costs associated with the regulation of private companies may be greater than they were under public ownership. Some commentators argue that public ownership may be more efficient than regulation of private industry where such monopoly conditions exist and, subject to the mechanisms used in structuring control, more effective in achieving public objectives (Trebilcock and Prichard 1983). Even where it is not possible to create market incentives in the product market, it is argued that the impact of transfer to private ownership creating new incentives for firms in relation to the capital and labour markets may be a valuable spur to efficiency.

2. THE CONTROL AND ACCOUNTABILITY OF PRIVATIZED INDUSTRIES

The foregoing analysis makes it clear that government has a wide range of choices associated with the privatization process. These choices involve not just the decision to transfer ownership from the public to the private sector, but also whether to restructure the industry, whether to introduce competition, whether to regulate the industries' prices and quality, and if so, how. Thus, privatization is a highly planned process, which may involve government in continuing to make a range of decisions in the period after privatization. The method pursued here is to examine the different spheres in which government decisions are made on privatization, by looking at the pattern of control and accountability of these industries in the product market, the capital market, and through regulation. Each of these spheres has an extensive body of economic theory associated with it. It is apparent, however, that government choices are dictated not just by economic theory, but also by a range of other political and economic factors.

2.1 The product market and industry structure

To advocate the advantages of the product market as a means of getting closer to both allocative and productive efficiency does not necessarily entail commitment to *laissez-faire* policies. If market incentives are real, they can, in theory, be harnessed towards achieving political objectives. The product market can be planned and structured for competition. Where this is not possible, other forms may be used to provide similar incentives. These forms include common carriage regulation, franchising, and contractual relations. All these forms of incentive are dependent on continuing state involvement, in terms of either competition policy and/or more direct regulation. While such policies may be identified as desirable theoretically, it is unclear in what political or economic conditions they are likely to be successful. The market structures in the sectors which have been affected by privatization have clearly been very diverse, both within and between sectors. So, for example, the privatized Rover Group competes with a number of competitors in what is a quite concentrated market. British Aerospace, too, is subject to a degree of international competition. British Gas, on the other hand, has a virtual monopoly of domestic supply, and the telecommunications sector is presently undergoing a transformation from the protected duopoly for the supply of fixed-link voice telephony services created at privatization of British Telecom in 1984 to a more liberalized market.

An important aspect of the economic debate has been to challenge the closure which results from characterizing an industry as a natural monopoly (Demsetz 1968; Helm 1987). In some cases artificial monopolies are identified as subsectors of industries in which a substantial degree of natural monopoly may be present, as with telecommunications apparatus and value-added network services, both liberalized under the Telecommunications Act 1981. Early on in the privatization programme Beesley and Littlechild examined potential market structures in various sectors in which there were nationalized industries, and developed a concept of 'appropriate privatization' (Beesley and Littlechild 1986: 48–55). They sought to identify those nationalized industries which could be sold and restructured to join or create competitive sectors. They distinguished good demand prospects from poor demand prospects, and markets where there was a potential for multiple suppliers from those where that potential was absent.

The group which Beesley and Littlechild argued demanded real attention as candidates for privatization and restructuring were those industries in which multiple suppliers were possible and demand prospects were good. In this group they placed electricity generation, telecommunications (excluding local), gas production, coal, and airlines. To date we have seen a degree of competition introduced into the electricity generation sector, through the break up of the CEGB into two generating companies, Powergen PLC and National Power PLC, and a company owned by the distribution companies to manage the electricity grid, National Grid PLC (Vickers and Yarrow 1991; Veljanovski 1990*b*: 30–4). In 1990 four new, smaller entrants to the generation market were licensed by the Office of Electricity Regulation (Office of Electricity Regulation 1991: 5). With regard to voice telephony, there remain technological problems to be overcome before the market for fixed-link voice telephony services can be fully liberalized. But the government has signalled an end to the duopoly policy, and now plans to 'consider on its merits any application for a licence to offer telecommunications services over fixed links within the UK' (DTI 1991: para. 3.6). This policy includes providing encouragement to the development of the assets of public sector utilities, such as British Rail's own telecommunications network, subject to restraints on unfair competition (ibid. para. 8.4). An important point here is that competition in these sectors is planned and structured. In this sense it is no different from creating a regulatory environment which emulates the effects of competition.

While some sectors seemed amenable to the creation of competitive conditions, in others this was less likely to occur. In the category 'good demand prospects, single supplier', Beesley and Littlechild placed electricity distribution and grid, local telecommunications, gas distribution, and airports. This group are quite capable of being sold, it was suggested, but are not capable of being restructured to allow competition, and are therefore likely to be subject to regulation to prevent monopoly abuse. Notwithstanding this analysis, the government is in fact attempting to promote competition in the local voice telephony market from the cable TV companies. Monopoly power is less of a problem in the single-supplier group with poor demand prospects, but they are not likely to be attractive candidates for full privatization. In this group we find rail, post, and waterways. The claim that monopoly is likely to continue in some sectors suggests a need in these sectors for different approaches. Just as competition can be planned, so can substitutes to competition be planned, in terms of contestable markets, franchising, rules requiring common carriage, and so on, in sectors where only one supplier is present.

The theory of contestable markets provides an argument that the product market may control business production and supply decisions, even though there may be no other companies at present supplying in that market (Vickers and Yarrow 1988: 53–61). This theory focuses on potential rather than actual competition, and thus places emphasis on the regulatory problem of the conditions of entry into, and exit from the market (Utton 1986: 196; Button 1985; Bailey and Baumol 1984; Baumol *et al.* Willig 1982). The argument is that where entry and exit are unrestricted and where existing suppliers price above marginal cost, then new entrants will appear, and excess profits will disappear. Existing producers subject to potential competition will produce efficiently.

Government policy on telecommunications has focused on the ultimate objective of removing entry barriers (DTI 1991; Utton 1986: 211; Beesley and Laidlaw 1989). But it is not clear how amenable a sector such as local networks is to the creation of a contestable market (Vickers and Yarrow 1988: 61; Beesley and Littlechild 1989). There may be too many political factors associated with continuing state involvement to make the market truly contestable. Remaining issues concern the propensity of the government to intervene, the ability of outsiders to obtain information, and the potential for anti-competitive practices. (On predatory pricing see Veljanovski 1987: 143 and Vickers 1985.) On the first point, if, for example, a change of government or a severe case of market failure were to occur in a service as basic as telecommunications, then intervention of a kind not now predictable might occur. The argument about government intervention is probably less strong in a case like telecommunications, where the publicly owned producers have been privatized, than in the case of industries still partly in public ownership—for example, urban transport (Utton 1986: 203). The theory suggests a need to pay attention to sunk costs; because if they are high, they may provide a barrier to entry, even where government has sought to deregulate entry barriers. Given the fairly heavy entry costs in terms of investment in capital equipment associated with telecommunications and this factor of uncertainty, we may doubt that the market will be perfectly contestable. An alternative mode of service provision suggested by the theory is that of continuing public ownership of capital, with facilities being leased to service-providing companies (Button 1985: 21). Such a policy is not inconsistent with organization of an industry on market principles. This potential suggests that the emphasis on ownership may be misplaced in terms of achieving the stated objectives of improved efficiency in key industries (ibid. 22).

The theory of contestable markets argues, then, for deregulation of entry barriers. An alternative approach is to permit private development —for example, of networks—but then require open access to those networks, a form of common carriage (Veljanovski 1987: 43). It is possible that equal access in telecommunications may develop towards a form of common carriage, although the regulatory and technical problems remain substantial (DTI 1991: para 7.12; Office of Gas Supply 1991: ch. 3). Oftel has proposed that British Telecom separate, for accounting purposes, its network infrastructure from its provision of services, in order to facilitate the regulation of access to the network on non-discriminatory terms (Carsberg 1992*b*). Other sectors which might be amenable to a common carriage policy include gas distribution and railways. The White Paper announcing the privatization of British Rail proposes initially to separate the British Rail's track and other infrastructure from service provision. Rail track will then lease the use of lines not only to British Rail's service divisions, but also to private companies (Department of Transport 1992).

A similar effect to contestable markets might be secured through franchising (Demsetz 1968: 86). Though both are theories of 'the hidden rivalry for incumbency', in the former that rivalry is always present, whereas in the latter it occurs before production begins only and at the time for renewal of the franchise. The former theory argues for taking down barriers to entry, whereas the latter recognizes that barriers may be necessary once the franchise is agreed (Williamson 1976). A whole range of criteria can be employed in selecting franchisees, as we have seen in relation to the new independent television franchises (Jones 1989). The government has indicated that the method by which passenger rail routes will be privatized will be to franchise routes presently operated by British Rail to private sector companies (Department of Transport 1992). The franchise conditions can act as a form of control over such matters as pricing, universal supply, and quality. However, the best potential for franchising is in conditions where there are many potential competitors, where sunk costs are not high, and where technological change is not rapid and uncertainty not great (Vickers and Kay 1990: 243). So, while this may be an appropriate regulatory form for commercial television, it is perhaps less appropriate to the public utilities. The problem of sunk costs in the utility sectors can be overcome in the way suggested above, by permitting equal access of all service-providers to a network which may be either privately owned, as in the case of telecommunications, or publicly owned, as in the case of the rail network. Other equipment such as rolling stock for railways may be leased, in the same way that passenger aircraft are presently leased to airlines.

It has been argued that the process of transferring ownership has focused too little on the relationship of the privatized industries to their consumers (Graham 1992; Saunders and Harris 1990). There is little scope for consumer representation in decision making by either the utility companies or the regulators (see Graham 1992 for a survey of legislative provision for consumer representation in the utility sectors). It might be argued, of course, that marketization of what were state monopolies does amount to an empowerment of consumers through the exercise of their preferences. However, where industries have remained highly concentrated, this argument loses some of its force, particularly where service-providers have proved resistant to treating the users of services as sovereign consumers. One response, adopted by both regulators and government ministers, has been to force a stronger consumer orientation upon public service generally, under the rubric of the Citizen's Charter programme (HM Treasury 1991; Barron and Scott 1992). In the utility sectors this resulted in a policy of removing the immunity from giving compensation previously enjoyed by the public utilities and the adoption of relations between consumers and industry involving clearer specification of quasi-contractual or contractual rights and remedies, greater use of performance indicators, and compulsory performance standards to be set by the regulators (Competition and Service (Utilities) Act 1992; Harden 1992; ch. 2; Graham 1992; Carsberg 1990: 93–4; Office of Telecommunications 1990: 10).

We find, then, that whereas early transfers of ownership revealed little concern with market structure and competition in the product market, government and regulators have more recently been more concerned with breaking up vertically integrated monopolies and with introducing a variety of forms of competition or surrogates to competition. The pattern proposed for the privatization of British Rail draws on a variety of restructuring techniques in a pragmatic way. At the time of writing it is unclear how the rail privatization will use the potentially contradictory techniques of open access to rail tracks and franchising of passenger services (*Independent*, 5 July 1992: 6; 15 July 1992: 20). As with earlier privatizations, the full implications for regulation and the character of continuing state intervention to provide for investment and consumer protection are only likely to become apparent with experience.

2.2 The capital market

Whereas the traditional focus of the relationship between markets and efficiency has been on the product market, much of the literature in the past twenty years has focused on the capital market and its impact on corporate decision making. In the capital market, again we find a number of norms, drawn from economics, under the rubric 'the market for corporate control', which seem to argue for restructuring of companies and regulation of securities markets. Regulation is needed in particular to facilitate disclosure of accurate information, prevent insider trading, and promote the free transferability of shares. Company law has traditionally emphasized the direct control of shareholders, who seek-profit maximization as the principal spur to efficiency in the company. However, the separation between ownership and control has long been recognized in the case of the majority of large companies. Limited liability means that the risk of the shareholder is limited to the value of the share and that the incentive for monitoring, particularly where portfolios are diverse, is diminished (Veljanovski 1987: 90–1). Individual shareholders, even if they were interested, might have very little impact on the decisions of managers. Institutional shareholders do seem to have some under-used potential for impact (Farrar and Russell 1984).

Government policy on privatization was ostensibly partly oriented towards harnessing the market for corporate control to the purpose of ensuring the efficiency of privatized industries. But, as a number of commentators have pointed out, the methods of privatization, the continuing governmental controls over a number of the privatized industries, and the inevitable uncertainty over the future of the industries have tended to provide obstacles to the free operation of that market (Caves 1990; Utton 1986: 103). Caves (1990: 160), for example, has suggested that in order to reduce free-riding by small shareholders, it would have been necessary to ensure that shares in the privatized companies were acquired in large blocks. The government's policy to promote wider share ownership, while it may not meet the objectives of harnessing the market for corporate control, may have the effect of requiring the companies to balance shareholders' interests in dividends against their interests in low prices as consumers of the utility service. In companies where the total numbers of shares are large, as in the case of the privatized companies, the scope for classical shareholder accountability is very limited. At best, we might see the impact of shareholders selling shares in large numbers rendering the company vulnerable to take-over, and, at the outside, institutional investors seeking to influence decision making (Prosser and Graham 1987: 38–41).

We find also that the free transferability of shares in many of these companies is compromised by the holding by government of golden shares, which allow in some cases the expropriation of shareholdings that have grown too large and in other cases restrictions on transfer of shares. The golden share is a special rights, redeemable preference share. The Articles of Association of the company, prepared by the government, state that certain actions will be regarded as alterations in the rights of that share, and therefore require the consent of the shareholder. Matters which have been included include sales of a specified proportion of assets of the company and build-up of shareholding by foreign investors (Prosser and Graham 1991: ch. 5; 1987; 1988). Other related techniques include entrenching limitations on shareholdings in the Articles. As Prosser and Graham (1987: 38) point out, the potential here is to replace the market for corporate control by negotiation with government (cf. Caves 1990: 159, which advocates a substantial retention of shares in the privatized industries by government as enhancing the operation of the market for corporate control).

Managerial freedom may to some extent be restricted by the right of the government to appoint one or two of the directors in some of the privatized companies. The appointment of government-nominated directors has a long pedigree in companies set up by the Companies Act, in which the government has a substantial interest, financial or otherwise. On privatization of a number of companies, the government has retained the right to appoint directors, although there seems to be no principled basis on which this has occurred (Prosser and Graham 1987: 34). The inactivity of such directors, combined with their duty in law to act in the best interests of the company, rather than of a particular shareholder, has meant that this device has had little perceptible impact. Employees' involvement in the transfer of ownership of public corporations, and therefore in the control and accountability of the companies after privatization, has varied in degree. In the early privatizations, about 90 per cent of employees took advantage of the opportunities given to acquire shares in the companies for which they worked (J. Moore 1986b: 88). Emphasis on the incentive effects of privatization gives employee participation a special role. Employees may be in a good position to assess the potential efficiency gains after privatization, and if they hold a substantial number of shares in the company, may have sufficient incentive to seek greater involvement in the governance of the company (Caves 1990:163). Employee share ownership has also been claimed to have a good effect on industrial relations (J. Moore 1986*b*: 89). However, much must depend on the underlying strength of the industry. So, for example, the decline of employment and employee power in the mining industry is likely to continue if that industry is privatized as under public ownership.

2.3 Regulation

Public regulation of private sector enterprises through the use of independent regulatory agencies does not have a strong tradition in Britain. This may, of itself, result in a timidity in passing governmental powers to agencies that would not be found in jurisdictions with greater experience of such forms, such as the United States. It should be added that the style of regulation in the United Kingdom differs markedly from that in the United States. UK regulatory procedures are designed to encourage consensual decision making between regulator and regulatee, and are subject to only minimal rights of consultation with interested parties, and only minimal opportunities for judicial review (Selzer 1991). The use of the regulatory agency form preceded the development of privatization in the 1980s. Examples included the Office of Fair Trading, the Health and Safety Executive, the Monopolies and Mergers Commission, and the Independent Television Commission. Horizontal forms of regulation have been most evident, as with competition and occupational health and safety. Competition policy in the UK has essentially been concerned with the keeping under review both levels of industrial concentration and the development of anti-competitive practices (Whish 1989; Craig 1987). Alongside the strategies of deregulation and privatization pursued by the Conservative government elected in 1979 was the introduction of powers for the Secretary of State to refer public sector bodies to the Monopolies and Mergers Commission for the purposes of an efficiency audit (Competition Act, 1980, sect 11; Chiplin and Wright 1982; Whish 1989: 104–6). This provides an example of the adaptation of regulatory techniques developed in the private sector to the public sector, a transfer also attempted with the creation of VFM (value-for-money) audits in the National Audit Act 1983 (McEldowney 1991).

Techniques of public regulation of private sector enterprises have assumed new importance with the creation of a number of new regulatory offices, the Office of Telecommunications, Office of Water Supply, Office of Gas Supply, and Office of Electricity Regulation, plus the National Rivers Authority, as part of the privatization programme. Regulation may be seen as the quid pro quo for the grant of monopoly status and special powers, such as those contained in the

Telecommunications Code, the Gas Code, and the Public Electricity Supply Code (McAuslan and McEldowney 1988). These new agencies have been created in those industries which retain substantial monopoly characteristics—telecommunications, gas, electricity, and water—with the stated objectives of promoting competition or, where this is not possible, providing a surrogate to competition, particularly through the regulation of pricing and quality. Related to this has been an objective of ensuring the continuing fulfilment of social obligations. Social objectives for an industry may be a regulatory concern irrespective of levels of competition in the market. However, even where the pursuit of economic objectives is paramount, the means for their pursuit is not capable of precise a priori formulation. Hence regulators have substantial amounts of discretion, and the regulatory process is characterized by a substantial degree of learning on the part of the regulator and bargaining with industry and other interests. Prosser (1986: 144) suggests that the open-endedness of such regulatory decision making is the crucial argument for greater openness, allowing all information to be brought forward and the basis of regulatory policy to be clear. Widespread public concern about high profits and high executive salaries in the utility companies has reflected badly on their regulators. There are indications from all four of the regulatory offices that tougher regulatory patterns are likely to emerge in the future (Veljanovski 1991a; Carsberg 1992a, 1992b; *Guardian*, 10 June 1992: 11; *Independent*, 11 June 1992: 29).

The design and implementation of regulatory structures presents a number of difficulties. Chief among these is the task of obtaining information in order to regulate (Utton 1986: 217). It is the asymmetry of information between regulator and regulatee which, it is argued, renders this regulatory function amenable to agency costs analysis. Obtaining information as to industry costs is considerably easier where there are a number of companies in the same market, even though they may have regional monopolies, as with electricity distribution and water supply (Prosser and Graham 1991: 188). Weaknesses in the Director General of Telecommunications' (DGTs) powers, especially with regard to the acquisition of accounting information and performance indicators, were not repeated with regard to OfWat and Offer (Water Act 1989, sect 33, Electricity Act 1989, sect. 28; Prosser and Graham 1991: 217). The Competition and Service (Utilities) Act 1992, has substantially improved the ability of all the regulatory offices to collect information and to set performance indicators (Graham 1992).

The main instrument of regulation has been the licence or authorization granted to the industry actors. In the case of the Public Telecommunications Operators licence issued to British Telecom, it is the instrument used to set out obligations on universal supply, supply of call-boxes, emergency services, pricing, and interconnection (DTI 1984). We may conceive of three stages in the life of these authorizations: grant, continuation, and modification (Prosser 1989: 145–6; Beesley and Littlechild 1989: 454). In each case the right to grant authorizations and to set conditions is held by the Secretary of State, though in some cases that authority may be delegated to the regulatory office, as has happened in the case of generation licences under section 6(1) of the Electricity Act 1989. One function exercised here is control over entry to the industry; a second is to set the conditions under which those companies permitted entry are required to provide services. Powers to enforce the authorizations are held by the director-generals of each industry. Here, clearly, information about the continuing operation of each company is important. The modification of authorizations, designed to deal with change in each industry, are made on the recommendation of the directors-general, subject to the consent of the companies involved. Where the company fails to agree to a modification, then director-general must make a reference to the Monopolies and Mergers Commission (MMC). The MMC inquiry starts from first principles, examining whether the company is acting in the public interest, and if not, whether the proposed authorization modification will improve things. The fact of this inquiry being a new consideration of the issues, with public interest criteria applying and the time that this involves, means that there is a strong incentive for the director-general and the company to agree on the modification and negotiate until agreement is found.

Price controls based on caps linked to the Retail Price Index (RPI) plus or minus a given figure (RPI – X or RPI + K), which were imposed on the utility companies, have provided a major focus for observation of the new regulation. As Beesley and Littlechild have pointed out, the setting of X by the Secretary of State initially is a decision which has regard to all the parameters of regulation, as all the other authorization conditions are set at this time (Beesley and Littlechild 1989: 457). On resetting the price, there is therefore much less room for the director-general to manœuvre. This is, first, because other authorization conditions are not to be reset at this time, and secondly, because the director-general needs to balance the interests of shareholders and customers, which the government, as owner at the time the authorization is given, does not have to do. On this analysis, the calculation becomes a fairly precise calculation of the price increases which will allow the companies to maintain a rate of return that will keep shareholders happy and allow increased costs to be adequately reflected in the price to customers. Scope for bargaining remains in relation to productivity improvements, the rate at which competition is allowed to develop, and the extent to which the director-general has information about the company (ibid. 461). The resetting of

X for British Telecom in 1989 at 4.5 apparently did not adversely affect
the share price of the company. However, the 1992 price review proposals
were followed by a fall in the share price of 7.5 points (*Financial Times*,
10 June 1992).

Relations between the directors-general and the utility companies have
varied. For a long period British Telecom and Mercury had fairly smooth
relations with the DGT. So, for example, British Telecom agreed to further reductions in its prices on the RPI – X model, the figure for X set in
1984, 3, having been increased in 1989 to 4.5 and from August 1991 to
6.25 (DTI 1991: para. 6.27). Oftel's 1992 British Telecom price review evidences a significant break with past patterns of consensual indirect regulation. The then DGT, Sir Bryan Carsberg, issued a consultative
document in the usual way, and received many detailed comments from
interested parties. However, when Oftel's final proposals were published,
they proved to be tougher and more extensive than many commentators
expected. British Telecom indicated that it found the proposals unaccept-
ably harsh, but the DGT pre-empted British Telecom's concern by saying
that it was not appropriate to negotiate over the proposals. If British
Telecom could not accept them, then they would be referred to the
MMC. Subsequently it was suggested that Oftel did in fact negotiate over
some of the less central elements of the package (*Evening Standard*, 15
July 1992: 27). The package of proposals was concerned both with supporting the trend towards greater competition in the telecommunications
market, while at the same time preventing abuse of monopoly position.
The package of price reductions for the basic basket of services was to be
fixed at RPI – 7.5, in a way which prevented a rebalancing such that the
price of any service increased at a rate above the rate of inflation.
Furthermore, bulk discounts were to be removed from the basket with
considerable financial consequences. Overall, the price controls proposed
to come into place in August 1993 are designed to reduce British
Telecom's rate of return from 20 per cent to a figure between 16.5 and
18.5 per cent, depending on how much competition develops in the industry. Even more controversial than this is the direct intervention of Oftel
in British Telecom's investment programme. A condition of the pricing
package is that British Telecom must virtually complete the digital network by 1997. This form of direct intervention in investment decisions,
normally associated with public ownership, may have considerable implications in the balance between regulator and regulatee if repeated in the
other utility sectors. A further radical aspect of the proposals mentioned
above is the separation of network provision from services for accounting
purposes, a proposal designed to deny British Telecom the advantages
associated with vertical integration (Carsberg 1992*a*, 1992*b*). British Gas
and the director-general of Gas Supply have also had tense relations, the

new price cap for British Gas having been agreed only after the director-general threatened to refer all its tariffs to the MMC (*Independent*, 30 Apr. 1991).

It is apparent, then, that the control and accountability of the privatized utility companies constitute a phenomenon of great complexity. In both structuring the industries and regulating them, the government and the regulators tread difficult paths, attempting to balance a range of diffuse interests which include shareholders, creditors, and domestic and commercial users. The pattern of control and accountability which results is dynamic. Ownership patterns have been subject to a greater concentration of shares with institutional investors, with smaller proportions being held by small individual investors. Industry structures have been fluid, with new competitors entering various parts of the telecommunications market, and now even the voice telephony market, and energy suppliers increasingly competing for large customer contracts. As the regulatory offices have learnt more about the industries they regulate and achieved greater expertise and confidence, they have shown themselves more willing to take on their regulatees, rather than follow the pattern of consensual regulation apparently anticipated by the privatizing legislation. This dynamic pattern pays lip-service to theories of industrial economics. However, it is apparent that the decisions and outcomes, in terms of ownership, industry structure, and regulation have been determined by a much broader range of political and economic factors. The shift in policy emphasis away from transfer of ownership *per se* towards restructuring of industries and tougher regulation may reflect the political failure of the earlier privatizations and the greater success associated with experience.

14

Risk, Trust, and the Market for Corporate Control

JOSEPH McCAHERY

INTRODUCTION

In the 1980s the American corporate economy experienced a massive increase in liquidity. This increase was linked to two sources: (1) an increase in internally generated funds within firms which were employed for the purposes of strategic acquisitions; and (2) the introduction of high-yield bonds which made possible the acquisitions of large corporations by relatively small firms or groups of investors (Jensen 1987). As a result of this massive increase in liquidity, there was a huge wave of hostile take-overs (Jarrell *et al.* 1988). The emergence of a 'self-regulating' market for corporate control redefined the traditional relationships among shareholders, managers, and non-equity stakeholders.

Business scholars, lawyers, and economists alike argue that the market for corporate control fundamentally changed the legal and corporate landscape in the United States and, to a certain extent, Britain in the 1980s (J. Gordon 1991; Coffee 1991; Jensen 1987; Coffee 1987; Chiplin and Wright 1987). In support of this proposition, evidence is offered regarding the scale, intensity, and efficiency gains of the merger activity. For example, Jensen observes that during the mid to latter half of the 1980s, corporate control transactions exceeded the 100 billion dollar mark each year (Jensen 1987: 314). These take-overs were dominated by a particular driving force: the desire to bust up the conglomerates formed during the merger wave of the 1960s and 1970s, which contributed to the furious pace of the market activity in the mid-1980s.[1] The conglomerate structure was an attractive target because it was easier to value (J. Gordon 1990).[2] However, there were only a small number of

[1] During the 1960s and 1970s most mergers were conglomerate, not horizontal (Scherer 1986). It is well documented that the conglomerate strategy was a dismal failure: '[L]arge scale movement of U.S. manufacturing toward unrelated diversification is now thought by many observers (including Porter) to have been unsuccessful. The high level of divestiture of peripheral businesses by diversified corporations beginning in the mid-1970s is almost surely a response to that failure' (Shleifer and Vishny 1988: 13).

[2] To be sure, there were other considerations behind these acquisitions—tax gains, management entrenchment, strategic investments, etc.—although the dominant consensus is that

conglomerates which were actually dismantled and whose assets were spun off to their most valued user (Gilson and Kraakman 1991); further-more, directors and managers themselves, in response to the stock-market's judgment that the conglomerate merger wave of the 1960s was, in effect, an economic mistake (ibid.), restructured their asset portfolios by spinning off unrelated divisions which were obtained during the con-glomerate acquisition phase. There is evidence to suggest that manage-ments' motive for restructuring the corporate asset and ownership structure reflects their desire further to entrench themselves, by improving their bargaining position, at shareholders' expense (Dann and DeAngelo 1988).

The changes involved in these transactions have been the subject of intense debate (see generally Bhagat *et al.* 1990; A. Auerbach 1988). Economists have attempted to determine whether take-over activity pro-motes economic efficiency or not (Franks *et al.* 1991). More specifically, some economists have attempted, with varying degrees of rigour and suc-cess, to measure the relative efficiency of take-overs as a means for rede-ploying assets. Indeed, one school of thought, heavily identified with the liberal wing of the Democratic Party in the USA, argues that take-over activity damages the productivity of firms, causing managers to plan for the short term, resulting in a reduction of expensive (but necessary) investment in human capital, R & D, and fixed capital and a long-run decline in economic productivity (see, e.g., Shleifer and Summers 1988; Shleifer and Vishny 1988).[3] These critics argue that proponents of the market for corporate control rely on an especially narrow conception of

---

the 1980s movement was motivated by the liquidation value of the target's assets. Certain commentators note, however, that the 1980s take-over movement was primarily motivated by firms acquiring businesses with similar assets. On this view, corporate managers, despite the threats of take-over and other disciplinary and market pressures, invested firm resources, even if they were not *ex ante* value-maximizing, in order further to entrench their firm-specific investments (Shleifer and Vishny 1989: 126). Also, a study by Bhagat *et al.* (1990) of 62 hostile take-overs between 1984 and 1986, in which the price paid or offered was higher than $50 million, shows that while tax savings, lay-offs, and strategic investment cuts were important reasons for the efficiency improvements in the post-take-over experience, 60% of the efficiency gains, according to the authors, came from transferring the target's assets to their most valued use.

[3] Coffee (1984: 1148 n. 5) summarizes dissenting views; see also (Tirole 1988: 43–4). Take-overs, according to Tirole, often produce perverse incentives for managers, and as a result are inefficient, e.g., the existence of the threat of take-over reduces a manager's incen-tive to make long-term investments, since she will not have an opportunity to capture her future rents. Moreover, the increased risk injects a new level of insecurity into the firm for junior and senior management. In response, managers disinvest in firm-specific assets, and are over-concerned about their career prospects, which may lead them to make decisions which are contrary to the interests of the residual risk-bearer. Finally, because the relation-ship between worker and manager may be short, the element of trust may not develop between them.

efficiency,[4] limited to notions of improvements in management or gains from organizational synergy. Herman and Lowenstein (1987) for example, argue that acquisitions motivated by the undervalued market values of the firms do not function solely to remove inefficient managements or to improve the deployment of assets, but rather reflect an operational flaw in the share market and its valuation process. Furthermore, these critics argue that the initial vision of the control market (offered by Manne 1965), which characterized the control market in terms of competing managers attempting to acquire assets in order to put them to their most efficient use, has been fundamentally reoriented by several factors, essentially by the competitive nature of the market and the attraction of premium short-term earnings.

Shleifer and Vishny (1988), for example, have endorsed the externalities perspective, arguing that most transactions have both winners (shareholders of the target, raider, etc.) and losers (non-management constituencies such as employees, suppliers, communities, and creditors). In the wake of the hostile take-over, they argue that acquiring shareholders appropriate stakeholders' *ex post* rents in the implicit contracts, which accounts for the efficiency gains.[5] They argue that the existing efficiency studies on take-overs are theoretically suspect, because they evaluate the wealth effects solely in terms of shareholder wealth. Embracing the property rights view of the firm (which conceives of the firm in terms of a set of *ex ante* incomplete contracts, in which the ownership of the asset confers certain *ex post* rights, which affect the bargaining power of the players and the *ex post* distribution of the organization's quasi-rent),[6] Shleifer and Vishny go on to argue that shareholders, when making a hostile purchase of an asset, are not in fact acquiring the rights to maximum feasible profits, but rather, are obtaining control over an asset which cannot assure them a satisfactory return on their investment.

Other theorists, by contrast, argue that take-overs improve the overall

---

[4] e.g., L. Summers (1990) argues that the reallocation of assets, which he speculates must logically involve the transfer of earnings from where they carry a low price/earnings ratio to where they carry a high ratio, must result in increased value only for those agents involved in the transactions. He cautions that the alleged efficiency gains which occurred as a result of take-over activity in the 1980s should be set against the background of a share market which tripled. Summers argues that the real source of value may be traceable to the ability of the acquirers to obtain reasonably cheap sources of financing for purchase of the stocks at an attractive rate. However, it is not at all clear that the value captured in such take-overs derives from efficiency gains, since other sources of value (e.g., lost tax revenue or undervalued human resources) may be very high, and dwarf the efficiency effects.

[5] This argument has also been advanced by Shleifer and Summers (1988). For critical accounts of the logic of this claim, see Holmstrom (1988) and Williamson (1988*b*).

[6] The property rights theory of the firm has been developed in Grossman and Hart (1986); O. Hart and Holmstrom (1986); Tirole (1988); O. Hart (1989); Milgrom and Roberts (1990); Kreps (1990); Holmstrom and Milgrom (1991). For a critical appreciation of the property rights standpoint, see Holmstrom and Tirole (1989) and Williamson (1990, 1991*b*).

productivity of the economy. Proponents of the market for corporate control offer diverse reasons for the efficiency gains that result from hostile take-overs. For example, Jarrell *et al.* (1988) argue that shareholders of target companies clearly gain significant wealth. In particular, some empirical work suggests that the source of value in hostile take-overs is not traceable to the stock-market underpricing stock or short-term myopia (J.C. Stein 1988). Furthermore, empirical evidence shows that labour cost saving following hostile take-overs is a marginal component of the apparent wealth gains from take-overs.[7] There is considerable controversy over the tax gains in take-overs. However, the view that tax gains are embodied as trapped equity has attracted few new proponents since recent share repurchase data failed to confirm the tax gains hypothesis (J. Gordon 1990). Commentators generally agree that the major source of value results from the reallocation of assets following the completion of the take-over (see, e.g., Bhagat *et al.* 1990: 34–44; Jarrell *et al.* 1988: 57–8). Furthermore, the evidence of the 1980s seems to show that friendly take-overs largely function in order to reallocate assets to firms operating in related businesses. The value gains from these strategic acquisitions may result from efficiency gains in production and distribution, as well as from other gains such as white collar lay-offs, tax savings, and R & D cutbacks (Jarrell *et al.* 1988: 57).

Against this background, the efficiency consequences resulting from these transactions are directly realized by the wealth transfers to the shareholders. The external costs appear to be low compared to the efficiency gains. L. Summers (1990), however, suspects that a closer empirical investigation might reveal that the efficiency gains obtained from horizontal acquisitions, which were the main type of transaction in the 1980s, are more closely tied to other sources of value, which would mean higher external costs.[8] Furthermore, it is difficult to ascertain whether the post-merger efficiencies are the result of increased market concentration and market power or the result of lower transaction costs. Theorists on both sides of the divide concede, however, that the strategic combinations of the 1980s resulted in abnormal increases in stock-market prices, which indicates that there was a source of value created. Central to my discussion is the claim made by proponents of the implicit con-

---

[7] See Bhagat *et al.* (1990: 52–4) arguing that savings are especially important in the case of leveraged buy-outs (LBOs) and management buy-outs (MBOs), Gilson et al. (1987); A. Auerbach and Reishus 1988 (dismissing the role of taxes as a source of value based on the tax procedure of combining losses with profits). But see L. Summers (1990) (rejecting Auerbach and Reishus's investigation, since everyone agrees that the ability to combine losses with profits is insignificant).

[8] Certain theorists have argued that the value gains from hostile take-overs might reflect a market overestimation of the value of the strategic acquisitions, and therefore the level of gains could be questionable (Bhagat, *et al.* 1990: 57–8).

tracts theory that take-overs are motivated by the wealth gains from breaching implicit contracts. In particular, Coffee argues that much of the shareholders' wealth gains are the result of the rents captured from stakeholders (Coffee 1987: 111; see also Shleifer and Summers 1988: 42–3; but see Holmstrom 1988: 57–8).

The debate among economists is concerned with the existence, size, and location of the wealth gains. My focus in this chapter concerns the related, but rather different, legal issues: specifically, the strategic relationship between managers and shareholders in the firm and how the 1980s market changed that conflict.

Hence, I wish to consider the primary justification for the market for corporate control: the market as an effective check on managerial discretion. In section 2, I examine the historical dimension of the debate, concentrating on the managerial theorists and their explanation of why managers prefer to satisfice rather than maximize profits. In the next section, I link the discussion of managerial theories with Coffee's differential risk hypothesis. Coffee's theory is analysed in detail, since it constitutes the controversial claim for the 1980s hostile take-over movement that the asymmetry of risk between manager and shareholder explains the rapid changes in the market for corporate control. I attempt to show that Coffee's model of risk asymmetry provides only a partial explanation of the 1980s merger movement. I argue that the conflict between manager and shareholders is an unsteady game, which depends on risk, resources, and time, and that the competition for control over the firm is dependent upon the outcomes of this continuous struggle, which often involves political lobbying by threatened managers to protect their firm-specific capital from expropriation (Romano 1990). Critical discussion of the differential risk model is particularly relevant to recent debates regarding the impact and justification of statutes protecting stakeholders who are not equity participants in the firm (Coffee 1990; Rock 1992). The new normative vision of corporate control challenges the shareholder maximization norm by emphasizing the legally enforceable obligations of stakeholders. The articulated political logic of the stakeholder coalition model is qualified and supported by the device of the implicit contract (Rock 1992: 545–8).

2. THE HISTORICAL ANTECEDENTS

In this section I survey the development of the modern firm. This is a well-travelled path (Bratton 1989*b*). The aim of this discussion is to demonstrate that the problem of control within the firm is long-standing and is connected with the modern changes in the internal organization of the firm.

The early development of corporate theory was concerned with the question of how to resolve the alleged problems which occur as a result of the separation of ownership and control of the firm. The consolidation of the corporate firm in the 1920s, and the survival of such firms following the crash and the great depression, was the historical background against which the emergence of managerialist theories of the firm can be understood. In the United States, the growth of the firm was facilitated by the departure from the unanimous shareholder approval rule, which introduced the flexibility necessary for management to consolidate small firms into large, multi-divisional ('M-firm') companies (Note 1989a: 824). The rapid growth in firm size was accomplished principally through public issuance of shares which, over time, further diminished the leverage of shareholders to alter management's power within the firm. As a result, the changing position of the shareholder altered the legal theory of the corporation, giving management enhanced control and relative independence from individual shareholders.[9]

The growing importance of the firm, the increasing dominance of managers and the passivity of shareholders, and the failure of neo-classical theory to explain the development of the firm formed the practical and conceptual background against which Berle and Means wrote *The Modern Corporation and Private Property*. In their classic work, they observed that shareholders were effectively powerless to exercise control over the firm, because ownership was so dispersed and because the residual risk-bearers were, in effect, incapable of co-ordinated action against incumbent management.[10] The decline of the single-owner firm, as the story goes, dissolved the significance of the individual entrepreneur as both residual risk-bearer and manager. Thus, with the 'splitting of the ownership atom', the professional manager commanded greater control over the firm's resources (Coleman 1990: 457).

[9] Dan-Cohen (1986) provides support for this account. He states that research conducted since Berle and Means's classic study 'confirms the radical separation of stock ownership from control in the large corporations which these authors have emphasized' (Dan-Cohen 1986: 18 n. 20; see also Blumberg 1975). Moreover, Dan-Cohen notes that, along with the decline in the classical picture of the corporation, there has been a dramatic decline in the significance of the individual shareholder. The extant empirical studies indicate that, historically, investment funds available to corporations were generated either from a firm's internal free cash flow or by institutional investors. Thus, the historical insight which follows is twofold: first, the splitting of the ownership atom provides a degree of autonomy from the individual shareholder; and secondly, the individual shareholder is no longer anchored to a single firm, but rather is spread across many firms.

[10] Berle and Means detected that shareholders have a collective action problem. The dispersion of shareholders leads to rational apathy, in which each shareholder has a preference, in the absence of incentives, to avoid the costs of monitoring management. There can be little doubt that by the 1920s and 1930s management and shareholders had reached an implicit agreement that managers would 'maintain stable dividends in return for the freedom to pursue a "growth" strategy' (Bratton 1989b: 1492–3). Bratton argues that this agreement permitted managers to raise capital internally, and thereby avoid market review of their performance.

Due to the change in investment patterns, Berle and Means suggested that there is a problem of corporate control.[11] Recently, Bratton (1989*b*: 1491–4) has interpreted the Berle and Means thesis as offering a combined institutional and contractual mechanism for confronting the problem of the fractured ownership structure. For Berle and Means, management is responsible for deployment of the firm-specific factors of production, whereas shareholders functioned as residual risk-bearers and suppliers of equity. In turn, the share market functions as the institution of mediation between management and shareholder, providing both monitoring services and exit for any discouraged shareholders. Hence, the corporation is conceived as a bureaucratically controlled organization which is tied essentially by contract to shareholders via the securities market. Bratton argues, however, that the contract is implicit, since there is no effective means of enforcement. Thus, Berle and Means set forth the fundamental premiss of managerialism: the growing separation of ownership and control of the corporation displaces the owner-entrepreneur from the helm of the firm, which is now taken by the manager.[12] The separation of functions has created a series of potential conflicts within the firm (Coleman 1990: 456–65).

---

[11] Williamson (1971: 346) notes that the corporate control issues which Berle and Means pointed to have been alleviated as a consequence of the changes in organizational structure of the firm. In particular, Williamson (1983: 360–1) argues that most large firms in 1932 were large functionally organized (U-form) business firms. The expansion of U-form firms '(1) results in greater control-loss experience, and (2) the utility function of the firm is augmented to include the expense-preference inclinations of the functional divisions'. Williamson argues that the reshaping of the U-form firm into a divisionalized (M-form) firm, in which strategic and operating purposes were separated, significantly reduced the inefficiency in information, and reduced the opportunism of management, by introducing a firm-wide competition for resources which, at the same time, facilitated the selection of investments that created greater returns to residual risk-bearers. However, Coffee challenges Williamson's explanation for the M-form on the grounds that the development of the conglomerate had more to do with management's preference for growth than with the lowering of transaction costs (Coffee 1987: 89).

[12] Coffee (1987: 81) observes that nearly everyone who has written on the firm since the 1930s has employed Berle and Means as a conceptual springboard to introduce the modern picture of the firm. He notes, however, that most writers depart from the Berle and Means characterization of managers as potentially autonomous. In effect, the vision of the firm offered by Berle and Means is a gross exaggeration of reality, since the separation of ownership and control did not entirely release managers from activity in the interest of the residual risk-bearer. Coffee certainly argues persuasively that managers over time have rationally chosen less autonomy (in the form of bonding and monitoring devices) in order to increase the value of the firm. Generally, he is claiming that shareholders rationally rely on managers to offer guarantees in order to attract external capital, since the economic welfare of managers depends on their ability to attract future shareholders. The second point of departure from the Berle and Means thesis, and one endorsed by Coffee (1990), is that the image of the shareholder as owner of the firm should be replaced by a conception of the firm understood in terms of an equilibrium position achieved through successive rounds of strategic bargaining between shareholders, creditors, and managers. Coffee's theory of the firm, which will be

2.1 Origins of corporate control

Following Henry Manne's (1965) paper 'Mergers and the Market for Corporate Control', the study of the market for corporate control officially began. Manne articulated a powerful challenge to the conventional 'managerialist' approach to the study of merger activity, which understood merger activity in terms of increased managerial power, by stating the simple proposition that the corporate merger might serve to discipline management discretion. Following Berle and Means's (1932) explanation that the firm is characterized by the separation of ownership and control, Manne argued that the disciplining of inefficient management is best handled by an outside take-over by shareholders; hence, the stock-market operates as an external monitor of management, in that the share value of the firm reflects the relative efficiency of the management. Thus, the market for corporate control operates to discipline managements which fail to act in the interests of shareholders. Managers who do not reduce the agency costs to shareholders are subject to the threat of take-over, which clears the way for more responsive managers to organize better returns for investors.

Yet Manne's neo-classical approach to the shareholder–manager conflict was not the dominant explanation for merger activity in the 1960s and 1970s. Rather, as Bratton has noted, the managerialist interpretation was the dominant theory of merger activity during that period. Seeing management as being at the helm of the firm, managerialists argued that, by virtue of their expertise in decision making and control over the firm's information rents, managers possessed considerable discretion. The managerialist view was premissed on certain behavioural assumptions. H. A. Simon (1955), for example, argued that managers operated in a world of bounded rationality, and, as a result, managers satisfied rather than profit-maximized. On this view, because the external constraints on managers are weak, shareholders' return to capital is necessarily sub Pareto-efficient. Thus, the separation of ownership and risk-bearing functions provides the space for managers to design strategies which work against the welfare interests of the residual risk-bearer.

The Berle and Means thesis also provided the basis for the more developed managerial theories of the firm of the 1950s and 1960s, which attempted to explain the workings of the management-controlled organization on the basis of various hypotheses. The managerial discretion hypothesis essentially holds that the profit motive does not explain the structure, organization, or performance characteristics of management

explored in some detail later, operates within the orbit of the managerial game-theoretic conception developed by Aoki. Like Aoki (1988), Coffee emphasizes the importance of *ex ante* relative bargaining power in the *ex post* distribution of the residual.

(Aoki 1984: 35). Instead, it is argued that managers maximize their own interests, based on the pursuit of power, prestige, and higher remuneration associated with the growth of the firm. The managerial utility hypothesis assumes that management is resourceful and capable of using its position within the firm to grab a significant portion of the firm's rent.[13] Early theorists of the firm, for example Baumol and Williamson, observed that management had only a minimal constraint on its opportunistic use of the firm's capital. In fact, Marris offered perhaps the most interesting analysis of the managerial utility function, stating that managers used their power to expand the firm beyond the size which maximizes shareholders' wealth. On this theory, managers deploy the firm's free cash flow to expand the growth of the firm, and lessen the degree of managerial insecurity within the firm.

Marris was the first to claim that managers' security-seeking behaviour is constrained by the threat of hostile take-over (Aoki 1984: 39). The work of Marris and the economic managerialists can best be understood in terms of managers attempting to diversify their portfolio within the firm (Coffee 1987: 81). Thus, a growth policy pursued by senior managers (and supported by junior executives) is a rational strategy if, and only if, it succeeds in reducing psychic tension and the personal risk of their firm-specific investments (Aoki 1984: 41). Marris argued that the threat of take-over was the best constraint on manager's pursuit of their growth policies. However, he stated that the market for corporate control was not fully constraining, because the take-over threat did not threaten all goals such as growth which were favoured by incumbent managers. Because of market and organizational failure, Marris argued that the modern firm tends to deviate from the model profit-maximizing firm.[14] Marris's managerial growth model was heavily criticized by Solow (1971) as being indistinguishable from value-maximizing models, because firms

---

[13] Dennis Mueller notes that since profits are to some degree the property of the residual risk-bearers, managers are forced to grab the firm's residual funds in a manner that appears from the outside to be a legitimate transaction cost. Thus, because there are few ways legitimately to absorb pecuniary funds, Mueller contends that managers most often take residual profits in a non-pecuniary form (D. Mueller 1986: 44). In order to maximize their managerial utility function, Mueller claims that managers will, in the context of uncertainty, seek to acquire information so as to increase the probability of their obtaining their personal pecuniary and non-pecuniary objectives.

[14] Marris and Mueller (1980) argue that Marris's original thesis, that there is 'considerable slack in the take-over mechanism', has been confirmed by all available empirical studies conducted up to the time they drafted the article. Based on pre-1980s take-over data, they argue that the market for corporate control has failed to drive out non-shareholder welfare-maximizing behaviour and the opposite result has been instantiated (Marris and Mueller 1980: 44). This argument has been endorsed from a slightly different vantage-point by Shleifer and Vishny (1988).

with different goals will respond in precisely the same manner to changes in data; i.e., tax rates, interest rates, wages, and firm subsidies. This criticism, while analytically telling, misses the most crucial insight provided by the model: namely, that managers of large corporations prefer growth over profitability, and that this preference is evidenced in the expenditures directed toward mergers (Shleifer and Vishny 1989; P. Auerbach 1988: 122; Williamson 1987*b*: 160).

2.2 The new management environment thesis

How insightful is Marris's model today? Coffee (1987: 88), for example, has recently argued that despite the model's dated theoretical assumptions (that firms are static structures and that the external constraints on managers are weak), Marris accurately described managers' preference for growth over short-run maximized profits of the firm. In support of this proposition, Coffee argues that the recent trend toward the bust-up take-over in the late 1980s is ironically telling evidence in support of the managerial growth hypothesis. Coffee speculates that the reasons for the bust-up trend are connected to the fact that firms in the 1960s and 1970s had grown to a sub-optimal size, or that managers failed to pay out more of the residual cash flow to shareholders in the form of dividends.[15] By contrast, he offers a more subtle and original interpretation for the 1980s era of bust-up mergers. He argues (Coffee 1987: 78) that the emergence of the hostile take-over in the 1980s '[a]ltered the character of the American corporation, both in terms of its goals, span of operations, and the behaviour of its managers and in terms of its ability to compete with foreign rivals'.[16] In particular, he argues that the 1980s movement constituted a return 'to the apocryphal era that Berle and Means assumed once existed where managers were in fact dutiful agents to shareholders' (Coffee 1987: 83).

---

[15] To a certain extent Coffee relies on Jensen and Meckling's (1976) thesis in support of this observation. Unlike property rights theorists, who attach theoretical significance to the distribution of resources in calculating the costs of co-operation between owners of property rights, Jensen and Meckling are concerned with how to align principal and agent interests. For them, agency costs are inevitable, since contracts are not costlessly written or enforced. Against this background, the rational interest of the agent is to reassure investors that the firm has an institutional structure which reduces agency costs, since their information rents depend on future shareholder support. The market for corporate control operates to reduce agency costs. The threat of take-over is thought to be sufficient to overcome an agent's shirking tendencies. More recently, Jensen has argued that the central conflict between principal and agent is over the firm's free cash flow: managers tend to retain the free cash flow for their own use, and shareholders attempt to get management to disgorge the capital as dividend, and this conflict partially explains the recent trend in hostile take-over activity (Jensen 1987: 314).

[16] A recent empirical study, however, indicates that hostile take-overs do not significantly restructure the firm (Bhagat *et al.* 1990: 57).

Coffee's argument proceeds on two analytically related levels. First, he suggests, following Jensen and Williamson, that the central legal conflicts between shareholders and managers have been resolved by a series of bargained compromises which obviate the concerns expressed by Berle and Means.[17] Secondly, Coffee argues that the central conflict between managers and shareholders concerns the degree of leverage or risk in the firm.[18] Coffee makes a major contribution to the theory of the firm by showing how the concern for risk is central to both managerial and nexus-of-contracts theories[19] and by connecting this problem to the larger areas of conflict in society regarding the debate over socially acceptable levels of risk.[20]

[17] The proposition that most legal conflicts between shareholder and manager have been resolved is not entirely persuasive. Let us consider the assumptions Coffee makes. Like transaction cost and property rights theorists, he assumes that certain terms of the employment contract between managers and shareholders are incomplete. Coffee stresses that if parties find it in their interest to agree, given imperfect knowledge of the gains from strategic behaviour and the *ex post* costs of negotiations, they will be disposed to co-operate. However, this cooperative game framework is limited, since a player's normative assumptions about strategic costs will affect that player's normative position with respect to a parties disposition to co-operate (Katz 1990; see also Elster 1989).

[18] Unlike contractarians who are concerned only with welfare, Coffee (1987: 113–14) directs his analysis to the distinctively normative question of whether the law should encourage wealth transfers from non-shareholder to shareholder classes. His concern is normative, because he is guided by the fairness of the actions of shareholders and the relative positions of the parties. To be sure, Coffee, like contractarian theorists, is not anxious to craft public policy interventions that sub-optimally redistribute assets. Rather, his justification for addressing the conflict in the first place is to offer a structure whereby the parties might design welfare-maximizing private agreements.

[19] The corporate law world is dominated by the nexus-of-contracts view of the firm. More a metaphor than a theory (Bratton 1989c), it has become almost mandatory to refer to the corporation as a nexus of contracts, which involves treating the firm as a legal fiction. The strength of this approach is that it brings into focus the fact that the firm is constituted by a series of contractual relations between employees, managers, suppliers, creditors, shareholders, and bondholders (Jensen and Meckling 1976). This approach has recently come under attack from a variety of perspectives. Property rights theorists, e.g., argue that the nexus-of-contracts perspective does not explain the firm, but, rather, 'leaves the question open why certain standard forms are chosen . . . [and] begs the question of what limits the set of activities covered by a "standard form"' (O. Hart 1989: 1764). In the context of corporate law, certain critics have noted that the metaphor does not correspond to corporate practice (see Bratton, Ch. 2 in this volume). Further, the nexus-of-contract vision suffers from many technical problems when applied to corporate contracts; thus Kornhauser (1989: 1452–7) argues that the conditions of 'full information' and 'costless contracting' which define the ideal contract for Easterbrook and Fischel (1989) are undermined by the complexity of corporate decision making.

[20] The 1980s take-over wave created a ground swell response in state assemblies for the protection of non-shareholder ('stakeholder') constituencies—i.e., managers, creditors, bondholders, and communities—which were harmed as a result of the transfer of risk. The promulgation of non-shareholder constituency statutes extended the traditional doctrine of fiduciary duty, which provides that a director's only duty is to the shareholder, to a new class of beneficiaries (see Rock 1992; Gavis 1990).

2.3 Risk and the firm

In this section I will begin by analysing Coffee's risk aversion model, so as to develop some general points about the bargaining problem between managers and shareholders.

It was the higher level of risk created by the junk bond funding of hostile take-overs that threatened the position of stakeholders in the firm during the 1980s. As a response to this situation, Coffee advanced the general proposition that non-shareholders' interests should be protected from the effects of corporate restructuring. His proposition is based on a normative argument which claims that the *ex post* distribution of the shareholders' take-over premium is justified on efficiency and equity grounds. Coffee defines risk here in terms of the unbargained-for contingency which certain stakeholders are unable to insure against in the context of a hostile take-over. He challenges the alleged efficiency effects created as a result of increased risk in the firm. In terms of the efficiency claim, Coffee insists that the increased leverage does not lead to the most efficient redeployment of assets, through either financial restructuring or the market for corporate control. Secondly, the effect of the greater leverage creates diseconomies at both the state and the community level. Coffee's argument is based on a normative concern: namely, how to protect those stakeholders in the firm who have failed to safeguard their firm-specific assets from post-contractual opportunism in the form of wealth-maximizing *ex ante* agreements (see generally Shleifer and Summers 1988).

Let us first consider Coffee's proposition that the struggle over the level of risk is the fundamental conflict between shareholders and managers in the firm. Risk is an important concept in economic theory. It is normally defined as 'that part of future uncertainty that is relatively systematic and predictable, but which is still dangerous because it can bring financial ruin' (Shepard 1990: 251). Simply stated, risk is defined in terms of the probability of some hazard occurring. Another aspect of risk is its severity. The analysis of risk is not confined to economics, however. Indeed, risk theory has been extended to the institutional analysis of modernity in general. For example, sociological theorists offer a wider conception of risk, defined in terms of disappointment. Consider, for example, Niklas Luhmann's (1975) theory of risk. For Luhmann, risk is a key concept for explaining how a social system, defined in terms of an autopoietic system which is recursively organized and self-referentially closed, learns and evolves. Risk is connected to trust, which presupposes an awareness of risk. For Luhmann, a person who consciously engages in a course of action in order to avoid disappointment embraces trust. So, for example, a litigant who selects a course of action, such as pursuing a legal claim to its conclusion in the face of a settlement proposal, and is upset by the outcome, may be disappointed if she acknowledges that she was partly to blame. As a result of disappointments, the system learns.

To be sure, Coffee's use of risk is complex. I would argue that it is located somewhere between the sociological and economic approaches we have just discussed. For Coffee, risk is understood in the context of a bargaining process. The firm is defined as a bargaining site on which several co-operative arrangements are possible, and the parties have conflicting preferences over them. Coffee rejects the fashionable view that the conflict between managers and shareholders is based on an attempt by the shareholders to monitor and control moral hazard, which is inevitable, given the problem of bounded rationality and the existence of transaction costs. The threat of a hostile take-over induces managers, who are normally risk-averse, to take higher risks, in order to avoid losing their future information rents. On this account, risk is understood in terms of contingency.

Coffee argues that the economists' moral hazard explanation is too coarse-grained to explain the increase in leverage. In its place he offers certain results from prospect theory. That theory provides that players will select low-risk strategies only if they are currently performing above their aspiration level, and, correspondingly, will alter their risk preference to a high-risk strategy when they are operating below their aspiration level. This insight is applied to the corporate decision-making context to explain the higher incidence of leverage in the firm. Taking his cue from the managerialists, Coffee contends that managers were able to price-satisfy until the late 1970s, because they met their expectation levels and could select low-risk strategies based on growth. He argues however, that the completion of the corporate control market changed that pattern and that, as a result, most managers, even those operating highly efficient firms, have altered their preference for low-risk strategies in order to avoid forced exit and the loss of their future rents.

Coffee maintains that under certain assumptions posited by modern financial ('portfolio') theory, that rational shareholders hold well-diversified portfolios and that fully diversified institutional investors dominate the share market-place, rational managers tend to be highly risk-sensitive compared with shareholders, who are theoretically risk-neutral (Posner 1986).[21] Three arguments are offered in support of this

---

[21] Economists argue that shareholders do not suffer the most risk, because they are able to spread their risk across investments through a portfolio strategy. The dispersed nature of shareholding creates the classical free-rider problem: given the diffused shareholding in the firm, how do shareholders induce managers to act in their interests when the rational shareholder has no incentive to monitor management. Agency theorists argue that the executive labour market and the market for corporate control are the strongest mechanisms for curbing managerial misconduct.

proposition. First, managers have an implicit contract for quasi-permanent employment, based on their assessment of their relative merit and their expectations of the growth of the firm. Moreover, managers highly value this employment relationship, and fear the potential loss of the firm's rents. Secondly, the manager has a high level of personal, as well as asset-specific, wealth invested in the firm and, as a result, is over-invested in the firm as compared with the shareholder with her diversified risk. Thirdly, managers may face personal and criminal liability for bankruptcy, fraud, or securities manipulation, whereas shareholders are, for the most part, effectively shielded. On this theory, managers have little shield against firm-specific risk, so are highly risk-averse; whereas shareholders are theoretically risk-neutral. However, Coffee argues that this asymmetry is not wholly undesirable, since it reduces the moral hazard problem. Coffee seems, in the end, to support the increased level of shareholder power but, at the same time, wishes to protect those interests most exposed to the new level of risk.

Before addressing the asymmetry hypothesis, I want to mention some of the implications of Coffee's managerial risk hypothesis for an understanding of the problem of moral hazard and, more concretely, the market for corporate control. As regards moral hazard, Coffee contends that managers, because they are over-invested in the firm, have an incentive to entrench themselves further, rather than make *ex ante* value-maximizing investments. Echoing the managerialists, Coffee believes that two propositions appear to follow: (1) the introduction of high risk into the firm is an incentive for managers to maximize growth size and not to maximize profits (Coffee 1987: 83); and (2) managers tend to minimize risk by financing growth though internalized funds, and generally avoid, as far as possible, external contracts for finance (see generally Gintis 1990). Thus corporate managers are committed to non-value-maximizing decisions, which explains certain general features of modern corporations: (1) their excessive earnings retention; (2) managers' preference for fixed, as opposed to entrepreneurial variable, wage contracts.[22] The main point to be made here is that managers, because they are unable to diversify their risk, deploy the firm's assets sub-optimally (O. Hart 1989: 1769).[23] Indeed, Coffee parts company with the managerialists in part because of

---

[22] This argument appears odd, since it seems that most managers do not actually select their own form of compensation package. Indeed, the agency literature argues that principals and agents draft *ex ante* agreements which include incentives, in order to align agents' interests. On this theory, even under an optimal incentive scheme, managers will tend to pursue their own interests.

[23] Hart argues that since moral hazard is ineluctable, expropriation problems can be avoided either by writing *ex ante* profit-sharing agreements or by parties sharing investment expenditures. Both suggestions may be insufficient to avoid moral hazard, since verifiability and ownership problems may create differentials.

their failure to appreciate the external, market pressures on managers to make efficient decisions. He argues that the managerialist growth hypothesis explains the conglomeration movement of the 1960s and 1970s and the fierce defensive response of managers in the 1980s to avoid the harsh effects of the restructuring movement.

2.4 Ex post settling up

Let us now ignore the moral hazard question and ask how the implicit contract provides a justification for *ex post* redistribution of the shareholders' take-over premium. Here Coffee is drawing on the economic theory of the firm which characterizes the firm as a nexus of contracts. In this model, the firm is defined as a set of explicit and implicit contracts. Most of the terms of these contracts are incomplete, since they cannot be costlessly drafted and enforced (Charny 1991; Williamson 1985). A contract may be incomplete for another reason; for example, in that it is insensitive to economically relevant future events (Ayres and Gertner 1989: 92 n. 29). Over the length of these agreements, the parties will bargain over the incomplete terms (Charny 1991; Milgrom and Roberts 1990). In this model, managers and shareholders develop a set of expectations which are the result of continuous bargaining. In cases where the parties are unable to agree or clarify their differences about a missing term, the court is called in to fill in the gap (Ayres and Gertner 1989). Coffee contends that in the event of a hostile takeover the missing term for managerial compensation should be interpreted by reference to what the parties would have bargained for *ex ante*. This approach is flawed. That is, the simple bargain framework may lead to results which are either inefficient or unfair (Ayres and Gertner 1989; Charny 1991). To be sure, Coffee fully admits this strategy is limited. In the alternative, he offers an argument for a broader extension of fiduciary duties towards stakeholders generally. The difficulty with this argument is that it encourages managers to further protect their interests at the expense of shareholders. A more explicit argument against extending fiduciary duties to stakeholders is that it offers protection to groups who can obtain contractual protections and, as a result, it diminishes shareholder protection (Stetson Law Review Symposium—J. Macey 1991: 40–41).

On the first level, as noted above, Coffee draws on the implicit contracts literature to justify the *ex post* distribution. To be sure, he acknowledges that this literature was originally devised to explain why employers of low-wage labour made adjustments to demand by changing the quantities of labour rather than the price (Coffee 1987: 84). Here, Coffee attempts to extend the concept of the implicit contract to explain one feature of the internal managerial labour market—namely, the tendency of risk-averse managers to trade off some portion of their current wages in exchange for increased job security. This strategy has limitations. Collins (in Ch. 5 of this volume) complains that the contractualist approach attempts to explain internal wage variations in terms of supply and demand. However, he argues that internal market wage rates are set not merely by market forces, but by reference to social and administrative norms. Collins's point is that the internal labour market wage might be tied to a norm, rather than to the fluctuations of supply and demand. He attempts to generalize this claim, but his attempt is only partially effective, since it assumes that all internal labour market wage rates are set by either norm or organization. To be sure, certain segments of the labour market will be market-influenced, and this seems especially true in the case of professional markets where there are sellers' propensities (Gilson and Mnookin 1990: 222–5).

The differential risk model has been challenged from a different perspective by Oliver Williamson (1987*b*: 159). In the first instance, the concept of an implicit contract is questioned, since it appears ambiguous and conceptually confused. More centrally, Williamson contends that the contractual problems of the firm are best understood in terms of *ex ante* contracting problems. Employing insights from transaction cost theory, the contracting problems between managers and shareholders can be addressed either in terms of incentives, including severance payments, or by recourse to a governance structure which can help resolve disputes. With this background, Williamson contends that in the context of a hostile take-over, in which the earlier contractual equilibrium has been disrupted, risk-averse managers are more likely to protect their firm-specific investment from hazard by recourse to contractual mechanisms. Williamson argues that the successor management should not be expected to renegotiate on the same terms, even if certain changes have occurred. To be sure, Williamson notes that the changed environment will produce at least one of three different changes: (1) a reduction in managers' firm-specific investment; (2) increased inducements to accept higher levels of hazard; or (3) insurance against loss of the firm's rent. It seems to me that Williamson's arguments are powerful, but could be usefully supplemented by an additional set of arguments against Coffee's implicit contracts thesis.

Coffee challenges certain aspects of Williamson's claims. First, Williamson's approach is unsatisfactory, since it assumes that the level of firm-specific capital explains the actions of managers. In particular, it is not at all clear that all managers have a particularly high level of firm-specific capital in the firm; furthermore, the existence of the executive labour market indicates that managerial skill is transferable, and not tied to a specific firm (Coffee 1987: 91). Coffee's major point is that the success of the firm in creating contractual incentives for managers to align their interest with that of the principals makes them more risk-averse, and explains their preference for growth and their aversion to debt.

The resort by Coffee to the implicit contract model invites a final comment. Rather than limit himself to a narrow claim that certain managers might be entitled to a premium share for an unforeseen risk, Coffee attempts to extend the point to address the normative question regarding whether anything should be done to offset the increased risk which certain groups, including the state and the community, have absorbed as a result of the hostile take-over. In order adequately to address this question, Coffee attacks the neo-classical vision of the firm and the shareholder sovereignty doctrine. Both theories place the shareholder-principal at the centre of the firm, and state that, as the risk-bearing entrepreneur, the shareholder is entitled to control over the residual, and is the only group in the firm which is owed fiduciary duties. I suspect that Coffee's use of the implicit contract hypothesis requires some unpacking on this point.

Coffee, in the main, aspires to offer a theoretical account of the firm which might provide an alternative foundation for corporate law. This approach is based on the following claims. First, as mentioned earlier, Coffee defines the firm as an imperfect and unstable risk-sharing arrangement, which translates into a more flexible vision of the firm. The principal is displaced from the centre of the firm, and the *ex post* struggle over the residual profit is not determined by one party but is a bargained-for outcome (Coffee 1990; Rock 1992: 545–9). Following the insights of the implicit contract thesis, Coffee argues that the shareholder is not the only risk-bearer in the firm. Because managers are risk-averse and are unable to get full insurance, they are highly exposed and, as a result, unable to protect their firm-specific assets. Against this background, managers make implicit contracts to protect this investment, which are breached by the hostile take-over. Arguing from fairness, managers should be compensated in the form of *ex post* devices like the golden parachute. The *ex post* devices are defended on the grounds that it is difficult to evaluate managers' behaviour *ex ante*, and that by offering *ex ante* incentives managers, might have an incentive to act opportunistically.

Coffee's account is not fully convincing. At this point, I will consider the economic arguments that Coffee employs in support of his claim justifying *ex post* distribution of the premium share. First, it might be equally well argued that the management compensation package negotiated by managers, in most instances, would include an insurance premium against the risk of forfeiture of future information rents. This would most certainly be the case for those managers hired since the hostile take-over market reached maturity in the early 1980s (Eisenberg 1987). Even if certain senior and junior managers did not sign complete contracts, one would expect that the principal calculated the costs for all imaginable future hazards into the terms of the contract (ibid.).

Coffee justifies the *ex post* compensation for managers in terms of efficiency. The claim here is that take-overs are necessary to reduce opportunism, but that management should receive a share of the take-over premium in order to compensate them for the unbargained-for risk as well as to smooth the transition. The efficiency grounds for this proposition are challenged by Brudney (1988: 153), who rightly argues that 'the case for management's need for more protection at take-over time is hard to see in light of the immense discretion that it has during the operation of the company to reward itself generously for its sacrifice in limiting its talents to firm-specific dimensions'. Brundey's point is that the aim of take-overs is not to supply management with more rewards, after it acts against shareholders' interests.

Two observations are relevant to our discussion. First, managers tend to make manager-specific contracts because they are harder to monitor and punish.[24] These implicit contracts are usually based on the reputation of the manager, and are part of the manager's own human capital (Aoki 1988; Kreps 1990; but see Williamson 1992). On this theory, if a manager can arrange for implicit contracts with the firm's most valuable employees and suppliers, he can extract a higher wage from shareholders. The degree of entrenchment depends on how highly the firm's assets are dependent on the incumbent manager's skills and knowledge. On the other hand, if the board removes the manager, he is able to exit with his contracts and commit himself to another. As a result, the fact that the incumbent firm stands to lose certain rents if the manager exits indirectly commits the shareholder to a reward rather than a punishment policy.

This model explains managers' objectives in terms consistent with those elaborated by Coffee. Shleifer and Vishny (1988) contend, like Coffee, that managers tend to further entrench themselves because they are over-invested in the firm. At every level of selection there is always a group of employees that have an interest in entrenching themselves. As a result, managers that are inefficient are least likely to be able to move between firms and have an interest in taking actions that are value-reducing to shareholders. The main insight is that managers collecting rents will attempt to do whatever they can to collect their future rents. Thus they will tend to make value-enhancing investments beneficial to the share-holder only if this choice further entrenches them. Several insights suggest themselves. First, Coffee, like Shleifer and Vishny, believes that the hostile take-over is an inefficient weapon for disciplining managers, and may have the opposite effect. Second, a highly organized group of managers

---

[24] Manager-specific investments include acquiring and divesting businesses which add to managers' position and making implicit contracts with the firm's employees and clients.

will mobilize, as they did in the 1980s, to influence legislation which protects them from potential loss of their firm specific capital (Macey 1988). Taking these points together, the effectiveness of incumbent management to protect its interest should not be underestimated.

3. CONCLUSION: TRUST AND IMPLICIT CONTRACTS

The diffential risk hypothesis attempts to justify *ex post* compensation to managers on the grounds of efficiency gains. In particular, Coffee claims that *ex-post* compensation is necessary to pay off the losers, in order to reduce the inefficiencies that result from managements' defensive responses to hostile take-overs, and at the same time to maintain the loyalty of managers. Such payments should protect the most risk-averse managers and restore the equilibrium between the various interests in the firm. However, Coffee does not explain the basis for such implicit contracts. This question has been addressed by theorists who rely on a notion of trust or reputation.

Proponents of the rational reputation or trust approach explain, like Coffee, that complete contingent claims contracting is expensive, hence shareholders prefer to rely on implicit contracts with stakeholders (Shleifer and Summers 1988: 37–9). The problem is to explain what motivates stakeholders to sink investments in firm-specific capital if there is no mechanism to sanction shareholders who breach their promises to stakeholders.

Trust is relevant to implicit contracting, because it recognizes that individuals act opportunistically, and it explains the circumstances in which individuals will honour a promise or agreement (Elster 1989: 274–5; Dasgupta 1988: 53). The concept of trust is defined in term of credibility.

A related approach in terms of rational reputation (Kreps 1990) is based on insights from non-co-operative game theory. This assumes a continuous bargaining game with a high probability of repeated bargaining rounds. Kreps argues that managers honour implicit contracts because it gives them a good reputation: 'I will begin by trusting you hoping that you will honour that trust. Indeed, I will continue to trust you as long as you do not abuse that trust. But if ever you abuse that trust, I will never again trust you' (Kreps 1990: 102). In a repeat game, if the manager adhered to the implicit contract in the earlier round, the manager will continue to honour the contract, since it generates a reputation for trust and hence increased capital for the firm. Limitations to the Kreps model are that it assumes that the only reason to trust a manager is her reputation (Shleifer and Summers 1988: 39), and assumes that a shifting constituency such as shareholders knows what a manager did in the earlier round (Williamson 1992: 167).

The role of trust has been applied to the take-over context by Shleifer and Summers (1988). They argue that hostile take-overs disrupt the implicit long-term contracts between shareholders and stakeholders. They refer to psychological evidence which they claim shows that people trust others for reasons other than reputation. Since this cannot explain trust, they argue that shareholders tend to select trustworthy managers, because this maximizes utility. While it is not clear what the selection mechanism may be, they claim that managers must pass through a 'loyalty filter' before promotion to positions of trust. Applying this model to take-overs, they argue that the extent to which managers are able to defend the implicit contracts made with stakeholders depends on their level of entrenchment and their willingness to honour those agreements. Shleifer and Summers see take-overs as rent-seeking devices, and challenge the view that net efficiency gains are achieved. While they concede that there may be some efficiency gains, they contend that there may be greater long-run efficiency losses due to the loss of trust which facilitates long-term contracting.

This argument turns on the view that shareholders prefer trustworthy managers who will entrench themselves and honour implicit contracts with stakeholders. Holmstrom persuasively challenges this claim, arguing that the fact that a manager is trustworthy does not ensure commitment (Holmstrom 1988: 57–8). Further, it seems that the entrenchment claim fails to explain why the present shareholders do not capture the rents from the implicit contracts. Holmstrom prefers to explain managerial behaviour in terms of managers' rational concern for their careers. Hence, they act to maximize their position within the firm, and respond only to the groups with the most voice or the greatest power. However, this self-interest model does not square with trust.

Finally, a major difficulty with the breach of trust claim is that it is without empirical support. As we have seen earlier, the recent empirical studies analyzing the large gains in shareholder wealth that arise from take-overs shows that the primary source of wealth is related to the anticipation of the post-take-over divestitures of the target firm's assets. Added to this point is the finding by Bhagat *et al.* (1990) that the reduction in labour costs and transfers from bondholders amounted to an insignificant aspect of the wealth increase overall. Based on these considerations, my conclusion is that the implicit contracts model is inaccurate in empirical terms and its normative foundations are questionable.

15

Banks and Corporate Control in Germany

THEODOR BAUMS

1. INTRODUCTION

In their seminal treatise of 1932 Berle and Means described the separation of ownership and control in the big American corporations with widely dispersed ownership. The small investor in the public corporation does not engage himself in the affairs of the corporation, and does not exercise his rights as a shareholder. When shareholdings are dispersed, a collective action problem leads to 'rational apathy' on the part of the small investor. In this case it is better for the investor to rely on the control and monitoring of management by other participants ('free-riding') or on legal provisions, like fiduciary duties, or, if necessary, he 'votes with his feet'. In these companies management is not effectively controlled by shareholders. As a result, the 'market for corporate control' developed to discipline management. Much empirical research appears to confirm the view that the hostile take-over is a rather costly and blunt solution to the problem of how to correct management failure (Eisenberg 1989: 1497).

With the decline in the effectiveness of the control market at the end of the 1980s, there have been attempts by institutional investors, such as investment and insurance companies, trust departments of commercial banks, and especially all institutions which administer pension funds, to exercise control over management, and ameliorate the problems of Berle and Means-type corporations. Recently, corporate theorists have argued that the emergence of active institutional monitoring not surprisingly suggests a changed relationship between liquidity and control, which gives way to much greater equity holdings by financial institutions and the possibility of greater control over the investment decisions of the firm (Buxbaum 1990, 1991; Roe 1991; Gilson and Kraakman 1991).

Against this background, it might be interesting to compare the development of capital market monitoring and its impact with other, foreign institutions and approaches. The Japanese system, for instance, seems to

Helpful comments have been given by Richard Buxbaum, Robert Cooter, Paul Davies, Melvin Eisenberg, Mark Roe, and Kenneth Scott. Financial support by the Volkswagen–Stiftung Hannover is gratefully acknowledged.

work completely differently, and the same is true of the German environment (Roe 1991: 59–61). The German system tends to rely on its banking institutions for external finance. Because of this dependence banks exercise considerable control in the largest corporations. As to the structure of these corporations, the two main differences in the German system compared with those of the USA and the UK are:

The *Aufsichtsratssystem*. There is a management board and a separate supervisory board in large corporations. Management is appointed and dismissed by the supervisory board (Meier-Schatz 1988).

There is *no management-controlled proxy system* in German company law. The stocks of the small investors in the shareholders' meetings are mainly voted by banks.

This latter function of banks already points to their dominant role in governance of the top 100 firms in Germany. On top of that financial institutions may hold shares in non-bank firms on their own account, act as creditors of these firms, and be linked to them by a network of interlocking directorates.

This extremely influential position, especially of a small group of banks, has been scrutinized and discussed over the past decade.[1] The Monopolkommission, a commission of scholars which advises the government on antitrust issues, has repeatedly suggested that the powers of banks, especially their equity investment power, be limited.

This chapter deals with the role of the banks in the German system of financial monitoring and corporate control. Its purpose is twofold: in the first part (Section 2) I introduce certain data regarding the various instruments available to banks by which they influence or even control firms. In the following sections (3 and 4) I analyse the proposal of the Monopolkommission to limit shareholdings to 5 per cent, and argue that the suggestions are at least premature. The chapter concludes with some remarks on the possible impact of the forthcoming EC directive concerning take-overs on bank–firm relationships and on the issue of the financial control of the corporation by banks.

2. THE INSTRUMENTS OF CONTROL

2.1 The meaning of 'control'

'Control' is especially necessary for partners who stand in a long-term contractual relationship such as a labour or credit relationship. Banks as

---

[1] Cf. esp. the biennial reports (*Hauptgutachten*) of the Monopolkommission and the basic report of the Gessler Commission (1979); for a short survey, see Krümmel 1980 and Immenga 1978.

financiers, for example, often face, after the conclusion of a credit contract, the problem of unforeseen developments and actions of the debtor which may endanger the accomplishment of the contract. As these problems and developments cannot be solved contractually *ex ante*, and contracting for every contingent development may be too costly, incentives for the debtor and rights of 'control', like informational rights and other rights, for the creditor are necessary. They supplement the necessarily 'incomplete' contract.[2] 'Control' in this technical sense simply refers to the exercise of rights or the influence available to one of the partners to make sure that he receives what he is entitled to or what he may expect to obtain from his partner.

In the main, there are two different relationships in which control of a firm by a bank may be important. First, as already mentioned, the credit relationship is key, since firms borrow from banks. The 'incomplete' character of the credit contract requires the lending bank to monitor the borrowing firm. German banks may hold shares in firms on their own account, and banks and firms are often linked to each other by a personal interlock. What do these devices contribute to the necessary monitoring of the borrowing firm? Are there gains from these additional instruments for the lending bank as well as for the borrowing firm? (See below, Section 3.)

Second, we will focus our attention on the relationship between the owners or shareholders of a firm and its management. What does it mean for this relationship, for the principal–agent problem between shareholders and management, when a bank stands in a long-term business (credit) relationship with a firm, when a bank is represented on the board of this firm, and, above all, when a bank votes stocks of this firm as a trustee of its shareholders? Our discussion will show that there are still quite a few puzzles to be solved before policy recommendations can be made. (See below, Section 4.)

Before looking for an answer to these questions, the various instruments by which a bank can execute its control over a firm will be described in more detail. Four different devices can be identified: the means available to a creditor, to a bank as a stockholder, to a bank as a voting custodian, and, finally, to a bank which is represented on the supervisory board of a firm.

2.2 Banks as creditors

Debt and control. Does bank debt play a role in corporate control, and what are the incentives for it and the monitoring devices of a creditor?

---

[2] On incomplete contracts, see O. Hart and Holmstrom 1987 and the references therein; see further Aghion and Bolton 1988, 1989; Hellwig 1989.

First, creditors scrutinize the project or the firm they are asked to finance before the conclusion of the contract. As a result, the decisions of the owners or managers are submitted to an additional control or even are corrected. This will be repeated before every extension of the credit. Second, the claim of the creditors for fixed payments, irrespective of the unsteady flow of returns to the firm, gives the debtor's owners or managers, the incentive to achieve the goal of repayment. Otherwise, they face the recall of the credit, or perhaps even the bankruptcy of the firm, or a reorganization under a new management. In the case of bankruptcy, control over the assets of the firm is completely taken over by the firm's creditors.[3] Third, a bank as creditor monitors the firm continuously, by evaluating its reports and balance sheets, by dialogue with its decision-makers, by collecting other information, by representation on the firm's board, and by other means. Certainly, the incentive and control effects of debt wholly depend on the respective relationship between creditor and debtor, as well as on the amount and the maturity of the debt. We do not have to go deeper into this here, because discussion of the control structure of debt and its role in corporate control is broadly treated in modern finance theory, and is not a particular German issue. One special type of a bank–firm relationship, however, with a credit link between them at its core, must be mentioned. These 'housebank' relationships between banks and firms used to play an important role in Germany, at least historically (Tilly 1989; Fischer 1990: 6–16), and the question is whether this is still the case today.

Housebank relationships. A housebank relationship has some special traits (Fischer 1990: 3–4):

— It is a long-term relationship between a bank and a firm. This means that the bank has thorough information about the firm, which creates a special confidential relationship between them.
— The housebank has the biggest share in the credit and other financial businesses of the firm.
— The housebank has a special responsibility for the firm in times of financial distress, especially for the rescue and reorganization of the firm.
— The special role as housebank is documented by the representation of the bank on the supervisory board (*Aufsichtsrat*) of the firm.

Factually, housebank relationships no longer seem to be typical for German corporate finance, and hence are not of much interest for our discussion of banks and corporate control. In his recent study of house-

---

[3] According to German bankruptcy law, the bankruptcy of a corporation leads to its dissolution and liquidation. Reorganizations of firms can be arranged privately, very often under the leadership of a bank or a group of banks.

bank relationships, Fischer concludes that exclusive relationships between banks and firms are the exception rather than the rule. They can be found between small firms and banks. However, for the most part, publicly held corporations, with widely distributed stocks (which to a large extent are voted by banks), have five to ten so-called main-bank relationships and quite a lot of further connections with other banks. In addition to this, they increasingly use the international capital markets either on their own or with the support of foreign institutions (Fischer 1990: 21–2, 102–3; Gessler Commission 1979: 93).

2.3 Banks as shareholders

The second means of control consists in the rights and facilities of a shareholder. According to German banking law, credit institutions may acquire and hold stocks in non-bank firms on their own account. There is no rule which limits such holdings to a certain percentage of the firm's capital. At the same time, a controlling participation in a firm which is a lender may not exceed 50 per cent of the capital of the bank.[4] All investments of a bank in stockholdings and other non-liquid assets may not exceed the capital of the bank. This latter rule, is not applicable, however, to portfolio investments (up to 10 per cent of the capital of the respective firm), to stocks which a bank has acquired for placement purposes, or to holdings in firms which the bank has acquired to avoid losses in its credit business, provided that the bank does not keep such a holding for more than five years.[5] The Second Banking Directive of the EC lowers these limits: it states that in future, each holding may not exceed 15 per cent, and all holdings together may not exceed 60 per cent of the capital of the bank.[6] In practice, these new rules will not mean much change for German banks and their equity holdings.

By the end of 1989 German credit institutions together held 4.69 per cent of all shares of the domestic publicly held companies (*Aktiengesellschaften*),[7] and 7.8 per cent of the shares in the domestic privately held companies with limited liability (*Gesellschaften mit beschränkter Haftung*).[8] These numbers include subsidiaries such as corporations that own banks' premises and so forth. To be sure, these numbers are

---

[4] German Banking Law (*Kreditwesengesetz*), sect. 13(4), 19(1) No. 6.
[5] Banking Law, sect. 12.
[6] Official journal of the EC, No. L 386 (30.12.1989).
[7] The total number of all publicly held companies at the end of 1989 was 2,373, of which 535 were listed on the German stock-exchange.
[8] The total number of all privately held companies at the end of 1990 was 430,000. Source: Deutsche Bundesbank, written testimony for the hearing before the Committee for Economy of the Federal Parliament (*Bundestagsausschuss für Wirtschaft. Anhörung vom 16. Mai 1990*), 16 Ap. 1990: 9.

not very revealing. For example, they do not tell us whether and in which groups or banks the ownership of these holdings is concentrated; in how many cases these holdings are mere portfolio investments, rather than controlling blocks of shares; whether they were acquired only for a short term, for placement or trading purposes, or as a long-term investment; or what the structure of the ownership for the rest looks like—whether it is widely dispersed or concentrated. Other recent data, which, however, are also not comprehensive and sufficient for our purposes (Bankenverband 1989), indicate that in 1989 the ten biggest banks held equity stakes in non-bank-firms in 101 cases. However, these data only cover firms with a nominal capital of more than DM 1,000,000 and holdings of more than 10 per cent of these firms' capital. Among these firms were thirty-eight enterprises with publicly traded, stock-exchange-listed shares. In nine of all (101) cases the shares of the banks exceeded 50 per cent; in twenty-nine cases it lay between 25 and 50 per cent; and in sixty-three cases between 10 and 25 per cent.[9]

2.4 Banks as voting custodians

Regulation. As the separation of commercial banks and securities firms is unknown in German banking law, banks are allowed to trade securities like stocks, and do so. Together with these services, they offer their customers custodial service for those shares (a depot), administer them (cash in dividends, e.g.), and vote them at shareholder meetings. Normally, banks do not charge extra fees for this latter service.[10] Shares of German publicly held corporations are predominantly bearer shares; smaller shares are mostly contained in one single global document. If a shareholder wants to get actual stock certificates, he will have to pay for them. To vote the deposited stocks, the banks need a special written power of authority. There is no limit which would allow the exercise of voting rights only up to a certain number of votes for a single bank. Alternative forms, like written voting or a proxy for the management, are not permissible according to German corporate law. The power of authority for the bank may not last for more than fifteen months, and it is revocable at

---

[9] The biennial reports of the Monopolkommission always contain an analysis of the capital and personal interlocks between the 100 biggest German firms, among them (in 1988) 9 banks; cf. the most recent report in *Bundestags-Drucksache* 11/7582: 203 ff. According to this report, the three big private banks (Deutsche Bank, Dresdner Bank, Commerzbank) in 1988 had equity stakes in 15 of the biggest 100 German firms, with an average of 15.9% of all shares of the respective firms.

[10] There are several possible explanations for this. e.g., cross-subsidizing to keep competing institutions out of this field or gains from the business with the respective firm. The most likely explanation seems to be that the basic fees for the depot services cover the costs of voting the stocks too, for these costs are almost the same whether a bank votes 10 or 1,000 shares.

any time. Before a shareholder meeting, banks have to recommend to their customers how to vote, and ask for special instructions. In practice, such instructions are given extremely rarely.[11] If the shareholder does not give his bank special instructions, the bank votes according to its recommendations. In its own shareholder meeting, however, a bank may only vote stocks if the shareholders give explicit instructions.[12] The three big private banks (Deutsche Bank, Dresdner Bank, and Commerzbank) are themselves publicly held companies with widely distributed shares, which are voted by the respective bank itself or by the other banks.

Statistics. There are several older empirical studies on banks as custodians for shareholders.[13] The most recent one, though it is not comprehensive, was published by Gottschalk (1988). From the list of the 100 biggest firms in the Federal Republic in 1984, he selected those companies of which more than 50 per cent of their stocks were either widely held or owned by banks. These thirty-two companies with a (nominal) equity capital of DM 29.5 billion in 1986 represented about a quarter of the nominal capital of all German publicly held companies. Among them were seven of the ten biggest firms of the Federal Republic.

The study adds up the voting power of the banks' own shares, their depot shares, and shares held by investment companies, which are a bank's subsidiary. The study gave the following results. All banks together on average represented more than four-fifths (82.67 per cent) of all votes which were present in the meetings. With one exception, they always had at least a majority (more than 50 per cent) of the present votes. The consequence of this is that they were able to elect the members of the management board, and that changes of the articles and by-laws of the corporation could not be effected against their votes. In twenty-two, or two-thirds of the firms, the banks voted more than three-quarters of all present stocks, and thereby could change the articles and by-laws. No other shareholder could block these decisions. It has to be added that most of these corporations (on the voting of these very banks) adopted a provision in their by-laws to the effect that no shareholder may vote more than (usually) 5 per cent of all stocks of the company (Baums 1990; i.e., the so-called *Höchststimmrechte*). This rule, however, does not apply to banks in their capacity as custodians, if they vote for different customers.

The breakdown in Gottschalk's study shows that the voting rights are

---

[11] Only in 2–3% of all cases (Immenga 1978: 103; Gottschalk 1988: 296).

[12] Cf. sect. 128, 135 *Aktiengesetz*.

[13] Monopolkommission 1978: 283 ff.; Gessler Commission 1979: 111, 559. The Gessler Commission concluded that in 1974–5 in 74 stock-exchange-listed companies (with a nominal capital of at least DM 50 m.) 52.5% of the present shares were voted by banks or investment companies as custodians, and another 10.2% as owners (Gessler Commission 1979: 290–1).

highly concentrated in the three largest private banks. Together these
three banks on average voted about 45 per cent of the represented stocks
in the general meetings of the respective thirty-two companies.[14] In
almost half these cases (fifteen firms), they together had the majority; in a
further one-third (ten firms), they had a blocking minority. Whether one
can speak of co-ordinated behaviour of these banks in the voting process
(Immenga 1978: 103–4; Gottschalk 1988: 300) has not yet been proved
empirically. The Gessler Commission noted that 'the banks mostly vote
in the same sense' (Gessler Commission 1979: 171). As these numbers do
not identify single bank–firm relationships, it is not clear to what extent
these stakes in single firms are stable over a longer period of time, and
whether banks try to keep their respective holdings in certain firms at
least at certain levels.

2.5 Personal interlocks

Regulation. Banks can influence or strengthen their influence on firms
through setting up interlocking directorates. Members of the managing or
supervisory board of a bank can be members of the supervisory board of
a firm, be it as a consequence of the equity participation of the bank or
its position as custodian of the shareholders, or as a consequence of its
business relationship, especially a long-term credit relationship, between
the bank and the firm. It is a question of the influence of the bank, on
the one side, or the independence of the firm and its management, on the
other, whether a representative of a bank is brought into the boardroom
because the bank or the firm, its shareholders or its management, asked
for it. The possibilities of receiving information on a firm or monitoring
it which are generated by such a relationship depend wholly on the legal
and factual rights and the means of the respective organ of the firm and
the position which the representatives of the bank have in it.

In partnerships and private corporations, to which the co-
determination laws do not apply, the duties of the board of a firm and its
members can be regulated to a considerable extent by charter or by-laws.
On the other hand, in publicly held companies and those private companies to which the co-determination laws are applicable, the composition
of the supervisory board, its tasks and duties, its internal rules as well as
its rights *vis-à-vis* the management board, are almost entirely mandatory.
The members of the supervisory board are elected by the shareholders,
apart from those elected by the employees. A single person may not be a
member of more than ten boards at the same time; this rule, however,

---

[14] This corresponds with the data of the Bundesbank, according to which, by the end of
1988, the three *Grossbanken* held 43% of all depot shares in their custody; *Die
Aktiengesellschaft 1989*, AG Report, p. 412.

does not restrain the institution which he represents. There is no rule in German law which prohibits membership on boards of competing firms.

The supervisory board appoints the members of the managing board, and dismisses them, though only for cause. It has to monitor the management. In practice, however, it acts as an advisory committee, rather than a monitoring panel, except in times of financial distress of the firm. To accomplish its duties, the board has a right to comprehensive information. The management has to report to it periodically on all important questions. Apart from that, the supervisory board can always ask the management for reports. The supervisory board checks the annual reports and balance sheets of the firm. The board can ask the management that certain important transactions, like, for instance, credits above a certain amount, not be carried out without its previous approval. When there is a resolution before the board on this subject, the representative of the crediting bank would, according to German law, not be prohibited from voting. Board members have the duty to treat information confidentially.

Statistics. There are no comprehensive data on personal interlocks between firms and banks in Germany. The Gessler Commission scrutinized no more than 336 banking institutions (of more than 5,000 in 1974). These institutions held 1,709 board memberships, of which 1,308 were in non-bank firms (Gessler Commission 1979: 122–6, 440–5, 585–98). Further studies checked all publicly held companies, all co-determinated companies, all companies which were quoted on a stock-exchange, and the biggest (by sales) 100 firms.[15] The most recent study on this subject has been done by the Monopolkommission.[16] It refers to interlocking directorates between banks and firms with regard to the 100 biggest firms as measured by their value-creating potential (*Wertschöpfung*). Among those 100 biggest firms were nine banks. In 1988 the representatives (mainly members of the management and supervisory boards) of these nine banks held ninety-four seats on the supervisory boards of ninety-six (of the biggest 100) firms, which equals 6.4 per cent of all board seats in those firms. The Deutsche Bank alone held thirty-five of the respective seats.

3. CONTROL AND THE CREDIT RELATIONSHIP

A discussion concerning the advantages and disadvantages of various links between banks and firms and their combination should commence

---

[15] Cf. the survey in Fischer 1990: 148–9 with further references; see further Immenga 1978: 108–9; Bankenverband 1989: 20; Gottschalk 1988: 299 ff.
[16] *Bundestag-Drucksache* 11/7582: 216 ff.

with an analysis which distinguishes the different relationships which are likely to be influenced by these various links. The following discussion addresses two questions: (1) What does the use of the various instruments and devices of control available to banks mean for the credit relationship between the bank and the firm? (2) What does it mean for the principal–agent problem between shareholders and management?

3.1 The proposal of the Monopolkommission

The Monopolkommission has repeatedly suggested that the equity holdings of banks be limited by law to 5 per cent of the shares of a firm, comparable to the legislation for bank holding companies in the USA.[17] The proposal rests upon various antitrust considerations and arguments, like restraint of competition on the markets for enterprises because of the long-term holdings of the banks, the negative impact on the competitors of the firms with a close bank relationship, restraint of competition in the markets for financial services because of the influence of certain banks as shareholders, and the like. In relation to these arguments one may ask why the regular provisions of antitrust law are not sufficient to deal with these problems. For example, why is the acquisition of a firm's stock by a bank not treated as a vertical merger, and thus submitted to the regular control of mergers? The Monopolkommission holds that this regular treatment is not justified, and that mergers between banks and firms should be generally restricted. It argues that mergers between, for example, two industrial firms may lead to synergies, economies of scale or scope, or other advantages. Because of these possible advantages in 'regular' merger cases, mergers are not generally limited; rather, possible detrimental impacts of a merger on competition have to be considered and weighted in every single case by the instrument of administrative merger control. These considerations are not applicable, however, to mergers or acquisitions of stocks of a firm by a bank. There are no such economically advantageous effects conceivable.[18] In its most recent report the Monopolkommission simply states that the influence of banks on the firm in which it holds an equity stake is questionable.[19]

The argument of the Monopolkommission is astonishing, for at least two reasons. First, its proposal to limit equity stakes of banks in nonbank firms does not touch explicitly on the role of banks as custodians.[20] But, as the statistical overview has shown, the influence of banks on (publicly held) corporations by means of their role as custodians is much more important on average than their influence by means of their own

[17] *Hauptgutachten* 1973/75: 296; *Sondergutachten* 1989 18: 145 ff.
[18] *Hauptgutachten* 1973/75: 296.   [19] *Sondergutachten* 18: 145.
[20] Cf. *Hauptgutachten* 1976/77: 339–40.

holdings. If, for example, banks use their influence on firms to create an exclusive business relationship, and thus restrict their competitors from access to the respective firms, the proposal to limit equity holdings of banks is not very helpful, since their influence on the firm as voting custodians and through personal interlocks may be much more important.

Apart from that, looking at the relationships between banks and firms merely from an antitrust point of view is itself questionable. Before policy recommendations can be made, it is necessary to look more closely at the relationships between the bank and the firm, and the possible advantages or drawbacks of a tighter relationship for the bank and the firm. The following remarks try to deal with this.

3.2 Debt–equity combinations

Asymmetric information. Before the conclusion of a contract, creditors face the problem of asymmetric information. This involves the prospects, the probability of risks and expected returns, and the underlying firm-specific factors (former performance of the firm, ability and skills of the management, etc.), and thereby the ability of the debtor to pay the interest and the capital back. Furthermore, even after the completion of a contract, informational problems will arise with regard to developing risks, which may threaten the payments on the credit.

It is often argued that an equity stake of the bank in the borrowing firm will improve the flow of information for the bank, and reduce the problem of asymmetric information (Cable 1985; Pozdena 1987, 1990a, 1990b; McCauley and Zimmer 1989; Berglöf 1990). This proposition is doubtful (K. Scott 1991). Consider two banks, X and Y. X simply lends money to a firm as a creditor, whereas Y splits the same amount of money up into a credit and an equity investment in a firm. To be sure, if Y has held its equity stake in the firm for a certain period of time before it lends money to the firm, Y very likely has an informational advantage compared to X. But Y would have this advantage, too, if it competed with X after having had a long-term credit relationship with the firm before without an equity stake. But if both X and Y are starting from the scratching there is no informational advantage for Y, at least not before the conclusion of the contract. This is evident for information which cannot be given by the other owners or the management at this time at all (because they do not have this information themselves, e.g.); and it is normally true, too, for such information as can be disclosed at this time. Things look different in the latter case only if the other owners or management are aware that they are more likely to be 'punished' by a shareholder (Y) than a creditor (X) for withholding information or giving wrong information. This is indeed highly likely should Y acquire the majority of the shares, but rather less likely in the case of a mere creditor or a minority shareholder. But the acquisition of a majority is a rather rare case for a bank.

There are similar considerations with regard to information asymmetries during the credit relationship. For example, a shareholder who owns the majority of the shares and manages the subsidiary with his staff certainly will have superior information compared to a mere creditor. This, however, is not the typical case for a bank, and there are other serious dangers and drawbacks connected with it, which will be mentioned later. Apart from the exceptional case, the comparative informational advantages of a shareholder over a bank lending a comparable amount are questionable. For the most part a shareholder will not get earlier or broader information than the bank. It may be different when the shareholder is represented on the board of the firm. As such, board membership does not depend on an equity stake in the firm. It would appear that it is personal interlocks between banks and firms, rather than stockholdings, that eliminate or lessen the 'informational asymmetry' between creditor and borrowing firm.

Risks and losses for the creditor. Mere informational symmetry is not sufficient to exclude or minimize the risks and losses for the creditor during a credit relationship. [The combination of equity and debt is said to be advantageous also in this respect.] An equity share provides the bank with an enhanced ability to monitor and influence the management. An equity holding could therefore lead to a better and less costly supply of capital for the firm. The system may impose less costs on capital than a fragmented financial structure in which banks are not allowed to acquire equity shares in firms.[21] To evaluate this argument, we should first distinguish between the different risks and possible harms which can be minimized by the creditor taking an equity stake in the borrowing firm. The main dangers in this respect seem to be:

— distribution of assets to shareholders or transactions with affiliated firms which could jeopardize the accomplishment of the contracts with the firm's creditors;
— mistakes and failures of the management that endanger the prospects of the firm and its position;
— undertaking of more risky projects after the conclusion of the contract.

The first group of possible harms to the creditors is at the core of traditional company law and the law of groups. There are mandatory rules which regulate transactions between a firm and its shareholders and

[21] Cf. McCauley and Zimmer 1989; Pozdena 1990*b*; Neuberger and Neumann 1991; K. Scott 1991.

between affiliated firms. In this respect there seem to be no major advantages from an own equity stake for a creditor except in the case in which he acquires the majority of the shares of the borrowing firm and thereby is able to obviate such practices. This is, not feasible normally, however, because the threshold is usually too high, and there are new inherent risks for a creditor connected with a controlling equity stake (which will be mentioned later). Apart from that, an equity–debt combination would not create an institutional improvement, because the other creditors and shareholders now face the risk that the management will treat the equity creditor more favourably.

Similar considerations can be made in the second case. To improve its influence on the management of the firm and its overall operations by means of an equity stake, a bank would have to acquire a share in the firm which would give it the right to appoint or dismiss the management and to monitor it continuously.

There are at least two instances in which an increased risk accrues after the completion of the contract. As the owners of the firm have to pay back only the capital and fixed interest, the surplus stays with them. In a firm with limited liability, the owners may take on more profitable and— at the same time—more risky projects according to the motto 'Heads I win, tails you lose'. This incentive may be particularly strong if the owner's equity stake is a small proportion of the overall capitalization. Secondly, a firm in financial distress may have an incentive to take increased risks, because in the case of a reorganization or bankruptcy the managers would lose their firm-specific capital. The firm would lose its reputational asset.

The creditor bank can try to get around the first of these two problems by drafting contractual provisions in the debt contract (viz., call provisions). This is not always feasible, however. If the bank participates as an equity-holder, the incentive for the owners to take on riskier projects fades, since they are required to share the surplus with the creditor. The second problem can be solved only if the bank acquires an equity stake which is sufficiently large to give it influence on the management and the overall operations of the firm.

Until now it has been argued that the different risks and possible harms to a creditor can be minimized, to a certain degree, through an equity participation of the bank in the firm. However, the equity stake should be large enough to give the bank the ability to effectively prevent possible harms and losses. In regard to large firms, the threshold will normally be too high to obtain enough influence to improve the behaviour of the firm and, if necessary, oust the management. Apart from that, a bank as a (major) shareholder would perhaps, on the one hand, reduce its risks as a lender. On the other hand, it would face new costs and risks. A shareholder does not have a claim to fixed payments irrespective of the outcome of the efforts of the management; he has to monitor the management on an ongoing basis, and incurs all problems and costs of this principal–agent relationship. Furthermore, there are inherent risks connected with a debt–equity combination. First, such a stake leads to a commitment which can be detrimental, especially in a crisis of the firm. The bank may run into the problem of whether it should, to rescue its equity stake, 'throw good money after bad'. There is still another risk. If the firm goes bankrupt, not only the bank's equity stake, but also the credit capital which was extended to the firm by the bank as a major shareholder, will be subordinated to other debt, even if its loan was secured by collateral. It seems safe, in the end, to conclude that debt–equity combinations are not generally a superior solution as compared with a mere credit relationship. This proposition is corroborated by the results of a poll of credit institutions which was done by the Gessler Commission, which found that banks acquire shares and take on participation for other reasons than the wish to improve monitoring and control of management (Gessler Commission 1979: 78–9).

Commitment of the firm. Fischer has recently analysed long-term exclusive relationships between a bank and a firm. In certain cases, such as, for instance, a rescue operation or a new venture, returns may accrue not just in the near future, but during later periods of the life of the respective enterprise. However, credits may not be available if the bank anticipates that it will not be compensated completely for having taken on the risks of providing the firm with the necessary funds, perhaps because it is aware that, after a certain period, when the returns have not yet been fully reaped, the firm will switch over to other competitors. That may happen even if long-term contracts cover the whole period of time. For example, it may be impossible to specify and enforce provisions concerning the sharing of returns that may accrue much later. According to Fischer, exclusivity serves as a commitment device, since the financing bank obtains an information advantage over outside financiers. This informational advantage commits the firm to the bank by reducing the strength of competition from outside financiers. This again supports the financier's initial willingness to supply funds to the firm, support a rescue operation, or provide start-up capital to it (Fischer 1990; Hellwig 1990).

Can this analysis be used to explain equity participations too? Can such an equity stake in a firm serve as a commitment device in cases in which long-term binding contracting about future returns between a firm and its financier is not feasible? Thus, in a system which allows banks to acquire and hold shares in firms, funds could be provided to firms by banks in situations in which in a different legal system finance would not be available.

Certainly an equity participation may well, depending on its size, create a commitment on the part of the firm. But, as already mentioned, it also creates a commitment by the bank, which at the same time exposes the bank to other, additional risks. And in cases in which there is no necessity to exclude other competitors, the equity participation of a bank may be detrimental if it excludes or restrains competition (Immenga 1978: 117–18).

So far, the analysis has shown that there seem to be only limited cases, if any, in which a debt–equity combination is a superior solution to straight debt finance. Further research is required to deal with the other reasons for which banks engage in equity participation. The reasons for taking an equity position should be clear. In some cases, the acquisition of shares is merely a transitory action, be it a special finance service either for the respective firm (placement) or for third parties (bank as a mandatary; acceptance as a pledge). In these cases, the shares either give the bank no influence or voting right in the respective firm at all, or the bank can exert this influence only over a short period of time. There are three cases which deserve particular attention in regard to corporate control: (1) the acquisition of shares in a firm which is being reorganized; (2) the acquisition of shares in firms with low own equity capital (including venture firms); and (3) finally those cases in which a bank acquired an equity stake in a firm at first for other purposes, and then decided to keep it. We lack a clear empirical picture of these cases, and require a more sensitive theoretical explanation to questions mentioned earlier. Against this background, policy recommendations like that of the Monopolkommission, which proposes to restrain bank's shareholdings to 5 per cent of the firm's capital, seem premature.

3.3 Official interlocks

The role of representatives of banks on supervisory boards is often analysed from the standpoint of conflicts of interest (Lutter 1989) or antitrust considerations.[22] I will confine my remarks here to the questions which affect interlocking relationships between a bank and a firm, and the impact they have on their credit relationship. A further question is whether this influence is detrimental to the firm, its shareholders, and other creditors or not.

First of all, the role of bank representatives on supervisory boards is generally highly appreciated, since they have specialized knowledge, especially in the field of finance. Moreover, banks often provide an assistant

---

[22] Most recently *Monopolkommission Bundestag-Drucksache* 11/7582: 216–25.

and facilities which support them in their work as a board member. The bigger banks have large departments which specialize in analysing the financial markets as well as the financial needs of their client firms. This information, too, is available to the representatives of these banks. An interesting question is whether bank representatives on the board of an enterprise are better monitors of management than an independent board member because they have independent outside information about the firm from the bank's credit department. As there is no 'Chinese Wall' concept in German law, the information from the credit department is available to the representative of the bank on the board of the (borrowing) firm. To be sure, for the firm, the question is whether this advice and information are neutral and independent, and whether this service is available on the market, or whether the firm could gather the necessary information itself.

The next question concerns whether the board membership of a bank's representative also improves the information of the bank? It has been observed that a bank could improve its information by virtue of its membership on the supervisory board of the firm. Thus, the bank could gain an informational advantage over its competitors, or harm the interests of other creditors of the firm (Immenga 1978: 111). Others consider the improvement of the information rather positively (Mayer and Alexander 1990: 23). Positive or not, the factual basis for these conclusions seems to be doubtful. The question is, does a bank get broader or earlier information from its representatives on the board than it would otherwise get as a major creditor? Fischer's survey shows that a bank does not expect to get any better or more thorough information from its representatives on the board than it already has (Fischer 1990: 80–1, 149). Indeed, members are required to keep the information they get on the board confidential. Board members normally are well aware of the confidentiality requirement and of their respective duties. Different problems may arise in a small bank, where the director or officer of the bank who sits on the board of a customer firm operates the credit department of the bank at the same time. A recent comparative study on firms in the UK and Germany challenges the claim that German firms rely more heavily on bank credits than do British firms. The study indicates the opposite (Mayer and Alexander 1990: 23). Further, this result does not support the thesis that the membership of bank representatives on the boards of firms improves the information of the bank significantly.

However, this does not lay to rest the question of informational advantages achieved through representation on the board. There are several reasons for this. First, the participation of a bank officer in the boardroom may reduce the riskiness of the information received as a creditor. The positive 'slant' in discussions with an outside lender may be contradicted in the boardroom discussion of a company's problems. With a representative of the bank in the boardroom, those talking with the bank's loan officers probably have less incentive to 'slant' the information. Second, if we define 'information' in a broader sense, which could include better knowledge of the persons who run the firm, understanding the firm's problems—in short, familiarity with the firm and its leading persons—then this may well have influence, and may even create a 'commitment' of the bank. We must turn to this point in more detail.

This aspect of 'commitment' was mentioned earlier. The question there was whether an equity participation can assure the bank that the firm will stay in a long-term relationship with it, and it was argued that such an equity stake may create a reverse commitment of the bank to the firm as well. Likewise a board membership may create a commitment of the bank to the firm. The membership on the board documents a special relationship between a firm and a bank to the other participants and the public. Board members take on a responsibility for the firm. As the board member representing a bank is somehow identified with the institution behind him, this responsibility extends to the bank itself. Furthermore, a board membership may create or strengthen personal relationships with owners or managers of the firm, and improve the understanding of influential bank representatives of interior problems of the firm and knowledge about the ability and skills of the management. These factors taken together may well create a commitment of the bank to the firm, which may be advantageous, especially in times of financial distress.

4. CONTROL, SHAREHOLDERS, AND MANAGERS

We now turn to examine the relationship between the owners or shareholders of a firm and its management. In practice, this question is of particular interest for the big firms with widely distributed ownership. The following considerations are confined to this type of firm. What does it mean for this relationship, for the principal–agent problem between shareholders and management, when a bank votes stocks of such a firm as a trustee of its shareholders, and, at the same time, stands in a business (credit) relationship with the firm, has an own equity stake in it, and/or is represented on its board?

Our analysis first examines the role of banks as voting custodians, and then asks whether this task is impaired or improved by its other roles.

4.1 Banks as 'delegated monitors'

In his important article on the theory of financial intermediaries, Diamond (1984) studied the role of banks in relations between creditors and borrowers. Diamond offers a model in which there are no banks. In such a world, firms must raise the external capital directly from private lenders, and there are high costs for searching and, on the side of the lenders, prohibitive information and monitoring costs. If a bank collects the capital from the lenders as deposits, and funnels it to the borrowers, there will be, of course, additional transaction costs at first. But they will be outweighed under certain circumstances. In its relation with borrowers, a bank can reap scale economies. Furthermore, in the relation between the bank and its depositors, the latter will not, according to Diamond, have an information and monitoring problem. The bank promises fixed interest rates to them on their deposits irrespective of the outcome of its credit business. Thus, the 'creditors' no longer need any information about the performance of each single credit relationship. And the information relevant to monitoring the bank, is, for the most part, unnecessary, since the bank lessens the risks of each of the single credit contracts by diversification, by sustaining relationships with numerous borrowers.

Is this analysis of the role of banks as credit intermediaries transferable to their role as custodians? Is this also an efficient arrangement of 'delegated monitoring'? Here, the small investors in a public corporation face similar informational and monitoring problems. A single institution, like a bank, can do this at least as effectively as thousands of small shareholders, but considerably more cheaply. Therefore, Diamond's analysis can be transferred at the very least to the relationship between the deposit institution and the corporation, particularly because the bank can monitor management more efficiently and reap scale economies. A problem arises only when the bank, in fulfilling its tasks as a custodian, pursues its own interests as a credit institution or a shareholder. This point will be addressed below.

However, here the parallel ends. It is not applicable to the relationship between the shareholders and the bank. Whereas the bank in Diamond's case 'transforms' the deposits into credits, and the outcome of the credits, business, and hence of the informational and monitoring efforts of the bank does not (apart from the case of bankruptcy of the bank) touch the depositors any longer, it is different in our case. Here the investors are immediately affected by the activity of the depot institution. Hence, for them, the problem, of if and how the bank fulfils its task *vis-à-vis* the management as their custodian remains.

To conclude, there are two questions we have to deal with: first, if a bank acts as a custodian for shareholders, do its own interests impair the fulfilling of its task? Second, how, in the relationship between the bank and the shareholders, can the necessary monitoring, the 'control of controller', be established?

4.2 Conflicts of interests; control of controllers

In the literature we find quite a lot of suggestions concerning the question of whether and why conflicts of interests arise when a deposit institution is a lender to the firm and at the same time has a direct equity stake in it, and why these conflicts could harm shareholders' interests. The general suspicion is that a share-custodian bank which at the same time offers credits or financial services to firms will not take its responsibility as a monitor of management very seriously, because it will be eager to develop or maintain a business relationship with the firm. On the other hand, one may argue that institutional shareholders with a block of shares large enough that the management must respect their wishes and with additional business relationships with the firm are better monitors than other institutional shareholders, because they are 'tied' to the firm, cannot 'vote with their feet', and hence have a strong incentive to vote and to monitor the management. Then the question remains as to whether the interests of a bank as a creditor and as a custodian of the shareholders are essentially different. A bank as a creditor probably prefers a secure and steady business policy to a profitable, innovative and perhaps more risky policy (Gessler Commission 1979: 101 ff.; Steinherr and Huveneers 1990: 22 ff.). A more detailed criticism in this context states that banks as creditors and custodians for small shareholders influence the dividend policy of the firm to secure the payments of their credits. Therefore they could have an interest in high retentions (Immenga 1978: 121). On the other hand, high retentions will make firms increasingly independent of external finance and, thereby of banks (Wagner 1986; Drukarczyk and Preuschl 1989).

Recently, a critical role was played by some banks when they suggested and supported the introduction of limited voting rights for shareholders (*Höchststimmrechte*). This rule is thought to be an impediment to take-overs. It may be acceptable for an institutional investor—for instance, a pension fund—to vote with the management on anti-take-over amendments, if it decides that this is in the interest of its shareholders or beneficiaries. With banks, however, the situation is somewhat different. They face the suspicion that they introduce this amendment into the by-laws of the company to preserve their business and personal interests (their credits, their own shares, and their position as deposit bank for a large amount of shareholders), and to achieve this, are willing to accept even a decrease in the value of the shares they vote as custodians (Baums 1990).

The Gessler Commission concluded that there are no preferable solutions at present other than the custodianship of banks, and that the banks generally did well in their capacity as institutional custodians, although specific improvements are necessary (Gessler Commission 1979: 287 ff.; Körber 1989). Here we need empirical studies on how banks behave in situations where there are, or could be conflicts of interest; and more theoretical work is needed on the effects of institutional monitors, especially banks, on the behaviour of management and the issue of corporate control.

The second related question concerns the 'control of controllers,' and cannot be answered here. Here, too, the report of the Gessler Commission contains quite a few ideas which have not caught on so far, such as disclosure of direct interests of a bank (e.g., a credit relationship with the firm or an equity stake in it) to the investors, the necessity of special instructions by shareholders in situations with conflicts of interest, the establishment of a supervisory board in the trust department of banks with investors as members, and others. Furthermore, comparative studies, like those on the duties of the management of pension funds or the trust departments in commercial banks in the USA, could provide us with further ideas (cf., e.g., Krikorian 1989; McGill 1989; Buxbaum 1991; Gilson and Kraakman 1991).

5. MARKETS OR INSTITUTIONS FOR CORPORATE CONTROL?

Many of the questions addressed in this chapter cannot be answered satisfactorily at this time. A comparison with other legal systems which have developed different instruments of corporate control is almost impossible at present. The heading of this paragraph does not aim at such a comparison, but seek to address a further question: How will the introduction of take-over rules in the European Community, the creation of a framework for public take-over bids, which have been almost unknown in Germany until now, and with that, the introduction of a 'market' for corporate control by the threat of a hostile take-over, influence the corporate control by institutions like banks? Do market-oriented and institution-oriented systems of corporate control exclude each other? Or can these instruments supplement each other? Can there even be a competition for the better, more efficient system? One argument in the literature predicts that the development of a take-over market, with hostile take-overs and the threat of such, will destroy long-term relationships and mutual commitments between banks and firms or impede their development, respectively (Cable 1985; Franks and Mayer 1990). This would not only affect the conditions of finance of the firms; it would probably also destroy the means and structures of control which are connected with it.

But one can make a different prediction. It is not very likely that there will be a take-over market in Germany in the future, one comparable to those in the UK and the USA, not even after the adoption of the EC framework. There are numerous institutional specialities which are likely to impede this (the two-boards model with co-determination, strict mandatory rules which protect the fixed equity capital of firms, anti-take-over rules in the by-laws like the *Höchststimmrecht* and others, influence of banks). Apart from that, take-overs as a means to correct management failure seem to be a rather costly, blunt instrument 'of last resort' (Eisenberg 1989). Perhaps we can instead improve monitoring and control by shareholders to the point where take-overs as a means of management control will not be necessary.

PART IV

Corporate Groups

16

Corporate Groups and Network Structure

JOHN SCOTT

I. INTRODUCTION

A starting point for many of the chapters of this volume is the 'contract' model of the enterprise, and the associated idea of the 'nexus of contracts' in corporate affairs. According to this viewpoint, relations between executive managers and the financial institutions which hold the company shares and which provide loans can be interpreted in contractual terms. Corporate entities can, on this basis, be seen as comprising complex networks of interests. Such a viewpoint does not go far enough. Several of the chapters in this section show that when a business operates through two or more companies, lawyers have considerable difficulty in recognizing a 'group' of companies as a legal entity. For this reason, an approach which reduces all business relations to contractual relations among individuals has a great appeal. But this is to side-step the problem, rather than to solve it. Our theories of how businesses operate must recognize the reality of corporate groups and a whole range of inter-corporate relations. It was the great French sociologist Emile Durkheim who criticized social contract and utilitarian theories for their neglect of what he called 'the non-contractual element in contract' (Durkheim 1893). By this he meant the framework of non-juridical norms and practices which structure legal relations. A sociological perspective on business affairs, then, must highlight the influence of such factors on corporate control and business decision-making.

My principal research concern for a number of years has been the analysis of business ownership and control. I began with a study of Scottish companies (J. Scott and Hughes 1980), and then undertook an investigation of large British companies (J. Scott and Griff 1984), which subsequently became part of a wider European investigation (Stokman, *et al.* 1985). On the basis of a comparative survey of evidence from many countries (J. Scott 1985), I have most recently undertaken a comparative study of Britain, the United States, and Japan (J. Scott 1986, 1991*a*).

These investigations had two objects first, to explore the networks of commercial, capital, and personal relations within which enterprises are embedded; and second, to critically examine the managerialist thesis of the separation of ownership from control. These two aims were complementary. Showing the theoretical and empirical inadequacy of the managerialist position has involved documenting the crucial role which is played by inter-corporate relations in the structuring of corporate power.

It is from the stand point of these concerns that I approach the issues of 'group' organization, 'corporations', and 'contracts' which are the themes of this book. As a sociologist, I am struck by the fact that many of those who write from a legal stand point have, by and large, accepted a particular economic model of the firm. In this model the assumptions of managerialist theory go largely unquestioned, and the enterprise is treated as a sovereign agent. My aim in this chapter is to suggest an alternative view, albeit one which complements the legal model. I hope that my outline of a sociological model of corporate relations will point to some unexamined issues in current legal considerations of group organization.

2. POWER IN CORPORATE RELATIONS

Central to any understanding of modern business is the analysis of power (Levine and Roy 1977). In classical economic theory, however, the issues of power and constraint hardly arose. Economic analysis was predicated on the role played by the individual entrepreneur in organizing production. Classical economists assumed that 'entrepreneurs' headed firms which they personally owned; and they could see no obvious reason to modify this view when analysing the behaviour of the modern, large-scale business corporation. Power, then, was simply irrelevant, as entrepreneurs simply responded to market requirements in an objective and rational way.

Critics of classical economics have pointed to fundamental changes in the structure of the capitalist economy during the twentieth century which have forced the issues of power and constraint into a central position. Two competing alternatives to classical economics have been proposed by its critics: the liberal theory of management control and the Marxist theory of finance capital. According to managerialist theory (Berle and Means 1932), the rise of the modern corporation has brought about a divorce of ownership from control. Family capitalism, it is held, was destroyed by a massive increase in the scale of economic activity, and, as a result, professional, salaried managers have become the most important participants in corporate control. The growth in the scale of business enterprise has meant that businesses can no longer be financed solely by individual entrepreneurs and their families. Capital has had to be raised through the stock-exchange from large numbers of individuals, no one of whom can exercise any significant power of control over the corporations in which they invest.

Galbraith (1974), for example, has argued that the expanding scale of production required an expanding pool of capital, and so produced a tendency for family holdings to become ever more fragmented over time. As a result, each individual shareholder became less influential in corporate affairs. At the same time, knowledge and expertise acquired a critical importance in business decision making, and large corporations had to devise ways of accumulating and co-ordinating such knowledge. Hence, managers were recruited who possessed the particular knowledge which the corporations required, and the managerial hierarchy was transformed into a 'technostructure'. On this view, then, it is the technically qualified managers who hold power in the modern enterprise.

The Marxist theory of finance capital (Hilferding 1910), on the other hand, holds that property has remained of critical importance to corporate control. The corporate form of the joint stock company had, indeed, been the basis of a fundamental transformation of capitalist relations; but the outcome was not a managerial system, but a system of finance capital. This theory sees not the individual entrepreneur of the nineteenth century but the financier as holding sway in the large enterprise. The increased dependence of enterprises on the stock-exchange and on bank lending has meant that those who occupy key positions in the financial system—the finance capitalists—are able to exercise virtually all the powers inherent in the capital mobilized by that system. Menshikov (1969), for example, argues that the joint-stock company has allowed a massive concentration of economic activity through the formation of competing 'financial groups', within each of which individual enterprises are linked by ownership and by interlocking directorships, to one another and to a bank which co-ordinates their activities. Through direct holdings and through their links with a bank, the very rich capitalist families function as finance capitalists who have dominated these groups. A financial oligarchy of wealthy financiers is to be found exercising power at the heart of the corporate system.

The exercise of power in business is, in fact, more complex than is envisaged in any of these theories. Ownership and control involve relations of power and constraint, and they must be understood in terms of networks of inter-corporate relations. In order to appreciate this, some important conceptual distinctions must be made. Berle and Means (1932) correctly used the word 'control' to describe a structural relation of constraint, rather than the actual exercise of decision-making power. They argued that the joint-stock company, or the 'corporation' in American terminology, introduced a dissolution of the unity which formerly existed between the ownership of assets and the ability to use those assets. For this reason, the question of power in a joint-stock company is always a question of 'control' rather than of legal 'ownership' *per se*. In a joint-stock company, the owners of shares are owners merely of the right to receive an income and to vote in corporate affairs. It is the company itself which owns the assets and is, therefore, legally responsible for them. Those who supply the capital ('the owners') do not necessarily stand in a direct relationship of control over the uses to which the corporate assets are put. This is not to say, of course, that share ownership becomes irrelevant to control. Far from it. The point is simply that the former legal unity of the property relationship has been dissolved by the introduction of the joint-stock company, and any *de facto* re-unification depends upon the particular economic and social constraints under which the corporation operates.

Control, therefore, has to be seen as a structural relation similar to property. While property is a *de jure* legal relation, control is a structural relation through which a particular category of owners have the *de facto* capacity to mobilize the powers vested in the company itself. The concepts of majority and minority control, for example, point to structures of relations which give particular groups of agents (the 'controllers') the potential to exercise the *de jure* powers of ownership which are vested in the corporation. The controllers are able to determine the composition of the board through their dominance in the affairs of the Annual General Meeting. Because they are able to determine the composition of the board, they are also able to constrain the actions of the executives in the formulation and implementation of corporate strategy.

Control, in this sense, is dependent upon the structure of share ownership, and is rooted, ultimately, in the legal rights which are attached to share ownership. 'Control' refers to the power potential which is accorded by a structure of company law within a wider framework of property law. But control must be distinguished from 'rule' (J. Scott 1990). Where 'control' is a structurally defined capacity, 'rule' refers to the actual exercise of the powers of decision making.[1] The rulers of an enterprise are those who actually decide upon its corporate strategy and set the framework within which its operations will take place. Their focus is the corporate boardroom and the constitutional arrangements which surround it. The rulers comprise the 'dominant coalition: they are the active leadership group within the enterprise' (Child 1972; see also R. A. Gordon 1945). The leadership groups of corporations are diverse in their composition, and may include some executives who have had decision-making powers delegated to them by the controllers, some inside and out-

---

[1] The failure to make this distinction between control and rule has been the source of much confusion in research and analysis, including my own discussion in J. Scott 1985. This section draws on the longer discussion in J. Scott 1990.

side interests who have been able to usurp such powers, as well as the shareholding controllers themselves and their representatives.

In the British and American economies, the distinction between 'control' and 'rule' is related to the distinction which Mintz and Schwartz (1985: 3–16) have made between 'discretionary decision-making' and 'institutional constraint'. Those who dominate discretionary decision making, they argue, always do so subject to the constraint which is inherent in the structure of control. Corporate decision-makers, the rulers, assess the constraints facing an enterprise, and come to a judgment about the optimum strategy to pursue. It is through such constraints that control can be effected without direct involvement in decision making.

Berle and Means (1932) were writing at a time at which company shares were being dispersed from concentrated family blocks to mass individual holdings. They did not foresee that the trend over the second half of the century would involve a growth in 'institutional' shareholdings. Financial institutions such as banks, insurance companies, and pensions funds have become the most important shareholders in large enterprises, squeezing out family controllers and individual shareholders alike. It is now the strategic actions of the financial intermediaries in Britain and the United States which are most influential in determining the constraints under which enterprises act. The financial institutions determine the conditions under which all other enterprises must act.[2] It is important, therefore, to assess the implications of this trend for corporate control and rule. Orthodox Marxist writers, for example, have seen this trend as leading to the formation of bank-dominated business groups under the leadership of finance capitalists. My own view on this matter is somewhat different, though these Marxists have correctly recognized that the growth of institutional shareholdings has fundamentally undermined the managerialist model of the business enterprise.

A principal concern of this book is the question of 'group' organization in business. Hadden's chapter makes a useful distinction between what he calls the 'total group' and the 'network group'. The total group, he argues, is the characteristic form of business enterprise in Britain, the group involving a parent company and its wholly owned subsidiaries. In the network group, on the other hand, a collection of semi-autonomous enterprises are mutually linked through intersecting minority shareholdings and smaller share participations. The network group, what Teubner (Chapter 3) has called the 'hydra-headed' group, has frequently been

---

[2] It is important to note here, of course, that control, as I have defined it, is only one aspect of the overall structure of constraints under which enterprises must act. Other constraints derive from bank-lending operations (which reinforce the pattern of financial hegemony), commercial relations and personal relations, as well as such factors as political constraints. Commercial, capital, and personal relations are discussed in J. Scott (1991a).

identified as characteristic of Japanese business. It has generally been held by non-Marxists that such network groups do not exist in Britain or the United States. Marxist writers, however, have seen them—in the form of the financial interest group—as a universal characteristic of the advanced capitalist economies. My research was intended, in part, to investigate whether 'network groups' could, in fact, be found in Britain.[3]

Such groups are, of course, difficult to identify in either legal or socio-logical terms. By virtue of their hydra-headed nature and the fact that their links run outside the group to other enterprises, it is difficult to establish with any precision the boundaries of a group. Using the tech-niques of social network analysis (J. Scott 1991b), however, it is possible to try to map the structure of inter-corporate relations and to uncover any 'network groups' which might exist. Research using these techniques (J. Scott 1986) has found that inter-corporate relations are extensive among large enterprises in contemporary Britain, but that there do not seem to be any 'network groups' of the type found in Japan.

3. BUSINESS GROUPS IN BRITAIN

While 'network groups' seem to be absent from the contemporary British economy, this has not always been the case. From the late nineteenth century until at least the 1930s, there were large corporate groups in heavy industry, in road and rail transport, in shipping, and in the financial sector. The investment trust sector has been characterized by group organization for much of its history, continuing right up to the present day. These groups were built around inter-corporate sharehold-ings and interlocking directorships.

The earliest forms of inter-corporate shareholding in Britain had their roots in the practice of syndicate financing, whereby a number of investors each took investment holdings in one or more other companies. This was spearheaded by the medieval merchant houses, which used this system to form trading companies and to undertake shipping ventures, and it was in this way that a number of London merchant houses formed the Bank of England in 1694. This same practice was the basis of the massive expansion of British overseas investment during the nineteenth century, more and more of the investing merchant houses adopting a cor-porate form (Chapman 1984: ch. 9). The crucial innovation made during this period, however, was the investment trust company, which allowed a considerable ramification of these systems of inter-corporate share-holding.

---

[3] The 'total group' is, in sociological terms, a single enterprise. In the remainder of this chapters I refer to the 'network group' simply as a 'group'.

Investment trust companies and similar investment vehicles began to appear during the 1860s, and their founders acted as promoters in the organization of investment syndicates. Investment trusts were not generally formed as single, isolated ventures. Rather, the trusts were elements in complex investment systems. A group of investors would each invest in a number of associated investment trusts, each of these being linked by the common administrative and management services which were provided by a firm of lawyers, accountants, or stockbrokers, or by a merchant bank. The trusts subject to common management and administration would then undertake co-ordinated investment in a collection of target companies. The strongest investment groups were those in which the constituent trusts took cross-holdings in one another's capital. In this way the legal independence of the separate trusts within a group masked the reality of co-ordinated syndicate investment (see Figure 16.1). Thus, syndicate financing led to a hierarchical structure of inter-corporate shareholdings, which allowed the formation of extensive investment groups.

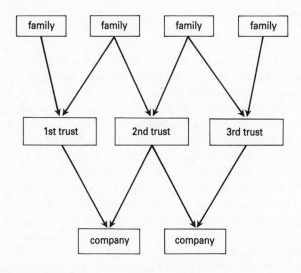

Fig. 16.1. Simplified model of an investment trust group. The arrows denote shareholding relationships.

This financial innovation of the late nineteenth century was the basis on which the principles of inter-corporate shareholding could be extended to other areas, giving those who headed the hierarchical investment groups a power out of all proportion to their personal ownership or office holding. Their power depended, crucially, on the access to financial resources which they were able to gain through the system of inter-corporate shareholdings. I shall illustrate this through two case studies.

3.1 The Kylsant group

Owen Philipps, later Lord Kylsant, was a leading figure in the British shipping industry from the First World War until the 1920s. His oldest brother John, later Lord St Davids, was a key figure in Kylsant's rise to power.[4] St Davids became active in the investment trust sector during the 1890s, building up cross-holdings among the trusts which he formed and co-ordinating their investments in shipping, railways, cement, electricity, and transport. Kylsant set up various shipping companies with the backing of his brother's companies, and in 1903 he became a director of the important Royal Mail Steam Packet Company.

Kylsant used the Royal Mail company as the cornerstone of his business operations, co-ordinating the activities of various shipping and investment companies in order to purchase controlling stakes in yet other companies. His principal business method was to alter the capital gearing of the companies so as to create a small number of voting shares and a much larger number of non-voting shares and loan certificates. In this way, he could maintain control with a small percentage holding of the total capital, and he rapidly built a huge and complex business group through the use of inter-corporate holdings. In 1925, for example, Kylsant and his associates owned 33 per cent of the voting capital of the Royal Mail company, and a further 33 per cent was owned by associated group companies. Group organization involved the circulation and re-circulation of capital among the various members of the group. Each company paid dividends to all others, and so success was self-reinforcing.

Unfortunately, this same system also allowed failure to reverberate through the whole group. In 1927 Kylsant agreed to purchase the White Star Line from its American owners, but the need to finance this acquisition coincided with other financial difficulties in the group. A depression in West African trade had caused a slump in the profits of one of the larger group companies, and this, in turn, resulted in smaller earnings for those group companies which depended on its earnings. A circulation of profits was turned into a circulation of losses. The resulting slump in share prices could not be resolved through capital reconstruction, as the bulk of the capital was held within the group. Pressure from loan stock-holders and bankers led to an inquiry which showed that the extent of the group's difficulties had been concealed through inadequate published

---

[4] To avoid confusion, I shall refer to the brothers as 'Kylsant' and 'St Davids', though John received his title in 1908 and Owen in 1923. For further background, see Green and Moss (1982) and Davies (1981).

accounts. Kylsant was imprisoned for breaches of the Companies Act, while his group was broken up and restructured by the Bank of England and other leading investors.

3.2 The Philip Hill group

Philip Hill was born in 1873, and began his business career as an estate agent. His offices were in the West End of London, not in the City, and he operated in commercial property independently of City banks and institutions. Through his involvement in commercial property, he came into contact with the Beecham family, pharmaceutical producers and music lovers, who had put together a syndicate of businessmen to purchase the Covent Garden Opera House and the surrounding land. Philip Hill secured the separate flotation of both the pharmaceutical and the Covent Garden companies, using the profits to form a small investment bank in 1932.

Hill rapidly acquired a reputation in the poorly developed area of corporate finance. With backing from Eagle Star Insurance, also isolated from the City establishment, Hill became involved in the formation and flotation of a number of companies, including a brewery, a pharmaceutical retailer, the Hawker Siddeley Engineering Company, and the Rank food concern. In each case, Hill and his associated companies would retain a stake in the companies which they advised.

Hill's business was secure enough to survive his death in 1942, the alliance with Eagle Star ensuring that there was continuity of leadership. Sir Edward Mountain of Eagle Star reconstructed the group by separating the banking and investment interests of Philip Hill into distinct companies, each of which had a reciprocal shareholding with his own company. This gave the group great stability, and allowed it to expand and diversify during the post-war period. A new chief executive, Kenneth Keith, was recruited, and he enlarged the group through the acquisition of two merchant banks, one of which was a member of the City's Acceptance Houses Committee. This gave the group access to one of the central forums in the City, and the group's expansion culminated in the acquisition of the prestigious banking business of M. Samuel in 1965. The banking side of the group, under the name of Hill Samuel, and the investment side, under the name Philip Hill Investment Trust (PHIT), remained tied through cross-holdings until the early 1980s, when Hill Samuel and PHIT were split, following the retirement of Kenneth Keith, and when Eagle Star was acquired by BAT Industries.[5]

The Hill Samuel group was tied to its industrial clients through rela-

---

[5] Hill Samuel was subsequently acquired by the banking group TSB.

tively small strategic holdings. But, with one or two important exceptions, it did not form them into the kind of pyramidal structure of group control that was achieved by Kylsant. Philip Hill and his successors saw a looser structure of participation and influence as being more stable in the long term. A tight form of inter-corporate shareholding was, however, important at the financial heart of the group. The Samuel family shared minority control of Hill Samuel, and the Mountain family was influential in the control of Eagle Star; but the key to understanding group control was the pattern of inter-corporate holdings. PHIT and its associated investment trusts shared minority control of Hill Samuel, and had a holding in Eagle Star; while Hill Samuel had holdings in both Eagle Star and PHIT. The basis of the Hill Samuel holdings, however, were not those which it owned in its own right, but those which it managed on behalf of its investment clients; its allied unit trusts and the pensions funds of numerous industrial companies (including those in which Hill Samuel had long-standing participations) were important means for buttressing the group structure.

4. BRITAIN AND JAPAN COMPARED

These examples of group enterprise built through inter-corporate shareholdings show certain obvious similarities to contemporary forms of group enterprise in Japan, South Korea, and Taiwan (Numazaki 1986; Hamilton *et al.* 1987; Lee *et al.* 1987). Access to financial resources allowed companies to be formed into a structure in which capital and control were highly geared. In this way, Lord Kylsant, Philip Hill, and various other British business leaders could build large business groups. But this pattern never became typical or widespread in British business. Only within the investment trust sector did loose business groupings have any lasting importance. Elsewhere, group enterprise was a relatively marginal and short-lived feature of business operations. Despite the emergence of such groups as those of Kylsant and Philip Hill, therefore, inter-corporate shareholding in Britain did not ultimately develop in the direction of enterprise groups and aligned shareholdings of the Japanese type. Why was this?

The reason must be sought in the organization of the stock-market and the financial system. The *zaibatsu*, and later the *kigyoshudan*, in Japan achieved a tight, stable group structure, because commercial banking operations and the provision of loan stock were themselves elements in the structure of group enterprise. Each of the large groups had a bank, an insurance company, and other investment institutions among its key members, and so was able to achieve a high level of financial autonomy.

This was never the case in Britain. Instead, group enterprise in Britain has always operated within a pre-existing environment of independent and competing providers of capital. This has meant that individual enterprises have had access to alternative sources of capital on a scale not found in Japan. It has not been possible, in general, for British enterprises to be tied into relations of tight financial dependence on one particular bank. They have always been able to avoid such dependence by securing alternative sources of capital.

The impetus to inter-corporate shareholding in Britain, therefore, was different from that in Japan, and it reflected the distinctive features of British capital mobilization. While inter-corporate shareholdings have existed in all the advanced capitalist economies, they have taken different forms under distinct national conditions. Common to all capitalist economies are two processes which can be termed the size effect and the wealth-limit effect. As businesses increase in size, they become too large for any individual, family, or group of related individuals to provide their capital. The need for large enterprises to draw on extended pools of capital as they increase in size is what is meant by the 'size effect'. The joint-stock form allows the size effect to operate, resulting in a dilution of the original ownership stake as more and more individuals become shareholders in the company. At this point the wealth-limit effect begins to operate. Those with sufficient wealth to invest in company shares form a very small proportion of the population, as it is only the members of the higher classes who have enough wealth to allow for personal investment. It is not possible for them to provide sufficient capital for all the expanding joint-stock companies. The capital requirements of an economy organized around large-scale enterprise cannot be met through personal investment.

These two factors operate together to weaken personal ownership and control in large-scale enterprises. Enterprises must seek alternative, non-personal sources of funding. This general tendency is common to all advanced capitalist economies, though it varies in strength from one to another. National variations in the move away from personal ownership depend on the overall significance of large-scale business in the national economy and on the size and riches of the wealthy classes. Personal investment is much more marked in the United States, for example, than it is in Britain (J. Scott 1986: 143–5), because the greater significance of large enterprises in the American economy is matched by the existence of much larger numbers of wealthy families.

The gap between the scale of business enterprise and the personal wealth of the higher classes in Britain has been filled by companies seeking funds from the already established financial system. As the banks and insurance companies of the City gradually became more willing to invest in company shares, inter-corporate shareholdings became an important feature of British business. These shareholdings took the form of 'institutional' capital, which made it both difficult and unnecessary to build enterprise groups. Financial institutions were independent foci of action, with interests opposed to those of the business groups which did emerge. Whenever groups needed outside capital, this was available only on the terms proposed by the institutions. The rescue and reconstruction of the companies in the Kylsant group, for example, involved its breakup into separate enterprises, each of which was financed by a diverse collection of institutions.

Inter-corporate shareholdings in Britain, as the key forces in the transition from personal to impersonal possession, took an increasingly institutional form after the Second World War. The particular form of 'citizenship' that was established in Britain involved a pattern of welfare provision through forms of pension and insurance funding, which strengthened the position of the financial institutions (Hannah 1986). The state encouraged the formation of schemes whose investment funds provided profits to pay the pensions of members. This system of pension provision strengthened institutional capital in Britain, and ensured that inter-corporate shareholdings continued to take an institutional form.

These factors were not absent in Japan, but they were overshadowed by other factors. Under the post-war American occupation, the old *zaibatsu* business groups were reconstructed. The wealthy controlling families were forced to sell their shareholdings, and the overall level of personal investment, which was already very low, was much diminished. The operation of the wealth-limit effect was, in this way, especially marked. For this reason, mobilization of capital by the banks was to play a crucial role in post-war Japanese reconstruction. In this way, the surviving elements of group enterprise were strengthened, as banks lent mainly to those companies with which they had been involved in the former *zaibatsu*. The new type of group organization that emerged, called *kigyoshudan* by business observers, was built up as banks and other companies set up cross-holdings with other group members. Inter-corporate shareholdings in Japan, therefore, produced a system of impersonal possession based on 'corporate' capital (Okumura 1979; J. Scott 1986, 1991*a*).

5. CONSTELLATIONS OF INTERESTS

If contemporary business organization in Britain does not involve the formation of 'network groups', how is the network of inter-corporate shareholdings to be interpreted? Large enterprises with dispersed capital are embedded in extensive networks of connection. They do not have the sovereign autonomy depicted in managerialist theory; but neither are they elements in the financial groups depicted in Marxist theory. My research has shown the crucial importance of the inequalities which exist among shareholders in these enterprises. In those companies with dispersed capital, the great bulk of voting power is in the hands of a small set of corporate interests—principally banks, insurance companies, and pension funds. The members of this set, generally numbering around twenty, constitute the major constraint on managerial autonomy; and they play a fundamentally different role in corporate affairs from all other shareholders.

I have introduced the concept of 'control through a constellation of interests' to describe the specific features of modern corporate control in Britain and the United States (J. Scott 1985: 49—51). Large enterprises with dispersed capital are controlled by a small but diverse constellation of institutional shareholders. The set has sufficient shares for control, but neither the capacity nor the willingness to act in a co-ordinated way as a cohesive controlling group. At any particular time an enterprise will be constrained by the interests of the shareholders which make up its controlling constellation. The dominant shareholders constrain the activities of the enterprise which they control; but their competing interests and their lack of unity give the enterprise considerable autonomy of action within these constraints. Their power is a negative constraining power through which, in the typical case, management seeks to discern and take account of their interests without the need for any positive and deliberate intervention.

The constellations which constrain each enterprise are true corporate entities, though they are not reflected in legal terminology. They are able, on occasion, to co-ordinate their actions, but they do not form tight coalitions or 'concert parties'. The various constellations which can be identified in an economy such as that of Britain overlap considerably in their membership, and this highlights the importance of studying inter-organizational networks. The overlapping constellations create a complex network of constraining shareholdings, which underlies the specific contractual relations which enterprises establish with one another. The structure of this network is 'invisible' from the standpoint of any particular enterprise, and it has no legal status or existence. It is, nevertheless, a crucially important 'non-contractual' factor in setting the pattern of constraints under which the management of enterprises must operate.

American researchers (Mintz and Schwartz 1985; see also, J. Scott 1986) have argued that those institutions which occupy central positions in the inter-corporate network comprise a group of dominant, or 'hegemonic', controllers, who are able to determine the overall flow of capital in the economy. The directors of these dominant institutions are involved in an additional network of relations, a network of interlocking directorships, from which emerges an 'inner circle' of corporate decision-makers who dominate corporate affairs (Useem 1984).

Control is vested in the institutions, and enterprises must adapt themselves to the institutions' interests, particularly as they are presented to them by the representatives of the institutions who sit on their boards. At the same time, each controlling constellation is beset by conflicting interests, and so a 'space' for managerial autonomy is created. It is for these reasons that actual patterns of rule vary from one enterprise to another. The actual power-holders in an enterprise are a loose and shifting coalition of people drawn from those who represent the financial institutions and those who occupy positions of managerial authority. The autonomy which they can achieve in corporate rule is limited by the structure of control under which they operate. Under some conditions, executives may be able to usurp many of the powers of control, and so be able to rule in an autocratic way; but this is constantly likely to be undermined by an assertion or reassertion of institutional control by those who represent the controlling institutions on the company board.

We are faced with a very complex situation in which the question 'Who rules the corporations?' is too simplistic. Corporate rule is always and necessarily exercised by particular people; but in a system of impersonal possession they do not act in their personal capacity, but as representatives of their employing organizations. In such modern systems, complex networks of relations are established, within which corporate groups and other structures may emerge. Legal theory, by and large, has confined its attention to the 'total group' headed by a parent company. Far less attention has been given to the various forms of 'network group' and the looser network structures that have been discussed in this chapter. If we wish to develop an adequate economic or legal theory of the modern business enterprise and the modern economy, we must begin to build an adequate sociological theory of business organization.

I have outlined some of the conclusions from my own sociological investigations, which point also to the structure of class relations within which corporate controllers operate (J. Scott 1991c). I hope that the discussion that will follow the publication of this volume will pursue the links between this sociological viewpoint on inter-organizational relations and the legal and economic models of contractual and market relations.

17

The American Law of Corporate Groups

PHILLIP I. BLUMBERG

I. ORIGINS OF ENTITY LAW

This chapter seeks to provide a summary review for European students of corporate groups of those significant developments in American judicial decisions and statutory law which I have termed 'the emerging American law of corporate groups'. I have written extensively of these developments in the five volumes comprising my series on *The Law of Corporate Groups* (Blumberg 1983, 1985, 1987*b*, 1989, 1992) and in various legal periodicals (Blumberg 1990*a*, 1990*b*, 1986), to which readers interested in more detailed discussion of these matters are referred.

However they may differ in other respects, the legal systems of the Western world without exception share the same fundamental concepts of corporation law. Reflecting their common legacy of medieval notions of Roman law (Buckland 1965: 54; Williston 1888: 164), Western legal systems share the same view of the juridical personality of the corporation. This is the view that a corporation is a separate juridical person with its own rights and duties, separate from those of the persons who may from time to time be its shareholders. This is entity law.

Centuries ago, the corporation thus conceived was recognized to have the capacity in its own name to acquire and hold property, to enter into contracts, to sue and be sued, and to have an existence with a duration independent of the persons comprising its shareholders. Further, it had its own seal, which under English common law, symbolized its distinctive juridical status (Coke 1628: iii. 6, 412; ii. 250a; Case of Sutton's Hospital, 1612: 970–1; Blackstone 1765–9: i. 470; Kyd 1793: ii. 103).

So much is clear. Limited liability is quite another matter. Although the limited liability of shareholders for the obligations of a corporation is frequently regarded as an essential concomitant of the separate personality of the corporation, both English and American history leave no doubt that it is a very different concept, and for a protracted period, was a

© The Blumberg Trust 1993. This paper is a revised version of the author's 1991 article 'Amerikanisches Konzernrecht', 3 *Zeitschrift für Unternehmens und Gesellschaftsrecht* 327. It has also been integrated in substantial part into the author's recent book, *The Multinational Challenge to Corporation Law: The Search for a New Corporate Personality*, Oxford University Press, New York, 1993.

highly controversial one. Centuries after the development of the concept of the corporation as a separate juridical person, limited liability was a disputed political issue in the United States. Even after Massachusetts, the largest industrial state of the time, gave what proved to be decisive recognition of limited liability in 1830, the political struggle continued for decades, with Rhode Island, the second largest manufacturing state, continuing with unlimited liability until 1847.[1] During this period, the ultimate acceptance or rejection of the doctrine was still in doubt.[2]

In fact, California retained its own unique principle of pro rata shareholder liability well into the twentieth century.[3] In addition, constitutional and statutory provisions throughout the United States imposing double or even triple assessment liability upon shareholders predominated until much the same time (Hurst 1980: 27; Cook 1926: i. 675 n. 1; see Blumberg 1987b: sect. 2.01.2).

During this formative period, American courts overwhelmingly held that corporations did not have the capacity to acquire or hold shares of another corporation in the absence of express authorization by statute or in their charter (e.g., *De La Vergne Refrig. Mach. Co.* v. *German Sav. Inst.*, 1899: 54–5; *Louisville and N.R.R.* v. *Kentucky*, 1896; see Fletcher 1980: sect. 2824–6; Blumberg 1987b: sect. 3.02.1). On frequent occasions in special acts of incorporation, the legislature included the power to acquire stock in a corporation's charter. In some instances, as in the case of banks and insurance companies, this was to encourage investment in the capital-poor country. More important were a number of statutes authorizing certain railroads, and later Western Union Telegraph, to acquire shares, evidently to facilitate extension of their lines. However, with some departures from the well-established rule, state legislatures consistently refused to include this power in charters of manufacturing corporations (Robinson 1910).

Thus, the corporate structures of the time, with rare exceptions, were simple. The corporation constituted the enterprise, while its shareholders were purely investors, not themselves engaged in conducting part of the enterprise.[4] The legal entity and the economic entity were identical; the corporation was the enterprise. All assets of the business were available for payment of the debts of the business, and limited liability protected

[1] Massachusets Act, 23 Feb. 1830, ch. 53, sect. 8 (*Massachusets Acts 1830*: 325); Rhode Island Act, June Session 1847, *Rhode Island Acts and Resolves* 30.

[2] Michigan in 1837, New Hampshire in 1842, Wisconsin in 1849, and Pennsylvania in 1853 all turned for a while to unlimited shareholder liability, but in the end each accepted limited liability (Blumberg 1987b: ch. 1).

[3] See art. IV, sect. 36, of the California Constitution of 1849; art. XII, sect. 3, of the California Constitution of 1879 (repealed 1930); and the California Civil Code, sect. 322 (repealed 1931); also Blumberg 1987b: sect. 2.01.1

[4] This refers to the conduct of economic activity on one's own account, not to participation in the management of the business of a corporation.

the investors from losses of the business in excess of their capital subscription.

In the United States, this changed dramatically in 1888–93 with the adoption by New Jersey of the first statutes authorizing corporations generally to acquire and hold stock in other corporations.[5] The New Jersey statutes authorized the holding company. In time, other states followed suit. Large-scale business increasingly became organized in the new form, which was eagerly sought by financial promoters as a technique for corporate acquisitions to replace the trust device, which was then under fierce attack. Corporate groups emerged. This has been described as a 'turning point' in the evolution of American business (Chandler 1962: 30).

With the ensuing growth of corporate groups, the simple two-part structure of the previous corporate world, consisting of a single corporation conducting the enterprise and its shareholders who were no more than investors, no longer fairly described the large corporations of the country. Instead, large corporations increasingly developed into complex corporate structures, typically consisting of a parent corporation, often sub-holding companies, and many operating subsidiaries, collectively engaged in conducting the enterprise.

By this time, it had been accepted for decades that the shareholder-investors in the older, simple corporation had limited liability for the debts of the corporation. When corporate groups emerged, limited liability obviously also applied to the shareholder-investors in the parent corporations of the new corporate groups. The addition of subsidiaries to the parent corporation in which they held shares did not change the investment nature of their relationship to the enterprise.[6]

But what of the new parent corporations? As an economic matter, they were collectively engaged in the conduct of the business of the group, along with their subsidiaries. They were part of the enterprise. On the other hand, as a conceptual matter, the parent corporations were shareholders in their subsidiaries, and it had become accepted that shareholders were not liable for the debts of the corporations in which they held shares. Which were to prevail: economic realities or legal concepts?

It is striking that this issue, which constitutes one of the major

---

[5] New Jersey Act, 4 Apr., 1888, ch. 269, sect. 1 (1888 N.J. Laws 385); Act of 17 Apr. 1888, ch. 295, sect. 1 (1888 N.J. Laws 445–6); Act of 9 May 1889, ch. 265, sect. 4 (1889 N.J. Laws 412, 414); Act of 14 Mar. 1893, ch. 171, sect. 2 (1893 N.J. Laws 301).

[6] No American decision has imposed enterprise liability on the public shareholders in a large American corporation. *Anderson* v. *Abbott*, 1944, is the only possible exception. The Supreme Court, by divided vote, construed the provision in the National Banking Act imposing double assessment liability on shareholders of national banks to apply to the public shareholders of a bank holding company with national bank subsidiaries. It should be noted that there was no indication that the holding company in question had been organized for other than legitimate business reasons, or as a device to evade the statutory provision.

challenges facing the law today, attracted no attention at the time. When it first came before the courts prior to the First World War, American law was experiencing the high tide of formalism, or conceptualism, as the only legitimate form of legal analysis. The bench, bar, and academy of the time still examined legal problems through a conceptualistic lens. On this view, the appropriate legal analysis was a syllogism. Shareholders were not liable for the obligations of the corporations of which they were shareholders. A parent corporation was a shareholder. Ergo, a parent corporation was not liable for the obligations of its subsidiary corporations of which it was the shareholder. Without further discussion and without apparent awareness that they were applying the traditional concept to a very different economic relationship, almost all American courts, through such formalistic analysis, uniformly disposed of cases seeking to impose liability on a parent for torts or contracts of a subsidiary. Courts and commentators alike were generally oblivious to the dramatic change in the underlying relationship.

For a brief period, there was strong recognition that railroad companies organized in 'systems' might be subject to tort liability on an enterprise basis without reference to 'piercing the veil'; but these decisions, including a notable Supreme Court opinion by Justice Brandeis in *Davis* v. *Alexander*, 1925, were not successful in developing a doctrinal framework that became generally accepted.[7] Instead, American law continued to apply entity law to corporate groups following (then) Chief Judge Cardozo's highly influential opinion in *Berkey* v. *Third Ave. Ry.*, 1926. In so far as limited liability was concerned, the legal position of a parent corporation as a shareholder was no different from that of any individual shareholder under the traditional doctrines.

In this manner, limited liability designed to protect persons who were solely investors and not themselves conducting parts of the enterprise was uncritically extended to parent corporations, although they manifestly constituted an important part of the enterprise, and although their shareholders—the ultimate investors—also were protected by limited liability.

2. ESCAPE FROM THE CONFINES OF ENTITY LAW

Notwithstanding their general acceptance, entity law supplemented by limited liability presented serious problems for the legal system. Even in

[7] '[W]here one railroad company actually controls another and operates both as a single system, the dominant company will be liable for injuries due to the negligence of the subsidiary company' (*Davis* v. *Alexander*, 1925: 117); see also *Lehigh Valley R. Co.* v. *Dupont*, 1904: 845–6; *Lehigh Valley R. Co.* v. *Krysienski*, 1906: *per curiam*; and other cases cited in Blumberg 1987b: sect. 12.02. 1.

the case of the 'simple' corporation owned by individual controlling shareholders, rigid application of the doctrine on occasion led to results which were clearly inequitable. As American courts fashioned an equitable remedy to deal with such cases, there emerged a body of law which may be called 'traditional piercing the veil jurisprudence'. Later, in part under the impetus of cases involving corporate groups, a liberalized version of 'piercing the veil' has also developed.

The piercing the veil decisions provide a rich source of enterprise law. This is known to almost all lawyers and scholars. Moreover, such decisions are joined by an impressive number of statutes, administrative regulations and decisions, and judicial decisions in allied areas, to provide a surprisingly wide demonstration of the growing application of enterprise principles in American law. This experience, which constitutes what I have termed 'the American law of corporate groups' is occurring across a wide spectrum of American law in the following areas:

(a) Piercing the veil jurisprudence: traditional and liberalized. Judicial doctrines, particularly liberalized applications, of traditional piercing the veil jurisprudence in matters involving corporate groups in private controversies at common law, particularly in tort.

(b) Unitary business doctrine. Judicial development of the 'unitary business' theory for determining the constitutionality of unitary tax apportionment.

(c) Judicial procedure. Judicial developments in the law of judicial procedure, often codified as judicial rules of civil procedure. This is particularly evident in such areas as jurisdiction, venue, *res judicata* and collateral estoppel, statute of limitations, discovery, and the scope of injunctions.

(d) Bankruptcy. Legislative and judicial developments in particular areas of the law of bankruptcy, particularly equitable subordination, substantive consolidation, and voidable preferences.

(e) Statutes of general application. Judicial and administrative developments in the construction and application to corporate groups of statutes of general application making no specific reference to corporate groups or enterprise principles.

(f) Statutes of specific application to corporate groups. Legislative and administrative developments in the enactment of statutes and regulations expressly adopting enterprise principles and applying to corporate groups, sometimes for pervasive industry-wide regulation, but most frequently for selected purposes in statutes otherwise resting on entity law.

This wide-ranging development of enterprise principles in American law reflects the increasing recognition by legislatures, administrative agencies, and courts alike of the limitations created by entity law impeding effective social ordering of the activities of corporate groups. Principles of entity law developed in the very different economic world of centuries ago ignore contemporary economic realities. In order to permit effective implementation of legal objectives, whether statutory or common law, in matters involving corporate groups, the increasingly anachronistic principles of entity law are beginning to yield in many areas to application of enterprise law. This is particularly true in the statutory area; but, as will be seen in the following summary review, it is evident elsewhere as well.

In view of space limitations, this review and the supporting citations are necessarily abbreviated; but the references to the earlier works of the author on which it is based will provide readers with detailed support for the points discussed.

3. PIERCING THE VEIL JURISPRUDENCE

The development of piercing the veil principles in the United States may be divided into two distinct phases: traditional piercing the veil jurisprudence and its modern, liberalized version, which is particularly evident in the judicial decisions in tort cases and in the construction of statutes of general application.

3.1 Traditional piercing the veil jurisprudence

The traditional doctrine was largely formulated in the context of corporations controlled by individual controlling shareholders. After such formulation, it was subsequently applied without significant change in cases involving corporate groups. It arose as a development in the law of equity to deal in isolated cases with particularly harsh consequences flowing from application of entity law.

Where abuse or misuse of the corporate entity could be demonstrated, particularly where factors long recognized as supporting equitable override of legal principles such as misrepresentation or fraud were involved, courts early responded by granting relief. By the outbreak of the First World War, this pattern had become a recognized aspect of American law, characterized in that familiar phrase 'piercing the veil' (Wormser 1912). With a wealth of case material, overwhelmingly involving individual controlling shareholders, traditional piercing the veil jurisprudence gradually emerged.[8] It had several variations: the 'instrumentality' doc-

---

[8] Several treatises had appeared on the topic by the 1930s: e.g., Anderson 1931; Powell 1931; Latty 1936; Wormser 1927. Although numerous articles have since appeared in American legal periodicals, the subject did not receive comprehensive treatise treatment until the publication of the volumes in the series comprising *The Law of Corporate Groups*.

trine, the *alter ego* doctrine, and the identity doctrine. Although their formulation differed, the variants were substantively the same.

Under traditional piercing the veil jurisprudence, the courts in 'rare' or 'exceptional' cases would impose liability upon a shareholder for obligations of a corporation where the following factors were present: (a) the control by the shareholder over the corporation's affairs was so intrusively exercised that the corporation was seen to be lacking separate existence;[9] (b) the corporation was utilized to commit some fraudulent or wrongful or inequitable or 'morally culpable' or 'fundamentally unfair' act to the detriment of creditors; and (c) the conduct resulted in loss to creditors.[10]

These courts were primarily concerned with a determination of the extent to which the corporate form had been respected or corporate formalities had not been observed. In such an event, the courts would conclude that the business and affairs of the corporation and the shareholder had become so intertwined that corporation and shareholder constituted only one entity. The corporation was then stigmatized as no more than the 'adjunct', 'agent', *'alter ego'*, 'conduit', 'department', 'instrumentality', 'puppet', or 'tool' of the shareholder, and liability was imposed on the shareholder.

This was jurisprudence by metaphor or epithet. It did not contribute to legal understanding, because it was an intellectual construct, divorced from business realities. The metaphors are no more than conclusory terms, affording little understanding of the considerations and policies underlying the court's action and little help in predicting results in future cases. The courts express their results in very broad terms that provide little general guidance. As a result, American lawyers are faced with hundreds of decisions that are irreconcilable and not entirely comprehensible. Few areas of American law have been so sharply criticized by commentators.

Fact-specific standards testing corporate separateness emerged, and in time became more and more complex. The fact-specific nature of these

[9] One frequently quoted expression of the standard is: 'Control, not merely majority or complete stock control, but complete domination, not only of finances, but of policy and business practices in respect to the transaction attacked so that the corporate entity had at the time no separate mind, will, or existence, of its own.' See *Lowendahl* v. *Baltimore & O.R.R.*, 1936: 157.

[10] This formulation follows the three-factor instrumentality doctrine. While the *alter ego* doctrine typically employs a different formulation, courts and scholars generally treated it as equivalent in substance to the instrumentality doctrine in all respects. Under the *alter ego* doctrine, piercing the veil is stated to be appropriate when (1) such unity of ownership and control exists that the two affiliated corporations have ceased to be separate and the subsidiary has been relegated to the status of the *alter ego* of the parent; and (2) where recognition of the two companies as separate entities would sanction fraud or lead to an inequitable result. The identity doctrine is much the same: see Blumberg 1987*b*: sect. 6.01–6.04.

standards made generalization of guiding principles almost impossible. Thus, it was acknowledged that no single factor was decisive, and that the outcome rested on the totality of all the circumstances. Some courts have referred to the fact-specific standards as 'laundry lists', a term which conveys a vivid sense of the courts' lack of confidence in the analysis.[11]

The second element in traditional piercing the veil jurisprudence was conduct detrimental to creditors. This was less elusive. Asset shifting, asset mingling, asset siphoning, or other types of asset manipulation; use of corporate funds for payment of the shareholder's obligations; and grossly inadequate capitalization were readily recognized as the type of wrongful conduct that would support relief when lack of separateness had been demonstrated.

Resting on formalism, traditional piercing the veil jurisprudence was invoked as a universal principle of law, and applied indiscriminately without regard to the area of the law involved in the particular litigation before the court. Accordingly, the courts relied on contract decisions to justify results in tort cases, on decisions in such common-law controversies to justify results in cases involving statutory law, and on decisions in substantive matters to decide issues of procedure. In the process, the underlying policies and objectives of the law in the area in issue were brushed aside. This highly objectionable indiscriminate application of the traditional doctrine has also been much criticized (e.g. R.W. Hamilton 1971: 985).

3.2 Liberalized piercing the veil jurisprudence

With the decline of formalism as the controlling force in American jurisprudence, the hold of traditional entity law on American courts in cases involving corporate groups is visibly, albeit slowly, weakening. In place of the rigid standards traditionally applied as a conceptual matter indiscriminately throughout the law, modern courts have become increasingly concerned with implementation of the underlying objectives of the law in the area involved in the case at hand. Tort cases are increasingly being recognized as involving different values and interests than contract. Substantive law is recognized as presenting different concerns than problems in judicial procedure. Even more widely, courts are acknowledging that the construction and application of statutes require a very different analysis than the settlement of controversies between private parties.[12]

---

[11] e.g., *Taylor* v. *Standard Gas & Elec. Co.*, 10th Cir. 1938: 704–5; *Fish* v. *East*, 1940: see Blumberg 1987b: sect. 7.01. See also *Second Serv. Sys.* v. *St. Joseph Bank & Trust Co.*, 1988: 414. (Application of a given metaphor is frequently reported to be based on consideration of a long list of factors; such a list means, effectively, no rule of decision and no guidance from the precedents for either courts or practitioners.)

[12] Contract distinguished from tort: e.g., *Edwards Co.* v. *Monogram Indus., Inc.*, 1984;

In responding to the challenge of defining enterprise principles and determining under what circumstances they best meet the needs of the legal system in a case-by-case process, American courts have made considerable progress in the difficult process of evolution of a doctrinal standard for application of enterprise principles. In the more forward-looking decisions which may be termed 'liberalized piercing the veil jurisprudence', decisions both in common-law controversies and in construction of statutes of general application[13] have moved well beyond the emphasis on the formalistic factors which constituted the core of traditional piercing the veil jurisprudence. The concern instead is with the economic realities: do the separate corporations actually function as integral parts of the group, or do they operate as independent businesses?

The factors defining the economic contours and the decision-making structure of the group which are becoming recognized as the central points for enquiry in determining the nature of the interrelationship between a parent corporation and its subsidiaries are the following.

Control. All cases in the area accept that the existence of the parent corporation's control over the decision making of the subsidiary, even when combined with the presence of common officers and directors, is not decisive in and of itself. They go further and inquire into the extent to which such control has been exercised. They are particularly concerned with whether the exercise is an 'excessively intrusive' intervention by the parent and its personnel into the decision making of the subsidiary when compared to 'normal' management patterns in the contemporary business world. The parent's exercise of control over day-to-day decision making of a subsidiary, for example, is widely recognized as one form of unacceptable exercise of control which will lead to imposition of liability (or other legal consequences)[14] on the parent.[15]

Control by the group over such matters as determination of general policy, planning, budgets and capital expenditures, executive salaries and

---

substantive matters distinguished from procedure: e.g., *Energy Reserves Group, Inc.* v. *Superior Oil*, 1978; statutory matters distinguished from common law: e.g., *Town of Brookline* v. *Gorsuch*, 1981: 220.

[13] As discussed below, statutes of general application are those that regulate conduct without any express reference to corporate groups. By contrast, statutes of specific application expressly refer to corporate groups.

[14] Enterprise principles have been selectively applied for various purposes in the area of judicial procedure, with legal consequences being attributed to a parent (or subsidiary) corporation by reason of activities of its subsidiary (or parent). These include such fields of procedure as jurisdiction, service, venue, corporate citizenship for diversity purposes, discovery, statute of limitations, injunctions, and *res judicata*. None of such decisions directly involve limited liability; see Blumberg 1983: *passim*.

[15] For a review of the crucial significance of 'control' over day-to-day decision making in the area of jurisdiction, even by courts otherwise ready to apply traditional doctrines of entity law, see Blumberg 1983: sect. 3.05.2.

bonuses, and group utilization of manuals and guide-lines setting forth mandatory group policies with respect to such matters as personnel, safety, purchasing, labour relations, public relations and affairs, accounting, finance, ethical standards, and the like have received differing receptions by different courts. As should be evident, the realities of the extent of exercise of control in the particular case present a difficult issue of considerable subtlety and complexity. The extent of the exercise of control, while not decisive, occupies a role of central importance among the factors considered by the courts.

Economic integration. Another factor of major importance is the extent of economic integration of the business conducted by the parent and subsidiary corporations of the group, particularly where the companies in the group collectively conduct complementary fragments of a common business. This includes such matters as the extent of intra-group purchases and sales reflecting integration of various stages of the production and distribution processes, group warranties, group purchasing, warehousing and marketing, group credit, and group property and casualty insurance.

Financial interdependence. The extent of the financial and administrative interdependence of the group and its constituent companies is an additional factor of significance. In these supporting areas, do the separate corporations function as an integral part of the group, rather than operate independently? Such financial interdependence arises where subsidiaries do not finance themselves independently, but meet their financing needs through direct borrowing from the group or by borrowing from third parties on the basis of guaranties by the parent corporation and other subsidiaries in the group. Financing by group affiliates using intra-group guaranties has become so common in the United States that it has generated a particular area of law of its own (Blumberg 1985: sect. 7.13b (Supp. 1990); Blumberg 1987*b*).

Administrative interdependence. Corporate groups increasingly seek to achieve economies of scale by centralizing administrative supporting services for the constituent companies of the group, either in the parent or in a service subsidiary organized for the purpose. These centralized supporting services include legal, tax, accounting, finance, insurance, engineering, research and development, public relations and public affairs, employee education and training programmes, safety, and similar activities.

Overlapping employment structure. This factor includes such matters as group personnel career patterns involving movement of employees from one group company to another, group employee training programmes, and group insurance, pension, profit-sharing, and similar benefit plans, and the like.

Common group persona. A final factor is the use of a common group persona in the conduct of the group business, whereby the constituent companies of the group utilize the same group trade name, trade marks, logo, colour schemes, and in some cases even colour and style of uniforms the world over.

These factors provide the most promising building blocks available at the present time for the construction of an American doctrine of enterprise law. An increasing number of courts, although still in the minority, have used these factors to identify whether a subsidiary is so integrally intertwined with its parent corporation and its group that enterprise treatment is appropriate. This standard reflects an economic pattern of integrated or unitary group functioning and goes well beyond the elements of control and of overlapping proprietary interest inherent in every parent–subsidiary relationship. American courts require such a demonstration before they will utilize enterprise principles in a legal order still wedded generally to entity law.

American law has thus seen the beginning of new judicial attitudes toward the application of piercing the veil jurisprudence to corporate groups, in which the rigid traditional doctrine is increasingly being modified to serve the needs of modern economic society. This process is still in the early stages, but it is already having its impact on the American legal system. In order to implement more effectively the objectives of the law in the particular area involved in the individual case, courts are sloughing off numerous elements of the traditional, rigid standards of conventional piercing the veil jurisprudence. Thus, compliance by a subsidiary corporation with the customary formalities for the conduct of corporate business, such as separate records, stationery, bank accounts, offices, and the like, and similar indicia of its 'real' existence as a separate corporation may not be deemed particularly important. Nor does adequacy of initial capitalization play a decisive role.

In traditional piercing the veil jurisprudence, the existence of some fraudulent, inequitable, or other morally culpable or fundamentally unfair conduct detrimental to creditors has been typically viewed as essential for application of the doctrine. Modern cases, even in common-law areas, are departing from this requirement in an impressive number of decisions (Blumberg 1987*b*: sect. 9.03), dramatically expanding the capacity of the legal system to disregard the confining limitations of entity law in order to achieve the objectives of the law in the area at issue. In the construction and application of statutes of general application, this development is particularly prominent.

4. THE UNITARY BUSINESS DOCTRINE IN THE UNITARY TAX CASES

One of the outstanding formulations of enterprise principles in American judge-made law is the unitary business doctrine developed by the Supreme Court in five decisions from 1980 to 1983.[16] These decisions considered the constitutionality of state taxation of local components of multinational groups, computed by unitary tax apportionment formulae taking into account the world-wide activities of the group of which the local activities were a constituent part. (See also Chapter 20 below.)

Under the unitary business doctrine, the Court has upheld the constitutionality of world-wide unitary tax apportionment so long as the in-state unit and the out-of-state affiliates included in the apportionment formula base are commonly engaged in the conduct of an integrated 'unitary business' and do not represent 'discrete' business enterprises. The Court has focused on the underlying 'unity or diversity of [the] business enterprise' and on the fact that, as an economic matter, 'a functionally integrated enterprise' is involved (*Mobil Oil Corp.* v. *Commissioner of Taxes*, 1980: 440–1). It has emphasized that 'the underlying economic realities of a unitary business' are decisive (ibid.).

In formulating the unitary business doctrine, the Court has stressed group involvement in the business of its components, requiring proof of 'substantial mutual interdependence' of the components and of the 'contributions to income resulting from functional integration, centralization of management and economies of scale' (*Container Corp of Am.* v. *Franchise Tax Bd.*, 1983: 179). The formal segregation of functional departments as independent profit centres (*Exxon Corp.* v. *Wisconsin Department of Revenue*, 1980: 224–5) is irrelevant where the departments are parts of a 'highly integrated business which benefits from an umbrella of centralized management and controlled interaction'. Such an interrelationship is demonstrated by such features as the availability of 'essential corporate services for the entire company including the co-ordination of . . . operational functions', the use of 'centralized purchasing', or a centralized marketing system involving '[a] uniform credit card system, uniform packaging, brand names and promotional displays' (ibid.).

This economic test supersedes the technical legal forms of separate organization[17] or functional administrative divisions when an integrated

---

[16] *Mobil Oil* v. *Commissioner of Taxes*, 1980; *Exxon Corp.* v. *Wisconsin Department of Revenue*, 1980; *ASARCO, Inc.* v. *Idaho State Tax Comm'n*, 1982; *F. W. Woolworth Co.* v. *Taxation & Revenue Dep't*, 1982; and *Container Corp. of Am.* v. *Franchise Tax Bd.*, 1983.

[17] '[O]ne must look principally at the underlying activity not the form of investment . . . the form of business organization may have nothing to do with the underlying unity or diversity of business enterprise' (*Exxon*, 1980: 440–1).

business is involved.[18] Indeed, a reluctance to have the incidence of taxation controlled by a taxpayer's selection of a particular legal or organizational structure for the conduct of its business is a major incentive for adoption of unitary apportionment in preference to other tax methods.

The doctrine has restrictions. First, in *F. W. Woolworth Co.* v. *Taxation & Revenue Dep't*, 1982, the Court refused to find that this well-known horizontally integrated group constituted a 'unitary business'. The Court stated that the necessary degree of 'functional integration' of the subsidiaries with the group and centralization of management did not exist where foreign merchandising subsidiaries autonomously and independently performed such major functions as selection of merchandise, store site selection, advertising, and accounting, without any 'centralized purchasing, manufacturing, or warehousing' or 'central personnel training', where financing was independent of the parent, where there was no exchange of personnel, and where these subsidiaries had their own accounting, financial staff, and outside counsel (ibid. 366–70).

Second, in *ASARCO, Inc.* v. *Idaho State Tax Comm'n*, 1982, the Court held that mere existence of 'control' by the parent is not sufficient; it must be exercised. This restriction is of limited significance, since in virtually all groups, the desire to exploit the opportunities made possible by common direction of the enterprise is responsible for the organization of the group in the first place.

The Court's formulation of the unitary business doctrine in such detail provides one of the outstanding examples of American judge-made enterprise law in the place of entity law, used in order to adapt the legal order to the challenges presented by an interdependent world economic society in which major economic activity is predominantly conducted by multinational corporate groups.

However, as illustrated in particular by *F.W. Woolworth Co.* the doctrine has its limitations for use beyond constitutional law. For purposes of determining the outer limits of state taxing power for constitutional purposes, the unitary business doctrine imposes relatively restricted boundaries in defining the type of multinational enterprises that states may constitutionally tax in this manner. Its applicability is limited to particular models of managerial direction and of economic integration. Further, it gives little emphasis to factors that have been recognized as significant in enterprise cases occurring elsewhere in American law, particularly financial interdependence, administrative interdependence,

---

[18] Cf. *Exxon*, 1980: 219–20, 224–5 (where it was found irrelevant that Exxon organized functionally into marketing, exploration, and production and conducted only marketing activities within the state, where the marketing was an integral part of a 'highly integrated business').

financial interdependence, group employment structure, and group use of a common public group persona.[19]

5. STATUTORY LAW: INTRODUCTION

As noted, the American legal system, like the legal systems of the Western world generally, is grounded on entity law—the view that each corporation is a separate juridical person even when owned and controlled by another corporation with which it conducts a common business enterprise. However, in an era of multinational corporations, in which the economies of the world are closely interlocked and major economic activity is overwhelmingly conducted by centrally controlled corporate groups consisting of scores or even hundreds of affiliated corporations functioning in many different countries, entity law—however accurately it reflected the economic society of the early nineteenth century when it matured—has become hopelessly anachronistic. The entity law concept of the corporate juridical personality no longer matches the economic reality. Legal systems the world over are accordingly struggling with the development of new concepts of corporate personality to deal with this urgent problem. Although this evolution is apparent in all areas of American law, it is most evident in statutory law, where legislatures, courts, and administrative agencies attempt to transcend the limitations of the corporate entity doctrine in order to achieve effective implementation of regulatory and revenue statutes.

This application of American statutory law to corporate groups provides a greater demonstration of the acceptance of enterprise principles than even the developments in various areas in American common law, procedure, and bankruptcy law. The development in statutory law arises in two quite different contexts.

First, there are the statutes of general application, prohibiting or regulating specified behaviour without any particular reference to corporate groups. In cases involving the application of such statutes to corporate groups, the courts (and administrative agencies subject to review by the courts) have the burden of construing and applying the statutes to determine under what circumstances such statutes should be given an enterprise, rather than entity, construction. Such statutes include the antitrust and trade regulation laws, the labour laws, the employment discrimination laws, the employee retirement laws, the environmental laws, and the patent, copyright, and trade mark laws, among others.

[19] In *F. W. Woolworth*, 1982: 365–6, the Court mentions the absence of such factors as contributing to the unconstitutionality of the state tax in question. However, it nowhere indicates that they are factors of particular importance.

Second, there are the statutes of specific application, in which Congress has expressly referred to corporate groups and has itself employed enterprise principles in the formulation of the regulatory programme or the tax laws. In this class of statutes, Congress has expressly adopted enterprise law, and the burden upon the courts is sharply reduced. These statutory provisions have provided the richest reservoir of utilization of enterprise principles in American law. These statutes include the bank, savings and loan, and public utility holding company acts, as well as statutes regulating railroads and trucking, air transportation, shipping, communications, securities, investment companies, and the tax laws.

6. CORPORATE GROUPS UNDER STATUTES OF GENERAL APPLICATION

In the area of statutes of general application, Congress has not expressly addressed the issue of the application of the statute to constituent companies of corporate groups. The text of the statute provides no unmistakable guide, and the courts have the burden of making the fundamental choice between enterprise or entity law in determining the appropriate construction and application of the statute in cases involving corporate groups. In approaching this task, American courts have a degree of freedom which is markedly lacking in other countries, such as Great Britain.[20]

In dealing with this important responsibility, American courts have utilized at least three different frameworks of analysis. Many courts continue to look at such issues through application of traditional piercing the veil jurisprudence as a transcendental doctrine underlying the legal structure as a whole, disregarding the fact that vital issues of public policy, not private controversies at common law, are concerned. Other courts are increasingly turning from the rigid formalistic analysis of traditional piercing the veil jurisprudence to focus on the concerns of public policy involved in statutory construction and implementation. They proceed by reliance both on a statutory variant of liberalized piercing the veil and on doctrines of liberal statutory construction. They emphasize

[20] Thus, the Supreme Court has acknowledged that 'silence in federal legislation is no reason for limiting the reach of federal law . . . The inevitable incompleteness presented by all legislation means that interstitial federal lawmaking is a basic responsibility of the federal courts' (*United States* v. *Little Lake Misere Land Co.*, 1973: 593). See also *C. T. Carden* v. *Arkoma Assocs.*, 1990: 1023 (O'Connor, J., dissenting: 'Application of statutes to situations not anticipated by the legislature is a pre-eminently judicial function'). Some English decisions refuse to apply enterprise principles to obvious utilizations of corporate structure, to evade the objectives of labour and employment discrimination statutes in a manner quite out of keeping with American law. See, e.g., *Dimbleby & Sons Ltd.* v. *National Union of Journalists*, 1984 (secondary boycott); *Haughton* v. *Olau Line (UK) Ltd.*, 1986 (sexual harassment). These cases are discussed in Blumberg 1989: sect. 13.06, 14.13.6.

the different nature of the responsibility before the court in cases involving corporate groups and individual controlling shareholders under
statutory law.

The courts turning away from traditional piercing the veil jurisprudence regard the application of statutes of general application to parent
and subsidiary corporations as a complex question turning on an evaluation of a number of interrelated issues of paramount importance. These
include such matters as the statutory language, the statutory history in
the light of the problem which Congress was addressing, the underlying
statutory objectives and policies, and the extent to which enterprise or
'group' construction of the general statutory provision is necessary or
desirable so as to include a parent corporation or subsidiary corporation,
or perhaps sister subsidiaries, in order to implement the statutory programme or prevent frustration of the statutory objectives or prevent evasion of the statute.

In order better to pursue such matters, courts refusing to be bound by
the rigid limits of traditional piercing the veil jurisprudence also typically
evaluate factors relating to the economic realities of the enterprise
involved in the litigation, including the supplemental factors already
noted, such as the extent of exercise of control by the parent corporation
or group, economic integration, financial and administrative interdependence, overlapping group employment structure, and use of a common
group public persona. In such an evaluation, the theoretical desirability
of application of enterprise principles or retention of entity law and limited liability[21] will necessarily differ from statutory area to statutory area,
as the underlying legal objectives and policies vary.

The unsuitability of traditional piercing the veil jurisprudence to statutory problems should be evident. Determination of the scope and relevance of general-application statutory law manifestly involves very
different values, interests, and policies. The courts should be concerned
with matters of public policy and public interest far removed from the
values and interests involved in common-law controversies between private parties. Transcendental jurisprudential doctrines developed in litigation at common law between private individuals and relying on matters
of corporate form and such considerations as the existence of conduct

---

[21] One of the anomalies of the survival of entity law in an age of multinational corporations is the existence of multiple layers of limited liability within the group. In addition to
protecting the shareholder-investors in the parent corporation, limited liability also protects
the parent corporation and each subordinate corporate layer of companies from liability for
the obligations of lower-tier corporate layers. In considering treatment of the component
corporations of the group as a juridical entity for certain purposes, it is not suggested that
any change be made in the protection of limited liability for the public shareholders of the
parent corporation. As noted above, no case in American law has apparently imposed such
liability, with the possible exception of *Anderson* v. *Abbott*, 1944.

unfair to creditors should represent no barrier to application of enterprise principles in construing the scope of statutes.

Entity law, which insulates a parent corporation from the regulatory obligations imposed on its subsidiaries and permits it to side-step regulatory obligations through the device of organization of a subsidiary, presents serious dangers for the effective implementation of the statutory programme, manifestly creates a high risk of frustration of the statutory objectives, and opens wide avenues for evasion and avoidance. Since the 1930s American courts and administrative agencies alike have, accordingly, struggled to formulate new legal concepts to overcome such limitations of entity law. They have done so through the utilization of enterprise principles, notwithstanding the lack of any express reference in the statute, in order to apply the statutory regulatory programme not only to the subsidiary corporation directly conducting the activity covered by the statute, but also to its parent corporation (or controlling shareholders) and in some cases to its affiliated corporations as well. They have done this notwithstanding the rigid limitations of traditional piercing the veil jurisprudence.[22]

In some cases, liberalized piercing the veil jurisprudence serves as the basis for an enterprise application of a statutory programme to the corporate group involved in the case at hand. In others, it coexists with, or merges almost imperceptibly into, a liberal construction of the statutory provision utilizing normal principles of statutory construction to apply to the parent and sometimes also to the other group components, as well as to the particular subsidiary involved.

Such liberal statutory construction reflects an increasing recognition of the economic reality that regulatory statutes concerned with business activity will often require application in major respects to corporations that are members of corporate groups engaged in the conduct of interrelated fragments of an integrated business under central co-ordinated direction. In the light of such recognition, courts are led to determine the outer reach of statutes in the light of the purposes and policies of the act, as well as of the nature of the legislative response to the social or economic problems at which the statute is directed. The text is to be read in the context of the full historical background. Such an approach inevitably

---

[22] e.g., *Town of Brookline* v. *Gorsuch*, 1981: 221 (Federal courts will look closely at the purpose of the federal statute to determine whether the statute places importance on the corporate form, an inquiry that gives less respect to the corporate form than does the strict common law alter ego doctrine'); *Capital Tel. Co.* v. *FCC*, 1974: 738–9 (test of 'alter ego under the strict standards of the common-law alter-ego doctrine which would apply in a tort or contract action' not applicable in statutory matters); *Kavanaugh* v. *Ford Motor Co.*, 1965; *SEC* v. *Elmas Trading Co.*, 1985: 234; *United States* v. *Firestone Tire & Rubber Co.*, 1981: 1039; *United Paperwkrs Int'l Union* v. *Penntech Papers, Inc.*, 1977: 620–1; see Blumberg 1989: sect. 2.05.3.

creates pressures on American courts to construe statutes in the manner that will best implement the statutory objectives, avoid frustration of the statutory programme, and prevent evasion or avoidance (for further discussion, see Blumberg 1989: sec. 2.05.04). Supreme Court decisions during the 1992–3 term, however, indicate that the current Court is paying increasing attention to the literal statutory text.[23]

7. CORPORATE GROUPS UNDER STATUTES OF SPECIFIC APPLICATION

7.1 Introduction

In other regulatory statutes, Congress has responded in a more sophisticated manner to the limitations of entity law and has specifically attempted to transcend its limitations. Such statutes are expressly made applicable not only to corporations conducting the activity being regulated, but also to other corporations in the corporate groups of which the corporations in question are components. These statutes may be termed 'statutes of specific application'.

The specific-application statutes fall into three groups. The first group (the 'pervasive statutes') include the regulatory statutes utilizing enterprise principles as the technique for the pervasive regulation of a few, key industries. These include such statutes as the Bank Holding Company Act, the Savings and Loan Holding Company Act, and the Public Utility Holding Company Act. In these, the statutory focus is on the group. Among other aspects of the pervasive nature of these regulatory programmes, the statutes regulate entry into the market and the scope of the enterprise. To accomplish such objectives, they are inevitably concerned with the group as a whole. Enterprise law underlies the entire statute.

The second group (the 'selective statutes') utilize express use of enterprise principles for selected areas of the regulatory programme, while relying on entity law in most other respects. Such statutes of specific application making selective use of enterprise principles include statutes regulating railroads and trucking, air transportation, shipping, communications, and securities. None of these statutes deals with such matters as the scope of the enterprise. Aside from the transportation industries, these programmes similarly do not restrict entry into the market. Unlike the pervasive statutes, the specific-application statutes focus on the regulated company, rather than on any group of which it is a part. They are not concerned with group affairs, except in a number of selected areas in which regulation of the activities of the regulated company is expressly made applicable to other companies within the group as well.

[23] e.g., *Estate of Cowart* v. *Nicklos Drilling Co.*, 1992; *Patterson* v. *Shumate*, 1992; *King* v. *St Vincent Hospital*, 1992.

The third group of specific-application statutes comprise the revenue laws. With very different objectives than the regulatory statutes, the revenue statutes deal directly with the problems presented by the component companies of corporate groups (along with other related taxpayers) in the implementation and prevention of evasion of the tax laws.

All the specific-application statutes attempt to supersede the entity law concept of the separate juridical personality of each corporation by introducing in one form or another enterprise principles to expand the statutory coverage to include interrelated corporations in areas where inclusion under the statute is deemed essential for effective implementation of the statutory programme. This presents the fundamental problem of definition: how is the corporate group or enterprise to be defined in order to include the component corporations of the group under the statute at issue?

It should be evident that any such definition of the corporate group or enterprise must be carefully tailored to the particular objectives of the statute in question, in order to serve its objectives most effectively. In the tax laws, for example, statutory provisions extending tax benefits to a selected class of taxpayers must manifestly be drafted very restrictively to confine the benefits to the interests intended. By contrast, other provisions in the tax laws intended to impose tax obligations or to prevent evasion of tax obligations must be drafted very expansively to achieve the impact desired. To ignore the implications of different statutory objectives in order to develop a transcendental concept of enterprise law to be applied throughout the legal system would thus be an error of first magnitude.[24]

Definitional standards must not only be realistic in terms of the activity or industry being regulated; they must effectively implement the particular objectives of the statutory programme in question. Regulatory programmes manifestly differ from each other. They differ in the underlying problems which they address, and they differ in the statutory objectives. This reflects such factors, among others, as the nature of the industries being regulated, their characteristic structural and operational features, their impact on the economy and the society, and the perceived abuses of unregulated activity.

---

[24] This is further illustrated by the experience of piercing the veil jurisprudence. The application of the rigid rules of traditional piercing the veil jurisprudence as a transcendental doctrine routinely applied in very different fields of the law is one of the major weaknesses of the doctrine. The reliance on piercing the veil decisions in one area of the law to reach decisions in a very different area, such as the indiscriminate invocation of decisions involving contract or tort or property or procedure in very different areas in which the law has very different objectives, has been much criticized. The lack of relevance of such indiscriminate utilization of piercing the veil jurisprudence is most evident in the application of the doctrine as developed in controversies between private individuals to questions of important public policy involving the construction and application of regulatory statutes.

With differing underlying problems and differing statutory objectives, the scope of the statutory regulatory programme and the standard for definition of the group will also differ. As a result, with the uniform application of a transcendental concept of enterprise applied in different statutory areas with different objectives patently unworkable, the American statutory experience reflecting such considerations has produced a rich variety of alternative definitional standards developed to serve varying statutory objectives.

Save for isolated and relatively unimportant exceptions,[25] the concept of 'control' is used as the decisive unifying factor throughout American law for defining the enterprise or the group for the purpose of determining the scope of American specific-application statutes. However, while control is the near-universal standard for defining 'enterprise', the formulation of the term differs materially in the various specific-application statutes, reflecting their basic differences. Such dramatic differences in formulation present an important problem in comparative law, which thus far has been almost entirely neglected in the literature.

What, then, are the various definitions of 'control' in the specific-application statutes, and what are the factors which appear to lead to the selection of one formulation rather than another?

7.2 STATUTORY FORMULATIONS OF THE CONCEPT OF 'CONTROL'

In approaching the crucial problem of defining the enterprise subject to the regulatory programme through the concept of control, two guiding rules would appear appropriate. First, the statutory formulation should effectively implement the objectives of the governmental regulatory programme under consideration. Secondly, the formulation should adequately respond to the special features of the economic and corporate organization of the industry being regulated.

Reflecting such fundamental factors, there are clearly discernible patterns in the formulation of the definitions of 'control' utilized in the statutes. In summary, it is apparent that regulatory statutes and revenue statutes adopt very different approaches.

Furthermore, the pervasive regulatory statutes and the selective regulatory statutes, while much more closely allied in their approach, also adopt somewhat different definitional patterns, reflecting the differences in their fundamental objectives.

---

[25] In special areas such those of labour, employment, and employment discrimination, American law utilizes the 'integrated enterprise' standard for limited purposes. Similarly, 'integrated enterprise' appears in isolated areas in the tax laws. However, as discussed, they do not lend themselves to broader application.

Pervasive statutes focusing on the group. In the specific-application statutes undertaking pervasive industry-wide regulation, the statutory focus is the group. The pervasive statutes all employ the following two elements[26] distinguishing their definitional approach from those of the selective specific-application statutes[26]:

(1) An expansive definition combining 'control', defined in much the same manner as in many selective statutes, with the somewhat more expansive term 'controlling influence', a term unique to the pervasive statutes.

(2) A presumption of 'control' arising from ownership or control of a specified percentage of the voting securities. The percentage giving rise to a presumption of 'control' ranges from as low as 10 per cent in the Public Utility Holding Company Act to 25 per cent in the Bank Holding Company Act and the Savings and Loan Holding Company Act.[27] Illustrative of the drafting pattern of these statutes is the relevant provision from section 2(a)(7) of the Public Utility Holding Company Act. It generally defines a holding company to include 'any company which directly or indirectly owns, controls, or holds with power to vote 10 per cent or more of the outstanding voting securities', as well as any person determined 'directly or indirectly to exercise (either alone or pursuant to an arrangement or understanding with one or more other persons) . . . a controlling influence over management or policies.[28]

In addition, the pervasive statutes, like many of the selective statutes, supplement their definition of 'control' to sweep under their regulatory programmes not simply the parent or subsidiaries of the regulated company, but sister subsidiaries in their group as well. The pervasive and many selective statutes accomplish this objective and expand the scope of coverage of the statutory programme by expressly including every company 'controlling, controlled by, or under common control with' the regulated company—in short, the group.

The common features evidenced by the three holding company statutes reflect a statutory focus on the totality of operations of the group.[29] This

[26] Bank Holding Company Act, 12 U.S.C.A., sect. 1841 (Supp. 1992); Savings and Loan Holding Company Act, 12 U.S.C.A., sect. 1467a (Supp. 1992); Public Utility Holding Company Act, 15 U.S.C., sect. 79a (1988). See Blumberg 1992: ch. 2, 3, 6.

[27] 15 U.S.C., sect. 79b(a) (7) (A), (B) (1988); 12 U.S.C.A., sect. 1841(a) (2) (Supp. 1992); 12 U.S.C.A., sect. 1467a(a) (2) (Supp. 1992).

[28] 15 U.S.C., Sect. 79b(a) (7) (A), (B) (1988).

[29] The Investment Company Act (ICA), 15 U.S.C., Sect. 80a (1988), is an anomaly. See Blumberg 1992: ch. 18. While investment companies are, of course, holding companies with portfolios of securities including the voting equity securities of other corporations, their resemblance to the holding companies regulated by the other holding company statutes ceases at this point. Under the other statutes, the holding company 'controls' its subsidiaries. They collectively constitute a corporate group, and the regulatory statutes impose controls over the group and the scope of its enterprise. By contrast, the regulated investment companies under the ICA do not usually 'control' their portfolio companies, which

reflects statutory objectives of high priority. One such priority is concern about the scope of the permissible activities of the group—that is, the permissible scope of the enterprise which it conducts. Such an emphasis may arise from quite different causes. In the case of the Bank Holding Company Act and the Savings and Loan Holding Company Act dealing with depository institutions, it reflects a concern that the lack of stability and financial soundness of one subsidiary depository institution may affect the stability and soundness of others. In the Public Utility Holding Company Act, it stems from a legislative objective to simplify the corporate structure of the industry and to achieve geographically integrated utility systems.

Whatever the particular concern, each leads to the same pressure to focus on the industry structure and on the groups that conduct, it, rather than simply on the regulated company and its activities. This common focal point explains the common definitional standards of the statutes and the elements distinguishing them from the definitional standards in the 'selective' statutes.

Selective statutes focusing on the regulated company. Other industry-wide statutory programmes, notably those regulating railroads and trucking, air transportation, shipping, communications, and securities, focus on the regulated company or activity, not on the group. Although dealing in a far-reaching manner with the problems of a particular industry, these statutes are typically not concerned with the scope of the enterprises of which the regulated companies are part, but deal primarily with the regulated company, often including such important public concerns as access to the market and the prices and operations of the regulated company as they affect consumers, employees, and the communities in which they operate.

Although such statutes do not focus on groups, the fact that large American corporations typically operate as members of corporate groups requires the statutes, nevertheless, to regulate selected areas involving the relationship of the regulated company to its affiliated corporations and its group. Thus, selective statutes all deal with such matters as the acquisition of control of a regulated company in order to regulate access to the market; the regulation of intra-group transactions to which the regulated

are typically independent companies whose securities represent only an 'investment' without 'control'. The ICA does not restrict the scope of the business conducted by the group and in other respects as well imposes less pervasive controls over the industry. The differences between the ICA and the pervasive holding company statutes are accordingly substantial. Nevertheless, although it focuses on the regulated investment company, the ICA in many respects resembles pervasive legislation. This probably explains why the statutory formulation of the ICA follows that of the holding company statutes, utilizing the supplemental concept of 'controlling influence' and a presumption of control arising from ownership of 25% of voting securities of any class. In such respects, it differs from every other selective statute.

company is a party, in order adequately to regulate pricing and return; and the establishment of accounting and reporting controls over the group as a whole, so as to obtain full disclosure of intra-group relationships. However, none of these statutes is concerned with the scope of the enterprise.

Accordingly, while such statutes also utilize the concept of control to deal with these matters, the statutory formulation of the term takes a different form. Instead of references to a specified percentage of stock ownership as giving rise to a presumption of the existence of control, as in the pervasive statutes, or to a specified percentage of stock ownership as an absolute objective standard, as in the revenue statutes, these statutes typically rely on a general definition expressed in functional terms and defer detailed formulation for administrative determination on a case-by-case basis. They do so to avoid having a fixed definition serve as a blueprint for avoidance of the statutory programme. The selective statutes not only avoid use of specified stock ownership percentages and presumptions. None seeks to expand the concept of control through use of the term 'controlling influence', as in each of the pervasive statutes.

In determining the existence of 'control', administrative agencies play a role of major importance. In *Rochester Telephone Corp.* v. *United States*, 1939, (139–40, 145–6) the Supreme Court gave 'control' an expansive meaning, holding that 'control' was a 'practical concept' 'to be determined by a regard for the actualities of inter-corporate relationships' and 'to encompass every type of control in fact'. In applying this conception, the Court firmly recognized the primary role of the administrative agencies. It held that an agency's determination of the existence of 'control' was a determination of fact and conclusive if supported by the record (see also *Gilbertville Trucking Co.* v *United States*, 1962: 125; *Alleghany Corp.* v. *Breswick & Co.* 1957: 163; *United States* v. *Marshall Transp. Co.* 1944: 38).

In the event that 'control' has been determined to exist, these statutes in the areas selected by Congress extend the scope of the regulatory programme through use of the familiar formulation imposing the programme, not merely on the regulated company, but on all companies 'controlling, controlled by, or under common control with' the regulated company. However, unlike the pervasive statutes, the selective-application statutes apply to the group as a whole only for limited purposes in carefully delineated areas, not generally.

Revenue statutes. The revenue statutes differ sharply from regulatory statutes in their approach. Whatever the particular objective underlying a particular provision,[30] the Internal Revenue Code ('the Code', cited as

---

[30] A particular tax may be a pure and simple revenue-raising imposition. It may also be a technique employed as an incentive or disincentive by which Congress attempts to

IRC) is, with unimportant exceptions, concerned only with revenue matters: the imposition of tax, the creation of exemptions or other special treatment with respect to taxes, and the prevention of evasion and avoidance of taxes. Effective implementation of these objectives in a world of corporate groups necessarily requires numerous provisions dealing with the many problems presented by the economic interrelationship of corporate groups and their components.[31]

In a revenue-raising system resting on returns filed by taxpayers, it is essential that the tax statute be, to the extent possible, comprehensible and capable of ready application. Although in many respects, as every American taxpayer knows, the Code utterly fails to achieve this objective, nevertheless, the aspiration has apparently been one of the factors shaping the drafting of the provisions of the Code dealing with corporate groups. The definitions utilized thus clearly reflect a perceived need for clarity and ease of application.

Although the details of formulation vary sharply, the various statutory definitions employed by the Code, like those of the regulatory statutes, overwhelmingly utilize the language of 'control'. However, the Code in its various provisions defines the term very differently from the regulatory statutes. Instead of the general functional definitions of 'control' uniformly used by the specific-application regulatory statutes or the presumptions utilized by the pervasive-application statutes,[32] the tax provisions, with isolated exceptions,[33] rely solely on numerical benchmarks of stock ownership, which serve as absolute objective standards.

In fact, although the Code consistently uses the term 'control', its use in many cases is a misnomer. In the regulatory area, 'control' is in all cases a term of art (see *B. F. Goodrich Co.* v. *Northwest Indus., Inc.,* 1969:57), referring to the capacity to determine, or in some cases influence, the decision making of another company. In the tax laws, it is never more than a term of drafting convenience, without intrinsic meaning of its own. It is merely a statutory drafting device, incorporating by reference an absolute, objective standard consisting of the particular

encourage or discourage particular economic activity. Whatever the motivation, in the end, the statutory provisions all focus either on the imposition of a tax or on an exemption or limitation with respect to such imposition.

[31] The Code, of course, also deals with matters involving the control of individual shareholders and other 'related' parties, which are beyond the scope of this volume.

[32] While some regulatory statutes do contain presumptions of control arising from specified numerical bench-marks of stock ownership, such presumptions supplement the general statutory conceptual definition. 'Control' under such statutes, unlike the Code, may be found to exist even though the amount of stock owned by the parent corporation (or other controlling shareholder) is less than the percentage required to give rise to a presumption.

[33] These exceptions are readily explained by the special contexts in which they are employed.

numerical bench-mark of stock ownership specified in the section. In many cases, the bench-mark utilized includes ownership of stock without voting rights and is, therefore, unmistakably not concerned with control over the decision making.

The various sections of the Code use many different numerical bench-marks of 'control'. In fact, the Code contains no less than nine major definitional models. As if this bewildering multiplicity was not confusing enough, each of the nine major models includes variations in its application, thereby creating additional sub-variations as well.

Some sections use a bench-mark of 'more than 50 per cent' of voting stock (e.g., IRC, Sect. 267(f), 954(d) (3), 957, 6038(1)). By use of a reference to a majority on the one hand and to voting stock on the other, this represents a standard concerned with control over the decision-making process; this test, while simplistic, is, of course, entirely consistent with the usage in the regulatory statutes.

In other provisions, however, the Code utilizes numerical stock ownership bench-marks of 'at least 50 per cent' or '50 per cent or less' (e.g., IRC, Sect. 246A, 279(i)), or 'at least 80 per cent' (e.g., IRC, Sect. 368(c), 582(b), 1504(a) (2), 1551, 1563). Even when related to voting stock rather than to all stock, none of these bench-marks appears to have been selected to establish an objective standard of control over decision making. The former standards are just a shade too low, and the latter much too high.[34]

Other examples in the Code of numerical bench-marks of 'control' which are clearly unrelated to control over decision making are even more common. Thus, in many provisions, the numerical bench-mark relates to 'the total value' of all the stock (e.g., IRC, Sect. 246A, 267(f), 382(1), 1504(a)(2), 1551, 1563), or the 'total number' of shares (e.g., IRC, Sect. 368(c)), and does not focus on voting stock at all. In such provisions, the Code, while speaking of 'control', is clearly concerned not with control over the decision-making process, but with the extent of proprietary interest or economic participation in the company, a very different matter.

The provisions of the Code fall into two classes. First, there are the provisions imposing tax and preventing tax avoidance—that is, provisions increasing the tax liability of taxpayers ('burdensome provisions'). Second, there are the provisions containing exemptions or restricting the application of burdensome tax provisions and provisions reducing the tax liability of taxpayers ('beneficial provisions').

The provisions in the Code utilizing numerical bench-marks of stock

---

[34] As a realistic matter, of course, 'control' over decision making in the typical large public corporation with thousands of shareholders may rest on ownership or control of significantly less than a majority of the voting shares; see Loss and Seligman 1989: iv. ch. 5.

ownership as the test of 'control' as a standard for their application divide into two basic groups, reflecting these underlying statutory objectives. As might be expected, the numerical bench-marks used for beneficial provisions are set high, at 80 per cent of stock ownership, to restrict the favoured taxpayers to the narrow class intended (e.g., IRC, Sect. 368(c), 582(b), 1504(a)(2), 1551, 1563). Conversely, the burdensome provisions use a lower 50 per cent bench-mark,[35] to widen the scope of the provision and implement the statutory revenue-raising objectives. While there are occasional exceptions to this division, they are not significant.

The striking aspect of the Code is that it relies almost exclusively on absolute, objective numerical bench-marks. Only in a few isolated sections does it use a general functional test of a broad, expansive nature, comparable to the standards customarily employed in the specific-application regulatory statutes. The principal section of the Code proceeding in this manner, section 482, is one of the major weapons of the Internal Revenue Service in dealing with tax manipulation in transactions between parties under common control; and it is highly appropriate for the Code to depart from reliance on numerical bench-marks in such a provision.[36] The other two instances (e.g., IRC, Sect. 267) are relatively unimportant.

It is quite clear that the statutory drafting reflects an overriding priority for clarity and ease of application, in order to facilitate business planning and tax reporting. Where there are exceptions, as in the area of tax manipulation attacked by section 482, for example, the parties seeking to evade or minimize tax liabilities are hardly in a position to complain of any lack of clarity in the application of the broadly worded provision.

In summary, the utilization of 'control' for tax purposes is a very different matter from the use of the concept in the specific-application regulatory statutes. While its inclusion in this review is essential for a complete understanding of the American statutory scheme, there are few lessons which may be learned from this area in considering the problems in the definition of 'control' for purposes of imposing enterprise principles in other areas of the law.

Other standards than 'control'. In addition to definitions resting on 'control', the statutory law experience provides isolated examples of other techniques for defining the corporate group for the purposes of applying

[35] These bench-marks take 3 forms. As noted, sometimes the standard is 'at least 50%', sometimes it is '50% or more', meaning that 50.00% is required; and sometimes it is 'more than 50%', meaning that 50.01% is required.
[36] Sect. 482 gives the Commissioner of Internal Revenue the authority to reallocate income, deductions, and credits of 'organization, trades, or businesses . . . owned or controlled directly or indirectly by the same interests in order to prevent evasion of taxes or clearly to reflect their income'. This is further discussed in Ch. 20 below.

enterprise principles. Such alternative approaches are provided by the handful of doctrines turning on the integration of operations of the affiliated corporations, rather than simply 'control'. One of these innovative developments is the 'integrated enterprise' doctrine[37] developed by the National Labor Relations Board for determination of a 'single employer', for resolution of certain labour relations matters under the National Labor Relations Act (a general-application statute). This standard has also been utilized in judicial decisions in such related areas as employment and employment discrimination law and has even been incorporated into statutory law in the Age Discrimination Amendments Act, 1984 (29 U.S.C., Sect. 623(h) (1988); see also Blumberg 1989: ch. 13–15). The isolated provisions of the regulations under the IRC utilizing 'integrated enterprise' as their standard provide another example.[38] These standards resemble in some respects the unitary business doctrine developed by the Supreme Court in testing the constitutionality of state unitary tax apportionment discussed above (Blumberg 1983: Sect. 22.03.5; 1989: Sect. 5.02).

Each of these solutions has only limited usefulness however, outside the immediate area in which it has been employed. The 'integrated enterprise' standard in labour, employment, and anti-discrimination laws focuses primarily on labour operations and ignores the other dimensions of the enterprise. Similarly, the 'integrated enterprise' standard under the IRC is used only in obscure sections for very restricted purposes[39] and is manifestly unsuited to wider application. Although these alternative approaches are not particularly helpful, their identification of integration of operations as the decisive factor for imposition of group liability in the areas to which they apply provides support for the judicial decisions utilizing this consideration as one of the key elements making for judicial utilization of enterprise principles in a particular area.

Summary. The specific-application regulatory statutes provide extensive guidance on the nature of control over corporate decision making with their examples of alternative models of defining 'control'. Although they provide a surprising number of different formulations of 'control', the

---

[37] The 'integrated enterprise' standard consists of four factors: (a) interrelation of operations, (b) centralized control of labour relations, (c) common management, and (d) common ownership or financial control. See 21 N.L.R.B. Ann. Rep. 14 (1956), adopted in *Radio & Television Broadcast Technicians Local Union* v. *Broadcast Serv. of Mobile, Inc.*, 1965 (*per curiam*).

[38] See Temp. Treas. Reg. under IRC, Sect. 367(b), Sect. 1.367(a)3T(e) (3) (1990). An 'integrated enterprise' standard was also used in 1917 for purposes of the First World War excess profits tax; see Treas. Reg. 41, art. 77.

[39] Thus, the regulations under Sect. 367(b) deal only with a third-order problem. Sect. 367(b) itself is an exception, in a very limited area, to the general provisions of the Code. The integrated business standard serves only in a still more limited area as the basis for an exception to the exception.

fact is that the formulations strongly resemble each other, and the differences appear to relate only to relatively infrequent marginal cases.

In evaluating the numerous, not dissimilar statutory model provisions available, American scholars are fortunate that the very same ground has already been explored in the securities area by a distinguished group of judges, scholars, and practitioners led by the senior scholar in the area, Professor Louis Loss, in the preparation of the Federal Securities Code.[40] Section 202(29) of the Code defines 'control' as follows:

(a) 'Control' means the power, directly or indirectly, to exercise a controlling influence over the management and policies of a company . . . (either alone or pursuant to an arrangement or understanding with one or more other persons), whether through the ownership of voting securities, through one or more intermediary persons, by contract, or otherwise.

(b)(1) A person who (either alone or pursuant to an arrangement or understanding with one or more other persons) owns or has the power to vote more than 25 per cent of the outstanding voting securities . . . is presumed to control.

(4) Any such presumption may be rebutted by evidence.[41]

This definition, including utilization of the more expansive term 'controlling influence' and a presumption arising from ownership of 25 per cent of voting securities, substantially follows the model provided by the pervasive statutes. Such utilization of a 25 per cent bench-mark as a rebuttable presumption of control accurately reflects the reality of the American corporate world. It is widely recognized that in the large public corporation with its stock widely distributed among tens or hundreds or thousands of shareholders,[42] stock ownership in an amount much less than the mathematical certainty of a majority of the voting shares will suffice for 'working control'. At least in cases where there is no other bloc of shares of comparable size, a holding of even less than 25 per cent will normally mean 'working control'.[43] The Code reflects this common

[40] American Law Institute, Federal Securities Code (1980). While the Code has not been enacted by Congress, as originally hoped, it has been warmly received and invoked by the courts. See generally Loss and Seligman 1989: i. 278–85.

[41] Federal Securities Code, sect. 202(29)(A),(B) (1980). The ALI; Principles of Corporate Governance: Analysis and Recommendations, sect. 1.05 (Proposed Final Draft, 1992) adopts substantially the same definition of 'control'.

[42] As of 31 Dec. 1986 the number of shareholders of record of the 50 companies listed on the New York Stock Exchange having the largest number of shareholders ranged from a high of 2,782,000 to a low of 124,000 (*N.Y.S.E. Fact Book*, 1987: 26). Since these figures reflect only shareholders of record, and do not take into account beneficial owners, the actual number of shareholders is even higher.

[43] See *Essex Universal Corp* v. *Yates*, 1962: 580 (Clark, J., concurring) (28.3% represents working control). See also Loss and Seligman 1989: iv. ch. 5. However, this may change in the future with the larger and larger accumulations of shares in the hands of pension funds and other institutional investors. It is estimated that institutional investors now hold more than 50% of the shares of companies listed on the New York Stock Exchange and more than 65% of the market value of shares included in the Standard & Poor's *500 Index*; see

understanding in order to simplify problems of proof, while preserving the opportunity to rebut the presumption in those cases where this might be possible.[44]

The American statutory experience further underscores the usefulness of supplementing such a definition of 'control', including its supporting elements—'controlling influence' and a presumption resting on a numerical bench-mark of stock ownership—with the familiar formulation in American specific-application statutory law under which the scope of the statutory regulatory programme is expanded to include not only the group component conducting the regulated activity in question, but also any person 'directly or indirectly controlling, or controlled by, or under direct or indirect common control with'[45] the group component in question.

When, however, one turns from specific-application regulatory statutes to other areas of the law where Congress or the legislature has not provided the definitional answer, the problem of the application of enterprise law is very different indeed. It is judicial, not legislative. The problem is no longer the relatively simple issue of draftsmanship of the appropriate statutory provision. It is the much more complex problem of the development of standards for the guidance of courts to determine their application of enterprise principles to the decision of a case at hand in the light of the objectives of the law in the area in question.

In the event that the courts do not conclude that the statutory text is so clear as to eliminate any issue of construction, the burden is on them to determine two fundamental issues. First, they must decide whether the adoption of enterprise principles or the retention of traditional concepts of entity law best serves the underlying purposes and objectives of the particular area of the law under consideration. Second, if they determine that enterprise principles should prevail at least in some cases, they must

Report of the Legal Advisory Committee to the New York Stock Exchange Board of Directors (1990).
 Take-overs may also produce exceptions. Thus, at the conclusion of the celebrated contest between Bangor Punta Corp. and Chris-Craft Industries, Inc. to acquire control of Piper Aircraft Corporation, Chris-Craft had acquired 42% of the Piper shares, but was still unable to acquire control because Bangor Punta had acquired more than 50% (*Piper Aircraft Corp. v. Chris-Craft Indust., Inc.,* 1977: 9).

[44] In particular specific-application regulatory programmes—for example, the Bank Holding Company Act, Savings and Loan Holding Company Act, and Public Utility Holding Company Act—the special features of the industry, reflecting among other matters regulatory controls rendering entry more difficult, may lead to use of a different percentage to give rise to the presumption (see above).

[45] See Securities Act, 1933, 15 U.S.C., sect. 77b(3), (11) (1988); Securities Exchange Act, 1934, 15 U.S.C., sect. 78c(a)(8) 78l, 78m (1988); Investment Company Act, 1940, sect. 2(a)(40), 15 U.S.C., sect. 80a–2(a)(40) (1988); Trust Indenture Act, 15 U.S.C., sect. 77jjjb 4 (1988); Federal Communications Act, 1934, 47 U.S.C., sect. 219(a) (1988); Cable Communications Policy Act, 1984, 47 U.S.C., sect. 533 (1988); Antidumping and Countervailing Duty Act, 1988, 19 U.S.C., sect. 1677(13) (1988).

then deal with the fundamental problem of determining when the relationship between affiliated corporations is so intertwined that the application of enterprise principles is appropriate. They must define the standard for application of enterprise law. While such an undertaking could be avoided by providing for the application of enterprise law in every parent–subsidiary relationship, such a far-reaching step, even if deemed desirable, is clearly not feasible at the present stage of American law.

The modern American experience in the formulation of concepts of enterprise for purposes of construing and applying general-application statutes and in common-law areas, particularly torts, is beginning to provide an answer to this definitional problem. As noted, the courts focus not merely on control, but on such aspects of the economic contours of the group as its extent of economic integration, financial and administrative interdependence, overlapping employee policies, and use of a common public persona.

8. JUDICIAL PROCEDURE

Enterprise concepts have made considerable inroads in American judicial procedure, although, as elsewhere, entity law generally prevails (Blumberg 1983). In some areas, such as the assertion of jurisdiction and the accompanying problems of service and venue, the contest between the conflicting doctrines is at its most controversial. In this area, the law had been dominated by the Supreme Court decision in *Cannon Mfg. Co.* v. *Cudahy Packing Co.* 1925 (336), enshrining entity law and formalistic analysis as the governing standard. Today, however, even many of the courts prepared to follow *Cannon* generally will apply enterprise standards in jurisdictional matters where the parent exercises day-to-day control over the subsidiary. Other courts have held *Cannon* obsolete in light of the Court's subsequent decision in *International Shoe Co.* v. *Washington*, 1945, establishing 'minimum contacts' with the forum as one of the fundamental constitutional standards for assertion of jurisdiction. In particular areas, such as antitrust, enterprise concepts have found wide acceptance. In the area of products liability, the 'stream of commerce' doctrine for assertion of jurisdiction has made the debate between enterprise and entity essentially irrelevant. Jurisdiction continues to be one of the most litigated areas involving the clash of enterprise and entity.

In a number of procedural areas, control is the decisive consideration and has led to full acceptance of enterprise principles. This is evident in such areas as *res judicata* and collateral estoppel, statute of limitations, and discovery. Other procedural areas in which enterprise notions have been accepted include the scope of injunctions. Judicial decisions in the area of the statute of limitations, discovery, and injunctions have been codified in the Federal Rules of Civil Procedure adopting enterprise approaches.[46] Entity law, however, clearly still prevails in such other areas as counter claim, set-off, and joinder.

9. BANKRUPTCY LAW

In a number of areas, American bankruptcy law has moved to an acceptance of enterprise law to a surprising extent. These include equitable subordination, voidable preferences, and to some degree substantive consolidation. While entity law continues to prevail elsewhere in bankruptcy law, there are signs of change, particularly in such areas as fraudulent transfers.

Equitable subordination of the claims of a parent corporation or sister subsidiary to the claims of general unsecured creditors in the bankruptcy of a subsidiary corporation provides an outstanding example of the movement of the law. In four landmark decisions,[47] the Supreme Court rejected the standards of traditional piercing the veil jurisprudence, and enunciated new standards for evaluating intra-group claims and claims of other corporate insiders. In place of entity law and piercing the veil as the governing standards, intra-group claims are now subject to special scrutiny and are evaluated according to equitable principles governing conduct by fiduciaries. The parent corporation or other insider must demonstrate not only the fairness of the inter-company transaction giving rise to the claim, but the fairness of its other interrelationships with the subsidiary (or controlled corporation) as well. This is no less than a conceptual revolution.

Section 547 of the Bankruptcy Code fully employs enterprise principles in dealing with voidable preferences. Under section 547, subject to certain limitations, any transfer of property by an insolvent debtor to or for the benefit of a creditor that is an 'insider' is voidable if the transfer is made within one year of bankruptcy. The statute defines 'insider' to include any 'person in control' or an 'affiliate'. It defines 'affiliate' to include persons owning or controlling 20 per cent or more of the voting securities of the debtor (i.e., a parent); or any corporation 20 per cent or more of whose voting securities are directly or indirectly owned or controlled either by the debtor (i.e., a subsidiary) or by an entity that directly or indirectly

---

[46] Federal Rules of Civil Procedure, 15 (statute of limitations), 33 and 34 (discovery), and 65(c) (injunctions).

[47] See *Taylor* v. *Standard Gas & Elec. Co.*, 1938; *Pepper* v. *Litton*, 1939; *Consolidated Rock Prods.* v. *Du Bois*, 1941; *Comstock* v. *Group of Institutional Investors*, 1948.

owns or controls 20 per cent of the voting securities of the debtor (sister subsidiary).[48]

Substantive consolidation, a judicial doctrine with no counterpart in the Code, is still another area receiving considerable development of enterprise principles. In substantive consolidation, the bankruptcy proceedings of interrelated companies are consolidated and administered jointly, with assets and liabilities of the affiliated debtors pooled and all inter-company claims and guaranties eliminated, as far as unsecured creditors are concerned. It is comparable to the Continental concept of extension of bankruptcy.

In the development of the doctrine, courts have emphasized that it reflects the 'prevalence' of parent and subsidiary corporations. Among the factors leading to such consolidation are the nature of creditor expectations, significant economic integration, intra-group financing and guaranties, difficulty in segregating and ascertaining individual assets and liabilities, commingling of assets and inter-company transfers, implementation of the administration, and increasing the feasibility of reorganization of the debtors. While injury to individual creditors from consolidation is recognized, it is, nevertheless, proper if creditors as a whole are benefited (Blumberg 1985: ch. 10).

10. PROBLEM AREAS

Discussion of the application of enterprise principles to corporate groups in selected areas of the law would not be complete without at least summary reference to some problem areas. These include the extent to which conglomerate enterprises and partly owned subsidiaries may present special features requiring special treatment. An even more troublesome area is the problem of extraterritoriality resulting from enterprise treatment of the foreign subsidiaries of multinational corporations.

10.1 Conglomerate enterprises

Conglomerates and other less than fully integrated groups present a more complex problem. In the formulation of enterprise principles, the economic integration of the group has played a significant role in the evolution of the law thus far. In economically integrated groups, the group may accurately be said to be collectively conducting a common business which has been fragmented among the various constituent companies of the group. In the event of the application of enterprise principles, the

---

[48] 11 U.S.C., sect. 101(2), 101(28)(B), (E), 547 (1988). See Blumberg 1985: sect. 9.02.

business enterprise and the legal unit for the purposes at hand would be the same—that is, economic entity and legal entity would be the same.

In conglomerate groups, the group conducts businesses that are in different industries. While their production and distribution functions may not be integrated, the subsidiaries are, nevertheless, integrated in other important respects. In financial matters, conglomerate groups function much like other groups, with a high degree of financial interdependence among the affiliated companies. The economic potential from internalization of the capital market function through substitution of the group for the market for financing purposes has in fact been recognized as one of the major incentives for the existence of conglomerate organizations in the first place (see Williamson 1970: 141–50; Van Horne 1974: 496–502).

In addition to financial interdependence, conglomerate groups similarly utilize the same patterns of administrative interdependence evident in other groups, with the constituent companies utilizing group resources providing an extensive series of essential supporting services. Financial and administrative interdependence provide opportunities of importance for economies of scale and other advantages of internalization.

The constituent companies in diverse industries organized in a conglomerate group constitute a 'firm' because of the opportunities for economies of scale and scope through financial and administrative interdependence. Nevertheless, conglomerate groups present at least two special difficulties for application of enterprise principles different from those presented by integrated enterprises. These are the impact on entrepreneurial risk taking and the possible externalization of costs.

One of the important advantages of limited liability is its encouragement of entrepreneurial risk taking and new investment. Application of enterprise principles to impose liability in the case of conglomerate groups thus might have undesirable consequences in tending to discourage expansion by the group into new businesses. This is a factor not present in the imposition of enterprise principles and the resulting loss of limited liability in the case of an integrated group where a single business has been fragmented among the members of the group, who continue to conduct it collectively under common control. In the latter case, entrepreneurial venturing into a new business is not involved at all. However, whatever the possible impairment of risk taking by conglomerate diversification, the fact remains, as some commentators have noted, that the various companies are not truly independent from a financial and commercial perspective, and that investments in them do not represent a full diversification of risk (Leebron 1991).

Another problem in applying enterprise principles in the case of conglomerate groups is the possible externalization of costs. In tort law, the application of enterprise principles has been recognized as particularly appropriate, because it means the imposition of the costs and risks of an undertaking on all the operations responsible with the ultimate social and individual costs of the product spread over the consumers of the products in question. In integrated enterprises, enterprise law appropriately makes all assets held by the subsidiaries conducting the fragmented parts of the business available for payment of the tort liabilities of the enterprise. The goal is to prevent externalization of the losses arising from such risks from the activity producing them.

The question arises whether conglomerate enterprises present a different situation. Where a group conducts a number of unrelated businesses, does the imposition of enterprise principles and elimination of limited liability within the group result in the automatic imposition of costs arising from the economic activity of the acquired company upon unrelated activities in other areas? If this were to occur, the imposition of enterprise principles with the objective of preventing externalities would in fact be creating other externalities for conglomerates.

This important question has two parts. The first question is whether the costs are being imposed outside the business of the 'firm'? This enquiry has already been discussed. As noted, although the component corporations of such groups lack the economic integration of the productive and distributive processes of integrated groups, they are tied to the group by both financial interdependence and administrative interdependence. Such linkages provide the necessary economies of scope and scale that make it economic for conglomerate enterprise to exist. Thus, despite the different industries served, the conglomerate enterprise is, none the less, a 'firm'.

A second, and independent, question is whether such costs may in fact be imposed on consumers of the products of the other unrelated subsidiaries? In the conglomerate, externalization could still arise if any of the costs imposed on the parent or sister subsidiaries arising from the exercise of enterprise principles were passed along to consumers of those affiliates, consumers in a different product or geographical market. Whether this would occur, however, depends on the extent of competition in the relevant markets. In the absence of monopoly elements, prices in such markets would be determined by the collective impact of costs of the various sellers in the industry and the nature of the demand. Any allocation to the affiliate in the market of enterprise liability costs would be irrelevant. The imposition of costs on the affiliates would affect their profitability, but it could not affect prices unless the affiliates possessed monopoly power. In such a case, however, the answer would appear to be the need for correction of the monopolistic elements in the market, rather than a change in the sweep of enterprise law for this particular consequence arising from market imperfections.

Thus, in summary, while conglomerate groups present a somewhat different balance of the comparable advantages and disadvantages of limited liability and unlimited liability from those presented by integrated groups, they do not appear to justify different liability rules on the basis of theoretical analysis. Nevertheless, it is necessary to observe that many of the reported decisions involving intra-group liability give considerable emphasis to the existence of economic integration as a factor of significance justifying employment of enterprise principles or piercing the veil jurisprudence. This at the least suggests that conglomerate corporations may present some unique aspects and that courts may distinguish even more sharply between conglomerate and integrated groups in the further development of enterprise law. The cases to date on this aspect of matters are simply too few to provide any guidance.

10.2 Partly owned subsidiaries

The existence of minority shareholders in partly owned subsidiaries may introduce still another new element. Most large American corporate groups function through wholly owned subsidiaries,[49] although the number of partly owned subsidiaries seems to be increasing, reflecting, among other matters, the increasing popularity of joint ventures as a technique for foreign investment. Under traditional doctrines of American corporation law, the parent corporation has fiduciary obligations to the minority shareholders of its subsidiaries. These fiduciary obligations require the subsidiary's board to conduct the affairs of the subsidiary in the best interests of the subsidiary and to maximize the return on investment of the subsidiary without regard to the interests of the group. Further, the parent corporation and the subsidiary's board of directors must respect fiduciary standards of fairness in all transactions between the subsidiary and the parent corporation or other companies of the group. They may not impose transactions on a subsidiary which are to the disadvantage of the subsidiary and to the advantage of the parent. Such fiduciary obligations manifestly constitute an important constraint in the direction of the subsidiary's business and affairs. However, these standards are loose and not particularly effective.[50]

[49] A survey as of 1976 of 180 USA-based multinational companies based on the Harvard Multinational Enterprise Project data showed that 8,059 subsidiaries of the 10,845 subsidiaries for which data were available (or 74.3 per cent) were wholly owned (Curhan *et al.* 1977: 143). Vernon's earlier study showed somewhat lower percentages for USA-based enterprises (65.1 per cent), lower totals for European-based enterprises (48.9 per cent), and much lower totals for Japanese-based enterprises (6.0 per cent) (Vernon 1977: 34; see also Blumberg 1983: appendix).

[50] Intra-group transactions to the benefit of the parent but not leaving the subsidiary at a disadvantage do not violate existing fiduciary standards in Delaware and New York, see, e.g., *Sinclair Oil Co.* v. *Levien,* 1971; *Case* v. *New York Central R. Co,* 1965. Whether such

While this factor will influence the direction of the subsidiary's affairs, it relates only to the internal governance of the subsidiary and does not involve the rights and liabilities of third parties. Accordingly, it is difficult to see its relevance in considering whether enterprise principles should be employed to impose liability upon a parent corporation or the group by reason of dealings between the subsidiary and third parties. Thus, while there is only limited authority available on this question, the decisions involving partly owned subsidiaries (or other controlled corporations) properly do not give this feature any particular significance.[51]

10.3 Multinational corporations and extraterritoriality

In the case of multinational corporations, application of enterprise law has serious consequences, which do not arise in the case of corporate groups operating in only one country. National doctrines of enterprise law inevitably present serious questions of extraterritoriality when applied to foreign, as well as domestic, member corporations of the group.

Such extraterritorial application of enterprise law by the home countries of parent corporations of multinational groups determining rights and obligations of foreign subsidiaries all over the world, often with objectives contrary to the national policies of the overseas host countries, engenders international confrontation where public law matters are concerned. The American attempts to enforce its boycott against the People's Republic of China and against the Soviet Siberian pipeline vividly illustrate the problems involved (*Société Fruehauf Corp.* v. *Massardy*, 1968; *Compagnie Européenne des Petroles S. A.* v. *Sensor Nederland B. V.*, 1982; Blumberg 1992: sect. 20.06.3, 21.05).

The reverse situation of the extraterritorial application of local law by host countries imposing obligations on foreign parent corporations and affiliated companies presents very different, but also significant, problems, both legal and economic (see Blumberg 1985: sect. 17.16, 17.23–6). The Deltec litigation in Argentina (J. Gordon 1974, 1979) and, to a lesser

a dubious result will survive future scrutiny remains to be seen. The American Law Institute recommends a general approach of fairness and reasonableness: ALI, 1984: sect. 5.10 (proposed final draft, 1992); see generally Fletcher 1980: 13, sect. 5810, 5811.

[51] See Blumberg 1987b: sect. 6.08. For the special purposes of particular statutes, wholly owned subsidiaries may be treated differently from partly owned subsidiaries. Thus, in the celebrated *Copperweld* decision, the Supreme Court held that a parent corporation could not conspire with its wholly owned subsidiary, in so far as violation of the sections of the Sherman Antitrust Act making unlawful conspiracies to monopolize were concerned. For these special purposes, the Court relied on enterprise principles, stating that 'a parent and a wholly owned subsidiary always have a "unity of purpose" or a common design' (*Copperweld Corp.* v. *Independence Tube Corp.* 1984: 771–2). Copperweld expressly reserved decision with respect to cases involving partly owned subsidiaries. For purposes of this particular statute, the question is more complex, and the law is still unclear (Blumberg 1989: sect, 7.02.3).

degree, the Bhopal case in India provide dramatic examples of the problem created by the absence of a world legal order. The imposition by a host country of liability for the obligations of a local subsidiary upon its foreign-based parent and affiliated companies will inevitably receive a hostile reaction in the home nation of the parent company, particularly a home nation not fully committed to enterprise law.

There are economic difficulties as well. Any application by host countries of enterprise law to local subsidiaries will make operation in such nations by multinational corporations less advantageous and discourage investment. In consequence, there will be pressures on undeveloped countries to adapt their legal structures to create a more attractive climate for investment.

Enterprise law thus has global implications of importance in the case of the far-flung foreign subsidiaries of the multinational corporations of the developed world. Until the emergence of a world legal order, extraterritorial application of enterprise law may be expected to create significant problems of its own.

11. CONCLUSION

The fundamental problem of the legal system in determining when enterprise principles should replace entity law in matters involving corporate groups goes far beyond the relatively simple question of the definition of the corporate group. It goes to the very nature of the legal system.

The legal system in the United States, as in the Western world generally, rests on a long-established doctrine of the corporate juridical personality which reflects concepts of entity law. In the centuries since the formulation of entity law and the more recent period in which entity law was strongly re-enforced by adoption of the supplementary principle of limited liability (Blumberg 1987b: ch. 1–5; 1986), the size, scope, and corporate and economic structures of business organizations have changed dramatically. Corporate groups of 'incredible complexity' (Blumberg 1983: appendix; Hadden 1984: 274) have replaced simple corporations owned by individuals. Multinational enterprises operating throughout the world have replaced local businesses. The corporate entity as formulated long ago in an economic world of simple corporations no longer accurately describes the contemporary large business, which typically includes scores or hundreds of corporations collectively conducting a common business under common control.

Entity law developed to serve the needs of the earlier period is no longer adequate in a world of multinational groups. In many areas, entity law has become anachronistic and no longer serves the ends of the law, however well it may have served such ends in the simpler corporate world of the nineteenth and earlier centuries in which corporate groups were essentially unknown. The challenge facing the developed world today is the adaptation of an outdated corporate legal system to serve contemporary needs.

American law is still in the relatively early stages of responding to this challenge. While entity law still generally prevails in most areas, American legislative, administrative, and judicial agencies are under increasing pressure to formulate and apply principles of enterprise law in many areas of American law. In view of the evolution of American enterprise law traced in the five volumes comprising the series *The Law of Corporate Groups* thus far,[52] it is clear that increasingly courts and legislatures are deciding in selected areas that enterprise principles should replace principles of entity law, in order to implement more effectively the underlying policies and objectives of the law in the area.

Such efforts are widely evident. The legislative acceptance of enterprise principles in major statutes of specific application and the judicial and administrative development of the doctrine in the construction and application of statutes of general application, as well as in particular areas of procedural law, bankruptcy law, and substantive common law, constitutes a surprisingly rich body of authority. Out of this development is emerging the American law of corporate groups.

---

[52] A sixth volume reviewing the position of corporate groups under state statutory law is under preparation.

18

Regulating Corporate Groups: An International Perspective

TOM HADDEN

I. THE REGULATION OF DIVERSITY

The corporate group, both national and multinational, is a significant institutional phenomenon in its own right. Its adoption as an almost universal form of business organization shows how flexible the corporate form has proved to be and how inventive the business community and its legal advisers have been in developing it. Group structures are ideally suited to the huge diversity of business requirements. They can ease the problems of operating in a large number of different jurisdictions. And they can, if desired, be used to shield the internal affairs of a business from unwanted governmental regulation.

The triumph of the corporate group over all other forms of business organization also raises a number of more general issues. What impact, if any, has the nature of the legal form had on the underlying economic development? To what extent have the business community and its legal advisers consciously sought to create a form of organization which is so inherently difficult to regulate? And what are the objectives and practicalities of regulation? Is there anything to be gained by seeking to limit the freedom of the business community to organize itself as it wishes?

It may assist in dealing with these questions to begin with some fairly general propositions on which there may be some consensus. The first is that the flexibility and potentially infinite variety of the corporate group is one of its most significant characteristics, and to some may constitute one of its most significant attractions. Any attempt to limit its flexibility is therefore likely to meet with strenuous opposition. The second is that neither of the two simplest approaches to the legal status of corporate groups—the maintenance of the traditional view that each constituent company in the group must retain an entirely separate legal personality, and the recognition of the group as a legal entity in its own right which submerges that of its constituent companies—is likely to prove either workable or acceptable. On the other hand, it is equally unrealistic to adopt the view that the relationships between the constituent parts of the group are entirely a matter for contractual agreement. Setting some limits to the range of permissible relationships, whether they are described as contractual or not, is an essential part of any scheme of legal regulation. The third is that there is a need for both national and international regulation to protect the legitimate interests of the principal parties involved in group transactions, notably those of external investors, employees, voluntary and involuntary creditors or consumers, and the host and home states of the enterprise involved. There is ample evidence, as will be seen below, of the ease with which group structures may be manipulated in order to avoid established controls and obligations to the disadvantage of one or more of these parties. The important question is whether and how far the various interrelated objectives of regulation can be more effectively achieved by structural as opposed to transactional controls—that is, by regulating the structure of the group as a whole, rather than particular transactions by or between its constituent companies.

To make any progress in answering these questions, it is essential, as in any other sphere of economic activity, to understand and be able to classify the various forms of group organization, the ways in which they may be manipulated or abused, and the objectives of national and international regulation. This in turn requires an understanding of the historical development of group structures and of their current use in the leading jurisdictions. This chapter therefore begins with an attempt to summarize the development and the main features of corporate group structures in the United States, Britain, Germany, France, Japan, and some other associated jurisdictions. In this light an attempt has been made to identify and classify some more general types of group organization. This is followed by a discussion of some of the principle problems and abuses to which they have contributed and of the legal rules which have been developed in an attempt to regulate them. The final section seeks to develop a more coherent approach to the objectives of regulation in respect of the main types of groups which have been identified.

2. INTERNATIONAL PATTERNS IN GROUP ORGANIZATION

In his latest book, *Scale and Scope*, Alfred Chandler (1990) draws some general conclusions on patterns of corporate organization and development in the United States, Britain, and Germany in the nineteenth and early twentieth centuries. Though his main focus is managerial organization, rather than legal structures, Chandler's work includes some useful details regarding the development of legal structures in the three countries. It also focuses attention on the way in which different legal regimes and traditions, notably in respect of the governmental response to com-

bines and monopolies, have influenced the patterns of group organization
and structure. The sketches which follow are based partly on Chandler's
work, partly on the legal analysis by Phillip Blumberg (1990*a*) of the
development of group law in the United States, and partly on other
accounts of some typical current group structures in Britain and some
other European countries, Australia and Canada, and Japan (Hadden
1983, 1984, 1992; R. Clark 1979; Henderson 1973; Hayakawa 1991).
Though most of the material is already well known, it does no harm to
recall the overall context in which the various forms of corporate groups
and the various legislative controls over them have been built up.

2.1 The United States

The formation of corporate groups did not become lawful in the United
States until the statutory bar on holdings of one company's shares by
another was removed, initially in New Jersey in 1888. But co-operative
combinations of leading companies through trade associations as a means
of market sharing and price fixing were already well established by that
date, and led eventually to the prohibition of such combines in the
Sherman Act of 1894. The interaction of these two statutory developments appears to have contributed to an initial burst of mergers in the
1890s and 1900s. Many of these were carried through by the creation of
new holding companies, which purchased shares in the participating companies. In the United States, in contrast to Britain, many of the new
holding companies appear to have developed the professional techniques
of group management from the outset. The reaction to this development
was the initiation of antitrust proceedings against some of the largest—
notably Standard Oil, American Tobacco, and Du Pont—and their eventual breakup in 1911, followed by the strengthening of the legislation and
its enforcement under the Clayton Act in 1914. Otherwise there was little
attempt to regulate the new form, though in the 1930s accountants began
to develop the techniques of consolidated group accounting.

The early part of the twentieth century also saw the development of a
second form of inter-company shareholding, that of investment companies or trusts. These shareholding companies purchased and held relatively small blocks of shares in other established companies for
investment purposes, and typically did not seek to influence or control
their management. Though there was initially no formal bar on the size
of holdings, and therefore no legal difference between these and other
types of holding company, specific regulations on the conduct of investment companies were introduced in 1940 under the Investment
Companies Act.

The major development in the middle of the twentieth century has been the internationalization of USA based corporate groups. In the early stages this typically involved the establishment of sales and distribution subsidiaries in major foreign jurisdictions. But this was soon overtaken by direct investment in production facilities, whether by establishing new subsidiaries or by the acquisition of established local companies and groups. The figures in *Scale and Scope* show clearly that between the early 1900s and the 1970s there was a progressive shift from establishing new companies to expansion by acquisitions (Chandler 1990: 160). Within the United States this trend led in the 1960s and 1970s to the development of conglomerate groups in which managers at group headquarters were less concerned with the overall planning of production and sales strategies than with setting targets for, and monitoring performance by, the constituent operating companies. But this trend appears to have been less common in respect of foreign-based subsidiaries. And more recently there has been a tendency for conglomerate groups to dispose of those businesses which do not fit with a more co-ordinated business strategy. In general terms it appears that most leading American groups have typically sought to achieve 100 per cent ownership in all their subsidiaries, and to avoid the creation or maintenance of unnecessarily complex corporate structures. As in Britain, co-operative relationships between established groups have typically been provided for by the incorporation of new joint venture companies.

One example of the streamlined corporate structure adopted by a leading US multinational is illustrated in Figure 18.1, which shows how the various acquisitions and foreign operations of IBM have been integrated in a functional structure designed both to reflect managerial controls and to minimize disclosure obligations on operating units.

2.2 Britain

Though there was never a statutory bar on the holding of shares in one company by another, the pattern of group development in Britain has in many respects been similar to that in the United States. However, there are some significant differences. Chandler's work shows that in the initial period of merger activity at the turn of the century, which, as in the United States, was a direct result of worries about the illegality of restrictive agreements between leading companies, there was a tendency for the newly formed holding companies to avoid interfering in any way with the established operations of their constituent subsidiaries (1990: 287–91). In Chandler's view, this was directly related to the continuing involvement of the founding families in most of the major industrial enterprises. There appears to have been a similar reluctance to disturb established corporate structures and managerial practices in many of the businesses which were acquired as the leading groups expanded by take-overs and mergers, rather than by direct investment. As a result, the leading British-based groups in the 1960s and 1970s appear to have operated with much more complex corporate structures and less coherent group management practices than their US and European counterparts, as indicated by the survey carried out by the Commission of the European Communities in the early 1970s (1976) and by research into some leading British groups in 1979 (Hadden 1983). When more streamlined divisional management structures were finally introduced in the 1970s, often on the advice of American management consultants, there was a tendency to superimpose them on existing corporate structures, thus increasing the apparent, if not the actual, complexity of the group.

Figure 18.2, showing the Rank Organisation as it was in 1979, may serve to illustrate some of these features of major British groups. It shows not only the underlying complexity of the legal corporate structure, in which many of the group's earlier acquisitions and its joint venture with the Xerox Corporation appear to have survived in their original somewhat haphazard form, but also how a more rational divisional structure had been superimposed on that legal substructure for managerial purposes.

The current tendency in Britain, as in the United States, is for holding companies other than pure investment companies to hold 100 per cent of the shares in all their subsidiaries. The terms of the City Code on Take-overs and Mergers are specifically designed to facilitate this, by prohibiting partial bids and requiring successful bids to be held open to allow initially dissenting shareholders to accept (City Panel on Take-overs and Mergers 1990: rules 31 and 36). There are also some well-established international combinations between leading British and Dutch companies, notably Unilever and Shell, in which parallel structures have been created in each country to achieve unified management in a group headed by separately quoted companies. In the 1970s and 1980s joint ventures between established groups for specific purposes, both within Britain and abroad, also became more common. These co-operative relationships have typically been formalized by incorporating new companies for each specific joint venture, which, as a result of the current definition of holding and subsidiary companies, may have to be treated as subsidiaries within both parent groups for some purposes.

2.3 Other European countries

There is much less detailed information on the development of group structures in other European countries in which multinational groups are based. The information in *Scale and Scope* on developments in Germany

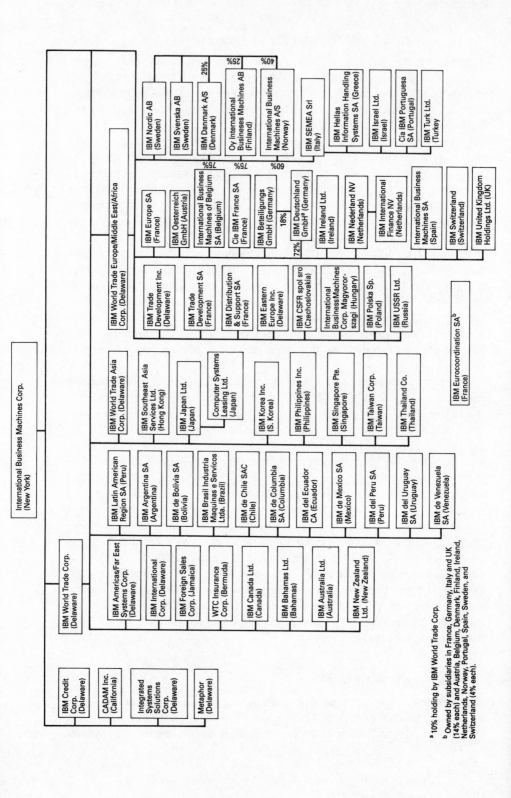

International Business Machines Corp.
(New York)

IBM Credit Corp. (Delaware)

CADAM Inc. (California)

Integrated Systems Solutions Corp. (Delaware)

Metaphor (Delaware)

IBM World Trade Corp. (Delaware)

IBM Latin American Region SA (Peru)

IBM Americas/Far East Systems Corp. (Delaware)

IBM International Corp. (Delaware)

IBM Foreign Sales Corp. (Jamaica)

WTC Insurance Corp. (Bermuda)

IBM Canada Ltd. (Canada)

IBM Bahamas Ltd. (Bahamas)

IBM Australia Ltd. (Australia)

IBM New Zealand Ltd. (New Zealand)

IBM Argentina SA (Argentina)

IBM de Bolivia SA (Bolivia)

IBM Brasil Industria Maquinas e Servicos Ltda. (Brazil)

IBM de Chile SAC (Chile)

IBM de Columbia SA (Columbia)

IBM del Ecuador CA (Ecuador)

IBM de Mexico SA (Mexico)

IBM del Peru SA (Peru)

IBM del Uruguay SA (Uruguay)

IBM de Venezuela SA (Venezuela)

IBM World Trade Asia Corp. (Delaware)

IBM Southeast Asia Services Ltd. (Hong Kong)

IBM Japan Ltd. (Japan)

Computer Systems Leasing Ltd. (Japan)

IBM Korea Inc. (S. Korea)

IBM Philippines Inc. (Philippines)

IBM Singapore Pte. (Singapore)

IBM Taiwan Corp. (Taiwan)

IBM Thailand Co. (Thailand)

IBM World Trade Europe/Middle East/Africa Corp. (Delaware)

IBM Trade Development Inc. (Delaware)

IBM Trade Development SA (France)

IBM Distribution & Support SA (France)

IBM Eastern Europe Inc. (Delaware)

IBM CSFR spol sro (Czechoslovakia)

International Business Machines Corp. Magyororszagi (Hungary)

IBM Polska Sp. (Poland)

IBM USSR Ltd. (Russia)

IBM Europe SA (France)

IBM Oesterreich GmbH (Austria)

International Business Machines of Belgium SA (Belgium) 75%

Cie IBM France SA (France)

IBM Beteiligungs GmbH (Germany) 18%

IBM Deutschland GmbH[a] (Germany) 72%

IBM Ireland Ltd. (Ireland)

IBM Nederland NV (Netherlands)

IBM International Finance NV (Netherlands)

International Business Machines SA (Spain)

IBM Switzerland (Switzerland)

IBM United Kingdom Holdings Ltd. (UK)

IBM Nordic AB (Sweden)

IBM Svenska AB (Sweden)

IBM Danmark A/S (Denmark) 25%

Oy International Businses Machines AB (Finland) 25%

International Business Machines A/S (Norway) 40%

IBM SEMEA Srl (Italy) 60%

IBM Hellas Information Handling Systems SA (Greece)

IBM Israel Ltd. (Israel)

Cia IBM Portuguesa SA (Portugal)

IBM Turk Ltd. (Turkey)

IBM Eurocoordination SA[b] (France)

[a] 10% holding by IBM World Trade Corp.

[b] Owned by subsidiaries in France, Germany, Italy and UK (14% each) and Austria, Belgium, Denmark, Finland, Ireland, Netherlands, Norway, Portugal, Spain, Sweden, and Switzerland (4% each).

Fig. 18.1. The structure of the IBM group in 1991. This chart shows a highly streamlined and functional corporate structure with a single, wholly owned operating subsidiary in most major jurisdictions co-ordinated through two major regional holding companies which form the basis for the regional breakdown of trading activities in the holding company's financial statements. *Source*: *IBM Annual Report* and *SEC 10-K Report* for 1991.

International Business Machines Corp.	(New York)
IBM Credit Corp.	(Delaware)
CADAM Inc.	(California)
Integrated Systems Solutions Corp.	(Delaware)
Metaphor	(Delaware)
IBM World Trade Corp.	(Delaware)
IBM Americas/Far East Systems Corp.	(Delaware)
IBM International Corp.	(Delaware)
IBM Foreign Sales Corp.	(Jamaica)
WTC Insurance Corp.	(Bermuda)
IBM Canada Ltd.	(Canada)
IBM Bahamas Ltd.	(Bahamas)
IBM Australia Ltd.	(Australia)
IBM New Zealand Ltd.	(New Zealand)
IBM Latin American Region SA	(Peru)
IBM Argentina SA	(Argentina)
IBM de Bolivia SA	(Bolivia)
IBM Brasil Industria Maquinas e Servicos Ltda.	(Brazil)
IBM de Chile SAC	(Chile)
IBM de Columbia SA	(Columbia)
IBM del Ecuador CA	(Ecuador)
IBM de Mexico SA	(Mexico)
IBM del Peru SA	(Peru)
IBM del Uruguay SA	(Uruguay)
IBM de Venezuela SA	(Venezuela)
IBM World Trade Asia Corp.	(Delaware)
IBM Southeast Asia Services Ltd.	(Hong Kong)
IBM Japan Ltd.	(Japan)
Computer Services Leasing Ltd.	(Japan)
IBM Korea Inc.	(S. Korea)
IBM Philippines Inc.	(Philippines)
IBM Singapore Pte.	(Singapore)
IBM Taiwan Corp.	(Taiwan)
IBM Thailand Co.	(Thailand)
IBM World Trade Europe/Middle East/Africa Corp.	(Delaware)
IBM Trade Development Inc.	(Delaware)
IBM Trade Development SA	(France)
IBM Distribution & Support SA	(France)
IBM Eastern Europe Inc.	(Delaware)
IBM CSFR spol sro	(Czechoslovakia)
International Business Machines Corp. Magyororszagi	(Hungary)
IBM Polska Sp.	(Poland)
IBM USSR Ltd.	(Russia)
IBM Europe SA	(France)
IBM Oesterreich GmbH	(Austria)
International Business Machines of Belgium SA	(Belgium)
Cie IBM France SA	(France)
IBM Beteiligungs GmbH	(Germany)
IBM Deutschland GmbH[a]	(Germany)
IBM Ireland Ltd.	(Ireland)
IBM Nederland NV	(Netherlands)

cont/

cont/

IBM International Finance NV	(Netherlands)
International Business Machines SA	(Spain)
IBM Switzerland	(Switzerland)
IBM United Kingdom Holdings Ltd.	(UK)
IBM Nordic AB	(Sweden)
IBM Svenska AB	(Sweden)
IBM Danmark A/S	(Denmark)
Oy International Busineses Machines AB	(Finland)
International Business Machines A/S	(Norway)
IBM SEMEA Srl	(Italy)
IBM Hellas Information Handling Systems SA	(Greece)
IBM Israel Ltd.	(Israel)
Cia IBM Portuguesa SA	(Portugal)
IBM Turk Ltd.	(Turkey)
IBM Eurocoordination SA[b]	(France)

[a] 10% holding by IBM World Trade Corp.

[b] Owned by subsidiaries in France, Germany, Italy and UK (14% each) and Austria, Belgium, Denmark, Finland, Ireland, Netherlands, Norway, Portugal, Spain, Sweden, and Switzerland (4% each).

up to the 1940s indicates that the absence of legal restrictions on market-sharing and price-fixing agreements meant that there was less incentive for the formation of large groups, but that when they were formed to assist in rationalization during recessions, the American practice of creating a strong managerial group headquarters was followed (Chandler 1990: 587–92). The German legislation requiring a strict separation of the management board from the supervisory board, on which representatives of banks and other leading companies have always been major participants, may also have contributed to the practice of maintaining co-operative relationships between larger numbers of smaller groups. This may have contributed to the development in Germany in the inter-war period of contractually based group relationships, known as *Vertragskonzerne*. Though it appears that this form of contractual group organization is now uncommon, the legal provisions for contractual groups are still prominent in German group law, and have created some major difficulties in the harmonization of this area of law within the European Community. The more significant practical feature of contemporary German groups, however, is the continuing influence exercised by leading banks in most major groups, both through their own relatively small shareholdings and through the much larger number of bearer shares which they hold and effectively control on behalf of other investors (see Chapter 15 in this volume). This has clearly contributed to the development of network theories of group structures by German authors (Teubner 1990*b*).

In other major European jurisdictions, such as France, Belgium, Holland, and Switzerland, the tendency for major groups to develop

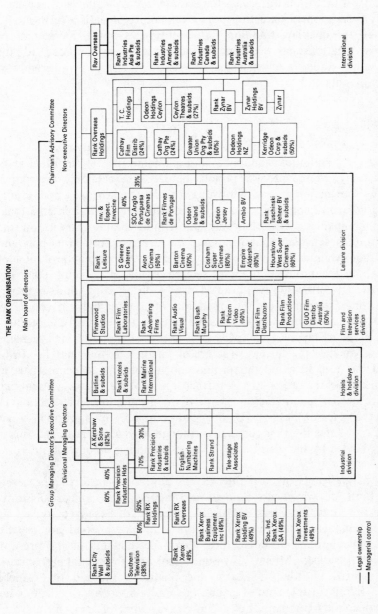

Fig. 18.2. The structure of the Rank Organisation group in 1979. This chart illustrates the complex relationship between the legal corporate structure of the group, which comprised some 160 active subsidiaries (not all shown on the chart), most of which were wholly owned, and the divisional managerial structure which had been superimposed on it and which in many instances cut across the formal legal structure. *Source: Hadden 1983: 64.*

complex networks of shareholders, including substantial cross-holdings with other leading companies and financial institutions, is even more marked (Baums *et al.* forthcoming). The development in France of specific legal provision for *groupements à l'intérêt économique*, which have recently been adopted on a European Community basis, is a further indication of the civil-law tradition of permitting, if not encouraging, cooperative relationships between distinct groups, as opposed to the common-law tradition of regarding all such relationships as inherently or potentially unlawful.

2.4 Japan

The structure of corporate groups in Japan is more directly related to the statutory prohibition of monopolies and combines than in any other leading economy. In the pre-war period the Japanese economy was dominated by four major groups, known as *zaibatsu*, each headed by a family holding company and each containing its own banking and international trading companies. After the war the United States insisted on the breakup of these *zaibatsu*, and imposed the stringent Anti-Monopoly and Fair Trade Maintenance Act of 1947. The most stringent provision of this statute, the prohibition under section 10 of any holding company unless special permission was granted, was soon repealed. But the prohibition under section 9 on the operation of a pure holding company, which is defined as one whose principal activity is to control the business of one or more Japanese companies by means of shareholdings, remains in force. Much of the current structure of Japanese groups may be attributed to the need to avoid this prohibition, which has no counterpart in any other developed economy. A further legacy of the post-war American influence on the Japanese legal regime is the prohibition under section 11 of the 1947 Act on holdings by financial companies of more than 5 per cent of the shares in other companies, though it would appear that this is widely avoided by the distribution of excess holdings among related companies.

Two major forms of corporate groups have subsequently been developed, both of which are known as *keiretsu*, or families of firms (Henderson 1973; R. Clark 1979). The largest are usually described as being the modern equivalent of the pre-war *zaibatsu*, and are usually listed in two groups of three: three direct descendants of the pre-war *zaibatsu* (Mitsubishi, Mitsui, and Sumitomo) and three banking *keiretsu* (those centred on the Fuji Bank, the Sanwa Bank, and the Daiichi Kangyo Bank). In this type of group, or family, of companies there is no principal holding company, but a complex network of small intra-group holdings designed to avoid the impact of the 1947 Act but to facilitate a

reasonable degree of co-ordination. This is achieved partly through regular meetings of the chairmen of the leading family companies and partly
through interlocking directorships. The second and more common type of
group is known as an industrial *keiretsu*, and includes at least 100 major
groups. They are much more like British or American groups, in that
there is a clearly defined principal holding company and numerous dependent or controlled subsidiaries or associates. In order to avoid the impact
of the 1947 Act, however, the principal holding company must carry on
its own business and restrict its holdings in subsidiaries and associated
companies to a maximum of 50 per cent of its own assets and its
dividend income to a similar percentage. Controlling holdings are thus
lawful, and are regularly held by the leading company in the group. It is
less usual, however, for 100 per cent of the shares in a subsidiary to be
owned. As a result, there are external shareholders in many of the principal operating subsidiaries in these industrial *keiretsu* groups. The reason
for this pattern is not entirely clear. It may be because the sale of shares
in a subsidiary is regarded as a useful source of funds for the holding
company (Kojo 1992 personal communication). On the other hand it has
been reported that the level of internal trading within these groups is
much higher than that in the traditional and banking *keiretsu* (Hayakawa
1991).

An example of the links between the two main types of *keiretsu* is
given in Figure 18.3, for the Toyota group, adapted from unpublished
material of Hayakawa. This shows both the small, but cumulatively substantial, holdings in various group companies by the Sanwa and Mitsui
banking *keiretsu* and the typical structure of relationships between the
principal holding company, Toyota, its subsidiaries, and associated companies.

It is not entirely clear how far these structures are accepted by the
Japanese business community merely as way of avoiding the 1947 Act or
as economically desirable in their own right. There appears to be a general acceptance in Japan of the value of informal co-operative structures,
rather than the more formalized control structures preferred in the West.
But the formal prohibition of holding companies is widely regarded as a
historical anachronism. One reason for maintaining it may be a desire to
avoid an unnecessary confrontation with the United States. Another
explanation for its retention, though it is one which is not mentioned by
Japanese commentators, may be that it provides a convenient means of
discouraging external take-overs of Japanese companies. The provisions
of the 1947 Act are officially interpreted as permitting the establishment
of a single subsidiary in Japan by a foreign holding company in its main
line of business, but as preventing the development of any larger network
of holdings or of any form of conglomerate.

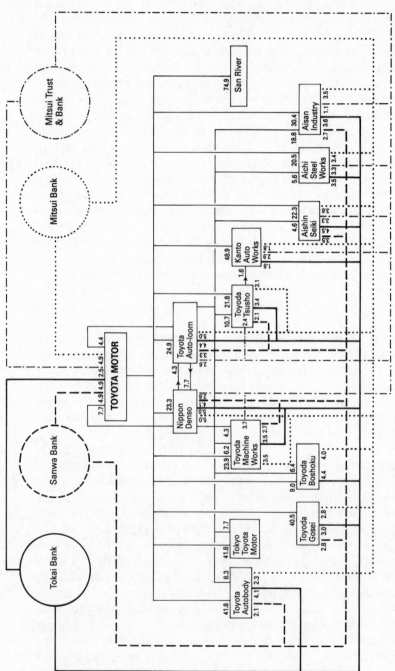

FIG. 18.3. The structure of the Toyota group in 1989. This chart illustrates both the internal structure of the Toyota industrial *keiretsu* and the way in which it was linked to the Mitsui and Sanwa banking *keiretsu*. Note the relatively small controlling holdings held by Toyota Motor in each of its main operating subsidiaries, and the pattern of holdings, each below the 5% level, but cumulatively substantial, by the banking *keiretsu* in each of those subsidiaries. The figures indicate per cent holdings. *Source:* Unpublished information supplied by M. Hayakawa.

2.5 Canada and Australia

In each of the jurisdictions discussed there is, of course, a huge range of different forms of corporate structures. In the account which has been given of patterns in the leading common-law jurisdictions, attention has focused on what appear to be typical structures for the most significant groups. In each of these jurisdictions, however, there are groups which diverge substantially from the prevailing patterns. Some British and American groups, for example, have not followed the general practice of seeking to achieve 100 per cent ownership of all their subsidiaries, and have instead exercised managerial control through a network of majority, or even minority, holdings. But such structures are the exception, and tend to be adopted by less significant groups at the margins of the corporate economy. In some other common-law jurisdictions, groups based on networks of holdings of less than 100 per cent are more common, and are adopted by some of the leading groups. Examples of this form of group structure for the purposes of this chapter will be taken from Canada and Australia, where such structures appear to be more common among

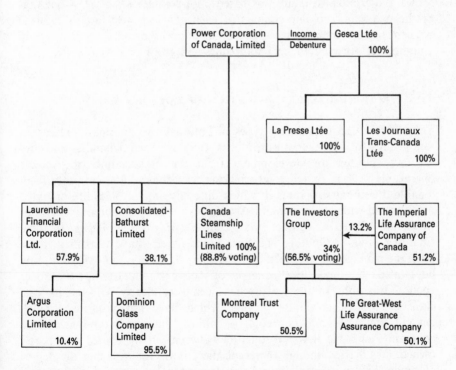

FIG. 18.4. Power Corporation of Canada, Limited: major investments, 25 March 1975. Common shares. *Source*: Royal Commission on Corporate Concentration (RCCC) research.

locally based groups, as opposed to those which form part of larger multinational groups.

In Canada the development of groups of this kind was highlighted by the Royal Commission on Corporate Concentration in 1978, notably in respect of the Power and Argus groups, which had established control over a significant number of Canadian companies through a network of majority and minority holdings (Canada 1978; Hadden *et al.* 1984). These are illustrated in summary form in the Figures 18.4 and 18.5, which are adapted from charts prepared by the Royal Commission.

In Australia, though most established groups have followed the British pattern of growth by the acquisition of 100 per cent control over most, if not all, their subsidiaries, some leading groups in the 1980s developed much more complex structures. One significant example, which has not attracted as much international attention as those Australian-based groups such as the Bond and Elders groups, which developed substantial non-Australian interests, but which has also run into very serious financial problems, is the Adelaide Steamship Company/David Jones group, which in the late 1980s ranked in the top ten Australian groups. As Figure 18.6 shows, the group's structure was based on a complex set of cross-holdings by the two major holding companies, each of which held just short of 50 per cent of each other's shares, as well as majority or minority holdings in a number of other public held companies and groups.

3. THE LEGAL CLASSIFICATION OF CORPORATE GROUPS

The classification of different types of national and multinational corporate groups for managerial purposes is well developed. Chandler and others have plotted the development from the organization of overseas operations by one or more international divisions to the currently fashionable divisional structures in which different product lines are operated on a world-wide or regional basis through semi-autonomous divisions which are treated as distinct profit centres (Brooke and Remmers 1978; Chandler 1990). Gunther Teubner and others have classified these different managerial structures as 'H-form', 'U-form', and 'M-form', and have also developed the concept of network relationships (Teubner 1990*b*). But none of these ideas has been very clearly reflected in legal classifications of corporate groups, which have not progressed much beyond the traditional concepts of holding, subsidiary, and associated companies and the newer distinction between wholly owned and partly owned subsidiaries, though more specific criteria for assessing the degree of ownership or control have been developed for taxation and certain other regulatory purposes.

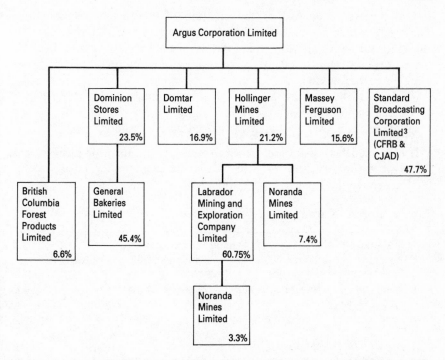

FIG. 18.5. Argus Corporation Limited: major investments. 25 March 1975. *Source*: RCCC research.

There is an obvious relationship between some of these legal distinctions and the various managerial classifications: the H-form structure is typically operated through a holding company which monitors the success of its investments in wholly or partly owned subsidiaries, the U-form structure through a pyramid of wholly owned and wholly controlled subsidiaries which are managed in a highly centralized and integrated manner and the M-form, usually, though not always, through wholly owned subsidiaries which are formally separated from group headquarters and run as semi-autonomous divisional units. The concept of co-operative or network relationships may also be linked to the looser group structures common in Japan and in some Canadian and Australian groups, or to the relationships involved in some joint ventures. But many of these more complex relationships and distinctions have not been reflected or developed in more strictly legal classifications for analytical or regulatory purposes.

There are several criteria on which more comprehensive classifications of group structures for legal purposes might be based. Some of the relevant axes of classification might be defined in terms of the degree of autonomy of parts of the group, whether in terms of formal ownership or formal powers of control or the creation of contractual relationships. These might then be related to the various types of managerial relationship outlined above and to the complexity of the group structure. Each of these axes is, of course, likely to constitute a continuum which might be represented as follows:

total autonomy—limited autonomy/control—total control
managerial—investment—co-ordination
simple hierarchical—partial/one way—complex/circular

It may then be possible to identify some typical, ideal, or ideal/typical forms of group structure on a socio-legal or economo-legal basis along the lines shown in Table 1.

Table 1. Forms of group structure

Type of economic relationship	Type of legal control		
	Shareholding	Directorships	Contractual
Managerial	Integrated group	Network group	Control contract group
Investment	Holding company		
Co-operative	Joint venture		Cartel

This simple example indicates clearly not only the huge range of possible categories of groups if all the axes of classification are used, but also that some potential categories do not appear to correspond to any typical group structures. Some of the resulting categories might then be used to identify significant types of group for regulatory and other legal purposes such as taxation, the attribution of liability, monopoly control, or outright prohibition. This clearly depends, however, on a much clearer analysis of the nature of the abuses or ill effects to be expected from each type and of the objectives of regulation.

4. POTENTIAL AND ACTUAL ABUSES

It has long been recognized by lawyers and accountants, and more recently by governments, that the development of corporate groups, and particularly of complex groups in which there is a network of majority and minority holdings and cross-holdings, creates the potential for a wide range of abuses. For the purposes of the present discussion it is not necessary to do more than summarize the major headings and to give a few examples.

Manipulation of control holdings. It is relatively easy within any corporate group in which there are external minority shareholdings in subsidiaries to exercise control over the whole group with a lesser shareholding, and thus a lesser commitment of capital, than would otherwise be necessary. The use of cross-holdings enables those who are in control of the group to entrench themselves with an even smaller commitment of personal or corporate capital. In the Adsteam/David Jones group illustrated in Figure 18.6, for example, the small personal holdings by leading directors were sufficient in conjunction with the cross-holdings of almost 50 per cent to ensure the continued control of the incumbent management.

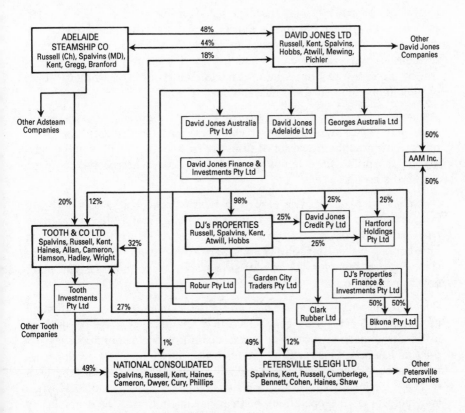

FIG. 18.6. The structure of the Adsteam group in Australia in 1989. This chart illustrates two significant features of this complex network group: (1) the high level of cross-holdings between the publicly held companies throughout the group; (2) the strategic position occupied throughout the group by three principal directors, whose small personal holdings in the two principal companies were sufficient, when added to the cross-holdings which they effectively controlled, to entrench their position. *Source*: Hadden 1992: 67.

Misleading accounts. The apparent profitability and worth of individual companies within a group can readily be manipulated by intra-group transactions designed to create profits, so as to conceal losses or otherwise affect individual balance sheets. The apparent profit or worth of the group as a whole as recorded in consolidated group accounts can also be manipulated in cases where the constituent companies operate with different accounting periods, again as in the Adsteam/David Jones group illustrated in Figure 18.6, or where associated companies which are not technically regarded as subsidiaries for the purpose of consolidation can be used as 'off balance sheet' vehicles to conceal or create significant transactions. Cross-holdings of any kind are a particularly serious problem, since they inevitably involve some diminution of apparent capital.

Oppression of minority interests. The usual problems of conflicting interests between directors and majority and minority shareholders are intensified within complex groups in which there are non-wholly owned subsidiaries and associated companies, since it is natural for those in control of the group to prefer the interests of the group as a whole to those of individual companies and shareholders.

Avoidance of liability. It may be possible within a group of companies to avoid liability to trade and other creditors and others affected by group operations, notably in respect of disasters such as that at Bhopal, by relying on the prima facie limitation of liability to each separate company within the group.

Avoidance of taxation. The ease with which profits and losses within a group may be manipulated by transfer pricing and other intra-group transactions makes it correspondingly easy to avoid taxation in high-tax jurisdictions by shifting profits to lower-tax jurisdictions or tax havens; similar group gains may be produced in respect of tax holidays and other governmental incentives to locate plants in particular jurisdictions.

Avoidance of antitrust, monopoly, and other regulations. The creation of groups and other forms of co-operative relationships may be used to avoid the impact of particular forms of antitrust and monopoly legislation, as has been illustrated by the historical development of group structures in almost every leading jurisdiction. Similar methods may be used to avoid the impact of certain forms of regulation in respect of take-overs and mergers or the operations of financial institutions—for example, by the warehousing of shares to avoid disclosure requirements, as in the Blue Arrow case in Britain (DTI 1990*b*), or the prohibition of holdings above a limited threshold, as in the case of financial institutions in Japan.

5. ESTABLISHED CONTROLS AND THEIR SHORTCOMINGS

All these forms of manipulation and abuse are well known to lawyers, accountants, and governments and a wide range of regulatory and anti-avoidance measures have been developed to deal with them. It would be impractical in this context even to attempt to summarize all the various measures which have been introduced in particular jurisdictions. Most have been introduced on an *ad hoc* basis in response to a specific problem or abuse, rather than in pursuit of any coherent legislative or regulatory strategy. But it is possible to draw a broad distinction between those which depend on controlling the way in which groups are structured and those which deal directly with the substance of the relevant transactions without reference to the structure of the group.

5.1 Cross-holdings

The most direct control over group structures is the limitation in most jurisdictions on the permissible level of cross-holdings between individual companies. In Britain, for example, there has long been a formal bar on the holding of shares by a subsidiary in its holding company (Companies Act, 1985, sect. 23). In Germany, cross-holdings are barred at a lower level between any company which holds more than 25 per cent in another company (*Aktiengesetz*, 1965, art. 19) (Wooldridge 1981). The initial justification for banning cross-holdings appears to have been concern over the inevitable depletion in apparent capital which any cross-holding involves. But cross-holdings may also be used to entrench control, and less directly as a means of supporting the share price in the relevant companies. A prohibition at the 50 per cent level, as in most jurisdictions, is clearly insufficient to prevent these potential abuses, as illustrated by the example of the Adsteam/David Jones group in Australia. It may even be argued that cross-holdings of any kind are inherently undesirable and so open to abuse that they should be universally banned at anything more than a minimal level. This would raise difficulties of equity in the context of contested take-over bids in which a target company might wish to buy shares in a bidding company as a means of defence or counter-attack. It might also be opposed by those who favour the development of certain forms of network groups. But this does not detract from the general consensus that there are some forms of intra-group cross-holdings, and therefore some forms of group structure, which should not be permitted.

5.2 Consolidated accounting

Statutory requirements in respect of the consolidation of group accounts are now almost universal, though legislation was introduced much earlier in this respect in common-law than in civil-law jurisdictions. The techniques of consolidated accounting were developed in the United States and Britain in the 1920s and 1930s, and the initial legislative requirements were in place by the 1940s (Walker 1978). But in some European jurisdictions action was not taken until the 1980s, under the terms of the Seventh European Community Directive (European Communities 1983c). A consolidation requirement does not in itself prescribe or prohibit any particular form of group structure. It operates by requiring the consolidation of the accounts of subsidiaries or associated companies which fall within the relevant definition of a group. In most common-law jurisdictions this has long been based on a control test, in terms of either a holding of more than 50 per cent of shares or the right to appoint more than half the directors. But this gives a good deal of latitude to network groups to avoid consolidation. A restrictive interpretation of the criterion in relation to the Adsteam/David Jones group, for example, meant that no consolidated accounts were published for the group as a whole. Under the Seventh Directive, however, the stricter tests of 'actual dominant influence' or 'unified management' have been adopted.[1] Even this would not cover some looser network groups of the kind which have been developed in Japan. There are additional shortcomings in the current rules for consolidation, in respect of equity accounting for investment in associated companies, merger accounting for acquisitions, and the disaggregation of information in respect of individual companies or divisions within a large or complex group. It is none the less clear in general terms that a precise definition of a group, and perhaps of different kinds of group, is required for accounting and allied purposes. It may also be argued that some types of network structure which make it difficult to produce a 'true and fair' statement of the affairs of the individual components or of the network as a whole should be prohibited on those grounds alone, at least in relation to publicly held companies.

5.3 Conflicts of interest and the oppression of minorities

There is a significant difference in approach between common-law jurisdictions and those civil-law jurisdictions which have adopted the German model in respect of conflicts of interest and the oppression of minorities

[1] For the British provision, see Companies Act, 1989, sect. 21, which replaces sect. 258 of the Companies Act, 1985.

within corporate groups. In common-law jurisdictions neither the courts nor the legislatures have sought to develop special rules to govern conflicts of interest between directors and shareholders at different levels in a complex group. Instead, they have merely taken account of the special situation within such groups in applying general rules governing the duties of directors, conflicts of interest, and the protection of minorities. For example, the concept of fraud on the minority in the United States and the statutory remedy in respect of oppression or unfair prejudice in Britain have been applied to protect minority shareholders in subsidiaries from discriminatory decisions by holding companies, even if those decisions were clearly taken in the interests of the group as a whole (*Sinclair Oil* v. *Levien*, 1971; *Scottish Co-operative Wholesale Society Ltd.* v. *Meyer*, 1959). Similarly, the growing number of statutory provisions prohibiting or imposing specific procedural safeguards in respect of potentially self-interested transactions have generally included related companies and their directors or shareholders in more general lists of persons or bodies with potentially conflicting interests. The only major deviation from this approach in common-law countries is the proposal by the Companies and Securities Law Review Committee in Australia that nominee or 'representative' directors of wholly owned subsidiaries should be expressly exempted from the ordinary rule requiring a director to act exclusively in the interests of his or her own company (Australia 1989: 65).

In German group law, on the other hand, a series of special rules and obligations has been developed for groups of different kinds (Hadden 1983: 33–4). For example, in integrated groups the directors of subsidiaries are authorized to subordinate the interests of their company to the group, though in return the holding company is liable for the debts of the subsidiary, while in a *de facto* group compensation by the dominating to the dominated company is payable in respect of such transactions. These different categories of groups are defined either in procedural terms, as in the case of a control contract group, or in structural or substantive terms, as in the case of a *de facto* group, or in both procedural and structural terms, as in the case of an integrated group. The continuing dispute over the adoption of the draft proposal for a Ninth Directive on Groups based on the German model (European Communities 1984) is centred on the respective merits of a structural approach and the common-law approach of applying general rules to group relationships without seeking to categorize different types of groups in any way. The absence of any great enthusiasm for the proposed Directive is perhaps an indication that for the limited purposes which it covers the structural approach is not widely accepted as being inherently superior.

5.4 Liability and insolvency

There is a similar difference in approach in respect of the liability of holding companies for the debts and obligations of other companies in a group. In common-law jurisdictions this issue is dealt with by applying general principles of company law to specific group situations. In the United States the main focus of attention has been on 'lifting the veil of incorporation' or subordinating debts owed by a subsidiary to its holding company under the 'Deep Rock' doctrine (*Taylor* v. *Standard Gas & Electric* Co., 1938). In Britain the main focus has been on the application of various statutory provisions based on the concept of fraudulent, and more recently wrongful, trading in advance of liquidation, and the potential impact of the new concept of 'shadow director' on holding companies 'in accordance with whose instructions' the affairs of a subsidiary are conducted (Prentice 1988).

In the German system some of these issues have been dealt with under the specific regimes provided in respect of integrated, control contract, and *de facto* groups, under which liability may be imposed on a controlling company for losses resulting from express instructions or negligent conduct on the part of group management (Hofstetter 1990).

The outcome under the two approaches is likely to be broadly similar in many cases. Neither has yet sought to impose group or enterprise liability in a strict sense. And neither has yet produced any clear guidelines on the difficult issue of the extent to which group liability may be imposed under a direct action in tort or delict against the principal group company in respect of disasters caused by the operations of a subsidiary (Muchlinski 1988). The basis of tortious or delictual liability in both systems is a deliberate or negligent decision or action either at an operational level in a subsidiary or division or at group level, as opposed to the existence of a particular corporate structure. There are none the less some arguments in favour of a structural approach to issues of liability. For example, in Australia the formal acceptance of general group liability for all debts and obligations of wholly owned subsidiaries has been accepted as a ground for exempting those subsidiaries from the obligation to publish separate annual accounts (Australia 1988). The structure of a group in terms of the ownership of assets and the flow of profits may be thought to be as significant a factor as the location or level of negligent conduct in determining the proper limits of liability.

5.5 Employee participation

The development of structures for employee participation in decision making, whether within individual companies or on a group level, is one of the most contentious and politically sensitive issues in corporate law and practice. Proposals for granting employees or their representatives a statutory role in corporate decision making at any level have been strenuously resisted in all common-law jurisdictions. In Germany and some other European civil-law jurisdictions statutory provisions for employee and trade union participation, typically at supervisory board level, within groups are well established, though there are widely varying views on their practical impact (Hadden 1982). For the purposes of this discussion it is sufficient to emphasize some general propositions on which there may be some consensus. The first is that many of the most effective structures for employee participation have been based on the creation of works councils at appropriate physical places of work or establishments, as opposed to the involvement of employee representatives in decision making at corporate or divisional levels. This form of participation, however, is likely to be restricted to issues of immediate concern within the work-place, rather than to address strategic managerial decisions which may have a more significant long-term impact on the interests of employees. The second is that it is difficult for the representatives of employees to participate effectively in managerial decision making at a strategic level without a good deal of training in managerial techniques, with the resulting risk that they become detached from the employees whose interest they are appointed to represent. Participation is in any event likely to be limited to a non-executive or supervisory role, whether as non-executive directors in the common-law system or members of the supervisory board in the German system.

The third proposition is that it is essential for employee representatives to be located in the managerial or supervisory structure at the point where major decisions are actually made. This means that provisions for employee participation must be centred on real managerial decision-making structures, rather than the formal corporate organization of holding companies and subsidiaries. It follows that if provisions for participation are to be based on corporate structures, those structures must reflect the real managerial organization of the group. This is relatively straightforward within a single jurisdiction. There is detailed provision in the German legislation, for example, for employee participation in works councils and on the supervisory board at group, as well as operating company, level (Hadden 1982). It is much more difficult to achieve a similar result at a multinational level, as has been shown within the European Community by the progressive dilution of the proposed Vredeling Directive and the lack of progress in securing acceptance for the proposed Fifth Directive (European Communities 1983a, 1983b). But this is essentially a political rather than a legal problem. There is little doubt that to secure effective employee participation in corporate decision making there is a need for some regulation of permissible group structures, not least in respect of looser network groups which might otherwise be able to avoid the impact of any legislation.

5.6 Taxation

The very great complexity of tax legislation in most jurisdictions makes it particularly hazardous to draw any general conclusions. It appears to be generally accepted, however, that for tax purposes the economic unity of corporate groups should be recognized. Accordingly, in most jurisdictions groups are permitted to offset profits and losses in constituent companies. The criterion of group membership for this purpose is usually a prescribed level of share ownership, though there is a tendency to extend this to cover actual control. All these provisions are in principle limited to group operations within the relevant jurisdiction, since tax authorities are primarily concerned with business conducted within their jurisdiction.

Tax authorities are also concerned with cross-frontier transactions, since it is so easy for multinational groups to shift profits and losses to the most advantageous tax regime. In most cases the authorities have therefore been granted powers both to take account of the operations of certain controlled foreign companies and to reopen the accounts of companies or operating divisions within their jurisdiction with a view to setting a 'proper' price for relevant transactions. This has led in turn to the adoption of a large number of international agreements in respect of 'corresponding adjustments' in other jurisdictions (OECD 1979, 1984; see further Chapter 20 in this volume).

As a result, tax authorities are typically less concerned with the regulation of the structures of corporate groups which are conducting business in their jurisdictions than with ensuring that all taxable profits arising there, whatever the structure of the business, are accurately recorded and reported. Though it might assist in this objective if all groups were required to create a single company or holding company through which all their operations in a given tax jurisdiction would be channelled, this is not strictly necessary. Companies are already obliged to prepare and submit accounts for tax purposes which are distinct from those which are presented to shareholders and are publicly disclosed, though it would be desirable if companies were expressly required to disclose any alterations or corresponding adjustments which have been required by the tax authorities and which affect previously published accounts.

5.7 Monopolies, mergers, and restrictive practices

The fact that the development of corporate groups in most jurisdictions was significantly affected by the desire of dominant enterprises to avoid the impact of laws on monopolies and restrictive practices has already been stressed. The creation of single corporate groups to encompass relationships which might otherwise have been held to be unlawful was one of the major factors in the early development of groups in the United States and Britain. The highly restrictive law on combines imposed by the United States is still a major influence in the structure of groups in Japan. It is hardly surprising, then, that current legislation on monopolies and mergers in most jurisdictions is specifically designed to cover anti-competitive practices, whatever the legal form used by those concerned. Though some practices which might well be held to be unlawful if agreed between independent enterprises may still be lawful if they are carried on under the umbrella of a single corporate group, there are now fairly stringent controls on the creation of such groups by take-overs and mergers. It is accepted that in the application of legislation in this sphere enforcement agencies and courts must consider the practical impact of the formal structures which have been adopted, as in the leading European Community cases of *Continental Can* v. *Commission of the European Communities*, 1973, and *Philip Morris* v. *Commission of the European Communities*, 1987.

The development of the concept of 'acting in concert' in the regulation of stock-market take-overs is a further indication of the predominance of substantial, rather than structural, criteria in this sphere, as in paragraph C1 of the current City Code on Take-overs and Mergers in Britain (City Panel on Take-overs and Mergers 1990). Regulatory legislation and other measures are thus applicable both to hierarchical and to network groups of all kinds. In some jurisdictions the regulatory authorities have power to prescribe corporate and other structures as a remedial measure when a breach of the law has been established or admitted. But it cannot easily be argued that the general regulation of corporate structures is essential to the achievement of the objectives of the legislation.

5.8 Regulation of external investment

A further form of regulation has been developed in some jurisdictions in which multinational groups have established subsidiaries. The objective is to ensure that the operations of the group within the particular jurisdiction are carried out in such a way as to advance the economic objectives of that state, as opposed to those of the multinational group. Various measures have been adopted to this end. Some countries, such as Ireland in the 1930s and more recently India and Nigeria, have required a certain proportion of the shares in the local subsidiaries of multinational groups be held by local individuals or interests. In others, such as India and Canada, measures have been introduced to require the involvement of nationals in the management of such subsidiaries, usually by requiring or encouraging their appointment as directors. Some state-socialist jurisdictions, notably the former USSR and China, also sought to develop what may be thought of as co-operative structures by requiring the establishment of joint ventures between state interests and the incoming multinational. The effectiveness and merits of this form of regulation are politically controversial in both home and host jurisdictions. In the present context it is sufficient to point out that all these approaches involve some structural regulation of the operation of the multinational. Controls on share ownership operate by ensuring that locally based subsidiaries are not wholly owned, and must therefore be dealt with, at least in theory, as units of operation whose interests must be considered separately from those of the group as a whole.

Controls on the nationality of management seek to achieve similar objectives by different means, though in formal legal terms this approach imposes fewer limitations on the way in which the operations of the subsidiary are conducted. Requiring incoming multinationals to enter into joint ventures with the state authorities is clearly the most far-reaching and potentially effective means of ensuring local control, though there is continuing dispute about the effects and effectiveness of structural regulation of this kind.

6. CONCLUSION: THE BALANCE BETWEEN STRUCTURAL AND NON-STRUCTURAL REGULATION

The answers to some of the questions posed at the start of this chapter will be clear from this brief and inevitably superficial survey of current controls over corporate groups in some leading jurisdictions. First, it is clear that legal regulation, particularly in respect of monopolies and restrictive practices, has had a substantial influence on the way in which corporate group structures have developed in most jurisdictions. Secondly, it is clear that at least some businessmen and their legal advisers have consciously used the corporate group as a legal form both to avoid existing regulations and to achieve objectives that would otherwise be unattainable. Thirdly, it is clear that the need to regulate corporate groups for a wide variety of purposes has long been accepted in every major jurisdiction. More generally, it appears that the answer to the question about the impact of the nature of the legal form on the underlying economic development is the usual and unexciting proposition that there is a complex and changing interrelationship between the two.

The answer to the more specific question as to whether the objectives of regulation can best be met by regulating the structure of the group or the particular transactions is similarly unexciting. It seems clear that some regulation of the permissible structure of corporate groups is necessary for some purposes, but not for others. It would be hard to deny the desirability of limiting, if not prohibiting altogether, anything more than marginal cross-holdings in order to prevent those in control of a group from entrenching themselves on a more or less permanent basis. Some regulation of corporate structures is also likely to be necessary to prevent some other forms of self-interested conduct or fraud by those in control, to ensure adequate and independent supervision of management, and to achieve the objectives of employee participation in corporate decision making. In the wake of the collapse of the Bank of Credit and Commerce International, the Bank of England has recently called for new powers to control the development of complex corporate structures by banks (Bank of England 1992). Such regulation may also be desirable, though less obviously essential, to ensure that shareholders and others are properly informed on what is happening within the group, as well as on the overall results on a consolidated basis. In all these respects a different approach is likely to be required in respect of hierarchical and wholly owned groups and looser network groups, some of which may need to be prohibited. On the other hand, the regulation of group structures would not appear to be necessary for the protection of minorities, for the imposition of group liability where that is appropriate, or for taxation or the regulation of monopolies and other anti-competitive practices.

The position in respect of the imposition of national economic objectives is less clear. For many purposes, this may be achieved as effectively by general legislation as by seeking to regulate the structure of a multinational's operations within the jurisdiction. But a structural approach may also be effective, provided that it is acceptable to the incoming group and does not deter investments which might have been made under less restrictive terms. In general terms, the position may perhaps best be summarized by stating that some regulation of corporate group structures is probably necessary for the purposes of the improvement or reform of corporate governance, but not for most other purposes.

19

Some Comments on the Law Relating to Corporate Groups

D.D. PRENTICE

The chapters by Phillip Blumberg and Tom Hadden respectively highlight what is a feature of modern economic life, and that is the pervasiveness of group structures. Hadden rightly points out the complexity of these and, what is more important, their variation. For example, in Germany and Japan the banks play a role in the affairs of companies that is not the case in the UK. Also, the *keiretsu* system in Japan (discussed by Hadden) produces the type of interlocking structure that breaks down the distinction between shareholder, supplier of goods and services, supplier of labour, and provider of finance (see Viner 1990: 27).

The ownership structure of a group is not a guide to the management structure; for example, even where the parent has 100 per cent subsidiaries, the management philosophy of the group may be such that the parent exercises a very loose control. Thus, Shell America is in its own right the seventh largest oil company in the world, and the degree of control that can be exerted over it by its parent will undoubtedly be influenced by this; its sheer size will result in it enjoying a considerable degree of autonomy. Some wholly owned subsidiaries are set up for regulatory reasons; for example, British Telecom, among other things, manufactures telephone equipment in competition with other manufacturers, and the regulatory authorities require it to conduct this activity through a separate company so as try to regulate the cross-subsidization between its monopoly activity (telecommunications) and its manufacturing activity.

Given the complexity of the group phenomenon and the adventitious nature of many group organizations, it is futile to try to put forward a uniform definition of what constitutes a group which will be appropriate for all situations. Also, from the point of view of a lawyer, this type of question simply makes no sense in the abstract. To be answerable, the question has to be asked in the context of a given legal system and for a given legal purpose.

Nevertheless, the group phenomenon obviously exists, and the question arises as to what are we to do about it. In the UK—and judging by

Blumberg's chapter, this also appears true of the USA—it is not that we do not have a law relating to groups, but that we have an abundance of law in this area (cf. Petite 1984: 84). There are laws relating to consolidation of accounts, disclosure, taxation, directors' dealings within the context of groups, minority shareholder oppression, and insolvency. An important feature of this legislation is that it often does not address the issue of groups as such, but rather deals with what are some of the salient regulatory problems of company law and in the process also covering the issue of groups. In my view, this is the preferable way of dealing with the problem. It does not entail that the issue of groups does not in some situations have to be specifically addressed; only that this should be the exception rather than the rule. Once the various regulatory issues have been addressed, then there will be little left to be mopped up by a law which specifically addresses the problem of groups.

We may consider one example, among many possible ones, of how this operates. Both Hadden and Blumberg, in this volume, address the difficult matter of parent liability for the debts of a subsidiary. Probably the underlying justification for imposing such liability is that the parent will normally exercise complete *de facto* control over the subsidiary and, accordingly, the subsidiary should be seen as nothing more than an emanation of the parent, which should therefore be liable for its debts. This argument could, of course, also apply to a company that is under the domination of a single shareholder. Even if one wants to go down the route of developing what Blumberg refers to as 'enterprise' law, difficulties remain. In particular, (1) how does one deal with exit—that is, a situation where the subsidiary leaves the group but with a liability which existed at the time it was a member of the group? (2) How does one deal with entry—that is, the acquisition of a subsidiary which has certain liabilities at the time it joins the group? (3) Why should the creditors of the subsidiary find that their claims have to be pooled with the claims of the creditors of the parent or of other members in the group, should the group get into financial difficulties? (4) Would group liability unreasonably increase the costs of lending to groups, since the lender would be interested in the total health of the group? (5) If, as pointed out above, control is important, why not also apply 'group law' to an individual who is a dominant shareholder.

We may consider more closely the recent changes in English law relating to the insolvency of a subsidiary, mentioned briefly by Hadden. These resulted from the concerns expressed in a 1982 official report (UK 1982) typical of this type of exercise: little theory, no systematic collection of data, but the members of the Committee were able, well-informed market professionals. One of the concerns of the Committee was that the corporate form was being 'misused' in that companies were continuing to trade in circumstances where there was no reasonable prospect that they could pay their debts. Implicit were a number of propositions which were not clearly articulated: first, that limited liability provides a perverse incentive to continue trading where the assets of the company are only sufficient to meet the claims of some or all of the company's creditors and hence the shareholders as residual claimants have everything to gain but nothing to lose from continued trading; second, and implicit in the Committee's concern, that those dealing with the company would not be adequately compensated through the price mechanism for the risk of dealing with an entity which enjoys limited liability. Although both these assumptions give rise to complex questions, we may assume that both are correct.

These concerns were addressed by a legislative provision (Insolvency Act, 1986 sect. 214) that directors can be made liable for debts of the company of which they are directors where (1) the company goes into insolvent liquidation, (2) the directors knew, or ought to have known, that the company could not avoid insolvent liquidation, and (3) the directors failed to take every step that they ought to have taken as reasonable directors to avoid loss to the creditors. This is referred to as 'wrongful trading' and its essence is negligently trading at a time when the company was not in a position to pay its debts.

In relation to groups, what is important is the definition of 'director'. It includes not only elected directors, but more importantly for our purposes, also a shadow director defined as a person in accordance with whose instructions the board of the company is normally accustomed to act (Insolvency Act, 1986, sect. 251). This could include a parent company depending on the extent to which the parent has decided to exercise its dominance. The definition could also include the dominant shareholder, or for that matter a company's bank which, as a secured creditor, exercises detailed control over a company's affairs (Prentice 1990).

There are many other examples of this type of unstructured approach in English company law; however, I would suggest that it has wider implications. It indicates that we should not attempt to define what constitutes a group for all purposes but that we should deal with each regulatory issue on an *ad hoc* basis. These issues will often implicate the group, but they will often involve others as well. Sometimes only the group phenomenon will be involved and therefore the issue of definition of what is a group for a particular regulatory purpose will have to addressed. An example of this would be consolidated accounts: it may be that there could be certain presumptions of parental liability in a given situation which can be rebutted (see, e.g., Hofstetter 1990: 583).

This does not involve a wholesale rejection of the idea of the enterprise but rather a more selective use of the concept. In particular, it entails that each issue will have to be dealt with on an *ad hoc* basis and the starting-point should be the nature of the regulatory problem which often will involve matters wider than those of the group.

20

Transfer Pricing and the Antinomies of Corporate Regulation

SOL PICCIOTTO

I. INTRODUCTION

The issue of transfer pricing, the pricing of internal transactions between affiliates within corporate groups, especially transnational corporations (TNCs), is firmly at the centre of the triangular relationship state–firm–market. It is therefore not surprising that it should be simultaneously a continual focus of political controversy, an arcane technical specialism, and a conundrum for economic and legal analysis. This chapter aims, by tracing the historical development of the taxation of transnational corporate groups, to indicate some of the dynamics involved in legal regulation by the state of capitalist property institutionalized in the corporate form.

The chapter first sketches out the historical emergence of the corporate form as part of the process of development of a regulatory framework for liberal capitalism, and indicates some of its contradictions, in particular in relation to the problem of corporate groups. It then traces the development of corporate income taxation as a specific type of regulation, and considers how it has interacted with the historical growth of TNCs as international corporate groups, before focusing in particular on the problem of intra-firm transfer pricing.

As earlier chapters have shown, the freedom for a company to own shares in another (corporate affiliation) permits great flexibility in corporate structures, but also enables manipulation of legal personality which can undermine the effectiveness and fairness of regulatory regimes. Hence, the general principle that each company is considered to be a separate legal person has become riddled with *ad hoc* exceptions where it has been accepted as necessary to 'lift the corporate veil'. This is a typical pattern in liberal forms of regulation, as the elaboration of complex forms for economic activity within the framework of general rules undermines the principles of equal treatment and freedom of economic action subject to predictable rules, on which liberal legitimation relies. While the proliferation of specific rules limiting the freedom of corporate affiliation is acceptable to the pragmatist (e.g., Prentice, Chapter 19 in this volume), others argue in more stirring terms for a fundamental reformulation of corporate law which can more adequately reflect and regulate the complex modern corporate groups (e.g., Blumberg, Chapter 17 in this volume; Wedderburn 1984: 87). However, the complexity and variety of business relationships formalized through corporate and contractual links cannot be adequately encapsulated by a single general legal principle (as pointed out in Chapter 18 by Hadden).

An approach typical of liberal regulation is to limit the freedom offered by facilitative law by reference to an 'anti-abuse' principle, based on the notion of substance over form—in this case, for example, by a presumption of unity of a corporate group where there is 'control'. Although this helps to identify the problem, it does not necessarily facilitate its solution. Unless 'control' is defined in specific legal terms (e.g., 51 per cent of voting shares), in which case the rule is easily avoided, it requires reference to extra-legal factors, which can be criticized as creating uncertainty. Furthermore, the main core of corporate law also intersects with other areas of regulation of the corporation itself (such as competition, employment, environmental, and tax law), each of which raises specific issues. Hence, the main trend has been towards the elaboration of specific solutions, which, however, are difficult, if not impossible, to rationalize within a general corporate law theory. Within these specific spheres there is a similar dynamic of the attempt to maintain liberal forms in the face of political pressures, and the consequent growth of complex modes of regulation.

This is the familiar phenomenon described in the sociology of law as 'legalization' or 'juridification', sometimes referred to as the 'regulatory crisis', which has been variously theorized and analysed (for a survey see Teubner 1987*b*). My perspective is that legal formalism, which is characteristic of liberal regulation, is not the apotheosis of modern law as propounded by Weber, but a specific mode of legitimation based on the attempt to maintain a radical separation of the political and the economic aspects of social relations. Hence it is not surprising that it becomes overlaid with other forms, usually of various bureaucratic administrative types, whether informal or formalized; and that general legal regimes (e.g., contract, delict, incorporation) become overlaid with particularized, technical administrative regulatory regimes (e.g., consumer codes, securities market rule books, corporate guide-lines, etc.).

At the same time, as Dezalay argues in Chapter 11 of this volume, the myriad fragmented regulatory regimes have been brought into increasing conflict and competition due to the globalization of economic and social relations. This brings into even greater prominence the professionals who act as mediators, both in adapting forms of capitalist property and transactions to the patterns of regulation and in helping to structure and give legitimacy to the regulatory and normative regimes. However, I argue that the emerging transnational regulatory regimes will continue to lack important elements of legitimacy unless they can accept and incorporate greater transparency, openness, and responsiveness to broader social needs (Picciotto 1991).

2. REGULATION AND THE CORPORATE FORM

The categories of the firm, the state, and the market are often treated by theories of the firm and of corporate or economic regulation in a structuralist manner, as autonomous and exclusive entities, although interacting with each other. On closer examination, however, it becomes clear that in practice they are intricately interrelated: each helps to constitute and reproduce the other, and all in turn are particular expressions of the changing and contradictory forms of broader social relations. Thus, 'market' relations are better thought of as social relations mediated by commodity exchange and circulation; and their existence and reproduction are dependent on the definition and guarantee of property rights through the state, on state backing for fiduciary money, and on the state's underpinning of a wide range of economic regulation, from systems of measurement and general rules of contract and other legal obligations to an increasing number of specialized regulatory regimes, including that of the corporate form. Indeed, far from state 'intervention' being the exception in capitalist societies, it is an essential and continually renewed factor in creating and maintaining their economic and social relations and overcoming their contradictions and crisis tendencies. Yet state regulation, since it is mediated through the forms of money and law, constantly runs up against the limitations of these forms, which reflect their origin in the characteristic separation of the economic and political aspects of social relations at the root of capitalist society (see generally S. Clarke 1991).

2.1 The development of the corporate form

The institutionalization of corporate capital dates from the last third of the nineteenth century, when the emergence of large enterprises was facilitated by the creation in the main capitalist countries of a liberal right to incorporation (usually by registration) and the subsequent hesitant, conflictual, and contradictory development of general principles of company law. Incorporation became no longer a political privilege but an economic right. This transformed and liberalized the much older notion of the corporation, which required a special state grant or charter, and which was as much a political as an economic entity (e.g., the old mercantile trading companies such as the East India companies). In Britain, the general right to incorporate was introduced following the emergence of a market in shares (mainly for railway companies, previously formed by statute). The acceptance of shares as a specific form of property in turn entailed the transformation of the separate entity concept; the company came to be seen not merely as an entity formed of (and thus in addition to) its members, but as formed by (and thus quite separate from) them (Ireland *et al.* 1987). A further key step was the acceptance of the capacity of a corporation to own shares in another corporation, which sanctioned the development of corporate groups, and permitted much more complex business structures than could be created by the trust device. However, the combination of the principle of separate personality, reinforced by limited liability, with the right to corporate affiliation, inevitably created problems for other aspects of corporate regulation, such as taxation.

Legal concepts and forms did not develop logically or automatically as a consequence of economic changes; rather, they were developed by specific individuals and groups as part of the processes of creation and shaping of markets and economic relations (cf. Dezalay, Chapter 11 in this volume). Professionals acting on behalf of business, especially lawyers, were active in developing and exploiting the possibilities of the new corporate form, and worked to secure legitimation and acceptance by legislatures and courts of liberal and formalist principles of company law. Thus, in Britain, it was after the protection of limited liability had been extensively exploited and developed by lawyers on behalf of private companies and sole traders, and against some judicial opposition, that the House of Lords sanctioned the sole-trader company in the famous Salomon case (Ireland 1984).

An important means of securing such acceptance was, and continues to be, inter-jurisdictional manœuvring, or exploitation of the 'Delaware effect'. In the USA, it was initially New Jersey that became a magnet for incorporation, especially in the 1890s, after James Dill, then lawyer for Rockefeller's Standard Oil trust, helped persuade its legislators to adopt the provision which permitted a New Jersey corporation to own shares in another.[1] Subsequently, Delaware, a smaller state for which even quite low corporate franchise taxes could be a great boon, took the lead (Buxbaum, in Horn and Kocka 1979; Buxbaum and Hopt 1988: 115–16).[2]

---

[1] In Europe, by contrast, the permissibility of corporate affiliation seems to have been less in issue (Lutter 1990).

[2] Buxbaum shows that in the USA it was initially the acceptance as legitimate of the use

2.2 Separate entity and legal formalism

The separate entity doctrine in company law is an excellent exemplar of the central dilemma of legal formalism. Liberal forms of regulation of economic activity require general but precise rules which give maximum freedom for social actors to engage in and plan economic transactions within a predictable framework, resting on indirect enforcement, relying on voluntary compliance, supplemented by inducements and retroactive sanctions on detected breaches. Pure liberalism envisages a radical separation of legal form and economic substance; laws should be addressed to the generality of legal subjects without regard to their economic or social status, and their freedom to act should not be hindered either by state requirements to obtain prior permissions or by retrospective legislation. The aim is to establish and maintain a 'level playing-field', or equality in the conditions of competition (Marx 1976:621), which is in the general interest of all economic actors. However, competition is not a static equilibrium, but a process of equalization among unequals, which also continually creates differentiation, as each entity seeks to discover or invent, and then protect, some advantages over competitors. In the economic arena, businesses seek production, marketing, or managerial advantages. In the political-legal arena, they seek regulatory advantages, lobbying legislatures for favourable provisions, as well as finding and exploiting ambiguities in rules, originating novel devices, and modifying transactions to minimize the adverse effects of regulations.

Hence, there is a central contradiction involved in attempting to establish conditions of equality for entities that are in social terms very different—and indeed, unequal.[3] Furthermore, the process of competition tends to exacerbate inequalities, and further undermines the general and non-discriminatory character of legal forms, leading to political pressures for state intervention to redress inequality and re-establish the viability of

of the corporate form to facilitate the exploitation of the rapidly growing US continental markets which 'provided the motive force' for breaking down state restrictions on foreign (i.e., out-of-state) corporations (Buxbaum and Hopt 1988: p. 40); once a corporation could choose its governing law by choosing its state of incorporation, attempts at more stringent controls in state laws were vain (p. 119), and the strong tendency to coalescence of state laws (towards a liberal model) was due in no small part to 'the magnetic pull of Delaware's jurisprudence as the touchstone of appropriate company law' (ibid. 128).

[3] Note that this is not merely a contradiction between substantive economic inequality and formal political equality, but the fragmentation of a social being into a political citizen on the one hand and a buyer/seller or economic entity on the other. This is important, since a standard argument of liberalism is that formal law is possible as laws are essentially procedural, and do not address economic substance. In fact, however, not only political, but also economic, relations appear as formal relations of equals, since price reflects value if a bargain is 'fair'; however, social inequalities create both economic crisis tendencies and political conflicts. Money and law, as the mediators between the economic and political aspects of social relations, are both (although in different ways) affected by and involved with, these crises and conflicts.

regulation. Both the effectiveness and the equity or fairness of regulation are undermined by the exploitation of formalism for particular advantage. Nevertheless, the maintenance of a generally formalist framework for regulation is an essential part of the legitimation of liberal capitalism, since the only alternative is considered to be the arbitrary exercise of authority. However, the framework undergoes a continuous process of redefinition, as political processes result in the constant refinement of the rules which specify the terms and conditions of interaction of legal subjects. Thus, the continual efforts to provide a fair and competitive framework for business entail a continual redefinition and reform of regulation, including the legal conditions for the creation of business organizations such as the company and the partnership, and the incidences of their operation.

Furthermore, although formalist regulation aspires to be self-regulating, by giving legal subjects freedom to decide for themselves on the specific content of their transactions, the competitive nature of economic relations not infrequently results in a conflict, a breakdown of the transaction, or a need for monitoring. Although the roles of the adjudicator and the administrative regulator, within a formalist system, consist in principle of resolving individual problem cases by logical application of the abstract rule to the particular circumstances of the case, it is illusory to believe that this is a matter of formal logic; the application of a rule or principle to real-life situations inevitably entails its interpretation, development, and adaptation, to a greater or lesser degree. Thus, regulation is a dynamic social process. Most important, although legal rules appear to be, and are treated by positivism as being, a comprehensive and internally logical system, they are in reality highly permeable and flexible. This is not only due to the inevitable ambiguities of language, but more fundamentally because of the abstract, formal nature of rules within a liberal regulatory system (McCahery and Picciotto, forthcoming).

From this perspective, social science is concerned not with discovering the formal legal rules which most appropriately regulate the substance of economic 'reality', but with considering the interaction of political and economic processes, as mediated and expressed in legal forms, which also help to create and legitimize the structures within which social relations develop.

3. TAXING INTERNATIONAL CORPORATE INCOME

Since the beginning of this century, direct taxes on income have formed a key source of the revenue of capitalist states. Their legitimation has rested on the liberal principle that the tax burden should fall equally on all citizens, and that its enforcement should interfere as little as possible with private economic activity. However, the application of this principle is deeply problematic, especially in relation to the two central issues which came to the fore once the income tax became a mass tax: the threshold of taxable income and the progressivity of tax rates. Does an equal burden imply a uniform rate? Or should ability to pay be reflected in progressive rates (vertical equity)? Equality is also generally assumed to entail taxation of income from all sources accruing to any entity, not only to individuals, but to all legal persons, including corporations (and in some systems, business establishments). Again, this is problematic: since different types of income (wages, rent, business profits, interest, dividends, etc.) in the hands of different entities (individuals, companies, businesses) have different economic implications, there may be justification for treating them differently; but such disparate treatment could be said to reduce the 'neutrality' of a tax system and encourage avoidance by the 'artificial' transformation of one type of income into another. Further, there is the problem of 'double taxation', the application of 'substantially similar' taxes to the 'same' income stream. But can this be said to arise, for example, if dividend income taxable in the hands of shareholders is paid from profits already taxed in the hands of the company? The issue of integration of personal and corporate income tax continues to be a live one today (which I will address further below). The very definition of income raises complex philosophical, economic, political, and legal questions. (For a general discussion of these issues, see Musgrave and Musgrave 1984: ch. 11.) The resolution of all these controversies has relied primarily on the political processes of the state, mediated by the law.

3.1 National jurisdiction and international co-ordination

A central feature of capitalism is that the state is national, whereas economic activities are to a significant extent international. However, the international state system should not be thought of as an aggregation of separate units, but rather as a network of interlocking jurisdictions. The modern nation-state is certainly defined in terms of its territory, and its legitimate enforcement powers are, in the last analysis, confined to that territory. However, to the extent that social and economic relations transcend national boundaries, state claims to jurisdiction inevitably overlap; and significant conflicts are caused by the frequent existence of power for more than one state to enforce such claims against some of the persons or property involved in trans-territorial transactions (Picciotto 1983). This became apparent very early in relation to income taxation. Although it could be asserted that this was a territorial tax, since 'either that from which the taxable income is derived must be situated in the UK, or the person whose income is to be taxed must be resident there' (Lord Herschell, in *Colquhoun* v. *Brooks*, 1899: 499); nevertheless, it could pro- duce extensive overlapping taxation, since it could be levied both on busi- ness profits at source, as well as on residents in respect of their world-wide income. As income taxes were introduced by more states, and the rates increased to finance the first Great War, businesses engaged in international activities quickly became aware of the importance of the rel- ative incidence of taxation on their competitive position. Pressures from business resulted in some unilateral measures by states to mitigate the problem, notably the introduction of the foreign tax credit by the USA in 1918.[4]

However, it became clear that unilateral provisions would be inade- quate without measures of international co-ordination,[5] and the business pressures became internationalized into a campaign against 'international double taxation' through business lobby groups. Studies and proposals were prepared at the request of the League of Nations Finance Committee, which were discussed by an intergovernmental conference in 1928. The initial expectation was that, provided governments could reach political agreement on the principle that each person's income should be taxed only once, a technical solution could be found relatively easily to the allocation between states of rights to tax; but this hope proved short- lived. Political agreement required an international consensus on legit- imizing principles for such an allocation, while income taxation had developed on a national basis, as part of the political processes involved in the consolidation of the various nation-states in the period 1865–1914; and these in turn were shaped by each state's particular international eco- nomic and political relationships. Thus, Britain put forward persuasive arguments for the simple principle that each state should tax only its own residents; however, while this would enable the UK (historically the major exporter of capital) to maintain its principle of taxation of all resi-

---

[4] Revenue Act, 1918, sect. 222 (individuals), sect. 238 (corporations). It was extended in 1921 to allow a credit against US tax liability for taxes paid by foreign subsidiaries, in respect of dividends remitted from them, but in the same proportion as that of the non-US to US source income. The justification for the credit given to Congress in 1918 was directed at the position of individuals, arguing that the thousands of US citizens working in Canada or Latin America on behalf of US business would be discouraged or might give up their cit- izenship if they were liable to US as well as local income taxes; although it was pointed out that rich US citizens living abroad on US investments, such as the Astor family in Britain, would pay tax in both countries (appendix to *Congressional Record, 65th Congress, 2nd Session 1917–18*: 677). However, no explanation was given in the debate for the credit for corporate income tax, although it was undoubtedly of great importance for US firms oper- ating abroad: an example of corporations benefiting from the 'legal person' analogy.

[5] The unilateral foreign tax credit has the major drawback that it encourages other coun- tries to increase their taxes on investors from abroad, since it is the home country's treasury that absorbs the burden, provided the tax qualifies for credit and does not exceed the home country rate.

dents on all their world-wide income, it meant that countries which were net importers of capital must discriminate in favour of foreign residents and grant them exemption. Unsurprisingly, the UK managed to conclude only one treaty embodying this principle, with the Irish Free State in 1926.

Instead of a single multilateral convention, the 1928 meeting agreed the texts of several model treaties recommended as a basis for bilateral negotiations between states according to their tax systems. The negotiation of such bilateral treaties helped to produce a degree of convergence of the principles of national income taxation and broad agreement on the allocation of tax jurisdiction between states, and contributed to further refinement of subsequent generations of the model.[6] The flexibility of the method of a model treaty adaptable to particular circumstances facilitated the rapid growth of a network of such bilateral agreements, especially after agreement on the landmark US–UK treaty of 1945. Nevertheless, the treaty system provides only a limited form of co-ordination, since the specialists involved in the development of the model provisions have balked at trying to formulate internationally agreed principles for the definition and allocation of the tax base of internationally organized business.

Thus, the model treaty makes no attempt at an agreed definition of taxable income, nor at any criteria for its international allocation; instead, it classifies and assigns taxation rights according to types of tax and the relationship of each state to the particular taxpayer (Rosenbloom and Langbein 1981: 366). Broadly, it is the state of residence that has the primary right to tax any legal person; the source state is permitted to tax business profits only if attributable to a permanent establishment[7] within its territory. Hence, under the treaty regime, each state can apply its own system of taxation to the business profits of any separate company resident[8] within its territory, as well as to the profits attributable to any branch or other base falling within the definition of a permanent establishment. 'Withholding' taxes on payments constituting returns on investment (dividends, interest, fees, and royalties) are subject to negotiated

---

[6] The descendant of the League of Nations' model treaties is the Model Double Taxation Convention on Income and Capital of the OECD, which, together with its authoritative commentary (OECD 1977) is the dominant text of reference; its articles and commentary are now being revised on a rolling basis by the OECD Fiscal Committee. Although capital-importing countries, especially those of the periphery, have held out for a stronger principle of source taxation of income, the UN model developed by its Group of Experts made relatively few changes to the OECD model (see Picciotto 1992a: ch. 2, sect. 2).

[7] The definition of a 'permanent establishment' is broader in the UN than the OECD model, but is commonly the subject of bilateral negotiation; for example, as to whether it includes a construction site or an oil rig in place for less than a year.

[8] Defined by the model treaty in terms of the location of its place of 'effective management'.

limits, frequently reduced to zero, especially between related entities, since in principle it is the country of residence of the recipient that has the right to tax such investment returns.

This allocation of rights to tax was aimed mainly at relieving 'juridical' double taxation; that is, the application of similar taxes to the same income of a single legal person. Business, however, pressed for the elimination also of 'economic' double taxation; that is, where the 'same' income stream is taxed in the hands of different legal persons. Different views can be taken on whether there should be such relief: for example, in relation to the tax on the profits of a company and the income tax on the dividends paid to its portfolio shareholders; hence, different national systems of corporate–personal tax integration have been introduced especially since the 1960s, while some countries (notably the USA) still adhere to the 'classical' principle of treating the two as separate taxes and hence provide no relief. These national differences greatly complicate the problem of international co-ordination (OECD 1977: 97–103; Ault 1978). Since there are inadequate political processes for finding international solutions to such problems of equity, bilateral negotiations for coordination by treaty tend to focus on bargaining over national interests, although the interest in revenue must be balanced against that in attracting investment.

3.2 Limits of international co-ordination

The bilateral treaty network is clearly a clumsy method for trying to achieve regulatory harmony between tax systems. In particular, the increasing sophistication of forms of financing corporate investment poses continually new issues in ensuring and reconciling national and international tax equity. Yet the international liberalization of capital movements has made such harmonization increasingly urgent. In recent years, notable problems have included the treatment of foreign exchange gains and losses, the capitalization and deductibility of brand names and goodwill, the treatment of myriad forms of loan capital (especially those with a partial equity character), particularly in debt-financed acquisitions and buy-outs, and the tax treatment of commercial banks' provisions against the risk of sovereign debt default. Without adequate international harmonization, national measures to solve such problems while ensuring fair taxation of income from capital create the risk of a capital outflow. Yet so entrenched are systems of income taxation in national political processes that there seems very little prospect of major moves towards their harmonization.[9] However, there are processes of emulation and

[9] e.g., a move towards a consumption basis for the corporate income tax, by exempting interest and dividend income and allowing full deduction of all business purchases, but not

national adaptation, based on discussions among global networks of specialists, since tax systems and changes, especially by the dominant states, exert a pull on other states due to the high mobility of capital (Razin and Slemrod 1991).[10] Otherwise, the co-ordination of tax administration has relied on arrangements for administrative co-operation between officials of the major states; and although this has been strengthened in recent years, and reinforced by the increasingly important mediating role of the professional specialists acting for business, it remains a secretive and bureaucratic process the lack of legitimation for which has become a serious handicap (Picciotto 1992*a*: ch. 10).

Even within the European Community, taxation is one of the most jealously guarded areas of national 'sovereignty'.[11] However, the Single Market programme gave a boost to several measures to improve coordination of corporate taxation, following which Commissioner Scrivener set up a Committee of Experts under Onno Ruding, to consider whether 'existing differences in corporate taxation and the burden of business taxes among member countries lead to major distortions affecting the functioning of the internal market'. Nevertheless, the Committee's proposals for establishment of 'minimum standards' for the definition of the corporate tax base and a band for tax rates (EC Commission 1992) met with a cool response from the Commission, which said that 'The committee's recommendation concerning the three corporation tax aspects of the rates, the tax base, and the systems . . . frequently go beyond what is strictly necessary initially at Community level'; and that 'it is important not to be carried away by a drive for harmonization which is not justified on economic grounds and which would not be consistent with the principle of subsidiarity'.[12]

---

allowing deduction of interest payments as an expense, could reduce a key source of inequity and avoidance resulting from the different tax treatment of loan and equity finance, and thus bring the effective tax rate on domestic capital into line with that applied *de facto* on international investment (see below); but it could not be done by one state unilaterally (Bird 1988: 296).

[10] e.g., the trend from the mid-1980s to more 'neutral' income tax systems with fewer allowances and lower marginal rates, leading in turn to increased reliance on sales taxes or VAT.

[11] Harmonization of indirect taxes was accepted as necessary for the establishment of the Common Market in the Rome Treaty (Articles 95–9); otherwise the 'elimination of double taxation' within the Community was envisaged as a matter to be dealt with by treaty among the member states (Article 220), and hence outside the EEC institutional framework altogether. Fiscal provisions are expressly excluded from the provisions of Article 100A added by the Single European Act, permitting qualified majority voting for measures aimed at the establishment and functioning of the internal market. Nevertheless, agreement was reached in mid-1990 on three measures, and the Commission is pressing on with other proposals, aimed mainly at harmonizing the treatment of payments between related companies within a corporate group (EC Commission 1991; and see Picciotto 1992*a*: ch. 3, sect. 2b).

[12] However, the Commission did state its intention to consult member states on post-1992 plans for corporate taxation, covering a number of specific points, including 'thin

On the other hand, politically inspired national measures, aimed at blocking tax avoidance due to exploitation of disjunctures between national taxes and inadequate international harmonization, can be attacked by other states and international investors as being in breach of international treaty obligations. Thus, the US Congress has been criticized for 'overriding' treaties as a consequence of several measures stemming from the 1986 Tax Reform Act aimed at ensuring taxation of a 'fair' share of international business (Picciotto 1992*a*: ch. 11, sect. 2b).

Academics have argued that a stronger institutional framework for international tax co-ordination should be established, perhaps by a somewhat more politicized multilateral forum of the GATT type (Vann 1991). However, the preference of both tax officials and the professional advisers employed by or acting for the large international corporate groups or TNCs has been to maintain the present arrangements, in which the principles established in the treaty network are the basis for a process of secretive negotiation between these tax professionals.

4. INTERNATIONAL TAX PLANNING AND INTERMEDIARY COMPANIES

Hence, it is clear that intergovernmental arrangements have failed to provide either principles or an adequate mechanism for the definition and allocation of international business income. Instead, the processes of legitimation of income taxation have remained largely national; to ensure fairness and 'equality' in taxation, countries can claim to tax both the local profits of all entities even if foreign or foreign-owned, as well as profits derived from investments abroad by their individual and corporate residents. The tax treaty system has merely mitigated the resultant possibility of overlapping taxation. In order to facilitate international investment, taxation at source by a host country is limited to defined types of income, including business profits of an enterprise or those attributable to a permanent establishment; while payments abroad, to an entity resident in a treaty country (especially if made to related entities within a corporate group), are normally exempt; and if the home country does not exempt investment returns, it must at least grant a credit for the appropriate foreign tax paid. Since this means that the investor should pay the higher of the home or foreign country tax rates, it aims at tax equity between home and overseas investment (capital export equity).

capitalization'; i.e. to seek a common EC definition to govern under what conditions tax authorities should treat interest payments as dividends when the payments are made by highly leveraged companies within a group to another group member (Announcement of 24 June 1992).

4.1 Havens and regulatory arbitrage

However, representatives of corporate capital, and in particular the TNCs, far from pressing for a higher degree of harmonization, have accepted this form of co-ordination, and indeed have opposed attempts at strengthened regulatory co-operation. Instead, they have developed legal structures for transnational corporate capital which take advantage of the ambiguities, disjunctures, and loopholes in the international tax system. Indeed, the growth of the TNC, in the characteristic form of an international network of related companies carrying on businesses in different countries in a more or less integrated way, is to a significant extent attributable to the opportunities it has to take advantage of regulatory differences, or 'regulatory arbitrage'. Thus, theories of the multinational enterprise, focusing on firm-specific advantages, have recently moved away from explanations based on industrial structure, such as economies of scale, which could be realized through contracting, and have emphasized instead the advantages of the organizational form—for example, in controlling the appropriation and diffusion of new technology, but most importantly in taking strategic investment decisions (Williamson 1985: ch. 11). In particular, TNCs can benefit from the diversification of financial risk and the internalization of the management of arbitrage opportunities arising from the diversity of currency exchange rates, financial markets, and regulatory regimes, of which taxation is especially important (Rugman 1979; Lessard 1979).

It should be emphasized that from the point of view of the firm, its aim is merely to mitigate the potentially harmful effects of overlapping and conflicting regulation, and to be a 'good corporate citizen' in each country where it has operations. Nevertheless, the superiority of the TNC as an organizational form lies precisely in the special advantages provided by its unity in diversity. Its centralization of strategic decision making enables the firm to structure its activities so that the whole is far more than the sum of its parts. This relies quite importantly on locating different entities so that their interactions are synergistic. The formation of intermediary entities (usually subsidiary companies), to act as bases or conduits for transactions, is often the key to taking advantage of regulatory differences. The use of such entities can make it possible to use legal personality to avoid adverse national regulation or the harmful effects of two overlapping systems.

In the case of taxation, it can be said that virtually any jurisdiction can be a 'haven' in relation to another, if their tax laws interact in such a way as to make it possible to reduce overall tax liability. Historically, however, certain jurisdictions have been sought out and their facilities developed to facilitate avoidance of tax which would otherwise be payable in relatively high-tax countries. This was pioneered in the 1920s and 1930s, mainly for family fortunes, in places such as the Channel Islands (in relation to the UK), Switzerland and Luxembourg (for Germany, France, etc.), and Panama, the Bahamas, and Newfoundland (for the USA). In the post-war period, the use of intermediary companies formed in convenient jurisdictions to exploit tax advantages quickly became standard practice as part of the growth of TNCs. It became reinforced with the rapid expansion of offshore financial centres from the late 1950s. This actually resulted from the measures taken by national central banks, who sought to stem large-scale capital flows by operating differential regulatory regimes, thus facilitating the growth of eurocurrency markets for financing international transactions (Mendelsohn 1980: 34).

TNCs could justify the use of tax mitigation strategies due to the inadequate resolution of international tax equity problem through the tax treaty system. In particular, they objected to the principle of capital export equity, which was used especially by the USA and the UK to limit international relief to the tax credit. Lobbies for international investors pressed for the full exemption of foreign profits. It could indeed be argued that the principle of capital export equity was inappropriate for foreign direct investment via TNCs, since it assumed that international investment flows were essentially portfolio investments by an investor who chose whether to place money at home or abroad, and repatriated profits directly when earned. In fact, after 1929, international portfolio investment largely dried up, and the resumption of international investment after 1945 not only took the form of direct investment by TNCs, but it was also mainly financed from foreign loans and the reinvestment of retained earnings (Barlow and Wender 1955). But it was hard to grant exemption of foreign income without its being exploited to reduce taxes on profits from exports, which could be channelled to foreign sales subsidiaries.

Tax planning strategies, developed and justified as necessary to mitigate inequitable taxation on international investment (e.g., Bracewell-Milnes 1980), have succeeded in significantly reducing the overall tax 'exposure' of internationally organized corporate groups. Liability to home country taxes on foreign earnings could in practice be deferred, by retaining earnings in subsidiaries incorporated or resident abroad.[13] This was an important factor for TNCs, which financed much of their growth from retained earnings. By channelling payments from foreign operating subsidiaries through intermediary conduit companies formed in countries with appro-

---

[13] US tax applies to foreign business only of companies incorporated in the USA; while for the UK this applies to residents, using the test of 'central management and control', generally interpreted as meaning where the board meetings were held, as being the location of key investment decisions (see Picciotto 1992a: ch. 1, sect. 2a).

priate tax treaties[14] and accumulating them in offshore holding companies ready for reinvestment, TNCs could minimize their liability to home country taxation on investment returns. Liability to source taxes on business profits could be reduced by forming base companies in suitable low-tax locations through which operating companies could be charged for services such as R & D, insurance, shipping, or even the supply of inputs for assembly or manufacturing. Since payments for such services and supplies, as well as interest on loan capital, are normally deductible, they can reduce taxable business profits; and if routed through conduit companies, withholding taxes can also be reduced or eliminated (see Picciotto 1992*a*: ch. 6, sect. 3, on intermediary company strategies).

4.2 The avoidance game

The development of these structures was possible due to the indeterminacy of the regulatory regimes. Indeed, the question of the extent to which the exploitation of tax deferral is legitimate has been the focus both of considerable ideological debate, as well as of practical negotiations between the managers and professionals representing TNCs and the officials and legislators of national states. Initially, national tax authorities used their discretionary powers[15] to target the 'abuse' of deferral; but as the issue became politicized, more explicit regulatory measures were enacted, originating with the Subpart F provisions of the US tax code enacted in 1962.[16] This targeted the accumulation of earnings in tax-haven holding companies, by taxing the US shareholders of foreign companies falling within the definition of a 'controlled foreign corporation' (CFC)[17] on their share of certain categories of undistributed profits.[18]

---

[14] A notable example is the Netherlands, which, due to its exemption of income received from a foreign related company and its wide network of tax treaties, became a popular location for the formation of the 'Dutch mixer' holding company.

[15] The British Inland Revenue has long used provisions enacted in 1951, which required Treasury permission for any company not only to transfer its residence abroad, but also to issue any shares or loans through a non-resident company over which it had control, as the basis for negotiation of an acceptable rate of remittance of foreign earnings by British-based company groups (Picciotto 1992*a*: 102–3). (From 1956 to 1965, however, British-resident companies trading wholly abroad were exempt on their undistributed earnings, under special overseas trade corporation provisions.) The US tax code contained a similar provision dating from 1932, which required IRS approval for a transfer of assets to a foreign corporation if such transfer might be considered part of a plan for avoidance of foreign taxes (later sect. 367 of the Tax Code); and the IRS took the view that setting up a foreign business so as to facilitate tax deferral might come under this section (Picciotto 1992*a*: 110–11).

[16] This is a good example of juridification.

[17] A foreign corporation over 50% of the voting power of which is owned by US persons (including corporations), each of which owns directly or indirectly over 10%.

[18] The main categories are: (*a*) 'foreign base company sales income', essentially income from the sales of goods to or from an affiliate, if neither the manufacture nor the use of the goods takes place in the country of incorporation of the CFC; (*b*) 'foreign base company

These provisions had a dual effect: they targeted some types of retained earnings in foreign subsidiaries of corporate groups substantially controlled from the USA as immediately liable to US tax; but at the same time, they legitimized tax deferral on retained earnings which did not fall within, or could be channelled outside, these complex definitions. They did not end the deferral debate, but had the effect of converting subsequent proposals to end deferral into bargaining over modifications of Subpart F between the various factions and pressure groups active in the legislative process, while the actual application of the provisions could be the focus of the game of avoidance and bargaining conducted by TNCs' tax strategists and the IRS.[19]

Although the ending of deferral has regularly been advocated by economists (e.g., Alworth 1988), and has been put forward several times by the US Treasury, the failure to achieve it results not only from powerful lobbying, but from the recognition that the internationalization of capital has made it impossible to take unilateral moves in this direction, even for the world's major power. Policy-makers became aware that TNCs had considerable flexibility in determining their capital and cost structures (Lessard 1979), so that taxation of international investment was no longer merely a matter of equal treatment of inward and outward investment flows, but now concerned the cost of capital to, and allocation of investment by, internationally integrated firms with the ability to locate intermediary affiliates in convenient jurisdictions.[20] The ending of deferral could not be considered in isolation from the broader issues of definition of the tax base, and could not be done unilaterally (Hufbauer and Foster 1977). Even the unilateral measures against CFCs entailed dubious assertions of jurisdiction (Park 1978): it might be acceptable for the US to tax profits from the foreign sales of goods manufactured in the USA channelled through a Bermuda sales subsidiary, but where the German manufacturing subsidiary of a US parent channels its sales via its Swiss affiliate, it is more likely German taxes which are avoided (Tillinghast 1979: 262–3).

Hence, the US measures against CFCs were subsequently followed by

service income', derived from rendering commercial or other services to an affiliate outside the country of incorporation of the CFC, and (c) 'foreign personal holding company income', which is passive investment income such as interest, dividends, or royalties, other than that produced from the conduct of a business (except for the insurance of US risks). If Subpart F income is 10% or less, it can be disregarded; if it is 70% or more, the CFC is taxed as if it were a US corporation; where Subpart F income is between 10% and 70%, the actual Subpart F income is taxed on a current basis.

[19] e.g., the use of a CFC for partial assembly or processing led to litigation (*Dave Fischbein Manufacturing* v. *Commr*, 1972) and detailed IRS rules; juridification often feeds on itself.

[20] Many analyses by economists of the taxation of international investment are totally unrealistic because they ignore this.

similar provisions, which have now been enacted by the main OECD countries, with some variations (Arnold 1986). Although there has been a considerable degree of emulation, the national provisions have been only loosely co-ordinated internationally, mainly to try to agree on basic principles to ensure their compatibility with tax treaties (OECD 1987; Picciotto 1992*a*: ch. 7, sect. 2). Countries enacting anti-CFC provisions have generally accepted three broad principles, which were also articulated by the OECD Fiscal Committee as necessary to ensure that such measures are used only 'to maintain equity and neutrality of national tax laws in an international environment': (a) that they should target only 'passive' income, and not extend to 'real industrial or commercial activity'; (b) that they should only apply to low-tax regimes; and (c) that they should not normally treat a base company as non-existent (OECD 1987: paras. 34, 47).

This still leaves considerable scope for tax reduction by operating some service activities through a company incorporated in a convenient tax jurisdiction, especially to service activities on transient global sites—for example, in businesses such as construction, shipping and oil drilling. Above all, CFC measures find it hard to deal with financial services such as banking and insurance carried out by 'captive' subsidiaries. Under many CFC provisions they are regarded as producing 'passive' income only if the services are provided in respect of the home country business of the shareholder or related companies. If a significant proportion of such services is provided to unrelated third parties—for example, by using pooling arrangements (common, e.g., in reinsurance)—then the 'captive' could be regarded as carrying on an independent business. Furthermore, the parent company may benefit by 'secondary sheltering' of tax-exempt income; the simplest means is by an 'upstream loan' (which is not a taxable receipt, as a dividend would be—and indeed, the interest may claimed as a deduction). Although this was described as 'a rather naive and straightforward form of tax avoidance' by the OECD Committee (OECD 1987: para. 72), and some countries such as the USA have provisions to tax such loans in some circumstances, it can be hard to counteract (e.g., if the related company arranges the loan 'back-to-back' through a third party). The UK Inland Revenue was forced to withdraw its 'upstream loan' proposals due to arguments that it would interfere with the carrying out of the central treasury function of UK-based TNCs, which might therefore move this function and the important associated financial business out of London (IFS 1982).

More recently, the emphasis has been on combating the avoidance of source taxation, either by refusing deductions from business profits for certain types of payment or by refusing exemptions from withholding tax to certain types of recipient. In setting up a subsidiary, especially if wholly owned, there are clear advantages in a high ratio of debt to equity: not only are interest payments usually tax-deductible, but they are also more flexible and easier to repatriate than dividends. Even better are hybrid forms of financing, such as convertible bonds or participating loans, which can be structured so that they are treated as debt in the payer's country (and the interest deductible) but equity in that of the recipient (thus qualifying for a tax credit); or the use of dual-resident companies, whose accounts can be consolidated with those of related firms in two jurisdictions, thus allowing a 'double-dip', or deduction of the same interest twice. The source state may take unilateral action by refusing the deduction, or even by recategorizing such payments as dividends.[21] However, such action may be attacked as impeding international investment, and if the payment is made to a treaty partner, the action may be invalid under the treaty provisions (Picciotto 1992*a*: 202–6). However, attempts so far to co-ordinate approaches to the treatment of capitalization, especially through the OECD, have borne little fruit.

Even more controversial have been moves by some states, especially the USA, to combat the use of intermediary 'conduit' companies by restricting the treaty exemptions from withholding tax to 'bona fide residents' of the treaty partner country. From the US point of view, it is quite legitimate to seek to prevent 'unintended beneficiaries' from taking advantage of tax exemptions granted by treaties merely by forming conduit companies; on the other hand, this can be regarded as amounting to pressures to 'rewrite the tax law of a foreign country which desires to attract foreign investment through tax benefits' or, in stronger terms, 'no more than a civilized version of gunboat diplomacy' (Oliva 1984: 299). However, the US financial gunboats have had only limited success in securing a renegotiation of tax treaties to include provisions against 'treaty shopping'. In order to reach agreement with countries such as Barbados, Bermuda, and the Netherlands Antilles, the 'limitation of benefits' clauses have had to be carefully drafted by the negotiators to embody a bargain whereby the havens accept co-operation with the US authorities and curtailment of their wide-ranging treaty-shopping possibilities in exchange for a more restrained but legitimized specialization—for example, in offshore reinsurance or banking. Instead of being tax avoidance 'supermarkets' (with the

---

[21] The boom in debt-financed company acquisitions (LBOs: leveraged buy-outs) finally led the US Congress to enact 'earnings stripping' provisions in 1989, to refuse deduction for 'excess interest' paid to a related person if the recipient does not pay US tax on such income and the payer corporation has a debt ratio over 1.5 to 1 and 'excess interest expense' (interest payments over a certain proportion of income). Lobbies on behalf of overseas investors objected that this entailed a breach of treaty obligations; but it at least provided a specific statutory rule (unlike the discretionary rules of thumb operated by other authorities), and thus some opportunities for avoidance.

risk of US retaliation), they would become specialized 'boutiques', each with its speciality.

However, this bargain failed to obtain domestic political approval on either side. The US Congress has been unhappy with the legitimation of treaty shopping behind the safe harbours of defined anti-abuse clauses, and has feared that a concession granted to one country would have to be extended to others; while the havens generally preferred the alternative of a free market in tax avoidance to reaching such an accommodation with the USA (Picciotto 1992*a*: ch. 7, sect. 3). Thus, the USA has been obliged to resort to terminating a number of its treaties with havens, joined by the UK, especially in relation to the Netherlands Antilles. This, however, proved an object-lesson in the constraints imposed by global capital markets on attempts to control them, even by powerful states. The US announcement of 29 June 1987 of termination of this treaty led to a sharp fall in the price of Netherlands Antilles Eurobonds,[22] threatening large losses to many US institutions holding them. Within two weeks the exemption of interest payable to residents of the Antilles and Aruba on existing Eurobonds was restored. Although joint action by the US and UK authorities had ended the exemption prospectively on many bonds issued after 1984,[23] it was still possible to make such payments via a Dutch holding company. In fact, instead of trying to beat the offshore centres, the US and UK authorities have effectively joined them since 1984, by allowing payments of interest gross to holders of international bonds, provided that the paying agent certifies that the recipient is a non-resident. In this way they hope to ensure enforcement of their own taxes and to provide inducements for international financial markets to locate in London and New York, where they may be more effectively supervised, while in effect offering arrangements facilitating the evasion of the laws of other countries.[24]

[22] This was because many such bonds had clauses providing for early redemption in the event of changes in the tax position, thus allowing refinancing at the lower prices then prevailing for new flotations.

[23] UK-resident companies were still allowed to pay interest gross to a Netherlands Antilles subsidiary to service quoted Eurobonds, provided the subsidiary was at least 90% owned by a UK-resident company not itself a 51% subsidiary of a non-UK resident (Income and Corporation Taxes Act, 1988, sect. 124). Presumably the Revenue felt it could adequately regulate the overall profits-repatriation policies of such UK-based groups by their other powers, described above.

[24] Where the country of residence of a company floating an international bond allows payment of interest gross to bondholders, in principle the latter should declare this income to their own tax authorities. However, evasion is facilitated by the issuing of most such bonds in bearer form; also, many such investments are made on behalf of clients by banks in Switzerland and elsewhere managing external discretionary accounts. It is commonly estimated that as many as half of all Eurobonds are held by individuals, motivated by the security of a hard-currency investment in a high-rated borrower, but also by the possibility of tax evasion. While these arrangements provide capital at extremely low cost for TNCs and

Clearly, the international tax system, based on the classification of legal persons as resident in particular countries and the allocation between states of rights to tax defined types of income, has become increasingly unworkable in relation to TNCs, which can centrally direct an integrated international strategy carried out through an international corporate network. Many of the structures developed by these groups have been within the grey areas of ambiguous legitimacy, and their representatives have generally reached an accommodation with relevant regulators, whose main concern has been to target 'abuse'.

Nevertheless, it is notable that enforcement has been more stringent, at least since the mid-1970s, and that arrangements for increasingly close international administrative co-operation have been developed, especially between the authorities of the main OECD countries, Moreover, these trends have continued even under right-wing, pro-business governments during the 1980s. This has been for two main reasons. First, the politicization of campaigns against 'the multinationals' from the late 1960s has sometimes strengthened populist pressures to reassert national 'sovereignty', and, when allied to middle-class taxpayers' revolts against the rising fiscal burden, have fuelled movements to increase the tax take from large—especially foreign—corporations.[25] Second, the opening up of global markets, increasing competition, and communications improvements have meant that many of the devices pioneered by large and 'respectable' corporations have become much more widely available and utilized by even quite small businesses, in circumstances much more clearly amounting to 'abuse'.

5. TRANSFER PRICE ADJUSTMENTS AND GLOBAL APPORTIONMENT

It was in fact recognized from quite early on that the taxation of related companies within a single corporate group should take into account its overall unity. Within a single tax system, affiliated corporations could be required to file a consolidated tax return, as was the case for US federal taxation from 1917.[26] However, consolidation requires the elimination of

other blue-chip borrowers, they contribute significantly to capital flight and tax evasion, especially from peripheral countries—e.g., in Latin America (Lessard and Williamson 1987).

[25] President Reagan's Treasury Secretary, Donald Regan, claimed that he shocked the President into initiating tax reform in 1983 by revealing that General Electric and 57 other big corporations paid less taxes than his own secretary (Regan 1988: 194).

[26] It may seem that there would be nothing to gain from shifting profits between entities liable to the same taxes; but, of course, advantage can be taken of different allowances and other such factors. Some national provisions allowing the adjustment of inter-affiliate pricing apply to domestic as well as international transactions (e.g., the US provisions in sect. 482). Elsewhere, a power to adjust may flow from anti-abuse provisions, or merely from basic principles; e.g., in the UK the courts held that undervalued transfers between related

all inter-affiliate transactions and the inclusion of the proceeds of sales only once made outside the group; hence it was impossible to consolidate affiliates which were subject to a different tax regime. It was nevertheless still possible for taxation of an affiliate to take into account its membership of a group, and try to devise principles for allocating profits and costs within the group.

5.1 Unitary taxation of groups

In principle, the most effective approach, short of full consolidation, would be to establish unitary accounts and allocate the global profits by an appropriate formula. Variants of this approach have indeed been used in determining inter-jurisdictional allocation, in particular in allocating profits of international businesses which are carried out through branches rather than subsidiaries, as is often the case with banking or insurance, as well as for state taxes within a federal system. Indeed, unitary taxation and formula apportionment became most developed within the USA, and have been used for state business franchise or income taxes since early this century. One of the pioneers in the application of the unitary approach to corporate groups was California, which had been concerned since the 1930s to prevent motion picture companies siphoning off profits through distribution affiliates in neighbouring Nevada.

Clearly, however, the unitary approach carries a significant risk of overlapping taxation unless there is some degree of harmonization of (*a*) the criteria for deciding when a business or group is unitary; (*b*) the principles for definition of the tax base (taxable profits); and (*c*) the formula for apportionment. Indeed, as state income taxes and the unitary system spread in the USA in the 1950s, a flood of cases challenged its constitutionality, as an impediment to interstate commerce; but these were generally rejected by the Supreme Court, provided the tax was non-discriminatory and bore a rational relationship to property values connected with the taxing state (*Northwestern Portland Cement* v. *Minnesota*, 1959). A degree of harmonization was achieved through the adoption of a Multi-State Tax Compact in 1966, which included a uniform Act (drafted in 1957) and established a Commission with the power to formulate regulations and ensure harmonized application (McLure 1984). The Act laid down a three-factor formula based on tangible property, payroll and sales, and a general criterion defining the 'business income' to which the formula applies; but it did not define a unitary business.

---

domestic companies are not sales in the course of trade, so can be credited at 'market' value (*Sharkey* v. *Wernher* 1955, and *Petrotim Securities* v. *Ayres*, 1963).

State unitary taxation became the object of international controversy in the 1970s, as many of the states began to apply formula apportionment to the world-wide profits of TNCs operating within the state. This appears to have originated in California, following decisions of its Supreme Court in 1963 upholding claims by US oil companies, which wished to be taxed on a unitary basis so that they could offset losses incurred elsewhere. This led to a more active use of the unitary method, which had previously been treated by the California authorities only as a back-up; it was also more broadly applied, since the Court rejected their view that unity existed only when operations were 'necessary and essential' to each other, preferring the broader test that they 'contributed or were dependent on' each other (Miller, in McLure 1984). Hence, from the late 1960s, foreign TNCs attracted to California by its booming economy suddenly found themselves required to file a combined report covering their world-wide operations, and liable to state tax on a proportion of their global profits, on top of the often considerable costs of start-up or take-over in that state.[27] This originated a campaign by business which has been waged for two decades. Economic as well as political pressures have obliged most of the US states at least to offer a 'water's edge election' limiting combined reporting to US operations. Support from the US federal government as well as other OECD states, and indeed from most national tax authorities, has ensured that official pronouncements of intergovernmental bodies have condemned world-wide unitary taxation. Paradoxically, however, this has increased the political pressure on the authorities to improve the effectiveness of enforcement of taxation of TNCs, thus shining a spotlight on the alternative arm's length method, to which formula apportionment is regarded as posing a major challenge.

5.2 Arm's length

The arm's length principle, as embodied in the model tax treaties (Article 9), permits national tax authorities to adjust the accounts of enterprises under common control if they consider that 'conditions are made or imposed between the two enterprises in their commercial or financial relations which differ from those which would be made between independent enterprises', in order to reallocate profit which would have accrued but for those conditions. This provision originated from an exhaustive study compiled for the League of Nations in 1931–3 by Mitchell B. Carroll, a US lawyer and delegate to the League's Fiscal Committee (Picciotto, forthcoming).

The reason for the study was that several states had taken action

---

[27] Verging on disaster in some cases, such as the ill-fated Barclays venture into California.

against foreign companies where they considered there had been tax evasion by the 'milking' of profits of their local branches or subsidiaries.
Thus, in 1915 the UK enacted provisions allowing a non-resident to be
assessed where due to its 'close connection and substantial control' it conducted business with a resident in such a way as to produce lower profits
to the resident than 'might be expected'. The Inland Revenue was
empowered to assess the non-resident in the name of the resident as
agent, on the 'true amount' of the profits, if necessary on the basis of the
percentage of the turnover of the business done in the UK. This measure
seems to have been taken in response to moves made by firms to reduce
their exposure to high wartime taxes. For example, Gillette had wound
up its UK subsidiary in 1912, and transferred its business to a separate
subsidiary formed in Massachussets; in 1915 it went further, and ceased
to trade directly in the UK, but licensed its UK business to a new company set up by its former UK managing director. An attempt by the
Revenue to apply the 1915 provisions to this licensing relationship, on the
grounds that the contractual relationship amounted to 'control', was
rejected by the courts as 'arbitrary taxation gone mad' (*Gillette Safety
Razor Co.* v. *Commrs of Inland Revenue*, 1920). Another action which
raised business hackles was the move by the French Treasury to apply its
tax on income from 'movable property' (i.e., securities) to dividend distributions by foreign companies with subsidiaries in France, in proportion
to their relative assets.

These claims to tax foreign entities ran counter to the approach
embodied in the model treaties agreed in 1928, which limited state taxation to residents. Better, instead, to focus on the adjustment of the
accounts of the resident entity so as to restore the 'diverted' profits. Thus,
a very broad provision had been enacted by the US Congress in 1928,
enabling the allocation of profits and deductions between entities under
common control wherever necessary 'to prevent evasion of taxes or
clearly to reflect the income'.[28] When the USA negotiated a treaty with
France in 1932 to try to remove the French tax on distributions by US
parent companies, both states were empowered to reallocate profits or
losses between related enterprises in the way permitted by this US provision, and the French therefore enacted a similar power in 1933.[29] In
Germany also, the federal income and corporate tax laws enacted in 1925
empowered the adjustment of the profits both of a branch and of a
locally operated subsidiary of a foreign company.[30]

---

[28] Revenue Act, 1928, sect. 45; this remains in force, with minor changes, as sect. 482 of
the Tax Code, a key provision in taxing TNCs.
[29] Loi du 31 mai 1933, Article 76; this remains in almost exactly the same wording as
sect. 57 of the Code Général des Impôts.
[30] Einkommensteuergesetz, 1925, sect. 33–4; Körperschaftssteuergesetz, 1925, sect. 13.
The scope of the provisions was greatly broadened by the famous decision of the

However, there has always been a central contradiction in the adjustment of accounts based on the arm's length principle. The starting-point was the desire to ensure that the affiliate show the 'correct' profit, and to restore any profit 'diverted' due to the control relationship. The criterion of 'correctness', embodied in the term 'arm's length', is a comparison with unrelated firms. Since the aim is to restore the accounts of the affiliate to what they 'should' be, the process focuses on adjustment of the payments made for intra-firm transactions, by comparison with 'market' transactions. The difficulty is that more often than not there are no comparable transactions between unrelated entities, since the very *raison d'être* of a TNC lies in its advantages as an integrated organization. In practice, therefore, the process has entailed negotiation and bargaining over the 'fair' profit allocation: the arm's length profit. Yet those involved, both officials and business representatives, have continually tended to reject the possibility of developing explicit criteria for profit allocation, and have preferred to focus on price adjustments. The effect is to depoliticize and technicize the process. But this has become increasingly difficult to maintain as the pressures to improve the effectiveness of taxation of TNCs, described above, have grown.

The experience of tax authorities reveals the difficulty of allocating profit by means of price adjustments. It was indeed already recognized in the country studies compiled in the Carroll report. Notably, the British Inland Revenue, which strongly advocated the separate accounting approach, using negotiation to agree a reasonable basis for pricing, nevertheless conceded that 'the fact that the revenue authorities have the alternative of basing profits on a percentage of turnover prevents the taxpayer taking up an unreasonable attitude' (League of Nations 1932: 191); and it estimated that in almost half the cases the assessment was explicitly based on apportioning the profits in relation to turnover, assets, or other appropriate factors.[31] Very little is publicly known about the more recent *Reichsfinanzhof* in the Shell case in 1930, using the 'organic unity' theory (*Organschaft*), originally developed to avoid the 'cascade' effects of turnover tax on sales between related companies, while giving it a wider interpretation, which the court argued was necessary in relation to the new global enterprises, which it described in stirring and prophetic terms. While the original concept required the 'complete financial, economic and organizational dependence' of the subsidiary, the court said that 'the power to command could not be concentrated in one place in the case of combines which circle the planet' (my translation).

[31] This was especially the case for businesses such as banking, insurance, and shipping, frequently carried out by branches rather than separately capitalized subsidiaries. Indeed, in the case of branches the model treaty (Article 7 (4)) still explicitly permits the apportionment of profits, if this has been customary; and the British provisions of 1915 which allowed this still survive (Taxes Management Act, 1970, sect. 20-1). By contrast, the provisions on related entities enacted in 1951 (now Income and Corporation Taxes Act, 1988, sect. 770-4) focus much more precisely on the adjustment of prices in specific transactions. However, the Revenue prefers to rely on the wording of Article 9 of the treaty, which (by virtue of Income and Corporation Taxes Act, 1988, sect. 788(3)) applies where the relationship is with an affiliate resident in a treaty country.

experience, since the British authorities have been very successful apparently in resolving cases by confidential negotiations with the representatives and advisers of enterprises: in three-quarters of a century there have been only two cases litigated in the courts, both dealing with the definition of 'control'.[32] Yet considerable sums are involved: settlements of transfer price cases were reported as giving an immediate yield of £71m. in 1987–8.[33]

By contrast, in the USA the procedures have become increasingly juridified, since the politicization of the problem in the 1960s. The IRS had already initiated an international enforcement programme in 1961 reactivating section 482; but, in view of its wide discretionary powers, was obliged to respond to pressures from taxpayers and Congress to issue detailed regulations (Bischel 1973: 492). Finally agreed in 1968, these regulations defined five categories of transaction (for loans, services, leasing, intangibles, and tangibles), and specified rules for determining prices for each. Thus, despite the very broad power in section 482 to allocate costs and profits, the regulations shifted the process very much towards the adjustment of prices for specific transactions (Langbein 1986). Furthermore, for each of the five categories of transactions they specified that the primary test of price should be the 'comparable uncontrolled price' (CUP), the price that would have been charged by uncontrolled parties dealing at arm's length. Yet, over twenty years of experience demonstrates that in a large proportion of cases, no comparables can be found. This has been shown by half a dozen studies, three carried out by the Treasury itself over the years, showing that in relation to tangibles, the CUP was used in as few as 15 per cent of cases and at the most in 41 per cent (US Treasury Department 1988: 22).

5.3 Collective costs and synergy profits

The central difficulty is that the integrated nature of the TNC means that it can economize by sharing many fixed and overhead costs. Further, the

[32] The *Gillette* case, 1920, already mentioned, and *C.I.R.* v. *Lithgows* 1960. A case reached the Special Commissioners in 1991, but was settled on terms which both sides claim as a victory (interview information). Under the Oil Taxation Act, 1975, which created the special petroleum revenue tax for oil exploitation, a special definition of transfer pricing was given, which explicitly provides that in determining the arm's length price it should be assumed that both buyer and seller should secure 'reasonable profit from transactions of the same kind carried out over a reasonable period' (Income and Corporation Taxes Act, 1988, sect. 771(6)(a)). These provisions have been considered by the courts in *Reg.* v. *A.G. ex parte I.C.I.*, 1985.

[33] This was the yield from the cases handled by the special unit in the international division, as reported in the Management Plan of the Board of Inland Revenue, 1988, although with the caveat that due to the complexity and uncertainty of the cases, 'yield fluctuates year by year, cannot be meaningfully forecast, and bears no relationship to the staffing resources put into them'. Routine cases are handled by districts, and oil by the Oil Taxation Office.

interaction of its operations generates profits from synergy which are not attributable to specific activities. By the same token, it has great flexibility in choosing how to spread such collective costs and benefits among members of the group. For example, a contribution to R & D can, if necessary, be 'bundled' into the price for raw material or component inputs; or, conversely, can be omitted or kept low. Not only is it very difficult to monitor intra-firm relationships by 'unbundling' (or 'rebundling') them as specific transactions; it is even more onerous to evaluate the qualitative and quantitative elements necessary to establish the comparability of similar transactions, even where the same item has been sold by the same firm to a third party.

This was largely admitted by the US Treasury, in its *Study of Intercompany Pricing* (White Paper), produced at the request of Congress in 1988, which proposed to restrict the use of the CUP to 'exact' comparables. This was substantially confirmed by draft amendments to the section 482 regulations issued in January 1992, which laid down that a 'matching transaction' could be acceptable if it concerned the same item 'under the same or substantially similar economic conditions and contractual terms'.

In fact, both these sets of proposals formalized a shift that had been taking place in the methodology used by the IRS for transfer price adjustments. This is towards 'rate of return' analysis, which entails defining the functions carried out by the related parties, measuring the assets or production factors utilized for those functions, and assessing a rate of return on such assets based on the 'comparable profit' of similarly situated firms carrying out such functions. This entails the use of microeconomic methods, which are dependent on the assumptions of the underlying theory justifying them. The marginal analysis assumptions of conventional micro-economics ignore the central factors of oligopolistic markets and organizational advantage, so their application tends to result in the identification of a large item of residual profit (Witte and Chipty 1990). In conjunction with the arm's length principle, the assumption is likely to be that, provided foreign subsidiaries show a reasonable rate of return on assets, synergy profits from integration are attributable to the parent company. It has been argued that a more sophisticated analysis based on transaction costs, rather than emphasizing production costs, would negate this assumption, since it would be clearer that this residual profit is a return to the organization as a whole (Langbein 1989). However, while such micro-economic analysis may improve the identification of profit, it does not provide criteria for its allocation.

Although this shift clearly backtracks from the attempt to fix arm's length prices, the US Treasury argues that it is compatible with the arm's length profit criterion in the tax treaties. In this they are likely to be broadly supported by other tax authorities (although some of the details of the proposed rules have been criticized), since most of them are empowered, or in practice seek, to achieve a 'fair' profit split. However, the business lobbies remain hostile. In the words of Wolfgang Ritter, writing on behalf of the Taxation Commission of the International Chamber of Commerce, this type of analysis: 'does exactly what unitary taxation does: instead of looking at the actual prices charged between related entities, it looks at the total profits earned by a number of entities and divides them up by reference to criteria determined by academic economists with no experience of the real business world' (De Hosson 1989: 73).

Paradoxically, however, it has been the representatives of business who have tried to persuade the tax authorities to accept the proportionate allocation of costs, especially in relation to central services and headquarters costs. This is because it is often hard to identify a specific benefit to a particular affiliate for services which benefit the group as a whole; the country of residence of the parent is unlikely to accept the brunt of the burden of such costs, yet from the viewpoint of the firm they must be deductible somewhere. While the OECD Committee inclined towards acceptance of cost sharing, provided certain criteria were met, there are still significant national divergences (OECD 1984: III). On the other hand, there has been sharp disagreement over the treatment of financing costs: both Japan and the USA require a single corporation to charge loan capital to branches on the basis of the average costs of external borrowing, and the USA has moved to extend this to affiliates falling within a defined affiliation rule;[34] but this was rejected by the other OECD states (OECD 1984: II, paras. 58–62). There is a clear anomaly in allocating joint costs proportionally, while attempting to tax the related entities as independent enterprises.

5.4 Profit split and formula allocation

There are clear advantages to taxing the separate affiliates of a TNC by starting from separate accounts and making adjustments as necessary. First, it is possible to use a much broader definition of 'common control' than is the case for consolidation (which generally requires majority ownership at least) or formula apportionment (which also applies only to unitary businesses). Although some countries look to formal legal powers of

---

[34] The IRS proposed to fix this as 80%; it was then reported that Ford Motor had decided to reorganize its financial subsidiaries so that they would be owned through a new holding company, 25% of whose shares would be placed with institutional investors (*Tax Notes*, 30 Oct. 1989: 531).

control,[35] which can create avoidance opportunities, others have broader definitions: the German transfer pricing rules apply even when the connection is through 'special channels of influence' (*besondere Einflussmöglichkeiten*) and 'identity of interests' (Radler and Jacob 1984: 10). Further, the adjustment of accounts of a local affiliate can be done by national tax authorities without resorting to a full examination of the entire group and without delaying the taxation of a profit made on an inter-affiliate sale until the final profit is realized by a sale outside the group.

The difficulty with separate accounting lies in establishing criteria for the adjustment. The aim has been to establish the 'normal' profit, and it seemed 'natural' that this could be done by adjusting the prices for specific intra-firm transactions in conformity with arm's length or 'market' prices. This was also highly desirable, since a reallocation of profit from one tax authority to another could result in double taxation unless it could be accepted by the other and followed by a corresponding adjustment. This appears more legitimate if done by adjustment of prices for specific transactions, based on such a 'natural' criterion, rather than as a profit split. Thus, a German Finance Ministry official has warned that the treatment of intra-firm transactions would be redolent of 'planned economy and sterile bureaucracy' if it were not firmly based on the principle that '[e]ven members of a group of enterprises are supposed to act in their pricing like participants of a free market' (Hoppner 1983: 212). By contrast, the German national report for the Carroll study recognized that although a global approach may be an unattainable ideal, a nationally based system could work towards it:

It may be said that the method of fractional apportionment (*Verteilung*) is preferable, both from the viewpoint of fairness, which is identical with just taxation, and from the viewpoint of diminishing as much as possible double taxation . . . In international intercourse, a uniform determination of total profits is not possible, in view of the fact that there is no harmony between the tax legislation of the various countries. It would be possible for each interested State, however, even in carrying out its own internal law, to determine the total profits in accordance with rules of assessment applicable in its case. The adoption of some system of reciprocal fiscal assistance might considerably lessen the difficulty of determining the total profits . . . An agreement regarding the principles of allocation would remain essential. Certain principles of allocation might be evolved in practical experience . . . but they would probably have to be different for the various categories of enterprises and . . . experience might lead to the establishment of certain well-defined allocation percentages (*Teilungsquoten*). (League of Nations 1933: iii. 122)

---

[35] Notably Japan and the UK. In *C.I.R.* v. *Lithgows*, 1960 the British courts held that family trusts are not under common control if even one trustee is different.

This analysis has proved remarkably prescient, as shown by the experience of the administration of the arm's length approach, some of which has been detailed above. The increased monitoring of intra-group transactions by national authorities since the mid-1970s has indeed led to a strengthening of arrangements for international administrative cooperation. These include procedures not only for the exchange of information, but also for the co-ordination of assessment of related entities. Thus, the USA has initiated programmes with over a dozen treaty partner states for simultaneous taxation of members of an international corporate group, on a bilateral, but also in some cases a multilateral, basis. By jointly agreeing to target one firm, usually based on indications of tax haven activity and possible non-compliance, a close co-ordination can be established for the parallel tax examinations of the related affiliates, making use of the information exchange procedures under the tax treaties. In addition to identifying avoidance or evasion, this process helps to align policies on the treatment of transfer pricing. Such alignment has also been facilitated by meetings of informal groupings of tax authorities, not only at the highest levels, but also at the working level of specialists, often focusing on tax treatment of specific global industries. Also, taxpayers may themselves initiate an international procedure through the 'competent authority' if they claim that double taxation will result from a transfer price adjustment by one tax authority, to request a corresponding adjustment by the other (see generally Picciotto 1992a: ch. 10).

The newest procedure, also initiated by the US authorities and on which considerable stress is being placed, is for 'advanced pricing agreement' (APAs). This allows, at the taxpayer's initiative, the negotiation of an agreed transfer pricing method which the tax authorities would accept, and which might remain valid, providing there is no change in the key parameters identified in the agreement, for several years. Since the procedure requires the same effort and level of disclosure as a contested audit, it is likely to be initiated only by firms at high risk of tax scrutiny. However, political pressure has led to a much more active programme of examination of TNCs, especially of foreign firms entering the US market which are popularly suspected of not playing fair. Of 45,000 foreign-owned subsidiaries in the USA 1,300 were under examination in April 1992, 220 of them under the IRS's Coordinated Examination Program, which systematically covers the largest corporations (US Treasury 1992). Thus, it is perhaps not surprising that by early 1992 some 40 APAs were already under negotiation. The aim of the IRS is to build up sufficient APAs to be able to establish bench-marks, which might be publishable, and thus reduce the administrative burden of auditing all firms individually.

Importantly, many APAs will entail bilateral, or even multilateral, negotiations with other tax authorities, otherwise the pricing agreed with the IRS may be disallowed elsewhere. Hence, the hope may be to build up a body of internationally agreed principles, firm by firm and industry by industry. However, by its nature, this process will be extremely time-consuming. Crucially, the need to preserve confidentiality, and hence the impossibility of publishing guide-lines until aggregate data can be used, will mean that a key role will continue to be played by the professionals at the heart of the system. Finally, it seems that this trend to individually negotiated agreements is further narrowing the gap between the arm's length approach (which, as we have seen, is increasingly based on profit split), and a global approach based on formula apportionment. Of the handful of APAs agreed by April 1992, two involved dealers in derivative products (Sumitomo Bank Capital Markets Inc., and Barclays Bank). Both were concluded on the basis of a formulary method for allocating expenses and income, and both had been agreed with other authorities (the UK and Hong Kong). This use of a formulary approach to reach agreement was described as a 'businessman's approach' by one (woman) professional involved (Turro 1992).

6. CONCLUSIONS: THE TRANSNATIONALIZATION OF REGULATION AND THE PROBLEM OF LEGITIMACY.

The example of international taxation throws light on the two interrelated processes of juridification of the regulation of corporate groups and the transnationalization of the processes of regulation. It can be seen that the freedom of incorporation and of corporate affiliation has been an important factor in the rise to dominance in the twentieth century of the TNC as the characteristic form of corporate capital. In particular, by exploiting the divergences between tax and other regulatory systems and the possibilities of formation of intermediary affiliates in convenient jurisdictions, TNCs were able to reduce significantly their tax exposure and the cost of their capital. However, the more widespread use of many of the facilities pioneered by the TNCs, and the increasing politicization of the issue of their regulation, led to the strengthening of national regulatory regimes and of international arrangements for co-ordination.

But, it is clear that these processes of bureaucratic bargaining and negotiation lack significant elements of legitimacy. The rejection of the unitary approach and formula apportionment has been based on the view that it would be impossible to achieve adequate international harmonization of the basic principles for definition and allocation of the tax base. The arm's length alternative, by providing a 'natural' criterion for interjurisdictional allocation, had the effect of depoliticizing and technicizing this process, while allowing national political processes to deal with the basic questions of income tax equity. However, the increased internationalization of economic and social relations has simultaneously put intensifying pressure on those national state processes, while bringing them into competition with each other, so that their harmonization has become both increasingly important and increasingly difficult.

The problem of legitimation can be seen in relation to both the criteria and the procedures for international allocation of income from international business. The politicization of the issue of taxation of TNCs, especially in the USA, has led to the elaboration of detailed rules for the treatment of foreign subsidiaries and of inter-affiliate pricing. But the increased sophistication of the methods used to evaluate transfer pricing, especially the application of micro-economic analysis, have merely revealed the extent of the problem, by identifying the residual synergy profits attributable to the organization as such. Furthermore, in relation to highly integrated international activities, such as global trading of financial derivative products, it has been conceded that unitary treatment and formula allocation are inevitable. While a pragmatic case-by-case approach may be possible initially, more general solutions will require a stronger political framework for legitimization.

Bibliography

Aaronovitch, S., and Sawyer, M. (1975), *Big Business* (London: Macmillan).

Abbott, A. (1988), *The System of Professions: An Essay on the Expert Division of Labor* (Chicago: University of Chicago Press).

Ackerman, B. (1980), *Social Justice in the Liberal State* (London: Yale University Press).

—— (1989), 'Why Dialogue?', 86 *Journal of Philosophy* 5.

Adams, R. (1975), 'Wage Determination: Reconciling Theory and Practice', 34 *American Journal of Economics and Sociology* 353.

Aghion, P., and Bolton, P. (1988), 'An "Incomplete Contract" Approach to Bankruptcy and the Financial Structure of the Firm' (Massachusetts Institute of Technology Working Paper No. 484).

—— (1989), 'The Financial Structure of the Firm and the Problem of Control', 33 *European Economic Review* 286.

Akerlof, G. A. (1982), 'Labor Contracts as Partial Gift Exchange', 98 (4) *Quarterly Journal of Economics* 543.

Albert, M. (1992), *Capitalismes contre capitalismes* (Paris: Seuil).

Alchian, A. (1950), 'Uncertainty, Evolution and Economic Theory', 58 *Journal of Political Economy* 211.

—— and Demsetz, H. (1972), 'Production, Information Costs, and Economic Organization', 62 *American Economic Review* 777.

Aldrich, H. and Whetten, D.A. (1981), 'Organization-Sets, Action-Sets, and Networks: Making the Most of Simplicity', in Nistrom and Starbuck (1981), 385–408.

Alexander, M. and Murray, (1992), 'Lawyers and Economic Power in Australia and New Zealand' (paper presented to the Conference on Legal Professions, Aix en Provence, June 1992).

American Law Institute (1984) 'Principles of Corporate Governance sec. 2.01(c)' (Tentative Draft No. 2).

—— (1986), 'Principles of Corporate Governance: Analysis and Recommendations' (Tentative Draft No. 5)

Alt, J., and Shepsle, K. (1990) (eds.)., *Perpectives in Positive Political Economy* (Cambridge: Cambridge University Press).

Alworth, J.S. (1988), *The Finance, Investment and Taxation Decisions of Multinationals* (Oxford: Blackwell).

American Academy of Political and Social Science (1900), *Corporations and the Public Welfare* (New York: McClure Phillips).

Anderson, W. (1931) *Limitations of the Corporate Entity, A Treatise of the Law Relating to the Overriding of the Corporate Fiction.*

Annable, J. E. (1984), *The Price of Industrial Labor* (Lexington, Mass. Lexington Books).

Antle, R. (1982), 'The Auditor as an Economic Agent', 20(2) *Journal of Accounting Research* 503.

Aoki, M. (1984), *The Co-operative Game Theory of the Firm* (Oxford: Clarendon Press).

—— (1988), *Information Incentives and Bargaining in the Japanese Economy* (Cambridge: Cambridge University Press).

—— (1990), 'Toward an Economic Model of the Japanese Firm,' 28(Mar.) *Journal of Economic Literature* 1.

——, Gustafsson, B., and Williamson, O. (1990) (eds.), *The Firm as a Nexus of Treaties* (London: Sage).

APB (Auditing Practices Board) (1991) *Proposals for an Expanded Audit Report* (Consultative paper) (London: APB).

—— (1992), *Investment Businesses* Practice Note 1 (London: APB).

APC (Auditing Practices Committee) (1988), *The Implications for Auditors of the Financial Services Act 1986* (Exposure draft) (London: APC).

—— (1989a), *Banks in the United Kingdom* (auditing guideline) (London: APC).

—— (1989b), *Building Societies in the United Kingdom* (auditing guideline) (London: APC).

—— (1990a), *The Auditor's Responsibility in Relation to Fraud, Other Irregularities and Error* (auditing guideline) (London: APC).

—— (1990b), *Communications between Auditors and Regulators under Sections 109 and 180(1)(q) of the Financial Services Act 1986* (auditing guideline) (London: APC).

—— (1990c), *The Auditor's Responsibility in Relation to Illegal Acts* (exposure draft of an auditing guideline) (London: APC).

—— (1991), *Client Assets: Guidance for Auditors of Investment Business* (Practice Note 3), (London: APC).

Arendt, H. (1958), *The Human Condition* (Chicago: University of Chicago Press).

Arnold, B. J. (1986), *The Taxation of Controlled Foreign Corporations: An International Comparison*, Canadian Tax Papers No. 78 (Toronto: Canadian Tax Foundation).

Ashenfelter, O., and Layard, R. (1988) (eds.), *Handbook of Labor Economics* (Amsterdam: Elsevier Science Publishers).

Atlan, H. (1979), *Entre le cristal et la fumèe* (Paris: Seuil).

Atleson, J. B. (1985), 'Reflections on Labor, Power, and Society', 44 *Maryland Law Review* 841.

Auerbach, A. (1988) (ed.), *Corporate Takeovers: Causes and Consequences* (Chicago: University of Chicago Press).

—— and Reishus, D. (1987), 'Taxes and the Merger Decision', in Coffee *et al.* (1987), 157–91.

—— (1988), 'The Effects of Taxation on the Merger Decision', in A. Auerbach (1988), 167–83.

Auerbach, P. (1988), *Competition: The Economics of Industrial Change* (Oxford: Blackwell).

Ault, H. J. (1978), 'International Issues in Corporate Tax Integration', 10 *Law & Policy in International Business* 461.

Australia, Government of (1988), National Companies and Securities Commission, Release 633 (Melbourne).

—— (1989), Companies and Securities Law Review Committee, *Nominee Directors and Alternate Directors*, Report No. 8: (Melbourne).

Ayres, C.E. (1973), *Prolegemenon to Institutionalism,* consisting of *Science, the False Messiah* (1927) and *Holier than Thou* (1929), in with a new introduction: (New York: Augustus M. Kelly).

Ayres, I., and Gertner, R. (1989), 'Filling Gaps in Incomplete Contracts', 99 *Yale Law Journal* 87.

—— (1991), 'Strategic Contractual Choice and the Optimal Choice of Legal Rules', 101 *Yale Law Journal* 729.

Baecker, D., Markowitz, J., Stichweh, R., Tyrell, H., and Willke, H. (1987) (eds.), *Theorie als Passion* (Frankfurt: Suhrkamp).

Bailey, E. E., and Baumol, W.J. (1984), 'Deregulation and the Theory of Contestable Markets', 1 *Yale Journal of Regulation* 111.

Baird, D. (1986), 'The Uneasy Case for Corporate Reorganizations', 15 *Journal of Legal Studies* 127.

Baldamus, W. (1961), *Efficiency and Effort* (London: Tavistock).

Baldwin, R. (1990), 'Why Rules Don't Work', 53 *Modern Law Review* 321.

—— and McCrudden, C. (1987) (eds.), *Regulation and Public Law* (London: Weidenfeld and Nicolson).

Bank of England (1992), *Bank Supervision and BCCI: The Response of The Bank of England to the Second and Fourth Reports from the Treasury and Civil Service Committee in Session 1991–92* (London).

Bankenverband (1989), *Zur Diskussion um die 'Macht der Banken'* (Cologne: Informationen des Bundesverbandes deutscher Banken).

Baran, P. A. (1973), *The Political Economy of Growth* (Harmondsworth: Penguin).

—— and Sweezy, P. M. (1966), *Monopoly Capital* (Harmondsworth: Penguin).

Barlow, E. R., and Wender, I. T. (1955), *Foreign Investment and Taxation* (Cambridge, Mass.: Harvard College).

Barron, A., and Scott, C. (1992), 'The Citizen's Charter Programme', 55 *Modern Law Review* 526.

Barron, P. (1984), 'Causes and Impact of Plant Shutdowns and Relocations and Potential Non-NLRA Responses', 58 *Tulane Law Review* 1389.

Bassett, P. (1986), *Strike Free: New Industrial Relations in Britain* (London: Macmillan).

Baür, J., Hopt, K., and Mailander, P. (1990), *Festschrift für Ernst Steindorff* (Berlin: De Gruyter).

Baumol, W. J. (1986), 'Williamson's "The Economic Institutions of Capitalism"', 17 *Rand Journal of Economics* 279.

—— Panzer, J., and Willig, R. (1982), *Contestable Markets and the Theory of Industrial Structure* (New York: Harcourt Brace Jovanovich).

Baums, T. (1990), 'Höchststimmrechte', *Die Aktiengesellschaft* 221.

—— Buxbaum, R., and Hopt, K. (forthcoming) (eds.), *Institutional Investors and Corporate Governance.*

Bebchuk, L. (1989), 'Limiting Contractual Freedom in Corporate Law: The Desirable Constraints on Charter Amendments', 102 *Harvard Law Review* 1820.

—— (1990) (ed.), *Corporate Law and Economic Analysis* (Cambridge: Cambridge University Press).

Beck, U. (1988), *Gegengifte: Die organisierte Unverantwortlichkeit* (Frankfurt: Suhrkamp).

Becker, G. S. (1976), *The Economic Approach to Human Behavior* (Chicago: University of Chicago Press).

Beesley, M., and Laidlaw, B. (1989), *The Future of Telecommunications: An Assessment of the Role of Competition in UK Policy* (London: IEA).

Beesley, M., and Littlechild, S. (1986) 'Privatization Principles, Problems, and Priorities', in Kay et al. (1986), 35–57.

—— (1989), 'The Regulation of Privatized Monoplies in the UK', 20 *Rand Journal of Economics* 454.

Bellamy, C., and Child, G. D. (1991), *Common Market Law of Competition* 3rd edn. (London Sweet and Maxwell).

Berglöf, E. (1990), 'Capital Structure as a Mechanism of Corporate Control: Comparison of Financial Systems', in Aoki *et al* (1990), 237–62.

Berle, A. A. (1931), 'Corporate Powers as Powers in Trust', 44 *Harvard Law Review* 1025.

—— (1932), 'For Whom Corporate Managers Are Trustees', 45 *Harvard Law Review* 1365.

—— (1954), *The Twentieth Century Capitalist Revolution* (New York: Harper and Row).

—— and Means, G. C. (1932), *The Modern Corporation and Private Property* (New York: Macmillan).

—— (1968), *The Modern Corporation and Private Property* rev. edn. (New York: Harcourt Brace).

Bewley, T. F. (1987) (ed.), *Advances in Economic Theory, Fifth World Congress* (Cambridge: Cambridge University Press).

Bhagat, S., Shleifer, A., and Vishny, R. (1990), 'Takeovers in the 1980s: The Return to Corporate Specialization' [1990] *Brookings Papers on Economic Activity, Microeconomics* 1.

Bhaskar, R. (1989), *The Possibility of Naturalism* 2nd edn (London: Harvester Wheatsheaf).

Bihr, A. (1992), 'Malaise dans l'etat-nation: mondialisation du marche, necessaire decentralisation', *Le Monde diplomatique*, Feb. 1992.

Bird, R. M. (1988), 'Shaping a New International Tax Order', [1988] *Bulletin for International Fiscal Documentation* 292.

Birley, S. (1985), 'The Role of Networks in the Entrepreneurial Process', 1 *Journal of Business Venturing* 107.

Bischel, J. E. (1973), 'Tax Allocations Concerning Inter-Company Transactions in Foreign Operations: A Reappraisal', *Virginia Journal of International Law* 490.

Black, B. (1990), 'Is Corporate Law Trivial?: A Political and Economic Analysis', 84 *Northwestern University Law Review* 542.

—— (1991), 'Shareholder Passivity Reexamined', 89 *Michigan Law Review* 520.

Blackstone, W. (1765–9), *Commentaries on the Laws of England* (Chicago: Chicago University Press, 1979 edn.).

Blasi, J. (1988), *Employee Ownership: Revolution or Ripoff?* (Cambridge, Mass.: Harper Buan).

Blois, K. (1972), 'Vertical Quasi-Integration', 20 *Journal of Industrial Economics* 253.

Bloomfield, M. (1921), *Labor and Compensation* (New York: Industrial Extension Institute).

Blumberg, P. (1975), *The Megacorporation in American Society: The Scope of the Corporate Power* (Englewood Cliffs: Prentice-Hall, Inc.).

—— (1983), *The Law of Corporate Groups: Procedural Problems in the Law of Parent and Subsidiary Corporations* (Boston: Little, Brown and Co.).

—— (1985), *The Law of Corporate Groups: Problems in the Bankruptcy or Reorganization of Parent and Subsidiary Corporations, Corporate Guaranties* (Boston: Little, Brown and Co.).

—— (1986), 'Limited Liability and Corporate Groups', 11 *Journal of Corporate Law* 574.

—— (1987a), 'Intra-Group (Upstream, Cross-stream and Downstream) Guaranties under the Uniform Fraudulent Transfer Act', 9 *Cardozo Law Review* 685).

—— (1987b), *The Law of Corporate Groups: Tort, Contract, and Other Common Law Problems in the Substantive Law of Parent and Subsidiary Corporations* (Boston: Little, Brown and Co.).

—— (1989), *The Law of Corporate Groups: Problems of Parent and Subsidiary Corporations under Statutory Law of General Application* (Boston: Little, Brown and Co.).

—— (1990a), 'The Corporate Entity in an Era of Multinational Corporations', 15 *Delaware Journal of Corporate Law* 285.

—— (1990b), 'The Corporate Personality in American Law: A Summary Review', 38 *American Journal of Comparative Law* 49 (Supp.).

—— (1992), *The Law of Corporate Groups: Problems of Parent and Subsidiary Corporations under Statutory Law Specifically Applying Enterprise Principles* (with Kurt A. Strasser) (Boston: Little, Brown and Co.).

—— (1993) *The Multinational Challenge to Corporation Law: The Search for a New Corporate Personality* (New York: Oxford University Press).

Bork, R. H. (1978), *The Antitrust Paradox* (New York: Basic Books).

Borrie, Sir Gordon (1991), 'Trading Malpractices and Legislative Policy', 107 *Law Quarterly Review* 559.

Bourdieu, P. (1989), *La Noblesse d'état: grandes ecoles et esprit de corps* (Paris: Editions de Minuit).

Bowles, S. (1985), 'The Production Process in a Competitive Economy: Walrasian, Neo-Hobbesian, and Marxian Models', 75(1) *American Economic Review* 16.

—— and Gintis, H. (1976), *Schooling in Capitalist America* (London: Routledge and Kegan Paul).

—— (1986), *Democracy and Capitalism: Property, Community and the Contradictions of Modern Social Thought* (London: Routledge and Kegan Paul).

—— (1990), 'Contested Exchange: New Microfoundations for the Political Economy of Capitalism', 18 *Politics and Society* 165.

Boyer, R. (1989), *Capitalismes fin de siècle* (Paris: PUF).

Bracewell-Milnes, B. (1980), *The Economics of International Tax Avoidance. Political Power versus Economic Law* (Deventer: Kluwer).

Bradley, C. (1990), 'Corporate Control: Markets and Rules', 53 *Modern Law Review* 170.

Bradley, K., and Gelb, A. (1983), *Worker Capitalism: The New Industrial Relations* (London: Heinemann).

Branson, D. M. (1989), 'Assault on Another Citadel: Attempts to Curtail the Fiduciary Standard of Loyalty Applicable to Corporate Directors', 57 *Fordham Law Review* 375.

Bratton, W. (1989a), 'Corporate Debt Relationships: Legal Theory in a Time of Restructuring', [1989] *Duke Law Journal* 92.

—— (1989b), 'The New Economic Theory of the Firm: Critical Perspectives from History', 41 *Stanford Law Review* 1471.

—— (1989c), 'The "Nexus of Contracts" Corporation: A Critical Appraisal', 74 *Cornell Law Review* 407.

—— (1992), 'Welfare and Goodwill in Corporate Fidiciary Law' (manuscript).

Brickley, J. A., and Dark, F. H. (1987), 'The Choice of the Organizational Form: The Case of Franchising', 18 *Journal of Financial Economics* 408.

Brodie, D. (1988), 'Individual Contracts of Employment (Part II)', 3 *Labor Law Journal* 663.

Brooke, M. Z., and Remmers, L. (1978), *The Strategy of Multinational Enterprises*, 2nd edn. (London: Pitman).

Brown, W. (1981) (ed.), *The Changing Contours of British Industrial Relations* (Oxford: Blackwell).

Brudney, V. (1966), 'Fiduciary Ideology in Transactions Affecting Corporate Control', 65 *California Law Review* 259.

—— (1982), 'The Independent Director—Heavenly City or Potemkin Village', 95 *Harvard Law Review* 597.

—— (1985), 'Corporate Governance, Agency Costs and the Rhetoric of Contract', 85 *Columbia Law Review* 1403.

—— (1988), 'Comment', in Coffee *et al.* (1988).

—— and Clark, R. (1981), 'A New Look at Corporate Opportunities', 94 *Harvard Law Review* 997.

Buckland, W. (1952), *Roman Law and Common Law*, 2nd edn. F. Lawson (Cambridge: Cambridge University Press).

Bunge, M. (1980), *The Mind–Body Problem: A Psychobiological Approach* (Oxford: Pergamon).

Bureau of Labor Statistics (1991), *Employment and Earnings* (Washington, DC).

Burns, T. (1969) (ed.), *Industrial Man* (Harmondsworth: Penguin).

Butler, H. N., and Ribstein, L. E. (1990), 'Opting Out of Fiduciary Duties: A Response to the Anti-Contractarians', 65 *Washington Law Review* 1.

Button, K. (1985), 'New Approaches to the Regulation of Industry', 148 *Royal Bank of Scotland Review* 18.

Buxbaum, R. (1990), 'Institutional Ownership and the Restructuring of Corporations', in Baür, *et al.* (1990), 7–29.

—— (1991), 'Institutional Owners and Corporate Managers: A Comparative Perspective' (University of California at Berkeley, Program in Law and Economics Working Paper Nos. 91–2).

—— and Hopt, K.J. (1988) (eds.), *Legal Harmonization and the Business Enterprise* (Berlin: Walter de Gruyter).

Cable, J. (1985), 'Capital Market Information and Industrial Performance: The

Role of West German Banks', 95 *Economic Journal* 118.

—— and FitzRoy, F. (1980), 'Productive Efficiency, Incentives and Employee Participation', 33 *Kyklos* 100.

Cadbury, Sir Adrian (1992), *Report of the Committee on the Financial Aspects of Corporate Governance, May 1992* (London).

Cain, G. (1976), 'The Challenge of Segmented Labor Market Theories to Orthodox Theory: A Survey', 14 *Journal of Economic Literature* 1215.

Campbell, D. (1990), 'Adam Smith, Farrar on Company Law and the Economics of the Corporation', 19 *Anglo-American Law Review* 185.

Canada Government of (1978), *Report of the Royal Commission on Corporate Concentration* (Bryce Report) (Ottawa).

Carey, W. (1974), 'Federalism and Corporate Law: Reflections upon Delaware', 83 *Yale Law Journal* 663.

Carnegie, A. (1889), 'The Bugaboo of the Trust', 148 *North American Review* 141.

Carsberg, Sir Bryan (1990), 'Injecting Competition into Telecommunications', in Veljanovski (1990a), 81–95.

—— (1992a), *Future Control on British Telecom's Prices* (London: Oftel).

—— (1992b), *Policy on Separation and Interconnection* (London: Oftel).

Casson, M. (1979), *Alternatives to the Multinational Enterprise* (London: Macmillan).

—— (1987), *The Firm and the Market* (Oxford: Blackwell).

Caves, R. E. (1982), *Multinational Enterprise and Economic Analysis* (Cambridge: Cambridge University Press).

—— (1990), 'Lessons from Privatization in Britain: State Enterprise Behaviour, Public Choice and Corporate Governance', 13 *Journal of Economic Behavior and Organization* 145.

Chamberlin, E. H. (1955) (ed.), *Monopoly and Competition and their Regulation* (Cambridge: Cambridge University Press).

—— (1962), *The Theory of Monopolistic Competition*, 8th edn. (Cambridge, Mass.: Harvard University Press).

Chandler, A. (1962), *Strategy and Structure: Chapters in the History of the American Industrial Enterprise* (Cambridge, Mass.: MIT Press).

—— (1990), *Scale and Scope: The Dynamics of Industrial Capitalism* (Cambridge, Mass.: Harvard University Press).

Channon, D. F. (1973), *The Strategy and Structure of British Enterprise* (Boston: Harvard University Press).

Chapman, S. D. (1984), *The Rise of Merchant Banking* (London: Allen and Unwin).

Charles, C. (1989), 'Pour une histoire sociale des professions juridiques', 76/77 *Actes de la Recherche* 117.

Charny, D. (1991), 'Hypothetical Bargains: The Normative Structure of Contract Interpretion', 89 *Michigan Law Review* 1815.

Child, J. (1972), 'Organisational Structure, Environment and Performance', 6 *Sociology* 1.

Chiplin, B., and Wright, M. (1982), 'Competition Policy and State Enterprises in the UK', 27 *Antitrust Bulletin* 921.

—— (1987), *The Logic of Mergers: The Competition Market in Corporate Control in Theory and Practice* (London: Institute of Economic Affairs).

City Panel on Takeovers and Mergers (1990), *City Code on Take-overs and Mergers* (London).

Clark, K. B., Hayes, R. H., and Lorenz, C. (1985) (eds.), The Uneasy Alliance (Boston Harvard Business School Press).

Clark, R. (1979), *The Japanese Company* (New Haven, Conn.: Yale University Press).

Clark, R. C. (1985), 'Agency Costs versus Fiduciary Duties', in Pratt and Zeckhauser (1985), 55–81.

—— (1989), 'Contracts, Elites and Traditions in the Making of Corporate Law', 89 *Columbia Law Review* 1703.

Clarke, J. B. (1898), 'Introduction', in Rodbertus (1898), 1–18.

Clarke, M. (1986), *Regulating the City: Competition, Scandal and Reform* (Milton Keynes: Open University Press).

Clarke, S. (1979), *Marx, Marginalism and Modern Sociology*, 2nd edn. (London: Macmillan).

——(1991) (ed.), *The State Debate* (London: Macmillan).

Coakley, J., and Harris, L. (1983), *The City of Capital* (Oxford: Blackwell).

Coase, R. H. (1937), 'The Nature of the Firm', 4 *Economica N.S.* 386.

—— (1976), 'Adam Smith's View of Man', 19 *Journal of Law and Economics* 529.

—— (1984), 'The New Institutional Economics', 140 *Journal of Institutional and Theoretical Economics* 229.

—— (1988), *The Firm, the Market and the Law* (Chicago: University of Chicago Press).

Coffee, J.C. (1984), 'Regulating the Market for Corporate Control: A Critical Assessment of the Tender Offer's Role in Corporate Governance', 84 *Columbia Law Review* 1145.

—— (1986), 'Shareholders versus Managers: The Strain in the Corporate Web', 85 *Michigan Law Review* 1.

—— (1987), 'Shareholders versus Managers: The Strain in the Corporate Web', in Coffee *et al.* (1987), 77–134.

—— (1989) 'The Mandatory/Enabling Balance in Corporate Law: An Essay on the Judicial Role', 89 *Columbia Law Review* 1618.

—— (1990), 'Unstable Coalitions: Corporate Governance as a Multi-Player Game', 78 *Georgetown Law Journal* 1495.

—— (1991), 'Liquidity versus Control: The Institutional Investor as Corporate Monitor', 91 *Columbia Law Review* 1277.

——, Lowenstein, L., and Rose-Ackerman, S. (1988) (eds.), *Knights, Raiders, & Targets* (New York: Oxford University Press).

Cohen, M. (1933) 'The Basis of Contract', 46 Harvard Law Review 553.

Coke, E. (1628), *First Part of the Institute of the Laws of England or a Commentary upon Littleton* (London).

Coleman, J. S. (1974), *Power and the Structure of Society* (New York: Norton).

—— (1982), *The Asymmetric Society* (Syracuse, NY: Syracuse University Press).

—— (1990), *Foundations of Social Theory* (Cambridge, Mass.: Harvard University Press).

Collins, H., (1986) 'Market Power, Bureaucratic Power and the Contract of Employment', 15 *Industrial Law Journal* 1.

—— (1987), 'Against Abstentionism in Labour Law', in Eekelaar and Bell (1987), ch. 4.

—— (1989), 'Labour Law as a Vocation', 104 *Law Quarterly Review* 468.

—— (1990*a*), 'Ascription of Legal Responsibility to Groups in Complex Patterns of Economic Integration', 53 *Modern Law Review* 731.

—— (1990*b*), 'Independent Contractors and the Challenge of Vertical Disintegration to Employment Protection Laws', 10 *Oxford Journal of Legal Studies* 353.

—— (1992), *Justice in Dismissal: The Law of Termination of Employment* (Oxford: Oxford University Press).

Commons, J. R. (1968), *Legal Foundations of Capitalism* (Madison, Wis.: University of Wisconsin Press).

Conant, C. A. (1900), *The United States in the Orient* (Port Washington, Wa.: Kennikat Press).

—— (1901), 'Crises and their Management', 9 *Yale Review* 374.

—— (1927), *A History of Modern Banks of Issue*, 6th edn. (New York: Putnam).

Contractor, F. (1981), 'The Role of Licensing in International Strategy', 16 *Columbia Journal of World Business* 73.

Cook, W. (1926), *Law of Corporations*, 8th edn. (Chicago: Chicago University Press).

Cooke, R. (1990), 'The Onerous Task of Detection', *Accountancy Age*, 15 Nov., 16.

Coombs, R., Saviotti, P., and Walsh, V. (1987), *Economics and Technological Change* (London: Macmillan).

Cooper, D., Radcliffe, V., and Robson, K. (1991), 'The Management of Professional Enterprises and Regulatory Change: British Accountancy and the Financial Services Act, 1986' (unpublished paper).

Cooter, R. (1982), 'The Cost of Coase', 11 *Journal of Legal Studies* 1.

Cornell, D. (1990), 'From the Lighthouse: The Promise of Redemption and the Possibility of Legal Interpretation', 11 *Cardozo Law Review* 1687.

Cotterell, R. (1987), 'Power, Property and the Law of Trusts: A Partial Agenda for Critical Legal Scholarship', 14 *Journal of Law and Society* 77.

—— (1988), 'Feasible Regulation for Democracy and Social Justice', 15 *Journal of Law and Society* 5.

Council of the Stock Exchange (1984), *The Yellow Book* (London: Stock Exchange).

Craig, P. (1987), 'The Monopolies and Mergers Commission: Competition and Administrative Rationality', in Baldwin and McCrudden (1987), 202–26.

—— (1991), 'Constitutions, Property and Regulation', [1991] *Public Law* 538.

Cressey, P., and MacInnes, J. (1980), 'Voting for Ford: Industrial Democracy and the Control of Labour', 11 *Capital and Class* 5.

Curhan, J., Davidson, W., and Suri, R. (1977), *Tracing the Multinationals* (Cambridge, Mass.: Bellinger).

Dale, R. (1991), 'Someone Must be in Charge', *Financial Times*, 22 July.

D'Amico, R. J., and Golon, J. (1986), 'The Displaced Worker', in Mills (1986).

Dan-Cohen, M. (1986), *Rights, Persons, and Organizations: A Legal Theory for Bureaucratic Society* (Berkeley, Calif.: University of California Press).

Dann, L. Y., and DeAngelo, H. (1988), 'Corporate Financial Policy and

Corporate Control: A Study of Defensive Adjustments in Asset and Ownership Structure', 20 *Journal of Financial Economics* 87.

Dasgupta, P. (1988), 'Trust as a Commodity', in Gambetta (1988*b*), 49–77.

Davies, P. N. (1981), 'Business Success and the Rule of Chance: The Extraordinary Philipps Brothers', 23 *Business History* 208.

Davies, P., and Freedland, M. (1984), *Labour Law: Text and Materials* 2nd edn. (London: Weidenfeld and Nicolson).

—— and Lord Wedderburn of Charlton (1977), 'The Land of Industrial Democracy', 6 *Industrial Law Journal* 197.

De Hosson, F. (1989) (ed.), *Transfer Pricing for Intangibles* (Deventer: Kluwer).

De Jong, W. H., and Shepard, W. (1986) (eds.), *Mainstreams in Industrial Organization*, Book I (Dordrecht: Kluwer Academic Publishers).

De Mott, D. A. (1988), 'Beyond Metaphor: An Analysis of Fiduciary Obligation', [1988] *Duke Law Journal* 879.

Deaton, R. (1989), *The Political Economy of Pensions* (Vancouver, BC: University of British Columbia Press).

Deggau, H.-G. (1987), 'Versuch über die Autopoiese des Vertrages' (unpublished paper).

Demsetz, H. (1968), 'Why Regulate Utilities?' 9 *Journal of Law and Economics* 55.

Department of Transport (1992), *New Opportunities for the Railways—The Privatisation of British Rail*, Cm. 2012 (London: HMSO).

Dertouzos, J., Holland, E., and Ebener, P. (1988), *The Legal and Economic Consequences of Wrongful Termination* (Washington, DC: Rand Corporation).

Dewey, J. (1926), 'The Historic Background of Corporate Legal Personality', 35 *Yale Law Journal* 655.

Dezalay, Y. (1991), 'Turf Battles and Tribal Wars', 54 *Modern Law Review* 792.

—— (1992), *Marchands de droit. La Restructuration de l'ordre juridique internationale par les multinationales du droit* (Paris: Fayard).

—— and Sugarman, D. (forthcoming) (eds.), *Professional Competition and the Social Construction of Markets* (London: Routledge).

Diamond, D. (1984), 'Financial Intermediation and Delegated Monitoring', 51 *Review of Economic Studies* 393.

Dioguardi, G. (1986), *L'Impresa nell'era del computer* (Milan: Il Sole 24 Ore W.m).

Dnes, A. W. (1988), 'The Business Functions of Franchising', 1 *Business Studies* 33.

—— (1991), 'The Economic Analysis of Franchising and its Regulation', in Joerges (1991*a*), 133–42.

Dodd, E. M. (1932), 'For Whom Are Corporate Managers Trustees', 45 *Harvard Law Review* 1145.

—— (1935), 'Is Effective Enforcement of Fiduciary Duties of Corporate Managers Practicable?', 2 *University of Chicago Law Review* 194.

Doeringer, P., and Piore M. (1971), *Internal Labor Markets and Manpower Analysis* (Lexington, Mass.: Lexington Books).

Dore, R. (1987), *Taking Japan Seriousy* (London: Athlone).

Dow, G. K. (1987), 'The Function of Authority in Transaction Cost Economics', 8 *Journal of Economic Behavior and Organization* 13.

Drucker, P. (1976), *The Unseen Revolution: How Pension Fund Socialism Came to America* (New York: Harper and Row).

Drukarczyk, J., and Preuschl, M. (1989), 'Zur Gestaltung der Ausschüttungskompetenzen in der Publikumsaktiengesellschaft' (University of Regensburg, Department of Business Economics Working Paper No. 3).

DTI (Department of Trade and Industry) (1982) *Insolvency Law and Practice* (Report of the Review Committee), Cmnd. 8558 (London: HMSO).

—— (1984), *Licence Issued by the Secretary of State to British Telecommunications PLC* (London: HMSO).

—— (1989a), *Report of Inspectors Appointed to Investigate Affairs of County Natwest Ltd and County Natwest Securities Ltd* (London: HMSO).

—— (1989b), *Summary Financial Statements for Listed Public Limited Companies* (Consultation Document, August 1989) (London: DTI).

—— (1990a) *Listing Particulars and Public Offer Prospectuses. Implementation of Part V of the Financial Services Act 1986 and Related EC Directives Consultation Document, July 1990* (London: DTI).

—— (1990b), *Report of Inspectors on Blue Arrow PLC* (London: HMSO).

—— (1991), *Competition and Choice: Telecommunications Policy for the 1990s*, Cm. 1461 (London: HMSO).

Dunning, J.H. (1981), *International Production and the Multinational Enterprise* (London: Allen and Unwin).

Durkheim, E. (1893), *The Division of Labour in Society* (New York: Macmillan, 1933 edn.).

Dyas, G. R., and Thanheiser, H. T. (1976), *The Emerging European Enterprise: Strategy and Structure in French and German Industry* (London: Macmillan).

Easterbrook, F. (1988), 'Corporations as Contracts' (unpublished paper).

—— and Fischel, D. (1989), 'The Corporate Contract', 89 *Columbia Law Review* 1416.

—— (1991), *The Economic Structure of Corporate Law* (Cambridge, Mass.: Harvard University Press).

Edwards, R. (1979), *Contested Terrain* (London: Heinemann).

Eekelaar, J., and Bell, J. (1987) (eds.), *Oxford Essays in Jurisprudence, Third Series* (Oxford: Oxford University Press).

Ehrenberg, R., and Smith, R. (1988), *Modern Labor Economics*, 4th edn. (Glenview, Ill.: Scott, Foreman and Co.).

Eisenberg, M. E. (1987), 'Comment: Golden Parachutes and the Myth of the Web', in Coffee *et al.* (1987), 155–8.

—— (1989), 'The Structure of Corporation Law', 89 *Columbia Law Review* 1461.

Elkouri, F., and Elkouri, E. A. (1985), *How Arbitration Works*, 4th edn. (Washington, DG: Bureau of National Affairs).

Elster, J. (1983), *Explaining Technical Change* (Cambridge: Cambridge University Press).

—— (1989), *The Cement of Society: A Study of Social Order* (Cambridge: Cambridge University Press).

Employee Benefits Research Institute (1990), *Quarterly Pension Investment Report*, vol. 4. (Mar.).

Enderwick, P. (1984), 'The Labour Utilisation Practices of Multinationals and

Obstacles to Multinational Collective Bargaining', 26(3) *Journal of Industrial Relations* 345.

Engels, F. (1976), 'Preface to the English Edition of Volume One', in Marx (1976), 106–13.

Englander, E. J. (1988), 'Technology and Oliver Williamson's Transaction Cost Economics', 10 *Journal of Economic Behavior and Organization* 339.

Epstein, R. (1984), 'In Defense of Employment at Will', 51 *University of Chicago Law Review* 947.

—— and Paul, J. (1985), *Labor Law and the Employment Market* (New Brunswick, NJ: Transaction Books).

Estreicher, S. (1988), 'Successorship Obligations', in Estreicher and Collins (1988).

—— and Collins, D. (1988), *Labor Law and Business Change* (New York: Quorum Books).

Etherington, N. (1982), 'Reconsidering Theories of Imperialism', 21 *History and Theory* 1.

—— (1983), 'The Capitalist Theory of Capitalist Imperialism', 15 *History of Political Economy* 38.

European Communities, Commission of (1976), 'Survey of Multinational Enterprises', (Brussels).

—— (1983*a*), 'Amended Proposal for a Directive on Procedure for Informing and Consulting the Employees of Undertakings with Complex Structures, in Particular Transnational Undertakings' (Brussels).

—— (1983*b*), 'Amended Proposal for a Fifth Directive on the Structure of Public Limited Companies and the Powers and Obligations of their Organs' (Brussels).

—— (1983*c*), 'Seventh Directive on Preparation and Publication of Consolidated Accounts', 83/349 EEC OJ L 193/1, 13 June 1983 (Brussels).

—— (1984), 'Draft Proposal for a Ninth Directive on Links between Undertakings and in Particular on Groups' (Brussels).

—— (1991), 'Removal of Tax Obstacles to the Cross-Frontier Activities of Companies' (Bulletin of the European Communities, Supplement 4/91).

—— (1992), 'Report of the Committee of Independent Experts on Company Taxation (Luxembourg).

Evan, W. (1966), 'The Organization Set', in J.D. Thompson (1966).

Faber, H., and Stein, E. (1989) (eds.), *Auf einem dritten Weg: Festschrift für Helmut Ridder* (Neuwied: Luchterhand).

Falim, P. D., and Sehgal, E. (1985), 'Displaced Workers of 1979–83: How Well Have They Fared?', 108 *Monthly Labor Review* 6: 3, 3.

Fama, E. (1980), 'Agency Problems and the Theory of the Firm', 88 *Journal of Political Economy* 288.

—— and Jensen, M. (1983), 'Separation of Ownership and Control', 26 *Journal of Law and Economics* 301.

Farrar, J. H., and Russell, M. (1984), 'The Impact of Institutional Investment on Company Law', 5 *Company Lawyer* 107.

—— Furey, N., and Hannigan, B. (1992), *Company Law*, 3rd edn. (London: Butterworths).

Feinman, J. M. (1976), 'The Development of Employment at Will Rule', 20 *American Journal of Legal History* 118.

Fenn, P., and Whelan, C. (1984), 'Job Security and the Role of Law: An Economic Analysis of Employment at Will', 20 *Stanford Journal of International Law* 353.

Fieldhouse, D. K. (1961), 'Imperialism: An Historiographical Revision', 14 *Economic History Review* 187.

Fine, S. (1967), *Laissez-Faire and the General Welfare State* (Ann Arbor; Mich.: University of Michigan Press).

Fischel, D., and Langbein, J. (1988), 'ERISA's Fundamental Contradiction: The Exclusive Benefit Rule', 55 *University of Chicago Law Review* 1105.

Fischer, K. (1990), 'Hausbankbeziehungen als Instrument der Bindung zwischen Banken und Unternehmen: Eine theoretische und empirische Analyse' (unpublished dissertation, Bonn).

Fish, S. (1989), *Doing What Comes Naturally* (Oxford: Oxford University Press).

Fitzpatrick, P., and Hunt, A. (1987) (eds.), *Critical Legal Studies* (Oxford: Blackwell).

FitzRoy, F. R., and Kraft, K. (1987), 'Efficiency and Internal Organisation: Works Councils in West German Firms', 54. *Economica* 493.

Fletcher, W. (1980), *Cyclopedia of the Private Law of Corporations*, (rev. edn.) (Chicago: Collaghan).

Förster, H. von (1985), 'Entdecken oder Erfinden? Wie läßt sich Verstehen verstehen?' in Mohlar (1985), 29–68.

Franks, J., and Mayer, C. (1990), 'Capital Markets and Corporate Control: A Study of France, Germany and the UK', 10 *Economic Policy* 191.

——, Harris, R., and Titman, S. (1991), 'The Postmerger Share-Price Performance of Acquiring Firms', 29 *Journal of Financial Economics* 81.

Freeman, R. B. (1976), 'Individual Mobility and Union Voice in the Labour Market', 66 *American Economic Review* 361.

—— and Medoff, J. L. (1984), *What Do Unions Do?* (New York: Basic Books).

Friedman, A. L. (1977), *Industry and Labour* (London: Macmillan).

Friedman, M. (1977), 'The Social Responsibility of Business is to Make Profits', in Steiner and Steiner (1977), 168–74.

—— (1982), *Capitalism and Freedom* rev. edn. (Chicago: University of Chicago Press).

Fudenberg, D., Holmstrom, B., and Milgrom, P. (1990), 'Short-Term Contracts and Long-Term Agency Relationships', 51 *Journal of Economic Theory* 1.

Fuller, L., and Perdue, W. R. (1936–7), 'The Reliance Interest in Contract Damages', 46 *Yale Law Journal* 52.

Galanter, M. (1974), 'Why the Haves Come Out Ahead: Speculations on the Limits of Legal Change', 9 *Law & Society Review* 3.

—— and Palay, T. (1991), *Tournament of Lawyers. The Transformation of the Big Law Firm* (Chicago: University of Chicago Press).

Galbraith, C., and Kay, N. M. (1986), 'Towards a Theory of Multinational Enterprise', 7 *Journal of Economic Behavior and Organization* 3.

Galbraith, J. K. (1974), *The New Industrial State* 2nd edn. (Harmondsworth: Penguin).

—— (1975), *Economics and the Public Purpose* (Harmondsworth: Penguin).

Gambetta, D. (1988a), 'Can We Trust Trust,' in Gambetta (1988b), 213–37.

Gambetta, D. (1988*b*) (ed.), *Trust: Making and Breaking Corporate Relations* (Oxford: Blackwell).

Gavis, A.C. (1990), 'A Framework for Satisfying Corporate Directors Responsibilities under State Nonshareholder Constituency Statutes: The Use of Explicit Contracts', 138 *University of Pennsylvania Law Review* 1451.

Gawalt, G. (1984) (ed.), *The New High Priests—Lawyers in Post-Civil War America* (Westport, Conn.: Greenwood Press).

Gerlach, M. L. (1989), *Alliances and the Social Organization of Japanese Business* (Berkeley, Calif.: University of California Press).

Gerrard, B. (1989), *Theory of the Capitalist Economy. Towards a Post-Classical Synthesis* (Oxford: Basil Blackwell).

Geser, H. (1990), 'Organisationen als soziale Akteure', 19 *Zeitschrift für Soziologie* 401.

Gessler Commission (1979), 'Bericht der Studienkommission Grundsatzfragen der Kreditwirtschaft' (Publications of the Federal Minister for Finance, Volume 28, Frankfurt).

Giddens, A. (1981), *The Class Structure of the Advanced Societies* 2nd edn. (London: Hutchinson).

—— (1984), *The Constitution of Society* (Cambridge: Polity).

Gilson, R. (1987), 'Evaluating Dual Class Common Stock: The Relevance of Substitutes,' 73 *Virginia Law Review* 807.

—— and Kraakman, R. (1991), 'Reinventing the Outside Director: An Agenda for Institutional Investors', 43 *Stanford Law Review* 863.

—— and Mnookin, R. H. (1990), 'The Implicit Contract for Corporate Law Firm Associates: Ex Post Opportunism and Ex Ante Bonding', in Aoki *et al.* (1990), 209–36.

——, Scholes, M., and Wolfston, M. (1987), 'Taxation and the Dynamics of Corporate Control: The Uncertain Case for Tax-Motivated Acquisitions', in Coffee *et al.* (1987), 271–344.

Gintis, H. (1990), 'The Principle of External Accountability in Competitive Markets', in Aoki et al. (1990), 289–302.

Goldberg, G. (1985), 'The Controversy on the Section 20 Contract Revisited', 48 *Modern Law Review* 158.

Goldberg, V. P. (1980), 'Bridges over Contested Terrain', 1 *Journal of Economic Behavior and Organization* 249.

Goode, R. M. (1988) (ed.), *Group Trading and the Lending Banker* (London: Chartered Institute of Bankers).

—— (1989), *Consumer Credit Law* (London: Butterworths).

Gordon, D., Reich, M., and Edwards, R. (1975) *Labor Market Segmentation* (Lexington, Ill: D.C. Heath).

Gordon, J. (1974), 'Argentine Jurisprudence: The Parke Davis and Deltec Cases', 6 *Lawyer of the Americas* 320.

—— (1979), 'Argentine Jurisprudence: Deltec Update', 11 *Lawyer of the Americas* 43.

Gordon, J. N. (1989), 'The Mandatory Structure of Corporate Law', 89 *Columbia Law Review* 1549.

—— (1990), 'Ties that Bind: Dual Class Common Stock and the Problem of Shareholder Choice', in Bebchuk (1990), 74–117.

—— (1991), 'Corporations, Markets, Courts', 91 *Columbia Law Review* 1931.

Gordon, R.A. (1945), *Business Leadership in the Large Corporation* (New York: Brookings Institution).

Gordon, R. (1984), 'The Ideal and the Actual in the Law: Fantasies and Practises of New York City Lawyers 1870–1910', in Gawalt (1984), 51–74.

Gottschalk, A. (1988), 'Der Stimmrechtseinfluß der Banken in den Aktionärsversammlungen der Großunternehmen', WSI-Mitteilungen 5/1988, 294–404.

Gould, S. J. (1982), *The Panda's Thumb: More Reflections in Natural History* (New York: Norton).

Gould, W. B. (1986), 'Some Reflections on Fifty Years of the National Labor Relations Act: The Need for Labor Board and Labor Law Reform', 38 *Stanford Law Review* 937.

Gower, L. (1950), 'Contract—Sale of Goods—Innocent Misrepresentations and Conditions', 13 *Modern Law Review* 362.

—— (1958a), 'The Contractual Effect of Articles of Association', 21 *Modern Law Review* 401.

—— (1958b), 'Rayfield v Hands—A Postscript and a Drop of Scotch', 21 *Modern Law Review* 657.

Graham, C. (1992), 'Consumers and Privatised Industries', 3(1) *Utilities Law Review* 38.

Green, E., and Moss, M. (1982), *A Business of National Importance: The Royal Mail Shipping Group* (London: Methuen).

Grochla, E., and Wittmann, W. (1975) (eds.), *Handwörterbuch der Betriebswirtschaft*, 4th edn. (Stuttgart: Springer).

Grossman, S. J., and Hart, O. (1986), 'The Costs and Benefits of Ownership: A Theory of Vertical and Lateral Integration', 94 *Journal of Political Economy* 691.

Gumbrecht, H. U., and Link-Heer, U. (1985) (eds.), *Epochenschwellen und Epochenstrukturen im Diskurs der Literatur-und Sprachhistorie* (Frankfurt: Suhrkamp).

Habermas, J. (1983), *Philosophical-Political Profiles*, trans. F. Lawrence (London: Heinemann).

——(1989), 'Morality and Ethical Life: Does Hegel's Critique of Kant Apply to Discourse Ethics?', 83 *Northwestern University Law Review* 38.

Hadden, T. (1982), 'Employee Participation: What Future for the German Model?', 3 *Company Lawyer* 250.

—— (1983), *The Control of Corporate Groups* (London: Institute of Advanced Legal Studies).

—— (1984), 'Inside Corporate Groups', 12 *International Journal of Sociology of Law* 271.

—— (1992), 'Regulating Corporate Groups in Australia', 15 *University of New South Wales Law Journal* 61.

——, Forbes, R., and Simmonds, R. (1984), *Canadian Business Organisations Law* (Toronto: Butterworths).

Hadfield, G. K. (1990), 'Problematic Relations: Franchising and the Law of Incomplete Contracts', 42 *Stanford Law Review* 927.

Hadley, A. T. (1896), *Economics* (New York: Putnam).

——— (1897) 'The Good and Evil of Industrial Combination', 79 *Atlantic Monthly* 377.

Hale, R. (1923), 'Coercion and Distribution in a Supposedly Non-Coercive State', 38 *Political Science Quarterly* 470.

Hall, B. (1990), 'The Impact of Restructuring on Industrial Research and Development' [1990] *Brookings Papers on Economic Activity, Microeconomics* 85.

Haller, M., Hoffmann-Nowotny, H.-J., and Zapf, W. (1988) (eds.), *Kultur und Gesellschaft* (Frankfurt: Campus).

Hamilton, G. G., Orru, M., and Biggart, N. W. (1987), 'Enterprise Groups in East Asia', *Shoken Keizai* 161.

Hamilton, R. W. (1971), 'The Corporate Entity', 49 *Texas Law Review* 979.

Hancher, L., and Moran, M. (eds.) (1989a) *Capitalism, Culture and Regulation* (Oxford: Oxford University Press).

——— (1989b), 'Organising Regulatory Space', in Hancher and Moran (1989a), 271–99.

Handler, J. (1988), 'Dependent People, the State, and the Modern/Postmodern Search for the Dialogic Community', 35 *UCLA Law Review* 999.

Hanf, K., and Scharpf, F.W. (1978) (eds.), *Interorganizational Policy Making: Limits to Coordination and Central Control* (London: Sage).

Hanks, J. (1988), 'Evaluating Recent Legislation on Director and Officer Liability Limitation and Indemnification', 43 *Business Law* 1207.

Hannah, L. (1986), *Investing in Retirement* (Cambridge: Cambridge University Press).

——— and Kay, J. (1977), *Concentration in Modern Industry* (London: Macmillan).

Hansen, F.R. (1985), *The Breakdown of Capitalism* (London: Routledge and Kegan Paul).

Hansmann, H. (1990), 'When Does Worker Ownership Work: ESOPs, Law Firms, Codetermination, and Economic Democracy', 99 *Yale Law Journal* 1749.

Harden, I. (1992), *The Contracting State* (Milton Keynes: Open University Press).

Harré, R. (1979), *Social Being* (Oxford: Blackwell).

Hart, H. (1954), 'Definition and Theory in Jurisprudence', 70 *Law Quarterly Review* 37.

Hart, O. (1989), 'An Economist's Perspective on the Theory of the Firm', 89 *Columbia Law Review* 1757.

——— and Holmström, B. (1987), 'The Theory of Contracts', in Bewley (1987), 71–155.

——— and Moore, J. (1988), 'Incomplete Contracts and Renegotiation', 56 *Econometrics* 755.

Hart, P. E., and Clarke, R. (1980), *Concentration in British Industry 1933–75* (Cambridge: Cambridge University Press).

Hastedt, H. (1988), *Das Leib-Seele-Problem: Zwischen Naturwissenschaft des Geistes und kultureller Eindimensionalität* (Frankfurt: Suhrkamp).

Hawkins, R. (1979) (ed.), 'The Economic Effects of Multinational Corporations', 1 *Research in International Business and Finance* (Greenwich, Conn.: JAI Press).

Hayakawa, M. (1991), 'Zum Gegenwartigen Stand des Konzernrechts in Japan', in Mestmacker and Behrens (1991), 391–418.

Hedlund, G. (1981), 'Autonomy of Subsidiaries and Formalization of Headquarter–Subsidiary Relationships in Swedish MNC's, in Otterbeck (1981), 25–78.

Hellwig, M. (1989), 'Banking, Financial Intermediation and Corporate Finance', (Basle WWZ-Discussion Papers No. 9015).

—— (1990), 'Asymmetric Information, Financial Markets, and Financial Institutions. Where are we Currently Going?', 33 *European Economic Review* 277.

Helm, D. (1987), 'RPI minus X and the Newly Privatized Industries: A Deceptively Simple Regulatory Rule', 7(1) *Public Money* 47.

Henderson, D. F. (1973), *Foreign Enterprise in Japan: Laws and Policies* (Chapel Hill, NC: University of North Carolina Press).

Herman, E. (1981), *Corporate Control, Corporate Power* (Cambridge: Cambridge University Press).

—— and Lowenstein, L. (1987), 'The Efficiency Effects of Hostile Takeovers', in Coffee *et al.* (1987), 211–41.

Hessen, R. (1979), *In Defense of the Corporation* (Stanford, Calif.: Hoover Institution Press).

Hilferding, R. (1910), *Finance Capital* (London: Routledge and Kegan Paul, 1981 edn.).

Hirschman, A. O. (1970), *Exit, Voice and Loyalty* (Cambridge, Mass.: Harvard University Press).

HM Treasury (1991), *The Citizen's Charter*, Cm. 1599 (London: HMSO).

Hoffmann-Riem, W., Mollnau, K. A., and Rottleuthner, H. (1990) (eds.), *Rechtssoziologie in der Deutschen Demokratischen Republik und in der Bundesrepublik Deutschland* (Baden-Baden: Nomos).

Hofstetter, K. (1990), 'Parent Responsibility for Subsidiary Corporations: Evaluating European Trends', 39 *International and Comparative Law Quarterly* 576.

Hollingsworth, R. J. (1990), 'The Governance of American Manufacturing Sectors: The Logic of Coordination and Control' (MPIFG Discussion Paper 90/4).

Hollington, R. (1990), *Minority Shareholders Rights* (London: Sweet and Maxwell).

Holmstrom, B. (1988), 'Comment', in A. Auerbach (1988), 56–60.

—— and Milgrom, P. (1991), 'Multitask Principal–Agent Analyses: Incentive Contracts, Asset Ownership, and Job Design', 7 *Journal of Law, Economics and Organization* 24.

—— and Tirole, J. (1989), 'The Theory of the Firm', in Schmalensee and Willig (1989), 61–133.

Hommelhoff, P. (1990), 'Produkthaftung im Konzern', 11 *Zeitschrift für Wirtschaftsrecht* 761.

Hoppner, H.-D. (1983), 'German Regulations on Transfer Pricing: A Tax Administrators Point of View', *Intertax* 208.

Hopt, K., and Teubner, G. (1985) (eds.), *Corporate Governance and Directors' Liabilities* (Berlin: Walter de Gruyter).

Hopwood, A. G., and Page, M. (1988), 'Changing Roles on the City Stage', *Accountancy*, June, 90–1.

Horn, N., and Kocka, J. (1979) (eds.), *Law and the Formation of the Big Enterprises in the 19th Century* (Göttingen: Vandenhoeck and Ruprecht).

Hornby, J. (1956), 'Houldsworth v City of Glasgow Bank', 19 *Modern Law Review* 54.

Horwitz, M. (1992), *The Transformation of American Law 1860–1960* (Cambridge: Cambridge University Press).

Hufbauer, G., and Foster, D. (1977), 'US Taxation of the Undistributed Income of Controlled Foreign Corporations', in *Essays in International Taxation* (Washington, DC: US Treasury).

Humphrey, C. (1991), 'Audit Expectations', in Sherer and Turley (1991), 3–21.

Hurst, J. (1980), *The Legitimacy of the Business Corporation in the Law of the United States—1780–1970* (Charlottesville, Va.: University Press of Virginia).

Hutchens, R. (1986), 'Delayed Payment Contracts and a Firm's Propensity to Hire Older Workers', 4 *Journal of Labor Economics* 439.

—— (1987), 'Test of Lazear's Theory of Delayed Payment Contracts', 4 *Journal of Labour Economics* 153.

Hutter, M. (1989), *Die Produktion von Recht: Eine selbstreferentielle Theorie der Wirtschaft, angewandt auf den Fall des Arzneimittelpatentrechts* (Tübingen; Mohr).

Hyman, R. (1975), *Industrial Relations: A Marxist Introduction* (London: Macmillan).

IFS (1982), *Institute for Fiscal Studies* (Report of the Working Party on Company Residence, Tax Havens, and Upstream Loans. IFS Reports No. 3) (London).

Imai, K., and Itami, H. (1984), 'Interpenetration of Organization and Market: Japan's Firm and Market in Comparison with the U.S.', 2 *International Journal of Industrial Organization* 285.

Imai, K., Nonaka, I., and Takeuchi, H. (1985), 'Managing New Product Development: How Japanese Companies Learn and Unlearn', in K.B. Clark *et al.* (1985).

Immenga, U. (1978), *Beteiligungen von Banken in anderen Wirtschaftszweigen*, Studien zum Bank- und Börsenrecht, vol. 2, 2nd edn. (Baden-Baden: Nomos).

Industrial Commission (1900), *Preliminary Report on Trusts and Industrial Combinations* (Washington, DC: US GPO).

Institutional Shareholders Committee (1991), *The Role and Duties of Directors—A Statement of Best Practice*, 18 May 1991 (London).

Ippolito, R. (1989), *The Economics of Pension Insurance* (Homewood, Ill.: Irwin).

Ireland, P. (1984), 'The Rise of the Limited Liability Company', 12 *International Journal of the Sociology of Law* 239.

——, Grigg-Spall, I., and Kelly, D. (1987), 'The Conceptual Foundations of Modern Company Law', in Fitzpatrick and Hunt (1987).

Jacoby, S. (1985), *Employing Bureaucracy: Managers, Unions and the Transformation of Work in American Industry 1900–1945* (New York: Columbia University Press).

Jarillo, J. C. (1988), 'On Strategic Network', 9 *Strategic Management Review* 31.

Jarrell, G., Brickley, J., and Netter, J. (1988), 'The Market for Corporate

Control: The Empirical Evidence since 1978', 2 *Journal of Economic Perspectives* 49.

Jensen, M. C. (1987), 'The Takeover Controversy: Analysis and Evidence', in Coffee *et al.* (1987), 314–55.

—— (1988), 'Takeovers: Their Causes and Consequences', 2 *Journal of Economic Perspectives* 21.

—— and Meckling, W. (1976), 'Theory of the Firm: Managerial Behavior, Agency Costs, and Capital Structure', 3 *Journal of Financial Economics* 305.

—— and Ruback, R. (1983), 'The Market for Corporate Control: The Scientific Evidence', 11 *Journal of Financial Economics* 5.

Jessop, B. (1982), *The Capitalist State* (Oxford: Blackwell).

Jevons, W. S. (1965), *Theory of Political Economy*, 5th edn. (Harmondsworth: Penguin).

Joerges, C. (1991a) (ed.), *Franchising the Law: Theoretical and Comparative Approaches in Europe and the United States* (Baden-Baden: Nomos).

—— (1991b), 'Status and Contract in Franchising Law', in Joerges (1991a), 11–66.

Johanson, J., and Mattson, L. G. (1989), 'Interorganizational Relations in Industrial Systems: A Network Approach Compared with the Transactional Approach', 18 *International Journal of Management and Organization* 34.

Johnston, J. S. (1990), 'Strategic Bargaining and the Economic Theory of Contract Default Rules', 100 *Yale Law Journal* 616.

Jones, T. (1989), 'The Deregulation of Broadcasting', 52 *Modern Law Review* 380.

Jovanovic, B. (1979), 'Job Matching and the Theory of Turnover', 87 *Journal of Political Economy* 972.

Kagel, J. H., Battalio, R., Rachlin, H., and Green, L. (1981), 'Demand Curves for Animal Consumers', 96 *Quarterly Journal of Economics* 1.

Kahn-Freund, O. (1946), 'A Review of the Report of the Committee on Company Law Amendment', 9 *Modern Law Review* 235.

Kalecki, M. (1954), *Theory of Economic Dynamics* (London: Unwin).

Kaneko, I., and Imai, K. (1987), 'A Network View of the Firm' (paper delivered to the First Hitotsubashi–Stanford Conference).

Kantorowicz, E. H. (1957), *The Kings' Two Bodies. A Study in Mediaeval Political Theology* (Princeton, NJ: Princeton University Press).

Katz, A. (1990), 'The Strategic Structure of Offer and Acceptance: Game Theory and the Law of Contract', 89 *Michigan Law Review* 215.

Kaufman, B. E. (1988), *How Labor Markets Work* (Lexington, Mass.: Lexington Books).

Kay, J., Mayer, C., and Thompson, D. (1986) (eds.), *Privatisation and Regulation—the UK Experience* (Oxford: Oxford University Press).

Kay, N.M. (1982), *The Evolving Firm: Strategy and Structure in Industrial Organisation* (London: Macmillan).

—— (1984), *The Emerging Firm: Knowledge, Ignorance and Surprise in Economic Organisation* (London: Macmillan).

Kaysen, K. C. (1957), 'The Social Significance of the Modern Corporation', 47 *American Economic Review (Papers and Proceedings of the American Economic Association)* 311.

Kenis, P., and Schneider, V. (1991), 'Policy Networks and Policy Analysis: Scrutinizing a New Analytical Toolbox', in Marin and Mayntz (1991*b*), 26–59.

Kirchner, C. (1985), 'Ökonomische Überlegungen zum Konzernrecht', 14 *Zeitschrift für Unternehmens- und Gesellschaftsrecht* 214.

Klandermans, P. G. (1984), 'Mobilisation and Participation in Trade Union Action: A Value Expectancy Approach', 57 *Journal of Occupational Psychology* 107.

Klein, B., and Saft, H. F. (1985), 'The Law and Economics of Franchise Tying Contracts', 28 *Journal of Law and Economics* 345.

Knyphausen, D. zu (1988), *Unternehmungen als evolutionsfähige Systeme: Überlegungen zu einem evolutionären Konzept für die Organisationstheorie* (Herrsching: Kirsch).

Köndgen, J. (1981), *Selbstbindung ohne Vertrag: Zur Haftung aus geschäftsbezogenem Handeln* (Tübingen: Mohr).

Körber, U. (1989), *Die Stimmrechtsvertretung durch Kreditinstitute*, Untersuchungen über das Spar-, Giro- und Kreditwesen Band, 55 (Berlin: Drucker and Humblot).

Kolko, G. (1963), *The Triumph of Conservatism* (New York: Macmillan).

Kornhauser, W. (1989), 'The Nexus of Contracts Approach to Corporations: A Comment on Easterbrook and Fischel', 89 *Columbia Law Review* 1449.

KPMG Peat Marwick McLintock (1990), *Audit and Auditors: What the Public Thinks* (London: KPMG).

Kratky, K., and Wallner, F. (1990) (eds.), *Grundprinzipien der Selbstorganisation* (Darmstadt: Wissenschaftlische Buchgesellschaft).

Kreps, D. (1990), 'Corporate Culture and Economic Theory', in Alt and Shepsle (1990), 90–143.

Krikorian, B. (1989), *Fiduciary Duties in Pension and Trust Fund Management* (Stoneham, Mass.: Butterworths).

Kripke, H. (1975), 'A Search for a Meaningful Securities Disclosure Policy', 31 *Business Lawyer* 293.

—— (1979), *The SEC and Corporate Disclosure: Regulation in Search of a Purpose* (Chicago: Law and Business, Inc.).

Krohn, G., Küppers, G., and Nowotny, H. (1990) (eds.), *Selforganization: Portrait of a Scientific Revolution* (Dordrecht: Kluwer).

Kronman, A. (1989), 'A Comment on Dean Clark', 89 *Columbia Law Review* 1748.

Krümmel, H.-J. (1980), 'German Universal Banking Scrutinized', 4 *Journal of Banking and Finance* 33.

Küpper, W., and Ortmann, G. (1988) (eds.), *Mikropolitik: Rationalität, Macht und Spiele in Organisationen* (Opladen: Westdeutscher Verlag).

Kuran, T. (1988), 'The Tenacious Past: Theories of Personal and Collective Conservatism', 10 *Journal of Economic Behaviour and Organisation* 143.

Kyd, S. (1793), *A Treatise on the Law of Corporations* (2 vols., London).

Ladeur, K.-H. (1989), 'Zu einer Grundrechtstheorie der Selbstorganisation des Unternehmens', in Faber and Stein (1989), 179–91.

—— (1992), *Postmoderne Rechtstheorie: Selbstreferenz—Selbstorganization—Prozeduralisierung* (Berlin: Drucker and Humblot).

Laffont, J-J., and Tirole, J. (1991), 'Privatization and Incentives', 7 *Journal of Law, Economics and Organizations* 84.

Lamoreaux, N. R. (1985), *The Great Merger Movement in American Business 1895–1904* (Cambridge, Mass.: Harvard University Press).

Landes, D.S. (1986), 'What Do Bosses Really Do?', 46 *Journal of Economic History* 585.

Landon, D. (1990), *Country Lawyers: The Impact of Context on Professional Practice* (New York: Praeger).

Langbein, S. I. (1986), 'The Unitary Method and the Myth of Arm's Length' 17 Feb. *Tax Notes* 625.

—— (1989), 'Transaction Cost, Production Cost, and Tax Transfer Pricing', 18 Sept. *Tax Notes* 1391.

Lange, O. (1960), *Political Economy*, Volume 1 (Oxford: Rosenberg and Sellier).

Lanoff, I. (1980), 'The Social Investment of Private Pension Plan Assets,' 31 *Labor Law Journal* 387.

Larenz, K. (1987), *Lehrbuch des Schuldrechts*, 14th edn. (Munich: Beck).

Latty, E. (1936), *Subsidiary and Affiliated Corporations* (Chicago: Foundation Press).

Lazear, E. P. (1979). 'Why Is There Mandatory Retirement?', 87 *Journal of Political Economy* 1261.

—— (1981), 'Agency, Earnings Profiles, Productivity, and Hours Restrictions', 71 *American Economic Review* 606.

League of Nations (1932), *Taxation of Foreign and National Enterprises. A Study of the Tax Systems and Methods of Allocation of the Profits of Enterprises Operating in more than one Country*, Volume 1 (France, Germany, Spain, the UK and the USA), C. 73. M. 38 1932 IIA 3 (Geneva).

—— (1933), *Taxation of Foreign and National Enterprises*, Volumes 2–4, C.425. M.217 1933 IIA 18 (Geneva).

Lee, H. K., Numazaki, I., and Ueda, Y. (1987), 'Comments on "Enterprise Groups in East Asia"', *Shoken Keizai* 162.

Leebron, D. (1991), 'Limited Liability, Tort Victims, and Creditors', 91 *Columbia Law Review* 1565.

Lehmbruch, G. (1985), 'Sozialpartnerschaft in der vergleichenden Politikforschung', 25 *Journal für Sozialforschung* 285.

Leinhardt, S. (1977) (ed.), *Symposium on Social Networks* (New York: Academic Press).

Lenin, V. I. (1964a), *Collected Works*, Volume 22 (London: Lawrence and Wishart).

—— (1964b), 'Imperialism: The Highest Stage of Capitalism', in Lenin (1964a), 185–304.

Lessard, D. R. (1979), 'Transfer Prices, Taxes and Financial Markets: Implications of Internal Financial Transfers within the Multinational Corporation', in Hawkins (1979), 101–25.

—— and Williamson, J. (1987), *Capital Flight and Third World Debt* (Washington, DC: Institute for International Economics).

Leubsdorf, J. (1982), 'Three Models of Professional Reform', 67 *Cornell Law Review* 1021.

Levine, J. H., and Roy, W. S. (1977), 'A Study of Interlocking Directorates', in Leinhardt (1977).

Levy, F., and Murnane, R. J. (1992), 'US Earnings Levels and Earnings Inequality: A Review of Recent Trends and Proposed Explanations', 30 *Journal of Economic Literature* 1333.

Llewellyn, K. (1931), 'Some Realism about Realism', 44 *Harvard Law Review* 1222.

Lorenzoni, G. (1990), *L'Architettura di sviluppo delle imprese minore: Costellazioni e piccoli gruppi* (Bologna).

Loss, L., and Seligman, J. (1989–), *Securities Regulation*, 3rd edn. (Boston: Little, Brown and Co.).

Lufkin, J., and Gallagher, D. (1990) (eds.), *International Corporate Governance* (London: Euromoney Publications).

Luhmann, N. (1975), *Trust and Power* (London: Academic Press).

—— (1981*a*), *The Differentiation of Society* (New York: Columbia University Press).

—— (1981*b*), 'Organisation im Wirtschaftssystem' in Luhmann, *Soziologische Aufklärung*, Volume 3 (Opladen: Westdeutscher), 390–414.

—— (1985), 'Das Problem der Epochenbildung und die Evolutionstheorie', in Gumbrecht and Link-Heer (1985), 11–33.

—— (1987), 'Die Differenzierung von Politik und Wirtschaft und ihre gesellschaftlichen Grundlagen', in Luhmann, *Soziologische Aufklärung* Volume 4 (Opladen: Westdeutscher), 32–48.

—— (1988*a*) 'Organisation', in Küpper and Ortmann (1988), 165–85.

—— (1988*b*), *Die Wirtschaft der Gesellschaft* (Frankfurt: Suhrkamp).

—— (forthcoming), *Social Systems* (Palo Alto, Calif.: Stanford University Press).

Lukes, S. (1973), *Individualism* (Oxford: Blackwell).

Lupton, T. (1963), *On the Shop Floor* (Oxford: Pergamon).

Lutter, M. (1989), 'Bankenvertreter im Aufsichtsrat', 145 *Zeitschrift für das gesamte Handelsrecht* 224.

—— (1990), 'Enterprise Law Corp. vs Entity Law Inc.—Phillip Blumberg's Book from the Point of View of a European Lawyer', 38 *American Journal of Comparative Law* 949.

Luxemburg, R. (1913), *The Accumulation of Capital* (London: Routledge and Kegan Paul, 1973 edn.).

Macaulay, S. (1963), 'Non-Contractual Relations in Business: A Preliminary Study', 28 *American Sociological Review* 55.

—— (1985), 'An Empirical View of Contract', [1985] *Wisconsin Law Review* 465.

—— (1991), 'Long-Term Continuing Relations: The American Experience Regulating Dealerships and Franchises', in Joerges (1991*a*), 179–238.

Macey, J. (1984), 'From Fairness to Contract: The New Direction of Rules against Insider Trading', 13 *Hofstra Law Review* 9.

—— (1988), 'State Anti-Takeover Legislation', [1988] *Wisconsin Law Review* 467.

—— (1989), 'Externalities, Firm-Specific Capital Investments and the Legal Treatment of Fundamental Corporate Change', [1989] *Duke Law Journal* 173.

—— (1992), 'Organisational Design and Political Control of Administrative Agencies', 8 *Journal of Law, Economics and Organization* 93.

MacIntyre, A. (1988), *Whose Justice? Which Rationality?* (London: Duckworth).

MacMillan, K., and Farmer, D. (1979), 'Redefining the Boundaries of the Firm', 27 *Journal of Industrial Economics* 277.

MacNeil, I. (1978), 'Contracts: Adjustments of Long-Term Economic Relations under Classical, Neoclassical, and Relational Contract Law', 72 *Northwestern Law Review* 854.

—— (1980), *The New Social Contract: An Inquiry into Modern Contractual Relations* (New Haven, Conn.: Yale University Press).

MacPherson, C. (1987), *The Rise and Fall of Economic Justice* (Oxford: Oxford University Press).

Majone, G. (1990) (ed.), *De-Regulation or Re-Regulation* (London: Pinter).

Malcomson, J. (1984), 'Work Incentives, Hierarchy, and Internal Labor Markets', 92 *Journal of Political Economy* 486.

Mandel, E. (1978), *Late Capitalism* (London: Verso).

Manne, H. G. (1965), 'Mergers and the Market for Corporate Control', 73 *Journal of Political Economy* 110.

—— (1967), 'Our Two Corporation Systems: Law and Economics', 53 *Virginia Law Review* 259.

Manning, B. (1987), 'State Competition: Panel Response', 8 *Cardozo Law Review* 779.

Mansfield, E. (1982), *Microeconomics, Theory and Applications* 4th edn. (New York: W W. Norton).

Marglin, S. A. (1974), 'What Do Bosses Do?' 6 *Review of Radical Political Economics* 60.

Marin, B., and Mayntz, R. (1991a), 'Introduction: Studying Policy Networks', in Marin and Mayntz (1991b), 11–23.

——(1991b) (eds.), *Policy Networks: Empirical Evidence and Theoretical Considerations* (Frankfurt: Campus).

Marris, R. (1964), *The Economic Theory of Managerial Capitalism* (New York: Free Press).

——and Mueller, D. C. (1980), 'The Corporation, Competition, and the Invisible Hand', 18 *Journal of Economic Literature* 32.

——and Wood, A. (1971) (eds.) *The Corporate Economy* (Cambridge, Mass. Harvard University Press).

Martin, K., and McConnell, J. (1991), 'Corporate Performance, Corporate Takeover, and Management Turnover,' 46 *Journal of Finance* 671.

Martinek, M. (1987), *Franchising: Grundlagen der zivil- und wettbewerbsrechtlichen Behandlung der vertikalen Gruppenkooperation beim Absatz von Waren und Dienstleistungen* (Heidelberg: Decker).

Marx, G. (1981), 'Ironies of Social Control: Authorities as Contributors to Deviance through Escalation, Non-Enforcement and Covert Facilitation', 28 *Social Problems* 221.

Marx, K. (1974), *Capital*, Volume 1 (London: Laurence and Wishart).

—— (1976), *Capital*, Volume 1 (Harmondsworth: Penguin).

—— (1981), *Capital*, Volume 3 (Harmondsworth: Penguin).

—— and Engels, F. (1976a), *Collected Works*, Volume 6 (London: Lawrence and Wishart).

—— (1976*b*), 'Manifesto of the Communist Party', in Marx and Engels (1976*a*), 477–519.

Mathewson, G. F., and Winter, R. A., (1985), 'The Economics of Franchise Contracts', 28 *Journal of Law and Economics* 503.

Maturana, H. R., and Varela, F. J. (1980), *Autopoiesis and Cognition* (Dordrecht: Riedel).

Mayer, C., and Alexander, I. (1990), 'Banks and Securities Markets: Corporate Financing in Germany and the UK' (City University Business School, London, Working Paper).

Mayntz, R. (1992), 'Modernisierung und die Logik von interorganisatorischen Netzwerken', 32 *Journal für Sozialforschung* 19.

McAuslan, P., and McEldowney, J. (1988), 'Towards a Legal Framework for a Privatized Electricity Supply Industry: The Input from Public Utilities Law', 9 *Urban Law and Policy* 165.

McBarnet, D. (1984), 'Law and Capital: The Role of Legal Forms and Legal Actors', 12 *International Journal of the Sociology of Law* 233.

McCahery, J., and Picciotto, S. (forthcoming), 'Creative Lawyering and the Dynamics Business Regulation, in Dezalay and Sugarman (forthcoming).

McCain, R. A. (1980), 'A Theory of Co-determination' 40(1–2) *Zeitschrift für National-Oekonomie* 65.

McCauley, R., and Zimmer, S. (1989), 'Explaining International Differences in the Cost of Capital: The U.S. and U.K. versus Japan and Germany' (Federal Reserve Bank of New York, Research Paper No. 8913).

McCubbins, M. D., Noll, R. G., and Weingast, B. R. (1987), 'Administrative Procedures as Instruments of Political Control', 3 *Journal of Law, Economics and Organization* 243.

McEldowney, J. (1991), 'The National Audit Office and Privatisation', 54 *Modern Law Review* 933.

McGill, D. (1989) (ed.), *Proxy Voting of Pension Plan Equity Securities* (Homewood, Ill.: JRWJN).

McLure, C. E. (1984), *The State Corporation Income Tax. Issues in Worldwide Unitary Combination* (Stanford, Calif.: Hoover Institution Press).

McPherson, M. (1983), 'Efficiency and Liberty in the Productive Enterprise: Recent Work in the Economics of Work Organization', 12 *Philosophy and Public Affairs* 354.

Meade, E. S. (1903), *Trust Finance* (New York: Appleton).

Meidner, R. (1978), *Employee Investment Funds* (London: Allen and Unwin).

Meier-Schatz, C. (1988), 'Corporate Governance and Legal Rules: A Transnational Look at Concepts of Internal Management Control', 13 *Journal of Corporation Law* 431.

Mendelsohn, M.S. (1980), *Money on the Move. The Modern International Capital Market* (New York: McGraw-Hill).

Menshikov, S. (1969), *Millionaires and Managers* (Moscow: Progress Publishers).

Mestmacker, E-J., and Behrens, P. (1991) (eds.), *Das Gesellschaftsrechts der Konzerne im internationalen Vergleich* (Baden-Baden: Nomos).

Meyer, J., and Rowan, B. (1992*a*), 'Institutionalized Organizations: Formal Structure as Myth and Ceremony', in Meyer and Scott (1992), 21–44.

—— (1992*b*), 'The Structure of Educational Organizations', in Meyer and Scott (1992), 71–97.

—— and Scott, W. R. (1992) (eds.), *Organizational Environments: Ritual and Rationality* 2nd edn. (London: Sage)

Milgrom, P., and Roberts, J. (1990), 'Bargaining Costs, Influence Costs, and the Organization of Economic Activity', in Alt and Shepsle (1990), 57–89.

Miliband, R. (1983), *Class Power and State Power* (Cambridge: Polity).

Miller, P. and Rose, N. (1990), 'Governing Economic Life', 19 *Economy and Society* 1.

Millon, D. (1990), 'Theories of the Corporation', [1990] *Duke Law Journal* 201.

—— (1991), 'Redefining Corporate Law', 24 *Indiana Law Review* 223.

Mills, S. M. (1986) (ed.), *The Changing Labor Market: A Longitudinal Study of Young Men* (Lexington, Mass.: Lexington Books).

Mintz, B., and Schwartz, M. (1985), *The Power Structure of American Business* (Chicago: University of Chicago Press).

Mintzberg, H. (1983), *Structure in Fives: Designing Effective Organizations* (Englewood Cliffs, NJ: Prentice-Hall).

Mishel, L., and Frankel, D. M. (1991), *The State of Working in America 1990–1991* (Sharpe, Armonk, NY: Economic Policy Institute).

Mitchell, A. (1990), 'Bankruptcies Raise Questions over Auditors', *Financial Times*, 6 Dec.

Modjeska, L. (1985), 'The Reagan NLRB, Phase I', 46 *Ohio State Law Journal* 95.

Mohlar, A. (1985) (ed.), *Einführung in den Konstruktivismus* (Munich: Oldenbourg).

Monopolkommission (1977), *Mehr Wettbewerb ist möglich 2. Aufl. Hauptgutachten 1973/75* (Baden-Baden: Nomos).

—— (1978), *Fortschreitende Konzentration bei Großerman ßunternehmen Zweites Hauptgutachten 1976/77* (Baden-Baden: Nomos).

—— (1989), *Zusammenschlußvorhaben der Daimler-Benz AG mit der Messerschmidt-Bölkow-Blohm GmbH Sondergutachten 18* (Baden-Baden: Nomos).

Moore, J. (1986*a*), 'The Success of Privatisation', in Kay *et al.* (1986), 94–8.

—— (1986*b*), 'Why Privatise?', in Kay *et al.* (1986), 78–93.

Moore, S. (1978), *Law as Process: An Anthropological Approach* (London: Routledge).

Moran, M. (1986), *The Politics of Banking*, 2nd edn. (London: Macmillan).

—— (1989), 'Investor Protection and the Culture of Capitalism', in Hancher and Moran (1989*a*), 49–75.

—— (1991), *The Politics of the Financial Services Revolution: The USA, UK and Japan* (Basingstoke: Macmillan).

Morck, R., Shleifer, A., and Vishny, R. W. (1990), 'Do Managerial Objectives Drive Bad Acquisitions', 45 *Journal of Finance* 31.

Morgan, C. (1989), 'Where to Draw the Lines of Duty', *Accountancy Age*, 26 Oct.

—— and Patient M. (1989), *Auditing Investment Businesses* (London: Butterworth).

Morris C. (1933), 'The Basis of Contract', 46 *Harvard Law Review* 553.

Muchlinski, P. (1988), 'The Bhopal Case: Controlling Ultrahazardous Industrial Activities Undertaken by Foreign Investors', 50 *Modern Law Review* 545.

Mueller, D. (1986) (ed.), *The Modern Corporation* (Brighton: Wheatsheaf).

—— and Fitzroy, F. (1986), 'Cooperation and Conflict in Contractual Organizations', in D. Mueller (1986), 52–77.

Mueller, R. K. (1986), *Corporate Networking* (New York: Collier-Macmillan).

Musgrave, Peggy B., and Musgrave, Richard A. (1984), *Public Finance Theory and Practice* (New York: McGraw-Mill).

Nagel, B. (1989), 'Der faktische Just-in-Time-Konzern-Unternehmensüber-greifende Rationalisierungskonzepte und Konzernrecht am Beispiel der Automobilindustrie', 42 *Der Betrieb* 1505.

Neale, A. D., and Goyder, D. G. (1980), *The Antitrust Laws of the United States of America*, 3rd edn. (Cambridge: Cambridge University Press).

Nelson, Robert (1987), *Partners with Power. The Social Transformation of the Large Law Firm* (Berkeley, Calif.: University of California Press).

Nelson, Richard R. and Winter, S. G. (1982), *An Evolutionary Theory of Economic Change* (Cambridge: Cambridge University Press).

Neuberger, D., and Neumann, M. (1991), 'Banking and Antitrust: Limiting Industrial Ownership by Banks?', 147 *Journal of Institutional and Theoretical Economics* 188.

Newman, S., and Yoffee, M. (1991), 'Steelworkers and Employee Ownership', 3 *Journal of Employee Ownership Law and Finance* 51.

Nicholson, N. (1981), 'Motivation: A Test Case for the Integration of Psychology and Industrial Relations', in Thomson and Warner (1981).

Nistrom, P. C., and Starbuck, W.H. (1981) (eds.), *Handbook for Organizational Design* (Oxford: Oxford University Press).

Noll, R. G. (1989), 'Economic Perspectives on the Politics of Regulation', in Schmalensee and Willig (1989), 1253–87.

Norton, S. W. (1988), 'An Empirical Look at Franchising as an Organisational Form', 61 *Journal of Business* 197.

Note (1976), 'Protecting Intangible Expectations under Collective Bargaining Agreements—Overcoming the Proscription of Arbitral Penalties', 61 *Minnesota Law Review* 127.

Note (1985), 'Golden Parachutes and the Business Judgment Rule: Toward a Proper Standard of Review', 94 *Yale Law Journal* 909.

Note (1989a), 'Corporate Theory', 64 *New York University Law Review* 806.

Note (1989b), 'Employer Opportunism and the Need for a Just Cause Standard', 103 *Harvard Law Review* 510.

Note (1991), 'State Legislative Attempts to Mandate Continuation of Collective Bargaining Agreements during Business Change: The Unfulfilled Expectations and the Pre-Empted Results', 77 *Cornell Law Review* 47.

Numazaki, I. (1986), 'Networks of Taiwanese Big Business', 12 *Modern China* 4.

OECD (Organization for Economic Cooperation and Development) (1977), Committee on Fiscal Affairs, *Model Double Taxation Convention on Income and Capital* (with Commentary) (Paris: OECD).

OECD (1979), *Transfer Pricing and Multinational Enterprises* (Paris: OECD).

—— (1984), Committee on International Investment and Multinational

Enterprise, *The 1984 Review of the 1976 Declaration and Decisions* (Paris: OECD).

—— (1984), *Transfer Pricing and Multinational Enterprises: Three Taxation Issues* (Paris: OECD).

—— (1987), Committee on Fiscal Affairs, *International Tax Avoidance and Evasion: Four Related Studies. I. Tax Havens: Measures to Prevent Abuse by Taxpayers; II. Double Taxation Conventions and the Use of Base Companies; III. Double Taxation Conventions and the Use of Conduit Companies; IV. Taxation and the Abuse of Bank Secrecy* (Paris: OECD).

Offe, C. (1985), *Disorganized Capitalism* (Cambridge, Mass. MIT Press).

Office of Electricity Regulation (1991), *Annual Report 1990* (London: HMSO).

Office of Gas Supply (1991), *Annual Report 1990* (London: HMSO).

Office of Telecommunications (1990), *Annual Report 1989* (London: HMSO).

Okumura, H. (1979), 'Stockholdings and Monopoly Problems in Japan', *Shoken Keizai* 129.

Oliva, R. R. (1984), 'The Treasury's Twenty-Year Battle with Treaty-Shopping: Article 16 of the 1977 US Model Treaty', 14 *Georgia Journal International & Comparative Law* 293.

Olson, D. (1982), 'Union Experiences with Worker Ownership: Legal and Practical Issues Raised by ESOPs, TRASOPs, Stock Purchases, and Cooperatives', [1982] *Wisconsin Law Review* 729.

Otterbeck, L. (1981) (ed.), *The Management of Headquarter–Subsidiary Relationships in Multinational Corporations* (New York: Gower).

Ozanne, R. (1967), *A Century of Labor–Management Relations* (Madison, Wis.: University of Wisconsin Press).

Park, W. W. (1978), 'Fiscal Jurisdiction and Accrual Basis Taxation: Lifting the Corporate Veil to Tax Foreign Profits', 78 *Columbia Law Review* 1609.

Parrini, P., and Sklar, M. J. (1983), 'New Thinking about the Market, 1896–1904: Some American Economists on Investment and the Theory of Surplus Capital', 43 *Journal of Economic History* 559.

Parsons, T., and Smelser, N. J. (1956), *Economy and Society: A Study in the Integration of Economic and Social Theory* (London: Routledge and Kegan Paul).

Patrick, H., and Rosovsky, H. (1976), *Asia's New Giant: How the Japanese Economy Works* (Washington, DC: Brookings Institution).

Pausenberger, E. (1975), 'Konzerne', in Grochla and Wittmann (1975).

Pennington, R. R. (1990), *Company Law*, 6th edn. (London: Butterworths).

Perrow, C. (1988), 'A Society of Organizations', in Haller *et al.* (1988), 265–76.

Petite, M. (1984), 'The Conditions for Consolidation under the 7th Company Law Directive', 21 *Common Market Law Review* 81.

Phillips, D. (1979), 'Managerial Misuse of Property: The Synthesizing Thread in Corporate Doctrine', 32 *Rutgers Law Review* 184.

Picciotto, S. (1983), 'Jurisdictional Conflicts, International Law and the International State System', 11 *International Journal of the Sociology of Law* 11.

—— (1989), 'Slicing a Shadow: Business Taxation in an International Framework', in Hancher and Moran (1989a), 11–47.

—— (1991), 'The Internationalization of the State', 43 *Capital and Class* 43.

Picciotto, S. (1992*a*), *International Business Taxation* (London: Weidenfeld and Nicolson).

—— (1992*b*), 'International Taxation and Intrafirm Pricing in Transnational Corporate Groups', 17 *Accounting, Organizations and Society* 759.

—— (forthcoming), 'The Construction of International Taxation', in Dezalay and Sugarman (forthcoming).

Pigou, A. C. (1938), *Economics of Welfare*, 4th edn. (London: Macmillan).

Piore, M., and Sabel, C. (1984), *The Second Industrial Divide: Possibilities for Prosperity* (New York: Basic Books).

Pollard, S. (1965), *The Genesis of Modern Management* (London: Edward Arnold).

Pontusson, J. (1984), *Pension Funds and the Politics of Capital Formation in Sweden* (Stockholm: Almquist and Wiksell).

Popper, K., and Eccles, J. (1977), *The Self and its Brain: An Argument for Interactionism* (New York: Springer).

Posner, R. A. (1976), *Antitrust Law* (Chicago: University of Chicago Press).

—— (1986), *Economic Analysis of Law*, 3rd edn. (Boston: Little, Brown and Co.).

Powell, F. (1931), *Parent and Subsidiary Corporations* (Chicago: Callaghan).

Powell, W. W. (1987), 'Hybrid Organizational Arrangements: New Form or Transitional Development?', 30 *California Management Review* 67.

—— (1990), 'Neither Market nor Hierarchy: Network Forms of Organization', 12 *Research in Organizational Behavior* 295.

Pozdena, R. (1987), 'Commerce and Banking: The German Case', *Federal Reserve Bank of San Francisco, Weekly Letter*, 18 Dec.

—— (1990*a*), 'Banking and Venture Capital', *Federal Reserve Bank of San Francisco, Weekly Letter*, 1 June.

—— (1990*b*), 'Why Banks Need Securities Powers' (Federal Reserve Bank of San Francisco, California Working Paper).

Prais, S. J. (1981), *The Evolution of Giant Firms in Britain*, rev. edn. (Cambridge: Cambridge University Press).

Pratt, J., and Zeckhauser, R. (1985) (eds.), *Principals and Agents* (Cambridge, Mass.: Harvard University Business School Press).

Prentice, D. D. (1988), 'Insolvency and the Group: Some Aspects of Current British Law', in Goode (1988).

—— (1990), 'Creditors' Interests and Directors' Duties', 10 *Oxford Journal of Legal Studies* 265.

Prichard, J. R. S. (1983) (ed.), *Crown Corporations in Canada—The Calculus of Instrument Choice* (Toronto: Butterworths).

Prosser, T. (1986), *Public Control of Nationalised Industries* (Oxford: Blackwell).

—— (1989), 'Regulation and Privatized Industries: Institutions and Procedures', in Hancher and Moran (1989*a*), 135–66.

—— and Graham, C. (1987), 'Privatizing Nationalized Industries', 50 *Modern Law Review* 16–51.

—— (1988), 'Golden Shares, Industrial Policy by Stealth', [1988] *Public Law* 413.

—— (1991), *Privatising Public Enterprises* (Oxford: Oxford University Press).

Putterman, L. (1982), 'Some Behavioral Perspectives on the Dominance of

Hierarchical over Democratic Forms of Enterprise', 3 *Journal of Economic Behavior and Organization* 139.

—— (1984), 'On Some Recent Explanations of Why Capital Hires Labor', 22 *Economic Inquiry* 171.

—— (1986) (ed.), *The Economic Nature of the Firm* (Cambridge: Cambridge University Press).

Radler, A., and Jacob, F. (1984), *German Transfer Pricing/ Prix de Transfert en Allemagne* (Deventer: Kluwer).

Raff, D. M. G., and Somers, L. H. (1987), 'Did Henry Ford Pay Efficiency Wages?', 5 *Journal of Labor Economics* 557.

Rappaport, L., and Cannon, J. (1989), 'Counseling Corporate Clients in the Uses and Implications of Leveraged ESOPs', in *21st Annual Institute on Securities Regulation*, ii. 747–838 (New York: Practicing Law Institute).

Rasmussen, E. (1989), *Games and Information* (Oxford: Blackwell).

Rawls, J. (1971), *A Theory of Justice* (Cambridge, Mass. Harvard University Press).

Razin, A., and Slemrod, J. (1991), *Taxation in the Global Economy* (Chicago: University of Chicago Press).

Regan, D. H. (1972), 'The Problem of Social Cost Revisited', 15 *Journal of Law and Economics* 427.

Regan, D. T. (1988), *For the Record. From Wall Street to Washington* (London: Hutchinson).

Reich, M., Gordon, D., and Edwards, R. (1973), 'A Theory of Labor Market Segmentation', 62 *American Economic Review* 359.

Reinsch, P.S. (1900), *World Politics* (New York: Macmillan).

—— (1902), *Colonial Government* (New York: Macmillan).

—— (1905), *Colonial Administration* (New York: Macmillan).

Renner, K. (1904), *The Institutions of Private Law and their Social Functions*, 1949 edn. (London: Routledge and Kegan Paul).

Reynolds, R. L., Masters, S., and Moser, C. (1986), *Labor Economics and Labor Relations* 9th edn. (Englewood Cliffs, NJ: Prentice-Hall).

Richardson, G. (1983), *Policing Pollution* (Oxford: Clarendon Press).

Rifkin, J., and Barber, R. (1978), *The North Will Rise Again: Pensions, Politics and Power in the 1980s* (Boston).

Robbins, L. (1935), *An Essay on the Nature and Significance of Economic Theory*, 2nd edn. (London: Macmillan).

Robinson (1910), 'The Holding Company (pt. 1)', 18 *Yale Law Journal* 390.

Robinson, J. (1955), 'The Impossibility of Capitalism', in Chamberlin (1955), ch. 3.

—— (1969), *The Economics of Imperfect Competition*, 2nd edn. (London: Macmillan).

Rock, E. (1992), 'Corporate Law through Antitrust Lens', 92 *Columbia Law Review* 497.

Rodbertus, K. (1898), *Overproduction and Crises* (New York: Burt Franklin).

Roe, M. (1991), 'A Political Theory of American Corporate Finance', 91 *Columbia Law Review* 10.

Röhl, K. F. (1987), 'Die strukturelle Differenz zwischen Individuum und

Organisation oder Brauchen wird ein Sonderprivatrecht für Versicherungen und andere Organisationen?', in *Festschrift für Ernst C. Stiefel* (Munich: Beck), 574–605.

——(1990), 'Zu einer Jurisprudenz der Organisation', in Hoffmann-Riem, *et al.* (1990), 266–83.

Roemer, J. (1988), *Free To Lose* (London: Radius).

Romano, R. (1990), 'The State Competition Debate in Corporate Law', in Bebchuk (1990), 216–54.

Rosen, S. (1985), 'Implicit Contracts: A Survey', 23 *Journal of Economic Literature* 1144.

Rosenberg, A. (1984), 'Student Note: Automation and the Work Preservation Doctrine', 32 *UCLA Law Review* 135.

Rosenberg, H. (1943), 'Political and Social Consequences of the Great Depression of 1873–1896 in Central Europe', 1–2 *Economic History Review* 58.

Rosenbloom, H. D., and Langbein, S. I. (1981), 'United States Tax Treaty Policy: An Overview', 19 *Columbia Journal of Transnational Law* 359.

Roth, G. (1987), 'Die Entwicklung kognitiver Selbstreferentialität im menschlichen Gehirn', in Baecker *et al.* (1987), 394–422.

——and Schwegler, H. (1990), 'Self-Organization, Emergent Properties and the Unity of the World', in Krohn *et al.* (1990), 36–50.

Rothschild, K. (1971) (ed.), *Power in Economics* (Harmondsworth: Penguin).

Roy, D. (1969), 'Making-Out: A Workers' Counter-System of Control of Work Sanction and Relationships', in Burns (1969).

Rubin, P. A. (1978), 'The Theory of the Firm and the Structure of Franchise Contracts', 21 *Journal of Law and Economics* 223.

Rugman, A. M. (1979), *International Diversification and the Multinational Enterprise* (Lexington, Mass.: Lexington Books).

Rumelt, R. P. (1974), *Strategy, Structure and Economic Performance* (Boston: Harvard University Press).

Ryan, P. (1989), 'Corporate Directors and the "Social Costs" of Takeovers— Reflections on the Tin Parachute', 64 *Tulane Law Review* 3.

——(1991), 'Strange Bedfellows: Corporate Fiduciaries and the General Law Compliance Obligation in Section 2.01(a) of the American Law Institute's Principles of Corporate Governance', 66 *Washington Law Review* 413.

Salais, R., and Thevenot, L. (1986) (eds.), *Le Travail. Marché, règles, conventions* (Paris: Economica).

Sandel, M. (1982), *Liberalism and the Limits of Justice* (Cambridge: Cambridge University Press).

Sapelli, G. (1990), 'A Historical Typology of Group Enterprises: The Debate on the Decline of Popular Sovereignty', in Sugarman and Teubner (1990), 193–216.

——(1992), 'Netzwerke, Kulturen, Betrieb', in *Netzwerk-Dimensionen: Kulturelle Konfigurationen und Management-Perspektiven* (Bergheim; Datscon).

Sappington, D. E. M., and Stiglitz, J.E. (1987), 'Privatisation, Information and Incentives', 6 *Journal of Policy Analysis and Management* 567.

Saunders, P., and Harris, C. (1990), 'Privatization and the Consumer' 24 *Sociology* 57.

Schanze, E. (1991), 'Symbiotic Contracts: Exploring Long-Term Agency Structures between Contract and Corporation', in Joerges (1991a), 67–103.

Scharpf, F. W. (1989), 'Politische Steuerung und Politische Institutionen', 30 *Politische Vierteljahresschrift* 10.

Scheffler, E. (1987), 'Zur Problematik der Konzernleitung', in *Festschrift für Reinhard Goerdeler* (Düsseldorf: IDV), 469–85.

Scherer, F. C. (1986), 'On the Current State of Knowledge in Industrial Organization', in De Jong and Shepard (1986), 5–22.

—— (1988), 'Corporate Takeovers: The Efficiency Arguments', 2 *Journal of Financial Perspectives* 69.

Schmalensee, R., and Willig, R. (1989) (eds.), *Handbook of Industrial Organisation* (North-Holland: Elsevier Science Publishers).

Schmid, W. (1983), *Zur sozialen Wirklichkeit des Vertrages* (Berlin: Drucker and Humblot).

Schmidt, J. (1985), *Vertragsfreiheit und Schuldrechtsreform* (Berlin: Drucker and Humblot).

—— (1989), ' "Sozialsysteme" und "Autonomie" ', in *Festschrift für Günther Jahr* (Cologne: Heymann), 34–94.

Schneider, V. (1988), *Politiknetzwerke der Chemikalienkontrolle: Eine Analyse der transnationalen Politikentwicklung* (Berlin: Nomos).

Schwartz A. (1989), 'A Theory of Loan Priorities', 15 *Journal of Legal Studies* 209.

Sciarra, S. (1991), 'Franchising and Contract of Employment: Notes on a Still Impossible Assimilation', in Joerges (1991a), 239–66.

Scitovsky, T. (1952), *Welfare and Competition*, rev. edn. (London: Allen and Unwin).

Scott J. (1979), *Corporations, Classes and Capitalism* (London: Hutchinson).

—— (1982), *The Upper Classes* (London: Macmillan).

—— (1985), *Corporations, Classes and Capitalism*, 2nd edn. (London: Hutchinson).

—— (1986), *Capitalist Property and Financial Power* (Brighton: Wheatsheaf).

—— (1990), 'Corporate Control and Corporate Rule', 41 *British Journal of Sociology* 351.

—— (1991a), 'Networks of Corporate Power', *Annual Review of Sociology* 17.

—— (1991b), *Social Network Analysis* (London: Sage).

—— (1991c), *Who Rules Britain?* (Cambridge: Polity).

——, and Griff, C. (1984), *Directors of Industry* (Cambridge: Polity).

——, and Hughes, M. (1980), *The Anatomy of Scottish Capital* (London: Croom Helm).

Scott, K. (1991), 'Comment on Neuberger and Neumann', 147 *Journal of Institutional and Theoretical Economics* 202.

Sealy, L. S. (1967), 'The Director as Trustee', [1967] *Cambridge Law Journal* 83.

—— (1984), *Company Law and Commercial Reality* (London: Sweet and Maxwell).

Securities and Investment Board (1990), *Statements of Principle Issued under Section 47A Financial Services Act 1986 on 15 March 1990* (London).

—— (1991), *Core Conduct of Business Rules Issued on 30 January 1991* (London).

438   *Bibliography*

Segal, M. (1986), 'Post-Institutionalism in Economics: The Forties and Fifties Revisited', 39 *Industrial and Labour Relations Review* 388.

Selzer, I. M. (1991), 'Regulatory Methods: A Case for "Hands Across the Atlantic"?' in Veljanovski (1991*b*), ch. 3.

Sharpe, L. J. (1985), 'Central Coordination and the Policy Network', 33 *Political Studies* 361.

Shepard, W. (1990), *The Economics of Industrial Organization* (Englewood Cliffs, NJ: Prentice-Hall International).

Sherer, M., and Turley, S. (1991) (eds.), *Current Issues in Auditing*, 2nd edn. (London: Paul Chapman).

Shleifer, A., and Summers, L. (1988), 'Breach of Trust in Hostile Takeovers', in A. Auerbach (1988), 33–56.

Shleifer, A., and Vishny R. (1988), 'Value Maximization and the Acquisition Process', 2 *Journal of Economic Perspectives* 7.

—— (1989), 'Management Entrenchment: The Case of Manager-Specific Investments', 25 *Journal of Financial Economics* 123.

Shorter, E., and Tilly, C. (1974), *Strikes in France, 1830–1968* (Cambridge: Cambridge University Press).

Siegfried, K.-J. (1987), *Rüstungsproduktion und Zwangsarbeit im Volkswagenwerk 1939–1945* (Frankfurt: Campus).

Simon, H. A. (1955), 'A Behavioural Model of Rational Choice', 69 *Quarterly Journal of Economics* 99.

—— (1957), 'The Compensation of Executives', 20 *Sociometry* 32.

—— (1991), 'Organizations and Markets', 5 *Journal of Economic Perspectives* 25.

Simon, W. (1988), 'Ethical Discretion in Lawyering,' 101 *Harvard Law Review* 1083.

Singer, J. (1988), 'The Reliance Interest in Property', 40 *Stanford Law Review* 611.

Sklar, M. J. (1988), *The Corporate Reconstruction of American Capitalism 1890–1916* (Cambridge: Cambridge University Press).

Smith, A. (1776), *The Wealth of Nations* (Oxford: Oxford University Press, 1976 edn.).

Smith, T. (1990*a*), 'Evidence of Fraud Office's Performance', *Accountancy Age*, 2 Aug.

—— (1990*b*), 'Regulation Requires a Rigorous Regime', *Accountancy Age*, 28 June.

Solow, R. M. (1971), 'Some Implications of Alternative Criteria for the Firm', in Marris and Wood (1971), 318–42.

Spencer Brown, G. (1969), *Laws of Form* (London: Allen and Unwin).

Stein, B. (1990) (ed.), *Proceedings of the New York University 43rd Annual Conference on Labor* (Boston: Little, Brown and Co.).

Stein, J.C. (1988), 'Takeover Threats and Managerial Myopia', 96 *Journal of Political Economy* 61.

Steindl, J. (1976), *Maturity and Stagnation in American Capitalism* (Oxford: Blackwell).

Steiner, G. A., and Steiner, G. F. (1977) (eds.), *Issues in Business and Society*, 2nd edn. (Chicago: University of Chicago Press).

Steinherr, A., and Huveneers, C. (1990), 'Universal Banks: The Prototype of Successful Banks in the Integrated European Market? A View Inspired by German Experience' (CEPS Research Report No. 2).

Stephen, F. (1984) (ed.), *Firms, Organization and Labour* (London: Macmillan).

Stetson Law Review Symposium (1991), 'Corporate Malaise—Stakeholder Statutes: Cause or Cure?', 21 *Stetson Law Review* 1.

Stewart, J. (1991), *Den of Thieves* (New York: Simon and Schuster).

Stichweh, R. (1987), 'Den frühmoderne Staat und die europäische Universität', 6 *Rechtshistorisches Journal* 135.

Stock Exchange, Council of (n.d.), *Admission of Securities to Listing* (London: Stock Exchange).

Stokes, E. (1969), 'Late Nineteenth Century Colonial Expansion and the Attack on the Theory of Economic Imperialism: A Case of Mistaken Identity?', 12 *Historical Journal* 285.

Stokes, M. (1986), 'Company Law and Legal Theory', in Twining (1986), 155–83.

Stokman, F., Ziegler, R., and Scott, J. (1985), *Networks of Corporate Power* (Cambridge: Polity).

Stone, K. (1975), 'The Origin of Job Structures in the Steel Industry', in D. Gordon *et al.* (1975).

—— (1981), 'The Post-War Paradigm in American Labor Law', 90 *Yale Law Journal* 1509.

—— (1988), 'Labor and the Corporate Structure: Changing Conceptions and Emerging Possibilities', 55 *University of Chicago Law Review* 73.

—— (1990), 'Legal Regulation ' of Economic Weapons: A Comparative Perspective', in B. Stein (1990).

—— (1991), 'Employees as Stakeholders under State Nonshareholder Constituency Statutes', 21 *Stetson Law Review* 45.

Stout, L. (1988), 'The Unimportance of Being Efficient: An Economic Analysis of Stock Market Pricing and Securities Regulation', 87 *Michigan Law Review* 613.

Sugarman, D. (1991), 'Lawyers and Business in England 1750–1950' (paper presented to the seminar of the European Working Group on Corporate Professionals, Vaucresson, June 1991).

—— and Teubner, G. (1990) (eds.), *Regulating Corporate Groups in Europe* (Baden-Baden: Nomos).

Summers, C. (1959), 'Collective Agreements and the Law of Contracts', 78 *Yale Law Journal* 525.

—— (1982), 'Codetermination in the United States: A Projection of Problems and Potentials' *Journal of Comparative Corporate Law and Securities Regulation* 155.

Summers, L. (1990), 'Comment', [1990] *Brookings Papers on Microeconomics*.

Sweezy, P. M. (1956), *The Theory of Capitalist Development*, rev. edn. (New York: Monthly Review Press).

Swensen, P. (1989), *Fair Shares: Unions, Pay, and Politics in Sweden and West Germany* (Ithaca, N Y; Cornell University Press).

Tattersall, J. (1991), 'Auditing in the Financial Services Sector', in Sherer and Turley (1991), 201–10.

Taylor, F. W. (1910), *Principles of Scientific Management* (New York: Norton, 1967 edn.).

Taylor, P., and Turley, S. (1986), *The Regulation of Accounting* (Oxford: Blackwell).

Teubner, G. (1979), 'Die Gesellschaft des bürgerlichen Rechts: Kommentierung zu 705ff. BGB', in Wassermann (1979), 718–49.

—— (1980), 'Die Generalklausel von Treu und Glauben: Kommentierung zu 242 BGB', in Wassermann (1980), 32–91.

—— (1987*a*), 'Episodenverknüpfung: Zur Steigerung von Selbstreferenz im Recht', in Baecker *et al.* (1987), 423–46.

—— (1987*b*), 'Juridification—Concepts, Aspects, Limits, Solutions', in Teubner (1987*c*), 3–48.

—— (1987*c*) (ed.), *Juridification of Social Spheres. A Comparative Analysis in the Areas of Labor, Corporate, Antitrust and Social Welfare Law* (Berlin: de Gruyter).

—— (1988*a*), 'Enterprise Corporatism: New Industrial Policy and the "Essence" of the Legal Person', 36 *American Journal of Comparative Law* 130.

—— (1988*b*), 'Hypercycle in Law and Organization: The Relationship between Self-Observation, Self-Constitution and Autopoiesis', *European Yearbook in the Sociology of Law* 43–70.

——(1990*a*) 'Die "Politik des Gesetzes" im Recht der Konzernhaftung', in Baür, *et al.* (1990), 261–79.

——(1990*b*), 'Unitas Multiplex: Corporate Governance in Group Enterprises', in Sugarman and Teubner (1990), 67–104.

——(1991), 'Beyond Contract and Organization? The External Liability of Franchise Systems in German Law', in Joerges (1991*a*), 105–37.

——(1993), *Law as an Autopoietic System* (Oxford: Blackwell).

Therborn, G. (1975), *Science, Class and Society* (London: Verso).

Thompson, E. P. (1967), 'Time, Work Discipline and Industrial Capitalism', 38 *Past and Present* 56.

Thompson, J. D. (1966) (ed.), *Approaches to Organizational Design* (Pittsburgh: University of Pittsburgh Press).

Thomson, A. W. J., and Warner, M. (1981) (eds.), *The Behavioural Sciences and Industrial Relations* (Aldershot: Gower).

Thorelli, H. B. (1986), 'Networks: Between Markets and Hierarchies', 7 *Strategic Management Journal* 37.

Thornley, J. (1981), *Workers' Co-operatives: Jobs and Dreams* (London: Heinemann).

Tichy, N. M. (1981), 'Networks in Organizations', in Nistrom and Starbuck (1981).

Tillinghast, D. R. (1979), 'Taxing the Multinationals: Where is the US Headed?', 20 *Harvard International Law Journal* 253.

Tilly, R. (1989), 'Banking Institutions in Historical and Comparative Perspective: Germany, Great Britain and the United States in the Nineteenth and Early Twentieth Century', 145 *Journal of Institutional and Theoretical Economics* 189.

Tirole, J. (1988), *The Theory of Industrial Organization* (Cambridge, Mass.: MIT Press).

Trasher, M. (1983), 'Exchange Networks and Implementation', 11 *Policy and Politics* 375.

Trebilcock, M. J., and Prichard, J. R. S. (1983), 'Crown Corporations: The Calculus of Instrument Choice', in Prichard (1983), ch. 1.

Treiman, D., and Hartmann, H. (1981) (eds.), *Women, Work, and Wages: Equal Pay for Jobs of Equal Value* (Washington, D.C.: National Academy Press).

Turk, F., and Willman, P. (1983) (eds.), *Power, Efficiency and Institutions* (London: Heinemann).

Turner, D. F. (1964–5), 'Conglomerate Mergers and Section 7 of the Clayton Act', 78 *Harvard Law Review* 1313.

Turro, J. (1992), 'IRS Inks Two Pricing Agreements in Derivative Products Area', 55 *Tax Notes* 725.

Twaalhoven, F., and Hattori, T. (1982), *The Supporting Role of Small Japanese Enterprises* (Schiphol).

Twining, W. (1986) (ed.), *Legal Theory and Common Law* (Oxford: Blackwell).

US Department of Labour (1988), 'Letter on Proxy Voting by Plan Fiduciaries (Avon Products)', 15 *BMA Pension Reporter* 391.

US Treasury Department (1988), *A Study of Intercompany Pricing. Discussion Draft* (White Paper), Oct. 1988 (Washington, DC).

—— and Internal Revenue Service (1992), *Report on the Application and Administration of Section 482, April 1992* (Washington, DC).

Useem, M. (1984), *The Inner Circle* (New York: Oxford University Press).

Utton, M. (1986), *The Economics of Regulating Industry* (Oxford: Blackwell).

Van den Bulcke, D. (1986), 'Autonomy of Decision Making by Subsidiaries of Multinational Enterprises', in Vandamme (1986), 219–41.

Van Horne, J. (1974), *Fundamentals of Financial Management*, 2nd edn. (Englewood Cliffs, NJ: Prentice-Hall).

Van Zandt, D. (1989), 'The Relevance of Social Theory to Legal Theory', 83 *Northwestern University Law Review* 10.

Vanberg, V. (1982), *Markt und Organisation* (Tübingen: Mohr).

Vandamme, J. (1986) (ed.), *Employee Consultation and Information in Multinational Corporations* (London: Croom Helm).

Vann, R. J. (1991), 'A Model Tax Treaty for the Asian-Pacific Region?', *Bulletin for International Fiscal Documentation* 99, 151.

Vardaro, G. (1990), 'Before and Beyond the Legal Person: Group Enterprises, Trade Unions and Industrial Relations', in Sugarman and Teubner (1990), 217–51.

Veblen, T. (1970), *The Theory of the Leisure Class* (London: Allen and Unwin).

Veljanovski, C. (1987), *Selling the State* (London: Weidenfeld and Nicolson).

—— (1990a) (ed.), *Privatization and Competition* (London: IEA).

—— (1990b), 'Privatization: Monopoly Money or Competition', in Veljanovski (1990a), 26–51.

—— (1991a), 'The Regulation Game', in Veljanovski (1991b), ch. 1.

—— (1991b) (ed.), *Regulators and the Market* (London: IEA).

Vernon, R. (1977), *Storm over the Multinationals* (Cambridge, Mass.: Harvard University Press).

Vickers, J. (1985), 'The Economics of Predatory Prices', 6(3) *Fiscal Studies* 24.

Vickers, J. and Kay, J. (1990), 'Regulatory Reform: An Appraisal', in Majone (1990), ch. 10.

—— and Yarrow, G. (1988), *Privatization: An Economic Analysis* (Cambridge, Mass.: MIT Press).

—— (1991), 'The British Electricity Experiment', 12 *Economic Policy* 189.

Viner, A. (1990), 'Mergers, Acquisitions and Corporate Governance in Japan', in Lufkin and Gallagher (1990).

Vogel, K. (1983), 'Administering Labor Contracts Using Transaction-Cost Economics', 5 *Law & Policy Quarterly* 129.

Wachter, M. L., and Cohen, G. M. (1988), 'The Law and Economics of Collective Bargaining: An Introduction and Application to the Problems of Subcontracting, Partial Closure and Relocation', 36 *University of Pennsylvania Law Review* 1349.

Wagner, F. (1986), 'Ausschüttungszwang und Kapitalentzugsrechte als Instrumente marktgelenkter Unternehmenskontrolle?', in *Kapitalmarkt und Finanzierung*, Schriften des Vereins für Socialpolitik, Volume 165 (Berlin: Drucker and Humblot), 410–25.

Walker, R. (1978), *Consolidated Statements* (New York: Arno Press).

Wallerstein, I. (1974), *The Modern World System* (New York: Academic Press).

—— (1979), *The Capitalist World Economy* (Cambridge: Cambridge University Press).

Wassermann, R. (1979) (ed.), *Alternativkommentar zum Bürgerlichen Recht*, Volume 3: *Besonderes Schuldrecht* (Neuwied: Luchterhand).

Wassermann R. (1980) (ed.), *Alternativkommentar zum Bürgerlichen Gesetzbuch*, Volume 2: *Allgemeines Schuldrecht* (Neuwied: Luchterhand).

Wayne (1991), 'Seeking to Stay Out of Proxy Battles', *New York Times*, 8 Apr. 1991, D1, col. 3.

Weber, M. (1925), *Wirtschaft und Gesellschaft* (Tübingen: Mohr, 1972 edn.).

—— (1978), *Economy and Society: An Outline of Interpretative Sociology* (Berkeley, Calif. University of California Press).

Wedderburn, K. W. (later Lord) (1957), 'Shareholders' Rights and the Rule in Foss v Harbottle', *Cambridge Law Journal* 194.

—— (1984), 'Note on Multinational Services Case', 47 *Modern Law Review* 87.

—— (1985a), 'The Legal Development of Corporate Responsibility', in Hopt and Teubner (1985).

—— (1985b), 'Trust, Corporation and the Worker', 23 *Osgoode Hall Law Journal* 203.

Weiler, P. (1990), *Governing the Workplace: The Future of Labor and Employment Law* (Cambridge, Mass.: Harvard University Press).

Weinstein, J. (1968), *The Corporate Ideal in the Liberal State, 1900–1918* (Boston: Beacon Press).

Wells, D. A. (1889), *Recent Economic Changes* (New York: Appleton).

Whish, R. (1989), *Competition Law* 2nd edn. (London: Butterworths).

Wickens, P. (1987), *The Road to Nissan* (Basingstoke: Macmillan).

Williamson, O. E. (1964), *The Economics of Discretionary Behavior* (London: Kershaw Publishing).

—— (1970), *Corporate Control and Business Behavior* (Englewood Cliffs, NJ: Prentice-Hall).

—— (1971), 'Managerial Discretion, Organizational Form, and the Multi-Divisional Hypothesis', in Marris and Wood (1971), 346.

—— (1975), *Markets and Hierarchies: Analysis and Antitrust Implications* (New York: Free Press).

—— (1976), 'Franchise Bidding for Natural Monopoly—In General and with Respect to CATV', 7 *Bell Journal of Economics* 73.

—— (1980), 'The Organisation of Work: A Comparative Institutional Assessment', 1 *Journal of Economic Behavior and Organization* 5.

—— (1981), 'The Modern Corporation, Origins, Evolution, Attributes', 19 *Journal of Economic Literature* 1537.

—— (1983), 'Organizational Form, Residual Claimants, and Corporate Control', 26 *Journal of Law and Economics* 351.

—— (1984a), 'Corporate Governance', 93 *Yale Law Journal* 1197.

—— (1984b), 'Efficient Labour Organization', in Stephen (1984).

—— (1985), *The Economic Institutions of Capitalism* (New York: Free Press).

—— (1986), *Economic Organization: Firms, Markets and Corporate Control* (Brighton: Wheatsheaf).

—— (1987a), *Antitrust Economics* (Oxford: Blackwell).

—— (1987b), 'Comment: Shareholders and Managers—A Risk-Neutral Perspective' in Coffee *et al.* (1987), 159–67.

—— (1988a), 'Comment,' in A. Auerbach (1988), 61–7.

—— (1988b), 'Corporate Finance and Corporate Governance', *Journal of Finance* 567.

—— (1988c), 'The Logic of Economic Organization', 4 *Journal of Law, Economics and Organization* 65.

—— (1990), 'The Firm as a Nexus of Treaties: An Introduction' in Aoki *et al.* (1990), 1–25.

—— (1991a), 'Comparative Economic Organization: The Analysis of Discrete Structural Alternatives', 36 *Administrative Science Quarterly* 269.

—— (1991b), 'Economic Institutions: Spontaneous and Intentional Governance', 7 *Journal of Law, Economics and Organization* 159.

—— (1992), 'Markets, Hierarchies and the Modern Corporation: An Unfolding Perspective', 17 *Journal of Economic Behavior and Organization* 315.

——, Wachter, M. L., and Harris, J. E. (1975), 'Understanding the Employment Relation: The Analysis of Idiosyncratic Change', 6 *Bell Journal of Economics* 250.

Willis, R. (1988), 'Wage Determinants: A Survey and Reinterpretation of Human Capital Earnings Functions', in Ashenfelter and Layard (1988).

Williston, S. (1888), 'History of the Law of Business Corporations before 1800 (pt. 2)', 2 *Harvard Law Review* 149.

Willman, P. (1983), 'The Organisational Failures Framework and Industrial Sociology', in Turk and Willman (1983).

Willoughby, W.F. (1898), 'The Concentration of Industry in the United States', 7 *Yale Review* 72.

Witte, A. D., and T. Chipty (1990), 'Some Thoughts on Transfer Pricing', *Tax Notes*, 26 Nov.

Wolf, G. (1990), 'Gestalten von Komplexität durch Netzwerk-Management', in Kratky and Wallner (1990), 103–26.

Wooldridge, F. (1981), *Groups of Companies: The Law and Practice in Britain, France and Germany* (London: Institute of Advanced Legal Studies).

Wormser, I. (1912), 'Piercing the Veil of the Corporate Entity', 12, *Columbia Law Review* 496.

—— (1927), *The Disregard of the Corporate Fiction and Allied Corporate Problems* (New York; Baker, Voorhis & Co.).

Wright, C.D. (1886), *Industrial Depressions* (Washington, DC: US GPO).

—— (1897–8), 'The Relation of Production to Productive Capacity II', 24 *Forum* 660.

Index